EVERYTHING
IS CINEMA

EVERYTHING IS CINEMA

THE WORKING LIFE OF
JEAN-LUC GODARD

RICHARD BRODY

METROPOLITAN BOOKS   HENRY HOLT AND COMPANY   New York

Metropolitan Books
Henry Holt and Company, LLC
Publishers since 1866
175 Fifth Avenue
New York, New York 10010
www.henryholt.com

Metropolitan Books® and ® are registered
trademarks of Henry Holt and Company, LLC.

Library of Congress Cataloging-in-Publication Data

Brody, Richard, 1958–
    Everything is cinema: the working life of Jean-Luc Godard / Richard Brody.—1st ed.
        p.   cm.
    ISBN-13: 978-0-8050-6886-3
    ISBN-10: 0-8050-6886-4
    1. Godard, Jean Luc, 1930– —Criticism and interpretation.   I. Title.
    PN1998.3.G63B76 2006
    791.43023'3092—dc22
    [B]   2006047347

Henry Holt books are available for special promotions and
premiums. For details contact: Director, Special Markets.

First Edition 2008

Designed by Meryl Sussman Levavi

Printed in the United States of America

10 9 8 7 6 5 4 3 2 1

To Maja, for my very being

CONTENTS

PREFACE

IN THE SPRING OF 2000, JEAN-LUC GODARD RECEIVED ME in his office in Rolle, a town on Lake Geneva in Switzerland, where he has been living and working for the past thirty years. Rolle is set on a sharply rising slope between the lake and the highlands. It is a sedate town. The main street has one traffic light. Mont Blanc hovers weightlessly in the distance.

When I arrived, Godard was seated at a broad, uncluttered trestle desk in a spacious office on the main floor of one of Rolle's few modern buildings. He has one wall of compact discs, another of books and pictures, and from his chair, he faces out onto a roomful of video equipment that would do a small TV station proud: sturdy industrial metal racks holding tape decks, switchers, meters, monitors, a bulky sound console squat on the floor, dozens of cables and wires and plugs strung from one board to another, and a computer. A television monitor was on: Godard was keeping an eye on the men's semifinal matches at the French Open.

He welcomed me with the description of a cartoon he recalled from the pages of *The New Yorker,* the magazine for which I had come to interview him. The drawing shows a unicorn wearing a suit, seated at a desk, and talking on the phone. The caption reads, "These rumors of my non-existence are making it very difficult for me to obtain financing." To Godard the cartoon seemed exemplary of his own situation. Happily, though, he continues to exist—and also to work—at an extraordinarily high level of artistic achievement. Somehow, this fact is disturbingly unknown, except among a small coterie of film lovers. His work continues to be the subject of academic conferences and journal articles, and the intermittent DVD releases of his films are greeted by flurries of eager Internet postings among the tight circle of his devotees. But Godard's name is no longer common currency in the film industry, or for that matter on the cultural radar. While enormous attention is given to filmmakers of more modest ability, Godard has become almost forgotten. But unlike Orson Welles, who struggled to make anything of value in his later years, or D. W. Griffith, whose career was stopped cold by changing fashions, Godard continues to develop. His obscurity is not hard to fathom—his work is demanding, but acceptance of its demands yields singular rewards, and, as the later chapters of this book will argue, his more recent films are indeed works of art fully equal—and in some respects, superior—to the early pictures that made his reputation and established his celebrity.

Godard is undoubtedly best known for his first feature film, *Breathless,* which he made in 1959. A highly personal yet exuberant refraction of the American film noir, *Breathless* was gaudily emblazoned with its technical audacity as well as with Godard's own artistic, literary, and cinematic enthusiasms. Even now, *Breathless* feels like a high-energy fusion of jazz and philosophy. After *Breathless,* most other new films seemed instantly old-fashioned. The triumph of Godard's longtime friend François Truffaut at the 1959 Cannes festival with *The 400 Blows,* had announced to the world the cinematic sea change effected by a group of critics-turned-filmmakers already known in France by the journalistic label of *la nouvelle vague,* the New Wave. But *The 400 Blows* was only the setup. *Breathless* was the knockout blow. If *The 400 Blows* was the February revolution, *Breathless* was October.

After *Breathless,* anything artistic appeared possible in the cinema. The film moved at the speed of the mind and seemed, unlike anything that preceded it, a live recording of one person thinking in real time. It was also a great success, a watershed phenomenon. More than any other event of its time, *Breathless* inspired other directors to make films in a new way and sparked young people's desire to make films. It instantly launched cinema as the primary art form of a new generation.

In the 1960s, Godard's films were eagerly anticipated events—in France, in the United States, and around the world—and each new release seemed to leave the last far behind. Writing in February 1968, Susan Sontag called Godard "one of the great culture heroes of our time"[1] and compared the aesthetic impact of his work to that of Picasso and Schoenberg. Mercurial, puckish, combative, and increasingly politicized, Godard was hailed during his 1968 speaking tour of American universities as being "as irreplaceable for us as Bob Dylan."[2]

Yet when Godard came to the United States that year for a celebrity tour of American universities, he was actually in a state of crisis and doubt. Even as his fame and his inventiveness increased through the 1960s, he became confused and uncertain in his work, which was being pulled in opposite directions by its fictional and nonfictional elements, by its personal and political implications. As the pace of social change outstripped his ability to invent new forms to engage it, Godard became increasingly strident in his response to the world around him. In his frustration, he also became increasingly hard on himself. Indeed, his films became public confessions and self-flagellations, but they were executed so effervescently, so inventively, so cleverly—with such a flamboyant and youthful sense of freedom—that they were most often received by critics and viewers as virtuosic displays of experimental gamesmanship.

The last of this torrent of films, *Weekend,* concludes with two title cards: the first reads "End of Film"; the second, "End of Cinema." When Godard finished filming *Weekend,* his fifteenth feature film in eight years, he advised the regular members of his crew that they should look for work elsewhere. He spent the next few years seemingly underground, working in a frenzied yet sterile engagement with one of the doctrines of May 1968, a nominal Maoism. After years of intellectual woodshedding and a period of artistic and physical convalescence (following a serious motorcycle accident), he returned to the French film industry in 1979. The films and videos he has made since that return are works of an even greater originality and a more reflective artistry than those of the 1960s, but Godard has never recovered his place at the center of his times.

IN A CERTAIN SENSE, Godard has been a victim of his own artistic success. As he fulfilled, after long delay, the underlying promise of the French New Wave—to turn movies into an art form as sophisticated and as intellectually powerful as literature or painting—his work became far too allusive and intricate for the wide range of moviegoers. In the earlier films, splashy borrowings from American movies and the presence of pop culture icons and iconography of the day went a long way to keep Godard in fashion even when his approach to them reflected the challenging philosophy of Jean-Paul Sartre or Claude Lévi-Strauss. Yet in his later work, Godard became even more intensely serious and demanding. His previous films represented a dismantling of movie conventions and forms; in his subsequent work he took on the colossal task of an aesthetic reconstruction of the cinema based on its excavated historical elements. Holding the present day up to comparison with the high points of cultural history, Godard found it wanting; his critique—indeed, utter rejection—of the contemporary culture of mass media made many people, especially the younger generations raised on that culture, simply wish that he would lighten up.

Lightening up is a notion profoundly at odds for a filmmaker who has made the greatest possible claims on behalf of the cinema's unique relation to reality and to history, of its power to transform whatever comes within its purview. As Godard told me, "Everything is cinema." Indeed, for Godard,

the cinema is the art of arts, encompassing and channeling the full spectrum of what is human, from the broadest political currents and the other
art forms to the most intimate reaches of his own life. For Godard, the cinema has always been inseparable from his personal experience—and his
own identity has been inseparable from the cinema. His initial enthusiasm
for movies had the force of a religious conversion, and his critical account of
the medium's unique psychological power derived from his own overwhelming encounter with it. As a filmmaker, he invented ingenious and
ever-more-elaborate means by which to relate both the substance and the
form of his work to his own inner and outer life, whether through his relationships with his performers (including his two wives, Anna Karina and
Anne Wiazemsky) or with his collaborators (including his longtime companion, Anne-Marie Miéville), or through his own forthright yet shifting
presence in the films.

Moreover, no other director has striven so relentlessly to reflect in his
work the great philosophical and political debates of the era: World War II
and its political aftermath in France; the uses and abuses of existentialism in
the postwar years; the structuralist revolution; the demise of Stalinism and
the rise of the New Left; the growth of modern consumer society and its political fallout in May 1968; the vast sea change and social heritage of the late
1960s; the hopes and disappointments of the Mitterrand era; Holocaust consciousness and the recuperation of historical memory; new fronts of battle
after the end of the Cold War; and the current era of big media and what
might be called the American cultural occupation of Europe. But despite
Godard's ongoing attention to the crucial questions of the day, his approach
to them has in recent years become so intricately interwoven with his advanced aesthetic methods, so rarefied, Olympian, and oblique, that many
critics and viewers have instead rejected these later efforts outright, asserting that he has somehow grown detached from political reality.

In fact, Godard's later work is marked by his obsession with living history. But this obsession has brought with it a troubling set of idées fixes, notably regarding Jews and the United States. In recent years Godard's vast
aesthetic embrace of the entire Western canon, from Greek mythology and
New Testament prophecies to twentieth-century modernism, has gone hand-
in-hand with his borrowing of some of the prejudicial assumptions of that
cultural aristocracy. Contemplating the contemporary world in the light of
lost traditions, Godard has adopted traditional attitudes as well, including
several shared by some of the most discredited and dangerous ideologies of
his times. Yet these invidious views have eluded widespread discussion,
largely due to the abstracted forms in which his films embody them, their
quiet place beside his more brazen media provocations—and, perhaps,

to the ready audience that the films still find among the cultural avant-garde. Godard's edgy relations with the media may have rendered his deepening isolation inevitable. From the start of his career, Godard made use of the press to help effect the personalization of his work. He turned the elements of his celebrity—in particular, the interview—into a parallel art form that illuminates and informs his films. He continues to fascinate the French press and remains an object of its attention; and he retains his fascination precisely by remaining himself, by not tailoring his public statements and behavior to the deferential or cautious norms of the media. Indeed, the more stringently he criticizes the fashions and conventions of public discourse, the more interesting he becomes to the objects of his opprobrium.

With his critique of the media, however, goes a deep understanding of the mechanism of celebrity and its crucial significance, especially now, in the creation and decadence of art. Godard's analysis of the media, which is an integral part of his work, is centered on what he considers their noxious effect on culture, on human relations, and particularly on the cinema. And because his faith in the cinema has been so great, and because he conceives his own identity in relation to it, Godard has taken on great personal, political and historical burdens in the name of the entire cinema. Thus, his later works and his public image have been marked by a sort of self-deprecating humility, even penitence. His blend of fierce prophecy and long-suffering sainthood have given his fame an odd twist. Though Godard remains a celebrity of sorts, especially in France, he has an air of taboo about him, like a great Dostoyevskian sinner who has come through his ordeals sanctified.

IF EVERYTHING IS CINEMA, then approaching Godard's vast work in any meaningful way necessarily means being prepared to deal with everything: politics, art, philosophy, history, nature, beauty, lust, torment, money, love, and the random element. True to the films, *Everything Is Cinema* is a book of correspondences, an attempt to discover and to observe the associations of the crucial elements in Godard's life, work, and times. It is a book that moves from his very first critical articles through all of his major films, all the while showing how his art is intertwined with his personal and intellectual experience and is inseparable from the social, aesthetic, and philosophical currents of the era.

Jean-Luc Godard is an artist as dominant, as crucial, as protean, and as influential as Picasso, but he is a Picasso who vanished from public consciousness and from the encyclopedias after the first heady flourish of Cubism. My hope is to provide guideposts that will help readers and movie watchers accompany Godard from his time of promise through the early years of flamboyant innovation, but also far beyond—on the long, lonely, yet exhilarating and indeed epochal journey of his artistic life.

EVERYTHING
IS CINEMA

A photograph of Jean-Luc Godard at age ten, as it appears in his film *JLG/JLG* (1994) *(TCD-Prod DB © Gaumont / DR)*

one

"WE DO NOT THINK, WE ARE THOUGHT"

IN THE SECOND EDITION, DATED JUNE 1950, OF A THIN newspaper-like magazine published in Paris, *La Gazette du cinéma*, a nineteen-year-old writer made a modest debut. Jean-Luc Godard's article, simply titled "Joseph Mankiewicz," was a short and breezy overview of that director's career, though, as in the following reference to the director's recent film, *A Letter to Three Wives*, it was devoted less to his films than to Mankiewicz himself: " 'One can judge a woman's past by her present,' Mankiewicz says somewhere: this letter to three married women is also three letters to the same woman, one whom the director probably loved."

In an eight-paragraph jaunt, the young writer lightly sketched a conception of the cinema that was as intensely personal as it was revolutionary: he suggested that films are one with the world offscreen. Casually, and without any theoretical fuss, he treated films as something more than creations that bore the mark of their makers; he considered them inseparable from the lives of their creators.

Godard's piece on the front page of the next issue of *La Gazette*, "For a Political Cinema," is as provocative now as it seemed at the time. In it, he put forth an aesthetic framework that daringly overrode basic ideological distinctions in the name of specifically cinematic values.

One afternoon, at the end of the Gaumont newsreel, we opened our eyes wide with pleasure: young German Communists were marching in a May Day celebration. Suddenly, space was only the lines of lips and bodies, time only the raising of fists in the air . . . By the sole force of propaganda that was animating them, these young people were beautiful.[1]

Godard compared these young people to St. Sebastian and to the youths in classical Greek sculpture: the state of possession, albeit an intellectual one, that resulted from the thrall of ideology seemed to him to resemble religious devotion and thus to confer on its subject a transcendent serenity. He added that in Soviet films, "the actor infallibly returns to what he originally was, a priest. *The Fall of Berlin* and *The Battle of Stalingrad* are coronation masses." Godard treated expressions of Communist and Christian faith as equivalent, and admired the similar power of Nazi propaganda films, which had so recently been pressed upon Parisian moviegoers by German occupiers:

> We could not forget *Hitler Youth Quex,* certain passages of films by Leni Riefenstahl, several shocking newsreels from the Occupation, the maleficent ugliness of *The Eternal Jew.* It is not the first time that art is born of constraint.

Godard praised these films not for their political message but for their psychology: they depicted people under the influence, and it hardly mattered whether that influence was political or religious. He took all fanaticisms to be alike and to be equally beautiful. Without equating the far left and the far right politically, Godard equated them aesthetically.

The essay ends with an exhortation: "French filmmakers in search of scripts, how have you unfortunate souls not yet filmed the assessment of taxes, the death of Philippe Henriod [*sic*], the wonderful life of Danielle Casanova?" Henriot, the Minister of Information in the Vichy government and a frequent and familiar orator on French radio under occupation, was killed in 1944 by Resistance fighters. Casanova, the founder of a Communist youth newspaper in the 1930s, was a Resistance fighter who died at Auschwitz. Godard endorsed as equally cinematically fertile the actions of a collaborator, of a resister, and ordinary parliamentary infighters, and he took the adventures and anecdotes that arose in the course of contemporary and recent history to be the cinema's natural subject. The passions to which the characters in such films would bear witness were those that belonged to the real world, as verified by the reality from which they derived. The cinematic fictions that the young Godard dreamed of arose from the documentary impulse.

Moreover, his idealistic depiction of the young fanatic was a touching, if oblique, self-portrait. He was leading a life of singular and exalted purpose: his monomaniacal fervor was ignited by movies, and he gave remarkably definitive expression to it in the following issue of *La Gazette*.

The October 1950 edition featured a brief note by "H.L."—Hans Lucas, "Jean-Luc" in German, a pseudonym that Godard occasionally adopted through 1955—on a documentary film about Alexander Calder's mobiles. One mercurial sentence sums up with a self-revealing clarity the adolescent

Godard's relation to the cinema: "At the cinema, we do not think, we are thought."[2] This observation was less an avowal of passivity than of the will to self-transformation through movies. It indicates Godard's consuming submission to cinema and the extent to which he experienced it as a personal epiphany, indeed a transfiguration. Godard had reached the essence of the experience at once, and conveyed it in an unabashed confession. In a single aphorism, he broke down the barriers of aesthetic distance and contemplation that separate the cinema, its viewers, and its makers. At the earliest stage of his work, Godard's existence and that of the cinema were already fused.

These three articles delineate a coherent and comprehensive cinematic philosophy, one which Godard would realize and rework in a wide variety of forms in a filmmaking career that began in 1954 and continues to this day. The ideas that they sketch are the unity of the filmmaker with the film, the inseparability of both from the social world at large, the credence of a devout moviegoer in the reality of the world as presented in the cinema, and the aesthetic fecundity of this fanatical submission. The viewer who was "thought" at the cinema was Godard himself; the filmmaker who was one with his film would be Godard himself; and his films would be the seemingly infinite variations on the theme of his singular faith in the cinema and in its ability to preserve and to reflect both the reality of the filmmaker and of his times through the intersection of personal stories and political history.

But each of these principles came with a price tag. Godard's submission to the cinema risked alienation from life. Films conceived as the expression of fanatical devotion to the cinema risked becoming a closed circuit of self-satisfied self-reference to the exclusion of reality. The identification of the film and the filmmaker risked the creation of a cult of personality that would detract attention from the filmmaker's work. And the avidly omnivorous, ideologically indeterminate recording of political currents ran the risk of detachment and ambiguity. Over time, Godard would recognize all of these risks and, in his work and his life, would attempt to confront and to overcome them.

THE STORY OF Jean-Luc Godard's work is one of a conversion to the secular religion of art and, specifically, to the art of cinema. For this art form, for this sort of passion, the holy city was, and remains, Paris.

The movies started in France, with the work of the Lumière brothers,[3] and the special relationship of Paris to the movies is in large part due to that city's central role in French civilization. For France, Paris is three things in one: it is the country's New York, Washington, D.C., and Hollywood—the cultural, political, and cinematic capital. The three domains are much more strongly interconnected in France than in the United States, and activity in any one of the three fields is quickly reflected in the other two. As a result, in

France the movie business has also been, all along, both a strain of high art and a sensitive political barometer.

French filmmakers participated in, and often emerged from, literary circles, and Parisian artists took a serious interest in the movies almost from their inception. It was the French critic Ricciotto Canudo who called the cinema the "sixth art" in a 1911 essay (and the "seventh art" in 1919). Charlie Chaplin and D. W. Griffith were French cultural heroes as early as 1916, and artists of all sorts, especially the surrealists, took the cinema very seriously. Jean Cocteau made a film in 1930; Salvador Dali collaborated with Luis Buñuel on *Un Chien andalou* and *L'Age d'or;* the film director Sacha Guitry was first a famous playwright; the greatest French prewar filmmaker, Jean Renoir, who made his first film in 1925, was the son of Auguste Renoir, the artist. Unlike American writers, for whom working on movies usually meant going to Hollywood and setting literature aside, such French writers as Cocteau, Jean-Paul Sartre, André Malraux, Jean Giraudoux, and Jacques Prévert were active in the cinema without having to distance themselves, geographically or practically, from the literary scene.

Postwar Paris was teeming with movies, especially American movies. Having been deprived of Hollywood productions under the German occupation, moviegoers were hungry to see those that had been made during World War II as well as the latest ones, and they flooded the screens. These films too were taken seriously, and nowhere more so than in a magazine called *La Revue du cinéma,* which was published by France's most prestigious literary publisher, Gallimard. When the fifteen-year-old Jean-Luc Godard came to Paris in 1946 to attend the prestigious Lycée Buffon, he entered a lively and burgeoning cinematic scene, one that was energized both by the quantity of films available and by the quality of thought in circulation regarding the "seventh art." It was enriched by contact with the literary, artistic, and intellectual elite that embraced it, and was riven by political controversies that mirrored the political divisions of postwar France—some of which were aroused by the cinema itself.

GODARD WAS BORN on December 3, 1930, in the elegant seventh arrondissement of Paris. His father, Paul Godard, a doctor, moved the family to Switzerland four years later. His mother, Odile, née Monod, was the daughter of one of the most prominent bankers in France, Julien Monod, a founder of the Banque Paribas. Monod was also an extremely literate man, a close friend of the writer Paul Valéry and, after Valéry's death in 1945, his literary executor.

Family documents include a letter that Valéry wrote to Odile Monod in April 1928, on the occasion of her engagement to Paul Godard. She was eighteen years old at the time; her fiancé was twenty-seven. Her parents opposed the marriage; Paul Godard, though Protestant like the Monods, was not of their social station. Nonetheless, the couple married in 1928. They settled temporarily in Paris, and their first child, Rachel, was born on January 1, 1930. (Valéry's letter to the newborn, dated January 6, 1930, is published in the collection *Lettres à quelques-uns.*) Godard also has two younger siblings, a brother, Claude, born in 1933, and a sister, Véronique, born in 1937.

The most comprehensive research on the subject of Godard's family and youth has been done by Colin MacCabe, who was, in the late 1980s and early 1990s, Godard's authorized biographer; the results of his research were published in 2003, in his *Portrait of the Artist at Seventy.*[4] Paul Godard worked at a private medical clinic, La Lignière, near Gland, on the shore of Lake Geneva, between Geneva and Lausanne, and ultimately opened a clinic of his own, near Lausanne. Broken plaster in a wall there was said in family lore to have been made by young Jean-Luc's head during a transport of rage. To see a photograph of the wall is to fear for any child whose head might have done it.[5] His mother wrote of the toddler Godard's furious temper, calling him a *grand éclabousseur* (a great spatterer).[6]

The family was prosperous and cultured. Reading aloud from literature was a common form of domestic entertainment and ritual. Godard's grandfather, Julien Monod, enforced humanistic rules, including the requirement that youngsters recite literature at the dinner table. Each year, on his maternal grandparents' wedding anniversary, young Jean-Luc was expected to recite Valéry's poem "Le Cimetière marin" (The Seaside Cemetery).[7] (Moreover, Godard recalled receiving Latin lessons from Valéry.)[8] Religion was part of the family's cultural heritage as well, and Godard recalled attending Protestant "temple" regularly though without doctrinaire devotion: he considered it a casual habit ("I went, the same way I played soccer or did gymnastics")[9] and, with his grandfather Monod, debated the minister's sermons.

When World War II started, nine-year-old Jean-Luc Godard was in Brittany on vacation with relatives, and it was only with some difficulty that he could return to Switzerland. Godard spent most of the war in Switzerland, though he and members of his family habitually crossed Lake Geneva in a small boat to make clandestine visits to their grandfather's estate on the French side of the lake.

During the war, Godard's parents worked with the Red Cross and, Godard came to believe, had knowledge of the concentration camps established by Nazi Germany. MacCabe emphasizes the pro-English sympathies of Paul Godard (who had studied in London and, during the war, sheltered an English prisoner of war), yet Godard often spoke instead of his father's pro-German sympathies, and, following his family's lead, he was rooting for the

Germans. He followed the course of the war on a map, with pins representing the movement of the opposing armies as reported in newspapers; he cheered on the advances of the German army and lamented its reversals, and later recalled, "When Rommel lost at El Alamein, I was deeply affected, a little as if my favorite soccer team had lost a game."

Godard's maternal grandparents were supporters of Vichy. Godard later described his maternal grandfather as "anti-Jew" and an "anti-Semite," and remembered hearing Julien Monod refer to his doctor as a *youpin* (kike).[10] At home, the family listened to Vichy-run radio, where Jean-Luc grew accustomed to the rhetoric of pro-German politicians and commentators and remembered, decades later, the rapt attention when speeches by Philippe Henriot were broadcast. The days of Henriot's assassination (in 1944) and of the execution of Robert Brasillach, the right-wing critic and novelist and anti-Semitic, pro-Nazi propagandist (in 1945), were days of mourning in the Godard house.[11]

Godard recalled spending about a year and a half, from the ages of twelve and thirteen, in wartime Vichy, where his maternal grandfather "knew some people." Godard recalled that he always had an "affinity" for Julien Monod, whose sympathies were clearly suggested by the reading that he shared with his grandson Jean-Luc, as Godard later recalled: "I read *Les Décombres,* by Lucien Rebatet, because my grandfather was ultra-literary . . . At night, we read aloud. We read Rebatet's novel."[12] Rebatet, who was convicted of collaboration in 1946 and spent six years in prison, was a vehement anti-Semite and actively endorsed France's pro-Nazi regime. *Les Décombres* (The Ruins), his lengthy screed about the decline of France—in his view, due largely to French Jewry and reversible by collaboration with Germany—was said to be "for the little Parisian collaborationist world, the great politico-literary event of 1942."[13]

The young Godard was an eager reader; his preferred fare was the children's adventure novel, such as *Le Voyage d'Edgar,* by Edouard Peisson, whose work was popular at the time. His mother was an avid reader of French classics; on his fourteenth birthday, she presented him with a copy of André Gide's *Les Nourritures terrestres;* his exalted experience with it converted him from his boyish taste for adventure writing to the literary novel. He was particularly fond of Gide's *Les Faux-Monnayeurs* (*The Counterfeiters*), and the novels of Georges Bernanos, Jacques Chardonne, Marcel Jouhandeau, Julien Green, and André Malraux. From his father, Godard acquired a taste for German romanticism, and as an adolescent, read works by Hermann Broch, Thomas Mann, and Robert Musil.[14]

Godard was not a frequent moviegoer in childhood (except during his stay in Vichy, where, he remembered, he often attended popular movies of the day)[15] nor was he particularly attracted to the medium, except as casual entertainment. He attributed his introduction to the cinema as an art form to reading—first from André Malraux's essay, "Outline of a Psychology of Cinema," which was originally published in *Verve* magazine in 1940, a copy of which his mother had saved and which he found by chance; and then *La Revue du cinéma*, which (after its first run of publication from 1928 to 1931) was relaunched in 1946, and which Godard read avidly despite being unable to see most of the films it discussed.[16]

In 1946, Godard went to study at the Lycée Buffon in Paris, where he intended to prepare for specialized mathematics exams to enter engineering school. Instead, he began to watch an endless number of movies, and several of his relatives recalled that he had already begun to write screenplays. His mother was able to arrange an introduction for young Godard to one of the editors of *La Revue du cinéma*, Jacques Doniol-Valcroze, who was the son of one of her childhood friends, though at the time nothing practical came of it.

Family connections afforded him a view of the most rarefied strata of artistic achievement and cultural sophistication that Paris had to offer. Through his grandfather's associations, Godard was lodged in Paris with the writer Jean Schlumberger, a friend of André Gide, who was a frequent visitor. The sixteen-year-old Godard also accompanied the two older men to a celebrated recitation by Antonin Artaud at the Théâtre du Vieux-Colombier on January 13, 1947.[17]

However, Godard failed his baccalaureate exam in 1948, and returned to Switzerland, where he studied at a high school in Lausanne and lived with his parents, whose marriage was breaking up. He was already interested in the movies, and frequented a café in Geneva, the Parador, with a group of bookish adolescents that included Roland Tolmatchoff, also a film fanatic, who later recalled: "I was encyclopedic, I could tell you who the set designer of a little American film from the '30s was, so we gravitated to each other because of the cinema."[18] (Another member of the circle was an extreme-rightist philosopher, Jean Parvulesco.)[19]

Meanwhile, Godard's older sister, Rachel, who was a talented artist (and ultimately became an art teacher), introduced him to modern art, and he tried his hand at painting, in an abstract style that was reminiscent of early Abstract Expressionism or the works of Nicolas de Staël. (His mother arranged for his canvases to be put on display at his father's mountain clinic.)

Godard went to a boarding school in Thonon, near Grenoble, to cram for the retest, which he passed. Returning to Paris in 1949, he enrolled in "propédeutique," the first year of studies at the Sorbonne, though Tolmatchoff recalled that Godard, who was already fanatical about movies, went with the intention of finding his way into the cinema. In Paris, Godard took courses in ethnology (in which he was awarded a "certificate") and in "filmology" (a sociological and linguistic approach to films, championed by the critic Henri Agel), but soon abandoned his studies (later explaining that he preferred "[Juliette] Gréco to Greek").[20] His family was ready to pay for him to study art, but he decided against it; he applied for admission to the most prominent Paris film school, IDHEC (Institut des Hautes Etudes Cinématographiques), but was rejected.[21]

He watched movies instead, and frequented the most important place to see them in postwar Paris, a museum-like facility called the Cinémathèque.

THE CINÉMATHÈQUE HAD been founded by Henri Langlois and Georges Franju in 1936. Langlois, born in 1914 in Ottoman Smyrna, was already a film buff at age four. Moving to Paris with his family in 1922, he haunted its numerous movie theaters, and when he was seventeen years old—in the early days of talking pictures, when old prints of silent films were being discarded as obsolete—he started to collect these relics and declared that he was founding a museum for their preservation and projection. (After the war, Franju became an important director, beginning with his 1949 documentary *Le Sang des bêtes* [Blood of the Beasts].)

Langlois's taste was remarkably wide-ranging and prescient. Though, in the 1930s, there were other film curators, including at New York's Museum of Modern Art, who sought to preserve silent films, Langlois rapidly went further. In 1939, Langlois—already an acknowledged expert—astonished MOMA's film staff by declaring that a new film which he had just seen at a nearby theater, the popular *Only Angels Have Wings,* was sure to be recognized eventually as an enduring work of art and should be acquired for the museum's collection at once. Like so many other Hollywood studio films of the sound era, this film, directed by Howard Hawks, has indeed come to be acknowledged as an artistic classic—and this recognition is due largely to Langlois's advocacy.

The process, however, was gradual, and was delayed by World War II, when Langlois saved prints, such as those belonging to Jewish producers, from confiscation and destruction (with the covert help of a German officer in Paris, Frank Hensel, who was also a film buff), and also held clandestine screenings of films which were forbidden by the German occupiers.

After the Liberation, Langlois's public screenings quickly became a focal point for film enthusiasts and artistic luminaries, including Jean-Paul Sartre, Simone de Beauvoir, Georges Braque, and André Breton. At his screening room on the avenue de Messine, they rediscovered films that had been rendered invisible by the war's restrictions, along with classics, familiar and hidden, old and new, from world cinema. In order to show the films while circumventing France's regulations concerning taxation and censorship (then, as now, films released in France were submitted to a review board for a "visa de contrôle"), Langlois—who also collected diverse forms of movie memorabilia, from classic posters to famous costumes—declared his collection the Musée du cinéma (Museum of Cinema), which offered its screenings to museum visitors for a trivial surcharge added to its admission fee.

As a collector, Langlois was an omnivore; as a curator, he was a critic of genius; as a film lover, he was a visionary. He was not at all modest about his intentions: he wanted his Cinémathèque to be "a sort of center where people come as they are and then leave different."[22] He offered his habitués a history of cinema based less on chronology than on thematic connections between films. For instance, from October 12 to 30, 1950, the Cinémathèque offered a series of rare silent classics, including Feuillade's *Vendémiaire* (1917), D. W. Griffith's *One Exciting Night* (1922), and *The Overcoat* (1926), by Kozintsev and Trauberg, along with two postwar films by Dovzhenko, science documentaries by Jean Painlevé, unreleased films by Joris Ivens, a wartime film by Leni Riefenstahl, an American independent film called *The Quiet One,* by Sidney Meyers, about a troubled child and the school that rescues him, and *Never Give a Sucker an Even Break.*

The creation of a new cinema was an inseparable part of Langlois's self-appointed mission, and, not content with the passive viewing of his literary habitués, he also saw to their cinematic efforts, providing Raymond Queneau, Jean Genet, and others with film stock for their own films (the one that has survived is Genet's *Un Chant d'amour* [A Song of Love], from 1950). Yet his screenings were Langlois's most important contribution to the creation of a future cinema. They offered young people a comprehensive overview of the cinema to date and oriented that history in terms of his own refined aesthetic taste; and Godard was one of the assiduous young habitués of the Cinémathèque whose enthusiasms Langlois cultivated.

THE POSTWAR PARIS in which Godard came of intellectual age was dominated by the influence of one thinker, Jean-Paul Sartre (1905–1980). During the war, Sartre had written a philosophical treatise, *L'Etre et le néant* (*Being and Nothingness*), published in 1943, in which he displayed his newfound absorption in the work of Martin Heidegger. There, Sartre sought to define human existence in terms of history—though not, as Heidegger did, abstractly, but in terms of the specifics of social life and the practicalities of political action. Though this massive tome brought Sartre a quiet renown in academic circles, his wartime experience as a playwright, a screenwriter, a journalist, and an organizer of a resistance group led him to consider how he, as a writer, could play a role in the history of his times.

Sartre later described his impression of the opportunity that the Liberation offered: "At that moment, as a way of adapting to what was taking place, I conceived the idea of a total public, something that no previous writer could ever have had. The writer could have a total public if he said to the total public what the total public itself thought, albeit not so well."[23] Immediately after the war, Sartre sought to achieve this identification of himself with a public that went far beyond élite literary circles: in order to become the defining thinker of his era, Sartre knew that he would need to become famous—and he understood that, as a result of the politicization of life during wartime, his postwar fame would continue to depend upon politics.

Starting in 1945, Sartre flooded Paris with his work. He cofounded with the philosopher Maurice Merleau-Ponty a monthly intellectual journal, *Les Temps modernes*—a reference to *Modern Times,* by Charlie Chaplin, who exemplified the artist who was simultaneously profound, original, emblematic of his times, a left-wing social critic, and undeniably, irresistibly popular. Sartre inaugurated the first issue with his "Présentation" (Introduction), in which he asserted the intrinsically political aspect of his own work, and of writing as such, in the ideal of "engaged literature":

> The writer is situated in his era: each word has reverberations. Each silence too. I hold Flaubert and Goncourt responsible for the repression that followed the Commune because they did not write a line to prevent it. Some will say that it wasn't their business. But was the trial of Calas Voltaire's business? Was the conviction of Dreyfus Zola's business? Was the administration of the Congo Gide's business? Each of these authors, at a particular circumstance in their lives, determined their responsibility as writers. The occupation taught us ours. Since we act upon our times by our very existence, we decide that this action shall be willed.

On October 29, 1945, Sartre gave a lecture sponsored by Club Maintenant (The Now Club) titled "Existentialism Is a Humanism." The event had been widely advertised; the hall was filled to capacity with a clamorous, at times rowdy, crowd; the speech was a raucous, much-reported success, and the printed text became an instant bestseller. As if overnight, in a success that almost a decade of philosophical and literary effort had prepared, Sartre became a celebrity and then an icon.

In the four years that followed, Sartre published fourteen books—novels, literary criticism, political commentary, plays, philosophical treatises, essay collections, transcribed colloquia—and generated a vast number of articles, interviews, radio broadcasts, journalistic reports, and public appearances. A public figure, indeed a world-renowned figure, as famous in the United States as at home, Sartre soon became something more: he became a brand name, exactly as planned.

In "Existentialism Is a Humanism," Sartre explained that his philosophy, which had been accused by Communists of subjectivism and by Christians of pessimism, was in fact "optimistic" and "a doctrine of action"—of political action which was favorable to the left. The conception of existentialism as humanism was, at the time, far from obvious: the bilious literary misanthropy of Sartre's prewar novels was familiar, as was the Nazi affiliation of Martin Heidegger, the philosopher who inspired Sartre's conjunction of philosophy and history. (Heidegger had briefly served as the rector of the University of Freiburg in 1934 and had publicly praised Hitler and the Third Reich.) But Sartre, during the war, had cast his lot with the left, and now was, in effect, reprocessing Heidegger's ideas in order to claim them for the left—and, at the same time, offering a new generation of leftists an avant-garde philosophy that seemed more exciting than another gloss on Marx.

As Sartre acknowledged, his sense of collective political enterprise, distilled in the notion of "engagement"—with political action as the defining trait of self-definition, and political inaction as a sin of omission—was a vestige of France's moral crises of World War II. His theory, a kind of metaphysical prolongation of the war and its occupation and resistance, was a rejection of modern liberal democracy (and its baseline ballot-box form of political participation), which had failed to recognize the German menace and to protect France from it. Sartre intended the "engagement" of a writer to signify the obligation to take sides, to convert writing into action—specifically, into a form of political action as defined by the one particular type of political commitment that was implied by Sartre's philosophy—on the far left.

In order to posit a prolonged resistance, the engaged thinker would also need to define it in opposition to a surrogate prolonged occupation. And the new occupation that Sartre perceived, and challenged, was American.

THE INFLUX OF American films quickly became a contested issue in postwar France. The "deserted and famished Paris" that Sartre described on August 20, 1945,[24] turned its eyes beseechingly to the last best hope for economic relief, the United States. Charles de Gaulle, France's postwar leader, sent former prime minister Léon Blum to negotiate a package of debt relief and other direct and indirect economic aid with James Byrnes, the U.S. secretary of state.[25] The so-called Blum-Byrnes Accords, announced on May 28, 1946 (after the resignation of de Gaulle as president on January 20, 1946), assured France of various forms of financial assistance from the United States. A sidebar agreement, announced two days later, concerned the cinema: it required each French movie house to show four weeks of French films per quarter. Though the measure seemed designed to protect the French film industry, its practical effect—as Byrnes and Blum knew—was that for nine out of every thirteen weeks, each screen would show American movies.[26]

The French film industry, and its unions, which were largely affiliated

with the Communist Party, protested vehemently that the accord would result in a drastic decrease in local film production. At an emergency meeting
of industry notables, the actor Louis Jouvet warned, "The alteration in our
public's taste would be irremediable and mortal. Raised on wines from Bur-
gundy and Bordeaux, our stomachs will have to become accustomed to
Coca-Cola."[27] A headline in the Communist daily *L'Humanité* trumpeted,
"The Franco-American Accords Condemn the French Cinema to Death."[28]
According to *L'Humanité*'s (unsigned) report on the emergency meeting,
"Evoking the struggle of the Resistance, the well-known artist André Luguet
energetically called for unity against the Blum-Byrnes accords."[29]

Communist opposition to the presence in France of American movies soon
intensified, for reasons having little to do with the cinema. When de Gaulle resigned as head of the postwar government in January 1946, he precipitated the
founding of the Fourth Republic, by referendum, on October 13, 1946.[30] The
new parliamentary system produced chronically unstable governments: in its
twelve years of existence, it yielded twenty-two heads of state, only two of whom
stayed in power for a year, and two of whom lasted as few as two days. Until the
Soviet invasion of Hungary in 1956, the Communist Party was the leading vote-
getter in France, receiving between 26 and 28 percent of the vote.

Yet, in the spring of 1947, under American pressure, the French government dismissed its Communist ministers (and was rewarded with the Mar-
shall Plan). From that point on, the Communists resisted American films
even more ferociously, as seen in *L'Humanité*:

THE CAMPAIGN OF LIES AND OF DEMORALIZATION
BY AMERICAN IMPERIALISM

> As for American films, the invasion of which was facilitated by the accords
> signed by Blum in Washington at the sacrifice of the French film industry,
> they strive toward the same goal: depraving our children by the glorification
> of gangsterism or erotic images, propagating the spirit of submission to the
> great benefit of religiosity.[31]

Like many other movie enthusiasts in Paris, however, Jean George
Auriol—founder and editor of *La Revue du cinéma,* the ambitious and sophisticated movie magazine that he had put out from 1928 to 1931 and that
he brought back to life in 1946 under the aegis of France's most renowned
literary publisher, Gallimard—thought otherwise:

> As for me, I've seen hundreds of American films, and everyone knows more or
> less what they represent in comparison to a French work: something lively, ac-
> tive, palpitating, diverting, often tonic, sometimes extravagant. A product that

is exciting, like champagne, coffee, or tea, in short, one of the rare gifts that our civilization can still offer us.[32]

Of the American films that had been embargoed during the war, none aroused more eager anticipation in Paris than Orson Welles's first feature, *Citizen Kane*. But when it was finally shown in Paris in 1946, Sartre took it upon himself to take the Wunderkind's reputation down a notch. Writing in *L'Ecran français* (The French Screen) in 1946, Sartre praised Welles's damning portrait of the plutocrat as an act of "anti-fascism," but he blamed the director for abandoning the "realist naiveté" of prewar Hollywood, asking, "Doesn't this film move us away from the cinema in general?" Though he recognized Welles's innovations in cinematic composition ("découpage") and technique, he nonetheless condemned them, declaring that Welles's characters were "presented in an intellective order" and thus were "dead": "The technical discoveries of the film are not designed to render life." Sartre saw in the popular American cinema a model for an authentically popular socialist realism for left-wing artists to adopt, and blamed Welles for not advancing it: "Since he isn't rooted in the masses and since he doesn't share their concerns, he will make an abstract, intellectual, conceptual film." Sartre's criticism was summed up in his finger-wagging warning: "For us, *Citizen Kane* is not an example to follow."[33] At least, not for French filmmakers who would come up to Sartre's standards for "engaged" artists.

The most significant response to Sartre came from a young critic, André Bazin, whose essay, "The Technique of *Citizen Kane*," Sartre himself published in *Les Temps modernes* in 1947.[34] Bazin praised the film for what he considered its singular artistic richness, and argued that Welles achieved this richness mainly by his use of the deep-focus technique. Bazin claimed that Welles, through this device, reinvented his art form "as Malraux, Hemingway, Dos Passos reinvented their own to their own ends." Indeed, his defense of the film depends mainly on his interpretation of Welles's reliance on this figure of style, which he described as "an endorsement of integral realism, a way of making reality homogeneous, of treating it as indivisible." Thus Bazin argued, in exact contradiction to Sartre, that Welles's methods were better suited to render life than any preceding ones, and that it was Welles's ability to do so which comprised his, and the film's, greatness.

Bazin, born in 1917, had planned a career as a teacher of literature but was kept from the classroom by his stuttering. Instead, he became an unofficial but enormously influential teacher of the cinema. A left-wing Catholic, he organized wartime film screenings and discussions for Work and Culture, a workers' education group that was affiliated with a labor union but was nonetheless officially tolerated by the German occupiers. Bazin's screenings and his extraordinary post-screening discussions attracted crowds, and served as a model for the film clubs that sprang up throughout France after the Liberation. Meanwhile, during the war and the German occupation—under which, as a result of German policy, French filmmaking flourished—Bazin had begun to write film criticism,[35] and after the war he published substantial and influential articles in La Revue du cinéma and Les Temps modernes.

Bazin's theoretical writings, which were launched in 1945 with the essay "The Ontology of the Photographic Image," revolved around his conception of the relation of image to reality—as he conceived it. He argued that, in photography, "an image of the world is formed automatically, without the creative intervention of man. The personality of the photographer enters into the proceedings only in his selection of the object to be photographed and by way of the purpose he has in mind." He claimed that photography "affects us like a phenomenon in nature"—and defined the cinema as "objectivity in time."[36]

Before Bazin, leading film theorists (most crucially, Sergei Eisenstein) had argued that the essence of cinema was the editing of film, the sequential ordering of different images in order to generate mental effects in the viewer. Bazin, however, asserted that film editing techniques serve mainly to falsify reality by breaking up space and time. Instead, he advocated the use of long, continuous shots in order to preserve spatial and temporal continuity; thus he extolled Citizen Kane's deep-focus technique, which permitted many planes of action to be seen clearly in a single frame and allowed them to unfold in a single uncut shot. Bazin evinced an extraordinary faith in the authenticity of the photographic and cinematic image, as well as an extraordinary humility before its power.

It is hard to imagine, however, that a critic who advocated the filmmaker's nonintervention and the effacement of the filmmaker's personality in favor of the "automatic" working of the camera could be much of an inspiration to fiery young aspiring artists. Indeed, another young critic, who, unlike Bazin, dreamed of making films, took up the charge of arousing a more inspiring and active view of the cinema—and this young critic's work got the teenage Godard's attention and aroused his interest.

MAURICE SCHÉRER, BORN in 1920, was a high school teacher, a novelist, and a film enthusiast who, in a trio of articles (one in La Revue du cinéma in 1948 and two in Les Temps modernes in 1948 and 1949), attempted to formulate an ambitious and comprehensive theoretical definition of the cinema that differed radically from Bazin's. In the first article, "Cinema, the Art of Space," Schérer rejected Bazin's emphasis on the representation of three-dimensional space within an image. Instead, Schérer argued that objects within that space, especially the "objects" known as actors, generated increased "meaning" from the way that a director placed them in space by means of film editing: "Movements and gestures whose meaning seemed contingent are in a sense—by their insertion into a certain spatial universe—grounded in necessity."[37]

In the second article, "For a Talking Cinema," Schérer called attention to a film's dialogue as one of the crucial elements that actors bring to life in the film's "spatial universe."[38] In the third, "We No Longer Love the Cinema," Schérer prophesied a new generation of film artists that his principles would spawn:

> We begin to envy the task that awaits the future filmmaker who . . . , in orienting our attention, as in the earliest days of the silent film but doubtless more subtly, toward the *acting* of the actor, will construct the basis of his new language out of the rich conjunction of their [*sic*] words, their expressions, their gestures and their movements.[39]

What was at stake was not merely theoretical or academic: Schérer was attempting to express his own experience of the cinema, his own ambitions, and his own tastes. He loved many films which are recognized to be classics but that Bazin, with his particularly literal concept of realism, dismissed. In his writings, Schérer explained the aesthetic virtues of a range of films neglected by Bazin, including those of Buster Keaton, many German "expressionist" films (especially F. W. Murnau's), and such recent American productions as the films of Preston Sturges, Jean Renoir (who had been active in Hollywood during and after the war), and, especially, Alfred Hitchcock (who, Bazin wrote in 1950, had "taken us in").

In practice, Schérer regularly put his enthusiasms on display at the Ciné-Club du Quartier Latin (CCQL), founded in 1947–48 by one of his students, Frédéric Froeschel. Schérer was the club's animating spirit and intellectual leader, and in practical terms, the moderator of its vigorous public debates after screenings. Having read Maurice Schérer's essays, Jean-Luc Godard began to frequent the CCQL.

Schérer, whose family was unaware of his practical activity in the field of cinema, adopted a pseudonym on the masthead of the CCQL's journal, *La Gazette du cinéma*. Indeed, Schérer's writings, with their emphasis on the speech and gestures of actors, foretold the films that he would make under that pseudonym—Eric Rohmer. Because of his important subsequent career as a filmmaker, the pseudonym ultimately usurped his given name.

AT THE CCQL and the Cinémathèque, Godard met another young regular at the screenings, François Truffaut. Born in 1932, Truffaut had dropped out of school at age fourteen, in 1946, in order to devote his time to watching films. In 1948, he attempted to found his own ciné-club, the Cercle Ciné-mane (The Cinemanic Circle), with little money and disastrous results. He proved unable to draw many cinéphiles to his Sunday-morning screenings, because of competition at the same hour from the screenings of Bazin's Work and Culture ciné-club (which Godard, a member, frequented).[40] The teenage Truffaut had the audacity to ask Bazin, a central figure in French film culture, to change his screening times. Though Bazin turned Truffaut down, he found the young enthusiast sympathetic and invited him to visit again.

This encounter would soon prove fortuitous for Truffaut. To keep his club afloat, Truffaut borrowed money from his father's colleague, then stole and sold a typewriter from his father's office—an incident later refashioned in his first feature film, *The 400 Blows*—to pay off his debt. Truffaut's father forced him to confess to his misdeeds in writing, and then conveyed the young man, and the confession, to the nearest police station.

From January to March 1949, Truffaut was confined in a juvenile detention center; a psychologist's consultation with André Bazin proved decisive in his release. Bazin vouched for Truffaut and, upon his release, hired him at Work and Culture as his personal secretary. Meanwhile, Truffaut kept up his moviegoing habits. At the Objectif 49 film festival held in Biarritz in July–August 1949, a kind of counter-Cannes begun by Bazin, Jean Cocteau, and others, Truffaut encountered Rohmer and, upon his return to Paris, began to attend the CCQL screenings and to partake vociferously in the post-screening discussions. His most vigorous debate partner, and soon his friend, was a young man three years his elder, Jacques Rivette.

Soon after arriving in Paris in late 1949 at age twenty-one, with years of ciné-club experience from his native Rouen behind him and his 16mm film, *Aux Quatre Coins* (To the Four Corners) in hand, Rivette found his way to the CCQL to hear Rohmer, whose writings he knew and admired. Soon, Rivette too became a regular in the post-film debates and quiz-competitions, at which, according to Rohmer, he was "unbeatable."[41]

As Rivette later recalled, the eighty seats of the Cinémathèque's small screening room, on the avenue de Messine (a quiet neighborhood in the eighth arrondissement), "were full only for *L'Age d'or, The Blue Angel*, or *Potemkin*, but were practically empty for the films of Griffith, Stiller, and Murnau."[42] Truffaut said that only "five or six" people showed up for a screening of the 1932 *Kühle Wampe* (by Bertolt Brecht and Slatan Dudow). When Langlois's screening room was full, the young men watched the films lying flat on their backs on the floor in front of the first row.[43]

Like Rivette and Truffaut, Godard virtually lived at the movies, though usually did not participate in the public discussions. He met Rivette in the front row of the Cinémathèque, where they sat, side by side, night after night, for several months, until Godard broke the shy silence by declaring (with the formal *vous*), "It seems to me that I recognize you."[44] The Cinémathèque, the CCQL, Work and Culture, and other film clubs and movie theaters were Godard's constant haunts, and Truffaut and Rivette became his constant companions there. It was standard practice for them to see three or four films per day, or to spend the entire day in a single theater. For instance, when Godard and Rivette went to see Orson Welles's *Macbeth* (which opened in Paris in June 1950), they entered the theater at 2 PM and stayed for repeated showings, until Godard left at 10 PM; Rivette, who was more enthusiastic about the film, stayed put until midnight.[45] Because films at the Cinémathèque often finished very late, after the métro's service ended for the night—according to Truffaut, Langlois was simply indifferent to such practicalities—the young enthusiasts, who could not afford a taxi, walked together through the night, talking about what they had seen.

Their obsession, in terms of quantity of knowledge and depth of understanding of the cinema, would leave its mark in the criticism, and ultimately the films, of these young enthusiasts. But Godard was the first to write about this obsession as the end in itself. He did so in *La Gazette du cinéma*, the monthly newspaper-style magazine that Rohmer had developed from the in-house "Bulletin" of the CCQL. Its archly lowbrow title disguised its intellectual ambitions. The prestigious *La Revue du cinéma* had been discontinued in 1948 (when Gallimard editor Albert Camus persuaded his bosses that the cinema was not a topic worthy of the publisher's ongoing subsidy) and *L'Ecran français* had become, in the wake of the controversies regarding the Blum-Byrnes agreements, closely aligned with the Communist Party and its doctrinaire anti-Hollywood line. *La Gazette* was an outlet for Rohmer's own writings (the first issue featured his "Technical Study of 'Rope,'" the film by Alfred Hitchcock, on the front page), and also featured the work of his young acolytes; the second issue, of June 1950, featured Godard's notes on Joseph Mankiewicz, as well as an essay by Rivette about Jean Renoir's *The Southerner*.

Yet Godard and his friends were not planning to be professional film critics; they planned to make films, and they were not alone in their desire to do so. Literary Paris had a passion for the cinema. During the war, Sartre had written the screenplay for a film called *Typhus*, Jean Giraudoux co-scripted Robert Bresson's 1943 *Les Anges du Péché*, and Jean Cocteau wrote dialogue for Bresson's 1945 *Les Dames du Bois de Boulogne* (based on a text by Diderot). In 1946, Cocteau directed *Beauty and the Beast*, and his diary of the shoot, published the same year, was read with fascination by Godard, Rivette, and the others of the CCQL.[46]

For the intellectual bohemians who flocked around the underground nightclubs, or "caves," of St.-Germain-des-Prés to revel in the aura of (the largely absent) Sartre and de Beauvoir, the 16mm (amateur-format) film was "the medium of choice," according to Anne-Marie Cazalis (whom Jean Cocteau had dubbed one of the two "princesses of Existentialism" alongside her friend Juliette Gréco). She said that for the young people in her circle, the 16mm film had taken the place of the novel as a means of artistic expression.[47] In "Birth of a New Avant-Garde," published in *L'Ecran français* of March 30, 1948, the novelist and journalist Alexandre Astruc, who also made 16mm films, prophesied the era of the "Caméra stylo," the "camera-pen" with which "an artist can express his thought, as abstract as it may be, or can translate his obsessions exactly as is done today with the essay or the novel." Astruc, who had a hand in planning *La Gazette du cinéma* (his "Notes on Film Direction" appeared on the front page of the first issue), argued that the cinema had already revolutionized intellectual history: "Today a Descartes would lock himself in his room with a 16mm camera and film and would write on film the discourse on method [*sic*]."

Godard exemplified the philosophical filmmaker of Astruc's fantasy. Astruc later wrote of finding the teenage Godard sitting at the Café de Flore (Sartre and Simone de Beauvoir's wartime base of literary operations) with a rose in his hand and declaring that he would be "the Cocteau for the next generation."[48] Godard's father, Paul, later recalled, "He liked Sartre enormously, he more or less lived in St.-Germain-des-Prés,"[49] the neighborhood of the Café de Flore and other cafés and clubs favored by Sartre's followers. Godard himself later recalled, "I had encyclopedic tendencies. I wanted to read everything. I wanted to know everything. Existentialism was at its peak at that time. Through Sartre I discovered literature, and he led me to everything else."[50]

Jean Douchet remembered him reading two books a day, but Truffaut described Godard's literary bulimia differently: "He would go to people's apartments and look at the first and last page of every book on the shelf."[51] Godard's approach to literature was perfect for a future filmmaker, inasmuch as it extracted from books the broadest story outlines and grandly aphoristic phrases, but, in its indifference to the intricacies of plot and fine points of character, it was antithetical to literary craftsmanship—as Godard quickly discovered.

Suzanne Schiffman,[52] Godard's classmate in "filmology" and a member of the Cinémathèque circle, recalled that Godard not only planned to become a writer (his dream was to have a novel published by Gallimard)[53] but declared himself to be one: "He claimed that he wrote thirty pages every morning."[54] But Godard saw something in the cinema that he found redemptive, namely, its mechanical, automatic quality. "When we saw some movies," he recalled, "we were finally delivered from the terror of writing. We were no longer crushed by the spectre of the great writers."[55] In thrall to the cinema, and unquestioningly accepting the reality that it presented, Godard saw his attempts at literary representation trumped definitively by the power of the camera—and yet, his primordial dreams would ultimately reveal themselves in a cinema haunted by the primal, originary force of literature.

Like his friends from the CCQL and the Cinémathèque, Godard planned to follow the example of Orson Welles and make his first feature film by age twenty-five. But the deep-rooted philosophical elements at the basis of his thoughts about the cinema required a slow and gradual growth. Where his friends, especially Rivette and Rohmer, quickly acted on the impulse to begin making films, Godard, for whom watching films was already being part of the cinema, waited, and instead helped his friends as best he could.

THE LEFT BANK bohemian ferment of the Latin Quarter and St.-Germain-des-Prés yielded strange artistic and political byways, and Godard, from his involvement in cinéphile circles, found himself in their bewildering midst. In 1949, Rohmer took up a collection at the CCQL for the benefit of an English filmmaker of his putative acquaintance named Anthony Barrier. This starving artist was, however, none other than Rohmer himself, who used the money to make a 16mm film, *Sexual Rhapsody* (the title in English), with assistance from Godard and Rivette.

In the summer of 1950, Truffaut made plans to shoot a 16mm film, but the project was unrealized. At the same time, however, Rivette tried his hand at another 16mm project with a title reminiscent of that of his earlier *Aux Quatre Coins.* "Godard saw to the production of my film, *Quadrille,*" Rivette later recalled. "He was also the producer: he put up the money for the 16mm black and white reversible[56] film." Explaining Godard's ability to do so, Rivette added: "Nobody had any money; he had a little bit more."[57] Though Godard got a little money from his family, he admitted that the money that went into Rivette's film came from stealing and selling books from his grandfather Monod's "Valérianum," his collection of first, private, and rare editions by Paul Valéry.[58] The film featured four actors: two women, Liliane Litvin and Anne-Marie Cazalis; one of the two men was Godard. According to Rivette, "It ran forty minutes and absolutely nothing happens. It's just four people sitting around a table, looking at each other." Suzanne Schiffman recalled, "At a given moment a guy slapped a girl and he walked out."[59] The film was shown at the CCQL, where, according to Rivette, "After ten minutes, people started to leave, and at the end, the only ones who stayed were Jean-Luc and a girl."

In a "16mm Chronicle," published in the November 1950 issue of *La Gazette du cinéma*—the last before the publication folded due to poor sales—Godard reproached Henri Langlois of the Cinémathèque for failing to program Rivette's film. He praised the film as "an homage to the Lubitsch of *Lady Windermere's Fan*," but did not mention his own participation in the film, behind and before the camera, or his friendship with its director.

The avant-gardism of Rivette's work arose from the Latin Quarter milieu that he frequented along with Godard. Asked whether the film was a surrealist provocation, Rivette later said, "No, Lettrist." As he explained, "The Lettrists were the successors to the surrealists and the precursors of the Situationists," and he added that the leader of the Lettrists, Isidore Isou, told him that the film was "ingenious."[60]

Isou (born Ioan-Isidor Goldstein in Romania in 1925) had emigrated to France after the war; a brilliant talker, he talked himself into a contract with Gallimard for his poetry; and he rendered himself famous, or infamous, in 1946 by gathering a claque of friends to disrupt a production of the Dadaist Tristan Tzara's play *La Fuite* (Tzara too was a Romanian Jewish immigrant, born Sami Rosenstock).[61] Isou (who died in 2007) thought that his movement, Lettrism, went further into authentic avant-gardism than did Dadaism or surrealism, inasmuch as he sought not merely to break up the meaning of sentences, but to break up words into letters, mere phonic elements, preferably of a primal violence: his performances and writings consisted of atavistic onomatopoieic eructations.

Isou and the Lettrists were denizens of down-at-the-heels cafés on the peripheries of St.-Germain-des-Prés and the Latin Quarter. His group of followers included members of the willfully abject "Club of Losers." One of them, Michel Mourre, a refugee from seminary, a teenage collaborationist in wartime, and a former right-wing strong-arm of the Latin Quarter, had come under the influence of the writings of Heidegger and concluded that the theological life had lost its meaning, and with it, life itself. Mourre recruited three other "Losers" to join him in disrupting High Mass at Notre-Dame on Easter Sunday, 1950. As they intruded on the service, Mourre shouted a speech that began, "God is dead!" but the organist played loudly to drown out the rest of it. The Swiss Guards on duty sprang into action and detained the four, who were arrested and remanded for psychiatric evaluation.

François Truffaut, who, while working with André Bazin, had parlayed his own gift of gab into journalistic connections, was assigned to cover the story for *Elle*, and sympathized with Mourre, who justified the demonstration in the name of an austere, arch-conservative moralism.[62] Truffaut brought the young firebrand into his own social circle; Mourre was present, along with Godard, Rivette, Rohmer, and Astruc—"the cream of 16mm and journalistic Paris," Truffaut wrote—at a birthday party that Liliane Litvin (one of the two actresses in Rivette's *Quadrille*) gave for herself on July 4, 1950.[63] It turned into a wild night: Godard left the party with Suzanne

Schiffman and, after wandering through Paris (leaving their friends to wonder what became of them), they turned up again the next morning.

Mourre's radical rightism responded to a crucial strain of thought in the CCQL circle. The young film-lovers' right-wing airs were due in part to the influence of Rohmer, who was himself a practicing Catholic and a conservative, but were also derived from their role in the artistic battles of the day. Since the main French adversaries of the American cinema were the Communist Party, and since the CP and the unions it dominated made it difficult for young people like those of the CCQL and the Cinémathèque to enter the film business, the young cinephiles who adored American movies and dreamed of making movies were necessarily anti-Communist. Nonetheless, their openly aggressive displays of newly resurgent right-wing sympathies, so soon after the far right had been tarnished by its wartime collaboration, revealed a pose of radical reaction that went far beyond the cinematic points of contention into outright provocation, outrage, and scandal.

In 1950, the CCQL showed a British film fantasy about a hypothetical conquest of Britain by the Nazis; in the middle of the screening, Frédéric Froeschel (the student who financed the CCQL) turned on the house lights and revealed a man standing before the audience in full Nazi military regalia and complaining loudly that he found the joke—the movie—in very bad taste; upon which the "officer" departed, the lights went out, and the screening continued.

The joker, Paul Gégauff, was a friend of Rohmer and Godard, and the nominal vice president of the CCQL. The joke in question derived from a costume party to which Gégauff was headed. He had in fact hoped to be accompanied to the gathering by a friend dressed in the striped clothing of a deportee and dragged at the end of a rope, but unsurprisingly, Gégauff found nobody willing to play along with him in this sordid game.

Born in 1922, Gégauff was a writer with a wartime past that he simultaneously sought to live down and boasted about: as a resident of Alsace, which Germany conquered and annexed, he was inducted into a Nazi youth organization, and wrote anti-Semitic articles for a local newspaper (a fact that was not revealed until after his death in 1983). Although never under suspicion for collaboration (indeed, Gégauff's first novels, in 1951 and 1952, were published by Les Editions de Minuit, a publishing house that began during wartime as a clandestine Resistance publisher), Gégauff's arch gestures seemed to confess to what he had not been accused of.

Gégauff led a flamboyant and sybaritic existence. He was said to have run through a lavish inheritance in two years of wild living.[64] Gégauff was a prodigious drinker and seducer. Indeed, his powers of seduction were the source of admiration among his associates; Charles Bitsch, who was one of the

members of the group from the CCQL, said that Gégauff "exerted a real fascination, especially on Godard and Chabrol."[65] Claude Chabrol, another
habitué at the CCQL and the Cinémathèque, diagnosed this fascination: "He
[Godard] was in love with a girl and I think that Gégauff laid her without
even trying. This shocked Jean-Luc, who was trying to go at things more
slowly." Chabrol described the resulting alignment: "Let's say that on one side
there was Momo [Rohmer],[66] Godard and Gégauff and on the other, Rivette
and Truffaut. I made my way between these tendencies."[67] Actor Jean-Claude
Brialy recalled that only two people in film circles, beside himself, called
Rohmer by the familiar "tu": Godard and Gégauff.[68]

According to Bitsch, Gégauff "wasn't a rightist by political conviction
but by the way he lived," although Bitsch found it annoying that Gégauff
"would say, very casually, 'the Germans,' 'the Russians,' 'the Jews.'" According
to Jacques Rivette, Gégauff "played the young fascist."[69] As the official CCQL
collaboration in Gégauff's practical joke suggested, right-wing affectations
were an integral part of the cinematic milieu that Godard frequented.

The CCQL was behind another, even more provocative, fascist practical
joke, which rippled far beyond cinephile circles. On October 6, 1950, the
club hired a sandwich-board man to advertise on the boulevard St.-Michel
in the Latin Quarter its screening that night of *Jew Süss,* the notorious Nazi
propaganda film from 1940, and outfitted him with a yellow star.

Although the film had previously been shown in film clubs without incident, the scandal-mongering advertising for the October 6 screening met
with vehement protest from across the political spectrum. Hundreds of protesters from organizations of Jewish students, Christian students, Resistance
veterans, Jewish survivors of concentration camps, and student members of
the three major parties—Communist, Socialist, and MRP (centrist)—persuaded the police that it was in the interest of public order to cancel the
screening.[70] The following week, a legislator in the National Assembly mentioned the intended screening of *Jew Süss* and other wartime propaganda
films from Japan and Italy, asked the minister of the interior "to put a stop to
it," and demanded an inquiry into the club's source of funds.[71]

The band's right-wing stunts and sympathies, so soon after the end of the
German occupation, suggested a willful association with evil, a punk-like
overturning of values. They also suggested the seemingly insurmountable distance between the young movie lovers and the official culture in which they
desperately sought their place. Although they were, in practical terms, outsiders, intellectually they were insiders whose autodidactic fury suggested their
craving for mastery of the canon. Godard's own political provocations, which
included his German pseudonym, Hans Lucas, and his article on political cinema, pointed to the underlying problem that the young future filmmakers of

the CCQL/Cinémathèque circle faced: despite their intellectual sophistication, they were condemned to anonymity, obscurity, marginality, unless they found a radical way to break into the French film industry, unless they found a way to attract attention.

Their method—the one that Godard himself undertook, at age nineteen—was criticism. It was a singular method, which served two purposes, revolutionary and didactic. Godard and his young film-lover friends were learning how to make films by watching films; they were giving themselves a conservatory education at the Cinémathèque and the CCQL. By writing about the films they saw, they did two things: they elaborated and refined their ideas about the cinema, in anticipation of the day when they could make films; and they created for themselves a public identity that would get them the chance to make films.

But the November 1950 issue of *La Gazette du cinéma*—which featured Godard's "16mm Chronicle" as well as his brief reviews of such films as Preston Sturges's *The Great McGinty*, Robert Siodmak's *The File on Thelma Jordan*, and the Danish *Ditte Menneskebarn*—proved to be the last: it sold too poorly to remain solvent, and for the time being, Godard and the other young enthusiasts around the CCQL had no outlet for their passion.

At that time, however, another publication was in the process of development. André Bazin would play a key role in its founding and editorial direction, and Rohmer would be an early contributor and elder statesman. Godard and his friends used this magazine, *Cahiers du cinéma*, as a base from which to launch their assault on the citadel of the French cinema. In the process, they changed the way that the French, and indeed the world, thought about movies, and helped to set in motion a generational shift that resounded far beyond their field of artistic endeavor.

Godard, 1951
(Courtesy of Véronique Godard)

two

"A MATTER OF LOVING OR DYING"

O N APRIL 2, 1950, JEAN GEORGE AURIOL, THE FOUNDER of *La Revue du cinéma*, which had ceased publication in 1948,[1] died in a car accident. Jacques Doniol-Valcroze, one of its editors, resolved to revive it, with the principal collaboration of André Bazin, but its financial track record did not immediately attract new investors. However, in the fall of 1950, a film distributor and theater owner, Léonide Keigel, decided to invest in the venture. Gallimard, the former publisher of *La Revue*, refused to cede the use of the title, but gave Keigel the right to copy the defunct magazine's format.

The first issue of the new monthly, *Cahiers du cinéma*, came out on April 1, 1951. Bazin, who was recovering from tuberculosis, was unable to participate in its day-to-day organization, and his name was left off the masthead of the first issue by Doniol's coeditor, Joseph Lo Duca, a film critic whom Doniol-Valcroze had hired for his extensive experience as a professional editor. The magazine began with a fund of goodwill based on its resemblance to *La Revue*, both in content and in visual style—like its predecessor, *Cahiers* was published on glossy paper and featured many photographs along with its articles. And these articles were substantial, as the new magazine attracted writers of diverse stripes, including Alexandre Astruc, the "filmologist" Henri Agel, and mainstream film journalists such as François Chalais and Herman G. Weinberg.

Jean-Luc Godard missed these events because in December 1950 he had taken leave of Paris. As a French citizen, Godard was subject to the French draft. In order to escape combat in Indochina, he claimed Swiss citizenship and joined his father and younger sister, Véronique, on a trip to New York.

His father was leaving Switzerland and heading for Jamaica because his marriage to Godard's mother had broken up, and his new clinic near Lausanne, Montbriant, had failed. Traveling by ship, Godard voyaged farther through Central and South America, stopping over in Panama, staying with relatives in Peru and Chile.

Godard's Swiss friend Roland Tolmatchoff recalled that the trip's proximate cause may have been the practical avoidance of French military service, but that its deeper inspiration was literary: "South America was because of [Jules] Supervielle, *L'Enfant de la Haute Mer* (The Child of the High Seas). It was very important for him, he talked about it a lot."[2] Supervielle's collection of stories, from 1931, presented a romantic view of South America.

Nonetheless, the romance of travel seems to have held little interest for Godard: a visitor who met him at his aunt's house in Lima recalled that the young man was uninterested in exploring the country and was absorbed in his books and his thoughts.[3] Though the trip may have had an artistic inspiration, it did not inspire him to much output. He even had plans to make a film, but nothing came of them. According to Truffaut and Rivette, Godard's return to Paris in April 1951 was accompanied by a change in his outward behavior. He was now taciturn. He barely said anything about the journey. Tolmatchoff's impression of Godard's reserve was even stronger: "I tried to speak with him about South America, but he didn't say anything. It's like a black hole, one wonders whether he really went. He did go, but I don't know what he did there. I even looked through his passports which were lying around . . . but I didn't find much."[4]

Upon his return to France, Godard threw himself back into helping others make films. In particular, he worked closely with Eric Rohmer on a short film that was conceived, written, and directed by Rohmer, but on which Godard nonetheless exerted a peculiar sort of authorship. Rohmer's short film, *Présentation* (Introduction)—the same title as that of Sartre's famous essay to inaugurate *Les Temps modernes*—was the first work in the professional, 35mm format by the young men from the CCQL and the Cinémathèque. It was built with and around Godard, who plays the lead male role of Walter, a young man who introduces one young woman to another in the hope of making each jealous of the other. One of them, Clara, is in a hurry and runs off. The other, Charlotte, is in a hurry too, but must return home for a moment, and Walter accompanies her. Because his shoes are wet and her kitchen floor is clean, she makes him drag the doormat indoors and stand on it—which he does the whole time he is at her home. Charlotte cooks herself a small steak and shares it with Walter (who remains rooted in place on the doormat). Their pointedly argumentative dialogue is ironic, flirtatious, and arch: "Don't you know that I love you very much?" he asks. "You're lying." "Perhaps, but I'll be faithful to you," he says. She responds, "That's idiotic; you know that I'm not." "I want to be faithful to you. I'd like to be dead, so that you'd think of me." "I'd think of you even less."

Walter takes Charlotte's face in his hands. They kiss, as she tells him that she does not love him and reminds him that he does not love her either. "Yes, I know," Walter answers, "but am I not sad?" "No, you're not, I'm sure of it. Come on, let's go, you always make me late." They leave Charlotte's immaculate little kitchen and trudge through the snow to the station as Charlotte's train arrives.

As he had done for Rivette, Godard paid for the film stock from his scant and dubiously gotten resources. He also helped Rohmer build the set for Charlotte's kitchen in a photographer's studio in Paris. Rohmer fondly recalled, years later, that Godard, who was young and athletic, had single-handedly lugged the refrigerator for the kitchen to the set ("I can still see Godard carrying it, falling over backwards").[5] Yet Godard's greatest contribution to Rohmer's film was not practical but moral, and was achieved through his on-camera presence.

In Rohmer's film, Godard is intense and romantic, with an ardent, tremulous gaze and precise gestures that suggest the mastery of great passions. His dark, wavy hair is thick, his hairline high and well defined, his jawline angular, his chin prominent. He is a handsome but intellectual leading man, burdened with too much inhibition to sweep Charlotte off her feet, too reflective to let himself get carried away, yet desirous of such abandon above all. Charles Bitsch, another young man of the CCQL and Cinémathèque circle, recalled Godard from that time as

> something of a dandy, with his dark glasses and his way of dressing. He was much better dressed than we were. He wore a tie, a checked vest, dark gloves—not Saint-Laurent, but with a certain class.[6]

Bitsch mentioned Godard's "way of talking very little" and added, "Seeing him, you would say that he isn't just anybody, he was a character." In choosing Godard to play Walter, Rohmer had indulged in typecasting. But he had also put Godard into a psychodrama, giving the amateur actor lines that coincided with his philosophical preoccupation with death—for it was at this time that Godard, thinking of making his own first film, wanted to interest a producer in an adaptation of Albert Camus's philosophical essay *The Myth of Sisyphus*, with specific reference to its famous first line, "The only serious philosophical problem is suicide."

Godard did not make this film. Instead, he addressed its existential theme in the pages of *Cahiers du cinéma*. He was the first of the younger critics from the CCQL/Cinémathèque group to be published in *Cahiers du cinéma*: although Bazin turned down his first article for the journal, a favorable review of Max Ophüls's *Le Plaisir*,[7] the January 1952 issue featured a brief review by "Hans Lucas" of an American melodrama from 1950 directed by Rudolph Maté, *No Sad Songs for Me*. One sentence in the article is loaded with references, allusions, self-promotions, and enough thematic material for an entire oeuvre:

> If destiny and death are the cinema's preferred themes, then there must be, in this carefully controlled presentation [*présentation*] which is mise-en-scène, the definition of the human condition.

In bringing together in a single phrase the title of his film with Rohmer, *Présentation,* and the title of André Malraux's novel, *La Condition humaine,* Godard announced outsized ambition and asserted that he had begun to fulfill it in the making of Rohmer's short film.

In May 1952, *Cahiers* reproduced the four-page screenplay for *Présentation,* credited to Eric Rohmer, along with a photograph of its three actors: though Godard is clearly recognizable, the caption lists him as "Nick Bradford," and the credits attribute the direction of the film to "Guy de Ray." A note in the same issue's "Cinema News" column declares, "After *Présentation,* Guy de Ray will shoot, with the collaboration of Hans Lucas, a cinematographic story, *Weekend of Love.*" This film did not get made either. For the time being, Godard's activities would not involve making movies; instead, they were centered around watching movies and writing about them for *Cahiers du cinéma,* and *Cahiers* itself was centered around André Bazin.

BAZIN THE ORGANIZER and Bazin the critic were, in effect, two different men. As a critic, he relentlessly pushed an idea that he developed into a doctrine, hardened to a dogma, and uttered as a prejudice. Yet as an organizer of ciné-clubs, he united lovers of movies and tirelessly proselytized for the cinema as such, and did so with extraordinary openness, tolerance, and generosity. At *Cahiers du cinéma,* Bazin did both: he continued to argue for his own theoretical notions, but he also gathered around him enthusiasts who disagreed with him—mainly Rohmer and the young men from the CCQL—and none did so more bluntly or brilliantly than Godard.

In March 1952, *Cahiers* included Godard's review of Alfred Hitchcock's *Strangers on a Train,* the first endorsement in the magazine of the director whom the CCQL habitués considered the exemplary artist of Hollywood's industrial system of film production—and *Cahiers* published it despite Bazin's distaste for Hitchcock's films. (An editor's note affirmed that Godard was arguing "against the Editors-in-chief.") In the September issue, Godard, again writing as Hans Lucas, offered a polemic that united his ideas in a remarkably sophisticated theoretical manifesto. He was not yet twenty-two years old. The title was "Defense and Illustration of Classical Découpage,"[8] and the object of his critique was Bazin.

In an article in the first issue of *Cahiers*, "To Be Done with Depth of Field," Bazin had attacked the "obsolete play of shot-reverse shot" (i.e., the standard Hollywood method for shooting and editing of dialogue sequences, with alternating shots of two characters seen from matching angles) and again argued in favor of long takes and great depth of field in order to maintain spatial continuity. He claimed that this practice constituted "dialectical progress in the history of cinematographic language."[9]

Godard challenged that notion head-on. Praising Otto Preminger and other American directors for their use of shot-reverse shot, he specifically locates in "that spatial discontinuity due to a change of shot, which certain enthusiasts of the 'ten-minute take' "—meaning Bazin—"feel obligated to disdain, the reason for the greater part of truth which this figure of style contains." Godard was claiming that spatial discontinuity itself generated a sense of "psychological reality, meaning that of the emotions." He argued that visual elements resulting from shot-reverse shot, such as the isolation of characters in the frame or the change in visual perspective, reflected the characters' differing mental points of view, their inner life. His prime example for his argument is the work of a director whom Godard referred to as "the greatest American artist—I mean Howard Hawks"—another Hollywood filmmaker whose films Bazin neglected.

Godard further argued that Bazin merely fetishized the technique of long takes and deep focus. In effect, he was accusing Bazin of a formalism that caused the elder critic to sacrifice the emotional life of the film to a theoretical prejudice. And the specific emotional life, the supercharged sentimentality, that Godard found exemplified in American melodramas, was not something that Godard apologized for as a base, kitschy, or guilty pleasure: on the contrary, he defended it as an attribute of high art and called attention to what he considered its latent philosophical import: "Do not smile at such passion inflamed by logic, one surely feels that what ensures its worth is that at each instant it is a matter of loving or dying."[10]

In effect, Godard's own revolution, though inspired by the philosophical modernism of Sartre and Camus, would be a conservative one, based

on the preservation, or restoration, of classical values. The cinema that Godard was praising aroused a direct emotional response through a traditional,
nineteenth-century-novelistic and naturalistic approach to character. For
Godard, paradoxically, this classicizing approach, as exemplified in such
Hollywood films as the harsh melodramas directed by Hawks or Preminger,
yielded a more authentically modern art—as a result of its forthright confrontation with the existential crises of death and the human condition—
than the more formalistic and overtly artful films of Welles, De Sica, or
Wyler, which Bazin endorsed. For Godard, the cinema would be the definitive repository of a traditional idea of humanity as represented in art.

Thus, Godard was stating his own case for existentialism as a humanism, one more concerned with the life and fate of individual characters than
with the politics of social conscience that Sartre proffered. But it was also,
for Godard, a humanism of a more venerable sort, akin to the Renaissance
humanism of classical learning. His early articles in *Cahiers* were filled with
citations. Godard cited not only films from among the vast number that he
took in, but also works from the literary and philosophical tradition that he
imbibed with a comparable intellectual voracity. The brief texts are span-
gled with references to Sartre, La Bruyère, Diderot, Gide, Madame de
Lafayette, Stendhal, Delacroix, Poussin, David, Mauriac, Fénélon, Corneille,
Baudelaire, Botticelli, Titian, Ingres, Dostoyevsky, Schumann, Manet, and
Aragon. Having quit his studies young, Godard was an autodidact, and in
his first days he exhibited his independent learning with the pride of a self-
made man. The exalted company of artistic notables was no accident: Godard considered the artists of Hollywood to be their peers, and conceived of
the cinema as a high art, despite its origins in the fiercely commercial
domain.

But Godard's coherent and lofty sense of the cinema and of his own
grand philosophical promise stood at this time in pathetic contrast to his
desperate life. When he came back to Paris, but did not return to the university, he lost his family support and lived on expedients, which included "borrowing" from his mother's best friend, his godmother, in Paris, and theft. He
stole first editions of Paul Valéry from his grandfather's collection, and other
first editions from Jean Schlumberger, selling them at the riverbank book-
stalls to pay for his moviegoing. He stole and sold a painting by Renoir that
belonged to his grandfather.

However, Godard, living a floating life in cafés and scrounging a living,
also associated with shallow provocateurs and publicity hounds who despised the complex, subtle, and introspective classicism that Godard intu-
ited. In St.-Germain-des-Prés, he spent his days with the current

avant-garde, the Lettrists and their even more radical dissidents (later the Situationists), who had begun to achieve an impressive public record of scandal and recognition. Isou's film, *Traité de bave et d'éternité* (A Treatise of Venom and Eternity), a vehement attack on the classical cinema, was shown privately at Cannes in 1951 alongside the festival;[11] even Rohmer, another St.-Germain-des-Prés adept, praised Isou's film in *Cahiers* while Godard praised it in private. In 1952, a film by the original Situationist, Guy Debord, *Hurlements en faveur de Sade* (Screams in Favor of Sade), made with a black screen and featuring a staged riot in the theater, was a succès de scandale. But theirs was an avant-garde of pure negativity that burst onto the scene with the sudden flame of gossip and outrage. Godard's project, in its philosophical complexity and neoclassical grandeur, was necessarily slow to develop, and was endangered by his proximity to dilettantes and poseurs. For a second time, he needed to get out.

IN THE FALL of 1952, tired of living on small change and on the edge of destitution, and in the hope of finding an alternate, more rapid, route into the cinema, Godard took money from *Cahiers*'s till and slunk back to Switzerland; there, with his mother's help, he found work with Swiss television in Zurich, but after stealing money from its safe, he went to jail for a few days,[12] then, through his father's intervention, was removed to a psychiatric clinic. Upon his release, toward the end of 1952, he moved in with his mother, who was living in Lausanne, and he wanted a job.

On Christmas Eve 1952, Godard made a new friend: his mother's lover, Jean-Pierre Laubscher, who, born in 1927, was eighteen years his mother's junior and three years Godard's senior. Laubscher recalled that on "December 24, 1952, his mother told me, 'Come at 5 PM'; Jean-Luc Godard arrived at 5:15. He already had his dark glasses—he said that the color values of black-and-white films are those which one obtains with dark glasses."[13] Laubscher, who had literary aspirations as well as practical plans to become an engineer, had been working since February 1952 as a laborer on the monumental Grande Dixence Dam, in the Valais, which, when completed, would be the world's tallest dam. Laubscher's uncle, an engineer, had gotten him the job. In October, carrying forty pounds of books up icy steps, Laubscher had slipped and broken his wrist; shortly thereafter, he met Godard's mother, Odile, who was working as a medical assistant in a physical therapy clinic. Nurse and patient got to talking about literature; he was a writer and enthusiastic reader, and she had letters of Valéry to show him. They soon took a studio together in Lausanne. Laubscher recalled that one day, when he came to the studio, "she said, 'Don't get undressed' because normally we made love immediately, 'Jean-Luc has sold all the first editions.' I went from bookstore to bookstore with my pay to buy them back. I gave them back to her."[14]

On April 27, 1953, Godard sent Laubscher a beseeching letter, in which he addressed him with the formal "vous":

> Dear Friend:
> My mother tells me that you would perhaps be able to get me hired for several months at the work sites where you yourself are working.

He asked Laubscher to send his response in care of his mother. Nothing came of this entreaty, but a lively friendship did develop between the two during Godard's stay in Lausanne, as evidenced in a letter of Monday, May 25, 1953, from Godard (where he uses the familiar "tu"), in which he addressed Laubscher as "my dear Elder." He wrote to "forewarn" Laubscher of his arrival for lunch the following Sunday and again to ask for work at the Praz Fleuri work site of the Grande Dixence dam.

The job Laubscher got him entailed hard manual labor: Godard had to carry a pick and a bucket and wear heavy boots. While working on the dam, Godard conceived the idea of making a film about it, and when his contract came to an end, Godard sought to "re-enlist" with the project in mind. On January 14, 1954, Godard wrote again to Laubscher, this time to ask about arranging for a transfer to some sort of office job, and mentioned his plan to shoot a film about the construction of the dam. His thoughts regarding film production were already strikingly practical: he intended to use the nonprofessional 16mm, a format which, he knew, could possibly be sold to English television and also shown to the dam's management "to see if they want a more beautiful one," because, he understood, "if the Dixence corporation is inclined to give me 5 to 6,000 francs to make a proper documentary, I could then make it in 35mm." Also, in deference to Laubscher's longer experience working on the dam, he asked Laubscher to be his partner.

Godard did get a cushier position at the work site, thanks to the unforeseen intervention of Eric Choisy, chief executive of the Grande Dixence Corporation, who looked out at a group of workers and, recognizing Godard—his cousin—among them, quickly arranged to have him transferred to the cleaner and calmer post of telephone switchboard operator.

Meanwhile, another one of Godard's Swiss friends, Roland Tolmatchoff, came to Godard's aid. At the time, Tolmatchoff owned a garage near the Grande Dixence work site; when he learned of the movie project, he suggested that Godard could more quickly earn the money for the film's budget by doing ten days of consecutive shifts—in other words, as Tolmatchoff later recalled, by working around the clock: "He spent the nights there on a cot, he got up when the telephone rang."[15] Then Tolmatchoff persuaded friends in Geneva who owned a 35mm movie camera to lend it to Godard for the shoot; one of them, Adrien Porchet, served as cinematographer.

IN APRIL 1954, Laubscher used vacation time to travel with Godard's mother to Paris, where he applied for admission to engineering school for the following year; on the basis of tests in math, physics, and chemistry, he was accepted. (One of her friends had a spare room where he would live.) On April 26, soon after Laubscher returned to work at the dam, Godard, who was on duty as the telephone operator, put through a call to him from Laubscher's mother, who reported that Odile Monod had had a scooter accident the previous night on her way to visit the caller herself after a terrible scene with her younger son—Claude Godard—and that she had died from her injuries.[16]

The funeral took place three days later at the Lausanne Crematorium. Godard left the work site and arrived at the Lausanne train station in order to be at the funeral, but members of the Monod family barred him from attending because of his stealing. That night, he dined with Laubscher and Laubscher's mother. He then returned to the work site and completed the film.

Godard was able to shoot on 35mm film on his low budget because he was spared the expense of renting a 35mm camera. He edited the film himself, on weekends, in an editing room in Geneva. The original commentary for "La Campagne du Béton" (The Campaign of Concrete or The Concrete Countryside), written by Laubscher and dated October 17, 1954, was two pages long and concise; it merely labeled the action. But Godard gave the film a rhyming title instead, Opération Béton (Operation Concrete), and rewrote the commentary. Though he kept several of Laubscher's felicitous turns of phrase, Godard's version, which he recorded in his own voice, greatly amplified the verbiage and resembled, instead of a series of photo captions, a person's enthusiastic, digressive account of his experience at work.

Exhibiting as great a devotion to the reality of the sounds as of the views, Godard rented a hefty professional sound truck, the heavy synchronized-sound equipment that was the film industry standard, to record location sound— an unusual procedure for documentaries at the time. He captures with striking clarity the overwhelming sonic energy of the thunderously cascading water, the rush of the wind, and the percussion of industrial noise.

The film credits mention two names: Godard and Porchet. Neither Laubscher the writer nor Tolmatchoff the assistant and fixer is named. As Godard had hoped, the company that administered the dam bought the film and used it for publicity purposes. A journalist who saw it commented enthusiastically on the film by "Jean-Luc Goddard" [sic] in a Swiss film magazine: "For two years, he tightened his belt to be able to show what he could do. Like a medieval artisan, he created his masterpiece in order to obtain his mastery. Now, he wants to make a more ambitious film."[17]

WITH THE MONEY earned from the sale of the film, Godard was able to quit his job on the dam. He moved to Geneva and produced an inexpensive short film in the nonprofessional 16mm format, *Une Femme coquette* (A Flirtatious Woman). Based on the story "Le Signe" (The Signal), by Maupassant, *Une Femme coquette* is a nine-minute tale about a woman (Marie Lysandre) who, seeing a prostitute beckon to passing men, decides to try the gesture herself. When a young man—played by Tolmatchoff—responds, she tries to dissuade him but he insists and, for fear of being accused of soliciting, she yields to his advances.

Maupassant's version takes place indoors: the woman signals from her window and the man comes into her apartment. In Godard's version, the two characters meet at a bench on the Ile Rousseau in Geneva. Godard turns the necessity of filming cheaply and rapidly, without movie lights, into an aesthetic virtue: the outdoor setting allows the man's obstinate advances to become physical drama, culminating in a chase scene, which Godard filmed with an exciting tracking shot in which the man pursues the woman by car as she runs along the walkway of a bridge.

Even more important than Godard's clever staging, however, is his theme, the question of imitation. *Une Femme coquette* is the story of someone who wants to try out a gesture she has seen, who is enticed by what she observes into imitation of it, and who, from the imitation, takes on the reality. It is a film about watching, about trying to live what one has watched, and about the inherent dangers of doing so. It is about fear and embarrassment, and about living with yourself after doing something you regret; it is about money and what to do with ill-gotten gains; it is about prostitution—about doing for money what is properly done for love—and how someone unintentionally practices it by merely imitating the gestures of a professional. Godard's first fictional film is about the perilous path that he was taking as he sought to enter the cinema, and it anticipates the moral dangers that awaited him there. *Opération Béton* had been a commercial project, undertaken with an eye toward its sale; *Une Femme coquette* was an extraordinarily personal and self-regarding work.

With two films in hand and some money left in his pocket, Godard was ready for another shot at Paris. He had been back to visit and had stayed in contact with his accomplices at *Cahiers,* in particular spending time with Rohmer and Gégauff, joined at times by Tolmatchoff (who occasionally drove him there).[18] On January 15, 1956, Godard met two friends in

Geneva—Hugues Fontana, whose wife had played a small role in *Une Femme coquette*, and Jean-Pierre Laubscher—and took them to dinner, declaring that he was leaving for Paris but would be back in four days. Laubscher recalled that he and Fontana knew Godard would not be back soon; indeed, he did not return to Switzerland for four years.

The Paris to which Godard returned was utterly changed from the city he had left in 1952. In his absence, his friends from the CCQL had begun to publish articles in *Cahiers du cinéma*, and they had caused a stir. In May 1953, Jacques Rivette followed Godard's praise of Alfred Hitchcock with an encomium to "The Genius of Howard Hawks," and Claude Chabrol, another longtime CCQL/Cinémathèque habitué, enthused over *Singin' in the Rain* in November. Then, in the January 1954 issue, François Truffaut's ferocious polemic, "Une certaine tendance du cinéma français" (A Certain Tendency of the French Cinema), sparked an intellectual controversy that definitively put the magazine and its contributors on the map of French cultural life.

Truffaut had presented a draft of "A Certain Tendency" to André Bazin as early as December 1952, but Bazin, who anticipated a scandal, demanded that Truffaut tone it down. Even toned down, it aroused shock and outrage. In it, Truffaut attacked the internationally respected films of the recent French cinema, the weighty literary adaptations (such as *La Symphonie pastorale* and *Le Diable au corps*) which garnered prizes at film festivals—the French "Tradition of Quality," as it was called—and declared them worthless, indeed pernicious.

Though Truffaut aimed his harshest attacks at these films' renowned screenwriters, such as Charles Spaak and the duo of Jean Aurenche and Pierre Bost (accusing them of a cynical amoralism that clashed with his own conservative values), he did so merely to set up his key polemical point: "directors are, and wish to be, responsible for the scenarios and dialogues they illustrate." Thus Truffaut, asserting directors to be the ultimate authors—"auteurs"—of their films, blamed them for the "vile beings," the "infinitely grotesque" characters that they brought to the screen from the scripts he derided. Truffaut went on to list the eight French directors he considered "INCAPABLE of conceiving" such characters and such films: Jean Renoir, Robert Bresson, Jean Cocteau, Jacques Becker, Abel Gance, Max Ophüls, Jacques Tati, and Roger Leenhardt. As if to make clear that his contrast of these worthy eight to the rest of the French film industry is not merely one of degree, Truffaut drew the battle lines in the strident terms of the Cold War: "I do not believe in the peaceful coexistence of the 'Tradition of Quality' and an 'auteur's cinema.'"

The *Cahiers* critics who had come from the CCQL and the Cinémathèque, and who came to prominence through Truffaut's fiery pen, were recognized for their heterodox love for American films and filmmakers, and the line that they defended was known as the "*politique des auteurs.*" According to this "policy" or "politics," the director's role is the central one in the art of the cinema, and the mark of the director's presence through his visual and sound style is the prime mode of perceiving a director's artistry. The "auteurists'" enthusiasm for the American cinema—as exemplified by Godard's praise of films by Hitchcock, Hawks, and Preminger, and Rivette's of Hawks—was not a blanket endorsement of the Hollywood studios' entire industrial output. Instead, through careful viewing and passionate critical discussions, they recognized the artistry of a handful of Hollywood directors whose work they understood to be art of the first order despite its origins in a restrictive commercial system. They asserted that these filmmakers, working in the studio system, were the artistic equals of the best filmmakers working anywhere else, and they took the filmmakers whose work they loved to be *auteurs*—the authors of their films, whose moral authority over their work and personal imprint on it made them the peers of novelists, painters, and composers. They considered these filmmakers to be artists of the same stature as those in any medium, and they considered them to be so whether they worked in France (like Jean Renoir), in Italy (like Roberto Rossellini), in Denmark (like Carl Theodor Dreyer), in Japan (like Kenji Mizoguchi), or in Hollywood (like Hitchcock or Hawks).

By 1954, the group had already made clear what it admired and supported; Truffaut's fierce article was the first to declare what it despised. Overnight, Truffaut had become the angry prophet of the French cinema, and he and his circle of friends rapidly became as famous for the filmmakers they rejected—more or less the entire squad of French mainstream directors—as for those they championed. Yet unlike the nihilism of the the Lettrists and their successors, Truffaut and his friends were not merely conducting a scorched-earth policy; they were clearing the ground for the recognition of their own artistic heroes, avatars of what they considered a truer and worthier classicism, as well as their own artistic models in view of the day when they themselves would become filmmakers. The enthusiasms of the young critics who had become known as "Schérer's gang"[19] permeated *Cahiers du cinéma,* which featured serious and enthusiastic critiques of American films by such directors as Nicholas Ray, Otto Preminger, George Cukor, and Fritz Lang.

The *politique des auteurs* served a theoretical purpose, but, as its name implied, it was also political in the general sense: it was the platform by which this group, whom actor Jean-Claude Brialy remembered as "revolutionaries,"[20] intended to "take over"[21]—that was, as Rohmer recalled, the phrase they used—the French cinema. Godard himself later emphasized the "politics" of the *politique*, likening the critical enterprise of the young *Cahiers* critics to the Resistance: he said that they considered the French cinema to be occupied by directors who "had no business being there,"[22] whom they intended to throw out, and whose place they intended to take. As Truffaut had written, the *Cahiers* group did not believe in "peaceful coexistence."

Soon after the notorious article was published, its publicity value became clear. Truffaut was invited by the editors of the weekly *Arts-Lettres-Spectacles* to join their film page: he would be published once a week, enjoy broad nationwide circulation, and be paid five times *Cahiers*'s per-page rate. But Truffaut's presence at *Arts* further inflamed the tensions between the *Cahiers* group and left-wing critics: *Arts,* a popular journal with a high intellectual tone, had a political agenda that was an open secret. Its publisher was the writer Jacques Laurent, who had held office in Vichy and was one of a group of right-wing writers derided as "Hussars" in a famous 1952 article by Bernard Frank in *Les Temps modernes.* Instead of expressing their political tendencies openly, these writers defended an apolitical literature and opposed what they considered the politicization of literature, by which they meant the affiliation of literature with the left. Rejecting calls for artistic attention to the sufferings of the poor and to political responsibility for them, the Hussars depicted with an unapologetic hedonism the sensual adventures of flamboyant bourgeois sybarites.

In another new film magazine, *Positif,* founded in Lyon in 1952 by left-wing film enthusiasts, the young *Cahiers* writers were derided as apologists for the "American way of life." In fact, the critics at *Cahiers* avoided politics, but not as a politicized repudiation of left-wing calls for "engagement." They wanted to talk about the cinema without being labeled as belonging to one or another side of a political conflict. As Fereydoun Hoveyda, who had started writing for *Cahiers* in 1954, recalled, almost everyone there was on the right (except Jacques Rivette and the older writer Pierre Kast), and Godard had the reputation as "rightist, almost fascist." But nonetheless, the writers avoided the subject of politics: "If we had accepted to write about the Algerian War, which was the major event at the time, it would have prevented us from talking to many people who were interested in the cinema."[23] As another writer for the magazine, Michel Dorsday, recalled, "The love of the cinema came first."[24]

Over the next four years, Truffaut published more than 500 articles (an average of more than two per issue) in *Arts,* and his combative reviews were often featured prominently on the front page. Thus the preoccupations, or obsessions, that "Schérer's gang" (also called by friends and foes alike the "Hitchcocko-Hawksians," when not simply labeled the "Young Turks") debated, theorized, and refined at the offices and in the pages of *Cahiers du cinéma* reached far beyond the specialized precinct of movie-lovers and became familiar to a wide French readership. Through Truffaut's writings, they gained a beachhead on the French cultural scene at large.

Yet it was also in the pages of *Cahiers* that the group found its most articulate opponent: André Bazin. In an article published there in 1957, Bazin challenged the *politique des auteurs* head-on, charging that "Hitchcock, Renoir, Rossellini, Fritz Lang, Howard Hawks, or Nicholas Ray appear, in the light of *Cahiers,* to be more or less infallible authors who never make a failed film"— and identifying in this trend the risk of "an aesthetic cult of personality."[25] He derided the group's emphasis on the stylistic subtleties of an auteur's mise-en-scène at the expense of the other aspects of a film, including its subject: "Auteurs, yes; but of what?"[26] He claimed that the cinema could not aspire to equality with literature, art, or music, because it is merely "a popular and industrial art," and declared that Hitchcock, Nicholas Ray, or Roberto Rossellini were not "on the same level of individuation"—i.e., did not leave as distinctive a mark on their work—as Picasso, Matisse, or other contemporary painters.[27]

Bazin was at odds with the young enthusiasts he had brought into the magazine. And no one in the group was more openly confrontational toward Bazin, and in sharper opposition to Bazin's ideas, than Godard. Indeed, as Godard developed his ideas about the cinema in preparation for his work as a director, he continued to wage a theoretical argument against Bazin at a deeper level than that of his colleagues. The December 1956 issue of *Cahiers* brought the conflict into the open: it featured an article by Bazin called "Montage Interdit" (Editing Forbidden) and one by Godard, "Montage, mon beau souci" (Editing, My Beautiful Concern).

Their exchange was a more pointed and passionate reprise of their earlier debates in the pages of *Cahiers,* and Godard's argument was even more radical than his earlier response. Starting out from his earlier premise—that editing brought about an acute psychological reality through its spatial discontinuities—Godard now explained classical film editing in terms of modern philosophy from Heidegger to Sartre, asserting its power "to make the heart prevail over intelligence in destroying the notion of space in favor of that of time." In a lapidary phrase, he asserted that "if direction is a look, editing is a heartbeat."

Where Bazin continued to praise the long take for its presumed fidelity to physical reality, Godard praised editing for rendering the subjective essence of reality: "A film ingeniously directed does indeed give the impression of having been laid end to end, but a film ingeniously edited gives the impression of having suppressed all direction." In other words, a well-edited film offered the most artless art: rather than presenting a good representation of reality, it seemed to provide the experience of reality itself.

Godard drew on his incipient experience as a filmmaker to assert that film editing is as crucial to the director's art as shooting: "One improvises, one invents in front of the Moviola as on the set." And finally, Godard reasserted the philosophical importance of editing, "montage," by suggesting that it is not merely a fact of the cinema but also a fact of life: "To direct a film is to plot [*machiner*], one says of a plot [*machination*] that it is well or badly laid [*montée*]." The action of life is "*monté*," edited. With this suggestion through wordplay, Godard asserted that Bazin, by repudiating editing, was in fact separating the cinema from reality.

WHEN GODARD RETURNED to Paris in January 1956, he had a plan for a feature film. If he would miss his deadline for making his first feature by age twenty-five, as Orson Welles had done, he at least was proposing to make a first feature that would rival *Citizen Kane* in outsized ambition. Godard had written a script based on Goethe's novel *Elective Affinities*. The title of the script was *Odile*—Godard's mother's first name, as well as the French translation of Ottilie, the name of a character from the novel, the story of which hit close to home: Edward and Charlotte, a wealthy couple living harmoniously on a large and serene rural estate, are visited by the man's friend, the Captain, and the woman's young protégée, Ottilie. Edward and Ottilie have an affair, and in the complications that ensue, Ottilie dies.

The script was 250 pages long—an extraordinary length, given the industry rule of thumb that a page of script translates into a minute of screen time—and the producer Pierre Braunberger, who read it, estimated that it would be extraordinarily expensive to shoot and would result in a five-hour film. Even for an established director, it would have been a difficult project to produce; for an outsider like Godard, it was impossible. But at the same time, he and his friends at *Cahiers,* all of whom were seeking to become filmmakers, took a lesson in the art of the possible from a director they admired and had come to know, Roberto Rossellini.

Rossellini, born in 1906, was the most important Italian director of the day, though few in Italy still thought so. Although he had made several patriotic films under official auspices during the war, the unauthorized film that he made in 1945 in the last days of the war, *Open City* (starring Anna Magnani in a drama about resistance fighters and collaborators in Rome under the German occupation), inaugurated the neorealist school of filmmaking.

This movement favored stories centered on the lives of working-class Italians, with particular attention to political and social problems, filmed on location, in a manner derived from documentary filmmaking. But in 1950, Rossellini made *Stromboli,* starring Ingrid Bergman (who soon also became his wife). With this film, and even more, with subsequent films that he made with Bergman (notably *Europa 51, Voyage to Italy,* and *Fear*), Rossellini abandoned the working-class politics of neorealism and located the new center of modern Italian life in the bourgeoisie. Replacing overtly political concerns with more abstract questions, Rossellini created a cinema of philosophical contemplation and symbolic abstraction in the framework of conventional melodrama. In effect, Rossellini made American-style films with European methods and ideas; and his new work, which was roundly derided by most of the European critics who had hailed the films of his first style, was appreciated, first and most vigorously, by the young critics at *Cahiers.* (Rohmer's enthusiastic endorsement of *Stromboli* on the front page of the May 1950 issue of *La Gazette du cinéma* set the tone for their views.)

One of the crucial aspects of the *politique des auteurs* as practiced by the young critics at *Cahiers* was its power to give them a personal "in" with filmmakers they exalted and whose work they praised. In 1955, Rossellini left Italy, where he was jeered, for Paris, where he found a more favorable reception. François Truffaut and Jacques Rivette, two of the critics who were championing his work, invited him for an interview, and Rossellini took a reciprocal interest in them—especially in Truffaut, the more prominent and outgoing of the two. Rossellini invited him to be his private secretary; he also got his French producer, Henry Deutschmeister, interested in a series of 16mm films to be made by Truffaut, Chabrol, Rivette, Rohmer, and the documentary filmmakers Jean Rouch and Alain Resnais. Rossellini exhorted them to write their scripts on the basis of practical research into local events. He wanted his young followers, in effect, to produce a new neorealist movement in France.

The collaboration fell through, due to Deutschmeister's hesitation and Rossellini's distraction (his own projects in Europe came to naught and he left for India to make a film there), but Godard's friends had done their research and had written their scripts. Now, with or without Rossellini and Deutschmeister, they were thinking like filmmakers and would realize their plans to make films.

Godard's massive script for *Odile,* with its literary romanticism, differed drastically from the small-scale, documentary-style stories that Rossellini had urged his young friends to prepare, and that he himself made. His 1953 film, *Voyage to Italy,* shown in Paris in 1955, was a revelation to Godard, from a practical standpoint. The film presents an English couple (Ingrid Bergman and George Sanders) who visit Italy in order to deal with a family inheritance, and dramatizes the stresses in their relationship as they travel through the countryside and experience its attractions and peculiarities. With its intimate fiction set in a landscape that Rossellini filmed with a documentary attentiveness and fidelity, *Voyage to Italy* inspired the Young Turks of *Cahiers* to consider the possibility of making highly structured dramas with spartan means. Specifically, Godard later recalled, he drew from the film a practical lesson: that to make a feature film, he needed only a pair of actors and a car. A low budget didn't entail the constrained subject matter of a low-budget film like Rivette's *Quadrille,* nor did the dramatic intensity of a script like *Odile* require access to outsized budgets and productions.

When Rossellini left Paris to make a film in India, he invited Truffaut to join him, but Truffaut refused; he didn't want to put his own career, which was still a dream, on hold. In mid-1956, Truffaut had the idea to make a small-scale film based on the true-crime story of Michel Portail, a petty criminal who, on November 24, 1952, had stolen the car of a Greek diplomat, shot a motorcycle policeman who pulled him over, and hid out for almost two weeks until he was found in a canoe docked in the center of Paris.[28] Portail was tried in November 1954 and sentenced to life imprisonment.[29] One aspect of the story that appealed to Truffaut concerned the killer's girlfriend, an American journalist with whom he had briefly lived a fashionable life and whom he attempted to find in Paris and persuade to run off with him. Instead, she turned him in to the police.

Truffaut (who had earlier sketched out the story with Chabrol) intended to direct the film on a low budget and in quasi-documentary style, and he called on Godard to help him rework the idea. The two met to talk it out on a bench at the Richelieu-Drouot station. (At the time Godard was working for a short-lived newspaper, *Le Temps de Paris,* as a gossip writer, having been hired through Truffaut's journalistic connections.) However, Truffaut failed to interest any producers in the story, largely, he believed, because of the political and bureaucratic difficulties in France of filming news-based stories.[30]

Instead, Truffaut turned to a purely commercial project, and he enlisted Godard's help with this too. On January 10, 1957, Truffaut signed an agreement with the producer Pierre Braunberger to write and direct a short film, *Autour de la Tour Eiffel* (Around the Eiffel Tower),[31] a rather heavy-handed comedy about a country girl who visits the big city for the first time, a peasant boy whom she meets en route to the Eiffel Tower, a livestock merchant who leads a cow through the city, a comedian (Raymond Devos) who erupts in an orotund comic monologue, and a prostitute whose profession the leading lady naively misunderstands.

At Truffaut's request, Godard revised the script, making its plot more elegant and its comedy wittier and more visually inventive. Instead of meeting a peasant boy near the Eiffel Tower, the country girl encounters an urbane young Parisian when he "narrowly misses her with his De Soto convertible." Godard devised a remarkable sight gag to crystallize their rapid courtship. As the pair ascend the tower, the country girl is transformed, floor by floor, through the power of film editing, into a sophisticated Parisienne: at the second floor, "she no longer has her braids . . . nor her peasant blouse nor her clogs"; after the couple race each other breathlessly up the staircase to the third floor, the young woman "is again metamorphosed, her hair short, a trace of lipstick on her lips, high heels, in a little dress by Guy Laroche."[32]

Godard conceived yet another unusual editing technique for the film. He planned to break the visual and narrative continuity by introducing into the story a literally documentary aspect: "With each specific action, a document (old film, photos, engravings, drawings) is inserted."

Truffaut worked up a budget and put together a cast, but then abandoned the project, which no longer resembled one of his. Its tone, simultaneously debonair and flippant, arch and gallant, profound and loopy, did, however, resemble the short films that Godard was about to make.

WORKING WITH ROHMER—FOR whose short adaptation of Tolstoy's *The Kreutzer Sonata* he had purchased film stock with the cash that he had brought back from Switzerland—Godard sketched out a series of short films revolving around a pair of young women, Charlotte and Véronique (Véronique being the name of Godard's younger sister). In the fall of 1957, Pierre Braunberger produced the first film in the series, *Charlotte et Véronique, ou Tous les garçons s'appellent Patrick* (All the Boys Are Called Patrick), directed by Godard from Rohmer's script.

The young man, Patrick, played by the actor Jean-Claude Brialy—who had become a friend of the *Cahiers* group—picks up two women in quick succession—one, Charlotte (played by Anne Colette, Godard's girlfriend at the time) in the Jardin de Luxembourg, and the other, Véronique (played by Nicole Berger, the producer's stepdaughter), just outside the gardens, moments after he says good-bye to Charlotte. Unbeknown to him, the two women are roommates. Back in their apartment, each admits to the other that she has fallen in love with a boy. They are amused by the coincidence that their new beaus are both named Patrick, and they compare notes. The next day, as they walk together near the park, they see Patrick and point him out to each other—just as he is picking up a third girl, whom he ushers into a taxi. Noticing them, he shrugs his shoulders as if to say, "Boys will be boys," and joins his new conquest in the backseat of the cab as it pulls out.

Little in the film suggests that Godard had any particular devotion to the story, which, in its gleeful fixation on the effortless *dragueur,* or pick-up artist, mainly suggests the strong impression made by Paul Gégauff on the austere, conservative Rohmer and the romantic Godard. Instead, Godard's directorial signature, his mark on the film, is its profusion of peripheral, almost encoded details: the film reads like a catalog of winks and nods to initiates, or rather, to his friends. From the dark glasses worn by all three characters as well as by a café patron who is a near-double for Godard himself, to the presence of books (Charlotte reads Hegel's *Aesthetics* in the apartment and Véronique carries a copy of *Cahiers du cinéma*), to the close-ups of a Picasso poster in their room and a Matisse postcard at streetside, to Véronique's question whether Charlotte's Patrick is Patrick "Valcroze" (as in Jacques Doniol-Valcroze, the coeditor of *Cahiers*), to the headline on the copy of *Arts* that Godard's stand-in is reading at the café—"The French Cinema Is Dying Under False Legends," a vituperative article from May 15, 1957, by Truffaut—to the "Japanese" phrase, "Mizoguchi Kurosawa," that Patrick tries on Charlotte, the film's principal mode of expression is in the collection of artistic and cinematic fetish objects it assembles. *Tous les garçons s'appellent Patrick* initiates the vast array of inside jokes, the personal museum of private associations, that would play a surprisingly large role in Godard's major films to come.

Eric Rohmer was surprised and dismayed by the changes that Godard had wrought upon his script and ended their collaboration. Rohmer then made *Véronique et son cancre* (Véronique and Her Dunce) without Godard, who, in turn, made another film in the series, *Charlotte et son Jules* (Charlotte and Her Lover), without a script by Rohmer—and virtually without money, décor, or action.

Anne Colette, who played Charlotte, had recently had a small role in a commercial film, *Sois belle et tais-toi* (Be Beautiful and Keep Quiet); Godard, unshaven and in sunglasses, had visited her on the set, where she introduced him to an actor playing a supporting role, Jean-Paul Belmondo, who had little experience in film but a burgeoning career in theater. Not long thereafter, Belmondo met Godard in the Brasserie Lipp, was put off by Godard's refusal to remove his dark glasses, and responded to Godard's suggestion that they work together with a casual "Yes": the actor assumed that this peculiar man would never get to make a film. Before long, Godard ran into the actor by chance and offered him 50,000 francs ($100) to appear in a film that Godard would shoot in his own apartment. Belmondo hesitated: he wondered whether the "film" was a pretext for a disagreeable proposition.

Charlotte et son Jules was shot in Godard's small hotel room, on the rue de Rennes. In a brief credit sequence, Anne Colette, eating an ice-cream cone, gets out of a sports car and signals to the young man behind the wheel to wait for her. Then, Jean-Paul Belmondo, alone in his room, responds to a knock at the door. Anne Colette enters (with her ice-cream cone), announcing, "It's me!" upon which Belmondo harshly responds, "I knew that it's you. I knew you'd come back. I told you so. You can't do without me. You're an idiot! You never listen." Thus begins his torrential, angry, reproachful, insult-filled, and crudely comical monologue, which runs the entire twenty minutes of the film.

Whenever Charlotte attempts to respond to what seem to be his questions, the young man, Jean, demands that she not interrupt him while he berates her for betraying him ("running off with a guy who charmed you for three minutes although you were in love with me for three years").

She intermittently looks out the window at the man in the sports car below, as Jean's monologue becomes increasingly wild and desperate and reaches a dramatic climax:

> I beg you, Charlotte, don't leave me! Besides, if you leave, I'll break your face! I've got connections too! I got a telegram from Hollywood. Yeah, for my novel. Stay with me, Charlotte. As soon as my book comes out, I'll buy you an Alfa-Romeo.

The clincher of the exchange and the resolution of the story is when he asks, "You can't do without me either. That's why you came back?" and she answers, "No, Jean, I came back to get my toothbrush!" and, taking it, leaves.

The film, an homage to Jean Cocteau, on whose *Le Bel indifférent* it was modeled, was an elaborate gag. The "indifference" it displays is Godard's own—indifference to cinematography and to story in favor of spoken text, as if the entire film were just a cartoon frame with a dialogue bubble that Godard filled to bursting. The image itself is conceptual placefiller, suggesting that the will to make a film could suffice as the matter for the film itself.

Charlotte et son Jules sat unfinished for months, until director Jacques Becker (a *Cahiers* favorite, best known for *Casque d'or* and *Touchez pas au grisbi* and whose *Montparnasse 19* Godard had fervently praised in the May 1958 issue) agreed to show it with his own next film.[33] The producer Pierre Braunberger then financed its completion, permitting Godard to proceed with the film's dubbing. However, by this time, Belmondo was doing his military service in Algeria; Godard had the idea to do the dubbing himself, and wrote to Belmondo to ask his permission to do so, promising him the lead role in his first feature film. Belmondo gave his consent, and indeed the voice with which the character Jean speaks in the film is Godard's own.

The madly romantic austerity of Jean's life resembled Godard's own. Roland Tolmatchoff described the circumstances in which he found his friend

when he came from Switzerland to pay him a visit: "In Paris he had a big Bogart poster on the wall and nothing else."[34] (At times, Godard could not even
afford a poor hotel room like the one in the film, and slept in the offices of
Cahiers or other publications he freelanced for.) Moreover, Tolmatchoff recalled that the same hectically romantic pursuit of a woman was also part of
Godard's store of experience: "In '57 or '58 he was in love with a girl who
lived in Madrid. He went there with nothing but flowers. He came back. He
told me, 'I called her, she said that she didn't want to see me anymore; I threw
out the flowers and I came back.' "[35] Godard's friends in Paris recalled that he
threw himself into sudden romantic pursuits that often ended badly; Truffaut
recalled that Godard "would meet a girl, and the next day he would be at her
front door with a bunch of flowers and a marriage proposal. It was always too
serious and too absolute; it never worked. He proposed forty times."[36] Gégauff bluntly described Godard in love: "He was always madly in love with the
stupidest shopgirls and went broke buying bouquets of roses and choco-
lates."[37]

The self-important dreamer and his romantic humiliation depicted in
Charlotte et son Jules comprised a self-deprecating self-portrait by Godard,
but, like the dramatics of *Tous les garçons s'appellent Patrick,* the film's personal and narrative aspects were subordinated to the proliferating allusions
in the torrential dialogue. Godard's next short film proved to be even less
dramatically viable and even more voluble than his previous efforts.

In February 1958, Truffaut persuaded Braunberger to produce, on short
notice, an improvised comedy in and around floodwaters that were at that
moment rendering the suburbs of Paris impassable. The story concerned a
young woman who needs a lift (the actress Caroline Dim) and her passing liaison with the young man (Jean-Claude Brialy) who provides it. While shooting the film, however, Truffaut felt embarrassed to be making a light comedy
in the presence of people who were struggling to save their homes, and as a result, he shot it hastily and unenthusiastically and then decided not to finish it.
But Godard, upon seeing the rushes, thought that he could do something with
them, and later in the year edited them into a relatively smooth continuity and
wrote dialogue and a voice-over that would be dubbed.

The text that Godard and Anne Colette recorded on December 17, 1958,
displayed a verbal extravagance that outdid even *Charlotte et son Jules* in the
coherence of its apparent randomness. His title alone, *Une Histoire d'eau* (A
Story of Water), was a pun on the title of the erotic bestseller *Histoire d'O, The
Story of O.* Godard's text, an arch and antic narration of the couple's comic
encounter, is a pastiche of references and quotations, of jokes and asides: Raymond Chandler, Edgar Allan Poe, Georges Franju; Aragon, Petrarch, and Matisse; "the Germans" ("I love the Germans—Max and Moritz, Goethe,

Wagner . . ."); five lines of Baudelaire; Degas and the Impressionists; Homer, Rasputin, a passage from Balzac ("That sentence isn't mine; it's from Balzac, in *La Duchesse de Langeais*"); a reference to one "Blondin" (a pun linking the famous acrobat of that name to the novelist and sportswriter Antoine Blondin); Valéry Larbaud, Paul Eluard, Jean Giraudoux in one sentence; patter and comedy from the music hall and the café, a brew of popular language and literary artifice reminiscent of Raymond Queneau, whose name is the text's first gag—"Que d'eau! Que d'eau!" (nothing but water)—and inside-film jokes.

In the texts of his short films as in his film reviews, Godard exhibited a prodigious recombinative intelligence, as in his extravagant and far-reaching wordplay, especially his puns, which made connections between similar-sounding signifiers in order to suggest comic relations between unrelated signifieds. It was a fitting linguistic habit for a critic who, from his first youthful efforts, wrote in praise of montage.

With their ornamental and digressive dialogue, *Une Histoire d'eau, Tous les garçons s'appellent Patrick,* and *Charlotte et son Jules* prove successively and increasingly the distinction between script and dialogue (or, for that matter, monologue). They reveal an increasing trend on Godard's part toward indolence and indifference, as if the richness of a film's text could take precedence over its casual production. He was using film merely as a set-up to express ideas directly: his three short films of 1957–58 were in effect blank panels of images on which Godard could all but inscribe his florid text.

Though Godard had long celebrated the artistic specificity of the cinema, literature still tempted him. If, in his abortive student days, he had dreamed and even boasted of writing a novel, he had abandoned that hope in favor of the cinema, but without abandoning writing—as his massive script based on *Elective Affinities* attested. His three short films of 1957–58 are not cinema but a substitute for cinema. In effect, they are conceptual gags that allowed Godard to exercise his powers of verbal invention. Godard had not yet mastered film technique well enough to wield its equipment pliably and spontaneously; it was only in his writing and in the theatrical delivery of his profuse verbosity that he was able to provide a simulacrum of the live event, of a creation on the fly and in real time, of a sheet torn from his notebook and passed along to the viewer with intimacy and a feigned offhandedness. Only the writing of his films' texts was able to provide him with proof that, for the brief duration of his slight creation, he existed.

Godard made short films but considered the genre inferior. Though he reported rhapsodically, from the Festival of Short Films in the French town of

Tours in December 1958, on a handful of films, and though he became fast friends with their directors—Jacques Rozier, Jacques Demy, and Agnès Varda (he already knew Alain Resnais, whose entry he also praised)—he nonetheless wrote demeaningly of short films as such. He granted their usefulness for directors "to prove their talent," but considered them, in comparison to feature films, to be "anti-cinema." The reviews were also a confession: Godard was desperate to make a feature film, because at the moment, he was mired in anti-cinema.

GODARD HAD BEEN able to put together *Charlotte et son Jules* using short ends of film stock sent to him by Claude Chabrol, who was the first of the *Cahiers* group to make a full-length film. Chabrol, who had been working in the publicity department of Twentieth Century-Fox's Paris office since 1955, was able to draw on an inheritance from his wife's family in 1957 to make *Le Beau Serge,* which was based on a script that he had written at Rossellini's behest. The film, which was released in 1958, was a modest success, and allowed Chabrol to self-produce a second feature, *Les Cousins,* later that year.

Chabrol left his position at Fox and turned it over to Godard, a small step that ultimately reverberated with great results. Fereydoun Hoveyda, then a *Cahiers* critic, later cited his colleagues' practical motive: "Chabrol, then Godard, went to work at Fox in order to find money for their films—in order to meet producers."[38] For Chabrol, the strategy didn't work, and he had to wait for a windfall; for Godard, the job with Fox proved profitable—albeit in a paradoxical way.

Godard's various responsibilities included the preparation of press kits for journalists, which gave him the chance to disseminate with a poker face colorfully false biographies of actors. He would also spend the day pursuing his own interests. Chabrol recalled that Godard used to keep the bathroom key in his pocket: "He would come into the office and look busy for an hour, and then say he was sick. Then he would lock himself in the lavatory and read scripts."[39] Godard enjoyed one of the position's principal benefits, the right to attend the company's private screenings, some of which were of American films not distributed in France, such as Otto Preminger's *Carmen Jones*[40] and Samuel Fuller's *Forty Guns,* about which he exulted, in the November 1957 issue of *Cahiers,* that this "brutal and savage Western . . . abounds with ideas of mise-en-scène the audacity of which calls to mind the extravagances of Abel Gance or of Stroheim, if not purely and simply of Murnau."[41]

Not all of the films that Godard saw at Fox excited him as much. After one screening, in early 1958, of a French film called *La Passe du diable* (Devil's

Pass), which was being offered to Fox for distribution, Godard confronted the producer and declared, "Your film is a disgrace."[42] The relatively young producer, Georges de Beauregard (born in 1920), who made films on small budgets under eccentric and risky circumstances and barely scraped by—and whose political sympathies were openly rightist—was curious about this audacious young man.

Then, in the summer of 1958, Godard, benefiting from the good fortune of another friend, François Truffaut, left Fox to take over for him as a film critic at *Arts*. Truffaut had gotten the chance, through the good offices of his father-in-law, the film distributor Ignace Morgenstern, to make his own first feature film, *The 400 Blows*. At the same time, Godard also took other small jobs in the film business, such as editing nature documentaries and working as a script doctor (in particular, adding dialogue), but he needed more work, and he called on Beauregard.

Coincidentally, Beauregard had something to offer: a businessman had stepped forward to finance screen adaptations of the exotic travel novels of Pierre Loti. The first film in the series, *Ramuntcho,* proved modestly successful. Now Beauregard was preparing a film of Loti's *Pêcheur d'Islande* (Iceland Fisherman), and recruited Godard to write the screen adaptation, paying him 400,000 francs (about $800) and sending him to the film's location, the seaside town of Concarneau, in Brittany, to glean local details to add to the script.

Pêcheur d'Islande did not at all interest Godard. The reluctant screenwriter added a love scene that would take place on top of a pile of mackerel, a scene that Beauregard considered a "comic masterpiece"[43] (and which seems strongly reminiscent of, and likely an homage to, the fishing scene in Rossellini's *Stromboli*); but he took off from Concarneau—heading back to Paris to resume his critical activities and to complete *Une Histoire d'eau*—leaving the script unfinished and owing Beauregard the reimbursement of his advance.

With Chabrol already shooting his second feature, *Les Cousins,* Truffaut preparing to make *The 400 Blows,* Rivette deep into the precarious adventure of *Paris nous appartient* (Paris Belongs to Us), a long feature film that he was shooting with donated services and supplies and no financial backing (and would soon interrupt), and Rohmer in possession of a script, *Le Signe du Lion* (The Sign of Leo), that Chabrol had agreed to produce, Godard was desperately scrambling for his own chance to make a feature film.

A letter he wrote to Truffaut—"Caro Francesco"—from Concarneau suggested how frantic Godard's efforts had become, as he proposed several projects that he hoped Truffaut's father-in-law would invest in: "Véronique pregnant . . . —Véronique and her kid—Véronique divorces, etc." He also

proposed adapting a novel by Georges Simenon, *Quartier Nègre,* and, alluding to his travels in 1950–51, said of the book's action, "It takes place in
Panama, which I know well. No kidding."

Morgenstern was not interested. Other producers to whom Godard
pitched his projects were not interested. Godard continued to work at his
patchwork of freelance assignments as critic, film editor, and script doctor,
and awaited his chance with mounting frustration.

IN OCTOBER 1957, the journalist Françoise Giroud, writing in *L'Express,*
coined the phrase Nouvelle Vague—New Wave—to name the generation of
French people between ages eighteen and thirty "that had not yet finished
high school at the end of the war."[44] She considered their concerns to be
more inward-looking and hedonistic, less political and collective, than those
of their elders, and she sensed that their ascendancy into positions of responsibility in France foretold significant social changes.

In February 1958, the film critic Pierre Billard, writing in *Cinema 58,* applied the term to young French filmmakers—and he meant it sarcastically:
"The caution with which this 'new wave' is following in the footsteps of its
elders is disconcerting." Several other young filmmakers, such as Louis Malle
(a graduate of the film school IDHEC), Edouard Molinaro, and Roger
Vadim, had managed to get films made, and Billard was right to lump them
with their established elders: they indeed displayed little originality to distinguish their films from those of their elders in the French film industry.[45] Of
the *Cahiers* group, only Chabrol had made a feature film, *Le Beau Serge*;
Billard hadn't seen it yet, and he mentioned it in passing alongside another
pair of "attempts at independent production," short films by Truffant and
Rivette. Chabrol's film was indeed not revolutionary in its aesthetic. However, there was in fact a revolutionary aspect to *Le Beau Serge* that distinguished it from the pack (although this distinction eluded Billard): Chabrol's
sober, professional competence had been won not in the film schools or
through long apprenticeship but simply from an absorption in the cinema as
an omnivorous viewer and as a critic.

A new generation of French filmmakers was indeed emerging, and, as
suggested by Françoise Giroud's sociological angle, they heralded epochal
change. But this cinematic New Wave would be properly defined not as a
generation but as a particular group of filmmakers with a common background at *Cahiers du cinéma*—and that handful of partisans was about to
force its way onto the world stage.

Truffaut began to film *The 400 Blows* on November 10, 1958; early in the
morning of November 11, André Bazin died of leukemia, which was aggra-
vated by the tuberculosis from which he had suffered grievously since 1950.

In April 1959, Truffaut's film, which he dedicated to the memory of Bazin, was chosen as one of the three that would officially represent France in competition at the 1959 Cannes festival—one year after administrators of the same festival had refused the director's journalistic credentials after his derision of the films shown there in 1957 as so many "false legends" from which the French cinema was "dying."

Godard wrote an ecstatically triumphant note in *Arts:* "What is important is that, for the first time, a young film has been officially designated by the public authorities to show the true face of French cinema to the entire world." He praised his fellow critics for having "waged . . . the combat for the film auteur":

> We have won in creating acceptance of the principle that a film by Hitchcock, for example, is as important as a book by Aragon. The auteurs of films, thanks to us, have definitively entered into the history of art.

But, Godard warned, "If we have won the battle, the war is not yet over."[46]

The screening on May 4 of *The 400 Blows* at the Cannes festival was an immediate success, winning acclaim from the audience and gaining in one stroke more publicity for the New Wave than all the films and articles that had preceded it. Truffaut won the award for best direction and now had no difficulty persuading Braunberger to allow him to make the film he wanted, an adaptation of David Goodis's novel *Down There* (which Truffaut would call *Tirez sur le pianiste* (*Shoot the Piano Player*). Godard, however, had not yet made his first film, and he sensed that Truffaut's success could open doors for him.

During the festival, Godard was in Paris, where he met Jean Douchet, a critic for *Cahiers,* by chance on the Champs-Elysées. Douchet recalled Godard telling him: "It's disgusting. Everyone's at Cannes. What the fuck am I doing here? I've absolutely got to get the money to go down there . . . Truffaut is a bastard, he could have thought of me . . ."[47] Godard knew that the moment had arrived for action; he again "borrowed" money from the till of *Cahiers* and took the train to Cannes at once. There, he set the wheels in motion: he asked Truffaut to let him use the story that they had worked on together in 1956 about the car thief, Michel Portail, who kills a motorcycle cop and tries to elude capture in Paris while seeking out his American girlfriend there. He pitched the story to Beauregard, who was also at the festival. On May 9, Truffaut and Chabrol both wrote to the producer, with Truffaut agreeing to write the screenplay and Chabrol offering to serve as "technical and artistic adviser" on the film that Godard would direct, called *A Bout de souffle* (*Breathless*).[48] But Beauregard, who was sixty million francs

($120,000) in debt from his two Loti productions, had little to contribute to the enterprise but his savoir-faire. A film distributor, René Pignières, of the Société Nouvelle de Cinématographie (SNC), reckoned there was money to be made distributing a New Wave film that would have Truffaut's and Chabrol's newly valuable names on it, and agreed to put up a small amount of money with which Beauregard would somehow be able to realize the project.

Godard directs Jean Seberg and Jean-Paul Belmondo in *Breathless;* Raoul Coutard holds the camera.
(© Raymond Cauchetier)

three

BREATHLESS

"A boy who thinks about death"

A REGULAR FEATURE OF *CAHIERS DU CINÉMA* FROM November 1955 onward was the "Council of Ten," in which critics from *Cahiers* and other publications rated new releases on a scale from "don't bother" (a dot) to "masterpiece" (four stars) and the scores were collated into a ranked list. Godard was first polled for the issue of August–September 1957 and soon became a steady participant. In July 1959, the list was headed by *Hiroshima, mon amour,* Alain Resnais's first feature film (from a script by Marguerite Duras), followed by Truffaut's *The 400 Blows* and Howard Hawks's *Rio Bravo*.

Only Godard had given all three films four stars, a gesture of recognition that their simultaneous release represented a landmark in cinema history: Hawks's film exemplified classicism, Truffaut's marked the French New Wave's arrival on the world scene, and Resnais's was a radical attempt at a cinematic modernism inspired by avant-garde literature. Godard, who was about to make his first feature film, conceived it in relation—and in opposition—to all three: against a dutiful approximation of Hawksian classicism; against Truffaut's naturalistic form of memoir-autobiography; and against Resnais's formalist modernism.

Once Beauregard's involvement in the project was confirmed and Pignières's promise of financing secured, Godard began to seek actors. He suggested to Beauregard[1] that efforts be made to hire an American actress, Jean Seberg, to play the American woman. As Godard knew, Seberg lived in Paris with her French husband, François Moreuil, a young attorney who also harbored directorial ambitions (and was a cousin of the American director William Wyler).

Seberg had become famous in 1956 when, while still a high school student in Marshalltown, Iowa, she was chosen by Otto Preminger in a much-ballyhooed nationwide talent search to play Joan of Arc in his film *Saint Joan*. Seberg was miscast—and then tyrannized—by Preminger. His notoriously harsh methods may have borne fruit with other, experienced actors, but Seberg could not bear up under his verbal assault, and her performance suffered: a Joan of Arc without self-confidence is no Joan of Arc at all. For the role, her hair had been cut martially short; and Preminger again imposed this style, both pixieish and provocatively androgynous, for her second film, *Bonjour Tristesse*, based on the bestselling French novel by the young writer Françoise Sagan.

Bonjour Tristesse, in which Seberg plays a teenage daughter who destroys her widowed father's chance at happiness with another woman, had been scorned in the United States. (The *New York Times* critic called it a "bomb" and Seberg a "misplaced amateur.") In France, where it was released in May 1958, *Bonjour Tristesse* was widely derided for what was taken to be Preminger's glossy Hollywood treatment of a novel that should have been reserved for a French director. The dissenting voice of enthusiasm for the film was that of François Truffaut, who exulted in the pages of *Arts* that Seberg had a "special quality of heartbreaking young beauty that somehow shone through her technically inadequate performances."[2] Godard placed the film third in his *Cahiers* ten-best list for 1958, behind Joseph Mankiewicz's *The Quiet American* and Ingmar Bergman's *Dreams*.

Seberg, who had been wounded by critics' uncomprehending response to *Bonjour Tristesse*, was immensely grateful to Truffaut for his praise. She thanked him in what she called a "fan letter," which she sent after the success of *The 400 Blows*. In the note, she told Truffaut: "of all the young directors I believe in you and Renais [*sic*]."[3] Her career had been hurt by the bad reviews and by the commercial failure of her films with Preminger: after making *Bonjour Tristesse*, Preminger had sold her contract to Columbia Pictures, which cast her in the minor comedy *The Mouse That Roared*.

Moreuil arranged a meeting between Godard and Seberg. She was unimpressed by the director, describing him as "an incredibly introverted, messy-looking young man with glasses, who didn't look [her] in the eyes when he talked," but she was encouraged by her husband to accept the role Godard was offering.[4] In any case, Seberg believed the project was more interesting than any she had been offered in the United States; meeting the director Samuel Fuller by chance in Paris, she told him, "It will be better than working with Preminger."[5]

Although Columbia had little work for Seberg, the studio was nonetheless reluctant to lend her out to unknowns. Godard tried to sway Columbia with a twelve-page telegram, giving the studio the choice of either one-half of the film's revenues outside France or fifteen thousand dollars. The decisive gesture, however, seems to have been that of her husband, who flew to Los Angeles and told the Columbia studio executives that Seberg would retire from acting if her request to film with Godard was not met. The studio executives agreed to terms with Beauregard on June 8. With little reason to believe that the film would generate much non-French revenue, they took the cash.

Godard had not forgotten his promise to cast Belmondo in the lead role of his first film. Although *Charlotte et son Jules* was still unreleased, Godard had in a way already publicly "discovered" the actor: writing in *Arts* in 1958 about the film *Un drôle de dimanche,* in which Belmondo plays a supporting role, Godard had likened him to two of the greatest French film actors, heralding him as "the Michel Simon and the Jules Berry of tomorrow."[6] Belmondo, who was already recognized as a comic theater actor, was beginning to get lucrative, if uninspiring, offers from the mainstream film industry. While Godard was preparing *Breathless,* Belmondo was offered a supporting role in a film by the veteran director Julien Duvivier, which his agent, Blanche Montel, encouraged him to accept. While waiting for Belmondo to decide, Godard considered offering the role to, among others, the popular singer and songwriter Charles Aznavour, whom Truffaut had met at Cannes and would soon cast as the lead in his second film, *Shoot the Piano Player.* Belmondo took Godard's offer, over the objections of Montel, who told him, "You're making the biggest mistake of your life." He signed a contract that paid him 400,000 francs (approximately eight hundred dollars), which barely covered his vacation on the Riviera before the shoot started.[7]

ALTHOUGH GODARD KNEW the story well, having worked on it with Truffaut, he was now at a loss as to how to tell it. His four short fictions had all been adaptations—*Une Femme coquette* of a Maupassant story, *All the Boys Are Called Patrick* of Rohmer's script, *Charlotte et son Jules* based on Cocteau's *Le Bel indifférent,* and *Histoire d'eau* using Truffaut's footage. His occasional work in the film industry had also been second-order—editing nature footage for the producer Pierre Braunberger and the publishing house of Arthaud, writing dialogue for scripts by the young directors Edouard Molinaro and Jean-Pierre Mocky, adapting the Loti novel for Beauregard. The stories he had proposed to producers had all been adaptations—*Odile* from Goethe, *Quartier Nègre* from a novel by Simenon, even *The Myth of Sisyphus.* Until now, he had been a critic, a writer who wrote in response to preexisting material; and he was having trouble getting a story going on his own.

On June 17, Godard sent a note to Truffaut from the Côte d'Azur to request help with the story: "If you have time to finish off for me in three lines the story begun one morning métro Richelieu-Drouot (those were the good Times[8]), although I haven't got Françoise Sagan[9] at my disposal, I'd be able to add the dialogue." Truffaut had formally ceded the story in question to Beauregard for the derisory sum of one million francs (two thousand dollars), a gesture of friendship to Godard for which the producer was grateful; but the story was at that point not a script or even a story outline.[10] Truffaut, who was also staying in the south of France with his mistress, Liliane David, wrote back with a promise to sketch out the story upon his return to Paris.

The outline was needed by Beauregard and Pignières for the latter to submit with his application to the government for the production subsidy to which he was entitled. Laws passed in 1948 to aid the French cinema in the wake of the Blum-Byrnes accord offered producers direct grants on the basis of their previous productions (and financed them with a special tax on ticket sales), and also provided inexpensive credit to producers from the French national bank. Pignières's track record allowed him to participate in this system, and on June 25, he submitted requests for a direct grant to foster production of *Breathless*.

Time was running out on this system of financing. On June 16, André Malraux, who had in January been named France's first minister of cultural affairs,[11] had announced a revision of the terms of government aid to the French cinema. Where the law had formerly granted financial assistance to producers primarily on the basis of the quantity of their previous releases— thus favoring the industry's commercial mainstream—now it would favor quality. The new system would be called the "advance on receipts," which granted producers financing on the basis of a script's quality (as determined by a board of industry reviewers).

A French cinema of artistic merit, Malraux contended, would reinforce French culture both within France and around the world. The new policy was based on Malraux's recognition that the cinema and its function had changed. As television became increasingly common in French households, demand for films was declining; the number of tickets sold in France had dropped from 411 million in 1957 to 371 million in 1958. Malraux recognized that, in order to remain viable, the French cinema would need to become part of the French cultural patrimony, and to be exported like Bordeaux wine or Camembert cheese; that if the French film industry was to have a future, it would be in the international market of art films.

But Pignières, when he submitted his dossier to the Centre National de la Cinématographie (CNC) on June 25, 1959, under the old system of aid for producers, was not claiming for the film any artistic merit; he was simply requesting quasi-automatic financial assistance for a commercial venture.

Beauregard's commerce, however, was singularly tenuous. The producer worked on a tightrope of solvency and did not always keep his footing. José Bénazéraf, a producer who shared an office with Beauregard at the time, summed him up in a phrase: "fragility and payment due."[12] Beauregard, he explained, "seems to have been persecuted by the constant lack of money. He put into a film everything he had and everything he didn't have."[13] Beauregard's two previous films (the Loti productions) had largely been financed by an independent backer, but did so poorly that Beauregard was left with a debt of 60 million old francs ($120,000). As a commercial proposition, *Breathless* could hardly do worse.

Godard's friends from *Cahiers* had made their first films without producers: Chabrol's first two films had been self-financed; Truffaut's company was funded by his father-in-law; Rivette's film, *Paris nous appartient* (*Paris Belongs to Us*), was self-financed (and was, at the time, unfinished, for lack of funds); Rohmer's forthcoming film was backed by Chabrol. Only Godard had a producer from within the French film industry. Beauregard, because of his trusting (and cavalier) temperament, granted Godard a liberty that was exceptional by industry standards but was still less than that afforded his friends by the autonomy of their productions. Compared to his cohorts, Godard was making his film in the face of opposition, which, although initially mild, would intensify during the shoot over matters of pure practicality.

IN PARIS, GODARD worked on the adaptation of *Breathless*. His original plan had been to use Truffaut's story outline and merely add dialogue to it. Instead, he remodeled the entire story, reconfiguring the action, adding and subtracting characters, and drastically shifting the emphases.[14]

Truffaut's new story outline differed in several respects from the version of the story that he had hoped to shoot several years earlier. His original plan ended in suspense, with the criminal aware that he was recognized by passersby from newspaper pictures: he knew that he was being looked at in the street, as Truffaut said, "like a star."[15] But when sketching out the subject for Godard, Truffaut replaced this personal touch with a clearer and more decisive ending, the criminal's bloodless suicide by aspirin overdose. Truffaut also cut a long flashback in the middle, concerning the backstory of the French criminal and his American lover in the United States several years earlier. He offered Godard a more straightforward and neutral story than the one he had planned for himself.

The new outline by Truffaut told a story of claustrophobia, of the increasingly frantic anguish of a young man who, having turned in despair to crime, sees the walls of the world close in around him—a parallel to *The 400 Blows,* and to Truffaut's own experience. It was mainly a manhunt, in which the point of view shifted between the police and the man being hunted.

Godard, however, removed all but a trace of the police side of the plot, focusing the action on the young man who is desperate in a big city, scrambling for help from his friends, who are all away or unable to help in time—an echo of the financial difficulties that Godard himself had endured.[16] And most importantly, in Godard's draft, the American woman comes into the plot near the beginning, and their love story dominates the film.

Also, Godard shifted the bulk of the action to his own stomping grounds—the Champs-Elysées (where *Cahiers du cinéma* was located), Montparnasse (the neighborhood of the hotel seen in *Charlotte et son Jules*), and St.-Germain-des-Prés—and even included in his treatment a geographical wink to Jean-Paul Sartre, showing the fugitive as he "crosses the boulevard Saint-Germain, passes in front of [the bookstore] la Hune and enters the courtyard of a building next to the Flore"[17]—the café made famous by Sartre during the war. Writing to Truffaut, Godard explained that "the action revolves around a car thief . . . in love with a girl who sells the *New York Herald* and takes courses in French civilization."[18] He similarly described the basic idea of the film he was about to make: "In general, the subject will be the story of a boy who thinks about death and that of a girl who doesn't."[19]

The film's autobiographical aspect is not found primarily in the plot, which does not depict (except in scattered details) incidents from Godard's own life. Instead, *Breathless* is autobiographical at a higher level of abstraction: the concerns of the "boy" reflect Godard's own. In making the film, Godard would find further, more radical, ways to redefine cinematic autobiography, but replacing autobiographical action with an autobiographical "subject" or idea was the first step.

The story of *Breathless* is centered on Michel Poiccard, who, with the help of a female accomplice whom he leaves behind, steals a car in Marseille from an American army officer and drives toward Paris where he plans to meet up with a woman named Patricia. He finds a pistol in the glove compartment. When a police officer on a motorcycle pulls Michel over for speeding, Michel—knowing that he will be arrested—shoots him and then flees on foot through open fields. Arriving in Paris, Michel finds Patricia selling the *New York Herald Tribune* on the Champs-Elysées; she is unsure whether she wants to see him again. He visits another woman, from whom he steals money, and proceeds in vain to a travel office in search of an underworld friend who owes him money. Making his way to Patricia's hotel, he sneaks into her room and waits for her in bed. In a twenty-six-minute sequence that takes place in the room and mainly in bed, they make love, fall asleep, wake up, and talk about love and life. There, Patricia reveals that she is pregnant by him. By the time they go out to the street, newspaper headlines blare that Michel is wanted for murder. Patricia helps him stay a step ahead of the police, and considers accepting Michel's offer to flee with him to Italy as soon as he collects the money he is owed. But when detectives find her at the *Herald Tribune* office and threaten her with criminal charges and deportation, she has misgivings. A friend finds Michel and Patricia an overnight hideout in a photographer's studio in Montparnasse; they install themselves there but when Michel goes out to buy food, Patricia calls the police and denounces him, then goes back and warns him. He flees, but, pursued by the police, he is shot in the back. He dies in the street, under Patricia's blank gaze.

The story resembles a classic American film noir, and indeed in a scene where Michel hides in a movie theater, the sound track plays a clip from Joseph H. Lewis's *Gun Crazy*, an American film from 1949 with a similar theme. But Godard approached the story in ways that departed radically from its genre models, and did so foremost by the methods with which he filmed it. His years as a critic and the philosophical inclinations that informed them bore fruit: despite his relative inexperience as a filmmaker, and his scant familiarity with the practical aspects of the cinema, he applied his ideas to the aesthetic and the technical elements of his film, and the results were revolutionary.

The shooting of *Breathless* took place in conditions that were in many respects unprecedented in the history of cinema. Godard was aware of their peculiarity; indeed, he would make sure that his way of making the film would be as much a part of its public identity as the story and the actors. Godard's novel method was not only the practical springboard for his formal and intellectual inventions, it was a part of them. *Breathless* would be an "action film" in the sense of "action painting": the act and the moment of making the film were as much a part of the work's meaning as its specific content and style. As such, it would be the first existentialist film.

THE CAMERAMAN, RAOUL Coutard, had worked on Beauregard's earlier productions. Michel Latouche had done the camera work on Godard's short films, and Godard had planned to ask him to shoot *Breathless*, but Coutard was Beauregard's choice. Coutard was gallantly prepared to feign a prior commitment so as not to compel Godard to work with him, but Godard asked Coutard to shoot test footage and was pleased with the results.[20] Prior to working with Beauregard, Coutard had been a documentary cameraman for the French army's information service in Indochina during the war, and Godard decided to rely on this aspect of Coutard's experience in conceiving the visual schema for the film.

Godard wanted *Breathless* to be shot, as much as possible, like a documentary, with a handheld camera and a minimum of added lighting. This decision had both an aesthetic component, making the film look newsreel-like, and a practical one, saving the time usually spent setting up lights and a tripod. For several sequences that featured tracking shots, Godard avoided the use of cumbersome tracking rails (on which a wheeled dolly rolls, bearing the camera). Instead, Coutard filmed from a wheelchair pushed by Godard; and for the first sequence with Belmondo and Seberg on the Champs-Elysées, Godard, planning to film unnoticed by passersby, put Coutard inside a deliveryman's pushcart into which two small viewing holes were cut in the front. An assistant pushed the cart and followed the unrecognized actors while Godard followed the action at a distance.

In order to film at night without added lighting, Godard drew on Coutard's earlier experience as a still photographer and asked him to name his favorite kind of film for low-light still photography. Coutard chose a film produced by the British firm of Ilford, but Ilford did not manufacture it in the 400-foot rolls that were standard movie stock—it was sold only in small canisters of 17.5 meters (approximately 46 feet), which fit 35mm still cameras.[21] Godard went to a photography supply store to buy out the store's inventory. He and Coutard extracted the rolls from their containers, and on location, two assistants were employed to load and unload the movie camera's film magazines with the tiny spools (which could be used for approximately thirty seconds' worth of filming).[22] After the shoot, Godard and Coutard used lightproof changing bags to splice the many short rolls together into longer ones so that they could be processed by the film laboratory.

Even film processing became an adventure of invention. Godard wanted to push-process the film, to develop it in a special chemical bath that would increase its sensitivity to light, further compensating for the absence of additional lighting. Laboratories, however, customarily processed film in far larger batches than the quantity Godard produced for *Breathless*. He persuaded the laboratory used by Beauregard to set aside a small and rarely used developing machine for the special chemical bath.

The choice of a lightweight handheld newsreel camera and an appropriate film stock and laboratory treatment allowed him to work more rapidly and casually than the norm. A letter that Godard wrote to the producer

Pierre Braunberger while the shoot was in progress is an invaluable record of his distinctive methods and his awareness of their significance. He told the producer:

> At the rushes, the whole crew, including the cameraman, finds the photography disgusting. I like it. The important thing is not that things be filmed in this or that way, but simply that they be filmed and not be out of focus.[23]

Godard's indifference to the specific image was no pretense but an accurate reflection of his conduct on the set. He habitually gave Coutard obscure, elliptical orders, as when he confusingly requested a close-up by asking that nothing be seen from the shoulders to the hips; when Coutard filmed something else, Godard said, "That's all right," and told him to move on to the next shot. As Coutard recalled, Godard often gave such negative instructions: "He said: 'I want this and that not to be seen,' and so you could pretty well figure it out . . . For instance, when he wanted a close-up, he said, 'I don't want to see the breast pocket on his shirt.' "[24] On another occasion, Godard asked Coutard where the "best place" for the camera was, and then, after getting Coutard's response, ordered that the camera be placed elsewhere. As Godard wrote to Braunberger: "My biggest job consists of keeping the technical crew away from the shoot. I am in a very bizarre state of mind, absolutely not crazed, and lazier than ever. I'm not thinking of anything."[25]

Godard kept the technical crew to the scant minimum, but nonetheless found their presence cumbersome. Union regulations required him to hire a makeup artist, but Godard prevented her from doing any makeup, though Seberg said that the makeup artist sometimes slipped her a powder puff.[26] The script supervisor was unable to keep track of continuity because Godard kept her away from the shoot; when the crew filmed the hotel room scenes, he made sure she stayed in the hallway. Godard's state of "not thinking of anything" made him utterly indifferent to continuity or planning; the result was a rare cinematic spontaneity, an "action cinema" akin to the "action painting" for which Abstract Expressionists were already famous. He was aware that the film would reflect the conditions under which it was made, and that his methods were inseparable from his aesthetic.

> Wednesday, we shot a scene in direct sunlight with Geva 36. Everyone found it awful. I find it fairly extraordinary. It is the first time that one obliges the film stock to give the maximum of itself by making it do that for which it is not made. It is as if it were suffering by being exploited to the outer limit of its possibilities. Even the film stock, you see, will be out of breath.

The movie and the film stock are, in this view, one; if the movie stock suffers, the film will reflect suffering; if the film stock is *à bout de souffle,* the movie will fulfill its title as well. Godard's notion of correspondence between the movie and life behind the camera is a stern aesthetic that unifies the film and the work that went into it, the film and its maker: it is as if the camera were turned as surely on the director and his crew as on his actors, as if the camera were running as much between takes as during them. This idea, which renders film technique personal and renders the personal a product of technique, would prove to be the most lasting effect of *Breathless* on Godard's work to come and a defining element of his contribution to cinema.

Godard included his friends in the film. He asked Jean-Pierre Melville— an independent filmmaker (born in 1917) who owned his own studio and made French crime movies with an American flair, including the legendary *Bob le flambeur*[27]—to play a voluble novelist whom Patricia would interview at Orly Airport for the *New York Herald Tribune,* and he named this character Parvulesco, after his Geneva friend, the right-wing philosopher. Godard wanted the scene to play like a real interview, and he asked Melville to improvise his answers—"to talk about women or anything I wanted, the way we did when we drove around at night."[28] Roland Tolmatchoff was supposed to come to Paris to play a gangster named Balducci (the last name of the film's publicist, Richard Balducci); when Tolmatchoff was unable to come on the appointed day, Godard asked Balducci to play a gangster named Tolmatchoff. He cast Jacques Rivette in a cameo role.

But the most unusual aspect of Godard's technique concerned the script, or rather, the lack of one. As Godard wrote to Braunberger, "At the moment we really are shooting from day to day. I write the scenes while having breakfast at the Dupont Montparnasse." He was not exaggerating. Before the shoot, Godard had begun to write a traditional screenplay, filling in dialogue for each scene (starting with the scene that occurs on the Champs-Elysées, where Belmondo finds Seberg selling the *New York Herald Tribune*). He attempted to write more dialogue (some of which he passed along to Seberg), but was dissatisfied with the results. In early August 1959, Seberg wrote to a friend, "Day by day, the scenario seems to be getting bigger and worse in every way."[29] Godard did not like the script either, so he got rid of it and decided to write the dialogue day by day as the production went along. Of course, the actors found this procedure odd. They hardly had time to learn their lines. The film, however, was shot without direct sound (the entire sound track, including the dialogue, was to be post-synchronized, i.e., dubbed), and so, when the actors' memory failed, Godard called their lines out to them while the camera was rolling. He wrote to Braunberger, "Seberg is crazed, and regrets doing the film. I start with her tomorrow. I'll say goodbye to you because I have to find what is going to be filmed tomorrow."

Having worked on Hollywood shoots, Seberg was shocked.[30] Belmondo was able to take the proceedings as something of a joke. Seeing himself at rushes in a hat and with a Boyard cigarette dangling from his mouth (Godard's brand, cheap, thick, yellow corn-paper cigarettes renowned for the pungency of their smoke), Belmondo feared for his career. Eventually, he felt reassured by the chaos of the shoot: Belmondo was sure that the film could not be edited into anything coherent and figured that it would never be released.

This idiosyncratic scripting produced a particular on-screen result. Godard's spontaneous method deliberately frustrated the actors' attempts to compose their characters in any naturalistic or psychologically motivated way. And to make sure of the spontaneity, Godard told Belmondo, "Don't think about the film tonight. We'll lose two hours tomorrow making you forget whatever you were imagining off by yourself."[31] In effect, Godard's actors were quoting Godard. Rather than becoming their characters, they were imitating them.

ON AUGUST 17, 1959, the first day of the shoot, the crew gathered at 6:00 AM at a café across from Notre-Dame. The action involved Belmondo, who in the story had just returned to Paris after killing the police officer on the rural highway. Godard asked him to enter a phone booth, say whatever he wanted, and leave the phone booth; Godard asked him to enter a café, place an order, and leave without paying. These brief sequences were the sole work of the day; such short work days would prove not atypical for Godard and his crew. The absence of additional lighting, the handheld camera, the lack of makeup, permitted the crew to work very rapidly. There were no cables or other equipment to limit the actors' freedom of movement; there was no crowd control, no attempt to modify the life on the street around the filming. Godard had calculated the rapidity of his methods, and counted on being able to fill a significant amount of screen time quickly, leaving the rest of his time free so that he could figure out the next day's program. He often discharged his crew after what was officially only a half-day's work, and on days when he did not feel inspired, he cancelled the shoot altogether. Beauregard assumed that Godard was slacking off and wasting money. One day when Godard called off the shoot on the pretext of illness, Beauregard found him at a café near the production office; a physical altercation resulted, and Coutard himself had to separate producer and director.

On September 3, 1959, four days into the third week of the shoot, Beauregard wrote to Godard complaining that "there have been eight half-days of work and of these half-days, the work has sometimes been only two hours." He threatened to report Godard to the CNC (which regulated contracts and employment in the industry) and to withhold his wages if he continued to work short days or to cancel shoot days. However, there was a method to Godard's apparent caprices, as he later explained: "I was also sort of the producer because I very quickly recognized that what's important in a film is to control the money; the money, meaning the time, meaning having the money and being able to spend it according to one's rhythm and one's pleasure."[32]

Godard's way of working not only contributed to the film's distinctiveness—but also proved to be the best kind of advertising. Months before the movie was even completed, *Breathless* was the talk of Paris, thanks to a magnificent publicity campaign orchestrated by the press agent, Richard Balducci, who had been hired by Beauregard. The usual puffery would not do for a first-time director working with a struggling producer and a fading starlet among a cast of unknowns. Instead, taking advantage of Godard's singular methods and the unique atmosphere that they generated on location, Balducci made them the subject of his campaign. In the process, Godard's way of working became, locally, as familiar as Jackson Pollock's method of drip painting. Balducci skillfully leaked information about the film, making a virtue of its peculiarities.

While shooting the film, Godard made sure that he would be recognized. He gave himself a crucial, albeit minor, role, something far richer than a Hitchcockian cameo: he plays a passerby who recognizes the nearby Michel Poiccard from his picture in the paper and shows detectives which way the accused criminal went.

The movie was publicized in three substantial articles that appeared in the mainstream press in the months following the shoot and before its release: first, an interview in *Radio-Cinéma-Télévision* with Truffaut, who put his celebrity to work on the film's behalf; second, a long and detailed report from location that ran in *France-Observateur,* written by a journalist who was "embedded" in the crew; and third, an interview in *L'Express* with Godard himself. All three played a role in the birth of a legend. The calculated methods of publicity had the effect of canonizing Godard as an auteur before he even had something to show.

On October 4, 1959, *Radio-Cinéma-Télévision* printed its article about Truffaut's involvement with the film (he had often written for the publication). Truffaut said that he had given Godard "about thirty" pages of a script treatment, and described its story as a sequel to *The 400 Blows:* "Imagine Antoine four years after the end of the film. After he runs away, he goes from reform school to reform school. He volunteers before he's drafted and, when he returns from a dreary war in Indochina, he becomes a car thief."

The association of *Breathless* with Truffaut's famous film was, of course, helpful to Godard, but as Truffaut told the interviewer, Claude-Marie Trémois, "The pretext is unimportant. What counts—and what is stunning—is what Godard has done with it." He spoke glowingly, if with a hint of ironic ambiguity, about the film-in-progress: "Godard is overflowing with ideas. The projection of rushes, which is usually so boring, is here exhilarating because he rarely does two takes of the same scene and when he does, it isn't really the same scene. It is a succession of discoveries." Indeed, Coutard later recalled, "Truffaut found it rather funny, the way we were shooting,"[33] yet in the interest of Godard's film, Truffaut mostly withheld his doubts from the press.

For the second article, Balducci had arranged for a journalist, Marc Pierret, to be planted with the crew as an assistant, with Godard's knowledge and consent, so that he could write about the experience. In a report that took two full pages in *France-Observateur*[34] of October 29, 1959, Pierret guided readers into the universe of Godard's production methods, and through Pierret, the public was also introduced to Godard's voice. The process that the *Cahiers* writers had helped to crystallize—the celebration of the director's personality through the recognition of its distinctive imprint on his films—was turned around by Godard. With other filmmakers, the film came first, followed by the recognition of the auteur's personality; with Godard, the person came first.

This process would serve as a template for Godard's career: interviews have provided him with a parallel sound track on the public record and a vehicle for the intellectual profusion that spilled beyond the confines of his films. In the 1950s, Godard had used criticism to pour forth his ideas with an arch and allusive brilliance; now that he was a professional filmmaker, interviews would play that role, and would do so even better—for Godard had long been recognized, by those who knew him, as a brilliant talker. And Pierret was merely the first of a long list of journalists who would adorn their pages with Godard's scintillating verbal sallies.

Pierret's questions teased out Godard's iconoclastic approach to the cinema. In one exchange, Pierret asks, "Do you love the cinema?"

> I have contempt for it. It is nothing. It does not exist. Thus I love it. I love it and at the same time I have contempt for it. A little like the way I have contempt for, and as I love, the actors who do cinema, who lend their face to all the caprices and obscure desires of the director.

While Bazin praised the cinema for its neutral fidelity to reality, Godard saw the medium's neutrality—its dependence on external reality—

equivocally. Godard had turned to the cinema by default, after painting and writing, and he did not only hold it in contempt—he held himself in contempt for not creating from scratch, as do writers, painters, composers, for having turned to a medium that by its nature is parasitic. Yet as he told Pierret, this medium that "does not exist" allowed Godard himself to exist: "I like to observe people in cafés, in the street. I don't do anything. I watch them. Then, I can re-create with actors the expressions, the mystery, which a sort of passivity or maladjustment helped me to discover."

Godard also spoke to Pierret of his unusual methods and alluded to the strain they were placing on his relation with Beauregard:

> I need a certain freedom. I get it by sowing a certain confusion. By playing around with the familiar ways. The producer thinks that I'm improvising, whereas I'm only adapting myself to his conditions in order to create a greater possibility of invention.

The journalist described Godard's "possibility of invention" as he observed the director at work late at night in a Latin Quarter pizzeria, near the end of the shoot, composing the film's crucial last scene: "The St.-Germain Pizza, 11 PM. J. L. Godard dines alone. Pieces of paper scattered around his plate of crudités. . . . It is not certain that Belmondo will be put to death. Godard is keeping it for the last days of the shoot."

In Truffaut's original idea, the ending follows the true-life story: the criminal is arrested; in Truffaut's sketch for Godard, the criminal commits suicide in police custody. In Godard's outline, the criminal tries to get away, taking money from his underworld friends and borrowing a car for his escape as Patricia looks on blankly. Now, during the shoot, Godard could not decide whether to follow the laws of genre (the criminal is punished) or to yield to the desire to grant him a light-footed escape.

Death, of course, won out; but rather than letting Poiccard expire bloodlessly, Godard put Belmondo through an agony that he filmed as something of a slapstick dance: Belmondo stumbles down the middle of the rue Campagne-Première in Montparnasse with blood oozing onto his white shirt.

In the long take, passersby, some bewildered, others bemused, can be seen on the sidewalk as they watch the action or gawk at the camera that trails the actor down the street as his overdone death canter tips the anguish of the moment into a comic theatrical approximation. Godard directed Belmondo quite vaguely, merely instructing him to run and to fall down; Belmondo chose to land poetically between the crosswalk markers—

although not for poetic reasons, but simply to avoid landing in the middle of oncoming traffic in the boulevard Raspail. So little attention was paid to crowd control that, as Belmondo completed the first take with his tumble, a policeman on duty reportedly leaped off a passing bus to aid the "victim," and exclaimed with surprise: "Oh, it's a movie?"[35]

According to Pierret, when Godard came in for a close-up of Belmondo at the moment of Poiccard's death, the director told the actor, "Try to die well: each second of this shot is worth a week in first run." This scene too was realized without crowd control, as crowds formed and pressed up against the director and the cameraman while filming proceeded.

Pierret's *France-Observateur* coverage was followed in late December 1959 with an interview of Godard by the journalist Michèle Manceaux that was published in *L'Express*. The interviewer encouraged the director to affect the role of the young outlaw. Manceaux remarked that Godard had also had his "four hundred blows"[36]: "He broke into a safe, got himself locked in an insane asylum, and even took off with the cash box at *Cahiers*." She asked Godard point-blank: "Why all this?"

> A need for liberty. I don't really know why. I broke into the safe because I was waiting for a girl who didn't show up and I really had to do something. Rebellion without a cause, as they say in America. I broke off with my whole family at that time. There are still moments where I need to be in contradiction: for example, I haven't insured my car. I get a kind of kick out of that.[37]

Godard's glamorized "rebellion" was patently relevant to his practice of film; the press had already made much of Godard's readiness to break the rules in directing, to do whatever wasn't allowed, and to sow a risky disorder on the set, as well as his willingness—or even desire—to endure the veiled disdain of those closest to him, such as Truffaut, as a result of it. The reports of his youthful delinquency reinforced the image of an artistic rebel with an ongoing need "to be in contradiction" with the way that others made films.

The *L'Express* interview also provided the occasion for Godard's first, and definitive, theoretical exposition of his idea of montage as the key element of the cinema: "I read three books a day. I didn't do anything else. As a freshman,[38] I started to go to the movies. But one day, I took off. I was twenty years old." Manceaux asked Godard whether he had ever considered becoming a writer.

> Yes, of course. But I wrote, "The weather is nice. The train enters the station," and I sat there for hours wondering why I couldn't have just as well written the

opposite: "The train enters the station. The weather is nice" or "it is raining." In the cinema, it's simpler. At the same time, the weather is nice and the train enters the station. There is something ineluctable about it. You have to go along with it.

Godard would repeat and rework this idea, in a variety of forms, for decades to come. Despite sounding like a joke or an incidental anecdote, this concept of the cinema formed the basis for a grand theory. Godard here laid out, minimally and powerfully, the notion he already asserted in his important writings of the 1950s, his view of montage as central to the cinema, indeed constitutive of it. His idea is to define montage as the simultaneous recording of disparate elements in a single image, the simultaneity in one image of two things that would happen sequentially on the page—the train entering the station, the rain falling. In his view, the cinema does automatically what literature wants to do and cannot: it connects two ideas in one time. Yet the organic montage that Godard considered inherent to the cinema mirrored his contempt for it: he depended upon the cinema's second-order or parasitic status in relation to reality, and upon the camera as a passive recording device. This device made him an artist, but, at least in principle, less of one than is a writer or a painter. Thus the cinema, for Godard, is at once a deliverance and a curse. In the cinema he would be both an artist and a slacker, a hero and a bad boy.

THE FIRST CUT of *Breathless* was two-and-a-half hours long, but Beauregard had required that Godard deliver a ninety-minute film. Godard asked Jean-Pierre Melville for advice on how to cut it down:

> I told him to cut everything that didn't keep the action moving, and to remove all unnecessary scenes, mine included. He didn't listen to me, and instead of cutting whole scenes as was the practice then, he had the brilliant idea of cutting more or less at random within scenes. The result was excellent.[39]

Godard (and the editor, Cécile Decugis, who essentially executed Godard's instructions) did not, for the most part, cut at random;[40] on the contrary, he responded to his enthusiasms, and removed all moments—within scenes, even within shots—that seemed to him to lack vigor. He kept in the film only what he thought was strongest, regardless of dramatic import or conventional continuity, thus producing many jump cuts, where characters and anything else that moves within the shot seem to jump from one position to another in a relatively fixed frame. Such cuts were generally considered to be a cardinal error of an amateurish film technique and were scrupulously avoided in the professional cinema. They were seen as both intrinsically funny, a kind of cinematic solecism, and unsettling in the way they break the cinematic illusion by presenting two obviously discontinuous times as immediately sequential. The jump cut, despite—and because of—its ill-repute, became one of the principal figures of the visual style of *Breathless.*

Godard also filmed from deliberately disorienting angles, filming the police chase of Michel from opposite sides of the road, so that the police car and Michel's car appear to be going in opposite directions rather than having one follow the other. He filmed a close-up of Michel's gun from the opposite side as he filmed Michel's body, thus having the gun point not at the policeman, but back toward Michel.[41] On another set, such brazen disregard for standards would have been cited by a script supervisor and a cameraman, who would have informed the director of his "errors." Here, these playfully defiant shots occur in the film's first minutes, as if to announce up front that the old rules would not apply to *Breathless* or to Godard.

Through these decisions, Godard removed the scrim of convention by which the cinema transmits time and space to the viewer; however, by flouting the principles on which the classical cinema is based, he in fact ended up emphasizing them. In appearing amateurish, the film calls attention to the codes of professionalism, and in the end highlights the fact that they are merely conventions: it denaturalizes them. *Breathless* presents standard aspects of the classic cinema, but mediated, or quoted. Paradoxically, this interpolation of Godard's directorial authority between the viewer and the action does not render the film arch, distant, or calculated, but rather produces the impression of immediacy, spontaneity, and vulnerability. Godard's presence is invoked as a sort of live-action narrator who calls the shots as they unfold, with as much potential for accident and error as any live performance. But here, the "errors" only reinforce the illusion of immediacy. The overall result is an accelerated and syncopated rhythm, made of leaps ahead and doublings-back, a sort of visual jazz (with Godard as the improvising soloist) that outswung the American detective and gangster films that had served as Godard's models.

The jump cut is a device that Godard subsequently reused only rarely. He soon devised other, and more sophisticated, methods for conjuring his presence in his films. It was not in Godard's work, but in the work of lesser directors, that the jump cut would become a cliché, and then a commonplace in television commercials and, later, music videos. The great importance of its appearance in *Breathless* was that it served as a starting point for Godard's more thorough reconsideration of technique and convention in editing: years later, after his work had changed direction more than once, Godard said of his editing technique in *Breathless:* "Thinking about it afterward, it gave me new ideas about montage."[42]

BREATHLESS IS NOTABLE for still another kind of montage, the assembly of allusions and references to film history. Not only did Godard film *Breathless* in the style of an American film noir, he stocked it with citations from the American cinema. *Breathless* is replete with visual quotations from movies by Samuel Fuller, Joseph H. Lewis, Anthony Mann, and from *The Enforcer*[43] (as well as from *Le Plaisir* by Max Ophüls). In lieu of credits—the film has none—the film bears a dedication to Monogram Films, an American "B-movie" studio; and the film shows posters for *Westbound,* by Budd Boetticher, a poster of Humphrey Bogart from *The Harder They Fall* (his last film), another poster for another western (starring Jeff Chandler) bearing the remarkable French title *Vivre dangereusement jusqu'au bout* (to live dangerously to the end), the original American title of which was *10 Seconds to Hell;* a clip from the sound track of Preminger's *Whirlpool.* Michel Poiccard himself is obsessed with American movies and takes on the gestures and the attitudes, the perpetual pugnacity and casual misogyny of the noir hero, specifically, the sneer displayed on-screen by Humphrey Bogart, as well as an aptitude for violence that seemed to him to constitute the genre and its promise, or myth, of freedom.

All of Godard's friends in the New Wave were deeply affected and influenced by the recent American cinema. However, the first films of the New Wave—those of Chabrol and Truffaut, as well as the early efforts of Rivette and Rohmer—hardly resembled it. As filmmakers, the group from *Cahiers* kept their relations with the films they loved tacit and implicit. Only Godard made a film that in story, in style, and in substance is directly derived from the American movies they admired.

Breathless openly bore the marks of its director's absorption of the history of cinema, and Godard went on to build his career as a filmmaker with an explicit and voracious aptitude for quotation. In *Breathless,* the technique only added to the immediacy of the effect, suggesting, as it did, that Godard dosed his film with quotations because they were what he was thinking about at the time of its making.

For Godard, the cinema's ability to combine two ideas in one image made it better than writing as a representation of his thought processes. The technical complexities of the cinema were nonetheless obstacles to a spontaneity of expression comparable to that of a writer, but Godard's unusual methods both made the medium more responsive to his immediate inclinations and made that spontaneity apparent in the film itself. The ultimate and most important effect of his decision to compose the dialogue, and to specify the action, as close as possible to the time of the shoot, was to displace the film from being revelatory of the fictional characters to being principally revelatory of Godard himself. Even as *Breathless* uncovers the psychology of its characters, it expounds the thoughts and preferences of Godard in the moment. The viewer's crucial and primary emotional identification is not with any filmed character but with Godard. The rapid, even irrational, transitions and juxtapositions of mood and tone are the cinematic equivalent of Godard's own stream of consciousness, one mind's montage of the thousands of hours of cinema to which Godard had subjected himself, with which he had forged his identity.

And Godard was thinking not only about films, but also about books, paintings, and music, elements of culture directly transmitted through the film by citations in images or on the sound track. Indeed, *Breathless* bore the burden of Godard's intense autodidacticism, with quotations from and references to literature (Faulkner, Dylan Thomas, Aragon, Rilke, Françoise Sagan, Maurice Sachs), paintings (Picasso, Renoir, Klee), and music (Mozart and Bach). The pieces of paper that Pierret, the journalist, saw scattered around Godard's plate of crudités included many quotations from literary sources that Godard had culled from his obsessive reading and which he liberally sprinkled throughout the film's dialogue. The result was a first-person documentary of a distinctive, indeed a unique, sort: this first-person cinema invoked not the director's experience but his presence.

And yet it was a presence that was defined as much by its displacement as by its manifestation. In this context, Godard's obsessive quotation, his past thievery, and his passive reaction to actors and circumstances—all second-degree actions—all appear as part of the same phenomenon: parasitism, literally, feeding on the side, nourishing oneself from another's product or earnings. Whether drawing from his grandfather or Beauregard, from the till at *Cahiers* or his pages of quotes, from the ecstasies of literature or the transcendent self-abnegation that was cinema, whether from the actors who peopled his film or the observed strangers in whose gestures Godard clad his actors, Godard as an original creator existed independently not at all. *Breathless* was both a work of existential engagement with the world—an engagement that was constant, essential, and involuntary, inasmuch as it was a collage of preexisting material—and therefore also a work of Sartrean bad faith, made by a thinker who did not think but was thought.

Breathless is essentially the film of an adolescent, the film to which Godard had been building since his early determination to make movies; it marked both the end of his adolescence and its culmination, and it is overfilled with stored-up ideas and desires. (Years later, when Godard was asked how he would account for the sense of urgency in *Breathless,* he answered, "Adolescence, youth, fear, despair, solitude.")[44] The film is infused with an exultation in despair, as seen in the dancelike movement of Belmondo to an inner dirge that he hears as up-tempo, or in his joy in his dark destiny, despite the gaudy ruin it promises. Truffaut saw it as the "saddest"[45] of Godard's films, as a film of "moral and physical unhappiness."[46] Critics less sophisticated than Truffaut recognized that the film transcended its own fictional or narrative contours to become a phenomenon, an act of self-assertion, a generational watershed.

Breathless is the cornerstone film of the French New Wave because it is the one that explicitly claims the group's intellectual heritage (American movies, modern literature, a polemical yet highly rhetorical critical style) while at the same time brandishing the group's hectic, threadbare, disreputable social circumstances. As Godard said, "We barged into the cinema like cavemen into the Versailles of Louis the Fifteenth."[47] *Breathless* identified the virtues and vices, the ideas and the practices of the New Wave with his own.

Moreover, with *Breathless,* Godard achieved for the cinema, himself, and his movement what Sartre had accomplished in the late 1940s for philosophy, himself, and existentialism: he made his movement the emblem of the times, defined his medium as the one of the moment, and personally became its exemplary figure. Godard instantly became the embodiment of cinema, the New Wave, intellectual fashion, and intellectualism as fashion. Sartre carried a generation with him in the name of the philosophy with which he was personally identified. Godard did the same for the cinema, his ideas about it, and himself; he not only depicted and enacted the struggles of his generation, he ignited its ambitions, turning it into a group that wanted nothing more than to make films, and to make them as he did.

THE SEMINAL IMPORTANCE of the film was recognized immediately. In January 1960—prior to the film's release—Godard won the Jean Vigo Prize, awarded "to encourage an auteur of the future."[48]

Then, after successful test screenings to full houses in Lyon and Marseille, *Breathless* opened in Paris on March 16, 1960, not in an art house but at a chain of four commercial theaters. In its first week of business, it attracted 50,095 spectators in those mere four theaters, and, in its entire Paris first run (which lasted seven weeks), 259,046 spectators. The eventual profit was substantial, rumored to be fifty times the investment. The film's success with the public corresponded to its generally ardent and astonished critical reception. Godard's new view of cinema and its broader implications were reflected, with a remarkable accuracy, in the reviews published at the time of its opening. Perhaps more than any other serious film in the history of cinema, *Breathless,* as a result of its extraordinary and calculated congruence with the moment, and of the fusion of its attributes with the story of its production and with the public persona of its director, was singularly identifiable with the media responses it generated.

Balducci had arranged for notables in and out of the cinema to see *Breathless.* Jean-Paul Sartre (who remarked, "It's really very beautiful"),[49] Sophia Loren, Marguerite Duras, Françoise Sagan, Jean Cocteau, Jacques Becker, and Carlo Ponti all saw early screenings. The film was a conversation piece in sophisticated circles by the time it opened. The most vituperative rejections of the film were from the left-wing film journal *Positif,* where Louis Seguin accused the film of purveying a "mythology" that was "rightist."[50] But most reviewers were aware that they were in the presence of something original and important; one critic set the tone for the film's epochal significance by referring back to Alexandre Astruc's 1948 article prophesying the coming age of the "caméra-stylo," the camera that a new generation of filmmakers would wield with the fluency, spontaneity, and intimacy with which writers write: Gérald Devries, in *Démocratie 60,* opined, "Here is, in fact, the first work authentically written with a caméra-stylo."[51]

Godard's film was recognized to be a part of the New Wave yet different from, and even opposed to, the work of his friends. In *Radio-Cinéma-Télévision,* Gilbert Salachas wrote, "What distinguishes *Breathless* . . . is a spectacular anarchy in the tone, the images, the language. This extremism in its originality is presented almost as a manifesto."[52] Critic and film historian Jacques Siclier declared, "In the light of *Breathless, The 400 Blows* looks like an obedient schoolboy's homework, Chabrol's films the product of a perfect academicism."[53]

Simone Dubreuilh of *Libération*[54] hailed Godard as "a young man who writes authentically everything that he is thinking directly in images."[55] Others, like Pierre Marcabru in *Combat,* recognized the correspondence between the film's substance and its director, and called attention to the implied continuity between the world off-camera and the one filmed:

> It seems that, if we had footage of Godard shooting his film, we would discover a sort of accord between the dramatized world in front of the camera (Belmondo and Seberg playing a scene) and the working world behind it (Godard and Raoul Coutard shooting the scene), as if the wall between the real and projected worlds had been torn down.[56]

The film was also recognized as the signal accomplishment of the New Wave: "Godard goes further than Resnais with *Hiroshima* and Bresson with

Pikpokett [*sic*]."[57] "The terms 'old cinema' and 'new cinema' now have meaning. . . . With *Breathless*, the generation gap can suddenly be felt."[58] With
Breathless, *Cahiers du cinéma* immediately became, in effect, the most important film school in France: the technical training formerly considered indispensable was now, virtually overnight, displaced by the wisdom offered
by Langlois at his unofficial conservatory.

THOUGH FEW YOUNG filmmakers would imitate *Breathless*, many would
imitate Godard himself, such as *Breathless* revealed him to be: an artistically
voracious autodidact devoted fanatically to the history of cinema.

Godard had been a critic for ten years before getting the chance to make
Breathless. By the time he made his first full-length film, he was intensely
aware of the role of the press in creating an idea of a film prior to its existence.
As the director of a film born of a unique mode of production and philosophical orientation, he also required the appropriate conditions for a correct
appreciation of his unusual work. He needed, in other words, to generate—
and to induce critics to employ—a method of criticism that was apt for his
own film. This was his self-appointed task as an interviewee. He needed to
speak directly to his viewers in order to orient their viewing, and he made
sure to become enough of a celebrity to get his voice quickly heard. Michel
Dorsday, of *Cahiers*, recalled that Godard "grafted" onto the film "the fame of
Jean-Luc Godard."[59]

The popular and commercial recognition of *Breathless*, and the intriguing stories surrounding its production, created a demand for Godard's presence in interviews. He was interviewed in *Le Monde* and in *Arts* at the time of
the film's release, as well as in Swiss journals shortly thereafter. These interviews were themselves a sort of virtuoso performance in which the director
both illustrated and extended the methods of his film into the press. In
Le Monde, Godard explained how he had worked:

> Based on this theme by Truffaut, I told the story of an American woman and a
> Frenchman. Things can't work out between them because he thinks about
> death and she doesn't. I said to myself that if I didn't add this idea to the
> screenplay the film would not be interesting. For a long time the boy has been
> obsessed by death, he has forebodings. That's the reason why I shot that scene
> of the accident where he sees a guy die in the street. I quoted that sentence
> from Lenin, "We are all dead people on leave," and I chose the Clarinet Con-
> certo that Mozart wrote shortly before dying.[60]

In fact, Michel sees a "guy" (played by Jacques Rivette) lying dead in the
street after a motor scooter accident (reminiscent of Godard's mother's

death) and walks on impassively, but remarks to Patricia later that day, "I saw a guy die." The next day, in bed with Patricia, he tells her: "Do you think of death sometimes? I think about it endlessly." Thus the "subject" of the film is indeed stated as baldly as possible—a boy who thinks about death—but the cultural artifacts that reinforce the subject and weave it into the fabric of the film are present as a sort of code, and Godard made use of the press to publish the decoder.

Godard's proposed interpretive method—and its difficult subtleties—did not go unnoticed. After seeing the film and reading the interviews, André Bessèges wrote in *France Catholique*:

> They are shown a "guy dying in the street," they are made to hear the clarinet concerto that Mozart wrote just before dying. The auteur assures us that it is to make us understand that his hero is obsessed with death. But one must have, to say the least, an acute sense of symbols, and also be an alert connoisseur of music, to catch onto those intentions.[61]

"To catch onto those intentions" required an initiation, an engagement on the part of the viewer. It also required the active role of the press in transmitting Godard's remarks in the context of reports on the celebrity's life. In a revealing moment in the film's long central scene in Patricia's tiny hotel room, Michel delivers a monologue on the women of different cities (a riff that Godard's voluble and opinionated friend Roland Tolmatchoff recognizes as his own) that concludes by praising the women of Lausanne and Geneva above all. At the sound of the word "Lausanne," the wail of an ambulance siren is heard sharply on the sound track. This sonic coincidence is no accident: the ambulance siren at that moment was added by Godard as a deliberate choice in the sound editing process (inasmuch as *Breathless* was shot silent and the sound track dubbed, all of the film's sounds were intentionally applied) and its presence is a reference to the death of Godard's mother in a motorcycle accident. Godard left the reference apparent to those who might perceive it but hidden from those who would not—yet given his sudden great celebrity, it was inevitable that the underlying facts would come out, and would render the passage explicable.

Godard slips into the film, and into the character of Michel Poiccard, such items of personal reminiscence as: the use of the Swiss numbers *septante* and *huitante* instead of the French *soixante-dix* and *quatre-vingts* for seventy and eighty, an ashtray that prompts mention of his grandfather's Rolls-Royce, a comment by Poiccard regarding the luxurious Parisian building where he was born (evoking Patricia's surprise at his déclassé status), numerous references to Godard's own Left Bank nightspots and Right Bank landmarks, a mention of a name (Zumbach) from a recent Swiss murder case, the names of Godard's Swiss friends.[62]

In a February 3 *Tribune de Genève* article, Godard, responding to a journalist's question about those names in the film which "come from the Geneva phone book," explained the story:

> Yes, those are old acquaintances. I thought those fellows would be happy I remembered them. And why make the effort to invent names? Besides, Tomatchov [*sic*] is unknown in Paris or Berlin. Only the initiated will smile at this sort of connection. Just like when I have my hero say that on average the girls of Geneva and Lausanne are better than those of other European cities.[63]

Journalists were part of Godard's system, providing skeleton keys to the work as they created the phenomenon on which they were reporting. Viewers and readers, upon their initiation into the film's esoterica, themselves popularized the advanced cinematic philosophy that *Breathless* represented, becoming the first citizens of the new republic the film heralded: the republic of media self-consciousness, of the fusion of communication with theories of communication, of criticism with art.

Having joined his critical theories to his work of art, Godard was aware of the conflict between symbolic expression in a heavily layered and ironic work of fiction, and direct, sincere communication. His next work, which he had announced while *Breathless* was still in progress, would be constructed around a first-person monologue, and was calculated to allay any doubts (including his own) on the subject of his sincerity.

Speaking during the shoot of *Breathless* with Marc Pierret, the journalist from *France-Observateur* who was planted in the crew, Godard announced, "I'll shoot my next film in Switzerland. With three times less money: an assistant, a cameraman, that's all. It will be something about torture." After the shoot ended, he told Michèle Manceaux of *L'Express* that it would be called *Le Petit Soldat.* But it was not the only new project with which Godard had gone public. Although *Le Petit Soldat,* the story about torture, would indeed become Godard's second film, it would, in a way, be his second second film.

His first second film had already been publicized, in August 1959, in the pages of *Cahiers du cinéma.* It was called *Une Femme est une femme* (*A Woman Is a Woman*), and was the story of a woman who tells her boyfriend that she wants to have a baby with him despite not being married. It was based on a story outline by the actress Geneviève Cluny, who had passed it along to the actress Michèle Meritz, who brought it to the attention of Claude Chabrol in 1957 while playing a small role in his *Le Beau Serge.* Chabrol showed the story to his assistant director, Philippe de Broca, and to

Godard, who decided to join forces to turn it into a full-length script. In the course of what de Broca recalled as their "fifteen abominable days" of work together, Godard took him to "disgusting cafeterias at impossible hours," and then announced that he—Godard—would write the story himself.[64] Cluny, however, decided to give her story to de Broca, who made it into his first film, *Les Jeux de l'amour* (*The Games of Love*), in the summer of 1959 (it was released in June 1960).

Godard, however, gave *Cahiers* an acerbic six-page divertissement called *A Woman Is a Woman,* which is a comic love triangle between a woman and two men but with the added fillip of a pregnancy by the wrong one of the two men. It ended with a pun, in which Josette's steady boyfriend calls her "infâme" (horrid), to which she replies that she is "*une* femme" (a woman). Godard's publication of his story in advance of the release of de Broca's film was a defensive maneuver to stake his claim to the story, which he would hold for the future; he would instead make *Le Petit Soldat* as soon as possible.

Starting another film as soon as possible was both to Godard's and Beauregard's advantage. Godard had wanted to sign for a second film before *Breathless* was released because he feared that, if *Breathless* failed, he might never get to make a second film. He was also jealous of Chabrol's output (three films since 1958) and wanted to catch up. As for Beauregard, signing on to another project at once would allow him to collect funds from automatic aid to producers, with which he could pay current expenses and debts.

By the end of 1959, with the reputation of *Breathless* growing, Beauregard took advantage of the moment to announce, in a gag of a two-page display ad in the trade journal *La Cinématographie française,* his forthcoming production of *Le Petit Soldat.*

The ad was a singular stunt—a text, written in the style of a classified ad, appearing in Godard's own distinctive handwriting, which read: "Jean-Luc Godard, who has completed 'Breathless' and is preparing 'Le Petit Soldat,' seeks young woman between 18 and 27 to make her both his actress and his friend," with Beauregard's company and telephone number listed at the bottom of the page. The prank seemed to be a smarmy attempt to use his growing fame to seek young women in the guise of an open casting call. In fact, Godard already had an actress in mind for the role in the film, a young woman who had rejected a role in *Breathless*—Anna Karina.

It is a story the actress has told often, each time a little differently, to *Cahiers du cinéma,* to journalists and interviewers (including to this author), to audiences in New York and in London, and most thoroughly, to Beauregard's daughter, Chantal, for her biography of her father.[65] For a small role in *Breathless,* Godard had been looking for a model, a cover girl for *Elle* magazine whom he had seen in commercials (shown not on television but in movie theaters). He made contact and asked her to come to Beauregard's office, where he offered her the role of the woman in St.-Germain-des-Prés from whom Belmondo steals money when he arrives in Paris. It required her to bare her breasts as she pulled her dressing gown over her head (giving Belmondo the moment to take cash from her wallet). For this reason, the actress refused the role (which Godard gave to Liliane David, Truffaut's mistress).

Now, while planning *Le Petit Soldat,* Godard sent the model a telegram asking to speak with her about a different role in a different film, possibly the lead. Given her experience with the director in Beauregard's office, she had some idea of what the role would, she thought, likely entail, so she ignored the message. But when she told two actor friends (Claude Brasseur and Sady Rebbot, both of whom would later work with Godard) about the note, they told her to respond at once, because they had heard rumors that Godard's yet-unreleased film was remarkable.

She met Godard at Beauregard's small office on the rue de Cérisoles. She took a seat. He walked around her several times and told her to come back the next day to sign a contract. She asked whether she would have to get undressed. He said, "No, it's a political film." She said that she wouldn't know how to give a political speech; he said, in a colossal deception, "There aren't any speeches, so come sign tomorrow." She could not sign, however, because the actress, Hanne Karin Blarke Bayer, known professionally as Anna Karina (a name bestowed upon her two years earlier, at the beginning of her modeling career in Paris, shortly after her arrival from Denmark, by Coco Chanel in the offices of *Elle*), was only nineteen, and a minor under French law regarding contracts. (Her mother promptly traveled from Denmark to Paris to sign on her behalf.)

Shortly after Karina's contract was signed, Godard's handwritten ad appeared in *La Cinématographie française.* The effect of this publicity stunt was to make her casting appear to be the result of a response to the ad. Unaware of the ad, Karina was returning to her apartment when her concierge reported the contents of an article in *France-Soir,* to the effect that Godard had met Karina through a want ad placed in the trade journal, looking for (as she said) his "actress and soul mate." Karina asked the concierge what this meant. To the concierge, it meant that the actress had slept with the director to get her role. The young actress, who was furious at what she considered a humiliating insinuation, returned to Beauregard's office in tears, ready to repudiate the contract and face the consequences. The next day, Godard sent her a telegram making poetic reference to her Danish nationality—"A character from Hans Christian Andersen has no right to cry"—which also suggested that through her association with him, she had embarked on a fairy-tale destiny. She ignored the telegram; the director appeared at her door with an enormous bouquet of roses to make amends, and apologized for the ad, which, he said, was Balducci's idea.[66]

Though Karina had already signed her contract, Godard began his effort to win her over to his cause. Karina recalled, "He invited me to a screening of *Breathless*. I didn't like it at all. Then we had dinner together. None of this appealed to me in the least. I was basically a little suspicious."[67] Nonetheless, she accepted Godard's request that she do a screen test:

> One week later, during the screen test, he interrogated me.
>> Do you like to read?
>> Which books?
>> Which music?
>> And what about boys. Do you like boys?
>> What kind of boys?
>
> Good Lord, what does he want from me? I didn't want to answer. First of all, I thought it was none of his business and besides, it seemed very strange. I was on the verge of tears.
>
> I said to him: Listen, this really is none of your business!
> He didn't insist.[68]

But of course, since Godard sought to eliminate the barrier between the personal and the artistic, between life on-camera and off, he would soon make it his business.

Anna Karina, during the shoot of *Le Petit Soldat*
(The Kobal Collection / Films Beauregard / SNC)

four

LE PETIT SOLDAT

"The sound of one's own voice"

T HE "POLITICAL" FILM THAT GODARD PLANNED TO MAKE
after *Breathless,* the film that would have to do with torture,
concerned France's war in Algeria.

That country, a French colony since 1830, had been fighting a guerrilla
war for independence since 1955. The position of French citizens and troops
in Algeria was growing untenable; they were coming under ever more violent
attack from an increasingly organized Algerian resistance, and the army responded with escalating brutality. France had a half-million troops in Algeria and had widened the war to target Algerian militants across the border in
Tunisia. Extrajudicial killings of Algerian activists by French agents had become commonplace, as had the assassination of French officials and notables
in Algeria by Algerian militants.

As the war in Algeria grew more difficult, the French government
seemed to hint at the possibility of autonomy for Algeria. In response, on
May 13, 1958, French military leaders in Algeria took over the French government in Algiers, and were attempting to carry out a military takeover of
France itself. The plotters demanded that General Charles de Gaulle, who
had resigned the French presidency in 1946 after parliamentary maneuvers
had limited his authority and who had been out of politics since then, return
to power. He and the National Assembly agreed; the result was the end of the
Fourth Republic, the unstable parliamentary regime that had yielded twenty-
two prime ministers between 1946 and 1958.

The sixty-eight-year-old general used force to put down the coup attempt
and governed with plenipotentiary powers for six months. In September

1958, the new French constitution, establishing the Fifth Republic (the current regime, which accords the president great powers), was voted in by a large majority, and de Gaulle himself was elected president (unopposed in a plebiscite) three months later. He was a paradoxical figure: though the army had imposed him on France as a bulwark against autonomy for Algeria, he had privately been advocating its independence for years. Nonetheless, de Gaulle was received by most French intellectuals and by the left as the instrument of the military insurrection and thus as the agent of a soft fascism.

He took over at a moment of crisis. Not only was the war itself going terribly for France, but in de Gaulle's first months in office, metropolitan France endured a campaign of terrorism by Algerian independence fighters: in August 1958, several policemen were ambushed, fuel stocks throughout France were destroyed, a police station was attacked; on September 15, 1958, an attempt was made on the life of Minister of Information Jacques Soustelle.

Some French citizens, especially intellectuals, had begun to collaborate secretly with the violent Algerian resistance and its campaign, in France and throughout Western Europe, against the French government. These activists, nicknamed the *porteurs de valises* (the baggage carriers), were organized and led, starting in 1957, by Francis Jeanson, a professor of philosophy and a colleague of Sartre's at *Les Temps modernes.* Jeanson's loosely assembled network hid and helped to finance agents of Algeria's Front de Libération Nationale (FLN). Within France and indeed elsewhere in Europe, the French secret police, aided by militant rightists, carried on their own dirty war to combat the FLN; targeted assassinations were carried out by the Red Hand, a clandestine group of vigilantes.

It was against this violent backdrop that de Gaulle gave a speech on French television on September 16, 1959, the day after the end of shooting on *Breathless,* in which he raised the possibility of Algerian self-determination. His extended time frame, however, which was intended to improve France's negotiating position regarding oil fields, military bases, and the status of French citizens in an independent Algeria, instead provoked greater violence from Algeria's independence fighters (who thought the pace too slow) and the defenders of the colony (who saw it slipping away). Despite his intention of setting Algeria free, de Gaulle intensified the fight against Algerian nationalists in the hope of establishing there a pacified and tractable state.

GODARD'S ABSORPTION IN the cinema to the exclusion of current politics was exemplified in his admission that during the attempted coup by the French military in May 1958, he was at the Cannes festival, oblivious to the crisis.[1] This remark paralleled the criticism that was widely leveled, particularly by the intellectual left, at the early films of the New Wave for their narrow concern with private and intimate subjects. At the very least, the Hitchcocko-Hawksians had done their best to maintain an apolitical stance—the war in Algeria was mentioned in *Cahiers du cinéma* only once, in passing—though the critics did not avoid politics in their personal lives. François Truffaut frequented the writer and convicted collaborator Lucien Rebatet (who had been an esteemed film critic under the nom de plume François Vinneuil); in *Breathless* Godard alludes to his friend on the far right, Jean Parvulesco; the *Cahiers* group included among its friends the rightist provocateur Paul Gégauff. The appearance of the actor Jean-Claude Brialy repeating Gégauff's stunt and turning up in a German military uniform in Claude Chabrol's *Les Cousins*—which, at the time of its release in March 1959, was the New Wave's biggest commercial success to date—prompted charges that the cinematic movement was a bastion of extreme rightism.

Godard himself had been attacked for what some saw as the politics implicit in *Breathless;* one Parisian critic had gone so far as to denounce "the type of anarcho-fascist ideal that is unleashed by the film."[2] Others paired it with Chabrol's films to suggest a connection in suspect political affiliations. Left-wing critics took Godard to task for Michel Poiccard's remark that he is "one of the few guys in France who really likes" the police; one likened Poiccard to "a paratrooper on leave";[3] another called him "one of those guys who writes 'Death to Jews!' on the walls of the métro and spells it wrong."[4] From Switzerland, the critic (and Cinémathèque Suisse founder) Freddy Buache claimed that "*Breathless* poses the first unambiguous prototype of the Fascist arrogance that is hiding in the hollow of the New Wave."[5]

Although Godard claimed that *Breathless* was "a film on the necessity of engagement," he also could not deny its lack of overt engagement with the politics of the day. Since he and the New Wave were so casually and widely charged with promoting political noncommitment, Godard self-consciously took on the most pressing contemporary political subject in order to show that the New Wave could also be openly political. Yet he would do so in a way that was so personal, and so independent of any prevailing orthodoxy, that his will to engagement would merely succeed in infuriating almost everybody and satisfying almost nobody. More than proof of an expressly political engagement, Godard's second film, *Le Petit Soldat,* was above all a revision, and a correction, of the autobiographical constructions of *Breathless.*

GODARD'S DECLARATION THAT he was planning to make a film that would be "something about torture" carefully omitted any allusion to Algeria,

though the implication was difficult to miss. A book published two years earlier made clear what was at stake. In June 1957, Henri Alleg, a French journalist in Algeria who had gone into hiding after writing in favor of Algerian
independence, was arrested by the French army and tortured in order to
compel him to divulge the names of Algerian fighters with whom he was
presumed to associate. Remanded to prison, he wrote a detailed account of
his experience of torture. His book, *La Question* (*The Question*), was published in January 1958 and posed the moral problem faced by France in attempting to suppress resistance to its colonization of Algeria. The book was
seized in the name of government censorship, as were most objective accounts of French actions in Algeria. It was a scantly publicized but well-
known fact that the French army practiced torture there, and did so not as
an aberration or as a violation of procedure, but under orders from top officers and with the knowledge and approval of civilian authorities. However,
during World War II, many members of the French Resistance had been tortured under German occupation, and many French people found it intolerable that liberated France would also engage in torture. The revelations of
torture by the French government now made many French citizens question
the cost of holding on to Algeria.

Jean-Paul Sartre reviewed Alleg's book in *L'Express* for March 6, 1958;
though the government seized the magazine from the newsstands, the
review—in which Sartre fiercely denounced France's practice of torture and
the colonial policy that gave rise to it—was quickly reprinted in a succession
of forms to stay a step ahead of the censors: first, according to the historian
Ronald Aronson, "as a pamphlet, confiscated, then appearing as a scroll that
could only be read with a magnifying glass, and finally being published in
Switzerland as a foreword to a reprinting of Alleg's text."[6] When Godard took
up the question of torture, and the question of Algeria, he was once again
following in Sartre's footsteps. Having made *Breathless*, which exemplified
existential engagement minus the politics, Godard would now make a film
on the subject of political engagement itself—and would contrast it negatively to a more subjective, personal form of engagement.

Godard was familiar with Alleg's book (and quoted from it on the sound
track of *Le Petit Soldat*), but he claimed to have had the subject in mind even
before the book's publication: "The film is born of an old idea. I wanted to
treat the theme of 'brainwashing' which I got from reading Koestler."[7] Godard acknowledged his debt to the anti-totalitarian writer even more
explicitly, claiming that the film was "*Zero and Infinity* [the French title for
Darkness at Noon] in the milieu of secret agents."[8] Godard planned a film
that would treat the subject of freedom in the face of violent constraint,[9] and

he spoke of the question not in terms of the war in Algeria but in broader abstract terms of pure freedom:

> My prisoner is someone who is asked to do a thing and who doesn't want to do it. Just doesn't want to, and he resists, on principle. That's how I see liberty: from a practical point of view. Being free is being able to do what you want, when you want.[10]

Godard's political film was born of an attempt to illustrate a philosophical point of crucial importance to Sartre's project; in taking on the question and nature of freedom, he was approaching the existential question par excellence. Indeed, he declared that the story's particular political context was incidental to the film: "It could as easily have been Hungarians continuing their fight on neutral terrain . . . I would have been able just as well to make it a story of drug trafficking."[11] He also said, "It's an adventure film. I could also have made a story around the theft of Sophia Loren's jewels. But why not choose what's going on, why consider current events taboo?"[12]

Of course, this rhetorical question was barbed: it was not filmmakers but the French government that considered current events taboo. His denial of the film's relation to the politics of the day served a practical purpose: a film about the war in Algeria would almost certainly be subject to government censorship. The decision by Godard and Beauregard to make the film in Switzerland was also no coincidence: they did not need to get authorization from France's CNC, a government agency, to shoot it. At the time, a film about the war in Algeria, especially one that had anything to do with torture, could never have gotten made in France.

As early as April 3, 1955, the French government had used the pretext of the Algerian uprising to justify wide-ranging censorship in all domains, including newspapers, books, magazines, and films. Issues of many prestigious national publications, such as *L'Express, France-Observateur,* and *Les Temps modernes,* were seized and destroyed. In the week in which *Breathless* was released, the French government seized the German newsweekly *Der Spiegel* at border crossings for an investigative report on the Red Hand. *L'Humanité* described the seizure of their issue of March 19, 1960: "In the early morning, under orders from the government, teams of policemen made the rounds of bookstores, depots, train stations, to remove the issue that had just come out."[13]

The CNC, which had refused authorization to shoot films that touched on contemporary politics in general, was implacable regarding the Algerian war in particular. As Jacques Doniol-Valcroze wrote in *France-Observateur,* "On the political scene, French censorship is *very* severe. We hardly notice it because, this state of mind being known, there is a preliminary auto-censorship and al- most all French films are devoid of political audacity."[14] *Le Petit Soldat* would be the first film by a recognized producer to deal explicitly with the war in Al- geria. Godard complained that "young directors, those less than forty years old, have the idea of censorship in their heads the moment that they make a film";[15] he said that "they shouldn't worry about it," and set out to show why not.

THE ACTION OF *Le Petit Soldat* begins on May 13, 1958, the date of the at- tempted putsch in Algeria, and ends later that month.[16] The story, set in and around Geneva, concerns a photojournalist, Bruno Forestier, who is involved with a right-wing paramilitary group working for the French government, which targets proponents of Algerian independence. The young man wants to leave the group and take refuge in Brazil; he falls in love with a young woman, Veronica Dreyer, who has worked with the Algerian freedom fighters, and he would like her to go with him. His comrades order him to murder a professor accused of aiding the Algerian resistance. He at first refuses, but is soon black- mailed and agrees to commit the crime. Before he can do so, he is captured by Algerian militants and tortured. He escapes to Veronica's apartment and, while preparing to flee with her, is pressed by his old friends to carry out the murder in exchange for diplomatic passports for himself and for her. He shoots the professor in the street, in broad daylight; in the meantime, his or- ganization kidnaps, tortures, and kills the woman he loves.

Godard filmed *Le Petit Soldat* in and around Geneva over a period of ap- proximately six weeks, beginning on April 4, 1960. The shoot had been scheduled to begin on March 21, but was delayed due to the opening of *Breathless* the previous week, which required Godard's presence for promo- tional purposes. This in turn rendered the shoot of *Le Petit Soldat* instantly and intrinsically newsworthy. Even before the shoot began, interviewers wanted to talk to Godard about his new project, and he obliged with several sweeping pronouncements. In an interview that appeared in *Arts* on March 23, Godard told Luc Moullet (a younger critic from the *Cahiers* group):

> One always does the opposite of what one says, yet it turns out the same way. I am for classical montage and I've done the most unorthodox montage. My next film, *Le Petit Soldat,* will be on the contrary very respectful of the con- ventions. It will displease those who admire *Breathless* and vice versa.

However, the "conventions" to which Godard's second film hewed were not those of technique but of narrative form. Where, in *Breathless*, Godard detaches the characters from the dramatic context to put forth an idea, put over a gag, or execute a gesture, in *Le Petit Soldat* he does not break with dramatic naturalism or deliver disruptive or digressive jokes. It maintains a unified tone of earnestness, romance, and adventure, and is far more of a classic film noir than *Breathless*. The political action of the story inclined Godard to work with aesthetic sobriety; the dazzlingly iconoclastic patchwork of his first film was altogether too brilliant and self-aggrandizing for a subject of such moral gravity.

During the shoot, Godard told a journalist, "I want to make a film even more stripped-down than *Breathless*."[17] Regarding *Le Petit Soldat*, Godard said, "I preferred to tell my story and to do fewer exercises of style."[18] Godard's seeming indifference to composition in *Breathless* was of course a studied indifference, in which the casualness belied a precise intention and became a sort of reverse aesthetic, an artifice of the anti-artificial. In the shooting of *Le Petit Soldat*, simplicity and sincerity were all: the film's audacity was built into the story.

And yet, *Le Petit Soldat* contrasted with *Breathless* in an aspect even more crucial than the film's politically sensitive context—namely, in Godard's heightened personal identification with the main character. *Le Petit Soldat* proved to be a far-reaching revision of the concept of cinematic autobiography.

GODARD AGAIN WORKED with Raoul Coutard, whose deft handheld camerawork, audacity with available light, and game willingness to abet Godard's quest for a personal cinematic technique had contributed much to the style and the tone of *Breathless*. A crucial addition to the crew was the new script supervisor, Suzanne Schiffman. She and Godard had known each other since 1949, when they were enrolled in a class on "filmology" at the Sorbonne. She had helped Rivette and Rohmer with their short films and, after working as the script supervisor on Rivette's first, desperate attempt to film *Paris Belongs to Us*, Truffaut hired her to do the same job on *Shoot the Piano Player* (filmed from November 1959 through January 1960). For years to come, Schiffman worked almost exclusively with Godard and Truffaut. With Truffaut, she learned the professional norms; for Godard, who was unconstrained by the usual notions of continuity, Schiffman instead served as something of a recording secretary, keeping "minutes" of the proceedings to help Godard and his editor complete the film.

Cécile Decugis, Godard's editor for *Breathless*, was unavailable: she had been arrested in July 1958 and charged with harboring a member of the FLN. While awaiting trial, she worked on *Breathless* and Truffaut's *Shoot the Piano Player*. On Wednesday, March 10, 1960, a military tribunal rejected her claim that she was unaware of her guest's political activities and sentenced her to five years in prison.[19] Godard sought a replacement as open to his methods as were Coutard and Schiffman, and asked the assistant editor, Lila Herman, whether she knew somebody, as Godard had put it, "who did not have too much experience, who had not been mistrained by feature films."[20] The young editor he chose to cut the film, and especially, to supervise the dubbing and edit the sound track, was Agnès Guillemot; like Coutard and Schiffman, she continued to work with Godard for years to come.

Godard cast as the eponymous little soldier a twenty-six-year-old actor named Michel Subor, after seeing him in Sartre's 1959 play, *Les Séquestrés d'Altona* (*The Prisoners of Altona*). Distributing his headshot door to door, Subor met Godard by chance in the corridor of the building that housed Beauregard's office. Godard invited him on the spot to do a screen test, which took place several days later on the set where Truffaut was filming *Shoot the Piano Player*.

Anna Karina played the role of Veronica Dreyer,[21] a young woman from Denmark of Russian extraction. Other parts were played by Roland Tolmatchoff, Jean-Pierre Laubscher, and Hugues Fontana,[22] as well as by Henri-Jacques Huet (who had a role in *Breathless*), Godard's friend László Szabó, a local professor of chemistry, a local car dealer, Beauregard himself (painfully nervous before the camera), and journalists who happened to be present at the shoot.

Godard had a great deal of trouble getting started on the film. As Schiffman later recalled, "The first week he went off to shoot with Coutard, an assistant, and Subor. I wasn't allowed to be at the shoot, so I could only ask, 'You shot how much?' and write down, '45 seconds.' "[23] Every day for a week, Godard and company had driven out to film the passage to Switzerland through a rural border crossing; every day, they came back having shot almost nothing. Like the rest of the crew, Schiffman had nothing else to do, she recalled. "But at 2 o'clock he came back to the office, or at 4 PM, we ate at 5 PM. He reshot the same shot for the whole week—but he convened us every day to make sure that we didn't think we were on vacation. Beauregard didn't understand."[24] Beauregard did not, however, attempt to call Godard to order as he had done on the shoot of *Breathless*, now that the director had made the producer's name and fortune.

As with *Breathless*, Godard wrote the dialogue every day. A Swiss journalist following the shoot explained, "For more than three weeks, Godard has been getting up each day at 6 AM. He no longer even has time to read *L'Equipe*," the sports daily. "He has to get right to his desk to sketch out the day's work."[25] Laubscher, who also worked as one of Godard's assistants, made a similar observation: "I went to pick him up at the Hôtel des Berges at six in the morning. He said, 'I'm not coming down, I don't have any ideas.' Coutard waited with his camera while Jean-Luc wrote the dialogue."[26]

Tolmatchoff, also an assistant on the film, related Godard's difficulty getting started to the tantalizing presence of Anna Karina: Godard, he recalled, was already in love with her, but she was there in Geneva with another man, Ghislain (Jicky) Dussart, Brigitte Bardot's photographer. Since *Le Petit Soldat* was being shot in sequence—in the chronological order of the story—the first scene, of Subor in a car at the border, did not include Karina, so the longer the first scene took to shoot, the longer the filming of Karina would be delayed.

Once Godard did get to shooting, however, he worked with even greater efficiency and audacity than he had on *Breathless.* The crew was smaller and more mobile. In Switzerland, Godard was not constrained to hire a union-minimum crew. This time, there was no need to splice together short rolls of photographic film: Agfa in Switzerland provided very fast black-and-white film in longer rolls, thus permitting night sequences and other low-light situations to be filmed in long takes. In one instance, Godard shot five scenes in a single evening, between nine and eleven o'clock, including a car crash, which was done in one take, without stunt drivers, in an unsecured street in central Geneva.

In fact, Godard filmed on location in Geneva as he had filmed in the streets of Paris for *Breathless,* but with a difference. At the end of *Breathless,* Godard had integrated incredulous or bewildered passersby into Belmondo's death-trot. They watched Belmondo lurching down the street, and they looked at the camera, thus putting visual quotation marks around the action. In *Le Petit Soldat,* Geneva and its inhabitants became unwitting, though crucial, participants in the film's action. Subor recalled,

> The murder at the end, we did it in the street with the camera hidden far away. I had a gun that was loaded with blanks. I fired. I fled. I was followed. A man cornered me. I pointed the gun at him. He stopped. I said, "It's a movie." He said, "You should have said so."[27]

While the effect of the chase on Subor was powerful (he was being pursued as if he were an actual murderer), it was something of a disappointment for Godard, who later admitted that he had wanted people to pounce on Subor *during* the take, not after it.

Godard's conception of the scene went beyond the desire for dramatic verisimilitude: it exemplified one of his key philosophical ideas about the cinema. "On the screen it appears almost unbelievable," he explained, "and yet the fact that this could have been filmed so that passersby suspected nothing proves the possibility and the veracity of such an action."[28] Godard's idea went beyond using documentary methods to convey a sense of reality;

rather, the fact that a given event could be filmed on location was, for Godard, proof that such an event could have happened in life as it appeared on film. This idea—a big one, which Godard would cite for years to come—was yet another response on his part to the writings of André Bazin, but a response that came from his practical experience with filmmaking: while for Bazin, reality was the touchstone of the cinema, for Godard the cinema was the touchstone of reality.

Godard radically integrated documentary into fiction in some of his most critical indoor scenes as well: while filming the torture of Bruno, Godard subjected Subor to near-asphyxiation with a water-soaked shirt wrapped around his face, telling the actor, "We're going to do it but not for long." For Subor's suicide attempt, Godard had the actor hold a real razor blade between his teeth and press its edge into his handcuffed wrists. For the scene of electrical torture applied to the toes via spring clips leading to a hand-cranked generator, Godard actually had László Szabó, who played the torturer, apply live current to Subor, who said that it gave him "a peculiar feeling."[29] The journalist Michèle Manceaux, who met Subor after the filming ended, wrote, "I saw Michel Subor still bearing the marks from the electrodes on his wrists and ankles."[30]

WHEN GODARD FINALLY began filming Karina, after a week's delay, the sequence that they shot, the scene of Bruno and Veronica's first meeting, was framed by a bet between Bruno and his friend Hugues, who introduces them:

> HUGUES: I'll bet you that you'll want to fuck her. She's got the same kind of mouth as Leslie Caron.
> BRUNO: No, I only sleep with girls I'm in love with.
> HUGUES: Well in that case, little man, I bet you that in five minutes you'll be in love.

Bruno bets Hugues fifty dollars and, after a few minutes' acquaintance with Veronica, silently pays him the money. The character's wordless confession was soon reflected in the director's own, off-camera approach to the actress.

Like Jean Seberg, Anna Karina was not a native speaker of French, and this fact was not incidental to Godard's choice of actress. He admired foreign actors speaking French in the cinema: "I liked people who had a foreign accent because it made their voice a bit different from French actors,"[31] and in *Le Petit Soldat,* he had Bruno say a line to that effect when Karina spoke ("A foreigner speaking French is always lovely").

Unlike Jean Seberg, however, Anna Karina had almost no experience as an actress. Not only did Godard make use of her occasionally faulty French, but he made her hesitations and her awkwardness an essential element of her performance. In her first major scene, Godard got around her inexperience with a script by letting her make up her own dialogue: Bruno's pretext for a rendezvous with Veronica is to photograph her, and Godard filmed their photo session with a personal intervention akin to psychodrama. In the scene, Bruno photographs Veronica while asking her questions. On the set, Godard stood behind the camera and asked the questions himself and Karina responded, unscripted—exactly as in Karina's screen test. Godard confirmed that he filmed the discussion between Bruno and Veronica

as if I, myself, interviewed her, Anna, not the character. And then I had Subor re-ask my questions in the film, and so it became a scene of fiction. Moreover, at the end, Anna says, "Oh, you're annoying me," well, I mean, it's what she was saying to me because she was fed up.[32]

The incipient relations between director and actress made it easy for Godard to identify with Bruno. And the fact that Bruno is a photographer made Godard's identification with him all the more apparent. As Bruno photographed Karina, he tossed off verbal riffs that echoed the sound of Godard's own voice: "When you photograph a face—look at me—you photograph the soul behind it . . . Photography is truth, and the cinema is truth twenty-four times a second."[33] The latter phrase became a famous and oft-repeated aphorism. Godard used it to adorn a two-page ad for the film that Beauregard placed in La Cinématographie française. But its meaning is paradoxical, suggesting that the staged, fictional images of cinema and the documentary images of the news photographer are equally true, equally revelatory of reality—in this case, of the reality of Godard's own life. As indeed they were, according to Anna Karina's recollection, decades later, of this particular scene: "It's a declaration of love. Jean-Luc took the place of the photographer and directed my gestures, the hair like this, the hands like that, the head at an angle . . . It's still very moving for me."[34]

During the scene, Karina had a visual lapse that called momentary but riveting attention to the actual situation, physical and emotional, in which she was being filmed. As Godard's questioning—through Bruno—grew more provocative and titillating (he asked to photograph her taking a shower and, when she demurred, asked whether she was "afraid" for him to see her body), she grew more flustered, until Bruno challenged her: "What do you think of me?" When she didn't answer, he persisted: "Why aren't you answering? It's as if you were afraid." Karina, obviously confused about whether Godard was posing the questions in Bruno's name or in his own, looked at Bruno but then reflexively shot a glance at the camera, where Godard was standing. As Karina recalled, the scene as played corresponded to the general facts off-camera: "We looked at each other a lot during the shoot, but we didn't do anything."

Then, one evening during the shoot, in Geneva, while Karina was at dinner with Ghislain Dussart, Godard came along: "Jean-Luc passed a note to me under the table: 'I love you. Rendez-vous at the Café de la paix, at midnight.' I packed my bags and I left everything, like a sleepwalker, swept away by him."[35] She also remembered how she found Godard at the café: "He was reading the paper. He wasn't surprised to see me. For me it was a thunderstroke."[36] Godard clinched their union by paying Dussart to get out of town.[37]

BECAUSE MICHEL POICCARD of *Breathless* is not an intellectual or an artist, he is less Godard's spokesman than the vehicle for his preoccupations. By contrast, Bruno Forestier is a character close to Godard: he is a maker of images and an intellectual; and he is the organizing consciousness of the film. Godard admitted, "The little soldier is more or less my spokesman, but not totally."[38] To one journalist he said, "It is easy for me to identify with him . . . Basically, I show a man who analyzes himself, who discovers himself to be different from the idea that he had of himself. Personally when I look in a mirror I often have the same feeling."[39]

Le Petit Soldat is a staging of that process: Godard attempting to see himself by means of the cinema. As Bruno photographs Veronica, he declares, "What's important is not the way others see you, but the way you see yourself." He says it while emphatically staring at himself in a mirror. Significantly, Godard does not contrast "the way others see you" with "the way you really are," but with "the way you see yourself." He does not compare appearance with reality, but appearance to others with appearance to oneself. This doubling of self—the development of self-consciousness through the self-image—defines the autobiographical in cinema as the filmmaker filming himself.

As Godard was completing the film, he declared to a journalist,

> I thought a lot about Malraux while making this film. I had heard him say in a lecture: "One day, I wrote the story of a man who heard the sound of his own voice, and I called it *La Condition humaine.*" In my film, the hero seeks constantly to recognize his own voice. Even his face, in the mirror, he no longer thinks it corresponds to him.[40]

In *Le Petit Soldat,* there is no shortage of Godard's own voice, transmuted into Subor's. Bruno speaks in eruptively verbose free-floating aesthetic reflections, sharp aphorisms, and historical speculations (Godard cited those of Malraux's *Les Noyers d'Altenburg* [*The Walnut Trees of Altenburg*] as a main influence), and the entire film is structured by the narrative frame of Bruno's voice-over commentary. Of the film's copious dialogue, Godard said, "There were passages where I let myself go."[41]

The film's multiple literary allusions were one way for Godard to let himself go. Early in the film, in voice-over, Bruno Forestier states his name. Forestier is the last name of two important characters in two major works of French literature that have significant similarities, and that were written and published within a year of each other. The authors, Jean Giraudoux and Jean Cocteau, were important references for Godard from the days of his earliest critical writings. Moments after Bruno Forestier introduces himself, he meets Veronica and, in voice-over, states, "The first time I met Veronica, she looked as if she had just stepped out of a play by Jean Giraudoux." Instead it was Forestier who had stepped out of a novel by Jean Giraudoux: *Siegfried et le Limousin* (to which Godard referred in his article "For a Political Cinema," in September 1950).

Siegfried et le Limousin, published in 1922, is set in the turmoil of Germany after the First World War, and features sharp intellectual dialogue, historical meditations, and learned yet witty philosophical asides. The novel, about a Frenchman who goes to Germany to seek a friend who disappeared there during the war, presents the crossing of the border as a change of identity, mentality, and inner music, and reveals Giraudoux's obsession with national identity, which he conceived in long and deep cultural terms. In the novel, Giraudoux harshly satirizes German Jews as rootless cosmopolitans without regard for regional tradition, and the novel ends with a fulsomely incantatory paean to the local names and age-old customs of which his characters' French identities are composed. Giraudoux—a conservative writer with an exquisite, arch style, something of a high bourgeois aristocrat of manners—was a prime literary model for Godard, and *Siegfried et le Limousin* would remain a key reference in his work for decades.

The second literary connection to the name of Forestier appears in another scene early in the film, when Bruno is trapped in the backseat of a car between two of his death-squad bosses, one of whom pulls from his pocket a copy of *Thomas l'Imposteur* (*Thomas the Impostor*) by Cocteau and reads aloud from it.

> Guillaume flew, leaped, sprinted like a hare. Not hearing the fusillade, he stopped, turned around, out of breath. Then he felt a terrible blow to his chest. He fell. He became deaf, blind. "A bullet," he said to himself. "I am lost if I

don't pretend to be dead." But in him, fiction and reality became one. Guillaume Thomas was dead.

Thomas l'Imposteur was one of two novels written by Cocteau in 1922 and published in 1923. The protagonist of the other, *Le Grand Ecart* (The Split[42] or The Great Divide), is named Jacques Forestier. *Le Grand Ecart* is the story of the love life of a sentimental yet vehement adolescent dandy whom Cocteau names in the novel's first sentence: "Jacques Forestier cried easily. The movies, bad music, a feuilleton, drew forth his tears." However, the "thin," "tormented," and "hirsute" Forestier had taken on "something of hardness" behind which:

> He could neither adhere to the right nor to a left which he found soft. But his excessive nature sought no middle ground.
>
> Also in virtue of the axiom: "the ends meet," he dreamt of a pure far-right, meeting up with the far-left to the point of being a part of it, but in which he could act alone.

Filming a right-wing militant in *Le Petit Soldat* with whom he closely identified, Godard—as he had done ten years earlier in his article "For a Political Cinema"—brought the two extremes together, both romantically (in Bruno's love affair with Veronica) and psychologically (in his increasing sympathy for pro-Algerian activists). This passage by Cocteau regarding Forestier's politics appears in *Le Petit Soldat,* only slightly transformed, as part of an eruptive monologue nearly seven minutes long that Bruno delivers in the presence of Veronica, after he is tortured and takes refuge with her. It is the scene in which Godard most completely "let [himself] go." Bruno's speech contains allusions to all of the film's most important and explicit literary references: Cocteau's Guillaume Thomas and Jacques Forestier, Malraux's *La Condition humaine,* the right-wing author Drieu La Rochelle, the left-wing writer Aragon. The monologue both embodies and refers to the imperative of self-consciousness, an obsession with talking, and, as in *Breathless,* features a boy who thinks about death.

Godard improvised his text and Subor improvised his performance. "Godard was behind the camera, he spoke it, I repeated it, sentence by sentence." As to the direction, Subor recalled: "He told me, 'You can move however you like.' "[43] Though the speech begins as a political reflection, it soon becomes a frantic, tormented search for self-understanding. Veronica prompts the tirade with her assertion that "against the Germans, the French had an ideal. Against the Algerians, they don't have one. They'll lose the war." Bruno disagrees, declaring himself "very proud to be French" and expressing an intellectualized cultural nationalism à la Giraudoux: "One defends ideas, one doesn't defend territories. I love France because I love Joachim du Bellay and Louis Aragon. I love Germany because I love Beethoven."

Bruno then takes up the question of death and suicide:

> Women, when they commit suicide, always throw themselves under a train or from a window. They are so afraid not to be able to go through with it that they throw themselves forward, so that it's impossible to turn back. Men never do that. It's very rare for a man to throw himself under a subway train and it's very rare for a woman to open her veins. I find it very courageous of them and at the same time very cowardly . . . Life is what counts for women, but death for men.

And from these existential questions, Bruno comes back to politics, only to give the subject an intimate spin:

> There is a beautiful sentence, I think it's from Lenin: "Ethics are the aesthetics of the future." I find that sentence very beautiful and very moving too. It reconciles the right and the left. What do people on the right and the left think about? What's the point of revolution today? As soon as a reactionary government comes to power, it applies a leftist policy and the other way around. As for me, I win or I lose, but I fight alone. Around 1930, young people had the revolution. For example, Malraux, Drieu La Rochelle, Aragon. We no longer have anything. They had the war in Spain, we don't even have a war of our own. Apart from ourselves, our own face and our own voice, we have nothing. But maybe this is what is important. To come to recognize the sound of one's own voice and the form of one's own face.

Godard's attempt, in this speech, to hear the sound of his own voice and to recognize his own face in the mirror ends with Bruno in front of a mirror: first looking into it, then turning his back on it and delivering the end of his monologue while staring into the camera. Godard described *Le Petit Soldat* as a film where "one has to yield up what one has in the guts, so to speak; and what one has in the guts is not necessarily made to be yielded up just like that."[44]

Forty years after the end of the shoot, Godard said about *Le Petit Soldat:* "It is perhaps too personal, it embarrasses me a little . . . because I was a little . . . yes, the character was, was not very sympathet—it should have been worked on more, he wasn't very sympathetic."[45] He had indeed "let himself go" and expressed ideas that he would rather have thought out more carefully. Bruno's cri de coeur is, in the end, an attempt to escape a narrowly defined political identity, but it was also an aestheticization of the issue at hand; it was noncommittal regarding the Algerian War. The great advance of *Le Petit Soldat* was also its limitation.

AS HAD BEEN the case with *Breathless,* Godard's spontaneous invention of dialogue on the set was made possible by the fact that *Le Petit Soldat* was filmed without direct sound[46] and was dubbed, thus allowing Godard to call dialogue to his actors while the camera was rolling. Yet in constructing the film's sound track, he made an ingenious and singular choice in the editing room in order to create the effect of filtering the action through Bruno's memory. Instead of re-creating the rich sonic texture of the city, Godard suppressed most ambient sound and couched the voices in a void, as if detached from the characters' surroundings. Agnès Guillemot, the editor, spoke of the unusual sound-editing procedure:

> I remember Godard asking me, for a scene of a car arriving at a railway crossing: "I only want the sound of the match." Ordinarily, one would have put the sound of the car in motion and then braking, the character reaching for his cigarette then lighting it.[47]

This practice lent the voices and the discrete sound effects a peculiar intimacy, as if, like Bruno, the viewer were experiencing not a moment in full but a particular, keen, and pointed detail as Bruno remembers it. Godard said of Bruno:

> One must be with him, must see things from his point of view, to the precise extent and time as the exterior story is told. The film is like a private diary, a notebook, or the monologue of someone who is trying to defend himself before an almost accusatory camera, as one does before a lawyer or a psychiatrist.[48]

Even the music points to the film's struggle with memory: where *Breathless* is filled with Martial Solal's bluesy swing, *Le Petit Soldat* is punctuated with the modernist composer Maurice Le Roux's fragmentary, atonal jolts of solo piano, aural pangs of conscience. The film's first lines, spoken in voice-over by Godard himself, establish the theme: "For me, the time for action is over. I have gotten older. The time of reflection is beginning."

THE MOST OBVIOUS cinematic point of reference for Godard's second feature film is Orson Welles's *The Lady from Shanghai* (1948), in which Welles plays Michael O'Hara, a young man who gets caught up in a plot from which he can extricate himself only at the cost of the life of the woman he loves. The last line of *Le Petit Soldat*—"There was only one thing left for me: to learn not to be bitter. But I was happy, because I had lots of time ahead of me"—is a loose adaptation of the last line of *The Lady from Shanghai*.[49] Godard said that he had originally intended to include an even more direct quotation from Welles's film, but then decided against it.

Another cinematic reference, however, had a far more pervasive influence on the film and on Godard's subsequent work: the French filmmaker Robert Bresson. Just after the end of the shoot, Godard told a journalist, "I really made this film under the influence of Bresson (*Pickpocket*) and of Malraux."[50] *Pickpocket*, Bresson's fifth feature film, released in December 1959, is loosely based on Dostoyevsky's *Crime and Punishment;* it tells the story of an intellectual pickpocket who justifies his crimes with Nietzschean theories of the superior man who is above the law, and of the simple, saintly, long-suffering woman who loves him. The film concludes with a spiritual transfiguration, and Bresson's aesthetic is up to his metaphysical ambitions. The style of *Pickpocket* is austere, abstracted, indeed exalted, but not weighty or gloomy: the precise gestures and uninflected diction of Bresson's amateur actors were perfectly adapted to the film's spare, unencumbered framing and its naturalistic sound track, and these elements were in the service of a sanctification—and a moral judgment—of the stuff of ordinary life. The influence of *Pickpocket*, in particular, was both a model and an intellectual challenge to Godard, and would exert an effect on Godard's work that was profound and enduring. Bresson's film obsessed Godard, who went to see it at least ten times, sometimes ducking into a theater just to see ten or twenty minutes of it. In 1983, Godard recalled, "I would surely like to be moved now as much as I had been moved by *Pickpocket*. One thought: ah, such a thing can be done!"[51] In his top-ten list for 1959 in *Cahiers*, he cited it as the best film of the year, ahead of *Hiroshima Mon Amour, The 400 Blows*, and films by Jean Renoir, Jean Rouch, and Georges Franju. In an interview as he prepared to shoot *Le Petit Soldat*, Godard suggested the grounds of his confrontation with the sublimity of Bresson's explicitly religious vision:

> The filmmaker, upon contact with life, discovers that the theoretical oppositions between contrary positions lack all foundation. It is false to say that there are classics and moderns, fascists and progressives, believers and atheists. There are people concerned with religion, politics, and literary problems, and people who aren't.[52]

Godard was claiming for his own relentlessly secular cinema the possibility of a secular exaltation equal to that of Bresson's religious work. He set out to make a film in which he would seek a Bressonian spiritual depth and intensity of inner experience without reference to God or religion.

WHEN ASKED TO what extent *Le Petit Soldat* was a political film, Godard answered, "One can say that the film is not political because I do not take a position for anyone and because the subject is not 'oriented' in the manner of Russian films."[53] Rather than engaging himself politically with a statement of position in the conflict, he simply sought to acknowledge in cinema that there was a conflict: he claimed that he did not "take sides" and was "for" both Bruno and Veronica. Godard presents both camps engaging in torture and reinforces this evenhandedness with a verbal gesture: both László of the FLN and Jacques of the Red Hand invoke the same phrase by Lenin to justify their actions: "Sometimes one must have the strength to cut one's way with a dagger."[54] Yet the balance—or detachment—of Godard's approach carried moral and personal risks. Godard sensed in advance the battles that would await him as a result of it: "I am sure that this film will not please anyone, because I show the hardness of both sides, because I don't take sides and I want only to treat seriously the character's problem."[55]

The enmity of the orthodox left toward the members of the *Cahiers* group did not abate now that they had become filmmakers. Because the left did not merely exhort filmmakers to cover certain subjects, but to advance a particular view of them, Godard had long taken the left to stand for constraint, unfreedom; whereas the right, in its avoidance of politics and explicit doctrines in culture, could more easily be identified with freedom of thought, if a self-centered one.

But the war in Algeria brought back into action the old fascist right. Rehabilitated Vichy collaborationists and their sympathizers were committing paramilitary murders of pro-Algerian activists throughout Europe. Anti-Semitic demonstrations and attacks, unrelated to the Algerian War, were on the rise; in the first months of 1960, such assaults were sufficiently numerous to be reported daily in *Le Monde* under their own rubric. The war in Algeria and the atmosphere in France made claims to aesthetic political detachment appear dubious. As a result, Godard sought to redefine his politics, to distance himself from the morass of neofascism that had emerged from behind the mask of world-weary romanticism, but to do so without yielding to the doctrinaire demands of the organized left.

Godard did indeed make a gesture in that direction: although in *Le Petit Soldat* he equated left and right and evenhandedly damned the moral compromises of both sides, he gave an interview in which he expressed a clear preference for one side over the other: "I think that people on the left are sentimental. Those on the right have formal ideas. Since I am sentimental, I am rather on the left. Especially in relation to my best friends, who are clearly on the right."[56] But even if Godard also sought to appease the French government in advance, in the hope of avoiding censorship, by declaring *Le Petit Soldat* "a Gaullist film because it objectively takes stock of things,"[57] the film was nonetheless a provocation aimed principally at the French government: by implicating France in a dirty war to which it had never admitted, *Le Petit Soldat* was an act of defiance that belonged naturally to the left. It was a singular rejection of the Gaullist regime's censorship, an attempt to break the silence about the war.

THE PRODUCTION OF *Le Petit Soldat* stopped for several weeks in order for Godard to attend the Cannes Film Festival. *Breathless* had been nominated as one of the three films to represent France at the festival; the ultimate decision, however, lay with the newly appointed minister of culture, André Malraux, who, without explanation, substituted *Moderato Cantabile,* adapted by the English theater director Peter Brook from the novel by Marguerite Duras. Godard's friends at *Cahiers* railed in print at such a historically shortsighted decision, but the decision stood; *Breathless* would be shown at Cannes, but out of competition.

Nonetheless, the screening of the film on May 9 was important for the world market. Godard attended, in the company of Anna Karina and Michel Subor. *Breathless* was shown several times, and was a very hot ticket for the gathered film professionals from around the world; it was also sold for distribution to many other countries, which proved more profitable for Beauregard than its first run in France.

After the screening, Godard, Karina, and Subor left Cannes to return to Geneva and finish shooting *Le Petit Soldat.* Godard and Karina were now a couple. At the end of the shoot, Godard drove back to Paris with her. Upon their arrival in the city, he asked Karina where he should drop her off. She responded, "You can't leave me, I've left everything for you, now I'm staying with you." But Godard did not have a regular apartment; he lived in a furnished hotel room, and he put her in the room next door. Karina later recalled, "There were two adjoining small rooms and . . . I felt from time to time someone in the night, slipping into my bed. It was Jean-Luc."[58] By day, he left her there while he went off to the editing room, and he asked her to find them an apartment.

WHILE AT CANNES, Godard was interviewed for French television by François Chalais, a journalist who had been Beauregard's friend since the early 1940s (when they both had low-level posts in the Vichy government), and who had written for *Cahiers* starting with its first issue in April 1951. Godard's talk with Chalais was shockingly unguarded:

> I have the impression of loving the cinema less than I did a year ago—simply because I have made a film, and the film was well-received, and so forth. So I hope that my second film will be received very badly and that this will make me want to make films again.[59]

Godard was now to get his wish, although not in the way he might have imagined.

Despite his claim that he didn't take sides on Algeria, many viewers felt that Godard was not at all evenhanded in his depiction of the conflict, and that, in showing the FLN committing torture, he favored the French. A journalist who spoke with industry insiders invited to private screenings of the film in the summer of 1960 reported that the adjectives he heard most often were *fascist, insolent, reckless.*[60] Godard later responded:

> Why did I show a scene of torture by the FLN? Because at that time, the opposite would have been too easy: at that moment, the FLN was more sympathetic and it was more meaningful for my treatment of torture to show them using torture and to leave only the suggestion that the French do the same.[61]

Of course, it was also inconceivable at the time that a film showing the French using torture would pass French censorship, whereas it seemed plausible that a film showing the FLN torturing would prove acceptable.

In 1916, France established a "Commission de contrôle," governed by the Ministry of the Interior and the police, which screened all films proposed for distribution and issued a "visa" to those judged appropriate for release. In 1960, that system was still in operation, under the aegis of the CNC, where films that failed viewing by a handful of the preliminary twenty-one members of the commission were then screened for the entire board.[62] The commission's judgment was remarkably politicized and censorious: for instance, in 1955, Alain Resnais was compelled to suppress in *Night and Fog* a documentary image of a French gendarme supervising deportees.[63] Some films were banned outright; for instance, in March 1960, *Morambong,* a French feature film shot in North Korea, was banned because the censors thought that it reflected negatively on UN troops.[64]

Godard and others who had seen the film privately knew that *Le Petit Soldat* would come under close scrutiny by the commission, and had sought to position the film favorably in the press. His repeated insistence that he did not take sides, and that his film was really "a Western with kidnappings and stuff like that,"[65] was an attempt to protect it from censorship. According to Michel Subor, Godard anticipated that the censors would require cuts but would permit the film's release.[66] As Godard told an interviewer: "Will my film be banned? I don't think so. It's an adventure film."[67]

But on September 7, 1960, the commission voted to deny the film a visa and banned its release both in France and abroad. The commission's vote, however, ultimately required the ratification of the minister of information, Louis Terrenoire. On September 12, Terrenoire announced his agreement with the commission's vote, for three reasons. First, because the film showed torture ("The fact that these tortures are carried out by the FLN in no way affects the judgments that must be applied against these practices and their representation on the screen")—meaning that the French government, which tortured but would not permit it to be said that it tortured, also required that torture be publicly condemned. Second, because the film's hero is a deserter from the French army. And, finally, because of "the words given to a protagonist of the film and by which the action of France in Algeria is presented as devoid of any ideal, whereas that of the rebellion is defended and exalted."[68]

The film was thus denied both the "visa d'exploitation" and the "visa d'exportation," which meant that it could not be shown anywhere in the world.

Beauregard and Godard attempted to defend the film in a joint communiqué. They stated that the torture scenes were only three and a half minutes long and were no more horrible than scenes in war or horror films, and that the film did not advocate desertion or insubordination. They also called attention to the fact that, in the scene where Anna Karina declares the French to be without an ideal in Algeria, Bruno contradicts her and declares himself "very proud to be French."[69] Elsewhere, Godard said that he would in any case willingly cut Karina's offending line.[70] Beauregard considered presenting the commission with a new version of the film, "with all references to the war in Algeria and to the FLN effaced,"[71] and even with a new title.

However, Beauregard and Godard had also foreseen the possibility of a total ban and had taken measures to protect against it. Several months earlier, Beauregard had sold foreign distribution rights in *Le Petit Soldat* to a Swiss company, which in turn had already made deals in foreign countries, including the United States. Godard, speaking with journalists, made the case that, since the movie had been shot in Switzerland by a director who was a Swiss citizen, on film stock that was bought in Switzerland, and since the film had indeed required an import visa to be brought into France for editing and dubbing, it was actually not French but was "Swiss merchandise" and thus was subject to French restrictions solely on its release in French territory.

Godard's strategic sense and legalistic argumentation were subtle and sharp, but they were trumped by main force. The response of the French government and its dubious defenders was swift. Jean-Marie Le Pen, who had not yet founded his far-rightist Front National party but who was a representative in the National Assembly, immediately wrote an open letter to Prime Minister Michel Debré requesting that Godard be expelled from France if the film were exported from Switzerland. He also recommended that France dissuade the Swiss government from authorizing such an export. In fact, Debré and his government threatened Beauregard with even more exquisite financial punishment, including refusal of authorization to produce other films.

Beauregard could not afford the risk: he had recently entered a coproduction agreement with a major Italian producer, Carlo Ponti, in a company called Rome-Paris Films, which put ample funds at his disposal for big-budget films. Beauregard backed down. Godard, for his part, feared other, less official, sanctions: as he admitted years later, "Since I had received death threats in my mailbox, I was pleased that it was banned."[72]

The film industry did not ignore the affront: articles challenging the ban appeared in leading journals, including *L'Express, France-Observateur,* and *L'Humanité.* Several film clubs organized a day of protest in Le Havre; and most significantly, *Cahiers du cinéma* (which had promoted the film with a still of Subor, handcuffed and attempting to slit his wrists with a razor blade held between his teeth, on the cover of its July 1960 issue) published the script of the film, in May and June 1961.

And yet, as outrageous as was the ban on *Le Petit Soldat,* it was far from the most contentious or aggressive act by the French government against those of its own citizens who opposed the ongoing colonization of Algeria. In the spring of 1960, many of the *porteurs de valises,* who worked with the network led by the activist (and philosopher) Francis Jeanson to harbor and transport members of the FLN, were arrested. In the wake of these arrests, the critic and novelist Maurice Blanchot, with the support and editorial contribution of a small group of like-minded intellectuals (notably, Claude Lanzmann), wrote a manifesto, intended as a petition, to support the right of French citizens to aid the cause of Algerian independence. The list of its first 121 signatories included Jean-Paul Sartre, Simone de Beauvoir, Pierre Boulez, André Breton, Marguerite Duras, Alain Resnais, Michel Leiris, Alain Robbe-Grillet, Nathalie Sarraute, Claude Simon, Simone Signoret, the historian Pierre Vidal-Naquet, and the classicist Jean-Pierre Vernant.[73] Resnais's wife—Florence Malraux, daughter of André Malraux, the minister of culture—audaciously added her name. Shortly after the publication on September 6, 1960, of the list—now known as the Manifesto of 121—forty others publicly added their names, among them François Truffaut,[74] Jacques Doniol-Valcroze, and Pierre Kast; then nineteen more, including producer Anatole Dauman, mathematician Laurent Schwartz, and Malraux's ex-wife, Clara.

The government responded with the strongest possible sanctions, threatening to fire any civil servant—teacher, professor, or employee of television and radio (which were still fully owned by the French government)—who signed. Furthermore, all signatories were banned from television and radio appearances, state-subsidized theaters, and government-aided films—which meant, for all practical purposes, all films. As one journalist, Madeleine Chapsal, noted in *L'Express,* "If the government really means to withdraw aid from all enterprises which employ a single signatory of the Manifesto of 121, the New Wave and its promise are finished."[75] After an international outcry against such restrictions—and offers from foreign countries to employ French artists denied the right to work at home, with the implication of a French McCarthyism—the government eventually backed down.

Godard refused to sign the manifesto. As Truffaut's wife at the time, Madeleine Morgenstern, later recalled, "He still hoped to have a visa de contrôle for *Le Petit Soldat,* and on top of that, he was a foreigner."[76] His signature could have resulted in expulsion from France; he also planned to make another film in several months—the comedy *Une Femme est une femme* (*A Woman Is a Woman*), the script outline of which had been published in *Cahiers* in 1959—and had reason to expect that, were he to sign, his authorization to direct would be denied. When asked in 1964 about his refusal, Godard explained it on purely temperamental grounds: "I didn't feel like it. I did what concerned me personally"[77]—apparently an unprincipled, adolescent stubbornness not unlike that of the little soldier himself—but his temperament clearly coincided with prudence and self-interest.

The ban on *Le Petit Soldat* provoked a scandal of only limited scope. Despite the outcry on the film's behalf, the government was intransigent, and in any case the angry response of Godard's friends and allies, though gratifying, was hardly thunderous. There were no mass protests in Paris, no strikes of the movie industry, no outpourings of popular support. *Le Petit Soldat* did not become a cause célèbre; the French cinema went about its business, and Godard had no choice but to go about his. He stoically absorbed the double blow—of the censorship and of the media nonevent—as an "enormous failure,"[78] and prepared to make a new film.

After seeing *Le Petit Soldat* in a private screening, Robert Bresson wrote an encouraging note to Godard in which he told him, "Continue." Godard continued.

Anna Karina continued too. When they moved in together after the end of the shoot of the film, Godard had advised her to give up acting. It was advice that he had already given her, in public, in *Le Petit Soldat,* when, speaking through Michel Subor as Bruno takes pictures of Veronica, he initiated the following on-camera dialogue:

> BRUNO: It's funny that you want to be an actress . . . Actors, I find it stupid.
> I despise them. You tell them to cry, they cry. You tell them to crawl, they
> crawl. To me, that's grotesque.
> VERONICA: I don't see why.
> BRUNO: I don't know, they're not free.

Yet Karina rejected his advice, at the first possible opportunity. After the director Michel Deville had seen a private screening of *Le Petit Soldat,* he offered her a leading role in a comedy that he was about to start filming in early September 1960, *Ce Soir ou jamais* (Tonight or Never). Godard told her that the script was bad and asked her mockingly how she could bear to say the lines, but Karina thought him to be "mad with jealousy."[79] And despite his displeasure, Godard, while fighting the censorship of *Le Petit Soldat* and preparing to make his next film, drove Karina to the studio each morning.

THE WAR, TOO, continued; in a four-day span in September, 326 Algerians were reported killed. After the French electorate voted overwhelmingly, on January 8, 1961, in favor of self-determination for the people of Algeria, the putschists-in-hiding came out to announce that their underground group, the OAS (Organisation armée secrète), would take up the fight more forcefully. In April, a group of French generals attempted another coup against French civil authorities in Algeria.

The FLN also continued its fight on French soil, assassinating several police officers. On October 17, 1961, a peaceful evening protest in Paris by Algerians who challenged a curfew that applied to Algerians only (in the wake of those killings) turned into a massacre: the police, tacitly unleashed by police prefect Maurice Papon, killed between two and three hundred people and dumped the bodies into the Seine.[80]

A campaign of bombings by the OAS, including two against Sartre and one against Malraux (which blinded his concierge's four-year-old daughter), aroused an outcry against the clandestine group's activities.[81] An anti-OAS protest on February 8, 1962, was attacked by the police, causing nine deaths. On March 18, the French government and the ALN (Armée de Libération Nationale, the armed wing of the FLN) signed an agreement that would result in an independent Algeria. On April 8, French voters approved the accord with 90.7 percent of the vote; on July 1, Algeria voted 99.7 percent in favor of independence and—after a nearly successful attempt by the OAS on August 22 to assassinate de Gaulle—Algeria became independent on September 9, 1962.

Soon thereafter, in December, the ban on *Le Petit Soldat* was lifted and the film was released the next month: with the war over, Algeria independent, and the OAS out of favor with the French government, no interest was served by withholding it. Although the political climate had calmed, the film still aroused the ire of the left, which felt that Godard was too complaisant with the violent reactionary and quasi-fascist underground that had pushed France repeatedly to the brink of civil war. As for the aesthetic of *Le Petit Soldat,* Godard had already superseded it; by early 1963, the film's moment had passed. The questions and controversies that Godard's subsequent work would arouse in the intervening two years were of an altogether different order, and *Le Petit Soldat,* if not unnoticed, was, at the time of its release, already an object of curiosity regarding a conflict that seemed to have faded rapidly into the historical distance.

On the set of *A Woman Is a Woman*
(© Raymond Cauchetier)

five

A WOMAN IS A WOMAN

"The moral of this story lacks cheerfulness"

GEORGES DE BEAUREGARD'S PARTNERSHIP WITH CARLO Ponti in Rome-Paris Films gave him access to more capital. It also made him eligible for the French government's new program of aid to French coproductions with foreign producers, a step intended to help internationalize the French film industry. Beauregard's first high-budget film, announced in the spring of 1960, would be Godard's third film, based on the story published in *Cahiers du cinéma* in August 1959: *Une Femme est une femme (A Woman Is a Woman)*. It was budgeted at 2,177,000 new francs[1] (approximately $435,000, or more than four times the budget of *Breathless*).

A Woman Is a Woman would be Godard's first Cinemascope (widescreen) and color film.[2] Not only were color film and processing substantially more expensive than black and white, but also, because there was at the time no color negative film as fast as the highly sensitive black-and-white stock Godard had formerly used, indoor shooting could not be done without a great deal of additional lighting. Therefore, the shoot schedule for *A Woman Is a Woman* would have to be longer than for Godard's first two films (to allow for the rigging of lights), and the crew would have to expand to include gaffers and grips (electricians and riggers). Moreover, despite Godard's resistance to putting heavy makeup on actors, the technique of shooting color film required its use, because film laboratory technicians needed a consistent skin tone to match the color from shot to shot.

In exchange for the cumbersome production methods that the larger-scale production would impose, Godard would get to play with a more sophisticated box of cinematic toys. In addition to color and Cinemascope, the film featured the direct recording of sound, as a result of which, Godard had to make the film with an unwieldy but quiet studio camera, the Mitchell, which weighed seventy pounds, far too heavy to be held by hand.[3] It was coupled with a sound truck, a large rig on wheels that recorded sound directly to 35mm film.[4]

Although Godard would make *A Woman Is a Woman* with the techniques of a Hollywood film, the result would be constructed in such a way as to lay bare the methods by which the beloved illusions are achieved. Godard's third film is the equivalent of a card trick performed with explanations. *A Woman Is a Woman* never rises to plausibility as an imitation of reality. Instead, the conjured reality that evokes emotion is not the drama itself, but the off-camera story of Godard and Karina, which the film reveals as a story of love and conflict, under the guise of a genre fantasy.

THE LEADING MAN of *A Woman Is a Woman* would be Jean-Claude Brialy, who had been a friend and "fellow traveler" of the *Cahiers* group since the mid-1950s (and who had starred in Godard's short film *All the Boys Are Called Patrick*). The second male role would be taken by Jean-Paul Belmondo, in a supporting part that was unsuited to his newfound stardom, but which he accepted out of gratitude to Godard.

When Godard first mentioned the role to Brialy in early 1960, he told the actor that his female costar would be Brigitte Bardot. However, Godard knew that Beauregard would not, in all likelihood, be able to afford Bardot's fee. Instead, Godard considered many actresses for the role, notably Marina Vlady, who had been a French teen star in the 1950s.[5] He even sent a telegram to Joan Collins, whom Karina recalled as Godard's "ideal, his favorite woman of the era."[6]

Ultimately, he offered the role to Anna Karina—but not until he saw her in the rushes of *Ce Soir ou jamais,* the comedy by Michel Deville which she was filming that fall. The contrast between *Le Petit Soldat* and *Ce Soir ou jamais* could not have been greater. Unlike Karina's debut feature, Deville's film was shot in a studio with a large crew, Karina had a script in hand, and she had to learn her lines before shooting. (In the event, *A Woman Is a Woman* would impose more conventional cinematic artifice on its performers than Godard's first two films had done.)

But there is a more critical reason that Godard cast Karina only after seeing her work for another director as a "professional" actress. Her part in Godard's third film is precisely that of a "professional," a striptease artist in a dingy little cabaret, who nevertheless takes her work seriously, planning her routines with care and never confusing her performance and her role as an entertainer with her private life. The character she was being asked to play in the film resembled the one she took on in life as a result of Deville's film, that of a professional performer.

A Woman Is a Woman was based on Godard's published story outline of the same title. A woman wants to get pregnant, but her boyfriend is not ready to have a child. She turns to his best friend, who has until then been flirting with her, and lets him seduce her. That night, to try to repair their relationship, the boyfriend agrees to sleep with her, so that his paternity, if not assured, would at least be possible.

Although Godard worked from his own preexisting script treatment, he again played the name game with his characters: the entangled trio, originally called Josette, Emile, and Paul, became Angela, Emile, and Alfred. Emile is the eponymous character by Jean-Jacques Rousseau, the child who would leave his books for an education in life.[7] Godard gave Emile the last name of Récamier, taken from Madame Julie Récamier, who ran one of the most famous salons in early-nineteenth-century Paris. Godard "amused" himself with the idea "that Anna would want to become Madame Récamier."[8] The choice of names, however, was not innocent: Julie Récamier was famous not for her wit but for her beauty. Angela is Anna as an angel (*ange*), an exculpation in advance of the character: she is not a schemer or a seducer but is innocent in both senses of the word, both unschooled and blameless. Emile's best friend, Angela's seducer—in Godard's first version, Paul, as in Gégauff, the ladies' man who was his friend—became Alfred Lubitsch, a Hitchcockian manipulator in a Lubitschian menage à trois like *Design for Living* (the 1933 film by Ernst Lubitsch that Godard cited as a model for the film's romantic schema).

Emile runs a small newspaper and magazine shop in Paris, in the old working-class neighborhood of Strasbourg-St.-Denis, centered on the rue St.-Denis, the street traditionally occupied by the sex industry. Angela—who is called Madame Récamier though she and Emile are not yet married—discovers from a device provided by a colleague at the club where she works that she is at the peak of her fertility cycle, and tells Emile that she wants a child at once. He is willing, but only after they are married. She suggests they get married as soon as possible (and, in a winking reference to Godard's life with Karina, that they write to her mother in Copenhagen for the necessary papers). He, however, is in no hurry to be married or to have a child, and besides, he has a bicycle rally on Sunday and does not want to tire himself with sex. She threatens to have a child with another man—with his best friend, Alfred (played by Belmondo), who has long been pursuing her. The next day, when Alfred shows her a photograph of Emile at a café with another woman, Angela lets herself be seduced. Emile, who discovers his betrayal, goes in despair to visit a prostitute. That evening, Angela confesses to Emile. They decide to resolve their crisis by making love, after which they will decree the child's paternity to be resolved in Emile's favor, and will live, so to speak, happily ever after. The pun with which the film ends, and which provides the title, concluded Godard's original treatment: "Angela, tu es infâme"—(Angela, you are horrid). "Non, je suis *une* femme" (No, I am a woman).

Karina was "thrilled" to be chosen by Godard for the lead in *A Woman Is a Woman,*[9] yet the unflattering correlation to her personal life with Godard seems too conspicuous to miss. Like Godard and Karina, the film's main characters, a man who is something of an intellectual and a woman who is an entertainer, a person of the body, formed a yet-unmarried couple.

Godard had sketched out the original version of *A Woman Is a Woman* long before he had met Karina, and had intended it to be a comic spectacle, not a film of confession and revelation. But the incidental adjustments to which he subjected the story rendered it autobiographical, specifically in regard to his relationship with Anna Karina. In the film, Godard revealed the emotional and artistic fault lines that threatened their relationship, and his diagnosis would prove painfully prophetic.

The subject of *A Woman Is a Woman* became Godard's own effort to make a film starring Anna Karina about their life together. The film's enduring importance is due to its peculiar reflexivity and the new aesthetic devices by which Godard realized it.

THE SHOOT WAS originally to have begun on November 21 on location in an apartment on the rue St.-Martin. Godard had offered the tenants, an elderly couple, ten thousand francs and lodging in a luxury hotel for permission to shoot there for approximately one month.[10] Days before the shoot was due to begin, the couple, hearing Godard describe the changes he was going to make to their apartment, withdrew their consent. Godard had mentally mapped out the film in relation to that particular apartment, and instead of looking for another, he decided to shoot those scenes on a studio set that replicated the apartment. Raoul Coutard, the cameraman, was pleased to have at his disposal a studio's technical resources—walls that could be shifted to facilitate camera moves, rafters from which lights could be hung. But Godard would have none of it; he specified that the apartment be reconstructed precisely, down to its inconveniences, with its walls and pillars fixed in place. As Anna Karina later recalled: "Every night, he locked the door behind him. Nobody could enter the apartment until he arrived in the morning to open it. He filmed in the studio as if he were on location. The others"— Coutard and the rest of the crew—"protested."[11]

The shoot began at the studio on November 28, 1960. But after several days of filming, Godard was dissatisfied; in particular, he said he did not like the way that Karina climbed into bed for a scene with Brialy. He attempted the gesture himself and, as Coutard recalled, declared: "It's crazy. We're trying to film Anna going to bed in her room and there's no ceiling. Anna has never slept in a room that hasn't got a ceiling."[12] Godard had a ceiling built, at great expense, telling Beauregard, "If there isn't a ceiling, Anna can't do the scene." But he admitted to a journalist a more practical reason for putting a ceiling in place: "Just to prevent the technicians from lighting the set from above. The lighting men were rather startled to have to work this way, but the effect was more natural."[13] Godard's pretext about Karina's performance in a ceilingless room and his simpler, more practical rationale boiled down to the same idea: Godard wanted the film to be not realistic but real. He was not interested in constructing a set that *resembled* an apartment; rather, he wanted to film in a place that *was* an apartment (or a replica of one). Whether the setting actually affected Karina's performance was beside the point; if Godard was satisfied with the authenticity of the space, he would be satisfied that whatever performance she rendered in it would be validated as authentic as well.

Godard's intentional allusions to his private life were imprinted in the film's first dramatic scene. When Angela brings lunch to Emile in his shop and peruses some magazines concerning pregnancy and childbirth, she takes them from a rack that prominently features a magazine called *Le Cinéma Chez Soi* (The Cinema at One's Home, or Home Movies). The ambition that Godard asserted in *Le Petit Soldat*—to film his own voice, his own look, and his own situation, albeit represented by another person—was now set forth in its ultimate form: what Godard wanted, ideally, was to make home movies in the guise of a fictional feature film, and to make a feature film that would fulfill the intimate function of a home movie.

THE SHOOT OF *A Woman Is a Woman* differed from that of Godard's first two films in one crucial respect: because the principal location (whether the apartment or the studio) would be available only for a brief period of time, Godard had to film the scenes in clusters, and the story out of sequence, as was typical for the industry. Yet Godard again wrote the dialogue at the last minute (as he said, "in the studio, while the actors were getting made up").[14] (To find out the day's agenda, the production manager, Philippe Dussart, fished Godard's notes from the garbage can.) But this time, because of the direct sound, Godard could not call the lines out to the actors without rendering the live sound unusable. The actors therefore had to learn their lines immediately. This made for a very demanding shoot—and not least, for Godard himself. Brialy admitted,

> I had complete confidence in Godard, but still, not to know anything a minute ahead of what one is going to shoot, it's stressful. And Godard doesn't say a word. He paces around on the set, looking off into space, his face blank, hermetic. The first three days, I don't know how I stood it.[15]

Moreover, the pressure of limited studio time did not allow Godard absolute freedom and caprice: for the most part, Godard stayed in the studio from noon until 8:00 PM and almost every day shot the three minutes of screen time that he needed to complete. It was the compulsion to push ahead, on the grounds of budgetary constraints, regardless of inspiration or the lack of it, that made Godard describe the film as having been directed "in a single brushstroke" and his work on it as "almost automatic writing."[16]

The stress of the shoot coalesced with the drama of one of the film's key moments: when Angela cries in despair over Emile's unwillingness to get her pregnant, she stumbles over her lines as she laments in close-up, "I think women who don't cry are stupid, trying to limit—no, that's not right, is it? No. I think that women who don't cry are stupid. Modern women just want to imitate men." Karina's tears fall all the more copiously as she struggles with her lines. In the editing room, Godard used both takes, the one where Karina blows the line tearfully and the one where she gets it right.

In the context of the story, the flub and the tears dramatize Angela's frustration with Emile, but in the context of the shoot, they lay bare Karina's frustrations with Godard's demands that she perform complicated scenes in direct sound with minimal preparation—a demand that was all the more difficult for Karina because she was an untrained and inexperienced actress. The shoot was stormy: on one occasion, Karina ran off the set and Godard ran after her. Brialy reported that the actress "began to assail our dear Godard with very crude words." He described their tormented union throughout the shoot: "They tore each other apart, argued, loved each other, hated each other, screamed at each other."[17] Godard was nonetheless especially solicitous of Karina on the set, and Brialy and Belmondo resented his exclusive attention to his lead actress, criticizing him for not even acknowledging them when he arrived at the set. The next day, Godard sarcastically greeted the actors with two bouquets of flowers.

GODARD'S FRIEND JEAN-PIERRE Laubscher reported for a Swiss newspaper on a day's shooting in a café on the rue du Faubourg-St.-Denis, where he elicited Godard's delicate yet precise judgment of the work at hand: "Ultimately, the moral of this story lacks cheerfulness."[18] Yet Godard filmed the scenes in a cheerful, overtly comic Punch-and-Judy manner that amplified the antic tone of the published synopsis. In the very first shot, Anna Karina enters and leaves a café and winks at the camera, the first of many occasions when the actors look into the camera and address the audience (Alfred watches Angela leave, for example, and tells the camera, "She leaves"; elsewhere, Angela orders Emile—or rather, Karina orders Brialy—to bow to the audience before playing a scene). The actors mug at the camera exactly as people do in home movies, and when they revert to their roles, they play them with the conspicuous theatricality of nonactors calling attention to the fact that they are performing. During the shoot, Brialy described to a journalist this mixture of tones: "We have to play the false situations truly, and the true ones falsely."[19]

This breaking of the fourth wall aptly joined with the chipper, exaggerated acting to convey a style appropriate to that of the music hall or the popular comic theater; in fact, the most significant change that Godard made to the story as written was to turn it into a musical comedy. Nothing in Godard's script treatment suggested that the film would be what Godard called "a musical comedy in the classical sense of the term, with dialogue scenes and then all of a sudden, scenes with songs."[20]

As he approached the shoot, however, Godard changed his ideas drastically—instead of filming a musical, he decided to make a film about the musical that he would not make.

> For me, it's a film on the nostalgia for musical comedy, as when Anna says: "Ah! I'd like to be in a musical comedy," it was rather in that vein. I had thought of it afterward, so I did the dialogue and then after, with [Michel] Legrand, we made music that gave the impression that the people were often singing. I mean, which is placed at the same time as, and under, the words in order to give them the tone of opera. It isn't a musical comedy, but it isn't just a talking film either. It's a regret that life is not lived in music.[21]

The film contains a great deal of music and a wealth of references and borrowings from musical comedies such as *The Pajama Game* (which Godard had praised at length in *Cahiers* in 1958). But instead of having his characters sing songs composed for the movie, Godard took advantage of every situation—music hall, café, jukebox, and radio—to bring music into the action, by having the actors hum, whistle, and sing, even a line or a phrase. There isn't very much singing in the film. Most of the music in the film was applied by Godard to the sound track in the editing room.

Indeed, the editing room is the principal site of Godard's innovation and invention on *A Woman Is a Woman.* The editing works against the conventional purpose of the process, which is to overcome any disparities in the footage, to emphasize the continuities and efface the discontinuities, to advance the illusion of a unified fiction. *A Woman Is a Woman* is constructed on exactly the opposite principle: it is constructed as a collage of its footage. Even in *Breathless,* Godard papered over many of his most audacious jump cuts with a continuous sound track. *A Woman Is a Woman,* on the other hand, features images that are not so much disconnected as simply unconnected, as well as breaks and jumps in sound that are as essential as those of the image. The editor Agnès Guillemot recalled that Godard "came up with the idea of alternating . . . shots with direct sound and shots dubbed with music underneath. And quite systematically. So there was always a shot dubbed with music followed by a shot with direct sound."[22] Godard edited the film precisely to call attention to the disparate places and times in which (and of which) the film was constructed, systematically unraveling the strands of image and sound that weave the cinematic illusion.

THE ODD PATHOS of *A Woman Is a Woman* is due to the contradiction on which it was constructed: originally a simple comedy, Godard ended up using the comic framework to express difficult truths about his incipient relationship with Anna Karina. Godard expressed a great deal, very early and very publicly, about their life together, but he did this by way of devices so distancing, distracting, and self-inhibiting as to doom the film in advance.

And yet it was in this failure that Godard succeeded, disturbingly, in putting on the screen his painfully intimate, confessional, and accusatory view of his home life with Anna Karina as he experienced it. The comic posturing of the actors in the film, the antic effort to simulate gaiety in this atmosphere, was Godard's way of conveying his frustrations. The central shot in *A Woman Is a Woman* is the one in which Emile comes home and finds Angela after she has made love with Alfred. He follows her through the apartment and around the dining-room table, and the camera watches him pursue her, until Emile disappears from view and Angela looks into the camera as she retreats from it, attempting to elude its gaze like a hunted animal. Godard's view through camera, which starts the shot in objective balance between Emile and Angela, comes to identify with Emile, and Anna Karina shrinks from its inquisitorial stare as does Angela from Emile's. In the shot's shifting point of view, Godard tips his hand in assimilating Emile's scrutiny of Angela to his own of Karina. The subtle device makes the stress of their work and life together apparent.

A *Woman Is a Woman* offers a Cinemascope spectacle that reveals the confinement within four walls of domestic life. In the street, the wide screen is full; at home, it is empty, the apartment's whitewashed, bare-walled breadth indicative of the dead living space that cried out for a joint activity to fill the couple's time together. Angela and Emile suffer a domestic void that, in this film as in all of Godard's films, is the curse of all couples who do not have a project of work together. Though the film has a conventionally happy ending, it foretells doom for the relationship of the professional performer and the bookish intellectual who lack a shared project of work, and predicts problems for Godard and Karina unless she put aside her desire to be a regular actress and continued to work with him toward a common end.

AFTER THE SHOOT ended in January 1961, Godard went to New York to promote *Breathless,* which would open there on February 8. He did interviews with the local press, in which he discussed his next project, a film on "French politics" that he decided to put off because of what he called "preventive censorship."[23]

When Godard returned to France, he received word that the brothers Hakim, producers of note since the 1930s, had bought the rights to James Hadley Chase's novel *Eva* and had signed Jeanne Moreau to play the lead role. The novel tells the story of a blocked writer who is both inspired and destroyed by a prostitute. Moreau, who was about to begin work on Truffaut's *Jules and Jim*—and who had done a droll cameo in *A Woman Is a Woman*—was asked to recommend a director. She recommended Godard.

The shoot of *Eva* was initially scheduled to begin in March; but first, life followed art: Anna Karina discovered that she was pregnant, and she and Godard decided to marry.

GODARD POSTED NOTICE of the impending marriage at the city hall of the Swiss town of Gland on February 4, 1961, just after his return from New York. The ceremony took place on March 3, 1961, in Begnins, Switzerland. The witnesses were Godard's friends Tolmatchoff and Fontana. The bride wore a wide dress to conceal her pregnancy, and the groom wore a bright green suit.[24] The exercise was repeated, three weeks later, in Paris, for the benefit of the press and the couple's Parisian friends; there the witnesses were Jean-Pierre Melville and Georges de Beauregard; the flower girl was Rosalie, the daughter of Jacques Demy and Agnès Varda.

In their brief time together, Godard and Karina had developed a couple's regular social habits, frequently meeting Demy and Varda to play cards on Sundays,[25] regularly joining Beauregard and his wife for Saturday lunch at an Italian restaurant (though according to the producer, Godard rarely spoke at these gatherings).[26] Godard and Karina partook of Parisian night life together, often in the company of Karina's friends, but he appeared uneasy with his new role.

Yet Godard's domestication was somewhat incomplete, as he had also developed the unusual habit of leaving home unannounced for such destinations as New York and not returning for days or even weeks. Karina tried to accommodate herself to Godard's habits, but they soon exacted a deep emotional cost. Karina was told by her doctors that her pregnancy was precarious and, on their advice, she took to bed. One night in the spring of 1961, Godard returned home to find her in great distress and covered in blood. She had miscarried, and her health was in danger: the fetus had been dead for three weeks. After a stay in the hospital, Karina recuperated at home.

> Jean-Luc was almost never there . . . Jean-Luc couldn't stay in one place, he left, sometimes he fled, and yet he loved me. Everyone called: "Where is Jean-Luc?" I received the tax collector, his friends Truffaut, Jean-Pierre Melville, Demy, Varda . . . who asked me, "Where is your husband?"
>
> I was embarrassed.
>
> "I don't know, when he left three weeks ago, he said that he was going out to get a pack of Boyards, I haven't seen him since." I was ashamed to say it.[27]

Upon his return—without a word of explanation—he attempted to make amends by borrowing money from Beauregard, renting a villa in the south of France, and inviting Karina's mother and stepfather to join her there. (Godard met them there shortly thereafter, bearing an emerald ring from Cartier for his bride.)

In the meantime, Godard's new project, *Eva*, had evaporated—or rather, Godard himself had evaporated it. He had asked the brothers Hakim to hire Richard Burton to play opposite Jeanne Moreau: "They said, 'We'll call him.' I said: 'There's the telephone.' 'Oh, yes, but it's not so simple, he may not be there.' I understood that they didn't want him."[28]

As for Moreau herself, Godard's unease with her was apparent. He had wanted the role to be played "like Rita Hayworth five or six years ago," in other words, as a brassy, streetwise seductress. But Moreau, a former member of the Comédie-Française, belonged to the artistic beau monde, and had worked with such directors as Jean Cocteau, Jacques Becker, and Michelangelo Antonioni. Since, with Moreau playing the lead role, Godard couldn't make *Eva* as he had planned, he completely reconceived the project.

Coutard, whom the brothers Hakim had wanted as Godard's cameraman, witnessed the shift that Godard was planning: "Then Godard proposed something else to them which was not *Eva,* it was something else, so they didn't do the film with him, and I didn't do it with them."[29] This "something else" that Godard proposed was to make the entire film in the office of the Hakim brothers, turning it into what he described as

> the story of a guy who was asked by a producer to write a screenplay about a woman, to find out whether he was really a writer. It becomes the story of a man who tries to write about a woman, but who doesn't manage to do it. Or maybe he manages, I don't know; in any case, that's the story that had to be told. I wanted to show the poem he wrote, and the analysis of the poem. He writes, for example, "I went out, the weather is nice, I met her, she had blue eyes," then he asks himself why he wrote that. Finally I think that he doesn't manage to do anything.[30]

An intriguing thought experiment in cinematic form, it was also an idea that would give Moreau nothing to do. Small wonder that the brothers Hakim were unwilling to produce it. Officially, the shoot was pushed back a month, then to September;[31] then Godard's name was removed from the project. In 1962, Joseph Losey directed the film, starring Moreau and Stanley Baker, with its novelistic structure intact.

Godard did not, however, abandon the underlying inspiration of the reconfigured story, and now anticipated filming it as a project of his own, minus any explicit relation to *Eva.* In an interview that appeared in *L'Express* in July 1961, Godard declared his intention to make a film about the "guy" who needed to prove his ability to write about a woman:

> What I also like is the idea of a journal. I would like, for example, to make a film about me, which would recount my life for, let's say, fifteen days, in which I would look for an idea, the idea for a novel. I think that's it. I would try to write a novel. I don't know whether I'll be able to do it or not. It would be my life in the process of trying to write a novel. The people I see, the ones with whom I talk. And then me, in the process of trying to write a novel. I will ask Sartre how one goes about writing a novel, so there will be the interview, etc.[32]

Godard's films to date had evinced the tension between cinematic form and direct address. The intended first-person transformation of *Eva* was Godard's attempt to do what he didn't with *A Woman Is a Woman*—to address his situation and to express himself in his own voice. He was unable to film his subverted version of *Eva*, but he found a way to rework *A Woman Is a Woman*, retrospectively, along the same lines.

After *A Woman Is a Woman* was finished, Godard made a phonograph record to promote it. Instead of simply copying the film's sound track, he made an original recording, interspersing brief clips from the film's dialogue and music with his own reflective, self-deprecating, punning, and revealing monologues, which he performed in an archly theatrical tone of voice.

> Angela thinks that death justifies men. But that life justifies women . . . Because she does not separate documentary from fiction. Exactly like me. And that's how Angela finally gets the impression that Alfred . . . Angela has the impression that Emile . . . In short, Angela has the impression that she's being taken for a ride. I mean: in a coach. And in fact, a little like Camille in the sublime film by Renoir,[33] Angela will wonder where theater begins and where life begins.

The record, which was never released commercially,[34] was Godard's vision of a cinematic utopia in which this hybrid form of narrative and direct address, art and criticism, documentary and fiction, would be an industrial possibility. It signalled his ongoing quest to bring these two strains of creation together. But most important, Godard's revision of the film was his own quietly devastating self-criticism, his admission of artistic failure. And indeed, the record is a more satisfyingly complete experience than is the film.

IN THE SPRING OF 1961, Godard awaited the release of *A Woman Is a Woman*. It was scheduled to be premièred at the Berlin Film Festival in June 1961, and to open in France in September, a prime season for the industry's major releases. But in the meantime, for the first time since he started to make feature films, almost two years earlier, Godard was at a loss for what to do next. For the moment, at least, the void would be filled by two short films—one in which he acted, the other which he directed.

Agnès Varda started to shoot her second feature film, *Cléo de 5 à 7*, on June 21. She planned an interlude toward the end of the film in which the main character would go to a theater's projection booth, where she would watch a movie. Varda derived her plans for the short film-within-a-film, a silent-comedy pastiche, from a visit that she and Jacques Demy had made to Godard and Karina when they were vacationing in the south of France. The four decided to try their hand at painting on canvases, and when Godard spattered his dark glasses, which he wore constantly, he took them off to clean them. Varda found his eyes "beautiful."

Thus I had furtively seen his big eyes and I wanted to see more of them. Hence my stratagem to make him act in this sketch in which he would take off his glasses.

So I turned him into a character à la Harry Langdon [the mild-mannered silent-era comedy star], running after his Anna Karina who is transformed from black to white when he removes his glasses.[35]

From the heights of a footbridge, Godard sees Karina carted off by ambulance. He calls out to her in anguish, chases the vehicle in vain, and at once plunges into depression, as shown by the enormous funeral wreath that he buys. Then, removing his sunglasses, he sees her return in good health to the scene of the accident, and charges at the ambulance driver, knocking him out and crowning him with the wreath before walking off into the distance arm in arm with his beloved.

This silent burlesque alluded to Karina's medical problems as well as to the couple's tempestuous relationship. It was as if everything that touched the couple turned to allegory.

IN MID-1961, TO capitalize on the fame of the New Wave, the producer Joseph Bercholz commissioned Godard and six other recently launched directors (including Chabrol and Demy) to direct the seven short films in a remake of the 1952 compilation film *The Seven Deadly Sins.*

Godard's sin was sloth, *La Paresse.* His first idea was to film a minimalist gag featuring Eddie Constantine, an American actor famous in France for his recurring role as the detective Lemmy Caution, lying on a bench for a single ten-minute take. However, it was difficult to pull off such a stunt—a long take requires careful preparation and exacting rehearsal. In effect, the execution of such a bravura representation of sloth would have required too much work, and so Godard turned the gag on its head: he made the film slothfully. He composed a series of variations on the actor's unwillingness to exert himself at all (such as refusing to get undressed in the company of a naked woman). The film's conventional lighting and conventional acting and conventional framings—in short, Godard's sloth—fulfilled his commission.

AT THE END OF JUNE 1961, Godard and Karina traveled to Berlin, where *A Woman Is a Woman* was showing in competition. Both Karina and the film won prizes, which augured well for the film's scheduled release in September. It was one of the more heralded releases of the *rentrée*—the new season after the monthlong August vacation—because, with the ban of *Le Petit Soldat,* it was the first film of Godard's to appear since *Breathless.*

A Woman Is a Woman would also be the public's first view of Anna

Karina (Michel Deville's *Ce Soir ou jamais*, the comedy in which Karina had performed in the fall of 1960, was still unreleased), and when it opened, on September 6, 1961, Karina became an instant star. Godard was given great credit for having discovered her and created her persona. One critic called her "an incontestable 'natural' who wins out over the professionalism of Brialy and of Belmondo."[36] Another called the film a "declaration of love" for the "gay, witty, ravishing" actress.[37]

The reviews were generally favorable. In *Le Monde,* Jean de Baroncelli exulted: "In its genre, *A Woman Is a Woman* is as original as *Breathless* could be."[38] Another critic bluntly declared that *A Woman Is a Woman* was Godard's "most ambitious film."[39] One critic, Claude Mauriac (son of the novelist François Mauriac), perceived that the film was a record of Godard's intensely personal allusions, and dared to say so:

> Jean-Luc Godard's extreme reserve lends a lighthearted tone to the most serious thing in the world for a man in love . . . Although he seems to make fun of himself and of us, Godard confesses his most intimate secrets.[40]

The positive reviews, however, did not translate into box-office success. Most reviewers unintentionally suggested the reason for this when they contrasted the popular genre with Godard's personal, artful, willful, albeit fascinating, approach to it. Beauregard and Ponti promoted the film as a Cinemascope-spectacular musical comedy. The film, however, did not correspond to the wider audience's notions of a musical comedy, and it attracted only 58,153 spectators in its first run, meager business for a film that cost the producers more than two million francs to make.

Godard blamed himself for having mixed the genres of musical and melodrama, the moods of artifice and realism, the tones of comedy and tragedy, and thus fostering vague expectations. He also blamed the distributor for an advertising campaign that sold the film as something it was not. Truffaut, however, offered a harsher explanation of why the film failed to please the general public:

> If one plays with sound and image in a too-unconventional way, people yell, it's an automatic reaction. They ripped up the seats in Nice because they thought that the equipment in the projection booth was bad. Of course, one can teach people in articles explaining to them what it's all about but, in the theaters where it was shown, the people were surprised. Godard went too far for them in the sound mix. When the girl comes out of the café, suddenly no more sound, there's silence. No problem: people think that the projector is

broken. . . . People expected to see a nice, classical story. A girl, two boys, in a neighborhood in Paris . . . The very story one expects to be told classically. They were flabbergasted.[41]

Truffaut's trenchant analysis highlighted essential differences between the two men. Truffaut thought of anticipating public reaction, whereas Godard thought solely of making the film as he saw fit. Truffaut's prudence was a commercially well-founded, if artistically dubious, response to the recent fortunes of the New Wave.

The box-office failure of A Woman Is a Woman was only the latest in a series of commercial disappointments for producers of films associated with the New Wave. Shoot the Piano Player barely broke even; Chabrol's fifth film, Les Godelureaux, was his third flop in a row (after A Double Tour and Les Bonnes Femmes). A spate of films by Cahiers critics, including Pierre Kast, Jacques Doniol-Valcroze, and Claude de Givray, fared poorly with the public, as did Jacques Demy's first feature, Lola, and films by other less heralded and less remembered directors. The French press, which had made much of the new directors' extraordinary early box-office successes, now trumpeted these commercial failures as proof that the New Wave had been overhyped and had already run its course.

Indeed, many in the French press seemed happy to report on the New Wave's calamities, after having done their best to cause them. No sooner had the Cahiers critics started making films than they, their work, and their alliance came under furious assault from all sides. Left-wing critics accused the movement of insufficient political commitment, or worse: Michèle Firk, reviewing Les Cousins in Positif, saw an apology for fascism;[42] another critic, writing in 1960 about Les Bonnes Femmes, was even more comically hysterical: "Some will say that Chabrol's direction is astonishing. During the war, plenty of people looked at the soldiers of the SS and said, 'They are so well-dressed, so well-disciplined, so polite.'"[43]

The right was no kinder: the editors of Arts, who had published Truffaut's verbal assaults on the beloved mainstream French cinema, now turned against the New Wave. They published a screed against the movement by the Old Wave screenwriter Michel Audiard, followed by a diatribe, in the guise of a review of Breathless, calling the new directors "Rebels without a cause, certainly, but not without a goal. The goal is to impose themselves on this hardly-comprehending society."[44]

As early as September 1960, Truffaut wrote that "the 'New Wave' is insulted more and more each week on radio, TV, and in the newspapers."[45] At the time, much of the hostility was due to the partisans of the old school who kicked back. But now, in 1961, Truffaut acknowledged the practical reasons for the French film industry's skepticism:

> At the beginning there was an excessive euphoria, then a moderate euphoria, and now a certain distrust, which is not at all abnormal when you consider that the "New Wave" has not had a real financial success for a year and a half, that is, since the release of *Breathless* . . . For eighteen months the film industry has been awaiting an indisputable success, that is, a film that would please both the critics and the public.[46]

The excitement of the New Wave's early days had sent producers scrambling to recruit their own young directors to make films for them, resulting in a remarkable proliferation of mediocre films by mediocre new filmmakers. As a result, in late 1961, the New Wave was in trouble, and an interviewer bluntly asked Truffaut about it:

> Q: All the newspapers are saying that the "New Wave" is finished; do you agree?
> A: It isn't as simple as that. First of all, it hasn't been said often enough: the "New Wave" is neither a movement, nor a school, nor a group, it's a *quantity*, it's a collective heading invented by the press to group fifty new names which have emerged in two years, in a profession which formerly accepted only three or four new names each year.[47]

Truffaut was actually conservative in his numbers: in December 1962, *Cahiers du cinéma* published an encyclopedic rundown of "One Hundred and Sixty-Two New French Directors" which listed "all filmmakers who have made their first feature film since January 1, 1959." Such numbers suggest that, from the first heady days of Truffaut's triumph at Cannes and the promise of artistic renewal, inflation had set in, and a shakeout was inevitable.

Most of the directors who figured on the *Cahiers* list (from Edmond Agabra to Henri Zaphiratos) soon dropped off the cinematic map. Even Beauregard had to cut back on production, shelving such promising projects as Rohmer's *Une Femme douce* (an adaptation of Dostoyevsky's novella *A Gentle Creature*, which would be filmed by Robert Bresson in 1969); a political musical by Demy, *Une Chambre en ville*, which he would make in 1980; and *George Sand*, by Varda. The open door through which young aspirants could dash into the French film industry was quickly closing. Defining the New Wave by the numbers would indeed lead to the conclusion that the New Wave ended in the early 1960s.

In the midst of the polemics and the hand-wringing over the well-publicized struggles of the New Wave, an amicable subterranean debate took place, in the back-and-forth of interviews in a variety of publications, between Godard and Truffaut over what the New Wave in fact was, and what could and should be done to rescue it. Their muted conflict began to open fault lines that suggested coming tectonic shifts in French cinema, culture, and society, and that also hinted at the eventual erosion and collapse of their personal relations.

Godard, looking beyond the short-term fortunes of filmmakers contending for a place in the industry, considered the New Wave as a historical phenomenon. He deemed the New Wave to be an ideal, an exclusive group, comprising the five Hitchcocko-Hawksians of *Cahiers*—Truffaut, Godard, Rohmer, Rivette, and Chabrol—who were united by their shared experiences at the CCQL and the Cinémathèque and by their critical viewpoint. He named other contemporary French directors whom he esteemed, including Resnais, Astruc, Varda, and Demy, but credited them with "their own fund of culture" which differed from the particular cinematic culture that he considered constitutive of that central New Wave "fraction," of which "*Cahiers* was the nucleus."[48]

For Godard, the historical and critical orientation that defined the New Wave was also marked by paradox, "by regret, nostalgia for the cinema which no longer exists. At the moment that we can do cinema, we can no longer do the cinema that gave us the desire to do it."[49] The New Wave, for Godard, was born of its distinctive relation to the history of cinema. Godard saw the Hitchcocko-Hawksian cinematic canon not as a series of models to imitate but as a source of inspiration, a point of departure—and a lost paradise.

For Truffaut as well, the *Cahiers* group was defined by its historical orientation, but in an entirely different way. He claimed that their cinematic canon provided a set of formulas to follow, and declared that the commercial prospects of the directors in his circle depended on their willingness "to continue to pretend to tell a mastered and controlled story which is meant to have the same meaning and the same interest for the filmmaker and for the spectator."[50]

In particular, Truffaut argued that the crisis of the New Wave was a crisis of the screenplay, or rather, of the lack of one. He blamed himself for the failure of his second film, *Shoot the Piano Player,* which he attributed to its flashbacks: "By working at it a little, one could surely have told *The Piano Player* chronologically."[51] He blamed Chabrol for the failure of his 1960 film *Les Bonnes Femmes*—specifically, for being unwilling "to imagine how Hitchcock would have undertaken a film like *Les Bonnes Femmes*"—and he described the film that Chabrol should have made, calling it *The Shopgirls Vanish.* The editors of *Cahiers* summarized Truffaut's remarks in a telling caption: "Let's Imitate Hitchcock."

Truffaut argued that the application of the Hollywood formulas that he and his *Cahiers* friends had absorbed as critics was the only way for the New Wave to reach the mainstream. But for Godard, if the New Wave (as he narrowly defined it) was to fulfill its original ambitions, the general conditions by which a mainstream—of cinema and of society—was constituted would have to change. If his cinema could not become the mainstream in French society, it was France, not he, that had to change.

Godard teased Truffaut publicly about his practical orientation, referring to him as "half producer, half director—in the morning he is a business man, in the afternoon an artist."[52] But Godard had a different—and, as it turned out, accurate—sense of the future of the French New Wave, and his idea of it was not, like Truffaut's, market-based but essentially political.

In the summer of 1961, with hopes for *A Woman Is a Woman* still high after its triumphant reception at the Berlin festival (which at the time ran from late June through early July), Godard gave an interview regarding its forthcoming release to Michèle Manceaux of *L'Express* and discussed his newfound recognition and social status.

I'm very much in favor of the word "artist." It's a beautiful word which has been despised. It was Alphonse Daudet, people with big hats, flowing ties, etc.

Today, directors are almost always dressed like everyone else. But to my mind, an artist is necessarily on the left. Even Drieu La Rochelle[53] was on the left. It's a state of mind. Khrushchev and Kennedy are equally on the right, they are totalitarian.

Being on the left does not mean showing a worker at work. A film like *Saturday Night and Sunday Morning* is what I call a rightist film. Reactionary, paternalist, in the sense that it imposes on the spectator an idea that the spectator enjoys. One speculates in advance on him.[54]

Godard saw and voiced the new and essential connection between art and politics, and its importance for the future of the New Wave and for his own. He defined the left as an aesthetic category and predicted that he and his handful of New Wave colleagues would find their cause advanced neither by the nominal political left, the old left that had been hostile to the New Wave, nor by the equally doctrinaire right, but by a new left that would find its most authentic expression and rallying point in a new culture—in the art of the cinema. And, of course, the crystallization of this new left and its entrance on the historical stage would be May 1968, which would finally, and definitively, enshrine the New Wave as the exemplary cinematic phenomenon of the era.

Godard recognized that the cultural politics of the 1950s were no longer relevant. In 1959, he had publicly echoed Roland Barthes's claim that "the talent is on the right."[55] Now, in 1961, Godard saw that the cinema that "speculates in advance" on the spectator, even in the name of Hitchcock, was necessarily reactionary; that art made in a spirit of aesthetic freedom and progress was inherently inclined to the left; that the right was necessarily hostile to such art; and that a new, post-Communist left would necessarily be favorably disposed to it. According to Godard, the recognition of directors as artists—the essential program of the New Wave—was indeed political in the broadest sense of the word: their program had, after all, been called the *politique des auteurs*. Before the *auteurs* and their acolytes could impose themselves on the cinema in particular, they would need to diffuse their influence through society at large.

The New Wave defied predictions of its early demise; in the early 1960s, when it seemed to be nearing the end, it had barely gotten started. The first burst of energy, the Big Bang from *Cahiers* into the French cinema, had been unleashed in 1959 and 1960. The rate of expansion of the New Wave's cinematic universe did slow appreciably in the following few years, but in the process, the movement crystallized, matured, spread beyond France into an international phenomenon, and indeed advanced, both practically and artistically, for many decades and arguably to the present day.

In the fall of 1961, however, this was not self-evident, and Godard's work too was slowed by the state of the local film industry. He had been considering the possibility of filming *La Nouvelle Histoire de Mouchette* by Georges Bernanos (a novel about a neglected, abused young girl who commits suicide, which would ultimately be filmed by Robert Bresson in 1966). However, under the financial and practical pressure of the moment, Godard changed his plans. On October 28, 1961, Truffaut wrote to a friend: "Godard is very dismayed by the failure of his latest film," *A Woman Is a Woman*, and "had decided against *Mouchette* and is looking for a project for Anna Karina who in a few months has become his sole reason for living . . . I believe— and so does he—that it would be to his advantage to adapt a major novel."[56]

A Woman Is a Woman represented Karina's coming-out, and the film's failure was a painful augury of the couple's life together. If Godard was hoping to make Karina a grand romantic heroine in a movie, it was to exalt her role in his life. In seeking a novel to adapt, Godard was conceiving a cinematic spectacle that would bring Karina the cultural cachet that she could never get from starring in films by more conventional, commercially successful directors.

But for the time being, Godard did not have a project in which to film

Anna Karina to her advantage, so she did not wait for more "home movies" but continued to establish herself as a professional. In line with the allegorical prognostications of *A Woman Is a Woman,* trouble resulted.

In September 1961, Karina began work on the second feature film by the director Jacques Bourdon, *Le Soleil dans l'oeil* (Sun in the Eyes). Most of the shoot took place on Corsica. The story concerned a Danish woman who goes to the island to follow a man, played by the young actor Jacques Perrin. The shoot itself was innocuous fodder for the popular press: when Godard traveled to Corsica to celebrate Karina's twenty-first birthday on September 22, *France-Soir* ran a photo of the actress blowing out candles on a cake as he and Perrin looked on. But shortly after the actress returned to Paris, in late November 1961, reports on the film became the pretext for the public revelation of intimate agonies, because the actress was hospitalized following an attempted suicide. The story that emerged in the coming days was the following:

During the course of the shoot, Karina decided that she would leave Godard to marry Perrin. According to *France-Soir,* Karina said, "I admire Jean-Luc very much. But he's of another generation. Whereas Jacques is my double."[57] On the night between November 21 and 22, Karina told Godard of her intention to leave him. In the resulting scene, Godard physically destroyed the possessions in their apartment—furniture, a tape recorder, his clothing (not hers, because, he told Jean-Pierre Melville, "it would have hurt her too much"),[58] fixtures, Karina's teddy bears—and left. Karina was reported to have taken an overdose of barbiturates. Perrin came to the apartment, found Karina ill, and called for an ambulance. She was hospitalized, then released on the morning of November 24 for rest and further medical attention at the apartment of the film's producer, Eric Schlumberger. Perrin and Godard both came to the actress's bedside (one account even has them meeting there).[59] "While the producer Eric Schlumberger calmly saw to the care of Anna Karina, Jean-Luc Godard looked for Perrin in the bistros of boulevard Exelmans to resolve the situation with dice. They finally challenged each other to poker, but the game was interrupted by a struggle with photographers."[60] That day, the physician attending Karina declared the environment "unfavorable" for her recovery and ordered her to rest in a clinic in Neuilly, a wealthy suburb of Paris. A week later, Karina was able to film the last sequences of the film, in and around Paris, together with Perrin.

The papers reported that Godard and Karina would divorce and that Karina would marry Perrin.

The resolution to this marital crisis proved to be the one hinted at in *A Woman Is a Woman:* a joint project. In January 1962,[61] it was announced (with evidence attached in the form of a tender photo of the couple) that

Godard and Karina had reconciled and that he would direct her in a new film, *Vivre sa vie* (literally, "To Live Her/His Life"; released in the United States as *My Life to Live*). The producer was to be Pierre Braunberger, who had brought masterworks by Jean Renoir to the screen in the 1920s and '30s, produced Godard's three short films from 1957 to 1958, and had recently made *Shoot the Piano Player*. Godard relied on a subject which he claimed to have gotten from Truffaut (and which Braunberger claimed to have proposed): the story of "a young woman who, to round off her monthly pay, takes to prostitution." Godard submitted a "screenplay" of several paragraphs to the CNC in the hope of obtaining an advance on receipts; his request was turned down. Instead, the budget went from low to minimal: 400,000 francs, even below that of *Breathless*. Godard decided that Karina need not be paid, since they were living together.

Nana walks the streets, followed by a potential client.
(Courtesy of the Everett Collection)

six

VIVRE SA VIE, LE NOUVEAU MONDE, LES CARABINIERS

"The definitive by chance"

AGNÈS VARDA'S ASSISTANT DIRECTOR ON *CLÉO DE 5 À 7*, Marin Karmitz, was a recent graduate of IDHEC, the main French film school. Godard met Karmitz, who was twenty-three, on that shoot and hired him as his assistant director on the short film *La Paresse*. Later, in the tumultuous days of late 1961, Godard called on Karmitz for assistance with three other matters.

First, Godard asked Karmitz to help Jacques Rozier complete his first feature film, *Adieu Philippine*, which had been shot in 1960 but remained unfinished. The film had been produced by Georges de Beauregard, to whom Godard had introduced Rozier after the success of *Breathless*, when the producer was flush with money and looking for new directorial talent, particularly new talent recommended by Godard. When Rozier failed to meet the distributor's completion deadline,[1] Beauregard washed his hands of the project and literally put the reels in the street. At Godard's request, Karmitz gathered and organized the footage, found an editing room, and helped Rozier finish the film in time for the Cannes festival in May 1962.

Then, Godard asked Karmitz to render a far more personal service: to come by his and Karina's house after their very public marital crisis "to calm things down a little, to gather the broken things," because, as Karmitz soon saw, the couple "had destroyed everything in the apartment." Finally, Godard asked Karmitz to lend him technical books from his days at IDHEC, and for a very specific reason: as Karmitz later recalled, "He said, 'I have to learn some technique.' He thought that the camera moved too much in *Breathless*."[2]

Whatever Godard found in Karmitz's books worked wonders. If 1961

had been a year of relative idleness, indecision, and despair, it was also a
helpful year of woodshedding. Godard's aesthetic self-criticism and his rethinking of technique combined with his responses to new circumstances—
including his marital storm and some published remarks about him by
Truffaut—to lead him to a new way of filming. This breakthrough resulted
in work that differed radically in content, tone, style, form, technique, and
philosophical import from his first three films. His new way of working
would prove in the long run to be even more influential than the heralded
methods of *Breathless*.

Indeed, Godard became so immediately prolific and so inventive under
the influence of these fruitful new ideas that 1962 could well be called his
first annus mirabilis. In that year, Godard would not only accelerate his pace
of production and juggle an extraordinary number of real or potential projects, but would also, in the process, openly define the New Wave as intellectual cinema. By championing the movement's ideals ever more vigorously, he
conspicuously pressed himself to its forefront—at the precise moment when
its survival was said to be in doubt.

THE ANNOUNCEMENT OF Godard's new project with Karina, *Vivre sa vie*,
was made in the first week of January 1962, and the shoot was scheduled to
begin on February 19. Godard had six weeks to pull the story together. He
struggled with the question of how to elaborate Truffaut's idea. The first effort he submitted to the CNC was a nine-paragraph note of intention. It was
no longer the story of a woman who turns to occasional prostitution to
round out her monthly budget. (That story would become, four years later,
the film *Two or Three Things I Know About Her*.) It was now the story of a
young woman, Nana, who works in a record store, and whom the film "will
follow for five or six months," during which time "Nana gives herself over to
prostitution, first as an amateur, then as a professional."[3]

Godard's choice of the name Nana as the prostitute was a reference to
both the novel by Emile Zola and the 1927 film produced by Braunberger,
directed by Jean Renoir, and starring Renoir's wife, Catherine Hessling. But
"Nana" is also an anagram for "Anna" (an "Anna-gram," a pun which works
in French, too), and the premise of the story is an unmistakable reprise of
the theme of *A Woman Is a Woman*, with its accusatory barbs at Karina. In *A
Woman Is a Woman*, Godard had treated the theme of the "professional" as
farce; now, in *Vivre sa vie*, he presented it as tragedy. In *Vivre sa vie*, Godard
explicitly sought the grandeur that had been missing from the previous film,
as well as what he expressly called "intellectual adventure,"[4] in the hope of establishing Karina as a serious actress.

From the outset, Godard sought to make explicit the philosophical depth and intellectual energy that would distinguish his film from whatever his competitors for Karina's performances could offer her. Indeed, the statement of intention in his note to the CNC was no mere sales pitch but, rather, a manifesto of his new cinematic conception, an attempt to realize an idea that he had been working on for more than a decade:

> Basically, I would like to try to reveal what modern philosophy calls existence in opposition to essence; but, at the same time, thanks to the cinema, to show that there is no real opposition between the two, that existence supposes essence and vice versa, and that it is beautiful that it be so.[5]

A hallmark of Sartre's philosophy was the idea that a person is defined by his actions, his outward reality. Sartre argued that the belief in an essence distinct from public and social phenomena was unfounded. Since the early 1950s, Godard had been arguing that Sartre's opposition of outer existence and inner essence was fallacious because it was transcended and resolved in the cinema. Godard had long been writing in defense of classical art and in praise of its attributions of psychology and of character, asserting that the cinema, which showed images of exteriors and social relations, automatically implied inner and metaphysical qualities.

In his first three feature films, Godard had attempted to work variations on themes by Sartre. Now, Godard's desire to make a sublimely tragic film that locates destiny in the essence of character would lead him to even more sophisticated contemplations of existential cinema.

GODARD WENT INTO production of *Vivre sa vie* with the low budget of 400,000 francs, of which he put up half, making him an equity partner on equal terms with Braunberger. With this film, Godard took a practical leap as great as his aesthetic one: he became a producer. He knew that his unusual methods of production, with his erratic shoot schedule and short days, invited conflict with producers. But he had another equally practical, yet more personal, reason, as he later recalled:

> Once I asked Rossellini: "When you get money to make a film, do you have to spend it all?" . . . And Roberto told me: "The best way is to make films that take place in the Middle Ages. During the week, everyone dressed only in potato sacks with two holes for the arms and a hole for the head. Above all, don't make films that take place on Sunday, because that's when they wore nice clothing. The rest you keep for yourself and your family."[6]

On the one hand, Anna Karina was the "family" who would enjoy the savings from Godard's frugal exertions; on the other, she would also, in effect, be wearing the potato sacks. Although the film would fulfill Godard's intentions of calling attention to her talents as a serious actress, Karina soon recognized its cost to her glamour and would resent it. A film that was intended to save the marriage proved to be a new source of conflict.

A fuller story outline—in effect, the script—that Godard elaborated on the basis of his original sketch concerns Nana, a young immigrant from Germany and an aspiring actress. She has left her husband, a struggling journalist, for a photographer who may help her break into acting. She has left her baby in the care of a nursemaid and is working as a sales clerk in a record store. She cannot earn or borrow enough to pay her rent; she fails at theft and, walking a street that prostitutes work, accepts a client. She then accepts others. She is introduced to a pimp, Raoul, who takes her on. She meets a young man, an artist, and wants to quit prostitution and to live with him. Raoul refuses to let her go; he punishes her for a minor "infraction" and sells her to another pimp, who shoots Raoul and is then shot by Nana. She takes up with another man and lives with him in a semblance of domestic happiness, prospering as a high-class call girl.

The most striking aspect of the outline is not the story but its construction, which Godard would reproduce in the film itself: it is broken down into thirteen discrete sequences, which Godard called "tableaux vivants," literally, living paintings. As he later explained, his idea with *Vivre sa vie* was "to also play on the word 'tableau' in theater and in painting. Since it's a 'tableau' [picture] of somebody, I had to do it with [theatrical] 'tableaux.'"[7] Godard had chosen *Vivre sa vie* to exalt the talent and the character of Anna Karina; as such, it was both a showcase for the actress and a portrait of the woman.

Godard got the idea for dividing the film into discrete sequences, or theatrical tableaux, from *The Threepenny Opera*. He had even planned to include a character taken directly from the film of that play, "a master of ceremonies who would say, 'Here is the sad story of Nana . . . Here is what happened to her one day,' etc."[8] Brecht was in the air, and in particular, in the air that Godard was breathing. The December 1960 issue of *Cahiers du cinéma* was entirely devoted to Brecht, in open acknowledgment of the potential cinematic application of his ideas. Shortly before making *Vivre sa vie*, Godard had seen a production of *Arturo Ui* at the Théâtre Nationale Populaire, and his outline for the film explicitly notes the influence of Brecht. The brief text ends with Nana as a "respectable" and prosperous prostitute crossing herself as she drives past Notre-Dame in her American car: "Nana, whom we saw with her real hair in the first sequences, then blonde in some of the following ones, now has a short coif-fure in the style of 1925. Music à la Kurt Weil [sic] emphasizes her Brecht-ian appearance."

Before shooting started, however, Godard purged the project of its plethora of Brechtian influences: though the film was indeed made in tableaux, the master of ceremonies making announcements between them was replaced by a black screen with white titles stating, like chapter headings, the actions and motifs in the sequence to follow. No Weill-like music is ever heard, and during the shoot (and to Anna Karina's great dismay), Godard cut the thirteenth tableau of a prosperous Nana, the "Brechtian" one, specifically to avoid the sort of political comment, or "social assertion,"[9] that he thought it suggested, and that was at the core of Brecht's theater. Instead, he would film an ending that he considered "typically theatrical,"[10] more in accord with the melodramatic conventions of the naturalistic theater. In place of so-cial satire, Godard wanted pathos, and he achieved it with an alternate end-ing: Nana's death, at the hands of pimps.

The main beneficiary of Godard's suppression of the Brechtian influence was Anna Karina. The expressionistic, demonstrative, savagely parodistic and yet detached acting style of the Brechtian theater would have worked at cross-purposes with Godard's intention of displaying Karina's gravitas in performance. It would have imposed on the actors an exaggerated and artifi-cial manner. For Vivre sa vie, Godard sought his actors' fully engaged emo-tional sincerity, and he made the film with a concentrated naturalism similar to that of Le Petit Soldat.

WHERE BREATHLESS AND Le Petit Soldat were stories about a man in love with a woman and A Woman Is a Woman was about the triangle of two men and a woman, Vivre sa vie was simply the story of a woman—it was Anna Karina's star turn, the movie in which she would occupy the center of a tragedy. No other role in the film approached hers in significance, and none of the other actors was familiar or charismatic enough to outshine her.

The week before the shoot began, Godard told an interviewer, "I will shoot on location, in natural settings, but without making a film of re-portage. It will rather be a work in the theatrical spirit."[11] Godard sought to capture realistic theater in its principal form: an interpretive performance sustained over time. To achieve this, Godard conceived scenes that could be shot in long takes, and he needed to film with direct sound. He used heavier equipment under more traditional conditions—precisely the equipment of mainstream filmmaking described in the books that he borrowed from Marin Karmitz. In Vivre sa vie, the camera was not waved around casually. Godard filmed Vivre sa vie entirely on location, but used unwieldy studio equipment to do so—the seventy-pound Mitchell camera; relatively slow black-and-white Kodak film, which required rigging movie lights; a sound truck—and the added personnel to handle it all. This more cumbersome apparatus and crew made their presence felt. Because it was now more arduous and time-consuming to set up shots, Godard could not easily change his mind about them and had to work more deliberately; because each setup took a long time to prepare, Godard saved time, and thus money, by shooting longer takes. Godard's attempt to join the laborious methods of studio filmmaking to the rapid exigencies of low-budget filmmaking and his own inclination for short work days—Braunberger recalled that the average day of shooting was three hours long—resulted in a film made up mostly of carefully composed and very long takes, many lasting more than three minutes. Rather than composing Karina's performance from moments edited together, from the "exchange of glances" that Godard had extolled in 1956, he would let her stage a sustained performance, which his camera would simply frame and allow to unfold in its own time.

Godard claimed that the emotional essence of the film was the equivalent of portraiture in painting: "I was thinking—like a painter, in a way—of confronting my characters head-on, as in the paintings of Matisse or Braque."[12]

> The greatest paintings are portraits. Look at Velasquez. The painter who wants to show a face shows only the exterior of people; and yet, there is something else going on. It's very mysterious. It's an adventure. The film was an intellectual adventure, I wanted to try to film a thought in action, but how to manage it?[13]

The different techniques demanded by *Vivre sa vie,* so unlike the scattershot methods that Godard had employed in his first three films, required a more composed, deliberate approach—which converted the mood of his images from something like jazz to something like classical music.

> It's as if I had somehow to extract the shots from the night, as if the shots were at the bottom of a well and I had to bring them up to the light. When I brought out the shot, I said to myself: everything is there, nothing to retouch, but there can be no mistakes about what has been brought out, about what has to emerge at the first stroke . . . It's a little bit like theater-vérité.[14]

Because Godard's first two films were shot largely with handheld cameras, he could not often look through the eyepiece. In *A Woman Is a Woman,* the choice of shots, made under studio time pressure, was often loose and haphazard. Now, for *Vivre sa vie*, Godard worked with Raoul Coutard to compose shots. The image-making of *Vivre sa vie* was imbued with the collective daring of the performer, director, camera operator, and the rest of the cast and crew, who maintained, together, the requisite perfection for long takes which often involved elaborate camera moves (on tracking rails) and choreographed action. The audacity and the tension on the set were essential elements of the film and Godard knew it: "For me, the ideal is to obtain at once what has to work, and without retouching. If it needs any retouching, it's a failure. The 'at once' element, that's chance. At the same time, it's definitive. What I want is the definitive by chance."[15]

Elia Kazan came to watch Godard shoot a scene of prostitutes and clients in a hotel, and spoke with Suzanne Schiffman between takes.

> It was a very long take, a fixed-focus shot. The camera didn't move, the actors entered and left the frame, they continued acting and talking outside the frame. Kazan asked me, "Which angle will he shoot the action from next?" "No, he never shoots a scene from more than one angle." Kazan didn't understand.[16]

To heighten the demands placed on the performers, Godard shot the entire film with synchronized sound recorded on location. Although several sequences were dubbed (very conspicuously, with the addition of voice-overs and, remarkably, in one scene, subtitles), most of the film used a single track of production sound, with its rich sonic environment of streets, stores, cafés, and the incidental clatter of daily life, with quietly melodramatic music (by Paul Misraki) occasionally added. The microphones available to Godard picked up a great deal of ambient sound, and thus their placement was crucial. The actors had to stay still in order not to leave the microphone's range. Anna Karina remarked on their effect on her performance: "In *Vivre sa vie*, I'm like a statue! Completely stationary! . . . In real life, I never stop moving."[17] The sonic effect was distinctive: the foreground voices, and particularly that of Karina, were endowed with a striking dramatic urgency, while the dense and lively background ambience seemed invested with the randomness of documentary reality. Manfred Eicher, the founder of ECM Records, said, "My greatest influence with regard to the work of sound was *Vivre sa vie* by Godard."[18]

Godard considered *Le Petit Soldat* to be like a "notebook" of visual jottings, whereas in *Vivre sa vie*, he said, "the camera is a witness."[19] Here, Godard signed his shots, in the way that a painter signs his pictures. The camera's weight, as Godard recognized, made itself felt in the film: the images seemed to have been composed with heavy dark frames around them.

Though many shots remained static, Godard achieved visual variety with a daring range of camera moves—traveling shots, sometimes lateral, sometimes plunging into the décor, sometimes moving with a pendular arbitrariness around stationary characters—and when the camera moved, it did so with a glacial, graphic precision. The singular visual construction of the world as seen by Jean-Luc Godard, the announcement of intellectual intent and content in the film's visual style, is on display in the film's first shot,[20] which runs one and a half minutes: Nana (Anna Karina) is seen from behind, at the bar of a café, as she talks with her husband, whom, it is soon understood, she has left for another man.

> PAUL: This guy, are you really interested in him?
> NANA: You know . . . I don't know, I wonder what I'm thinking of.
> PAUL: Does he have more money than me?

This shot, which Godard likened to "a musical score that begins very quietly, instead of starting with big chords,"[21] was his "first idea for the film." Indeed, he admitted, "I knew that *Vivre sa vie* was to start with a girl seen from behind—I did not know why. It was the only idea I had."[22] Although he offered specific justifications for this choice—"In my film one has to listen to people speaking, all the more so since they are often seen from behind and one is not distracted by the faces"[23]—there was another important motive: a cinematic response to and refutation of a remark made in the press by Truffaut about him and his way of filming.

GODARD'S NEW METHODS are part of an esoteric debate between friends which took place in a public forum. In an interview that appeared in *France-Observateur* in October 1961, Truffaut attempted to place the current situation in French cinema within an ambitiously broad view of film history, based on his overall notion "that there are two kinds of cinema: the 'Lumière branch' and the 'Delluc branch.'" Truffaut's idea was that the brothers Lumière "invented the cinema to film the nature of actions" whereas Louis Delluc, "who was a novelist and a critic, thought that one could use this invention to film ideas." Truffaut lined filmmakers up on one or the other side:

> The result? It's the History of Cinema, with the "Lumière branch": Griffith, Chaplin, Stroheim, Flaherty, Gance, Vigo, Renoir, Rossellini (and closer to us, Godard), and on the other side, the "Delluc branch," with Epstein, L'Herbier, Feyder, Grémillon, Huston, Bardem, Astruc, Antonioni (and closer to us, Alain Resnais). For the first group, the cinema is a *spectacle,* for the second, it is a *language.*

Truffaut explained that directors in the Delluc branch of ideas—from which he had excluded Godard—"film in a more concerted and more intellectual way, they film moral conflicts between characters who usually speak with their backs turned."[24]

Though Truffaut had grouped Godard with filmmakers whom they both admired fiercely, he had nonetheless trapped Godard in an ill-fitting rubric. Calling him a nonintellectual was an obvious, if unintentional, slight, and it was apparently due to Godard's one great failing: he had filmed his characters talking while they faced the camera. It was an error that Godard was determined to rectify: to get himself recategorized among the intellectuals, he would make a film of "moral conflicts between characters who speak usually with their backs turned." The first shots of *Vivre sa vie* were Godard's attempt to prove to Truffaut's satisfaction that he was the intellectual equal of Resnais and Antonioni.

The subject of the film's opening is derived with a self-punishing directness from Godard and Karina's life, with Nana telling her abandoned husband, Paul, "I want to die." She threatens him with further humiliation ("If we get back together, I'll betray you again"), and she blames him for preventing her from fulfilling her ambitions as an actress ("In any case, if I do manage to find work in the theater, it won't be thanks to you"). Paul is quietly aggressive, telling her that her work in the record store "suits [her] even less than the other stuff," and accusing her again:

PAUL: Besides, finally, you're leaving me because I don't have money.
NANA: Finally, yes, maybe . . .

The abandoned husband puts a new twist on the name games of Godard's films; he is the first in a series of new Pauls. In *Vivre sa vie* he was played by a counterpart of Godard, a film critic (of *Cahiers du cinéma* as well as *France-Observateur*), André S. Labarthe, who hoped to make films but had not yet begun to do so—in effect, by an unfulfilled Godard.

The film is pervaded by such associations to aspects of Godard and Karina's life and work together. Walking in a prostitute-filled street near the Porte Maillot, Nana is approached by a man, who asks her, "Will you take me along?" She says, "Yes," and thus begins her initiation, as an amateur, into prostitution. Nana's walk, a low-angle tracking shot facing her (the camera retreating as Nana advances), reveals over Nana's head a sign of a business on the street: Lucas Service (probably an auto-repair shop). "Hans Lucas" (German for Jean-Luc) was, of course, the pseudonym Godard used during his years as a critic and as the director of his first fiction film, *Une Femme coquette*. Nana thus takes her first step as an amateur prostitute under the sign of Lucas Service; Anna Karina puts herself in the service of Lucas, or Jean-Luc.

Vivre sa vie suggests a disturbing analogy between Karina as an actress and Nana as a prostitute—between prostitution and acting, in general. The film is studded with references to Nana's desire to pursue a career as an actress. She complains to her spurned husband, Paul, that he did not help her pursue her dream, and she mentions having appeared in a film with Eddie Constantine (as Karina had done in Varda's *Cléo*). As if to reinforce the analogy, the role of Luigi, one of the pimps, is played by Eric Schlumberger, the producer of *Le Soleil dans l'oeil,* the film which brought Karina together with Jacques Perrin.

In the film's eleventh, and penultimate, sequence, a young man whom Nana had met earlier has now become her lover. He sits on a bed, his face blocked by a book of Edgar Allan Poe's stories. The couple's dialogue of tender practicalities takes place entirely in subtitles, without spoken dialogue. ("What shall we do today?" "Let's go to the museum." . . . "Why don't you come live with me?" "Yes, I'll have to tell Raoul that it's over.") Then the lover's voice is heard as he reads aloud from his book. The voice is not that of the actor, Peter Kassovitz, who plays the scene alongside Karina. Instead, Godard lends his own voice to the character, and recites on the sound track several passages from Poe's story "The Oval Portrait," interrupting it with a statement of its theme, a revealing comment which is not found in the text: "This is our story: a painter who does the portrait of his wife." The passages he recites indeed concern a painting made by an artist whose wife sits as the model. The portrait has "a vital expression, absolutely equal to life itself";[25] however, when the painting was completed, the artist "trembled and was struck with fear. And crying with a shattering voice, 'Indeed, it is life itself!' he turned around suddenly to look at his beloved. She was dead."

In short, Nana was doomed; and Godard's prophecy for Nana was also Godard's doom, his fate to lose the woman he loved through the shared project of artistic work. His revised ending of the film makes this point. Instead of having Nana escape Raoul and take up with her new lover while working successfully as a high-priced call girl, Godard has Raoul sell Nana to another pimp. In one long and mournful take, Nana is dragged from the car by Raoul and used by him as a human shield when he is threatened by the other pimp. In a moment derived directly from a scene of Samuel Fuller's *Forty Guns,* the other pimp shoots Nana. Raoul himself shoots her again, to make sure that she cannot testify against him, and both pimps flee. Nana's death is stunning both in its catastrophic swiftness and in its choreographed precision. The film ends with Nana's body sprawled in a deserted street.

The ending is also stunning in its puritanical moralism, which would be a distinctive and seemingly incongruous aspect of many of Godard's films to come. The first shot of *Vivre sa vie* shows Nana brazenly admitting her adultery; the last one shows her lying dead on the pavement. The film is constructed as a cautionary tale of the wages of infidelity, Nana's fall being traceable directly to her betrayal of her husband.

Most of Godard's films for the next five years would issue the same warning to Karina: they would allude to her unfaithfulness and suggest its moral price. Wounded by Karina, Godard would spend years filming, in the most varied of guises and through the most diverse of cinematic and intellectual frameworks, the drama of a woman's faithlessness as a false step leading inescapably to disorder and tragedy, and presenting sincere monogamous love as inevitably redemptive. Godard, discussing the film shortly after completing it, judged Nana harshly: "She lets herself go: lack of character, mediocre intelligence, laziness."[26] Beneath the surface expansiveness of Godard's films from the 1960s is an implication of the harsh condemnation of sin, and of one particular sin. Under his praise of freedom is an ode to self-restraint. Within a Sartrean emphasis on the immanence of and confrontation with death is a call to save one's soul. Godard was making a case for himself as a conservative revolutionary.

NOT ONLY IS *Vivre sa vie* Godard's most classically tragic film; it is the one that has had the greatest practical influence on the subsequent history of cinema. The film defined and launched a new style that would be applied widely to productions of all sorts and from many countries. Whereas, in practical terms, *Breathless* encouraged young directors to infuse a Hollywood genre with their own self-conscious intellectualism, *Vivre sa vie* offered them a new paradigm altogether: it reoriented mise-en-scène from space to time.[27] Godard did not invent the long take, but in *Vivre sa vie* he invented the staging of lengthy dialogue scenes in artful framings. The films of Jean Eustache, the later films of Philippe Garrel, the films of Chantal Akerman, the subsequent films of Eric Rohmer, all of the modern verbal American cinema—Martin Scorsese, Woody Allen, Hal Hartley, Quentin Tarantino, Kevin Smith, Spike Lee—and even the flowing dialogue shots of Abbas Kiarostami, are derived from the long and carefully patterned talk-takes of *Vivre sa vie*.

Godard told a critic of *Vivre sa vie* who wondered why the characters talk so much, "As in life, people talk a lot when they have a lot to say . . . What I have to say, I don't say myself but I have my characters say it and that's why they talk abundantly."[28] After *Vivre sa vie*, any director who had something to say did not hesitate to have his or her characters say it in his or her stead, to feature the actors saying it in a way that emphasizes the taut string of their theatrical performance, and to use the frame of the image as an implicit proscenium arch to call attention to those performances.

VIVRE SA VIE was accepted by the Venice Film Festival, and Godard, Karina, and Braunberger introduced it there on August 28, after a conflict with Italian officials over several shots of nudity that Godard cut from the release print. The film was booed after the screening: the difference of tone from Godard's previous works, with their Hollywood stylings, was disconcerting. Nonetheless, it was "the object, the whole day, of all conversations" at the festival,[29] and the film was awarded two prizes: the Critics' Prize and the Special Jury Prize.

French journalists in attendance received the film with icy condescension. Bernard Dort, reporting on the festival for *France-Observateur,* charged Godard with filming "with an offhandedness approaching mannerism" and called the film "a work of shameful romanticism, open to all the mirages of spirituality."[30] In *Candide,* Pierre Billard wrote, "Godard's Nana astonished us for all of one morning."[31] However, when the film was released, on September 19, other, more perceptive critics made up for the slight with reviews ranging from respectful to rapturously enthusiastic. Claude Mauriac, in *Le Figaro littéraire,* recognized that "of all the films made to date by Jean-Luc Godard, *Vivre sa vie* is the most minutely composed."[32] Georges Sadoul, in *Les Lettres françaises,* declared, "After having seen it again in Venice, I consider it better than *Breathless.* For the perfection of its mise-en-scène, its classicism, the marvelous performance by Karina, yes, but above all for its emotion and for its message."[33] Jean Collet, of *Télérama,* called the film "a new masterpiece" and ranked it alongside the films of Rossellini and Bresson.[34] In *Cahiers du cinéma,* Jean Douchet declared it to be "a pure masterpiece, the first absolutely flawless film by Godard."[35] The "existential" element was duly noted by critics, too: Henry Chapier of *Combat* called *Vivre sa vie* "a deliberately 'Sartrean' film."[36] François Truffaut, who wrote an introductory note for the publication of a transcript of the film's dialogue and action in the October 1962 edition of *L'Avant-scène cinéma,* wrote discerningly of the film's extraordinary significance:

> There are films that one admires but which are discouraging: what is the point of continuing after them, etc. Those are not the best, because the best give the impression of opening doors and also of the cinema beginning, or beginning anew, with them. *Vivre sa vie* is among them.

The public responded favorably to the critical exhortations. *Vivre sa vie* attracted 148,010 spectators in its Parisian first run,[37] a commercial success (due in large part to the small budget) that Godard would rarely match with his subsequent films.

The film's overtly intellectual tendencies, however, resulted in a painful personal break for Godard with a friend. Although Godard had, at the time of his first films, enjoyed a close relation with Jean-Pierre Melville, that friendship faltered as Melville blamed the New Wave and its intellectual tendencies for the industry's problems. He called Godard's films "anything at all, shot any old way."[38] Melville's widow, Florence, recalled that the elder director told Godard at this time, "You are making a lazy man's cinema, this no longer deserves the name of cinema, you put down the camera and you have people talk, nothing more. For me, this isn't cinema."[39] Finally, in response to Melville's harsh criticisms, Godard declared, "There can no longer be a friendship between us, if one doesn't like one's friend's film, one can no longer be his friend."[40] And from that point on, Melville wasn't.

Godard knew what he had accomplished with *Vivre sa vie:* it was the first of his own films that he included in his year's ten-best list for *Cahiers* (at number six, modestly placed behind Truffaut's *Jules et Jim* and Rohmer's *Le Signe du Lion;* in first place was Howard Hawks's *Hatari!*). The director attributed a significant measure of the film's quality to the star's devotion to it, as well as his own: "The film was made in a sort of altered state, and Anna isn't the only one who gave the best of herself. Coutard succeeded in doing his best photography."[41]

All had not been paradise, however; not by any stretch. Braunberger had given Godard the key to his office, where the director was often found in the morning, having slept there after a scene at home. Karina attempted suicide again (delaying production for half a week), after Godard decided to change the ending of the film from the sardonically happy one where Nana lives to the tragic one where she dies.[42] Nonetheless, the film achieved Godard's purpose, and even sooner than might have been expected. It created horizons for Karina as a performer which might otherwise have remained closed for a long time to come.

Yet years later, Godard recognized that the film, with its visual and emotional austerity, contributed to their eventual separation: "She was furious afterward because she thought that I had made her look ugly, that I had done her a considerable wrong by having made this film; that was the beginning of our breakup."[43] Despite their mutual cinematic achievement, and the opening of new doors for Karina, they were not, Godard thought, the ones she wanted to pass through: "I think that she always regretted not making films in Hollywood."[44]

In the spring of 1962, immediately after making *Vivre sa vie,* Godard tried to find a way to make her wish come true. He had conceived another

musical extravaganza for Karina, costarring Gene Kelly. It would be filmed in
the United States and would be of unquestionable intellectual value, since it
would also, remarkably, costar William Faulkner. It would be the story, Godard said, of

> Anna herself, Anna who is an actress and who arrives in New York. She goes to
> see Gene Kelly and she says to him, "I am a French actress, I admire you, can't
> you find me some work?" Finally it's the discovery of America by this girl,
> from within seven or eight great genres of the American cinema. Then Gene
> Kelly says, "But no, my little girl, the musical comedy is finished, the great
> stage at MGM no longer exists." Then they go into the street and it becomes a
> little bit musical. Then, I don't know what, she needs money, she steals money,
> she meets people and it becomes a criminal episode. I would have wanted, for
> example, for her to get hired as a maid, or a gardener, or whatever, by
> Faulkner.[45]

Faulkner died on July 6, 1962, and Godard abandoned the project.

A more realistic proposition for Godard and Karina involved another
theater-based project, one that could not have been further from a Hollywood musical. In an effort to help Jacques Rivette get his directorial career
going after the commercial failure of *Paris Belongs to Us,* Godard had introduced him to Beauregard, and Rivette had proposed to the producer a film
of Denis Diderot's *La Religieuse.* The story, which Diderot began in 1760 and
took up again in 1781 and which was published posthumously in 1796, concerned a young woman who is interned by her parents in a convent against
her will and attempts to escape. She is subjected to attempts at seduction
both by a nun and a priest. Although the book was a recognized classic,
many Catholics still considered it offensive, and after his difficulties with *Le
Petit Soldat,* Beauregard put Rivette's project off.

However, in the spring of 1962, at dinner with Godard and Karina, Rivette suggested that the actress would be perfect for the part in *La Religieuse,*
if it ever got made. Godard brought the notion up with Beauregard, who was
skeptical that Karina, with her Danish accent, could play the lead in a film of
an eighteenth-century French classic. Nonetheless, Godard went into action,
introducing Rivette to the producer Eric Schlumberger, who submitted the
scenario by Rivette and the screenwriter Jean Gruault to the CNC for "precensorship." Predictably, the commission anticipated that the film would be
banned. Godard was not deterred. As Karina continued to study French diction with the text of *La Religieuse* in hand, Godard approached the theatrical producer and director Antoine Bourseiller[46] about staging the play in his
Théâtre des Champs-Elysées, with Karina in the lead role—and at Godard's

expense. As Bourseiller later recalled, Godard "knew that, if the play was put on, and if it wasn't censored, then when the film was made they could argue, 'You didn't ban *La Religieuse* in the theater, you can't ban it in the cinema.' "[47]

Bourseiller, who welcomed the chance to work with Godard and Karina, not only accepted *La Religieuse* but also raised the theatrical ante for the glamorous couple. In the summer of 1962, Bourseiller was scheduled to direct a production of *Pour Lucrèce*, by Jean Giraudoux, at a summer theater festival in Brittany. He offered Karina the lead role of Lucile, a woman of fierce rectitude who is tricked into believing herself to have been raped, and who, in her humiliation, commits suicide. He also offered a small part in the play to Godard: "I had very little money, and so, since I knew that Godard was going to come with Anna, I asked him to play the notary. He wasn't paid, of course."[48] When Godard accepted, Bourseiller changed the text of the play to amplify Godard's role; in the process, Bourseiller turned the couple's work together into self-dramatizing allegory. In Giraudoux's text, Lucile, after her suicide attempt, is found unconscious by her maid. In Bourseiller's production, Godard's character, the notary, would find Lucile in danger and would cry out, "Madame has taken poison!"

The play went off as planned, but one night, Godard took matters into his own hands: he spoke his big line over and over again, with as many different inflections and tones as he could muster, and the audience laughed uproariously. Karina was not amused: "He went on for five minutes. He played the clown. He ruined my show . . . He couldn't keep from upstaging the star. I was busy dying at the end of the play—in front of three thousand people."[49]

Karina was not long in finding a way of upstaging Godard in return.

When the couple got back to Paris, Godard started to plan a film of *Pour Lucrèce*, which he would shoot in early September, immediately after the presentation of *Vivre sa vie* at the Venice festival. It was to be a rapid production: as Raoul Coutard later recalled, "He wanted to shoot it in one week."[50] Godard would not film a staging of the play, but simply a reading of it, in the garden of the house in the suburbs of Paris where Louise de Vilmorin (the novelist, and André Malraux's mistress) lived. Godard told a journalist that the project was to take up where *Vivre sa vie* had left off, as a film of theatrical inspiration: he planned "simply to direct a voice on the screen, show someone more or less motionless on the screen speaking a fine text."[51]

Godard, who coproduced the film with the distribution company Cocinor-Marceau,[52] recruited a cast of well-known actors—Sami Frey, Marie Dubois, Charles Denner—which did not include Karina: she had left for Spain to play the title role in a big-budget historical fantasy, *Scheherazade*, directed by the Old Wave director Pierre Gaspard-Huit (who had been an object of derision for Godard and his friends at *Cahiers*).[53]

On the first day of the shoot, it rained. Godard asked Raoul Coutard, "Can we shoot anyway?" Coutard responded, "We can, but it would be comical to have people sitting on the terrace right outside the door in the rain, wouldn't it?" They went on waiting. Then Godard took Coutard aside and asked him, "What would they say if I said I was stopping the film?" Coutard answered, "They'd laugh." But Godard called an early lunch, and as Coutard later recalled, "Everyone was at the table, he gets up and he says, 'This is the meal for the end of the shoot.' Everyone laughed, but he was serious."[54]

It was an expensive decision, because as coproducer, Godard himself was responsible for paying off the actors and the crew. To raise the money rapidly in order to do so, he pressed Braunberger to buy back from him for thirty thousand francs (six thousand dollars) his half share of *Vivre sa vie*, the value of which Braunberger estimated at 100,000 francs (twenty thousand dollars), and which would soon become all the more valuable with the film's successful release and international sales. (The relationship ended badly: several years later, in the midst of a dispute, Godard called Braunberger a "dirty Jew," an insult that Braunberger said he could never forgive.)[55]

Then, making plain his motive for canceling the shoot, Godard left at once for Spain to join Anna Karina. (He even made a cameo appearance in the arrantly commercial *Scheherazade*.) Godard was distracted by her absence and all too mindful that it had been less than a year since the debacle of the shoot of *Le Soleil dans l'oeil* in Corsica—a date that Godard would soon commemorate on film.

IN THE FALL of 1962, Godard signed three contracts for films with three different producers—the short film *Le Nouveau Monde* (The New World) for a compilation by the Italian producer Alberto Bini; the medium-length *Le Grand Escroc* (The Great Swindler) for an international consortium of producers; and the feature *Les Carabiniers* for Beauregard. As a result, Godard was suddenly flush enough to produce *La Religieuse*, starring Karina and directed by Rivette, at Bourseiller's theater.

The play opened on February 6, 1963. It was not a financial success, but it won favorable reviews. The film historian Lotte Eisner called it the best stage production she had seen "since Brecht."[56] Moreover, Beauregard was enthusiastic about Karina's performance and the prospects for a future film, but censorship was still an issue. Rivette and Gruault rewrote the script, which Beauregard submitted to the precensorship board. It passed, but Beauregard found himself again on a financial downswing and could not afford to produce it. Meanwhile, in July 1963, Rivette agreed to take over the editorship of *Cahiers du cinéma* from Eric Rohmer, and thus *La Religieuse* was again placed on hold.

EARLY IN THE shoot of *Vivre sa vie*, in a café in the Latin Quarter, a journalist took Godard aside during the setup of an elaborate sequence and asked the director whether he had any "masters." "No," Godard answered, "or perhaps just one, because of his will to independence: Rossellini."[57]

Roberto Rossellini had been a crucial inspiration for the New Wave, first by example (*Voyage to Italy*, from 1953) and then in practice (his effort in 1955–56 to organize a series of 16mm features for the Young Turks of *Cahiers* and their associates). As Godard's friendship with Melville waned, his connection to Rossellini deepened. The correlation between Rossellini's films and his life could not have escaped Godard's attention: Rossellini's relationship with Ingrid Bergman was inseparable from their extraordinary series of films from the early 1950s, and their marriage foundered on the same shoals that Godard and Karina's was scraping against, in particular the actress's desire, in the face of the commercial limitations of her husband's films, to work with other directors in the mainstream of the industry.

Yet Godard and Rossellini had several major differences of opinion. Rossellini was hostile to cinephilia and to any veneration of the cinema as a means of artistic expression. In late 1962, at the time of the release of *Vivre sa vie*, Godard acknowledged this difference uneasily: "I love the cinema. Rossellini no longer loves it, he is detached from it, he loves life. Compared to Rossellini, I have the sin of the cinephile."[58] Moreover, Godard thought that Rossellini's dedication to ideas ran the risk of antiemotionalism, and he contrasted his own intentions with Rossellini's in this regard: "One might say Rossellini's failure is that the principal feature and beauty of his films is that they are shot from remote distances: he probably shoots them like this on the assumption that his underlying conception is the most important thing, but people seen from a distance are rarely very moving."[59]

Moreover, Rossellini and Godard disagreed about the importance of the recent works of a veteran filmmaker who had suddenly, in the early 1960s, become emblematic of the times—and who had taken over from Rossellini the vanguard position in the Italian cinema—Michelangelo Antonioni.

Although Rossellini's films had led Italian cinema out of the exclusive realm of the working class—the subject par excellence of neorealism—to depict the rise of the managerial middle class, he was unable to take, or even to understand, the next step, which was Antonioni's: to show a society of mass culture and media, of technology and ostensible progress, and to consider the transformations in individual consciousness that were taking place in this new world. Rossellini believed so strongly in the freedom of individuals that he could not make sense of the idea that people who could be alienated from themselves by the mass media, which he considered merely to be a form of rhetorical persuasion that should be rejected by claims of reason. He acknowledged that an artist might want "to talk of incommunicability, alienation," but thought that the artist was then obligated to tell the public, " 'One can indeed not be alienated, and one can also, indeed, communicate.' That is the function of the artist: to overcome things, to find a new language."[60] Rossellini blamed Antonioni for allowing his characters to wallow in their alienation, for giving viewers the idea that such alienation is inevitable, and for creating cinematic forms which enshrine alienation as an aesthetic mode.

In the fall of 1962, Jean Gruault brought Rossellini to a screening of *Vivre sa vie*. Not only did Rossellini privately reproach Gruault for having "made him waste his time," but the next day, when Godard drove Rossellini back to Orly Airport together with Gruault, the elder director did not hide his displeasure. As Gruault later recalled:

> On the road to the airport, [Rossellini] maintained a silence that was heavy with danger. Suddenly he proclaimed, in a deep, prophetic voice, like that of Cassandra announcing the fall of Troy or Isaiah threatening an impious people with the gravest harm: "Jean-Luc, you are on the verge of Antonionism!" The insult was such that the unfortunate Godard lost control of the car for an instant and almost sent us into the landscape.[61]

For Rossellini, the formal stylization of *Vivre sa vie* was Godard's admission that Nana's travails were inevitable, and her unwillingness, or inability, to explain her choices signified his rejection of reason and communication. Godard did indeed see more merit in Antonioni's films and their ideas than Rossellini did, and would in fact later attempt—avowedly—his own version of "Antonionism," though not yet; *Vivre sa vie* was not it.

Nonetheless, this shadow debate between Rossellini and Antonioni oddly dominated the three films that Godard made in late 1962 and early 1963. Godard called his extraordinary short film *Le Nouveau Monde* "anti-Rossellini." The medium-length film *Le Grand Escroc*, which is based on a Rossellinian idea, is a remarkably indifferent film emotionally. The feature *Les Carabiniers*, in which Godard adapts a work of Rossellini's, was as out of step with the moment as were Rossellini's own recent films.

IN MAY 1962, Godard had returned to Paris from the Cannes Film Festival with plenty of projects in mind and none in the offing, and rapidly sought to do something about it. He had heard from Gruault about a play that Rossellini was about to stage at the Spoleto festival—Beniamino Joppolo's *I carabinieri*, a biliously satirical view of war and its instigation—and decided to get hold of it. He dispatched Gruault to ask Rossellini for a tape-recorded description of the play's action, and he got Beauregard interested in producing it.

Godard used a typed transcript of Rossellini's narration as the basis for his first scenario, cutting and pasting parts of it into a notebook and adding his own handwritten annotations and interpolations. The story was a fable-like depiction of an isolated peasant family (a mother, her two sons, and her daughter) visited by two "carabiniers," who conscript the sons for war and entice them to go by dangling visions of wealth through plunder and happiness through cruelty. This version,[62] the notebook itself and its fifteen pages of text, was rejected by the precensorship board. Godard soon thereafter revised the story to emphasize what he called its fairy-tale nature.

> The several characters are situated neither psychologically, nor morally, and even less so sociologically. It all takes place at the level of the animal, and, moreover, this animal is filmed from a point of view that is vegetal, unless it is mineral, which is to say, Brechtian.[63]

This overtly theatrical version passed precensorship. But with its war machinery and its broader landscape, *Les Carabiniers* would be budgeted too high for Beauregard's modest means; as a result, the project was delayed.

AT THE VENICE Film Festival in September 1962, Godard received an offer from the Italian producer Alfredo Bini to make a short film that would be a part of a compilation feature on the theme of "the happy beginnings of the end of the world."[64] Three other directors also received such an offer, and the producer proposed to combine the last names of the four filmmakers—Rossellini, Godard, Pier Paolo Pasolini, and Ugo Gregoretti—to make the film's senseless but distinctive title, *RoGoPaG*. In the fall of 1962, after Rossellini had derisively dismissed *Vivre sa vie*, Godard described for interviewers from *Cahiers du cinéma* his plans for his contribution, *Le Nouveau Monde*.

> A man goes out in the street, everything seems normal, but two or three little details reveal to him that people, that his fiancée, are no longer reasoning normally. He discovers for example that a café is no longer called a café. And if his fiancée doesn't come to their rendezvous, it isn't because she no longer loves him, it's simply because she is reasoning in a different way. Their logic is no longer the same. One day he picks up a newspaper and sees that there was an atomic explosion somewhere, so he says to himself that he is undoubtedly the

only person left on earth who can reason normally. Things are the same, while being completely different.[65]

To this practical declaration, Godard added a barb: "It's anti-Rossellini, but that's how it is." Godard was clear on what he was doing: his project was indeed "anti-Rossellini" because it called into doubt (by way of an extreme allegory) the possibility of communication. Instead of making a film that verged on Antonionism, Godard made one that directly assumed Antonioni's themes, but raised their gravity to the level of a cosmic joke. Though the film is only a sketch, it is one of farsighted implications.

Godard got the idea for the film from a science-fiction story by Richard Matheson, *I Am Legend,* in which, after horrific wars, a man discovers himself to be the last human in a world filled with vampires.[66] At the very start of *Le Nouveau Monde,* the protagonist, upon awakening from a two-day sleep, learns from a newspaper of an atomic explosion over Paris and then begins to notice the changes that result from it. In lieu of a surprise ending, the film has a surprise beginning—the old world has already ended—from which derives a cinematic master stroke: every shot that follows is presumed to be postapocalyptic. Although filmed on location in Paris, the most ordinary elements—a windblown city square, a subway train, a traffic jam—are made to feel forbiddingly strange and altered.

This cinematic sleight-of-hand was amplified by a few choice pieces of stage business. Several younger critics from *Cahiers* show up in crowd scenes and publicly pop pills, as does Godard himself in one brief shot, in the middle of the Champs-Elysées. This plot turn allows for some crude but jolting optical effects that lop off the top of the Arc de Triomphe and the upper half of the Eiffel Tower.

In the film, a dark-haired man (unnamed throughout the film and played by Jean-Marc Bory) searches for his lover, Alexandra (Alexandra Stewart), after she fails to show up at their meeting in a café. He calls around and finds out that she had gone to a swimming pool. Tracking her down there, he sees her from afar and finds her kissing another man. "Little by little I became jealous," he admits. "Only now do I see how that stopped me from reasoning clearly. I ought to have understood that all this was only because of the end of the world."

Back at home together, he drinks a cup of coffee and awaits her explanation; she offers him a Coca-Cola.

"You didn't show up," he challenges.

"Yes, I did," she claims.

She pops a pill, then again offers him a Coca-Cola. They have an absurd dialogue of contradictions worthy of Ionesco or of Abbott and Costello, in which she says that she never saw the other guy before in her life; when he challenges her to be logical, she claims not to know what the word means. Taking stock of the changes that Alexandra and the city have undergone, the nameless man concludes:

> It was obvious that some obscure and terrible ill was slowly corrupting the human mind, even if everything seemed to be the same. The person I loved had suddenly lost every moral sense, or worse, lacked that sense of freedom which yesterday every last man still had.

The next day, at home again, the man reads another newspaper headline—"No Danger After the Atomic Super-Explosion, the Experts Declare"—and on the back of the paper is the headline, "The Paris of Tomorrow," over a scale model of an ultramodern city with glass arches, sleek bridges, and boxy International Style towers. After another spat of verbal illogic, Alexandra goes out and leaves the man behind. Looking mournfully out the window at a forbiddingly uniform group of modern apartments, he says in voice-over:

> The new world has begun, and a miracle has saved me. But I too may be contaminated by the ghastly mechanicalness, the death of logic. That's why I've written these words in this notebook. One day they'll be read with curiosity as the last testimony of the world of freedom.

As he speaks, a hand is shown writing these words in an extreme close-up of the notebook itself, in Godard's own distinctive handwriting.

The film is precisely situated in time: the headline declaring nuclear apocalypse over Paris is printed on a copy of *L'Humanité* dated November 24—one year to the day of Godard's showdown with Anna Karina and, in particular, of her release from the hospital after her suicide attempt.[64] Thus the man's opening monologue—"The city hadn't changed, but Alexandra had, and I didn't know it yet. It had been a year of fear, or rather, of feelings more intense than fear, for which there is no name on earth"—bears witness to Godard's own year of domestic anxiety.

The intensely personal and the cosmic are, from the outset, unified with an offhanded wink: nothing less, indeed, than "the end of the world" could have endangered their love. If Karina chose infidelity, it was proof that she had definitively lost her "sense of freedom," meaning her ability to reason and think logically; and such a thing would only be possible, let alone normal, in a world that had "suddenly lost every moral sense." Godard himself, "the only person left on earth who is able to reason normally," is also therefore

the last free person on earth—and the proof of his wife's loss of freedom is
her infidelity (because if she had been free, she would freely have chosen him
over his rivals).

Under the guise of a gag, the film is a cry of pain, despair, and incomprehension, aroused by the fear and misunderstanding that had come to mark
Godard's relationship with Karina. His uncertainty at home was a calamity
so great that he could attribute it only to a world-historical catastrophe.

LE NOUVEAU MONDE introduces two elements into Godard's films that remained tenaciously present in the decades to come: the Beethoven string
quartets and his own handwriting. Instead of commissioning music for the
film, Godard used excerpts from Beethoven's late string quartets—in particular, the Grosse Fuge and his final quartet, opus 135. It was music that he put
forth as a lasting challenge to the moral compromises and empty banalities
of the moment. Le Nouveau Monde was the first film of Godard's twenty-
five-year devotion to the Beethoven quartets as an element, even a building
block, of his films. The other element, the image of Godard's own handwriting on-screen, also served a fundamental purpose: it was his way of recording his presence and his thoughts on-screen without appearing as an actor.
Since the time of the unrealized reformulation of Eva, Godard had wanted to
film a writer writing, on-camera. Here, he found a way to do so.

Le Nouveau Monde has never received the recognition it deserves because it remains largely unseen. RoGoPaG, the compilation of four short
films in which it was included,[68] was completed in 1963, but was never released theatrically in France, where Godard's segment was first viewed on
television in 1980. RoGoPaG was shown in its entirety at the first New York
Film Festival in September 1963; it was received indifferently by critics and
Godard's sequence was booed by the audience, perhaps because of its apparent trivializing of nuclear apocalypse.

GODARD'S COSTLY ABANDONMENT of Pour Lucrèce in September 1962 had
a paradoxical benefit. After his return from Karina's Scheherazade shoot in
Spain, Godard approached Cocinor-Marceau, the distributor who had paid
an advance on that project, and proposed, as compensation, a new and more
conventional project: it would have a screenplay—and by Rossellini.[69] In this
way Godard was able to resurrect his plan to make Les Carabiniers. With advances from the distributor and its Italian partner supplementing funds
from Beauregard and Ponti's Rome-Paris Films, the project came back to life
in mid-September, and the shoot was scheduled for the end of the year.

The pedigree of Les Carabiniers was exactly to Godard's taste of the moment: it derived from the Brechtian theater but, with Rossellini's association,

had the imprimatur of the cinema. It was precisely the peculiarity of that double heritage that made the film an awkward exception among Godard's works.

As the project was advancing toward production, Godard spoke with interviewers from *Cahiers du cinéma* and told them the story of the film. It concerned two peasants who receive a draft notice from the carabiniers, the state police, who explain to them that in war, all is permitted—from stealing to killing, from petty thuggery to massacre. The peasants are suddenly enthusiastic and joyfully go to war in quest of booty. Then the war ends, and, as Godard said:

> The king does not win the war, but he signs a peace treaty with the enemy and those who fought for him are considered war criminals. Instead of collecting their wealth, the two peasants are shot. All will be very realistic, in a perspective that is purely theatrical; we will see war scenes . . . as in the films of Fuller, with some newsreel footage. But now that I've told it to you, I suddenly have less of a desire to make it.[70]

Godard's deflation was a kind of wisdom: indeed, unlike any of Godard's other films to date, this one exhausted its significance in the telling. This process, too, resulted from the influence of Rossellini, who, according to Godard, thought "that his underlying conception is the most important thing." While Godard's other films came to life during the shoot, both by way of the methods of production and the images that resulted, *Les Carabiniers* was predetermined by a script that was so strong and so thoroughly elaborated— and so allegorical and impersonal—that it dominated Godard's direction and ultimately crowded out his own view of reality.

The Brechtian influence, which Godard had purged from *Vivre sa vie* in the interest of sincere emotional engagement, returned with a vengeance in *Les Carabiniers*. The film is blaringly crude, a calculated assault on the sensibilities of viewers. The actors, Albert Juross and Marino Masé, and the women who play opposite them, Catherine Ribeiro and Geneviève Galéa, had little or no film experience, and Godard made sure that their performances showed it. The actors mug, cavort, gesticulate, pose, declaim, mime, and emphasize every intention with the harsh exaggeration of a puppet show. According to Charles Bitsch, who was Godard's assistant on the film and on most of Godard's films from the 1960s, the inexperienced actors' difficulty with dubbing their lines heightened the artificial declamation. And yet it is this tone which is precisely the film's lasting innovation and virtue: the blind flailing of characters venting their venality and stupidity, the raucously aggressive display of despicable and unredeemable qualities paraded before the audience with a sardonic sneer, the hectoring volume level of the sound track, with its war sounds and its shrill conflation of church and circus music. The ending, as Godard had originally planned it, would have gone even further in expressing this aggression. As he explained to an interviewer:

> I had shot another ending: when the story ends, the dead character would get up and say, in close-up: "Now go home in your little cars. Go take your tranquilizers, go dream of your paid vacations." It was a pure insult, a slap in the face . . . I made the entire film in that spirit. Against socialized society.[71]

He decided against this ending, but the anarchistic anger remains, and is the film's most memorable element. It is a rage directed in particular at bourgeois life in a modern, increasingly technological society, rejoining the critique of "the new world" in Godard's apocalyptic short film.

Les Carabiniers connects with *Le Nouveau Monde* in another, peculiar way. In Godard's first draft of the script, the daughter's name was Anne, which Godard crossed out in favor of Lucrèce, and then changed, prior to filming, to Venus. The underlying point is revealed in the daughter's name: Anne/Lucrèce loses her innocence when she exhorts her reluctant husband to fight for the king—not from belief in the cause but in order to win wealth for the family. This is the story as told in the first script: "Leonardo and Machiavelli hesitate a bit, but Lucrèce, the most rapacious, pushes them to accept the bargain, to go off to war as soon as possible."[72] Anne/Lucrèce forgoes her purity by sacrificing her Leonardo to her venal dreams. Godard's play with names serves to explain to Anna Karina why he couldn't go fight for her in Hollywood or on big-budget mainstream productions. (While *Les Carabiniers* was being filmed, Karina, who had just returned from filming *Scheherazade,* was pursuing her dream of theatrical renown and rehearsing the lead role in Rivette's staging of *La Religieuse.*)

IN *LES CARABINIERS,* Godard stands outside and above the stupidity of the world; the film's point of view is flattering to intellectuals and contemptuous of everyone else. *Les Carabiniers* is a film of demagogy that comforts the intellectual in his sense of moral and political superiority to the willing cannon fodder from the unwashed masses. This is, perhaps, why many intellectuals defended this film with a particular vehemence. In fact, according to Bitsch, *Les Carabiniers* was the film of Godard's that "aroused the most enthusiasm on the part of the crew."[73]

The strongest moments in the film are the confrontations of the rustic brutes with the modern world around them—the documentary side of the film's fictional premise. The bracing simplicity of the film's first shots, of a modern highway outside Paris, with its underpasses and its monotony as seen from the windshield of a moving car, promise far more of that confrontation than the film actually delivers.

Indeed, the film's political didacticism introduces a deception that is central to its premise. The carabiniers pay the soldiers a visit, and explain that they will be able to claim their spoils when the war ends. Michelangelo asks them how the soldiers would know when the war has ended, since "there's nobody here." The bumpkins' premedia isolation is the real subject of the film. It is the necessary context for the film's argument and it is the crucially Rossellinian element, but it is also what makes the film seem so weirdly disconnected from the realities of modern war and its propaganda.

LES CARABINIERS WAS released on May 31, 1963, and was subject to a rare and near-unanimous critical savagery. Even critics who had been stalwart supporters of Godard's work were hard on the film. Henry Chapier of *Combat* was one of the few to recognize its "thousand inventions," to praise its "ferocious" comedy as "healthy," and to salute Godard's "extreme liberty."[74] None, however, quite understood it: most criticized Godard for incidental matters. Stung by their reproaches, Godard took the unusual step of responding to the more egregious ones in the August 1963 *Cahiers*. But the damage had been done. The nonintellectual public may have taken the measure of the aggression and steered clear of the film. Bitsch recalled that when the film came out Godard was asked, " 'How did it go?' He said, 'About 31 people.' Everyone had expected the film to be acclaimed as the masterpiece that it is." One young man in Paris was the only paying customer at a theater where the owner refused to show the film unless someone else showed up. In first run, it attracted so few viewers—an estimated 2,000—that its box-office statistics went unreported.

Godard was angered by the film's failure.

> If *Les Carabiniers* had no success in Paris, it's because people are worms. You show them worms on the screen, they get angry. What they like is a beautiful war à la Zanuck. For three hours they kill lots of Germans. Then they go home happy, heroic. Real war, they don't want. It isn't war that is disgusting, it's ourselves. People are cowards.[75]

But Godard also took its failure to be a sign of his own failings, his own self-deception, telling the critic Jean Collet on September 12, 1963:

> I was taking more and more distance with respect to my characters. After *Vivre sa vie* and *Les Carabiniers*, I could not go any further in that direction. I had to reduce the distance. I finally got to the point of despising the cinema, of

saying to myself: it hardly matters how it's filmed, as long as it's true. I had lost my cinephile attitude. I was rejoining Rossellini, but what is right for Rossellini is not necessarily right for me because I was denying the cinephilia that led me to the cinema.[76]

Too much "distance," together with "denying the cinephilia," the Rossellinian influences, compounded by the Brechtian one, made *Les Carabiniers* a film of isolation; there was indeed almost nobody there, barely even Godard.

BY THE TIME Godard endured the brickbats of critics and the indifference of the public in the spring of 1963, he had already completed the third film in his unofficial Rossellini trilogy, *Le Grand Escroc*, in which he tipped his hat to Rossellini's ideas while leaving them behind. In October 1962, Godard agreed to make one of the short films in a compilation called *Les Plus Belles Escroqueries du monde* (The Greatest Swindles in the World), a French-Italian-Dutch-Japanese coproduction.[77]

The film, *Le Grand Escroc* (literally, "The Great Swindler" but also the French title for Herman Melville's *The Confidence-Man*), is another story that exhausts itself in the telling, an anecdote that Godard stretched into a twenty-five-minute shaggy-dog story. Although Godard showed Melville's book in the film's first scene, the story came from a news item about a man in Israel who printed counterfeit banknotes and passed them to beggars. The story was trivial; what mattered was the frame in which Godard set it—the cinema itself. The film is concerned less with the swindler than with the efforts of a cinema-verité documentary filmmaker to find and to film him.

The filmmakers in that movement used lightweight cameras and portable sound equipment to record reality as unobtrusively as possible and edited their footage with a minimum of voice-over commentary and overt intervention. Such films as *La Pyramide humaine* (by Jean Rouch), *Primary* (by Richard Leacock, Robert Drew, and D. A. Pennebaker), *Le Joli mai* (by Chris Marker), and *Showman* (by Albert and David Maysles) were bringing the movement a great deal of attention and critical respect. Rossellini was hostile to the trend, arguing that the filmmakers, in their desire to make films without apparent directorial self-assertion, had substituted mere verisimilitude for comprehension. "There is no technique for grasping reality," Rossellini said. "Only a moral position can do so . . . The camera's a ball-point pen, an imbecile, it's not worth anything if you don't have anything to say."[78]

Godard filmed *Le Grand Escroc* in Morocco in January 1963. It would mark the first time that he made his protagonist a filmmaker—a woman, played by Jean Seberg—and in so doing, he would satirize her in terms that echoed Rossellini's critique of cinema verité. Seberg plays a character with the same first name as her role in *Breathless*: Patricia Leacock, an American television reporter who goes to Marrakesh, Morocco, to do a "man-in-the-street" report. Walking through a souk, she stops at a stall to buy a traditional gown and is promptly arrested, for reasons unknown to her. In the police station, the inspector (played by Godard's friend László Szabó) explains that she had passed a counterfeit bill and asks whether she knew where it had come from. When she explains that she had come to Marrakesh precisely in order to do a report on a counterfeiter, the inspector engages her in a theoretical discussion about the word *report*. After her release, Patricia finds the swindler. He defends his counterfeiting as philanthropic, and likens her photographic report about him to his own benevolent swindle: "You are stealing something from me and you, too, are giving it to others."

Le Grand Escroc is itself something of a swindle, a casual goof filmed casually, although, as with any true artist, Godard was unable to make an ugly or pointless work. A long take of a car pulling into a huge public square, where the counterfeiter attracts a crowd with his fraudulent giveaway, is a striking realization of epic sweep with minimal means. A final flourish makes clear the deeper significance of the facile theoretical considerations that preceded it: the film concludes with a close-up of Patricia pointing her camera directly at the viewer, as Godard intones in his own voice the literary moral of the story, citing lines from Shakespeare that Patricia Leacock recalled:

All the world's a stage,
And all the men and women merely players:
They have their exits and their entrances;
And one man in his time plays many parts.

The last words of *Le Grand Escroc*, with Godard's voice on the sound track, suggest a critique of cinema-verité that is closer to Antonioni's than to Rossellini's: life is intrinsically theatrical and personal identity necessarily fabricated, multiple, and elusive, thus thwarting attempts to film them without artifice. And—going both Antonioni and Rossellini one better—the identity called into question by the last shot, which joined the fictional filmmaker's face and the actual filmmaker's voice, was Godard's own.

Stressful times at Cinecittà
(Strand Releasing / Photofest)

seven

CONTEMPT

"It's the end of the cinema"

IN 1963, TWO OF GODARD'S CINEMATIC WISHES WERE FUL-
filled; in both cases, the reality proved disappointing. Godard's
first contact with a Hollywood producer revealed to him the decadence of a system that had generated the cinema that he loved. The contradiction would prove unbearable. He had long wanted to work with Brigitte
Bardot, whose performance in Roger Vadim's *Et Dieu . . . créa la femme*
(*. . . And God Created Woman*) from 1956, had seemed to him and his
friends at *Cahiers* like a riotous, erotic intrusion of brash youth into the scle-
rotic French film industry. But working with Bardot, and dealing with her
demands and her celebrity, turned out to be difficult.

Toward the end of 1962, Georges de Beauregard learned that Bardot had
expressed in an interview a desire to work with Godard. The producer offered
her the lead role in Godard's adaptation of Alberto Moravia's novel *Contempt,*
about a screenwriter and his failing marriage. Earlier in the year, Godard had
discussed the project with Beauregard's partner, Carlo Ponti, who had the
film rights,[1] but it had stalled over casting issues (Godard wanted Frank Sinatra and Kim Novak, Ponti offered Sophia Loren and Marcello Mastroianni).
Bardot accepted the role, and on the basis of her involvement, Beauregard and
Ponti were able to raise a budget of $1 million, much of it from the American
film producer and distributor Joseph E. Levine, who had entered into a four-
film partnership with Ponti. For Godard, the sum was unprecedented.

Bardot signed the contract on January 7, 1963, while Godard was still filming *Les Carabiniers.* Much as he welcomed the opportunity to work with her, he
anticipated that her involvement would inevitably entail complications.

The celebrity of Bardot, known throughout France simply as "B.B."

(pronounced "bébé," meaning "baby"), was extraordinary. According to a 1957 poll, "She occupies 47% of French conversations; she is the number-one subject of discussion, ahead of politics, which gets only 41% of the votes."[2] She was a one-woman engine of gossip and scandal. Her relationships with Vadim and the actors Jacques Charrier and Sami Frey—as well as her suicide attempts—all fed her tabloid charisma.

There seemed to be no limit to Bardot's fame. In November 1961, the OAS, the French terrorist group fighting against Algerian independence, sent her a threatening letter demanding fifty thousand francs. Bardot's reaction was courageous and rousing: she gave *L'Express* the letter to publish and added a contemptuous response, which read in part, "I won't play along, because I don't want to live in a Nazi country."[3] Her defiance won the praise of such diverse figures as French president Charles de Gaulle, Jean-Paul Sartre's secretary Jean Cau, and the editors of the Communist daily *L'Humanité*.

When she signed on for *Contempt*, Bardot was both a celebrity and a national hero. She had also somewhat outgrown the movies that had made her famous. After her revelation in . . . *And God Created Woman*, the glorified starlet appeared in a series of trashy films. Following her appearance in early 1962 in Vadim's *Le Repos du guerrier* (The Warrior's Rest), she declared that she was taking an extended break, both to choose her projects more carefully and to escape the relentless hounding of the sensational press.[4] Bardot was twenty-eight; she was famous but not a respected actress. *Contempt* would mark her widely anticipated return to the cinema after the voluntary layoff. If she lent the New Wave her box-office power, Godard was lending her its artistic and critical allure.

The project had begun with Ponti's plan to produce a film for Godard that, he said, for once would have a real script, which the producer expected to be based on the novel. Godard called Moravia's novel itself the script and promised to follow it closely. That sufficed for Ponti, but not for Joseph E. Levine, who demanded something like a traditional film script. Godard complied, but in an unusual way: he waited until the casting was completed, and, instead of imagining the film on the sole basis of Moravia's novel, he wrote his script in specific relation to the actors who would play the main roles, and began it with a nineteen-page prelude regarding the characters and the performers.

The novel's plot concerned the making of a film, the conflicts between director and producer over the film, and the reflection of those conflicts in the relationship of the film's screenwriter and his wife. In his script, Godard's descriptions of his characters and the actors who would play them set up with literary flair his view of the story, which, of course, turned out to be another view of his differences with Anna Karina. The trouble, as he described it here, was the incompatibility of a reflective man and an instinctive woman.

Godard said of the film's main character, the screenwriter—the second in the series of Godard-like Pauls initiated in *Vivre sa vie*—"Paul Javal[5] is the first of my characters who is realistic, whose psychology can be explained—at a purely psychological level."[6] The character seemed realistic to Godard, of course, because it was so closely based on himself.

To play the role, Godard turned to a thirty-five-year-old French actor, Michel Piccoli, who worked mostly in theater, but whose performance in a 1957 French police movie, *Rafles sur la ville* (Roundups in the City), Godard had praised in *Cahiers*. The screenplay description of Paul is the longest and fullest. As the director's stand-in, Paul is the character whose mind Godard knew best. Paul is a writer who does small jobs in the cinema but really wants to write a play. His problems with his wife are caused by his overwrought analysis of clear emotions: "He does not know how to live in the fullness and the simplicity of the present moment, whence his disarray and irreparable blunders." One reason for this is his inability to experience his own life first-hand; instead he conceives it as a reflection of the cinema: "Paul almost always wears a hat, like the Dean Martin of *Some Came Running*."

Bardot would play Paul's wife, Camille, "a young woman of 27 or 28, French or of French origin," who is, as Godard wrote, "very pretty, she re-sembles Eve in a painting by Piero della Francesca."

> But as opposed to her husband, who always acts as a result of a series of com-plicated reasonings, Camille acts non-psychologically, so to speak, by instinct, a sort of vital instinct like a plant which needs water to continue to live.
>
> The living drama between her and Paul, her husband, comes from the fact that she exists on a purely vegetal level, whereas he lives on an animal level.[7]

In *Contempt*, Godard filmed a woman's emotions as an irresistible force of nature. Yet he claimed that Camille's "non-psychology" was less a function of the role than of the actress: "If I'd had another actress to play Camille Javal, the film would have had a much more pronounced psychological as-pect. But then the film would have been much more unbearable."[8] Unbear-able, at least, for Godard, who did not want to imagine that Camille could stop loving Paul on the basis of a rational decision rather than through the blind force of her nature.

Jeremiah Prokosch, the producer who hires Paul for a writing assignment, would be played by the American actor Jack Palance. Prokosch/Palance, Go-dard wrote in the script, has the face of "an Asiatic bird of prey . . . As with many producers, he likes to humiliate and to offend his employees and friends and always behaves with them, his entourage, like a little Roman emperor." Prokosch's fierce desires and flamboyant energy exert a powerful influence on the lives of Paul and Camille. He himself would suffer a fall, but not before bringing down everyone around him.

The most eminent of Prokosch's employees is the director, Fritz Lang, who plays himself as the director of the *Odyssey*, the film that Prokosch is producing and that Paul is hired to rewrite. Born in Vienna in 1890, Lang was one of the great directors of the silent era, with *Metropolis* and *Dr. Mabuse, the Gambler;* in the sound era, he made *M* and *The Testament of Dr. Mabuse* before leaving Germany for France in 1933. The next year, Lang went to Hollywood, where he had an impressive career, directing twenty-two films (including such classics as *You Only Live Once, Rancho Notorious,* and *The Big Heat*). In 1960, in West Germany, he made *The Thousand Eyes of Dr. Mabuse,* which turned out to be his last film, but at the time of *Contempt,* Lang still nourished hopes of directing another (in particular, a remake of *M* called *And Tomorrow, Murder*). In his script, Godard wrote of Lang's unimpeachable integrity:

> Thirty years ago, or almost, Goebbels summoned Lang to his office and asked him to run the entire German cinema. That evening, Lang packed his bags and crossed the border.[9]
>
> Paul will recount this to Jeremiah Prokosch, pointing out that one cannot get such a man to give in, unless he wants to.

Godard intended Lang to be "the conscience of the film, the moral hyphen that joins Ulysses's odyssey to that of Camille and Paul."

If Lang was the film's "moral hyphen," its linguistic hyphen would be Prokosch's secretary, Francesca Vanini (her last name derived from Rossellini's 1961 film of Stendhal's *Vanina Vanini*), the ubiquitous interpreter who serves as the link between the characters' polyglot dialogue—Lang's German, Palance's English, Piccoli and Bardot's French, and the Italian of the locals. The character was played by the Italian actress Georgia Moll, whom Godard had praised highly in 1958 for her multilingual role in Joseph Mankiewicz's *The Quiet American.* Francesca, like Lang, has emerged from the wreckage of history: "Francesca, [Prokosch's] press secretary, is as much his slave as his secretary. He saved her, at the end of the war, from a German concentration camp, and never lets her forget it."

The story of *Contempt* concerns Paul Javal's first big job: an offer from Jeremiah Prokosch to rewrite the script of the *Odyssey.* Paul, accompanied by Camille, arrives at a dilapidated lot in Cinecittà in Rome, unsure whether to accept the job of redoing the story according to the producer's psychoanalytical view: namely, that Ulysses left home to fight in the Trojan War and took ten years to return because he had not been getting along with Penelope. Prokosch is sure that the writer will accept the job, for the money. "How do you know?" Javal asks. The producer answers, "Because I hear that you have a very beautiful wife."

The couple join Prokosch for a drink at his villa. Camille, who senses the producer's intentions, accuses Paul of using her to ingratiate himself with Prokosch, who invites her to be his guest on location in Capri where Lang is shooting the *Odyssey*.

Back at their blandly modern apartment, Camille and Paul have a long domestic scene. A series of disputes—including whether she will accept Prokosch's invitation to go to Capri, whether Paul will take the job, and whether Camille loves him—culminate in Paul's slaps and Camille's flat declaration that she has contempt for him and no longer loves him.

The film then moves to Capri; Paul has taken the job, and Camille has gone with him to the producer's villa there. (Godard had secured as the main location the modernist masterwork Villa Malaparte, a flat-roofed structure built atop a promontory that is reached by a sweeping triangular staircase.) From the rooftop terrace, Paul sees Camille kissing Prokosch. He confronts Camille and then informs Prokosch that he will not do the script. Camille reproaches Paul for jeopardizing the project when they need the money, declaring again that she has contempt for him and no longer loves him. She leaves Capri with Prokosch.

In the producer's Alfa-Romeo, Camille tells Prokosch of her plans to find work in Rome as a typist. As the car lurches onto the highway, it is crushed by a truck; both Camille and Prokosch are killed. Back on the set, Paul, upon hearing the news, quits the project and plans to return to Paris to write his play. Fritz Lang continues to direct his film of the *Odyssey*.

GODARD'S MAJOR CHANGES to the novel's plot rendered the film all the more personal. First, he put the screenwriter to work not on a future film of the *Odyssey* (as in the novel) but as the rewriter of a film already under way, turning *Contempt* into a movie that shows the making of an international coproduction like *Contempt* itself. Second, though in Moravia's novel it is the director, Rheingold, who had artistic reasons for turning the *Odyssey* into a modern psychoanalytic study of an unhappy couple, in Godard's film it is the producer who wants to vulgarize the *Odyssey* as a modern romance for commercial reasons, and whose view Paul, the screenwriter, adopts. Godard—who had entered discussions with Carlo Ponti about the project shortly after the marital crisis of late 1961—presents himself as the worst sort of cinematic sinner, one who betrays his own artistic sense to insinuate himself into the mainstream film business, in the hope of making more money and making his wife happy. In *Contempt*, Godard suggests that, far from collaborating with Karina in the cinema, he felt he was supporting her by way of it, perverting his own artistic dreams to do so, and thereby losing the integrity for which she had loved him.

OF THE FILM'S million-dollar budget, Bardot got half. Much of the rest went to Palance and to Lang, leaving Godard with relatively little to make the film—which he did in five weeks, but not without great difficulty. According to Raoul Coutard, "A lot of excessive things come with a star like Bardot—not just her salary, but also her hair stylist, her wardrobe person, and the like. These things completely alter the entire organization of the film."[10] The shoot was also slowed by Bardot's resistance to shooting early in the morning.

The atmosphere on the set did not help. Godard was now operating under intense media scrutiny. Bardot was the principal target of Italy's paparazzi, who created an unnerving commotion. Godard had asked his friends Tolmatchoff and Laubscher to come along for moral and practical support as his "fixers." Tolmatchoff knew Bardot from the 1961 shoot of *La Vie privée* (*A Very Private Affair*), where he had assisted Louis Malle. Now serving as Bardot's driver in Rome, Tolmatchoff often had to "pull her from the claws of the paparazzi."[11] Godard had also asked Laubscher to shoot production stills, as he had done for *Le Petit Soldat* and *A Woman Is a Woman*. However, Bardot had brought her own personal photographer, Ghislain (Jicky) Dussart, who was also her confidant and unofficial bodyguard (and who had been Anna Karina's boyfriend before *Le Petit Soldat*). Dussart did not like the competition from Laubscher, and Bardot pressed Godard to send his friend away, which Godard unhappily did, telling him, "What can I do?"[12]

Charles Bitsch, Godard's assistant director, sensed that the actress was playing a temperamental game with the paparazzi, which interfered with the film: "There was a crazy pack of photographers hunting her, and she did not want anyone to photograph her; but she was contradictory: on the one hand, we had to call the police to protect her, on the other, she was angry when nobody asked to photograph her."[13] Godard's friend, the director Jacques Rozier, captured on film the efforts to fend them off. He had been commissioned by the cultural services of the French Ministry of Foreign Affairs to direct a short film about the making of *Contempt*, and he called it, simply, *Paparazzi*. It showed the photographers' relentless pursuit of Bardot and the resulting distractions (including Godard's own trek up a rocky hill to face down a pack of intruding shutterbugs). Rozier simultaneously made a second film from the set of *Contempt*, called *Bardot et Godard, ou le parti des choses* (Bardot and Godard, or The Point of View of Things), centered on a scene that Godard had attempted to film on a cliffside beach but which was washed out by the sudden arrival of high tides. Rozier, who admired the director and the actress, put their collaboration in a positive light, recording moments of complicity and happy relaxation on the set. He did not capture Godard's private response to Bardot, the uneasiness of their relationship, or its effect on the film.

BEFORE THE SHOOT, Godard occasionally met with Bardot and, afterwards, raved about her to Charles Bitsch, who later recalled that the director "got carried away like a child." Godard had told him, "What a life, what a marvelous woman!" The enthusiasm, however, did not survive the reality of the shoot: two days into it, Godard sought solace with Bitsch, complaining that he found the actress "unbearable" and "horrible." Bardot wore only miniskirts and refused Godard's request to wear longer ones. He asked her to moderate her high and tousled hairdo—which he called her "sauerkraut"—and she at first refused. Godard later told an interviewer, "When I asked her to lower her hairdo by two centimeters," he had to offer to walk twenty meters on his hands in order to persuade her. "It was a game." Recounting the story on TV in 1965, Godard reproduced the stunt, and added sarcastically, "A pleasant way to work, right?"[14]

The character of Camille was determined less by Bardot's temperament, however, than by Anna Karina's. Many of the lines spoken by Bardot in *Contempt* were things Karina herself had said to Godard.[15] In one scene, Bardot wore the short dark wig that Karina had worn in *Vivre sa vie,* and, as she later recalled, Godard even wanted her to walk like Karina: "Godard told me that I had to be filmed with my back to the camera, and to walk away from it, straight ahead. I rehearsed, and he wasn't happy. I asked him why. Because, he said, my manner was not the same as Anna Karina's!"[16]

Tolmatchoff sensed that Bardot was suffering greatly from her separation from her boyfriend, Sami Frey, who was shooting a film in Spain at the time. One night, she required thirteen takes of a long tracking shot that ended at the ticket booth of a small movie theater and, according to Tolmatchoff, was "sleepwalking" through the performance. "She was terribly distracted, and Godard told me, 'Take her for a ride in the car, here's the phone number at the theater, take her away, call me and let me know whether you're coming back or not.'" In the car, Tolmatchoff said, "She cried, I didn't know that it was possible to cry so much," and he telephoned Godard to call off the night's shooting: "She can't do anything, it's screwed for tonight."[17]

Coutard, who had worked with Godard on all of his previous feature films, found him in an exceptionally foul mood during the shoot of *Contempt;* Suzanne Schiffman thought that Godard "threw a few more temper tantrums than necessary."[18] As the crew approached the end of their time in Rome, Godard was behind schedule, having been slowed down by the media circus around Bardot and the inconveniences intrinsic to the big production itself, and he was advised by his production manager, Philippe Dussart, that the company was in danger of having to shoot overtime, at enormous cost (primarily Bardot's extra salary).[19] There remained a long scene to shoot— the confrontation of Paul and Camille at home—and Godard decided that he could make up for lost time by shooting it as fast as possible with as little preparation as possible. He asked Dussart to find him a modern apartment in Rome in which to film the scene.

The action was centered on the couple's discussion about whether Camille should accept Prokosch's invitation to come along to Capri, and quickly degenerated into open marital warfare. In his script Godard had anticipated the scene's unpredictability in an aside to Joseph E. Levine:

> This sequence will last about 25 to 30 minutes. It is difficult for me to recount precisely and chronologically what will happen in it . . . I have a pathological need for the presence of the characters . . . in order to imagine definitively all the details of this Sequence 5, which I can only describe to you for the moment in broad strokes; because, you know as well as I do, a sequence of twenty minutes straight hangs together only thanks to the details which make the characters exist; and details of this sort are not invented a priori on paper, or at least, almost never.[20]

As it turned out, the "details which make the characters exist" were those which Godard took from characters who already existed: from Anna Karina and himself. According to Piccoli, who played the screenwriter, "The male character in *Contempt* is [Godard]. He wanted me to wear his tie, his hat, his shoes."[21] Elsewhere Piccoli said that he also wore Godard's jacket and socks. "I am convinced that in *Contempt* he is trying to explain something to his wife," Coutard said. "It's a letter that cost Beauregard a million dollars."[22] The "letter" says something fairly simple: if Godard continues to accept projects that he despises—such as *Contempt* itself—but persuades himself to like it so that he can pay for the luxuries he thinks his beautiful young wife expects, Karina will ultimately despise him nonetheless. In general, the "letter" suggests, they would be fine if not for the cinema, where Godard's work curdles Karina's feelings for him and drives the couple apart.

The long and demanding apartment scene was filmed in a frenetic discharge of energy—almost the entire half-hour sequence was shot in five days,[23] "as if," Dussart said, "we were in a factory." The sequence turned on a single two-and-a-half-minute shot of the couple arguing while sitting at opposite sides of a coffee table, with a table lamp and its oversized conical shade between them. A lateral tracking shot moves back and forth between the two characters as Paul reasons intricately why he should refuse the job, Camille declares that she no longer loves Paul, and he desperately seeks to explain her rejection of him. Meanwhile, Paul flicks the remote light switch on and off, as pointlessly involved in its absurd mechanics as in those of his own vain rationalizations. (The movements of the camera were prepared, but not their timing: Godard improvised them during the shot, walking behind the camera and tapping a technician on the shoulder each time he wanted the camera to glide from one character to the other.) This shot makes the model apartment's modernist architecture and furnishings visually eloquent: they are part of the problem, as their inhumanly geometric contours contribute to the couple's incomprehensions and miscommunications.

GODARD'S TEMPESTUOUS devotion to Karina made itself felt during the shoot. He often returned to Paris to see her on weekends (Coutard knew, when he saw Godard with a clean shirt, that the director was preparing a quick getaway), and Karina came to Rome to pay him a visit. As she later recalled:

> It was mad love. Love, jealousy, revenge. We adored each other. We were rather passionate. We had crises of jealousy. Oh, there were some slaps. In Rome we went one evening to a nice nightclub, someone invited me to dance, I went, and when I came back, [Godard] gave me a slap in the face, in front of everybody, because I had danced with this other man. But I wasn't angry—it was proof of his love. I kissed him afterward, because it proved that he loved me.[24]

Karina's presence in Rome and her symbolic presence throughout the shoot was an obstacle to Bardot's performance; according to Piccoli, Bardot "no longer knew her place." She was unable to forge any kind of personal relationship with Godard, and she "detached herself . . . by locking herself in her hotel with her friends, her entourage, except during shooting hours, playing cards while waiting to be called to the set."[25] Asked about his relations with Bardot during the shoot, Godard answered, "None," and added, "She wasn't very interested in me and I wasn't very interested in her."[26] Outwardly, Bardot remained supportive of Godard, and Jacques Rozier recorded Bardot and Godard mounting the long staircase of the Villa Malaparte hand in hand, laughing. The producers were delighted to find Bardot so apparently pleased by the course of the shoot. But the director and the actress suffered a silent and mutual disillusionment.

Godard's relations with Palance were worse. When the actor accepted the role of the producer, it was with the expectation that the character would be Italian. He had had a bad experience with several Italian producers and now "wanted to do a satire and take a little revenge on those bastards," but the character of Prokosch disappointed him: "The role has been changed, now it's an American producer. I feel a little bit duped."[27] From the outset, Palance was bitter and unenthusiastic. His frustration burst into open conflict over Godard's hands-off way of directing actors. Suzanne Schiffman recalled a scene where Prokosch was supposed to call his secretary, Francesca: "Palance asked Godard, 'How should I call her? Am I angry?' " Godard answered, 'No, just do it,' and Palance responded, 'It's impossible to act like that.' He gave Godard twenty-five versions."[28]

Godard's seeming caprice was an essential part of his method. He had always directed, or nondirected, his actors in this way—Godard had "never explained anything to anybody," Schiffman said—but by now he understood the method's purpose and its price, telling a visiting journalist: "If I give them very few indications, they think that I'm asking nothing of them. Whereas it's exactly the contrary."[29] He was lucid on the subject of the inner meaning of his way of directing, which was part of his "existential" relationship to the actor as a person whose free will does not vanish on-camera.

> I do not direct them much. I seek to disconcert them. It's not a matter of brutalizing them . . . I leave them rather in the dark, I speak to them very little, I limit myself to placing them in a certain situation in such a way that they react according to their own inclination, like the man or the woman they really are. It's a free man that you have before you. He must bring with him his entire life. He doesn't stop living, being himself, when he arrives on the set. The actor must control his life, but that control must escape him. As for me, my role is to render them vulnerable.[30]

As Godard recognized, some actors "suffer a bit" from this approach— for instance, "real theater actors, like Brialy or my wife, Anna." Palance openly voiced his suffering: "We never know in advance what we're going to do. There's almost no dialogue. It's the worst experience I've ever had! It's madness!"[31] By the end of filming, Palance not only refused to speak to Godard (passing his remarks through the head set decorator) but also tried to keep him out of sight. Suzanne Schiffman reported that the choleric actor could not even bring himself to mention the director's name and haughtily decreed when Godard stood next to the camera, "I prefer that this person not be there."[32] It was Prokosch brought to life.

Godard's relations with his producers were hardly better. Prior to the shoot, Carlo Ponti had sought to replace Godard with Truffaut—as the latter recalled, because his recent *Jules and Jim* had done better than *Vivre sa vie*—but Truffaut refused.[33] As for Joseph E. Levine, he later complained that throughout the shoot, Godard did not respond to his telegrams, which were mainly exhortations to Godard to make the film more erotic.

IN THE FILM, Godard has Paul express a desire to "return to the cinema of Griffith and Chaplin . . . at the time of United Artists." According to Godard, this invocation meant two things: first, the union of "the industrial and aesthetic aspects of the cinema,"[34] which foreshadowed his own venture into the business side (which he had tested out during *Vivre sa vie*). Second, the idea of "auteurs and actors who joined together to produce films"[35] recalled the passionate partnerships he had formerly enjoyed as a young cinephile and critic.

Godard was now alone and suffered from his solitude. He missed the companionship, the constant discussion, and the common purpose he had known in the 1950s. During the making of *Contempt*, Godard spent lots of evenings in the offices of *Cahiers du cinéma* "to stay on top of things," even though it seemed to Karina that he went there "as other men went to the café or to the pool hall."[36] Yet even there the sense of fellowship was mitigated: it was where he went in the hours when he was *not* shooting a film. Godard also keenly felt his solitude in the marriage: despite the appearance of working with his wife, he later claimed that he had grown apart from Karina because he "couldn't talk about films with her."[37] On the set of *Contempt* in Capri, lonely and lashing out in frustration amid the organized chaos of a grand production, Godard sought to ease his solitude in the company of a visitor.

A young journalist from *L'Express*, Michel Vianey, who wanted to meet Brigitte Bardot, asked his editors to send him to Capri to report on the shoot. Vianey was no ordinary journalist, having had three novels published while still in his twenties. Godard welcomed him with unusual openness, as Vianey later recalled: "When I arrived, he came over, he said, 'I need to talk to someone.' " One of the things Godard talked about was the "great solitude of the director," because of the personal preoccupations of the cast and crew with such ancillaries as lunchtime and days off.[38]

Godard granted Vianey extraordinary access to the set. The resulting report, a cover story published in *L'Express* on May 30, 1963, featured long and revealing conversations with Godard, Lang, Palance, Bardot, and Piccoli, along with Vianey's keen observations of life on a film set. Godard sent Vianey a telegram to compliment him on the article, and upon returning to Paris, invited him to lunch. Their connection proved inspiring: several years later, it contributed greatly to one of Godard's projects. If the cinema did not provide Godard with people who shared his interests, he would go outside the cinema to find them.

IN ROME, GODARD's editor, Agnès Guillemot, began work while the shooting was still taking place.[39] Godard had hoped to present the film at the Venice Film Festival in late August, where the previous year *Vivre sa vie* had won a prize. A cut was shown in midsummer 1963 to the festival's new director, the critic and filmmaker Luigi Chiarini, as well as to several friends and journalists. The response was favorable: the film was invited to the festival, and several critics spread advance word of a noteworthy achievement.

The same cut was shown to the producers, and their response was quite different.[40] Ponti and Levine complained that the film as edited seemed different to them from what they had seen during the shoot. In particular, Levine and his American colleagues were disappointed that Bardot was not shown in the nude often enough (in that cut, twice: sunbathing prone on the roof of the villa in Capri, with only a book covering her buttocks,[41] and again, from afar, swimming in the Mediterranean). The producers rejected the cut, and they also refused to allow it to be screened in Venice. Moreover, Bardot, who had until now been very supportive of Godard in his dealings with the producers, agreed with them that the film was not really finished and should not yet be shown.

Godard took his case to the industry, buying a two-page spread in the trade publication *Le Film français* to publish an open letter to Luigi Chiarini ("I apologize twenty-four times a second for the behavior of these people who saw fit to refuse your kind invitation"),[42] and further took matters into his own hands, confiscating the edited work print (the spliced copy which would be the template for the finished film) and stapling the splices together, rendering it unprojectable. The producers threatened to reedit the film to their own satisfaction (which Ponti later actually did for the Italian release). Godard sent telegrams of protest to the producers, addressing them as "King Kong Levine" and "Mussolini Ponti," and he threatened to take his name off the film (which he did for the Italian release). Bardot also threatened to take her name off the credits if they recut the film (a gesture that won her Godard's lasting gratitude), but the producers refused to release Godard's version, and the standoff frustrated them, because they were eager to begin to recoup their investment.

On October 8, on a sidewalk near the Champs-Elysées, Godard had a heated discussion with Ponti's Paris representative, the sixty-nine-year-old Simon Schiffrin. Godard was arguing that the credits should appear in the film's four languages. Schiffrin (who six months later won an Oscar as producer of the best documentary short, a film on Marc Chagall) agreed with

Ponti that Godard should be banned from the editing room. Godard slapped him twice in the face, and the elderly man fell backward. Schiffrin filed suit against Godard, and won: on February 12, 1966, Godard was sentenced to pay a fine of five hundred francs (one hundred dollars).[43]

Though the film was not yet finished, a lascivious advertising campaign featuring Bardot went up on the walls of the Paris métro on October 23. The producers were getting impatient, and soon Levine's associates (or, as Godard said, his "yes-men") approached the director in an attempt to reach an agreement on the editing of the film. Godard recalled:

> "At the beginning of the film," they said, "we want a scene with Michel Piccoli and Brigitte Bardot, in bed, in the act of love. In the middle of the film, we want a scene with Brigitte Bardot and Michel Piccoli, in bed, in the act of love. At the end of the film, we want a scene with Jack Palance and Brigitte Bardot, in bed, in the act of love. That's all."
>
> I began by refusing to show Jack Palance and Brigitte Bardot making love.[44] As for the Piccoli-Bardot scene in the middle of the film, it appeared to me almost impossibly absurd, because *Contempt* is precisely the story of a woman who detaches herself from her husband and refuses to sleep with him in the conjugal bed! So I refused to do this scene, but I said to them: "You've given me an idea; I'm going to do something the opposite of what you want, which will please you nonetheless." The first scene they proposed, however, was quite in keeping with the spirit of the script, and I agreed.[45]

Godard's agreement, however, came with a poison pill: an additional budget of 100,000 francs (twenty thousand dollars), which covered an exact studio replica of the apartment in Rome where he had filmed and which he was sure the producers would reject. To his surprise, they accepted; for her part, Bardot went along too, but with a caveat: that she have a body double for some shots. An eighteen-year-old cabaret dancer was paid six hundred francs for the job. The supplementary shoot took five days, and each day of shooting required the producers' approval of the previous day's rushes.

To conceal the sleight-of-camera, Godard coiffed the model in a blond Bardot-like "sauerkraut" wig the tousle of which nearly covers her face. (Discussing the film soon thereafter, Godard came close to admitting the presence of a body double for some shots when he claimed to have filmed Bardot at "her real age, 29 years old," when "suddenly something happens and her face changes, you see a very young woman emerge, one of, I don't know, 20 or maybe 22.")[46] For the first scene, Godard filmed a single long take of Bardot from the side, nude and supine on the bed, in dim light except for the highlights on her buttocks. Talking with Piccoli (who is dressed and wearing a hat), she enumerates the parts of her body and asks him whether he loves all of them. He answers "yes" to each item on the list; she asks, "So you love me totally?" His answer: "Yes. Totally, tenderly, tragically." In the editing room, Godard tinted the first third of the shot in blue, left the next part in white light, then tinted the last third red (the blue-white-red of the French flag, as if advertising Bardot's rear end as a French national treasure).

The ribald scene is quite distinct from the rest of the film. Godard understood that "it doesn't explain anything special and doesn't change the meaning of the film."[47] Many critics who had little use for the rest of Contempt at least found this one scene to praise.[48]

The second nude scene, however—the one which Godard derived from the "idea" the producers gave him—is an extraordinary aesthetic conceit: at the moment that Camille flings herself on a sofa and disrobes (at a great distance) to let Paul make love to her, "but quickly," Godard shows Bardot (or her double) again posed nude and face-down, on a sofa and on a bearskin rug, and intercuts these shots with flash-images of Camille and Paul from other parts of the film, as the characters, in overlapping voice-overs, recite passages from the novel as a sonic montage of interior monologues and erotic fantasies. This subjective collage—which was different from anything that Godard had done to date—is so well integrated into the couple's long apartment scene that critics aware of Godard's dispute with his producers were unable to identify a second supplementary nude scene.[49]

It is impossible to judge the box-office effect of the added scenes, but even critics who had privately viewed the first, unaugmented cut at a screening for the Venice festival officials sensed that Contempt was aimed at a wide audience.[50] Godard acknowledged that the film was "a little more normal" than his others. Contempt was the closest thing to a conventional movie that Godard had made, and he knew it. Whatever his producers may have thought of Contempt, Godard had fulfilled their commission; it is a far less radical work of art than Breathless or Vivre sa vie. In 1985, Godard commented that it was "the only 'classical' film that [he] had the chance to make, within the system," and he called it "a somewhat Hollywood-ish film."[51] In 2000, he expressed his bewilderment that Contempt remains as popular as it does. (It was successfully re-released in France in 1981 and the United States in 1997, and was called by the critic Colin MacCabe in 1996 "the greatest work of art produced in post-war Europe".)[52] Godard suggested that the film's lasting renown is due precisely to its conventionality: "It's because it's a twopenny novel, it has a 'cheap novel' side."[53]

Nonetheless, Contempt is a significant achievement, primarily as a reflexive commentary, as an expression of Godard's own view of the cinema. Set in the ruins of two classical eras, the age of Homer and the age of the Hollywood studios, *Contempt* is Godard's first film of cultural nostalgia. Expanding on the sense of a culture threatened with imminent disappearance, a theme first exposed in *Le Nouveau Monde,* Godard dramatizes that possibility in action in *Contempt.* The film begins in the desolate wreckage of Prokosch's studio in Cinecittà, where the producer laments that the property has been sold and a department store will be built there. When he declares, "It is my last kingdom," his secretary's "translation" is, "C'est la fin du cinéma" (it's the end of the cinema).

This remark is not too different from what Godard told an interviewer in 1961: "Chabrol, I know, would like to make a picture in the Hollywood way, and so would I, because everything runs smoothly . . . except the producer. I'm sorry that Hollywood is dead now."[54] As Godard explained at the time of the release of *Contempt,* "The dream of the New Wave when we were film critics, when we started to make films, and my own dream, personally, was to shoot—and it's my dream to this day—was to shoot a five-million-dollar film on the big stage at MGM, in Hollywood. But it's a dream that I will never realize . . . because the big stage no longer exists."[55]

The Young Turks of *Cahiers* had come to know the American cinema in its postwar years of independent production, when many directors enjoyed a freer hand than in the prewar studio productions. It rightly seemed to them a sort of new Golden Age. That age, however, was short-lived. "Our tragedy," Godard said, "was thinking that we were coming in the middle of something when in fact we were coming at the end of it."[56] Godard accurately understood that the rise of the New Wave coincided with the demise of the studio system. The year 1960 seems to have been something of a divide,[57] after which the careers of many of the most important Hollywood directors, including those "discovered" and celebrated by the critics at *Cahiers*—Nicholas Ray, Douglas Sirk, Joseph Mankiewicz, Budd Boetticher, Fritz Lang—went into decline or ended altogether. *Contempt* is an elegy for the classical heights, in which the ancient Greek era appears like a palimpsest through the vanished age of Hollywood.[58]

REVIEWS OF THE film were mixed. On the one hand, Jean-Louis Bory, writing in *Arts,* claimed that "there has rarely been so profound an understanding . . . between an actress and a director."[59] Michel Aubriant, in *Paris-Presse-L'Intransigeant,* called *Contempt* "the densest and most stripped-down, in my view, of Godard's works, and one of the most enriching works of the French cinema in recent years."[60] In *Le Monde,* Jean de Baroncelli reserved special praise for the apartment scene: "The mise-en-scène is here truly, as Godard desires, the reflection of a thought."[61] On the other hand, Gérard Legrand complained in the pages of *Positif* that "Godard no more mastered the procedure in *Contempt* than elsewhere."[62] Robert Benayoun of *France-Observateur* called it "empty," "foolishly pretentious," and "intellectually null," and praised only the opening nude scene, commending Joseph E. Levine for requiring it.[63] In *Les Lettres françaises,* Georges Sadoul contemplated the film at length but deferred judgment: "I thus reserve the right to come back one of these weeks to this work, which is sometimes irritating but always fascinating."[64]

Several weeks after the film's opening, the editor in chief of *Les Lettres françaises,* the poet and novelist Louis Aragon, wrote an exultant "Homage to Jean-Luc Godard" in which he put Godard's achievement into a broad perspective:

> I've seen a novel of today. At the cinema . . . It's called *Contempt,* the novelist is someone named Godard. The French screen has seen nothing better since Renoir, when Renoir was the novelist Jean Renoir. I can't understand the reservations that I've read regarding this film, elsewhere and in my own newspaper. We've been asking for genius—well, here is genius.[65]

Contempt did business that would have been creditable for films made on a lower budget, but which was only modest for a million-dollar production: in its first run, it attracted 234,374 viewers,[66] still a larger audience than had seen Godard's previous films. It was very likely that some viewers came mainly to see the film's star in the nude; some audience members in the opening week whistled in the theaters (the local equivalent of booing).[67] Deemed a commercial disappointment, the film led to the breakup of Georges de Beauregard's partnership with Carlo Ponti, who withdrew from Rome-Paris Films. Joseph E. Levine offered to take Ponti's place as Beauregard's coproducer, but Beauregard turned him down. He was determined to be on his own again, and his work with Godard would go forward.

IN THE UNITED STATES a year later, the film also flopped at the box office, after devastatingly silly reviews in major publications; Bosley Crowther in the *New York Times* suggested that Godard "could put his talents to more intelligent and illuminating use," and Judith Crist in the *New York Herald Tribune* praised the opening nude scene and concluded that "charming as the Bardot derriere is, you can, under the Godard circumstance, have too much of a good thing very early on."

But a sea change in the American moviegoing audience, and therefore the American reception of *Contempt,* was taking place beneath the radar of the box-office reports, and several years later, Joseph E. Levine would bear witness to it, as reported in a 1967 profile of him in *The New Yorker*. Asked by the writer Calvin Tomkins about a recent speaking engagement at Dartmouth, Levine answered enthusiastically:

A thousand people showed up—practically the whole student body . . . Those kids were great. They asked me questions for two hours. And you know what film of mine they really wanted to hear about? *Contempt!* . . . I told them it was the worst film we ever made—maybe the worst film *anybody* ever made. We lost a million bucks on that lousy film, because that *great* director Jean-Luc Godard refused to follow the script . . . I said, "Listen, I'm very glad your fathers had enough money to send you to college, but if you liked that picture you haven't learned much." At the end, I said I was going to donate prints of some of my films to Dartmouth, the way I did last year to the Museum of Modern Art. "And I'm not only going to give you a print of *Contempt*," I said. "I'm going to give you the negative." They loved it.[68]

Karina, looking young and vulnerable
(Columbia Pictures / Photofest)

eight

MONTPARNASSE ET LEVALLOIS, BAND OF OUTSIDERS

"A simple, perfectly legible film"

LATE IN 1963, GODARD AND KARINA AGAIN SEPARATED, and he sought the usual means of attempting communication and reconciliation: the cinema. But the cinema, at the time of his wrangling over the completion of *Contempt,* and in the wake of the utter financial disaster of *Les Carabiniers,* was less receptive than usual to Godard's entreaties. He offered the Hakim brothers' production company a project called *La Bande à Bonnot.* The Bonnot Gang was a group of political anarchists who terrorized France from December 1911 through April 1912 with a series of bank robberies, brazen murders, and amazing escapes. Their capture was a public spectacle, with tens of thousands of people crowding to watch divisions of the French army and national guard surround and bombard the gunmen, who had barricaded themselves in several houses. Their legendary status in France was similar to that of Bonnie and Clyde's in America. The story's significance to Godard was suggested by the motive of the gang's leader, Jules Bonnot, an expert mechanic who turned to a life of vengeful crime in his despair over the loss of his wife to another man. Godard's project thus promised to be a radicalized view of marital infidelity and its price, but it also promised to be a big-budget costume production, and the Hakim brothers demurred.

At the same time, Godard was seeking to launch another large-scale commercial project, a new installment in the series of action-adventure films about the fictional secret agent Lemmy Caution, starring the rough-hewn, American-born Eddie Constantine, whose prior incarnations of this character made him one of France's most popular actors. Speaking to a journalist in October 1963, Constantine—who had appeared in Godard's short film *La Paresse* in 1961—explained his interest in agreeing to work with Godard: "He should be able to find new tricks for an old character."[1] But despite the film's evident box-office appeal, Godard and Constantine found, for the moment, no backers.

Godard was briefly without anything to do, but his friends' fortunes and misfortunes quickly brought him a project of slight cinematic merit but great personal significance. If nothing more, it offered proof of Godard's power to mold even the most recalcitrant forms to his own personal ends.

AFTER THE DEATH of André Bazin in November 1958, Eric Rohmer had taken over as the editor of *Cahiers du cinéma*. He had intended his editorship to be a way station on his route to a career as a filmmaker, but his first feature, *Le Signe du lion,* which had been shot in the summer of 1959, was not released until three years later. In 1962, Rohmer made a short film, *La Boulangère de Monceau* (The Bakery Girl of Monceau), with amateur equipment, on 16mm black-and-white film. The lead actor was Barbet Schroeder, a twenty-one-year-old critic at *Cahiers,* who joined Rohmer in founding a production company, Les Films du Losange. Soon thereafter, Schroeder gained crucial experience as an assistant to Godard on *Les Carabiniers,* and then oversaw the production of another 16mm film by Rohmer, *La Carrière de Suzanne* (Suzanne's Career).

Meanwhile, Rohmer's editorship of *Cahiers* was prompting some dissatisfaction. Despite the journal's favorable coverage of most of the New Wave films, it did not fight for the movement as a whole. Rohmer ran special issues on Brecht, on Joseph Losey, on the state of film criticism, on the Italian cinema, but none on the French New Wave. The New Wave was taking a beating in the general press, in other film journals, and at the box office, yet Rohmer's *Cahiers* did not stand up for it.

In the spring of 1962, after discussions with Godard, Truffaut, and Pierre Kast, Jacques Doniol-Valcroze drafted a lofty editorial in their name, calling for a new orientation of the journal as an "instrument of combat" for the New Wave. They wanted Rohmer to sign the document, to publish it, and to act on its fiery advocacy. Rohmer partially complied, publishing a tribute to the New Wave in December 1962 with a brief statement of purpose that featured part of Doniol-Valcroze's text. He also accepted a new editorial committee that included Godard and Truffaut. But in June 1963, still under pressure, Rohmer yielded the editorship to Jacques Rivette and left the magazine, as did his younger allies, including Schroeder. (One of the first combative acts of Rivette's refashioned *Cahiers* was to grant Godard space, in August 1963, to respond to the negative reviews of *Les Carabiniers*.)

Rohmer's departure from *Cahiers* was the best thing that could have happened to him (as he later acknowledged), inasmuch as it induced him to relaunch himself quickly as a filmmaker. He and Schroeder embarked on an ambitious feature-film project, *Paris vu par . . .* (Paris seen by . . . , released in the United States as *Six in Paris*), a compilation of six short films that would bring together three unestablished directors (Rohmer, Jean-Daniel Pollet, and *Cahiers* critic Jean Douchet, who had resigned along with Rohmer) and three well-known filmmakers (Godard, Chabrol, and Jean Rouch). The films were to be made with a minimal budget and crew on 16mm film; the project's unifying idea was for each film to be shot in a different part of Paris.

In late 1963, Schroeder happened to be in New York and staying with Albert Maysles, a pioneering director and cameraman of the American cinema verité movement, just as Godard was preparing to start work on his contribution. Schroeder had the sudden inspiration to pair Maysles with Godard. Schroeder mentioned this to Godard, who told Maysles to take the next plane for Paris, as the shoot would take place in a few days. As Maysles recalled: "He had it all set up, actors, script, lighting . . . I filmed it like a real event, as if it were a piece of documentary reality, so it had this quality of total spontaneity. As everything took place, I filmed it as I would a documentary—each moment a new discovery."[2] Godard stood on its head not only the method, but also the idea, of cinema verité—to document reality without directorial intervention—and put it to an end entirely his own.

The event that Godard staged for Maysles's camera was an anecdote—derived from a story by Jean Giraudoux—that Jean-Paul Belmondo had told Anna Karina in *A Woman Is a Woman*: A woman sends two "pneumatiques" (telegrams) to schedule dates with her two lovers, but is immediately seized with panic; she believes she has accidentally switched the envelopes and sent each man the billet-doux meant for the other. She goes to the first lover to confess her infidelity before he receives the other man's note, and he kicks her out. She crosses Paris to see the second lover, assuming that by now his envelope has arrived, yet she finds him calm and supposes that he is toying with her. She apologizes for her infidelity, and he shows her the letter he received—which is indeed the one she had written to him—and then he, too, turns her out. (In Giraudoux's story, from 1910, the protagonist is a man, the deceived lovers two women.)

To render the film neighborhood-specific, according to Rohmer and Schroeder's plan, Godard put the two boyfriends in two distinct parts of town, which became the film's title: *Montparnasse et Levallois*. Montparnasse is the modern artistic center of Paris, Levallois an industrial suburb just over the city line to the northwest—and they are at opposite ends of bus line number 94.

The film's title card indicates the nature of Godard's limited ambition in making this sketch—he does not credit himself as the director or author of the film; instead, the credits read:

MONTPARNASSE AND LEVALLOIS
AN ACTION-FILM
ORGANIZED BY JEAN-LUC GODARD
AND FILMED BY ALBERT MAYSLES

The young woman, Monika (Godard took the name from Bergman's film of that title, which is also the story of a defiant adulteress), is played by the Canadian actress Joanna Shimkus as a pert young woman dressed in chic new "mod" styles (dark tights and a short plaid skirt, a red sweater, and a trim trenchcoat). Monika sends the telegrams just outside the Montparnasse train station, tries to fit her hand through the slot of the mailbox to get them back (a detail from the Giraudoux story), and unable to do so, runs to see her nearby boyfriend in Montparnasse.

Philippe, a sculptor who works in metal (played by the sculptor Philippe Hiquilly) is a tall, laconic young man in denim, who moves purposefully through his garagelike studio, bearing a welding torch while Monika attempts to explain the mix-up. When she asks about one of his artworks, he says, "It's an action sculpture," and explains: "It means that chance enters into the creation of the sculpture. I take pieces of metal, I throw them, and the way they fall, I weld them. It makes for a very experimental kind of sculpture." His "action sculpture" is akin to Godard's "Action-Film"—and to round out the association with Godard, the sculptor also wears dark glasses (albeit industrial ones suited for his work with the acetylene torch) and smokes a cigar (which he lights with a casual blast from his torch).

After being roughly thrown out of Philippe's studio, Monika is next seen crossing an industrial road and passing a sign for Levallois-Perret. On a side street, she enters the cramped auto body shop belonging to Roger Delpirou, a short, gruff, middle-aged man (played by Serge Davri) who is alone at work on a sports car. He is a proud industrial craftsman who declares, "In my own way, I'm an artist." When Monika admits her infidelity and tries to make it up to him by beginning to undress and leading him to bed in his upstairs loft, he shows her his letter and throws her out the door: "Get out,

American!" "I'm not American, I'm Canadian," she responds. "It's the same thing, American and Canadian." "No, it's not." Both of the artists, manual laborers who work with heavy metal, have rid themselves of the bourgeois woman, the New World foreigner.

Giraudoux's original story was called "La Méprise"—literally, "The Mistake"—which happens also to be the feminine form of Le Mépris (Contempt), the title of the film Godard had just completed. Contempt concerns a man who has lost his moral clarity due to a tangle of confused thinking; Godard's film of "La Méprise" is about a woman who thinks confusedly due to her loss of moral clarity. The adaptation of "La Méprise," a small-scale, feminine version of Godard's previous film, was as much a letter to Anna Karina as Contempt had been.

Godard praised Maysles publicly for Montparnasse et Levallois.[3] In fact, Maysles's camera work is merely efficient and functional; but this inexpressive neutrality is itself the point of the film: thanks to Maysles, a famously objective observer, Godard could offer blandly documentary images as indisputable evidence that the woman was wrong—not simply in the practical error of her letters but in the moral error on which the story is based, her blithe infidelity.

Montparnasse et Levallois is not one of Godard's greatest works of art, but it is an extraordinary illustration of how he conceived cinematic form in terms of his own private allegories. Its uninflected images—and Godard's willingness to relinquish control of them to Maysles—suggest his growing doubt about how, and on what basis, to make films. The crisis in cinema history that Godard had asserted in Contempt left its first concrete trace on his filmmaking in this short film. It was a crisis that would mark his films all the more deeply in the coming years.

THE DESPERATE INDICTMENT of the New World as the source of modern decadence—a sadly comical reflection of the American stereotype of libertine France—hints at Godard's changing view of the American cinema and its role in the world. In late 1963, he joined the other former Hitchcocko-Hawksians (minus Rohmer) in a roundtable discussion (published in the December 1963–January 1964 Cahiers) in which everyone agreed that the collapse of the Hollywood studio system also meant the end of the American cinema as an aesthetic wellspring. Though six of the films on Godard's top-ten list for 1963 were from the United States—The Birds, The Chapman Report, Donovan's Reef, The Nutty Professor, Irma la Douce, and Two Weeks in Another Town—he said that films of such caliber had become the exception: "The reason we loved the American cinema was that out of 100 American films, there were, let's say, 80% good ones. Today, out of 100 American films,

80% are bad." When he first began making movies, he said, the American cinema "was the model to imitate. Today, it is the thing not to do."

This remark contained a hint of Godard's looming crisis: he now knew what not to do, but did not have a positive, constructive model to replace the one he had jettisoned. His films for the next few years would be, in general, decomposed rather than composed, and the collage-like fragmentation for which they were celebrated was in fact a despairing avowal of lost bearings.

Godard's immediate problem, however, was tied to the scramble for money: he needed financing and, despite the artistic decline of the Holly- wood studios, he understood that they were still, indeed more than ever, the place to go: "In reality, the American cinema has never been stronger. Its power is such that no film can succeed today if, sooner or later, it isn't bought by America or if, in one way or another, the Americans aren't in on it."[4] Un- able to find funding for his desired projects in France, Godard sought to set up his own production company—and to do so with Hollywood money. He recalled:

> I couldn't find any money. So I wrote to Columbia, Paramount, United Artists, asking could they give me $100,000 to make a picture. They said, "Well, that's a huge fee for a director."[5] And I said, "No, that's not for me, that's for the whole picture." Columbia was the only one interested.[6]

Godard offered the studio three projects from which to choose: one about "a woman leftist," one about a writer, and one based on a crime novel—specifically, the French translation of Dolores Hitchens's *Fool's Gold*, which he had read on Truffaut's suggestion that it would make a good subject for him. Unsurprisingly, the studio opted for the crime novel. Though it provided a rich trove of pulp for Godard to adorn as he had done with *Breathless*, he now intended to take a new approach to such lowbrow material.

In an interview, he announced his new plan: "I want to remain faithful to my two inclinations, let's call them the instinctive and the reflective. But to realize them separately, from one film to the next, rather than blending them in one same film." He wanted, on the one hand, "to tell little stories, to return to the tradition of *Quai des brumes* [a classic French crime drama from 1939], the genre of *The 400 Blows*, of *Shoot the Piano Player* and of *Jules and Jim*, or of American comedy," and on the other, "to make reflective films, without concessions." He admitted, "Before, I tended to stuff all this into the film of the moment. Now, I want it to be all one or all the other."[7]

By hailing Truffaut's three films as exemplars of "instinctive" and "non-reflective" cinema, Godard was damning them with faint praise. Yet by becoming his own producer, Godard was about to fall into the same trap in which he considered Truffaut to have been caught as the owner of his production company, Les Films du Carrosse: Godard would mix his artistic and his commercial motives, to similarly unhappy effect.

Just as he had done with *Vivre sa vie*, Godard took the step into production to reforge his marital bond with Anna Karina. He called the production company Anouchka Films, after one of his pet names for her.[8] It had been almost two years since Godard and Karina had worked together, in *Vivre sa vie*. She had since appeared in a series of commercial vehicles, from the pageantry of *Scheherazade* to the domestic comedy of *Un Mari à prix fixe* (A Prix Fixe Husband). Karina was a well-known actress but hardly a star, and despite the acclaim she enjoyed from several of these roles, she failed to reach the heights, artistically or commercially, that she had with Godard's films.

Much was riding on this adaptation of *Fool's Gold*: it was intended to establish the company that bore Anna Karina's name, to reestablish Godard as a commercial man of the international cinema, to bring her the sort of success that he thought she craved, and so, to secure his future life with her.

The novel was fairly typical for the hard-boiled genre, and the story Godard extracted from it was also typical: a sheltered young woman is befriended by a man to whom she reveals a stash of money in her guardian's house. The man turns out to be a petty criminal who divulges the secret to his friend, a bolder thief, and the two of them plot with the woman to steal the cash. Both are in love with her; she chooses the second, bolder one. His uncle, a retired gangster, sees a chance for one last big score and tries to move in on the scheme. In the end, the second man is killed, and the woman ends up with the first one.

Godard cast the intense and serious Sami Frey (by then Bardot's ex) as the first, more romantic criminal and the blunt and impulsive Claude Brasseur as the second, more aggressive one. His original title for the film referred to two of its three leads, *Arthur, Sammy and Anouchka*, but the studio rejected it; he offered as a substitute *Les Mimis* (The Cuties, or The Good-Looking Kids), which was also rejected; in the end, he settled for *Bande à part* (Band of Outsiders).

Though otherwise free from direct interference from Columbia's executives, Godard did too good a job of internalizing their standards and fulfilling their wishes. *Band of Outsiders* is one of Godard's least substantial and adventuresome films, as well as his most conventional one. It was recognized as such at the time by the critics most familiar with his work, and by Godard himself; and yet—or perhaps, as a result—it was eventually exalted as one of his great artistic triumphs by critics who were bewildered by his more audacious and original films. Its ongoing popularity is due precisely to the film's overt neo-classicism.

Columbia's executives considered the budget so small that, once they approved the project, they did not ask to see a script. However, the CNC did require a script for precensorship and authorization to shoot, and Godard arranged for his assistant, Jean-Paul Savignac, to write what Coutard, the film's director of photography, called a "junk script."[9] The forty-two-page-long text is not drastically different from the film; Godard's copy reveals the extent to which his approach to the shoot diverged from his previous work.[10] His annotations and diagrams, on the front and the back of most of the pages, not only fill in dialogue or modify situations but also map out camera angles, sketch rooms and furnishings, provide blocking for actors, and diagram seating arrangements and various movements and gestures. According to Sami Frey, "Everything was very precise, decided in advance—even the details."[11] The shoot lasted twenty-five days, and, according to Coutard, Godard worked methodically, making full use of the schedule.[12]

Despite the casual air of the camera moves, they were largely determined in advance. Coutard described the director's unusual procedures: "To Godard it was a given that we would work with a handheld camera, always following the actors—whereas in his other films the camera had moved freely, independent of the actors . . . First the actors' movements were pretty thoroughly prepared; Godard himself stood in the place of the camera. Then there were rehearsals with the camera, to synchronize the movements of the camera and the actors."[13] The film's look of offhand grace and spontaneity was in fact the product of careful forethought. *Band of Outsiders* is the first film in which Godard attempted to convey an impression that was essentially different from the reality of the shoot.

Godard took no chances with the material: he declared that he wanted "to make a simple, perfectly legible film."[14] The transparently masked content of the story is apparent in the names that Godard assigned to his fictional characters: Claude Brasseur's audacious thief became Arthur (Arthur Rimbaud); Frey's sensitive one became Franz (for Kafka, whom Godard thought Frey resembled); and Karina's character was named Odile Monod (Godard's mother's maiden name). Godard said that he took the name both from his mother and from the eponymous novel by Raymond Queneau (a copy of which turns up in the film), a roman à clef about the surrealists—another band of outsiders similar to the New Wave itself. Odile Monod Godard was an - accomplished and refined woman, nothing like the unpolished adolescent played by Karina; but it had been almost precisely ten years since Godard's mother's sudden and horrific end, and her name in the film suggests a touching conflation of the two women of Godard's life to date. The film is nowhere more personal than in this connection of love and death. Karina had survived a suicide attempt and was extremely fragile and desperate at the time of the filming:

> I had come out of the hospital. It was a painful moment. I had lost the taste for life at that time. In the meantime I had lost weight, I wasn't doing well, neither in my head nor in my body. It's true: the film saved my life. I had no more desire to live. I was doing very, very badly. This film saved my life.[15]

Godard amplified Karina's vulnerability in luminous close-ups and demanding long takes. Her struggle to hold herself together emanates a poignant frailty and translucency that arouses sympathy, less for the character (whom Karina rightly called "a crook, and none too clever")[16] than for the actress herself. Indeed, when the film was shown in the 1964 New York Film Festival on the same night as *A Woman Is a Woman,* many viewers even failed to recognize that the earlier film's exuberant dancer and the new film's yearning, tremulous adolescent were played by the same woman.

The film's basic triangle is established in the first sequence. Franz, accompanied by Arthur, drives a convertible sports car on a long, desolate suburban road along a riverbank and leaps from his seat to point out Odile, whom he sees riding by on her bicycle. Godard, in a voice-over commentary, sets the scene as both omniscient narrator and interested party: "My story starts here. Just about two weeks after having met Odile, Franz is driving Arthur out to Joinville to see the house." The story is a romantic disaster foretold, as Arthur soon announces brusquely to Franz, "I'll make her whenever I feel like it." And indeed, just after the two men track Odile down at a private English class in a comically grim, bare classroom where Franz had first met her, Arthur ensnares her with his aggressively seductive banter.

The English lesson they attend is a formidable, bittersweet comic set piece in which Godard shows off his classical culture as well as its inescapable personal relevance. The teacher is played by the veteran actress Danièle Delorme, who puts her theatrical diction to lofty use by reciting passages from *Romeo and Juliet,* translated into French, which her adult students must then translate back into English. With the canny choice of citations that comprise her text, Godard in effect rewrote the play to make it resemble the story of his life with Karina. The teacher begins with Act 5, where one lover finds the other dead.

> *I will kiss thy lips,*
> *Haply some poison yet doth hang on them*
> *To make me die with a restorative.*

Delorme then attributes to Juliet a line originally Romeo's, regarding "some vile forfeit of untimely death"—a line accompanied by close-ups of Karina and Frey, two actors who, in real life, had made widely reported suicide attempts.

The teacher's recitation comes to an end, during a shot of Anna Karina, with a line delivered in an undertone of afterthought, "O Fortune, Fortune! all men call thee fickle." It is as if Godard had made Delorme say this line both to the character played by Karina, Odile, whom Arthur will seduce, and to Karina herself, whose unstable relationship with Godard was the director's obsessional master plot.

Odile yields to Arthur, going off with him by métro as Godard, on the sound track, calls their trip to the St. Michel station a descent to "the center of the world"—a citation from Giraudoux's story "La Méprise." The sequence ends with Godard's masochistic shot of Karina in bed with Brasseur—rather, Odile in bed with Arthur—while Franz is shown at home, sleeping alone.

Ultimately, the impulsive Arthur is killed, and Odile ends up with Franz. Godard described this happy ending in terms of Odile's newfound maturity: "Odile obviously goes first to the more brilliant of the two. And then afterward, she discovers Franz, who is more solid, but who doesn't have appearances in his favor." He also spoke of Odile's dalliance with Arthur as a dialectical stage in her life with Franz: "They have come to terms with themselves. They needed Arthur to come into their lives for them to arrive at this point."[17]

As with the characters in the film, so with Godard and Karina: all's well that ends well, as art and life coincide. During the making of *Band of Outsiders,* he and Karina reconciled, moving into a new apartment in the Latin Quarter. Decorated in high style, the duplex was the subject of a celebrity–news photo spread in *Paris-Match.*[18]

THOUGH THE DRAMA of *Band of Outsiders* is conventional, Godard depicted it strikingly. Coutard's photography coalesced with Godard's careful choice of locations to produce an almost tactile attachment to place, from the gritty working district of the rue St.-Antoine in the eleventh arrondissement to the banks of the Marne on the road to Joinville, from the nocturnal glow of the place Clichy to the mysterious depths of the métro.

He also adorned it with several notable set pieces, such as the trio's attempt to set a new world record for the fastest dash through the Louvre and their snazzily foot-stomping, hand-clapping line dance in a café, a popular step called the Madison (which the actors, who were not natural dancers, rehearsed daily for a month). It also offers Godard's wistfully romantic tribute to Karina, set on a moving métro car, in which Odile speaks to Arthur of marriage (Arthur responds coolly); after they observe a melancholy traveler on the train, Odile, framed by Godard in a moody close-up, sings in a half whisper a poem by Aragon about romance among the struggling folk of the city. The camera's ardent gaze at Karina matched the sentimental nostalgia of Godard's tribute to survivors of the daily grind.

Godard likened *Band of Outsiders* to *A Woman Is a Woman* for its "common," working-class characters whom he presented as "somewhat cartoonish"[19]—in other words, relatively inarticulate people cut off from the filmmaker's own intellectual life and vocabulary. Soon after making the film, Godard did what he had done for *A Woman Is a Woman:* he immediately produced a revision that better reflected his deeper inclinations. For *A Woman Is a Woman,* that revision was the unreleased record based on the film's sound track; for *Band of Outsiders,* it was a text called "My Characters" that Godard wrote for promotional use.[20] In it, he fused the characters and the actors who play them—"Odile" Karina, "Arthur" Brasseur, and "Franz" Frey—spinning around them an elaborate web of literary and cinematic references as well as subtle psychological analyses that give them a depth and a "reflective" dimension that were missing from the film itself. Likening Odile to Hardy's Tess, to the Ottilie—in French, Odile—of Goethe's *Elective Affinities,* and to a host of characters and actresses from classic movies, Godard wrote that she "reacts to the entreaties of the world in a purely animal way, without obvious logical reason"—in other words, like Bardot's Camille in *Contempt.* Arthur, he wrote, "believes in stage sets and in appearances, in Billy the Kid as in Cyd Charisse," calling him "a boy for whom life is totally stripped of mystery, but with all the poetry implied by the word 'total.'" Godard reserved for Franz his own chosen destiny: "Franz is strong and original, in our era corrupted by the bureaucrats' I.B.M.s, for having kept intact the reserves of imagination lauded by the Surrealists."

In this elaborate retelling, Godard suggests regretfully what the film could have been, and was not. *Band of Outsiders,* which was conceived for practical ends, had a personal significance for him that exceeded its cinematic importance. He was the first to acknowledge the film's flaws, at first with hints and later unrestrainedly—and many of his most perceptive viewers also voiced their reservations.

WHEN THE FILM was shown at the Cannes festival, out of competition, in early May 1964, Godard did his duty as a producer with grim good humor, putting on the forced smile of the self-promoting salesman. He took out a two-page ad in the special Cannes issue of *Le Film français,* which featured the following bit of puffery: "What does the movie-going public want? said

Griffith. A revolver and a girl! It is in response to this desire that I have shot and Columbia is distributing *Band of Outsiders,* a story of gold which will sell lots of tickets. [Signed] Jean-Luc Godard."

However, Godard's cynicism was perceived at once: in an on-the-spot roundup of the films shown at Cannes, *Cahiers du cinéma*'s Luc Moullet, one of the subtlest and most enthusiastic of Godard's critics, wrote, "This offhanded overflight recalls Godard's sole failure, *Une Femme coquette* (1955), now forgotten."[21]

In early July, *Band of Outsiders* was shown out of competition at the Berlin festival, where it was received warmly, but at its screening at the Locarno festival on July 29, it was whistled at, booed. When it opened in Paris on August 5—during the great lull of the Parisian vacation period—not only did it fail at the box office, but it was rejected, either with open hostility or quiet bewilderment, by many critics who to that point had been among Godard's staunch defenders. A young *Cahiers* critic, Jacques Bontemps, concluded, with a shrug, that *Band of Outsiders* "remains on the margin"[22] of Godard's oeuvre. The wider press was less guarded. Claude Tarare, in *L'Express,* declared that "King Godard is naked."[23] And in *Les Lettres françaises,* Alain Vanier called the film the "self-criticism of an author in the process of plagiarizing himself."[24]

DURING THE SHOOT of *Band of Outsiders,* Godard, newly reconciled with Anna Karina, bought the rights to what he called a "Lolita-style"[25] crime novel, *Obsession,* by the American writer Lionel White, translated into French as *Le Démon de onze heures.*[26] It was the story of a young middle-aged executive who takes off with a teenage girl, his children's babysitter, on a cross-country spree of lust and crime. What Godard had in mind was to represent his own desperate obsession with Karina, starting from when she herself was a teenager. He wanted the film to star Michel Piccoli and the nineteen-year-old Sylvie Vartan, who was one of France's most popular female pop stars. However, Vartan turned Godard down, and he put the project aside. He also conceived a new film for Karina herself to act in, *La Boniche* (The Servant Girl), which she described as "the story of a little domestic maid who disembarks from the provinces, suffers a lot of misfortunes, and finally kills herself."[27] Its pointed personal allusions were painfully obvious. But the collaboration would be deferred, and the reconciliation short-lived. Karina accepted a role in Jean Aurel's *De l'amour,* which was filmed in April 1964, and a starring role in *Noël au soleil* (Christmas in the Sun) alongside the actor Maurice Ronet, who was also making his debut as a director. Karina and Ronet had an affair; Godard and Karina separated and filed for divorce.

As usual, Godard's response to the crisis was cinematic: he repudiated the careful methods and the neoclassicism of *Band of Outsiders* and renounced the separation of "instinctive" and "reflective" elements. He would again try to combine them. Closing the book on the failed experiment of trying to separate them, he placed *Band of Outsiders* in a different category from his other films: "That's why I called it 'Bande à Part.' It's really apart, it won't change anything, it's a diversion, *Bande à Part*."[28]

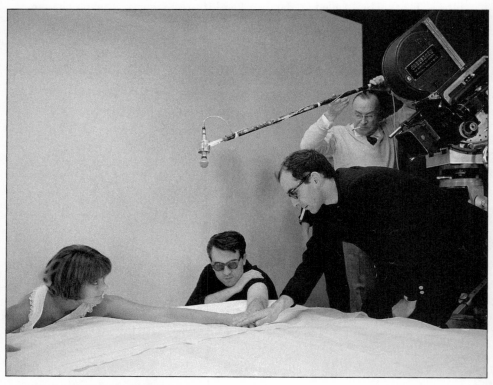

Filming close-ups of hands
(© Georges Pierre / Sygma / Corbis)

nine

A MARRIED WOMAN

"Even the sex life is not their own"

IN MAY 1964, WHILE AT CANNES PRESENTING *BAND OF OUT-*
siders, Godard told a journalist, "Why am I at Cannes? Well, because I was a little bit bored and a little bit sad, I came and I feel at
ease . . . I'm a little bit like those husbands who leave their wives to go to the
café and do some coffeehouse strategizing."[1] He was strategizing to get back
to work: at Cannes, Luigi Chiarini, the director of the Venice Film Festival,
expressed to Godard his regret at not being able to premiere *Band of Out-*
siders there (the festival would run from August 27 through September 10).[2]
In response, Godard offered to make another film that would be finished in
three months, in time to debut at Venice.

Once again, he turned to Columbia Pictures for financing and trotted
out the same two subjects that its executives had rejected earlier in the year, a
story about a female Communist student and another about a writer. He also
offered a third idea, a romantic melodrama about adultery, and this was the
one the studio selected.

The outward contours of the story, which Godard called *La Femme mariée*
(*The Married Woman*), gave his backers no hint of his actual intentions. To
the familiar and sentimental setup—the triangle of a woman, her husband,
and her lover—Godard added a twist: "She will find out from the doctor that
she is pregnant. But she has a lover, and she doesn't know whose child it is."
When asked by an interviewer which man the woman ends up with, he responded:

> I don't know yet. My heroine sends a letter to Marcelle Ségal [the advice
> columnist] at *Elle* . . . I really have sent a letter to Marcelle Ségal. The end of

my film will depend on her actual response. I think that the husband will win by a nose.[3]

This triangle, which was already familiar territory in Godard's work and life, was the mirror image of François Truffaut's most recent film, *La Peau douce* (*The Soft Skin*), about a man's extramarital affair. Godard greatly admired Truffaut's film and wrote to tell him so. He also sent along the story outline of *The Married Woman* so that Truffaut could see whether it seemed too similar to *The Soft Skin*—"in which case," Godard wrote to him, "I should film in another direction."[4]

The Soft Skin, made largely in Truffaut's own apartment, was based on the story of his own infidelity. Along with *The 400 Blows*, it is his most personal film. Its immediacy and intensity reflect Truffaut's urgent need to shoot it: he shaped the stuff of his life into a compact, classical melodrama that evoked the subject's strong emotions rapidly and clearly.

The Married Woman would be nothing of the sort. Godard used the classic subject to create an explicitly and stringently modernist film, and subordinated its melodrama to a surprisingly abstract style of filming. He made use of the story's built-in relation to the popular press—the letter to *Elle*—in order to express the Antonioniesque idea of communication breakdown and identity crisis in the face of media noise. Godard converted the familiar story of *The Married Woman* into his most aggressively philosophical film to date, one which unambiguously reflected a generational shift in intellectual matters and proclaimed his engagement with the most advanced thinking of the day: the social-scientific and linguistic elements of structuralism, as expressed in the work of Claude Lévi-Strauss and Roland Barthes. At the same time, Godard was also attempting to reconcile this new philosophy with existentialism and the work of his own intellectual hero, Jean-Paul Sartre, who was the structuralists' bête noire. *The Married Woman* is as much a melding of two conflicting philosophical arguments as it is a synthesis of two forms of expression dear to Godard—sentimental narrative and speculative essay.

The overtly theoretical aspect of *The Married Woman* contributed to its extremely close personal identification with Godard himself. Working amazingly fast to be ready for the Venice festival, Godard yielded to his own basic tendencies and made a film rich in philosophical argument and critical reflections. The more freely he indulged his taste for abstract thought, the more personal and intimate, the more confessional and autobiographical, the film seemed to be.

The Married Woman firmly established Godard as a politically and socially engaged artist. It placed him fully within his times and put his times clearly on his side. It also established the tonality for his work to come, both in its forth-right assertion of the cinema as an analytical instrument and in its unique permeability to the events, moods, and ideas of the day. Yet the specific view of the contemporary world that Godard offered was not favorable. Instead, he further developed the moralizing and puritanical critique of modern life that he had already expressed in *Le Nouveau monde* and in *Montparnasse et Levallois*—in other words, a critique of a world in which it was plausible for Anna Karina to leave him. Godard's intellectual and documentary engagement with his times would converge upon the burning point of his romantic agony, which it would reveal and salve, and to which it would offer the prospect—or the dream—of a favorable resolution, literally a conservative resolution.

If Godard's social outlook was conservative, his filmmaking was freneti-cally radical. The film's startling fragmentation and abstraction reflect the modern philosophy that was on Godard's mind—and his loss of faith in the familiar Hollywood styles. Paradoxically, the frustrating uncertainty behind its composition lent *The Married Woman* an air of desperate urgency that seemed not merely the filmmaker's but the era's.

GODARD HAD LIKED "for its principle"[5] a pair of films from 1963 called *L'Amour conjugale* (Conjugal Love), by André Cayatte: one of the films pre-sented the husband's point of view on the marriage, the other, the wife's. They both featured, in a supporting role, a young French actress of Russian extraction named Macha Méril,[6] born Macha Gagarine (a relative of the So-viet cosmonaut Yuri Gagarin). For several years, Méril had seemed to be on the verge of stardom but had not yet played a lead role. Godard contacted her agent and asked to meet the actress at her home. As Méril later recalled:

> He came over. He plopped himself down in a chair, and for an hour and a half he didn't open his mouth. Me, I talked, I told him my life story and he kept a terrible silence. I had the impression of confessing. He left, without even ut-tering the word "cinema."[7]

Starting with his choice of Méril, Godard wove into the fabric of *The Mar-ried Woman* an extraordinary set of similarities that linked the film's three lead actors to the trio on the other side of the camera whose story they enacted. Méril, born on September 3, 1940, was twenty-three, like Anna Karina. Strangely, not only Méril, but also the two leading actors—Philippe Leroy, the husband, and Bernard Noël, the lover—mirrored their real-life counterparts in age: Leroy was thirty-three, as was Godard himself; Noël and Maurice Ronet—Karina's lover—were both, at the time of the shoot, thirty-seven.

Beyond the coincidences of age, a distinct family circle of the cinema drew the performers into Godard's world of associations. Noël had appeared alongside Ronet in Louis Malle's *Le Feu follet* and, along with Ronet and Anna Karina, in Roger Vadim's version of *La Ronde*. As for Méril, she had played a major role in a comedy by Michel Deville, *Adorable Menteuse*, which was that director's follow-up to *Ce soir ou jamais*, in which Anna Karina had starred after *Le Petit Soldat*.

One further detail sharpened the parallel of art and life: the married woman's lover was, like Ronet, an actor.

MÉRIL WAS AWARE of the film's correspondence with the director's private life; she knew that her role in the film was no dramatic fabrication but was indeed modeled on the template of Anna Karina, and she was anguished by the all-too-apparent identification.

> I was not, I did not want to be, this woman, a product of Godard's resentment against this or that woman, because it was not me. And yet, I nonetheless had to be this woman who was not me, because I had been hired and because I had signed on for it.[8]

Méril was made uneasy not only by the role itself, but by Godard's unusual working methods on the film, which diverged from his previous practice of denying the actors control over their characters. After their first meeting, he told her, "It's perfect. You talk a lot. I won't have to write any dialogue."[9] His joke foretold the reality: during the few weeks of preparation for the film, Méril learned that much of her work would not be scripted at all, not even at the last minute. Godard planned to shoot some scenes for which she would invent her own dialogue as the cameras rolled, and others in which she and other actors would wear earphones through which Godard would pose questions that they would answer as they saw fit. Méril was not necessarily the best trained or most charismatic actress, but she was intelligent and articulate, and Godard chose her not merely to embody the title role but to find the married woman within herself and bring her to life.

THE FILM BEGINS with Charlotte's afternoon encounter with her lover, Robert, who is impatient for her to divorce her husband, Pierre, and have a child with him. Afterward, she collects her son (actually Pierre's, from his first marriage) from school, then goes to the airport to pick up her husband and his colleague, the filmmaker Roger Leenhardt; they all return to the couple's modern suburban apartment for dinner. After Leenhardt's departure, Charlotte and her husband playfully fight to the lubricious laughter of an "erotic" record and make love. The next morning, she stays home and super-

vises the maid, Madame Céline, who tells her a long tale of a sexual rendezvous (in a text that Godard derived from Louis-Ferdinand Céline's *Death
on the Installment Plan*). Charlotte then attends a fashion-photo shoot at a
swimming pool and listens in at a nearby café as two teenage girls chat about
their love life. She goes to the doctor and finds that she is pregnant; she does
not know which man is the father. Charlotte and her lover, Robert, meet at
Orly Airport, where he is about to fly to Marseille to perform in Racine's
Bérénice. In a room at the airport hotel, she questions him about love; she
finds his answers unsatisfying. They read together from the text of Racine's
play; as he prepares to leave for his flight, she cries and tells him, "C'est fini"
(It's over).

Godard's lofty approach to the story is announced in the film's first moments, as the austere credits are accompanied (as in *Le Nouveau Monde*) by a
Beethoven string quartet (one of five that would be interspersed throughout
the film) and include a title card that declares the film to be "Fragments of a
Film Shot in 1964." The promised fragmentation is apparent from the very
first shot, which begins with an undefined whiteness that is soon seen to be a
bedsheet, as a woman's hand, with a wedding ring on the fourth finger of the
left hand, slides across its surface; then a man's hand enters the screen per-
pendicular to the woman's bare arm and grabs it just above the wrist. The
image is a visual metaphor for Godard's view of the proceedings—the lover
has got the married woman in his grasp—and in the course of the film she
will recognize that his grasp, to which she willingly submits, is in fact a constraint from which she must liberate herself.

The movie's first five minutes are constructed mainly of such partial yet
intimate views of Charlotte and Robert, of close-ups of body parts: the back of
Charlotte's head and bare shoulders, her bare legs on the bed, a shot of her
navel and stomach as Robert puts his hands there and declares that he wants
her to have his child. These erotically suggestive shots, in which Charlotte's
erogenous zones are being caressed just beyond the screen's borders, are remarkably abstract and decontextualized. Robert's face is not seen until five
minutes into the film, and the setting, Robert's new apartment, is not seen for
another minute. Until then, the lovers' bodies, voices, caresses, and thoughts
remain detached from their surroundings and from the characters to whom
they belong.

These fragments of the body, which reduce the act of love to stylized
gestures and depersonalized poses, are the traces of an erotic disaster: the
bodies in question are examined with the restrained, almost vengefully clinical detachment of a scorned ex-lover. The scene is the anatomy of an affair,
as seen through the lens of a coldly repressed jealousy. By isolating the parts
of bodies from their characters, Godard suggests that the sexual acts are

being performed mechanically and unthinkingly, rather than as the actions of complete, responsible people.

The film comprises three long sequences centered on such intimately erotic yet abstract shots of lovers: one at the beginning of the film and another at the end, with Charlotte and her lover; and one in the middle of the film, showing her with her husband. (Godard joked that if nothing else, his film showed the main difference between a faithful and an unfaithful wife: the former gets dressed once a day, the latter twice.) But these movements and poses, considered apart from the people who make them, are also a sociological catalogue of the gesture repertory of modern love, a sort of public ritual performed in private. These scenes suggest that the quest for pleasure is not an authentic fulfillment of desire but rather conformity to a set of ready-made ideas imposed from the outside. And Godard conceived a remarkable cinematic device by which to show this.

Between some of the shots in Charlotte and Robert's opening fragmented love scene, Godard inserts extreme close-ups of text, such as a newspaper headline that reads, "The Secret Desires He Cannot Admit"; the title, "The Mistress"; a neon sign for the film *Hier, Aujourd'hui, Demain* (Vittorio De Sica's *Yesterday, Today, Tomorrow*);[10] a pan shot along the graphic logos of popular perfumes, *My Sin, Arpège, Scandale, Rumeur, Prétexte;* most provocatively, a tracking shot of an article about Truffaut's *The Soft Skin,* featuring a bold headline—"cet amour qui nous concerne" (this love that concerns us)—which Godard films with a pause on the first three letters of the last word *con* (cunt, in French) before going to the last five, *cerne* (to surround or confine)—"this love which cunt-fines us"; and the cover of a recent book by Elsa Triolet (Louis Aragon's wife), *The Age of Nylon—The Soul.*

Godard had always integrated documentary into his fictions, but *The Married Woman* actually shows documents in the literal sense. Having first tried out this strategy in *Le Nouveau Monde,* he relies on it amply in *The Married Woman* to embody his main idea: that the image- and word-drone of advertising and media are in control of the modern mind—in particular, of the married woman's mind—and that they insidiously plant in her and her peers a dangerous ideology, namely, the ideology of pleasure. Godard intersperses such documents throughout the film, mainly advertisements from magazines, but also ones from billboards, posters, neon signs, and other product logos—as well as related phenomena, such as characters speaking dialogue that Godard takes directly from advertising slogans or sales brochures, models cavorting salaciously for a fashion photographer, and sinuously alluring pop music.

These elements dominate a single bravura sequence in the middle of the film, in which Charlotte, during a visit to the swimming pool to meet colleagues involved in a photo shoot, sits at a table in a café and reads a copy of

Elle. As two girls at a nearby table discuss their hesitant steps toward a sex life, Godard shows the magazine's contents, in extreme close-up, as the pages slowly turn to reveal a plethora of gauzily seductive lingerie advertisements. Shortly thereafter, Godard pushes this method to its limits: the entire two-minute-and-forty-second duration of a pop song on the sound track—"Quand le film est triste" (When the Film Is Sad), sung by Sylvie Vartan—is accompanied on-screen by a montage of magazine advertising images chore-ographed in geometrically rigorous panning shots that move vertically and horizontally to show bulges in men's bathing suits, women in corsets and brassieres, garter belts strapped over inner thighs, heads tilted back in de-light to show well-formed cleavages, lips parted to receive lipstick, an endless procession of lace and gauze and curved and shaded flesh—and the eroti-cized and suggestive phrases printed to accompany them: "to please"; "beauty truth"; "scandal"; "youth"; "a love that . . ."

Godard described the point of this sequence:

> If I have shown . . . the place that magazine advertisements occupy in the life of this woman, it's because certain forms of advertising are going so far as to become people's own thoughts. The models that are proposed to people are becoming identical with the people themselves. Even their sex life is not their own, it's already displayed on the walls. People's existence is no more than the reflection of what they see, their freedom is a prefabricated thought.[11]

The profusion of images from the popular press, set to the bouncy charm of light rock, and the comical liveliness of the advertising copy mouthed by Pierre and Robert (extolling a luxury housing development, praising an electronic posture belt, "a French invention, perfected by Swiss specialists" that Charlotte borrows to "develop the bust") suggest, in their bubbly yet pathetic forms of popular expression, the enthusiastic playfulness of Pop Art. As such, Godard helped to inaugurate a poetry of the banal.

But unlike Pop artists, Godard did not revel in, or puckishly accept, the artifacts of mass culture or the impulses they expressed. Not only did he con-demn the ideology of pleasure that he found celebrated in the popular me-dia, but he offered as the explicit rebuttal to such blithe emptiness, the contemplative sobriety of high culture. Despite a rueful smile at the effluvia of popular culture, Godard held up Beethoven's quartets and Racine's dra-mas as models and guardians of aesthetic morality and moral aesthetics. As he told an interviewer:

> The characters in *The Married Woman* are ordinary people who do tradi-tional things in a world that has made them ordinary. But they are not

unhappy. They have nothing but psychological reflexes. Something in them has disappeared. It's a film in which something is missing. But this something is the subject of my film, the something that has been lost and must be found again . . . What they lack is conscience.[12]

The underlying story of *The Married Woman* is the woman's rise to conscience—and for Godard, the proof of its onset is her decision, after having learned of her pregnancy, to leave her lover and return to her husband. Charlotte's decision is foreshadowed moments earlier as she reads aloud with her lover, the actor, lines from Racine's *Bérénice,* a play in which Titus chooses his royal duty over his desire for Bérénice: "How will we bear it, my lord, that so many seas will keep me apart from you, that the day will begin and end without Titus being able to see Bérénice?" Charlotte's decision— hinted at by her tears and deftly delivered with the movie's last words, "C'est fini" (It's over), followed by the resolute final phrase of the last movement of Beethoven's last quartet—is her liberation, her ascendance to a self-awareness that she had lacked throughout the film.

ON DECEMBER 20, 1963, twenty-two officials and guards of the Auschwitz concentration camp went on trial in Frankfurt. The trial, which lasted until August 1965 and ended with eighteen convictions and four acquittals, featured a factually and emotionally overwhelming weight of evidence, provided by 359 witnesses, 211 of whom were survivors of Auschwitz. Despite the sharply detailed recollections of the witnesses, none of the accused admitted their crimes, and their defense attorneys attempted to shake the survivors' testimony on cross-examination.

In France, the Frankfurt proceedings were widely, sometimes luridly, reported in the press and were featured on many television programs. Yet the prompting of memory was matched by an ongoing calculated forgetting: maintaining the official myth that liberated France was a nation of resisters, France had not officially acknowledged its national role in deporting Jews from its territory to German concentration camps during the Second World War. In 1956, French censors compelled Alain Resnais to alter a shot in his film *Night and Fog* that showed the cap of a French gendarme who was overseeing a group of deportees assembled at a concentration camp in France.[13] Maurice Papon, who, as the chief of police in Bordeaux during the war, had personally signed orders of deportation of Jews, was the chief of police in Paris in the 1960s.

Godard introduced the Auschwitz trial into *The Married Woman* as a way of inserting his view of another sort of forgetting that, he suggested, had taken hold in France—the conjoined failures of historical and personal memory that resulted from the world of mass media and the ideology of gratification.

When Charlotte meets her husband, Pierre, and the film director Roger Leenhardt at the airport, the two men have just returned from Frankfurt, where they observed the trial. Leenhardt mentions it to Charlotte:

LEENHARDT: You've heard of Auschwitz?

CHARLOTTE: Oh, yes, thalidomide?

LEENHARDT: No, not exactly. You know . . . it's that old story, Auschwitz.

CHARLOTTE: Oh, yes . . . Hitler, yes.

LEENHARDT: Today, in Germany, I said to someone: "How about if tomorrow, we kill all the Jews and the hairdressers?" He answered, "Why the hairdressers?"

CHARLOTTE: Yes, why the hairdressers?

The subject of the threesome's after-dinner discussion is the Holocaust, in particular the difficulty commemorating it. Godard has Pierre tell a strange anecdote about a group of former concentration camp inmates who marched a decade later in their prisoners' garb and the absurdity of their making such a demonstration when they were obviously well-fed and comfortable. The tale suggests that Godard was making an uneasy distinction—which he would later reassert in other films and remarks—between the Holocaust as historical abstraction and the Jews who were its victims and survivors.

The subject of the conversation soon shifts to a theme that was then central to Godard: the question of memory in general, and in particular its implications for the betrayed husband and the unfaithful wife. Pierre tells Charlotte that he "remembers everything" about their life together, though, recalling her earlier infidelity, says: "Of course there are things that I'd like to forget, but . . ." Charlotte, by contrast, says that "memory is no fun, the present is more important," and explains why she feels that way: "In the present, I don't have the time to reflect, I can't think." She seeks sensation without reflection, and, in her affair with Robert, she gets it. By connecting the couple's discussion of memory, conscience, and infidelity to the theme of Auschwitz, Godard likens Charlotte's unreflective fealty to pleasure to complicity in crimes against humanity.

When Charlotte and her lover, Robert, join up at Orly Airport for their final tryst, they meet in the darkness of the movie theater there (to avoid the detectives she thinks her husband might have hired to follow her); the movie playing there is *Night and Fog*. The couple find each other in the dark and caress each other as Godard offers Resnais's images of the camp's towers and barbed wire and clips from the sound track featuring phrases from the writer (and concentration camp survivor) Jean Cayrol's commentary, which seem harshly apt for the lovers' Faustian bargain.

> Even a peaceful landscape, even a prairie with crows flying above, with harvests and hay fires, even a road with passing cars, peasants, couples, even a vacation village with a fair and a steeple, can lead very simply to a concentration camp.

For Godard, the lovers' adulterous embrace in a dark theater suggests the banality of evil.

GODARD MADE SURE that the viewer knew that, like Charlotte's husband, Pierre, he forgot nothing. Godard himself whispered on the sound track and interspersed throughout the film a series of phrases that hint at the married woman's thoughts:

> I hesitate. The following morning. He didn't know. In the clouds. Getting undressed. In your place, I wouldn't go. Tuesday afternoon. Very quickly. For several days. In January '64. And besides, it amuses me. It's nerves. Free of that hope. Nothing had changed. One last time. The new apartment. The telephone rings. It was a nice day. Neither to him nor to anyone. What good would it do? We'll go wherever you want. It had stopped raining. We heard nothing. One has to choose. At first, I said nothing.

These apparently haphazard gatherings of apposite phrases were Godard's version of Charlotte's stream of consciousness. It was as if he were sharing with an intimate stranger the self-lacerating confidences of what he had heard, seen, or imagined from his life together with Anna Karina.

Macha Méril noted Godard's unrequited obsession with Karina and recalled that, throughout the shoot of the film, Godard's secretary, Patricia Finaly, played the go-between.

> Godard wrote [Karina] letters every day, and [Finaly] was supposed to bring back letters that Anna had written to him—but she never wrote him a single one. For Godard it was like a bone stuck in his throat. He never understood what had happened, it had come on him from the outside.[14]

The Married Woman puts on fulsome display that "outside," namely, the world of exhortations and incitements to illicit pleasure conjured up by advertising. Godard could only assume that, were Karina authentically free, liberated from the false consciousness of media propaganda, she would discover within herself her authentic nature, her true desire, her natural virtue, and would come back to him.

THE STRIKING NEW aesthetic with which Godard renewed the personal aspect of his art was not lost on the sophisticated viewers in the front lines of advocacy for the film.

The generation that had recently come to the fore at *Cahiers du cinéma* during Rivette's tenure was perched on the leading edge of Parisian cultural and cinematic thought. The cinema and the city's intellectual life were more congruent than ever. By the early 1960s, the auteurist ardor of *Cahiers*'s former Young Turks had been validated by the artistic triumphs of their films (and despite box-office failures): the tastes and habits of the New Wave directors in their youth—extreme moviegoing, a love for classic American cinema, the high-toned discussion of ostensibly popular movies—were now common coin among serious young French people. Much of this had to do, again, with Henri Langlois.

In early 1955, Langlois had been informed that the Cinémathèque would have to leave its small quarters in the avenue de Messine, which was in an isolated residential part of Paris.[15] The new screening room, on the rue d'Ulm, was many times larger than the old one (with approximately 250 seats as opposed to nearly sixty) and was also in the middle of the Latin Quarter, a neighborhood crowded with schools and universities, cafés and nightlife, and, of course, young people.[16] The new space and setting encouraged Langlois to put on increasingly ambitious programs: his Ingmar Bergman retrospective in 1957 revealed the director to the French public, and his invitation to Louise Brooks to present a retrospective of her films in 1958 was, as she said, "the first time I had heard anything about myself in thirty years."[17] Buster Keaton was similarly moved by the twenty-minute ovation he received at the Cinémathèque's 1962 retrospective.[18] In the early 1960s, a ticket for any of the three nightly shows at the Cinémathèque was tough to get.

The burgeoning interest in both classical and aesthetically ambitious cinema opened up yet other new viewing options for the young film lover in Paris. The ciné-club movement, which had thrived after the war, again flourished, with French film clubs reporting over four million tickets sold in 1961. A new category of movie theater, which the government aided under the rubric of *art et essai* (art houses), was growing rapidly, more than tripling, from fifteen to more than fifty, between 1959 and 1962.[19] Godard noted that the art houses in the Latin Quarter were "always full to the rafters."[20]

In early 1962, *France-Observateur*'s critic Bernard Dort waxed sarcastic about the generation of young intellectuals for whom the cinema had become "a religion."[21] A year later, in the same magazine, Robert Benayoun wondered whether the rise of obsessive cinephilia among "students of law, philosophy, or philology" indicated that all were now living "in the *age of the cinema?*"[22]

Of the serious young people who were devoted to the Cinémathèque and its tributaries, the most intellectually adventuresome gravitated to *Cahiers.* Such younger writers as Michel Delahaye, Jean-André Fieschi, Jean-Louis Comolli, and Jean Narboni, who joined the magazine between 1960 and 1962, kept up with the demanding intellectual currents of the day— including the work of Heidegger, Barthes, Lévi-Strauss, Georges Bataille, Maurice Blanchot, Louis Althusser—without sacrificing their love of the cinema to any one theoretical line. When Rivette took over in 1963, he devoted much space to these writers and their advanced preoccupations, which he shared. He published interviews with thinkers and artists not obviously connected with the cinema, such as Barthes, Lévi-Strauss, and the composer Pierre Boulez. The young critics at *Cahiers* employed the new theoretical vocabularies, and Godard quickly picked up on them.

Godard used the language of structuralist philosophy to describe the analytical aspects of *The Married Woman* and their role in the making of the film:

> I have a fragmented and dislocated vision of the world. I wanted to translate only its most important signs. Thus, one can say "I love you" using only four letters. For the feeling, for the form to be felt, to come through, one needs only a minimum of signs. If one lets the meaning take the lead, the form disappears.[23]

Philosophically, Godard had used a structuralist approach for diagnosis in *The Married Woman,* but Sartrean methods—self-consciousness, historical consciousness, an appeal to conscience and the liberty it implies—for the cure. The cinematic terrain on which Godard had been negotiating these debates in recent years was the Italian cinema—the humanistic modernism of Roberto Rossellini versus the analytical modernism of Michelangelo Antonioni. Now, with the film's completion, Godard declared himself forthrightly in Antonioni's camp.

WHEN *THE MARRIED WOMAN* was shown at the Venice festival, on the evening of September 8, 1964, it was well received: "The ironic lines, the humorous scenes were underlined by the applause and laughter of the audience and set off only once by an angry whistle."[24]

Antonioni, whose *Red Desert,* his first color film, was also being shown in competition, came up to Godard after the screening and energetically shook his hand. Following the closing ceremonies, at which Antonioni won first prize, the Golden Lion, and Godard nothing, the triumphant director told the *Cahiers* critic François Weyergans, "Tell Godard that in my opinion he deserved the Silver Lion."[25] Godard, for his part, said that Antonioni fully deserved his award: "I saw that there was a difference in quality that was far from being in my favor."[26] Godard recognized in Antonioni's film something that he himself had wanted to do but couldn't: "When I saw *Red Desert* . . . I said to myself: this is the kind of movie I wanted to make with *Contempt*."[27] The thirty-three-year-old Godard approached Antonioni humbly to congratulate him on his achievement and also proposed to interview him for *Cahiers du cinéma*, a gesture that Antonioni graciously accepted.

Although Godard's film won no prizes, it was immediately praised by French critics. Claude Tarare of *L'Express* apologized in print for his prior fulminations against Godard and declared the new film to be "quite superior to *Breathless*."[28] In *Le Monde*, Jean de Baroncelli, whose admiration for Godard had long been hedged, now applauded unreservedly the personal, essayistic aspect of *The Married Woman:* "It is indeed a documentary. But this documentary is less about conjugal life than about Jean-Luc Godard himself, or more exactly, about the cinema according to Jean-Luc Godard."[29]

In *Cahiers du cinéma*, where *Band of Outsiders* had been received poorly, *The Married Woman* was immediately hailed as a major artistic and intellectual achievement. Jean-Louis Comolli wrote an unusually long and deeply engaged review, confirming the unity of Godard's cinema with his philosophical thought: "The shot takes about as much time to complete itself as the idea to formulate itself. That is to say that thinking and filming are one and the same thing for Godard."[30]

Other young writers at *Cahiers* praised the film even more vigorously when *The Married Woman* went into theatrical release, but that release turned out to be somewhat delayed.

IN SEPTEMBER, THE Commission de Contrôle (the censorship board) met to view *The Married Woman* and to vote on whether to permit its release. Godard had foreseen difficulties with censorship even while making the film, and included in it a classical citation to defend it in advance: Robert tells Charlotte of the theologian Bossuet's charge that "the representation of agreeable passions naturally leads to sin," and cites Molière's response that "the theater purifies love in order to prevent sin."

This defense proved unsuccessful: on September 29, the commission voted, by a count of thirteen to five, with two abstentions, to ban *The Married Woman* outright. The next day, its president, Henry de Segogne, wrote to the minister of information, Alain Peyrefitte, to explain the proposed ban.

- The title, "by the generalization that it implies, appears as a sort of insult to all women who find themselves engaged in that state"—the state of marriage. In other words, the title implied that all married women were adulterous.
- "*The Married Woman* is devoted almost exclusively, in a disguised but clever, and in any case perfectly suggestive, fashion, to the salacious illustration of scenes of sexuality." And it wasn't just a few scenes that the commission would have wanted to suppress, but rather, "it is half the film that would have to be cut."
- Above all, the commission and its president saw *The Married Woman* as a crucial test case and wanted to make use of it to set a clear example for the entire French film industry: "We must, I believe, draw the line."

De Segogne also told Peyrefitte that one member of the board was furious that the film had already appeared at Venice, thus giving it "publicity of a worldwide character." The commission's reasoning, so carefully detailed in the letter to Peyrefitte, was not made public. Instead, de Segogne simply announced the board's recommendation that the film be banned on the grounds of "images contrary to good morals." The ultimate decision, however, lay with Peyrefitte, who at the time was on a mission to New Caledonia. When he returned in early October, he watched the film and, keeping his opinions to himself, agreed to meet with Godard.

Thus began two months of debate, negotiation, and precisely the sort of scandal that the commission members feared. *France-Observateur* immediately made the proposed censorship a cause célèbre, publishing a fierce article by Michel Cournot in high praise of the film ("This film is materially formed of ideas, and, more than of cinema, one must think of Plato directly 'visualized' ").

> Perhaps never have the annoying and ultimately somewhat useless complications of adultery been shown so clearly. Never has adultery been so fittingly condemned. But Godard condemns it in beauty. The censors, for whom adultery signifies ugliness, do not see further, and they condemn beauty.[31]

The magazine accompanied Cournot's diatribe with an interview in which Godard compared the film's censorship with the shrugging tolerance of blatantly "erotic" films shown in "specialized" theaters, and contended that the political import of the film was the real problem: "The people of the commission have sensed that my film attacks a certain mode of life, that of air conditioning, of the prefabricated, of advertising." At the same time, he declared himself open to negotiation: "If you ask to cut the feet off of Rodin's

The Kiss, fine, it may be possible. If you ask to cut off the mouth, he'll say: It's not possible."[32]

On the afternoon of Tuesday, October 13, Godard met with Peyrefitte, who proposed several changes. First, the title would have to be changed. (Godard made a modest proposal: "We could call it, for example, 'No Admission Under 18 Years of Age.'")[33] Second, the minister proposed "cutting three minutes of the picture and several changes in the dialogue, notably the suppression of an allusion to concentration-camp inmates."[34] Godard told a journalist, "I have a month to think about it and to propose cuts and changes. Then, the new version will be shown again to the commission, which will deliberate."[35]

Godard indeed made what he considered "no great changes,"[36] and did so with an ironic good cheer. He refused to remove the references to concentration-camp inmates but did excise a short documentary interlude by Jacques Rozier about the "monokini," or topless bathing suit for women, a shot of Charlotte's panties falling to her feet, a shot of a bidet,[37] and the sound of a pair of scissors which Charlotte brought below her waistline (and below the line of the film frame) to trim her pubic hair.[38] He also changed the title of the film from *La Femme mariée* (The Married Woman) to *Une Femme mariée* (*A Married Woman*), which prompted one Swiss critic to wonder whether the French censors might next seek to change Molière's titles to "A Misanthrope" and "A Miser."[39]

On November 30, 1964, Peyrefitte wrote to Godard's company, Anouchka Films, to announce that at the plenary session of the Commission de Contrôle of November 24, the film, thus modified, had been granted a visa but would be forbidden to viewers under eighteen years of age.

THE FILM WAS released on December 5, to the energetically favorable critical response that could have been foretold from the advance word from Venice. Not only was the film itself praised, and not only did it do well—the next year, Godard told Helen Scott of the French Film Office in New York that the only films of his to have made money were *Breathless, Vivre sa vie*, and *A Married Woman*[40]—but Godard himself was now recognized and extolled as a representative of the highest intellectual and cultural values. Georges Sadoul of *Les Lettres françaises* praised the film lavishly and declared Godard to be both a great artist and a crucial thinker of the age:

> This *Married Woman* has become *Madame Bovary*, an object of scandal for expressing too directly the reality of its times . . . it is even more by his ideas than by his rhetoric that Godard belongs, profoundly and consciously, to our times. Yesterday, he asked himself questions. Today, he answers them.[41]

The acclaim grew rapidly and took diverse forms, as Godard's public appearances proliferated in the press and on television. He was already a recognized filmmaker and a celebrity; now he became an artistic phenomenon. In October, he was interviewed on film for a thirty-minute television program, *Jean-Luc Godard ou le cinéma au défi* (Jean-Luc Godard or the Cinema Put to the Test). The title was derived from a 1930 essay by Louis Aragon, "La Peinture au défi" (Painting Put to the Test), and the program began with Aragon speaking in praise of Godard. In January 1965, Godard was interviewed on French television by Jacques Doniol-Valcroze. Although the discussion with his elder friend and *Cahiers* colleague turned lofty, with long exegeses of Sartre and Bonnard, Godard also repeated for the studio cameras the trick that he had performed in Capri to get Bardot to change her hairdo: he walked on his hands.

In November 1964, *Les Lettres françaises* published an extraordinarily long and politically provocative interview of Godard with Gérard Guégan and Michel Pétris, a pair of young Marxist cinephiles.[42] Godard, who had long been attacked by the orthodox left, had nonetheless considered himself to be on the left, or rather, considered that the left should be defined by alignment with himself and his own progressive aesthetic. He once again denounced leftists who presumed to impose a narrow range of subjects on their political allies:

> One has the impression that people on the left always do things to clear their names. But one is free to do it or not to do it. I mean, it's not up to me to make a film about the longshoremen's strike in Nantes, because, really, I don't know anything about it, and I would do it badly. I can help some people to make it. There are certainly some people who should do it, and who would do it better than I would. But I can only make a mess of it.[43]

Guégan, Pétris, and their film-loving friends on the left were aware of the company that Godard kept—as Guégan later explained, "He was with Coutard, who had served in Indochina, which for us was the worst thing in the world, and with Gégauff, who had been in the SS and went around talking about it"[44]—but it didn't keep them from a higher appreciation of Godard's importance:

> For us it was as much a question of aesthetics as politics. For us it was modernity, it was people who to us seemed to be American. Our idea of a hero in the cinema was Farley Granger in *Johnny Guitar*. The actors [Godard] chose had the same style as the American actors we loved. He made us think irresistibly of American youth, the audacity, the vivacity.[45]

Indeed, young leftists in film circles may have taken vehement exception to American politics and the American film industry, but they continued to endorse with equal vehemence the styles, myths, and artists of the classical Hollywood cinema: in 1964, the young and leftist *Cahiers* critics championed such films as Raoul Walsh's *A Distant Trumpet,* John Ford's *Cheyenne Autumn,* and Howard Hawks's *Man's Favorite Sport?*

Guégan and Pétris were impressed not only with Godard's cinematic aesthetic but with his personal aesthetic as well, with the palpable fusion of the man—or his persona—with his work. "When we met him," Guégan recalled, "it was a shock: his sarcasm, his openness, his humor. He was someone who carried himself the way it seemed to us that an artist should carry himself, with a moral and physical elegance, with his yellow Boyard corn cigarette and his raincoat."[46] If Godard found a home on the left, it was because the left had changed: it had become a matter of form and style, of tone and mood, instead of simply an ideology, and had, as such, redefined its criteria and realigned its spectrum to include him—even realigned itself to accord with him. A new generation adopted him as its own. But in the 1960s, generations succeeded each other with a dizzying rapidity, and the new aesthetic left of 1964 would soon look as old-fashioned as the pro-Soviet apologists of the Communist Party and, as such, would give Godard another new worldview to film, to account for—and, so as not to be left behind, to adopt.

THE DATE OF the appearance of the interview of Godard by Guégan and Pétris, November 19, 1964, was a red-letter day in French journalism: it was the date of the first appearance of the transformed *France-Observateur,* now called *Le Nouvel Observateur.*

L'Express, which had been the intellectual magazine of choice in the early 1960s, had recently been transformed, under the tutelage of its founder, Jean-Jacques Servan-Schreiber, into a newsweekly that he openly modeled on *Time* magazine, with a sleek, crisp, rectilinear style of graphics, color photographs, and a reduced intellectual substance. Many of its best writers had no place in the strict new formula, which was unveiled in September 1964, and a void was created in the French press.

Jean Daniel, formerly a journalist with *L'Express,* sought to fill that void. He was tapped to transform *France-Observateur,* as he recalled, "in the style of 'New Journalism,' adapted to the doubtlessly growing demands of an increasingly educated public"[47]—a public that he understood to be that of the French "New Left,"[48] the upwardly mobile and aesthetically conscious left, a cultural left that was not of the working class but of the university and professional class, and that had the avant-garde artistic tastes that went along with it. Daniel built an imposingly literary magazine with progressive tastes in art, music, theater, literature—and inherited a movie section divided between two critics and their opposed views, the *Positif*-ist doctrinaire leftism of Robert Benayoun and the *Cahiers*-ist enthusiasms (and dazzling literary voice) of Michel Cournot. Benayoun had never seen fit to repent of his viciously ad hominem attacks against Godard; Cournot had led the charge in defense of *The Married Woman*. Daniel decided in favor of Godard and let Benayoun go.[49]

Le Nouvel Observateur rapidly became something of a house organ for Godard himself. The week of the release of *A Married Woman*, the magazine published both a highly literary celebration of the film by Michel Cournot in the form of an imagined interior monologue from Charlotte's point of view ("The bed is a white beach smoothed out by the sea, a stretch of earth that is soft on the knees . . ."), and also a two-page spread devoted to the film that Godard would soon start shooting, *Alphaville*.

AT THE SAME TIME, *Cahiers du cinéma* had also, for the second time in eighteen months, entered a new era, this one even more conspicuously new than that of Rivette's stewardship. Unlike Rohmer, who was a careful and frugal administrator, Rivette was a madly ambitious editor who would not let the reality of practical obstacles stand in the way of his projects. His double issue of December 1963 and January 1964 devoted to the American cinema was over 250 pages long and extraordinarily expensive to produce. By 1964, the magazine was in serious financial difficulty, and it needed outside help in order to stay afloat.

Daniel Filipacchi, the publisher of the popular teen magazine *Salut les copains* (Hi, Buddies),[50] was persuaded to buy a majority share of *Cahiers* in June 1964. He brought members of his own team onto the *Cahiers* editorial board and brought *Cahiers* into the visually splashy mode of modern publishing by way of a thorough redesign. The first issue of the newly formatted *Cahiers* appeared in November 1964. It was larger, more generous with photographs; the classic yellow logo was replaced by a streamlined yet freefloating pattern of title over picture; it featured a lively visual jazz of sans serif typefaces and an increased interplay and overlap of word and image. The layout was bold and full of contrast, with large blank spaces competing with dramatic two-page spreads.

The personnel and the thought behind *Cahiers* had recently been rejuvenated. Now the magazine was openly attuned to the energies of youth. As such, it too became a regular home in print for Godard. The inaugural issue of the new format featured Godard's interview of Antonioni. Godard participated in the January 1965 dossier on the economics of the French cinema. *A Married Woman* was reviewed twice in February 1965, and, after Rivette left the magazine in May 1965 and was replaced as editor by Jean-Louis Comolli, Godard's presence at the journal grew even stronger and more frequent: he granted a series of extraordinarily long interviews, he himself interviewed Robert Bresson, and he contributed a sort of "diary" as well as other occasional and incidental pieces to the magazine.

The two rhapsodic critiques of *A Married Woman* that *Cahiers du cinéma* published in February 1965 were distinctly different in tone and import. The first, by the art historian Michel Thévoz, industriously traced connections between Godard's work and trends in modern art, including Paul Klee, Pop Art, Rauschenberg, Picasso, and Dubuffet. The second, by Gérard Guégan, pointed far ahead to fault lines that would fracture the French New Left almost as soon as it got its footing: "On page 204 of Volume XXXVIII of his 'Works' (Russian edition), Lenin writes: 'Human consciousness does not only reflect the objective world, but creates it.' " Guégan, who called himself "a Marxist but not of the Party,"[51] picked up on Godard's conjoined aesthetic and social critique but also attempted to assimilate it into his own political doctrine.

This inner division of the left, the refabrication of a new Marxism in the rubble of an older one, had been present from the start. During his inaugural meeting with Jean Daniel regarding the refashioning of *France-Observateur,* Sartre told the incoming editor, "In general, you're on the left. Which is to say, that you place yourself in the interior of Marxism."[52] Daniel thought exactly the opposite and had set himself precisely the problem of "how to reconstruct the left (which at the time had vanished) without (and against) Marxism."[53] He sensed that Sartre's remark boded ill for the nondoctrinaire political movement that the magazine was intended to promote and to represent. And, although Godard was no Marxist, he too confronted the same aesthetic and political conflicts that Daniel was struggling to resolve.

SARTRE, WHO WAS ALREADY FAMOUS, had become all the more so since the publication, in March 1964, of his autobiographical book *Les Mots* (*Words,* or *The Words*).[54] The short memoir was rapidly acknowledged to be a literary masterpiece and was an instant bestseller. Sartre's newfound prominence on the French scene was further amplified when, in October 1964, he won and refused the Nobel Prize for Literature. And yet, as great as was his prestige and his fame, his philosophical influence among young people was seriously waning. Sartre was something of an anathema to the new philosophical generation. It was, after all, Roland Barthes who had provided the most serious modern theoretical opposition to Sartre's notion of engaged literature (in *Writing Degree Zero*), arguing that literary form took precedence over the explicit content of a book in defining its engagement with history. Similarly, Claude Lévi-Strauss concluded *La Pensée sauvage* (*The Savage Mind*), from 1962, with a chapterlong diatribe against Sartre, charging that Sartre, with his emphasis on conscience, was "a captive of his Cogito" (Descartes's assertion "I think, therefore I am") and that "in Sartre's system, history plays exactly the role of a myth."[55] For the younger generation of intellectuals, the ones who were immersed in structuralism and linguistic theory, Sartre was intellectually passé.

This was not so, however, for Godard, who, in the spate of interviews that he gave in the wake of *A Married Woman,* offered even more, even lengthier, references to Sartre than he had done before. Godard began his 1965 television discussion with Jacques Doniol-Valcroze by defining his entire filmmaking career, in particular his rapid and voluminous work, in terms of Sartre's 1957 essay on Tintoretto, "The Captive of Venice." In his interview with Guégan and Pétris in *Les Lettres françaises,* in November 1964, he cited Sartre as the prime reference and role model for his own efforts to unify his life and his work.

> What an artist creates is inseparable from his life, from life in general. What makes the difference between Sartre and [author André] Maurois isn't so much that one of them writes better or worse French, or things like that. It's that one of them doesn't separate life from literature, and the other one does.[56]

As early as 1962, Godard had told interviewers from *Cahiers du cinéma,* "Shooting and not shooting, for me, are not two different lives. Filming should be a part of life and it should be a natural and normal thing."[57] The theme of the inseparability of life and art had been Godard's since the time he began to think about the cinema, and had been an essential idea of his practice of cinema, from *Breathless* onward. Now, however, in 1964, Godard suddenly sought to weigh the two against each other. This is exactly what Sartre had done in his sole, signal interview regarding *Words:* "What I was missing was the sense of reality. I have changed since then. I have had a slow apprenticeship in the real."[58] For Godard, as for Sartre, the comparison was, for the most part, unfavorable to art. In late 1964, Godard said:

> I knew nothing of life, and it's the cinema that made me discover life . . . with people, men, women, houses, cars, work, workers. I discovered it as if I were in Plato's cave and then there was a little window in it and a film being projected. So one day I said: "Look, there is life; so I'm going to do cinema too in order to discover life." Now, I have the impression of having passed to the other side of the window, and to be looking and filming behind the screen. At

the time of *Breathless,* I had the sense, basically, of being in front of the screen, and now I have the sense of being behind it, of seeing life more head-on.[59]

ART, HOWEVER, has structure and form; life by its nature is formless, or at least, its forms are hidden from the eye and revealed only through research and thought—precisely the sort of quasi-scientific abstractions that Godard had applied to cultural effluvia and managed to bring to the screen in *A Married Woman.* The result, however, was the one that Godard announced in the film's credits: fragmentation. Godard explained to Guégan and Pétris that he had "abandoned [his] cinéphile habit"; he had left behind the model of the American cinema, which he now looked upon as an object of nostalgia. With no particular cinematic example or tradition to follow, Godard's films would lack a structuring principle. Both he and life were on the other side of the screen; but where was the cinema?

AT THE APOGEE of Godard's public renown, at the moment of his triumph as a cultural hero to the young and a new classic to his elders, he was increasingly lost as a filmmaker. He continued to make brilliant, personal films, even epochal films, and he did so at a furious pace that left his acolytes breathless. And yet, he would work with an increasing despair. Precisely as Godard's engagement with "life"—political, social, intellectual—and with the new complexities and incipient crises of the times was intensifying, he was in doubt regarding the cinematic form with which to represent it. As his films became ever more permeable with regard to the explosive tensions and wild energies of the day, they also became increasingly formless. The summit of Godard's fame and of his esteem as an artist and a cultural touchstone of the age was also the moment of his cinematic breakdown, which he displayed on-screen in real time.

Godard and Richard Roud at the first New York Film Festival, 1963
(Film Society of Lincoln Center)

ten

THE AMERICAN BUSINESS

A S EARLY AS JUNE 1960, THE LITHUANIAN-BORN FILM-
maker Jonas Mekas, who was also the lead film critic for the
New York *Village Voice*, wrote in *Cahiers du cinéma* that the
New Wave was a strong influence on American directors. He cited as evidence the work of several independent filmmakers, including John Cassavetes. Mekas claimed that the French New Wave had taught young
Americans to break taboos regarding so-called production values (i.e., the
industrial sheen of the commercial cinema) and to tell stories of their own
experience without regard to the conventions that marked the films of their
elders. The "first-person" cinema that Truffaut had called for in 1957 had
made rapid advances: in 1962, *Cahiers* critic Luc Moullet mentioned "German, English, Italian, American, Argentinian, Japanese, Russian, Polish, and
even Spanish New Waves";[1] to which he might soon have added the Czechs
and Brazilians.

But the New Wave's most powerful effect came when its American
acolytes assimilated the movement's underlying critical position and sought
a cinematic education similar to the immersion the New Wave filmmakers
had undergone. The New Wave was not just a personal cinema of youth; it
involved extensive reference to the history of cinema, and its resounding
worldwide influence entailed a reorientation of taste. In the United States,
this only happened when the *politique des auteurs* crossed the ocean,
prompting American intellectuals to embrace the heritage of the Hollywood
cinema.[2]

At first, the New Wave's admiration for seemingly routine thrillers, melodramas, comedies, and westerns by American directors—including Hitchcock,

Hawks, Nicholas Ray, Douglas Sirk, Anthony Mann, and Otto Preminger—
baffled most intellectuals, critics, and even industry professionals in the
United States, who considered these films merely popular commercial enter-
tainments. But a few energetic film programmers relying on the advice of a
few good critics, as well as by the farsighted support of a few large cultural
institutions, spurred a change in attitude. Primarily, the shift took hold
among young intellectuals and artists, largely through the work of one tire-
less proselytizer, Peter Bogdanovich, and the writing of one critic, Andrew
Sarris.

Bogdanovich, a young actor and precocious film buff (born in 1940),
had two pulpits from which to preach: he helped Daniel Talbot, the pro-
grammer at the New Yorker Theatre, organize revivals of classic American
films. At age twenty, he also had a radio show called *The Film Scene.* In 1960
the Museum of Modern Art asked Bogdanovich to organize an Orson Welles
retrospective for the following year. Then, under the personal influence of
Sarris as well as Eugene Archer of the *New York Times,* he programmed for
Talbot two series of "Forgotten Films"—forgotten because they had been
critical failures—which included such now-canonical classics as Hawks's
Bringing Up Baby and *Rio Bravo,* Hitchcock's *The Wrong Man,* Max Ophüls's
Letter from an Unknown Woman, and Ray's *Johnny Guitar.* These series were
great successes and brought Bogdanovich commissions from the Museum of
Modern Art to organize a six-month Hawks retrospective in 1962 and a similarly comprehensive Hitchcock retrospective in 1963; both were widely heralded and well attended.

New York audiences, which had embraced the first films of the French
New Wave, now began to turn their attention to the movies that had inspired them. But just as the postwar Parisian taste for popular American
films had been galvanized into a polemical line by the young *Cahiers* critics, New York's newfound enthusiasm for the classic American cinema
found its clarification and defense in the critical discernment and audacity
of Andrew Sarris.

Born in 1929, Sarris was a film critic alongside Mekas at the *Village
Voice* when, having familiarized himself from afar with the writings and
films of the *Cahiers* group, he went to Paris in 1961. There he met New Wave
directors and saw their films. He recognized the merits of the *Cahiers* agitations on behalf of American directors who had been so overlooked or dismissed at home. He was also present for the release of the surprising New
Wave works that were inspired by them, such as *Shoot the Piano Player* and
A Woman Is a Woman. As Sarris later described the experience, "I began
seeing a lot of American movies through French eyes . . . To show you the
dividing line in my thinking, when I did a Top Ten list for the *Voice* in 1958,

I had a Stanley Kramer film on the list and I left off both *Vertigo* and *Touch of Evil*."[3]

When Sarris returned to the United States, he brought to his American readership the enthusiasms he had cultivated in Paris. He wrote "a very *Cahiers du cinéma* review of *Psycho*," which received "a tremendous amount of hostile mail. The *Voice* had all these readers—little old ladies who lived on the West Side, guys who had fought in the Spanish Civil War—and this seemed so regressive to them, to say that Hitchcock was a great artist."[4] He decided to write an essay to introduce and defend the *politique des auteurs*. This in itself was a bold move. François Truffaut himself had never written the theoretical exposition of the *politique des auteurs* that he had promised *Cahiers* throughout the mid-1950s. Sarris's effort was even more daring: to satisfy himself that his essay was intellectually honest, he conceived and wrote it as a response to the antiauteurist essays of the *politique*'s most profound detractor and the man he considered the greatest film critic of all time, André Bazin.

The "little magazine" *Film Culture,* published and edited by Jonas Mekas, included Sarris's "Notes on the Auteur Theory in 1962" in its Winter 1962–63 issue.[5] In it, Sarris rightly admitted that his essay was "less a manifesto than a credo." He recognized that the underlying premise to what he called the "theory" ("auteur theory" being his own translation of the *politique des auteurs*) was one of taste: "These propositions remain to be proven and, I hope, debated. The proof will be difficult because direction in the cinema is a nebulous force in literary terms."

Sarris was offering an overview of the *politique* rather than an analysis of the films which inspired him to endorse it, and his essay is less a work of criticism than a prologue to future criticism. In his essay, he asserts the practical import of the *politique* for working critics: "Just a few years ago, I would have thought it unthinkable to speak in the same breath of a 'commercial' director like Hitchcock and a 'pure' director like Bresson." He continues:

> After years of tortured revaluation, I am now prepared to stake my critical reputation, such as it is, on the proposition that Alfred Hitchcock is artistically superior to Robert Bresson by every criterion of excellence, and, further, that, film for film, director for director, the American cinema has been consistently superior to that of the rest of the world from 1915 through 1962. Consequently, I now regard the auteur theory primarily as a critical device for recording the history of the American cinema, the only cinema in the world worth exploring in depth beneath the frosting of a few great directors at the top.

For Sarris, the auteur theory served the same purpose that it served his French counterparts: to fight for the recognition of the great Hollywood directors working within the structures (or strictures) of the studio system as the equals of the greatest directors working anywhere; and for the recognition of the cinema's artists as the equals of artists working in the traditional art forms. He offered three premises on which the theory rested:

- It is not a cult of personality, but a synoptic view of existing work—a guide to film history rather than a cheat sheet for judging new works in advance: "What is a bad director, but a director who has made many bad films?"
- It asserts "the distinguishable personality of the director as a criterion of value"—here Sarris argued for applying critical intelligence to Hollywood fare in order to discover the personal signature of filmmakers who were generally thought not to have one.
- It "is concerned with interior meaning, the ultimate glory of the cinema as an art. Interior meaning is extrapolated from the tension between a director's personality and his material." Sarris explains his quasi-mystical concept as "not quite the vision of the world a director projects nor quite his attitude toward life. It is ambiguous, in any literary sense, because part of it is imbedded in the stuff of the cinema and cannot be rendered in noncinematic terms." He attempts to capture this artistic essence with an uncharacteristically flamboyant aphorism: "Dare I come out and say what I think it to be is an élan of the soul?"

Here, Sarris's view echoed that of the French New Wave critics: he did not merely assert the equality of cinema to other arts, but suggested that there was something about cinema that distinguished it from the other arts. For Godard it was montage, for Rohmer it was the art of space; for Rivette it was "mise-en-scène." Overall, the *Cahiers* group—and especially Godard, who had made so much of the quasi-mystical thrall that the cinema induces ("at the cinema, we do not think, we are thought")—had not merely praised certain unrecognized directors, they had exalted the cinema as the preeminent modernist art form.

Sarris was caught in a difficult trap: although he could transfer Hitchcocko-Hawksian taste to the United States and and get his compatriots to see American movies through "French eyes," he could not reproduce the context in which those visions were expressed. First, Sarris did not write with the polemical aggression of the *Cahiers* critics, who commanded attention through their vehement attacks on the mainstream French cinema. Second, where the *Cahiers* critics were preparing the terrain for their own art, Sarris asserted the theory as a historical program, as a school for critics. Although he endured as much public opprobrium for his ideas as had the French pioneers, Sarris could not promise, as those critics did, to deliver the films that would confirm them.[6]

While André Bazin's objections to auteurism were tempered by his personal respect for the young critics at *Cahiers,* Sarris's detractors had no such inhibitions. The most talented and least temperate of them was Pauline Kael. In the early 1960s, Kael (who was born in 1919), lived in California. She wrote for a wide range of publications, from the popular (*Mademoiselle* and *Holiday*) to the serious (*The Atlantic Monthly*), and also did radio broadcasts. She responded to Sarris, in the spring 1963 issue of *Film Quarterly,* with a diatribe, "Circles and Squares" (referring to his incidental notion of three "circles" of directorial achievement), in which she argued with sarcastic condescension that the auteur theory was "a mystique, and a mistake."

Kael considered the auteurist critics' emphasis on visual style over subject to be a deliberate search for petty or recondite touches in avoidance of a responsible consideration of a film's overall artistic merit: "It's understandable that they're trying to find movie art in the loopholes of commercial production—it's a harmless hobby and we all play it now and then. What's incomprehensible is that they *prefer* their loopholes to unified film expression."

She blamed the auteur critics for their drive "to exalt products over works that attempt to express human experience," and she was sure that she knew the difference. Thus she condemned the auteurists' praise of films noirs (such as those of Samuel Fuller, Robert Aldrich, Otto Preminger, and Nicholas Ray) as anti-intellectual nihilism:

> These critics work embarrassingly hard trying to give some semblance of intellectual respectability to a preoccupation with mindless, repetitious commercial products—the kind of action movies that the restless, rootless men who wander on Forty-second Street and in the Tenderloin of all our big cities have always preferred just because they could respond to them without thought. These movies soak up your time. I would suggest that they don't serve a very different function for Sarris or Bogdanovich or the young men of *Movie*[7]—even though they devise elaborate theories to justify soaking up their time.

She complained that most of the auteurist critics, who were male, were a bunch of gentle intellectuals looking to pose as tough guys by absorbing and praising cinematic violence and as pocket nihilists by gagging their intellects with cinematic drivel. In so doing, she argued, they were betraying not only their adult responsibilities but also the significance of the French criticism that inspired them:

> The French *auteur* critics . . . adored the American gangsters, and the vitality, the strength, of our action pictures . . . Where the French went off was in finding elaborate intellectual and psychological meanings in these simple action films . . .
>
> Can we conclude that, in England and the United States, the auteur theory is an attempt by adult males to justify staying inside the small range of experience of their boyhood and adolescence—that period when masculinity looked so great and important but art was something talked about by poseurs and phonies and sensitive-feminine types? And is it perhaps also their way of making a comment on our civilization by the suggestion that trash is the true art form? I ask; I do not know.

Kael ignored the fact that the French Hitchcocko-Hawksians lavished praise on the films of Murnau, Eisenstein, Bresson, Ophüls, Rossellini, Renoir, Mizoguchi, Bergman, and other international directors working away from Hollywood and its traditions, as well as such American directors as Douglas Sirk, Stanley Donen, Frank Tashlin, and Vincente Minnelli, whose work had little to do with violent fantasies of cowboys or gangsters. (Sarris too, in his personal "pantheon" of twenty directors, featured many from the same international group, and only a handful from Hollywood.)

More important, Kael entered the movie theater, and the critical arena, with a pile of unacknowledged prejudices, which showed themselves in the vocabulary of her stern reprimands. She blamed the auteurists for their "fanaticism in a ludicrous cause" and set against it her own moderation:

> I believe that we respond most and best to work in any art form (and to other experience as well) if we are pluralistic, flexible, relative in our judgments, if we are eclectic. But this does not mean a scrambling and confusion of systems. Eclecticism is not the same as lack of scruple; eclecticism is the selection of the best standards and principles from various systems of ideas. It requires more care, more orderliness to be a pluralist than to apply a single theory.

Kael selected the "best" standards and principles on the basis of a prior standard, principle, or theory, this one hidden offstage, whether cleverly or naively. For all of her empiricism and eclecticism, Kael wrote under the unacknowledged weight of an unshakable set of fixed categories: she was sure that she knew art from trash, adolescence from adulthood, simplicity from complexity, dogma from experience, the masculine from the feminine, the immutable laws of genre. She believed that films could be judged insignificant because she so judged the "restless, rootless men" who, she presumed, favor them. When she praised American films, it was as invigorating "kitsch" which she took care not to mistake for art. Because she was certain that she knew "trash" when she saw it, she could not see through the Hollywood conventions to recognize the artistry of artists. Her lines of thought were more rigid, more exclusive, more arbitrary, more dogmatic than Sarris's—and yet, they were less subject to debate because they lurked invisibly under the guise of her presumed eclecticism and empiricism. The fixed categories of Kael's thought made her prolific, decisive, and recognizable.

In the process, Kael flattered her readers: in considering a film as "experience," she insured that the viewer's own preoccupations and pleasures remained at its center. Thus, whatever a film's significance as art or information, its principal purpose was to provide a favorable experience—to entertain. Kael offered the literary apotheosis of this view. Her supreme virtue as a critic was her ability to write persuasively of her own experience at the movies as it related to her experience of life in general. Kael was largely a first-person essayist who made use of movies to write brilliantly of the times and of herself; she was, in effect, a New Journalist in disguise. Her performance was essentially literary, and its cinematic import was often enough incidental; if she resisted auteurism in the cinema, it was in order to practice her own flamboyant authorship as a critic. Indeed, throughout her career, she wrote brilliantly about all aspects of the cinema—from the acting and the set design to studio politics and social trends—except the art of the director.

Moreover, Kael came up with a critical doctrine that went far beyond her claims to eclectic empiricism and justified her self-centered approach to film with a stark metaphor: "If a lady says, 'That man don't pleasure me,' that's it. There are some areas in which we can still decide for ourselves."[8] In a pleasure-seeking era, she wrote to justify her own search for pleasure, and to justify the reader who sought the same; thus, except to the extent that Kael was the Tom Wolfe of film criticism, she was its Helen Gurley Brown, liberating the partisans of traditional taste without liberating them from it.

KAEL ENERGETICALLY PRAISED some of Godard's early films and ultimately recognized his singular importance. However, in the early and mid-1960s, when Godard's works were still seeking a foothold in the United States, she praised most highly those films of his that were modeled on "mindless, repetitious" American action films: *Breathless* and *Band of Outsiders*. In her 1964 essay "Zeitgeist and Poltergeist," she relegated *Vivre sa vie* to the category of "art-house films," dismissed it as "confusing," and scoffed at any "existentialist point" that she might be missing in its ending.[9] She scoffed even more vehemently at Bresson and at what she called the "left-wing formalism" of Resnais and Antonioni. She did not like "*The Married Woman*" [*sic*], asserting that there Godard "seems to settle for arbitrary effects," and later stated that she simply "would not recommend" it.[10]

In 1968, Kael was hired as film critic for *The New Yorker;* she attributed her hiring to her writings about Godard. Her articles in praise of some of Godard's films, she said, caught the attention of William Shawn, the editor of *The New Yorker,* who, she said, "realized that there was something to Godard. And I had been writing very lovingly about Godard."[11] She had indeed been writing lovingly about his films, albeit intermittently and belatedly, starting in 1966, and her run of enthusiasm would be short-lived.

Paradoxically, it was Kael who, in blinding herself to the work of some of Hollywood's real artists, such as Howard Hawks, Nicholas Ray, and Otto Preminger, found herself backed into defending the mere competence of industrial skill against the heroic virtues of art. In the long run, Kael became an ever more staunch defender of ever more banal Hollywood movies, like *Fiddler on the Roof* or *Yentl*. Sarris, far from being the adolescent nihilist of Kael's surmise, came off as the true classicist, swaying the visionary subjectivity of the downtown film scene toward an appreciation of the highly organized art of a Hitchcock or a Hawks.

THE LINCOLN CENTER for the Performing Arts opened on the West Side of Manhattan in September 1962. In 1963, its leaders, recognizing the ferment in the world of cinema, established the New York Film Festival for the purpose of showing masterpieces of contemporary cinema from around the world which had not yet been seen in New York. Amos Vogel of the New York ciné-club Cinema 16 was asked to organize the festival. Richard Roud, an American who had been programming the London Film Festival since 1957, was invited to program it. The festival was to be relatively small and would offer no prizes. It was intended to be a "festival of festivals," not necessarily the place where films would premiere, but rather a selection of the putative best in a given year.

Roud was a Francophile who had come to know Henri Langlois during the late 1950s while working for the British Film Institute. He was keenly aware of the New Wave's importance in sparking enthusiasm for the cinema in New York and the rest of the world. Nonetheless, the first festival, which took place from September 10 to 19, 1963, did not feature a particularly strong dose of the New Wave. It did include such important films as Bresson's *The Trial of Joan of Arc*, Resnais's *Muriel*, Chris Marker's *Le Joli mai*, Luis Buñuel's *The Exterminating Angel*, and Ermanno Olmi's *The Fiancés*. The only film of Godard's to be shown was *Le Nouveau Monde*, included in *RoGoPaG*, and it was booed. The festival as a whole, however, was a great success: most of the films were well received, and the audiences were large, unusually young, and hip—especially striking for an uptown venue like Lincoln Center.

By the time of the second festival, in September 1964, the debate over auteurism dominated the cinematic discussion, and even if Sarris lost the rhetorical battles—his earnestly modest style could not stand up to Kael's belletristic vigor, and he resisted any temptation to respond in kind to Kael's ad hominem attacks—he won the youth of the city. The new critical discourse left its mark on the festival's program, which featured *A Woman Is a Woman* and *Band of Outsiders* (along with Buñuel's *Diary of a Chambermaid* and his 1930 *L'Age d'or*, Kenji Mizoguchi's 1955 *The Taira Clan,* and Bernardo Bertolucci's second feature, *Before the Revolution*). If the selection was somewhat more conservative overall, it was also more inclusive of the American cinema, featuring a pair of Hollywood films (Robert Rossen's *Lilith*, starring Jean Seberg, and Sidney Lumet's *Fail-Safe*) alongside the independent films *The Brig*, directed by Jonas and Adolphus Mekas, and *Nothing But a Man*, by Michael Roemer.

Both *A Woman Is a Woman* and *Band of Outsiders* were acclaimed when they were shown at Philharmonic Hall (today, Avery Fisher Hall) on September 25, 1964. Godard came to New York to present the films at a press screening (and then went to watch a double feature of westerns).[12] They were extremely well received by Andrew Sarris at the *Village Voice* and by Eugene Archer in the *New York Times*. Before the New York Film Festival, only two films by Godard had been shown in the United States (*Breathless*, in 1961, and *Vivre sa vie*, in 1963); from November 1964 to October 1965, four films by Godard (*A Woman Is a Woman, Contempt, A Married Woman,* and *Alphaville*) had their American releases. Susan Sontag's ecstatic essay "On Godard's *Vivre sa vie*" had been published in 1964 in a little magazine called *Moviegoer*:[13] Godard was taking his place in America's intellectual firmament.

As in France, *A Married Woman* received a particularly positive critical appreciation befitting its originality and complexity, with Stanley Kauffmann of the *New Republic* lauding it as the director's "best picture to be seen here since *Breathless*" and praising Godard for having "used his armory of experiment, trick, imaginative innovation for a perceptible and communicated purpose."[14] Brendan Gill, in *The New Yorker,* called it simply "the best of the Godard pictures" that he had seen. "In the past, his intrusions often proved a nuisance; here they become a welcome part of the whole."[15]

But Godard's trip to New York in September 1964, where his bark was being lifted by the rising auteurist tide, was not merely promotional; he had business to pursue.

SEVERAL WEEKS EARLIER, while at the Venice festival to present *A Married Woman,* Godard had read a script that François Truffaut had given him. It had been written by two young American journalists at *Esquire* magazine, Robert Benton and David Newman, and was called *Bonnie and Clyde.* The story concerned the Barrow gang and its two leaders, Clyde Barrow and Bonnie Parker, criminals who had rampaged through the South in the 1930s. Newman later recalled: "Back in the sixties, when we wrote *Bonnie and Clyde,* there was something going on about cinema—a word you never hear anymore in the States—that was almost like a religion. Not just for me but all my friends, everyone I knew."[16] Benton had been a lifelong lover of movies but considered that his view had been forever changed by the first New Wave films to be shown in New York: "There were other great directors, like Bergman and Antonioni, but the French New Wave was something different, it spoke to us differently"—precisely because its films recapitulated the genres and forms of the American cinema. Although Benton and Newman had known American movies, they had not, so to speak, known the American cinema, at least not as the French New Wave understood it. For this, Benton said, they had Andrew Sarris to thank:

> The only serious critic we had was Sarris. There was Pauline [Kael], there was [Vincent] Canby in *Variety* who took films seriously, there were others, but not with that kind of vision that went beyond individual films. Sarris brought about a shift in the point of view of what work was.[17]

The practical side of their cinematic reeducation was provided by Peter Bogdanovich, who was also a contributor to *Esquire.* As Robert Benton said, "Bogdanovich was in the process of doing his monograph on Hitchcock, so he'd call us, and say, '3:00 PM, *Rope.*' We'd see the film, and then we went back and worked on the script"[18] in *Esquire's* offices, while ostensibly working for the magazine.

Benton and Newman, inspired by the New Wave's artistic view of American gangster films, thought that they were writing a French New Wave film; indeed they wrote it with the idea that François Truffaut would direct it. Helen Scott, a confidante of Truffaut's who worked in the French Film Office in New York, read, admired, and translated the script treatment and sent it to Truffaut, who received it on January 2, 1964. In April, Truffaut went to New York and met with the writers, proposing many changes. By way of example for a revised ending, he screened for them the 1949 film noir *Gun Crazy:* Godard, who was in town to do research for a documentary on American women that he was planning to make for French television (which didn't pan out), was at the screening too.

In the summer of 1964, Benton and Newman traveled to Texas to do research and then rapidly wrote their full-length script, which they sent to Truffaut. Though he liked the story, he wrote to the producers on September 7, turning it down regretfully ("of all the scripts I have turned down in the last five years, 'Bonnie and Clyde' is the best"), because of his plans to film Ray Bradbury's novel *Fahrenheit 451* or another project featuring Jeanne Moreau. Truffaut did, however, add, "I took the liberty of letting my friend Jean-Luc Godard read Bonnie and Clyde and he, too, greatly liked the script."[19] Indeed, Godard had sent Truffaut a telegram from Venice: AM IN LOVE WITH BONNIE AND ALSO WITH CLYDE STOP WILL BE PLEASED TO SPEAK WITH AUTHORS IN NY STOP.[20]

Benton later recalled that despite Truffaut's rejection, the news that the script had gone to Godard made them happier than ever: although the pair felt a "great debt to Truffaut," he and Newman knew that "Truffaut was not great in the same way that Godard was great. He was not revolutionary in the way that Godard was revolutionary."[21]

In New York in September, Godard met with Benton, Newman, and the pair's producing partners, the brother-and-sister team of Elinor and Norton Wright, telling them, according to Benton, "I'm supposed to do a film called *Alphaville*. I don't want to do it. I'll go back and get out of it, then I'll be back and do this in December"[22]—in other words, three months later. According to the writers' joint recollection in 1972, Godard told the assembled group that he wanted to do the film "in three weeks from now."[23] In 2000, Godard recalled: "So I saw the producer, it was a Friday, and he asked me, 'When do you want to start?' I said, 'Monday,' and it didn't come about."[24]

Godard thought that the producers had the financing in place and were ready to start filming soon—whether in three months, in three weeks, or on Monday. But the producers were only, in effect, packagers, who planned to use the script to attract name actors, and the names plus the script to raise money for the film—but, rather than admitting their situation, they prevaricated. As

Benton later recalled: "Instead, the young man [Norton Wright] said, 'The weather won't be right in Texas at this time of the year.' They were just backing and filling; and Godard said, 'I'm talking cinema and you're talking meteorology.' "[25]

Godard told the producers that if the weather was bad in Texas, he could shoot the film anywhere, even "in Tokyo."[26] When they argued that it would be impossible to gather everything needed to shoot in three weeks, Godard told them, "If it happens in life, it can happen in a movie"[27]—meaning, in effect, that *Bonnie and Clyde* would be whatever Godard pulled together and called *Bonnie and Clyde,* whether or not it resembled what Benton and Newman had written.

Benton and Newman were game for anything Godard proposed; but the idea of a *Bonnie and Clyde* shot in Tokyo or New York was unacceptable to the Wrights. Godard left the meeting and that day (or the next) he called the writers from the airport and told them to get in touch with him when the producers' option expired.[28]

The producers, for their part, were unable to put together a package. When Warren Beatty got wind of the project, he not only coveted the role of Clyde but also decided to produce the film himself. The screenwriters' contract with him, however, stipulated that he meet with Godard before hiring another director. According to Benton, the meeting, which took place in London in 1966, was "a disaster," and Beatty hired Arthur Penn.

After *Bonnie and Clyde* opened in 1967, Benton and Newman met Godard in Paris. He told them, "*Now* let's make it."

WHEN GODARD RETURNED to Paris after the New York Film Festival, he made the film that he had been willing to put aside in favor of *Bonnie and Clyde—Alphaville,* starring the American expatriate actor Eddie Constantine.

eleven

ALPHAVILLE

"The capital of pain"

GODARD AND EDDIE CONSTANTINE HAD BEEN PLANNING to work together in late 1963, while *Contempt* was still unfinished. Their project was now reinvigorated by the fledgling producer André Michelin. Early in 1964, Michelin had hired Constantine to play the lead role in an American-style detective film, *Nick Carter va tout casser* (*License to Kill*). Constantine mentioned to Michelin his interest in working with Godard, then brought director and producer together. At that meeting Godard explained that he wanted to cast the star in a futuristic vampire film adapted from Richard Matheson's *I Am Legend,* in which, after horrific wars, a man discovers himself to be the last human in a world filled with vampires. Michelin was not enthusiastic. "So," said Michelin, "we looked for a subject."[1]

Godard then suggested putting Constantine—as the secret agent Lemmy Caution, the role for which he was famous—into a science-fiction film based on Brian Aldiss's 1958 novel, *Non-Stop,* about life inside a vast, city-like spacecraft, but he quickly realized that the story would be very expensive to film. Instead, he decided to come up with a story of his own which would nonetheless combine elements of Matheson's and Aldiss's plots.

At the Venice Film Festival, in September 1964, Antonioni had talked to Godard about his research for *Red Desert,* which involved interviewing cybernetics researchers who were experimenting with artificial intelligence. Godard's interest was piqued and he began to look into the subject while in New York. On his return, he told Michelin, "Over there I got in contact with electronics specialists and I was struck to see to what extent electronic brains, the calculation of probabilities, are becoming important

Eddie Constantine rescues Karina from a heartless dystopia.
(TCD-Prod DB © Chaumiane / DR)

in the lives of businessmen, even in the lives of heads of state."[2] Michelin put Godard in touch with a group of engineers from Bull, one of the leading French electronics companies. The theme was in extreme contrast to the romantic and violent adventures of a cinematic secret agent—and it was exactly this contrast that Godard turned into the subject of *Alphaville.*

Michelin asked Godard to write a screenplay, which would be used to obtain financing from German coproducers. Godard agreed, but then procrastinated. Godard's assistant, Charles Bitsch, stepped bravely in, as he recalled:

> I told Godard that the screenplay was due the day after tomorrow; he told me, 'So just write it.' 'But what should I write?' He said, 'Buy an adventure of Lemmy Caution; you read, you write.' So I wrote thirty-five pages, 'An Adventure of Lemmy Caution'; there were fights and pretty girls. Godard didn't read it. He gave it to Michelin. Michelin liked it and gave it to [his West German coproducers], who liked it.[3]

Bitsch's script was just a place-filler which kept the project afloat while Godard continued to meditate.[4] In December 1964, after the contracts were signed and the project announced, the *Nouvel Observateur* filled two pages with interviews of Godard, Constantine, and Karina, who, marital strife aside, was slated to play the female role. Under the two-page headline, "Alpha-Ville, a science-fiction adventure by J.-L. Godard," Godard described his film:

> A secret agent will arrive in a city, Alpha-ville. He will at first be bewildered, then he'll understand, from certain signs, that the inhabitants, the Literates,[5] are mutants. . . . Constantine, my Illiterate,[6] will notice that certain words have disappeared . . . Anna [a Literate] will not know the word "to love" . . . The Literates will not know the word "handkerchief" either, because they won't know how to weep . . . I will show a thought that tries to combat this, and which to some extent succeeds. Anna will finally be able to weep.

Anna Karina said of her role, " 'You are a Literate and you don't know how to weep.' That's how my husband explained his film to me. I didn't get it. In the story there is also an 'eternal programmatrix,' but it isn't me. I think it's a machine."

Constantine noted that Godard hadn't "written anything yet, but that's all to the good, because this is all too deep for me." But the actor did understand one essential aspect of his work with Godard: "The Americans just bought all my films in one blow, to show them on television. Because of the Godard film, of course . . . Without Godard, without the young, I'm ruined!"[7]

BETWEEN THESE INTERVIEWS and the start of the shoot, on January 4, 1965, Godard wrote his own story treatment. By that time, Godard was no longer Karina's husband, the couple's divorce having become final on December 21, 1964. Karina would remain in the film, however, and Godard did not give up hope: *Alphaville* would be another attempt, like *A Married Woman,* to show that Karina's true emotions had been distorted and suppressed by irresistible external influences and forces. The main drama of the film would be the effort of Lemmy Caution to teach Karina's character to say the words, "I love you." Through an extraordinary filter of genre, it would be a film in which Godard was desperate for life to imitate art.

Though Godard had been eager to drop *Alphaville* in favor of *Bonnie and Clyde,* he now infused it with his most pressing personal and aesthetic concerns. As Eddie Constantine later recalled: "He wanted to shoot this film, he needed it. He thought that if he didn't shoot it, he would never do anything again."[8] After *A Married Woman,* which the title card declared to be "fragments," Godard once again wanted to attempt to compose a film along the lines of a classical story, within a familiar genre, but without sacrificing (as he had done in *Band of Outsiders*) his spontaneous methods or his philosophical reflections. As it turned out, the armature of this story was strong and clear enough for Godard's frenetic and willful methods to have surprisingly little impact on the narrative flow of the finished product. *Alphaville* was, in some ways, Godard's last movie (without, of course, being his last film).

Godard considered his story to be, in its essence, a western, and it is indeed a variation on John Ford's *The Searchers,* in which a man enters enemy territory to rescue a woman who had been held there since early childhood. (It also resembles Orson Welles's *Mr. Arkadin,* another drama about a malevolent mastermind whose daughter the detective-surrogate loves.) But Godard set his film in something like an outer-space dystopia called Alphaville, in which life is governed by a giant computer and emotion is a crime punishable by death.[9] Godard understood the project to be "the development" of *Le Nouveau Monde,* with its view of a person projected into a society that had lost the meaning of its language and the truth of its feelings; the film would also be "the prolongation"[10] of *A Married Woman,* with its accusations of mind control and the repression of love in a centrally governed society.

Lemmy Caution's mission in Alphaville is to find two men—the secret agent Henri Dickson[11] and the scientist Leonardo von Braun.[12] But when he gets there he meets Leonardo's daughter, Natasha, played by Anna Karina, who had been born in the "Outer Lands" but was brought to Alphaville as a child too young to remember anything else; she works there as a "seductress," a prostitute. He falls in love with her, though she literally does not know the meaning of the word *love*, which is forbidden there (along with all other illogical thought). He confronts her father, destroys the computer that runs Alphaville, helps Natasha to recognize that she is in fact from the Outer Lands, takes her away from the ruined city, and teaches her the meaning of love.

The film is an allegory as radical as that of *A Married Woman*: Karina is held captive in an evil empire of mind control (indeed is an unwitting prostitute), but she would reclaim her virtue and be able to love the lucid and intrepid man who loves her—if only she were free. The film's scenario, with its action-genre clichés and simplistic onesidedness, is remarkably cartoonish. So much does it resemble a comic strip in tone that, to advertise the film to the industry as the shoot got under way, Godard had his assistant, Jean-Paul Savignac, distill the film's story into an actual comic strip that stretched over two pages of *La Cinématographie française*, and included a panel of Constantine and Karina face to face in the backseat of a car, with these words inked in: "I love you, beautiful and cruel Anna Karina!" "Me too, Lemmy, but I'm afraid!!!" [*sic*][13]

Alphaville was set in a transparently contemporary future that drew most of its traits from the alienating aspects of ordinary life; as Godard said, "We are already living in the future."[14] He filmed in the studios of French national radio, in the vast computer research complex of Bull (with its spinning reels of magnetic tape and the consoles of blinking lights of a powerful new computer called Gamma 60),[15] in the new modern office and residential complex of La Défense, just outside Paris, and on newly built roads running through tunnels glowing with eerie banks of lights.

As for the mind-controlling computer itself, "Alpha 60," it was, Godard said, "a little three-dollar Philips fan, lit from below."[16] The computer's muffled, uninflected voice was provided by "a man whose vocal cords were shot away in the war and who has been re-educated to speak from the diaphragm." The use of actual locations and objects to represent the dystopian future reflected Godard's tendentious view of the modern world: he said that *Alphaville* was "really about the present,"[17] of which the film's presumptive "future" was really just a *projectio ad absurdum* of what he saw occurring in the world in which he lived.

THE SHOOT WAS, even by Godard's standards, unusually stressful, because of his own anxieties and demands. He spent the first days driving around Paris with Constantine and Coutard but could not commit to attempting a single shot, even as the clock ticked on an international coproduction with one of the biggest stars in France. Then, as Constantine recalled: "He phoned me after three days: 'I have the story now, I'm going to write it.' In the morning he wrote, from nine o'clock to noon, at two o'clock we started to rehearse, and then at five we started to shoot."[18]

Godard made extreme demands of his crew and of Raoul Coutard in particular. To realize his idea of making the present look like a dystopic future, Godard used an unusual and risky photographic technique. He wanted to create a look of extreme high contrast without using any movie lights regardless of low-light conditions. Godard heard that the London-based film manufacturer Ilford (responsible for the sensitive film used in *Breathless*) now made a 35mm motion picture film that could be processed to achieve very high photosensitivity, and he visited the firm's laboratory in London to become acquainted with the techniques required to do so. To be sure of getting the darkness he wanted, he shot the film at night, allowing Coutard to add only an occasional incandescent lamp.

Coutard was leery of Godard's plans and warned him that the film would be black and unexposed. To protect himself against just this danger, Godard did an unusually large number of takes, shots, and angles. Suzanne Schiffman recalled:

> *Alphaville* was shot pretty much without any light, in the dark. Coutard said, "We'll put a little light, and I'll stop down the lens, it will amount to the same thing, it'll be very dark." Godard refused: always the need for the real. He shot without movie lights, with a special film that was very fast, but even so! . . . It became the joke of the film: "We won't see a thing!" "Yes, but we're shooting anyway." The result: three thousand meters of film were unusable. Godard did not redo everything. Some shots were eliminated, others were put into the film as is.[19]

The schedule proved to be very difficult for the crew. They were being paid the daytime rate despite shooting all night, and soon they went on strike. Godard, who had no budget to pay for the overages, was then compelled to shoot in the daytime with windows blacked out. Schiffman considered the results indistinguishable, but Godard cried that he was being "sabotaged" by his crew.[20] Coutard, considering that Godard felt, more than ever, the constraints imposed on his artistic creativity by the need to work with others, told Schiffman, "He'd like to swallow the film and process it out his ass—that way he wouldn't need anyone."[21]

The only person who submitted intrepidly and unquestioningly to Godard's methods was Eddie Constantine. One side of Constantine's face was heavily scarred, and in his prior films, he was usually slathered with makeup; often directors just avoided filming his scarred side. Godard, however, allowed no makeup, used harsh lighting, and filmed Constantine from any and all angles, revealing the actor's face in all of its craggy humanity. For Constantine, honesty was a professional risk. If in the end the gamble won the actor new admirers from a new audience, many of his longtime fans were not pleased.

FOR *ALPHAVILLE*, GODARD borrowed the cartoonish narrative style and apocalyptic tone (and a great grotesque of an actor, Akim Tamiroff, in the role of Henri Dickson) from the American low-budget science-fiction films of the 1950s. (Tamiroff also played a key role in Orson Welles's *Mr. Arkadin,* and his performance as Dickson, his final work, was largely modeled on it.) Godard also borrowed the coolly brutal heroism of American detective movies. He relied on the styles of the popular cinema to make his message as clear as possible: the film was a broadside and would look and feel like one. The film's main fund of references came from the German "expressionist" cinema of the 1920s and early 1930s, yet its relation to those works was more than mere *hommage*—it was a metaphorical threat, a stylistic warning (akin to the references to Auschwitz in *A Married Woman*) that the same social depravities were in the offing as those foretold by the menacing shadows and ferocious hauntings of the Weimar German cinema.

Godard called *Alphaville* "a film about light. Lemmy is a character who brings light to people who no longer know what it is."[22] It begins with light deployed in a system of signs: a close-up of a round traffic light that flashes against total darkness as if in Morse code. Lemmy Caution is seen in his car, in deep nocturnal shadows; he lights his cigarette with a Zippo lighter, which illuminates his face. Soon there is another close-up of a traffic light, then another of a glowing signal arrow pointing left. The lights from the windows of the railway cars on an elevated métro line, and the headlights from cars below, loom unnaturally and fantastically strange.

Godard's insistence on filming *Alphaville* with available light was not just a matter of hasty practicality or an artistic tribute to the gravelly images of the low-budget private-eye genre. It was also a metaphorical approach to a philosophical point about the cinema. As even amateur photographers know, scenes that look normal to the naked eye may come out on film as impenetrably dark. For Godard, *Alphaville* would be the transformation of ordinary unproblematic views into strange and alienating ones, by way of the movie camera. "The sensitive film gives the image a lunar aspect," Godard explained. "It was very important to me. I wanted an expressionistic style. In filming things that we see every day, I wanted them to arouse fear. Without cheating. The things are there. One looks at them. And suddenly, one discovers that they are not at all as one thought."[23] The camera in *Alphaville* shows not a distortion of reality but a hidden or inner reality: what appears to the naked eye as an adequate brightness is revealed in fact to be a dangerous darkness, exactly as a person of apparently healthy aspect can be revealed by X-ray or MRI to be seriously ill. Here, Godard used the movie camera as a scientific instrument, attempting to put his faith not in the way things appeared but in what filming them might reveal.

For the same reason, Godard created the film's imaginary futuristic inventions by using everyday artifacts in surprising ways: a high-style jukebox becomes a surveillance device; a small round traveling alarm clock is a cordless telephone; a set of apartment-lobby call buttons serves as a futuristic pay phone. The alienation through technology that *Alphaville* depicts as future dystopia is in fact that of the present day.

The provocation that Godard intended was political as much as social. Lemmy Caution, the agent, comes from what remained of the old world ("Nueva York," "Tokyorama," "Angoulême City"), introducing himself into the city-state of Alphaville under false pretenses as "Ivan Johnson," a reporter for *Figaro-Pravda*. The blend of Communist East and capitalist West recalls a remark by Godard regarding his opposition to "all forms of socialism, whether Kennedy's or Khrushchev's";[24] the idea was central to his conception of the film. When the critic Jean Collet said that the film reminded him of Georges Bernanos's book *La France contre les robots* (France Against the Robots), Godard responded avidly:

> I re-read this book, which I like a lot, before making *Alphaville*. There is even an entire sentence from the book in my film. What is magnificent, is that Bernanos wrote *France Against the Robots* at a time when electronic programming did not exist. And this book is current. Bernanos was a prophet.[25]

Despite the title, Bernanos's book is not futuristic; it is a frantic, rhetorical essay, written during World War II from the author's self-chosen exile in Brazil, extolling a distinctive French alternative to the ideological struggles of East and West. He decried the attendant militarism of that conflict, as well as both sides' thrall to technology and bureaucracy, and called for a France free of such burdens. Bernanos contemptuously denounced what he called the three great modern "Democracies"—"the English imperial Democracy, the American plutocratic Democracy, and the Marxist Empire of the Soviet Dominions"—as fronts for "a sort of State socialism, the democratic form of dictatorship," preferring "a French tradition of Liberty," exemplified by the revolution of 1789.[26] He further argued that "the Modern State, the Technological Moloch, in erecting the solid foundations of its future tyranny, remained faithful to the old liberal vocabulary, covering or justifying with that liberal vocabulary its innumerable usurpations." Bernanos considered mechanization and technology to be the avatars of this new universal tyranny, and thus feared America as much as he did the Soviet Union, wondering incredulously about "this Truman, this politician of business, without breeding, without a past, without culture, who must have blind confidence in the Civilization of Machines."[27] Bernanos asserted fiercely that "French civilization, heir to Hellenic civilization, has for centuries striven to form free men, that is, men fully responsible for their actions: France refuses to enter into the Paradise of Robots."

Like Bernanos, Godard was and remains a conservative revolutionary whose utopian visions are moralistic and aesthetic. Godard's insistence on Karina's character, Natasha von Braun, having been born in the Outer Lands and rediscovering her origins as a precondition for emotional fullness recalls Bernanos's nationalist, race-bound traditionalism and anticosmopolitanism. The pontificating computer Alpha 60, the electronic tyrant of Alphaville, declares, in lines that are also reminiscent of Bernanos: "In the so-called capitalist world or communist world there is no malicious intent to suppress men through the power of ideology or materialism, but rather the natural aim of all organizations to increase their natural structure." Like Bernanos, Godard considered both the capitalist and communist worlds to be equally inimical to the values of life, love, and, crucially, art.

When Lemmy finds the debilitated and destitute secret agent Henri Dickson, the broken spy laments what the "pure technocracy" of Alpha 60 has destroyed: "Artists, novelists, musicians, and painters. Today there's nothing. Nothing." An official "seductress"[28] (who, like all of Alphaville's seductresses, is tattooed with numerals on her neck) comes to Dickson's room and makes love to the old man, who collapses with the effort, as Lemmy Caution hears his dying words: "Conscience . . . conscience . . . destroy . . . make Alpha 60 destroy itself . . . tenderness . . . save those who weep." Dickson reveals a book hidden under his pillow: a collection of poems by Paul Eluard, *Capitale de la Douleur* (*The Capital of Pain*), which Lemmy slips into his pocket. In Alphaville, poetry will prove to be the pathway to conscience, to love—and to freedom.

Lemmy accompanies Natasha to a "gala" (on the way they step into an elevator showing a button for the "SS" floor—a gag based on the French word "sous-sol," or basement), where he learns that in Alphaville, those who weep are executed. The "gala" is an evening of public executions, by firing squad, of people standing on the edge of a diving board and falling

into the water, where they are retrieved—and then also stabbed to death—
by gracefully diving women bearing daggers slipped in the side of their
bikini bottoms.[29] Lemmy is told by a pair of officials that "generally there
are fifty men to every woman executed," and that their crime was "illogical
behavior."

With the tattooed numbers, the SS floor, the character von Braun (who
is also Professor Nosferatu), and a plethora of visual references to German
films of the 1920s, Godard repeats the analogy asserted in *A Married
Woman*: that the emotional failures of the modern world are akin to its failures of historical memory, that the modern world of technology, order, and
comfort is regimented like a concentration camp, and that the inability to be
true to the dictates of one's conscience in love is a moral failing at the level of
collaboration with a Nazi-like power. The private failure of love—Anna
Karina's failure to love Godard—is both the result of a plot almost cosmic in
its malevolent dimensions, and the sign of complicity, albeit unwilling and
unwitting, with an evil force.

Lemmy Caution, under interrogation by Alpha 60 (for which Godard
put Constantine in a glassed-in radio broadcast booth as microphones
glide around his head, while a table fan lit from below silently whirs to
sudden starts and stops), gives a perfect exposition of the film's aesthetic
politics:

> ALPHA 60: What transforms night into day?
> CAUTION: Poetry.
> ALPHA 60: What is your religion?
> CAUTION: I believe in the immediate givens of my conscience.

Lemmy's answers are a clear statement of Godard's own aesthetic politics. Poetry is the light that the modern world is lacking, and conscience has
the sacred status of faith and transcendent moral law. The book of poetry
Henri Dickson gives to Lemmy Caution, Eluard's *The Capital of Pain*, was
chosen by Godard in part because its title stood for Alphaville itself. But as
significantly, Eluard wrote and compiled the book in the early 1920s during
the agony of his jealousy over his wife Gala's affair with the artist Max Ernst,
and the poems relate to that particular pain.[30] The uses to which the book is
put in the film—as the prop that Dickson passes to Lemmy and that Lemmy
uses to teach Natasha about love, it becomes the film's MacGuffin—make
manifest the parallel between the creations of the two poets, Eluard and
Godard.

By means of the poetry Lemmy has given her, Natasha is able to understand
the word "conscience," even though it does not appear in the Alphaville

"Bible," the dictionary. He helps her to recover from the depths of her unconscious the memory of her roots: she realizes that she is originally from "Nueva York, where in winter, Broadway sparkles under snow as soft and as gentle as mink." Most crucially, when Natasha asks Lemmy the fateful question—"Love: what is it?"—Godard answers the question himself, cutting to an extraordinarily intimate close-up of Anna Karina, her face illuminated by velvety indirect sunlight, as she is saying and doing nothing, looking distractedly off-camera, almost out of character. It is a brief shot of breathtaking beauty that shows what love is: the emotion, on the part of a filmmaker, that gives rise to such an image.

Soon thereafter, Lemmy is captured by the evil mastermind von Braun/Nosferatu, who warns him of the fate that awaits him as a "romantic individualist": "You will suffer something worse than death: you will become a legend." Lemmy guns him down and escapes. After an antic chase, Lemmy and Natasha leave Alphaville together, with Lemmy at the wheel of his "Ford Galaxie" (actually a Mustang, though Godard himself owned a Galaxie). He warns her not to turn around—a command invoking less the myth of Orpheus than the destruction of Sodom and Gomorrah. Natasha slowly extracts from herself the three words: "I," "love," "you," and then links them together as a sentence, accompanied on the sound track by the soaring violins of conventionally romantic movie music.

In the world of Alphaville, poetry and love are illogical. The leap of faith called love flies in the face of all logic. As Lemmy has learned, in Alphaville fifty times more men are condemned to death for behaving illogically than women—men are fifty times likelier to fall in love than are women. Godard suggests that if women are so susceptible to persuasion against love—whether, like Charlotte in *A Married Woman*, by the industry of pleasure, or, like Natasha in *Alphaville*, by the regime of self-interest—it is because of their chilly natural affinity for inhuman logic, the Aristotelian "A is A," which, for Godard, is "a woman is a woman." For Godard, only a foolishly romantic man would, with his illogic, his poetry, and his heroism, seek to liberate a ruthlessly logical yet misguided woman, to call her to his impractical and unreasonable—but sublime, poetic, and artistic—faith in love. Only such a man would seek, through love, to arouse her conscience and awaken her consciousness. In *Alphaville*, the light of love is the light of enlightenment, depicted as a form of natural light that breaks through the fluorescent confinement of the technological tyranny.

As Lemmy and Natasha speed away from the nightmarish city, they leave the labyrinth of symbols behind and head into the reality of love—and into a brief but unmistakable scene of naturalistic, melodramatic representation. A romantic dream, *Alphaville* is also the end of romantic dreams in the hope of a couple's ordinary reality. As a genre pastiche, *Alphaville* is a clever but minor exercise in style, although its title remains an enduring catchword for heartless techno-dystopia. But it is as complex and moving an avowal of Godard's artistic, philosophical, and personal conflicts and contradictions as any he had yet offered.

IN FRANCE, THE critical response to *Alphaville* was overwhelmingly enthusiastic. Godard still had his inveterate detractors, both in the popular press of the right (such as *Le Figaro*) and in the specialized press of the left (for instance, *Les Temps Modernes*, where Arlette Elkaïm, the young lover whom Jean-Paul Sartre was in the process of adopting, gave Godard a schoolmarmish scolding: "It is true. The housing projects are sad and, in the evening, the people in the métro seem gloomy or dazed. But the computers have little to do with it"). The acceptance of Godard as an intellectual and cultural force—a process that had begun with *A Married Woman*—was itself a part of *Alphaville*'s reception (as, for instance, Anne Andreu noted in *Paris-Presse*, "the press has unanimously surrendered").[31] In an interview, Godard offered a pair of matched explanations for the film's wide acceptance:

> With *Alphaville*, people have the feeling that for the first time I mastered the subject [of the film]. There's an introduction, a development, a conclusion. I did my homework well. . . . I give people the impression of finally taking on big problems. *Alphaville* expresses ideas that are in the air. Let's say, ones that are to the taste of the day. I have, to some extent, cleared my name.[32]

With *Alphaville* attracting more than 150,000 French spectators by the end of 1965,[33] Godard had again achieved both commercial and critical success. (Though this was no help to Eddie Constantine, who said, "After *Alphaville*, there was total silence, nobody asked me to shoot films anymore.")[34] As nasty as the criticism by some of his opponents may have been, it could not touch him now: Godard had become a legend. He had, in the process, lost his wife and his faith in the cinema. If he did not "suffer something worse than death," he nonetheless suffered, and would now go on to stage that suffering in a series of cinematic self-scourgings.

AT THE THIRD New York Film Festival, held in September 1965, three Godard films were on view: *Le Petit Soldat*, *Montparnasse and Levallois* (included in *Paris vu par . . .*), and *Alphaville*, which was shown at the opening night gala benefit for the New York Civil Liberties Union, tickets for which were being sold for $12.50 and $17.50 (when normal prices were $2 and $4). The festival's programming was more audacious than ever: it was a true feast of modern cinema, featuring Carl Theodor Dreyer's *Gertrud,* two films by Jerzy Skolimowski, Luchino Visconti's *Sandra,* and Jean-Marie Straub's first feature film, *Not Reconciled,* along with such important redis-coveries as the five hours of Louis Feuillade's serial *The Vampires,* Michelan-gelo Antonioni's 1953 film *The Lady Without Camellias,* and Erich von Stroheim's *The Wedding March.*

Like most of the shows at the festival, the gala screening of *Alphaville* sold out. It was an event at which to see and be seen (the downtown-style patrons who bought the few non-gala tickets got to watch the post-screening reception through a glass wall). The reviews set a new and respectful tone. As in France, the essential story in New York was of Godard's canonization. Al-though several major reviews of *Alphaville* were reserved and baffled, Godard was now a recognized value of the modern art world, and the film was received as an important aesthetic event, essentially beyond the reach of criticism. The festival's success and enduring significance were due to its ap-peal to youth; as Robert Mazzocco wrote in the *New York Review of Books,* Godard is "completely infatuated with films and with film-making," and "imparts that infatuation to us—or at least, to the young."[35] According to the decidedly uninfatuated Mazzocco, *Alphaville* provoked controversy, but "no one, I think, doubted whether it was art." *The New Yorker's* Talk of the Town section presented the film's screening as a deadpan carnival of bohemian youth being served, and reported on Godard's own appearance, ideas, and attitude as a fact of culture that transcended the importance of any single film.[36] Indeed, the reception of Godard's films became the subject of meta-criticism in which critics critiqued each other's critiques of Godard and his films. Jonas Mekas wrote in the *Village Voice,*

Kael dislikes Godard . . . The press attacked Godard for "Alphaville." The members of the press conference and the symposiums attacked Godard. I never thought I would have to come to the defence [*sic*] of Godard. I thought Godard had enough friends. But even Andrew Sarris (who remains Godard's best defender) declared that he thought Godard was (in his last two films) on the wrong track and that he is beginning to detect something ominous about Godard.

Mekas then countered with prophetic vehemence, "Godard is saying: Go to hell. Everything is possible," and explained the hostility that his films had aroused: "Godard is ominous. Like any stark truth is ominous. Truth de-stroys untruth. Poets are ominous, sometimes."[37] Mazzocco reported that Pauline Kael had called *Alphaville* a "deadend." Though she may not have meant it as a compliment, she was, in a certain way, right: in making *Alphaville,* Godard had indeed come to the end of a certain road—the road of movies reminiscent of those made within the mainstream of the industry. Sarris was correct about finding something "ominous" in Godard's most recent work: by the time *Alphaville* was shown in New York in September 1965, Godard had driven past the end of the road and was venturing dangerously far into a cinematic wilderness.

twelve

PIERROT LE FOU

"Silence! I'm writing!"

GODARD'S NEXT FILM, *PIERROT LE FOU* (CRAZY PETE), brought his devotion to classical cinematic forms and moods to a spectacular end, and began a set of works marked by a hysterical, self-flagellating despair. In film after film, Godard's frustrated loves and cinematic uncertainties would play out as self-damaging fantasies and petulant conflagrations of violence. With the end of his marriage to Anna Karina came the end of his quest for a form in which to represent and reinforce it; his new formless way of filmmaking mirrored a frantic state of mind that left no illusion of balance, finish, or grace.

Pierrot le fou is based on a novel, *Obsession,* by Lionel White (translated as *Le Démon de onze heures*). Godard described it in February 1964 as being about "a guy who leaves his family to follow a girl much younger than he is. She is in cahoots with slightly shady people and it leads to a series of adventures." Asked who would play the girl, Godard responded:

> That depends on the age of the man. If I have, as I would like, Richard Burton, I will take my wife, Anna Karina. We would shoot the film in English. If I don't have Burton and I take Michel Piccoli, I could no longer have Anna as an actress, they would form a too "normal" couple. In that case, I would need a very young girl. I'm thinking of Sylvie Vartan.[1]

Godard thought that Burton looked much older than Karina, when in fact he was born in the same year as Piccoli, in 1925. But Burton and Vartan were unavailable, so Godard approached Jean-Paul Belmondo instead,

In *Pierrot le fou,* Karina meets a bad end.
(Janus Films / Photofest)

telling him, "I have to make a film, you absolutely have to help me."[2] But Belmondo, who was born in 1933, was and looked even younger than Piccoli. Thus, when Godard announced in New York in September 1964—while he was considering making *Bonnie and Clyde*—that the film would star Karina alongside Belmondo, he had succumbed to filming a "normal" couple and reoriented the subject accordingly.

> The presence of Anna and Belmondo changed everything. I thought of *You Only Live Once*. Now, instead of the couple from *Lolita* or *La Chienne*, I wanted to shoot the story of the last romantic couple, the last descendants of *La Nouvelle Héloise*, of *Werther*, and of *Hermann and Dorothea*.[3]

While the original story would have allegorized Godard's catastrophe with Karina as that of a man doomed by lust for a younger woman, the new approach portrayed them as a man and a woman joined as equals, who still come to doom. Godard would present himself as neither a predator nor a fool, but rather as a victim deceived and betrayed.

UNLIKE *A MARRIED WOMAN*, the new film would be expensive to make: Belmondo's salary alone was eighty thousand francs (sixteen thousand dollars), and this was a bargain rate that he offered against his agent's wishes to the film's producer, Georges de Beauregard. The shoot would require many locations and would be in color and widescreen. Also, as ever with Beauregard, the financing had to be cobbled together piecemeal, which caused delays. Godard returned to Paris and made *Alphaville*, while planning to direct this noirish love story as soon as the opportunity presented itself.

Godard needed a dummy script of White's novel to be submitted to the CNC as well as to coproducers and distributors, and for this job, he turned to a longtime acquaintance, Rémo Forlani, a friend of Truffaut's since the late 1940s. Forlani, a painter, was also a streetwise raconteur who had decided to try his hand at writing, and had been tapped through social connections to write several minor screenplays, the most recent of which attracted Godard's attention for reasons other than its artistry. It was the script for *Le Voleur de Tibidabo* (The Thief of Tibidabo), made in Spain in the fall of 1964. It starred Karina and her new lover, Maurice Ronet (who also directed).

When Forlani got back to Paris, Godard invited him to lunch and advised him to see Beauregard about the adaptation of *Obsession*. Then Godard, as Forlani later recalled, got to the main subject: pumping him for information about what went on between Karina and Ronet in Spain: "How many times she made the trip from Paris to Barcelona. And if they love each other a lot or just a little. And whether this skirt-chaser Ronet is making her happy or not."[4]

Forlani's script sets the story in France rather than in the United States, but otherwise hews closely to the contours of the novel. Pierre, a bourgeois Parisian man who lost his job and despairs of a dull marriage, flees a dismal cocktail party and takes off with Lena, his children's babysitter, for the south of France. Her former boyfriend, Joel, has underworld connections and causes trouble for the lovers on the run. When Joel catches up with them, Lena, pretending to visit Joel solely in order to square things with him for good, runs away with him and leaves Pierre behind. Pierre searches for them, finds them, kills them, calls the police on himself, and then—in Forlani's conclusion—rigs the hideout with dynamite, ending the story with a vast conflagration.

However, Forlani's text was a mere placefiller. Godard didn't plan to follow it (and Beauregard didn't expect him to do so), but he did make use of two elements from the script: the lead character's name, Pierre (changed from the novel's Conrad), which gave him a new title, *Pierrot le fou;* and the ending, with dynamite.

The title, which Beauregard announced in the February 27, 1965, issue of *La Cinématographie française,* aroused certain expectations: "Pierrot-le-fou" was the nickname the French press had given to Pierre Loutrel, France's Public Enemy Number One in the late 1940s, the leader of a violent, brazen gang of robbers. In the mid-1960s, he was still a legend in France, and journalists, learning of the film's title, anticipated a biopic of the criminal band—a kind of French *Bonnie and Clyde.*

Forlani's script helped Beauregard to raise the needed funds, but it also got Godard a scolding from the precensorship board at the CNC. The panel authorized Godard to begin shooting but cautioned him to direct with prudence a script which they called "a hymn to violence, to sensuality, to murder, without any redeeming moral." As it turned out, sensuality in *Pierrot* would prove no less sternly moralistic than Godard's previous work, and the many scenes of "violence" or "murder" would owe little to reality and much to Godard's own enveloping sense of despair.

GENERALLY TENSE AND choleric during shoots, Godard was also solitary and grief stricken during the filming of *Pierrot le fou.* The shoot was rendered all the more difficult by a number of exacerbating factors that played havoc with his mood, including his own doubts about how to make the film. As he later recalled: "When I began *Pierrot le fou,* one week before, I was completely panicked, I didn't know what to do. Based on the book, we had already established all the locations, we had hired the people . . . and I was wondering what we were going to do with it all."[5]

Complicating matters, Godard had chosen to film in a new widescreen process, Techniscope, which, according to Raoul Coutard, his cinematographer, brought with it a new set of inconveniences, including the need to shoot with high-contrast side-lighting—"otherwise we would get a flat image, without definition. So it implied working at certain hours, changing axes, changing angles because we weren't well-placed in the light."[6] The resulting constraints slowed the production down and stifled Godard's spontaneity.

By Godard's relatively Spartan standards, the shoot itself was unusually long—eight weeks, running from May 24 to July 17—and complex. Because "fast" (highly light-sensitive) color negative film did not exist, interiors required a great deal of lighting, hence additional crew members and time. Much of the shoot was outdoors, so the camera could not be placed on a rolling dolly or handheld in a wheel chair for traveling shots; tracking rails had to be laid down instead, a slow and labor-intensive process. The crew was large, the equipment cumbersome, the frustrations built-in. And the cost of keeping a large crew and shooting in a wide range of locations meant that, despite the indeterminate script, Godard had to keep to schedule.

Godard, who was indifferent to the novel's action and had lost faith in the noirish cinematic genre, added various forms of pageantry and burlesque to the already clotted plot. He recruited the comedian and monologuist Raymond Devos to do a solo turn and found a role for the popular dancer and choreographer Dirk Sanders and for his troupe of dancers. Godard had no intention, in this spectacle of despair, of sparing the spectacle; yet the cinematic excesses led to an even more intricate and burdened shoot.

Most crucially, the film starred a woman whom Godard loved and had lost. His wounded state of mind was apparent to his colleagues. His divorce from Anna Karina and her relationship with Ronet left Godard agonizingly alone, yet he was still bound to Karina, both by emotional and artistic bonds. Karina had a career apart from Godard but not a major one; and although Godard had proven that he could make films of prime importance without Karina, he had little interest in doing so. Asked by an interviewer before the beginning of the shoot about his choice of actresses, Godard answered in a way that suggested the complex and conflicting emotions—tenderness, jealousy, self-pity—that he then put on display in the film: "I need to love the people I film, that's why I always take Anna Karina."

He spoke of his divorce, joking that marriage is "an alliance for life . . . with the person with whom one is least-suited to live," and followed up with a striking interpretation of why his relationship with Karina had ended through infidelity.

Fidelity is a rule and like all rules, it can admit of certain exceptions . . . What I desire to do . . . I can put into my films and so have a calmer life. Before being a director I needed more things . . . For a woman it may be different inasmuch as she does not create, she needs to externalize herself more.[7]

In other words, Godard created drama in film, while Karina needed to create it in life.

GODARD'S SOLITUDE AND lack of emotional sustenance at this time revealed itself in his quest for company. A number of people whose presence he sought out came to figure significantly in the making of *Pierrot le fou,* in particular a couple whose evident harmony shocked him and exacerbated the pain of Karina's rejection.

Driving early in the morning in the south of France in the spring of 1965 in his Ford Galaxie convertible while scouting locations with his assistant director, Bernard Toublanc-Michel, Godard heard a song on the car radio and said that he wanted just that kind of music in *Pierrot le fou.* Toublanc-Michel replied that Godard was in luck: they were five minutes by car from the songwriter's house. They dropped in on Serge Rezvani, a painter who wrote songs under the nom de plume of Bassiak (a song of whose was famously sung by Jeanne Moreau in Truffaut's *Jules and Jim*),[8] and his wife, Danièle.

Rezvani played two songs. Godard immediately took both for the film (they would be sung by Anna Karina's character—once by her, once by a singing double), but he was also impressed by something other than Rezvani's songs. He asked the songwriter with astonishment, "You left Paris and you live here all year long, just the two of you with your dog and your cat?"[9] Soon thereafter, when Rezvani heard the film's story, he understood Godard's bewildered look at the contented couple in their rustic refuge—at the man who was an artist and the wife who was his inspiration and helper. That type of relationship was, in fact, the main subject of *Pierrot le fou;* in the film, Godard would show how the woman corrupts and undermines such a relationship. Gazing at the Rezvanis, Godard beheld, to his amazement, an artistic couple that was thriving. Godard's subsequent contact with the couple, Rezvani noted, showed how consumed he was by the problem—by his failure and their success.

The search for companionship led Godard to turn *Pierrot*'s shooting locations in the south of France into something of an unofficial salon. He frequently saw Serge and Danièle Rezvani before the shoot and then received them on the set. Rezvani, in turn, brought two friends, the critic Alain Jouffroy and Jouffroy's girlfriend, Laetitia, to meet Godard. A parade of journalists from a diverse list of local and international publications came to the set, and Godard received them with an unusually patient solicitude. He allowed Alain Bergala, a local student and cinephile, to film the cast and crew at work.[10] Claude Lanzmann, then a journalist, came by to do a report for *Elle* magazine.[11]

When the shoot came to Paris in early July, Godard sought out the journalist and novelist Michel Vianey (whose detailed report on the shoot of *Contempt* had pleased him) and invited him to the set. Earlier, Godard had asked Vianey to follow him around during the shoot of *Pierrot le fou* and to write a book about what he saw, but Vianey was unavailable at the time. Now Godard met Vianey in Paris and, on July 14, granted an interview in which he said: "If I shoot films, it's because I'm alone. I have no family. Nobody. It's a means of seeing people. Of going places."

In his loneliness, Godard also began to experience the role and the work of the filmmaker differently. He translated his personal solitude into a sense of artistic isolation, and responded by trying to involve his cast and crew more deeply in the filming than he had done before. As he told Vianey:

> I want everyone who works on a film to live it. They must continue to exist while they shoot. Personal problems count. Mine necessarily influence the film. So if a technician thinks about his wife during his work, so much the better, so long as it inspires him, helps him to frame a shot well. But if you don't tell them this, they stop existing, except when you push them.

Godard described a familiar exchange: "A shot is messed up. I complain. [They say] 'Ah, but you didn't tell us . . .' 'You should have found it by yourself.' 'Not at all. We're not paid for that.' And I think that it is precisely this that they're paid for. And so we quarrel."[12]

They certainly did. Godard's taciturn ferocity on the set was already legendary, but he raised it to a new pitch while making *Pierrot le fou*, and he knew it: "I get along very well with Belmondo. Except, sometimes, I lose patience. Even with Coutard. Lovers' quarrels. Indifference. It's getting worse."[13]

Godard made the same demands of Karina as of the rest of the cast and crew but expressed them with particular venom. Luc Moullet observed, "Anna Karina said, 'What should I do?' and Godard said, 'You have a mouth to talk with, don't you?'"[14] Alain Jouffroy recalled that "on the set, she fled from him."[15] Bitterness prevailed. Belmondo said they were "like a cobra and a mongoose, always glaring at each other."[16]

The tension was further heightened by the actors' difficulty remembering Godard's last-minute dialogue. Assistants carried cue cards with text written in blue and red letters as the camera rolled. After a fight one day with Karina over her unwillingness to sing,[17] Godard kicked the camera and caused it to fall, costing the crew the rest of the day's shoot and prompting a vehement argument with Coutard, who walked off the set. As Suzanne Schiffman recounted, Godard ran after the cameraman and called out, "Just because I yell at you today doesn't mean I'm not happy to see you tomorrow."[18]

Godard sought the input of the cast and the crew for the simple reason that while making the film, he was at a loss by himself: his North Star of cinematic navigation was gone, and he was at sea. Shortly after completing the film, he admitted as much to interviewers from *Cahiers du cinéma:* "In my other films, when I had a problem, I asked myself what Hitchcock would have done in my place. While making *Pierrot,* I had the impression that he wouldn't have known how to answer, other than, 'Work it out for yourself.' "[19] But Godard had trouble working it out without the example of the classic Hollywood films that had inspired and sustained him. His absorption of the entire canon of cinema was of no help to him, nor was his experience as a filmmaker. In making *Pierrot le fou,* Godard felt as if he were making his "first film."[20]

Yet this lack of mooring, this state of doubt and bewilderment, had surprising results, not all of which were negative. Godard advanced the plot of Lionel White's novel mechanically and with a conspicuous boredom, but filled in its interstices with a free and flamboyant array of images produced with untrammeled creativity: "The whole last part was invented on the spot, unlike the beginning which was planned. It is a kind of happening, but controlled and mastered. This said, it is a completely unconscious film."[21] In *Pierrot le fou,* Godard gave unusually free vent to his emotions, without the intervening forms of modernist social science (as in *A Married Woman)* or winks at genre conventions (as in *Alphaville)*—and those emotions were harrowing ones. *Pierrot le fou* was an angry accusation against Anna Karina and a self-pitying keen to bewail how she had destroyed him.

IN GODARD'S REVISION of Forlani's script treatment, the main characters' names were changed: Pierre became Pierre-Louis-Ferdinand—Pierre plus the name of Louis-Ferdinand Céline—and the woman, Lena, was renamed Marianne Renoir (Marianne being the name of the exemplary French revolutionary heroine, the Amazonian symbol of the Republic). The film is studded with references to Céline, including a recitation by Ferdinand from the posthumously published *Guignol's Band II: London Bridge.* While making *Pierrot le fou,* Godard was expecting to follow up with a vast film based on Céline's *Journey to the End of Night.* The project was the brainchild of the

Old Wave screenwriter Jacques Audiard, and Belmondo would star. Although the Céline film was never made, by Godard or anyone else, *Pierrot le fou* was itself a Célinian eruption of ecstatic rage at the state of the world and of his own existence.

It was also full of Godard's ambitious allusions to a kind of cinema he dreamed of but was not yet able to create. The first scene shows Ferdinand in the bathtub reading aloud to his young daughter a passage by the art historian Elie Faure: "Velázquez, after age fifty, no longer painted a definite thing. He drifted around objects by means of air and twilight, he captured in the shadows and the transparent backgrounds the colored palpitations that he made the invisible center of his silent symphony." The citation proved prophetic: Godard would be nearly fifty before he could achieve anything similar. In *Pierrot le fou* he was left, as he knew, just with doubt and fury, with methods too crude to convey his finer impressions.

In the film, Ferdinand is preparing to go to a cocktail party with his wife at the home of his in-laws ("Mr. and Mrs. Expresso"). After admitting to having sent the maid off to the movies to see Nicholas Ray's *Johnny Guitar*, Ferdinand sees the replacement babysitter—Marianne—arrive, and the two, who already know each other from long ago, exchange a magnetic glance. He will flee the cocktail party and, ostensibly driving the babysitter home, will take off with her into the night, never to return. Godard effected this crucially personal plot twist to the novel and to Forlani's script: the "Lolita-style"[22] moment of lust at first sight is converted into a romance of reunion (precisely as in *Johnny Guitar*). He turned *Pierrot le fou* into a story of separated lovers reconnecting.

Ferdinand's flight from home is a flight from civilization, and Godard takes care to define, in the most bilious terms, the sorry excuse for a civilization that Ferdinand has fled. He filmed the cocktail party as an inhuman environment of ugly, artificial people in ugly, artificial light, as a scream of revulsion, with actors posed flat against the wall and shot in a denaturing harsh front-lit overexposure that burns out humanizing details.

Yet from this morass comes a hero, a silent older man leaning against the wall and smoking a cigar. Ferdinand addresses him. He introduces himself, in English: "I'm an American film director. My name is Samuel Fuller. I'm here to make a picture in Paris, called *Flowers of Evil*."

Fuller, the director of *Forty Guns*, *The Naked Kiss*, and other violent action movies with extremely low budgets, was recognized in Paris as a great artist, but back home was treated like a schlockmeister. Unable to get work in the foundering studio system, Fuller went to Paris in 1965 on the promise of two young aspiring producers to finance his film version of Aristophanes's *Lysistrata* with the Baudelairean title *Flowers of Evil*.[23] Godard asked Fuller to play himself in *Pierrot le fou* and to answer questions that actors would ask him on-camera.

Belmondo asks Fuller, "What is cinema?" Fuller came up with a lapidary aphorism: "The film is like a battleground—there's love, hate, action, violence, death—in one word, emotions." He delivered it with his hard-boiled sidelong cackle, his cigar jabbing the air. Off-camera, Fuller's response brought tears to Godard's eyes. The American director in Paris was an artist in exile, and the irony of filming Fuller adrift in Paris and stuck at a cocktail party with his back against the wall and nobody to talk to was not lost on Godard, who outfitted the uprooted director in a pair of dark glasses like Godard's own. The director of primal aggression—whose film *Shock Corridor* Godard placed fifth on his *Cahiers* top-ten list for 1965—was a good fit for Godard's raw and raging movie.

THE MORNING AFTER Ferdinand's escape with Marianne, he awakens to her carefree love song by Rezvani, in an apartment filled with blood and corpses and the mark of political intrigue: daubed on the wall is a sign, OASIS, hinting at the OAS, the group of right-wing paramilitaries who had terrorized Algerians and French advocates for Algerian independence. For the film, Godard changed the novel's criminal subplot into a story of Marianne's shadowy role in a political underworld of violence and terror.

Fleeing the apartment in a stolen car, the couple reach the countryside and conceal their traces by setting the car on fire. Their realization that they have also burned up a suitcase full of cash that was in the trunk exposes the fault line along which the couple will come apart, as Marianne pouts: "Do you know what we could have done with that money? We could have gone to Chicago, Las Vegas, Monte Carlo. Pathetic jerk!" Ferdinand responds, "I'd have said, Florence, Venice, Athens."

Soon, after Ferdinand ditches another stolen car—Godard's own big convertible[24]—by driving it into the sea, the couple, broke and without a car, is compelled to put up where they are, in the wild. Marianne asks, "Where are we going?"

"To Mysterious Island, like the children of Captain Grant," Ferdinand tells her. "And what will we do there?" she asks. "Nothing. We'll exist."

Marianne's response heralds trouble: "Oh, boy, won't that be fun."

Yet their brief time together, in isolation at a wild seaside, is the crowning moment in Ferdinand's romantic dream of life and art coexisting. Seated on a high rock with a gaudy parrot perched on his shoulder, he keeps on his lap a notebook in which he constantly writes. This journal, seen in extreme close-up at different points in the film, is in Godard's own handwriting. As Ferdinand writes in it, he announces his vastly ambitious plans for a new form of the novel: "not to describe the lives of people," he tells Marianne, "but just life, life by itself; what is between people, space, sound, colors. I'd like to accomplish that. Joyce tried, but one should be able to do better."

Again Godard suggests a grand artistic dream of work more composed and more serene than the scattershot eruptions of *Pierrot*. But Ferdinand would not long enjoy the chance to fulfill it in idyllic partnership with Marianne, any more than would Godard with Karina. In *Pierrot le fou*, Godard brings together the beauty of nature and the life of shared purpose with the beloved woman as the basic preconditions of artistic creation. The problem of the couple—of Ferdinand and Marianne, of Godard and Karina—is made plainly and painfully obvious in the film's most famous moment, as Marianne wades through the water, repeatedly whining, "What can I do? I don't know what to do." Ferdinand, sitting on a boulder, tells her, "Silence! I'm writing."

Such a mode of existence, in which she provides moral and practical support for an artist in isolation from society, is not enough for Marianne, who demands a change: "I've had it! I've had it with the sea, with the sun, with the sand, and with eating from cans, that's it! I've had it with always wearing the same dress! I want to get away from here!" It is not enough for her to *be*; she cries, "I want to live!"

The couple returns to civilization and its corruptions, to what Marianne calls "a police novel with cars, revolvers, nightclubs." It is a return to sordid political violence, to living history, with its bloodshed, tumult, and imposed commitments—not just for Ferdinand and Marianne but for Godard himself.

Godard had imbued *A Married Woman* and *Alphaville* with allusions to Nazi Germany and its depredations, as they were both remembered and forgotten in the present day. But a current event elbowed the Nazi demon offstage: the American war in Vietnam. In March 1965, Jean-Paul Sartre cancelled a lecture tour of the United States because, according to Gallup polls, a majority of Americans supported the escalation of the Vietnam War—thus, he exclaimed, "dialogue is impossible." He explained, "I would not want to find myself in New York the day they are bombing Hanoi."[25] Sartre put the French left on alert that there was a new cause to take up.

Pierrot le fou is full of the Vietnam War, from a news report on the car radio to a movie-theater newsreel of the Vietcong raid on the American base at Da Nang. However, the war is just one in the litany of charges that Godard brought against the United States. Ferdinand and Marianne, intertwined on the beach in the moonlight, talk in a way that recalls the neutral French path that Godard had already begun to trace, along the lines of Bernanos, in

Alphaville. They look up at the "man in the moon," and Ferdinand explains that the man in the moon is actually packing up to leave:

> Because he's fed up. When he saw [Russian cosmonaut] Leonov coming, he was happy. You bet: finally there's somebody to talk to, after all eternity as the only man in the moon. But Leonov tried to cram the complete works of Lenin into his head. So as soon as [U.S. astronaut] White arrived, he ran over to the American side. But before he even said hello, the other guy shoved a bottle of Coca-Cola down his throat and made him first say thank you. So he's fed up. He'll let the Americans and the Russians fight it out, and he's taking off.

Yet at the scene's end, the political is ditched altogether, as Karina utters a line to Belmondo that was Godard's purest, most vulgar moment of wish-fulfillment: "Baise-moi" (Fuck me).

MARIANNE CLAIMS THAT her brother is an operative in a political gang involved in illegal arms deals; his henchmen kidnap her and use her to lure Ferdinand to their apartment. When he gets there, she has escaped, and in a scene recalling *Le Petit Soldat,* they torture him with a wet shirt on the face to find out where she is. Unlike Bruno Forestier in *Le Petit Soldat,* Ferdinand lacks courage and quickly gives them the information they demand—repeating it so there's no mistake.

Though freed by his captors, Ferdinand has lost Marianne, who, he assumes, will be killed as a result of the information he provided. He remains at the coast and scrapes by as a seaside laborer (working as a cabin boy for a woman claiming to be an exiled Lebanese princess—who plays herself in the film). Then Marianne reappears. As she and Ferdinand walk together along the beach, a pop dance troupe passes by, rehearsing a routine. Its director is Fred, whom Marianne says is also her brother.[26] Fred soon proves to be a faux brother, with whom Marianne runs away shortly thereafter, on a boat that leaves the dock moments before Ferdinand can board it.

Instead, Ferdinand takes a barge to the island of Porquerolles, sees Marianne and calls out to her, sees Fred and shoots him, then shoots Marianne. He brings her body to a villa on the island and finds an arsenal of explosives belonging to the arms runners with whom she had been working. He calls Paris to hear that his children are well; he paints his face in Yves Klein monochrome blue; he writes in his journal "LA RT" (*l'art:* art) and then puts in the middle the letters *mo* (*LAmoRT, la mort:* death); and, carrying two bound bundles of dynamite, Ferdinand climbs to the top of a rock formation, lets loose terrifying animal cries, and begins to tie the bundles of dynamite around his head. "What I wanted to say . . . oh . . . why?" Blindfolded by the dynamite, he tries to light matches; they catch and light the wick—"After all, I'm an idiot," he says. But then, regretting his decision, he tries desperately to snuff out the wick with his hands, yelling, "Shit! Shit!" Those are his last words on earth, as the dynamite explodes, in long shot, with the sea and the sky indifferent to the small human flame burning itself out in their dominion. The film's final words are by Rimbaud, its lines spoken in alternating voice-over by Karina and Belmondo:

> *It is found again.*
> *What?*
> *Eternity.*
> *It is the sea, gone*
> *With the sun.*

SHORTLY BEFORE THE release of *Pierrot le fou,* Godard admitted in an interview that upon completing the film, he had shown it to François Truffaut and asked him, "Is it a film? . . . I'm not asking whether you like it."[27] The interviewer, Gérard Guégan, pressed Godard for an explanation: "But what, in your view, is a film?" Godard explained again in terms of an imaginary talk with Hitchcock: "For *Pierrot le fou* . . . I have the impression that he would have said: 'Well, I'm sorry, but this isn't a film.' "[28]

When *Pierrot le fou* premiered at Venice, on August 29, 1965 (a mere six weeks after the end of principal photography), it was booed. At his press conference, Godard retreated behind a mask of sarcasm. ("Is your film a comedy?" "If you laughed, yes. If not, no.") Asked whether the death of Belmondo was a "conventional ending," he answered, "I don't know whether death is a traditional conclusion. In life, in general, that's how life ends." Asked whether the New Wave was dead, Godard answered, "No, since I'm still alive."[29]

The most derisive review came from Louis Marcorelles, writing in *Les Lettres françaises,* who criticized the film as "the affirmation of the nothingness of our existence, like the refusal to construct a film, to tell a story."[30] But Yvonne Baby of *Le Monde* understood its harsh reception in favorable terms: "What is original and new always arouses controversy. *Pierrot le fou* can't escape from this rule; it is being diversely received and no doubt will continue to be."[31]

The negative views of the film were indeed rapidly eclipsed by the audacious advocacy of Michel Cournot in *Le Nouvel Observateur* and of Aragon, also in *Les Lettres françaises,* who challenged the stone-faced clerics' haughty indifference and rose up on its behalf. First, Cournot, in his roundup of films from Venice, declared, "I feel no embarrassment declaring that *Pierrot le fou* is the most beautiful film I've seen in my life" and praised the film for its confessional intensity:

> People's private lives are not often my business. *Pierrot le fou* has come to scream in my face that a fairly young man whom I know, who has meant a lot to me, who has hushed his life behind great silences and a gentleness like the evening seashore, a . . . boy named Jean-Luc Godard, died, I don't know on which day last year, because he loved a woman madly, and because this woman left him.[32]

The next week, Aragon contradicted Marcorelles, his own employee, with a song of exultation that became a historic moment in French literary journalism. Aragon's oversized headline declaimed the question of the age: "What Is Art, Jean-Luc Godard?" In an excited rush of words that started on the front page and covered an entire tabloid-size inner page, Aragon answered: "There is one thing of which I am sure . . . : art today is Jean-Luc Godard." Aragon—admitting with a certain pride that *Pierrot* cites several lines from his novel *La Mise à mort* (The Execution)—asserted Godard's importance in heroic terms: "The game of saying who is Renoir and who is Buñuel does not interest me. But Godard is Delacroix."[33]

When the film was released, on November 5, 1965, Cournot raised the rhetorical stakes even higher, with an article that Godard recalled decades later for its literary flair and critical bravado: Cournot wrote about the film virtually in tongues, with each paragraph a stream-of-consciousness run-on sentence.[34] Samuel Lachize of the party-line Communist *L'Humanité* said simply, "*Pierrot le fou* is a date in the history of cinema."[35] The film was a tough ticket for weeks at the three theaters in Paris where it played. (One writer noted that it was the first time he had ever had to wait on line for a Godard film.)

However, the most important testimony to the singular power of *Pierrot le fou* was not that of critics or of the box office, but of young intellectuals on whom the film had a life-changing effect. It was, above all, young people—especially adolescents—who were struck by its importance, in the cinema and beyond (despite the film's being officially barred by the censorship board to viewers under eighteen). The philosopher Bernard-Henri Lévy said:

> I was in high school; I was seventeen years old. I went to see *Pierrot le fou* at least twelve times when it came out; I knew it by heart; I have recited it to my children . . . *Pierrot le fou* taught me love. Before, I loved women as did [Old Wave directors] Autant-Lara or Le Chanois. Instead of Micheline Presle and Gérard Philipe in *Devil in the Flesh,* it was Anna Karina and Jean-Paul

Belmondo at Porquerolles . . . I loved women more because of Godard's films. He pulled the struts out from under foolishness.[36]

Serge Toubiana, the director of the Cinémathèque in Paris and a former editor of *Cahiers du cinéma,* was a sixteen-year-old high school student in Grenoble at the time. The film "was really epochal" for him: "I had the feeling that with this film, the cinema became an art of my era, tied to my comprehension or incomprehension of the world."[37] For the filmmaker Chantal Akerman, born in 1950, *Pierrot le fou* was the determining moment in her artistic life: "I went to see the film because of its intriguing and funny title. When I came out of the theater, I was on my own little cloud. I didn't try to analyze the how and the why of it: I knew I would spend my life making films. Period."[38]

Shortly after the film came out, Godard and Michel Vianey were waiting in the lobby of a movie theater and a young woman approached them. Vianey described the scene. The young woman said:

"I just wanted to tell you how much *Pierrot le fou* overwhelmed us, my friends and me."

[Godard] looked at her kindly, moved his lips but didn't say a word.

"How much," she continued, "that film helps us to live, in a certain way, to understand life."[39]

Godard was aware of the power of *Pierrot le fou* and of its effect even on himself. As he told Vianey: "*Pierrot le fou* is a sort of voyage to the moon. A film is like a multi-stage rocket . . . The last stage went up very high . . . I haven't come back yet."[40] The next film he tried to make was conceived from this lofty new vantage—another story about a mortal crisis of an artist and his wife, who was also his model. Godard had wanted Serge and Danièle Rezvani to appear together in *Pierrot le fou* in a scene that would be filmed on the patio of their house. They agreed, but on the appointed day, Godard was shooting elsewhere and canceled. Shortly thereafter, he proposed something different: he wanted them instead to play the lead roles in an adaptation of Edgar Allan Poe's story "The Oval Portrait," the story Godard had read to Anna Karina on the sound track of *Vivre sa vie,* concerning an artist whose perfectly lifelike portrait of his wife seeps the life from her until it is completed and she dies. Rezvani and his wife refused Godard's offer; they were willing to take bit parts, but did not want to be lead actors. Rezvani, however, was well aware that the film they refused was to have been "complementary" to *Pierrot le fou.*[41] Godard greatly regretted not having been able to make the film. "It would have been extraordinary,"[42] he said.

The unrealized film of "The Oval Portrait" would have resembled a counterfactual version of *Pierrot le fou*—an exploration of what might have happened had Marianne been content to remain alongside Ferdinand as he worked, with her help, to fulfill his artistic projects. Godard was struggling to reach a compassionate understanding of what Marianne/Anna might have been thinking when she sought escape from the life of an artistic idyll—and the Poe story offered a reasonable answer: to save herself. (As explanations go, this one had the virtue, for Godard, of displacing the couple's problems from life to art, from Godard's person to a universal or quasi-metaphysical matter of fate.)

Instead, by the time that Godard made his next film, *Masculine Feminine,* in the gray chill of late fall, he had hardened the view of women that had led to the wrath of *Pierrot:* the woman does not think at all; instead, functioning as a force of nature (or the protagonist of her life's drama), she inevitably destroys those who seek to harness her energy, whether in life or in art. In practical terms, starting with *Pierrot le fou,* Godard would show the man dying at the end, not the woman.

MASCULINE FEMININE

"I no longer know where I am"

W HILE MAKING *PIERROT LE FOU*, GODARD HAD
looked for ways not to be alone. As he began work on his
next film, *Masculine Feminine*, he considered himself to
be more solitary than ever. Since *Breathless*, Godard had felt an increasing
sense of the loss of the fellow feeling and complicity of the auteurist "cell"
to which he had belonged throughout the 1950s; now, before the shoot of
Masculine Feminine, he expressed his longing for such shared purpose and
time with a heightened pathos. In the spring of 1965, in a preface to the
published script of Truffaut's *The Soft Skin*, Godard recalled his youthful
rambles with Truffaut:

> On a stifling Saturday in July, we set off from Clichy . . . the most beautiful
> square in Paris, François was sure of it . . . we had bought cigars next to the
> Atomic . . . then gone all the way to the Pax-Sèvres, where my godmother
> slipped us 10,000 francs, my month's allowance in advance . . . we went to
> see *The Red Angel* with Tilda Thamar . . . "what a beautiful woman!"
> François kept saying.[1]

In a note on *Pierrot le fou* that Godard contributed to *Cahiers du
cinéma* later in the year, he returned to the same theme: "One evening, two
or three cinéphile friends, because they were too poor to pay for a taxi,
were forced to cross the city on foot from the Cinémathèque to their garret
rooms."[2] The intensity, the constancy, and the fanatical unity of purpose of
the seminal years of the rising New Wave had become for Godard an object
of nostalgia.

Jean-Pierre Léaud talks, Chantal Goya listens; Marlène Jobert waits in the background.
(Royal Films / Photofest)

He was in need of sympathetic intellectual companionship, and during the making of *Masculine Feminine,* he sought it with the writer Michel Vianey. In October 1965, several days after returning from the New York Film Festival, Godard invited Vianey for lunch and asked him to do what he had been unavailable to do for *Pierrot le fou,* to follow Godard around and write a book about the making of the film. Surprised by the simplicity of the terms, Vianey repeated them back to Godard: "I'll observe you, I'll write everything that I see." Godard responded, "Yes, yes, exactly as you see it. I'll tell you everything, you'll be my confidant." In amazement, Vianey repeated, "I'll follow you everywhere?" "Everywhere."[3] Having invited Vianey to spend the next four months in his constant company, Godard also offered to pay Vianey for his time.[4]

Vianey closely observed the preparation, the filming, and the postproduction of *Masculine Feminine.* He visited Godard's office on the rue Edouard-Nortier in Neuilly to observe meetings with actors, went location-scouting with him, dined with him, and was present on the set for most of the shoot. Their frequent discussions gave Godard a chance to talk out his ideas as the shooting progressed. A novelist and a journalist, Vianey was a well-informed interlocutor on current themes. If *Masculine Feminine* shows a more concrete view of practical reality than any of Godard's other early films and conveys, or conjures, with uncanny precision, a sense of place, time, and historical moment, it is due, at least in part, to the film's development through Godard's ongoing dialogue with Vianey.

MASCULINE FEMININE RESULTED from the seed of an idea planted by the producer Anatole Dauman, one of the major figures in the French art cinema (he also produced films by Resnais and Bresson). In September 1964 he commissioned an erotic film from Godard, and in order, as the producer later recalled, "to excite him a little, and mindful of certain Swedish films that were doing unforgettably well at the box office in the United States,"[5] Dauman gave him a book to read on the trip: *Philosophy in the Bedroom,* by the Marquis de Sade.

Upon his return to Paris, Godard signed with Dauman for a short film called *Avec le sourire* (With the Smile), based on "Le Signe" ("The Signal") by Maupassant, the story from which he had made his first fiction film, *Une Femme coquette,* in 1955. The story concerns a woman who sees a prostitute attract a man with the slightest of gestures; she attempts the same gesture at her own window, and to her horror, a man assumes that she, too, is a prostitute. He comes to her room and insists on her services—which, in order to get him to leave before her husband's return, she provides. Dauman gave Godard an advance of five thousand francs (a thousand dollars), and bought the film rights from the executors of Maupassant's estate.

In *Une Femme coquette,* Godard had moved the action outdoors and staged the man's persistence as a car chase. Now, for Dauman, Godard sketched out a new and different adaptation, which treats the man's pursuit as comedy and follows it with a sardonic bedroom scene in which the comedy turns serious: the man corners the woman in her hotel room and, declaring that he "fully intends to fuck her," delivers a self-justifying erotico-philosophical discourse derived from *Philosophy in the Bedroom.*[6]

Godard agreed to make the film in December 1964, just before filming *Alphaville,* but, as Dauman later recalled, Godard changed his mind: "The day before he was to start shooting, Godard bluntly announced that he was in no condition to direct because of his blood pressure. I got worried: 'What is your blood pressure?' He replied: '120 over 80' "—that is, normal.[7] Dauman agreed to the postponement because he suspected that something would nonetheless come of the unfulfilled contract and its outstanding obligation.

Dauman was right. "Sure enough," he later recalled, "soon after that Godard came to see me with a disarming smile to announce that he was going to direct Jean-Pierre Léaud in some further adventures of Antoine Doinel in-between the episodes of Truffaut's series."[8]

The character of Doinel—the character played by Léaud in François Truffaut's *The 400 Blows* and the short film *Love at Twenty*—was on hold at the time, as were the careers of Truffaut and Léaud. Truffaut had put all other projects aside while waiting for *Fahrenheit 451* to be financed.[9] Léaud, who had been virtually adopted by Truffaut after *The 400 Blows,* had not acted in a film since *Love at Twenty,* in 1962. Born in 1944, Léaud had been a difficult adolescent. He had been kicked out of school and out of the home of a retired couple to whose care Truffaut had entrusted him. Living in a small studio apartment that Truffaut rented for him, Léaud worked as an assistant on *The Soft Skin* and on Truffaut's production of *Mata Hari.* Godard then hired him as an assistant on *A Married Woman* and *Alphaville.* Shortly after the shoot of *Alphaville* ended, in early 1965, Godard took Léaud to dinner and offered him the lead role in the film that would follow *Pierrot le fou.* He also asked Léaud to join him again as assistant on *Pierrot.*

Michel Vianey, who visited the shoot of *Pierrot* on location in Paris in the summer of 1965, described how Léaud's experience as Godard's assistant looked to him:

I remember him holding back the onlookers at the quai de Javel during the shoot of *Pierrot le fou*, being treated roughly by Godard who suddenly turned ferocious, his voice like a kick, "Good God, how many times must I, you're all such jerks," in a voice like a Gauleiter, and Léaud not sulking but coming back to him, obedient and zealous, hardly more irritated, at least outwardly, than a carriage horse brought into line by his coachman.[10]

Léaud, for his part, told Vianey that the experience brought him "a joy that was . . . incalculable," because, he said, he felt like "a student of Leonardo da Vinci who mixes his colors. Leonardo sees the colors. Well, well! and dips his brush in it. What happiness for the student, right?"

Léaud's fervent devotion to Godard and acceptance of his methods proved as essential to the new film as the off-screen presence of Vianey. Godard's nostalgic view of the intense companionship of his own youth gave rise to a fascination with youth as such, and through his work with Léaud, he made this the raw material of which *Masculine Feminine* was composed.

WHEN GODARD CAME back to Dauman with a project starring Léaud, he had in mind a feature-film adaptation of *two* Maupassant stories, "The Signal" and "La Femme de Paul" ("Paul's Wife"), which Godard described as "the story of a boy who is in love with a girl and it doesn't work out because this girl is in love with another girl."[11] Dauman bought the rights to film "Paul's Wife" and then recruited Swedish coproducers to the project, whose investment was contingent on a Swedish on-screen presence. Dauman went ahead and advertised his forthcoming project with Godard, titled "Paul's Wife, with the Smile," and featuring Michel Piccoli, "an unknown Swedish woman," Jean-Pierre Léaud, and "an unknown French woman."[12] (Piccoli, who would have played the client in "The Signal," did not take part in the end.)

The casting was not the only factor up in the air. Several days after joining the project, Vianey went to Godard's office to pick up a copy of the screenplay. To his surprise it was just a few pages long.[13] The text begins:

This film tells the story of Paul and Madeleine. They met in the office of *Age tendre*, a magazine, where he files photographs and she, together with some girlfriends, belongs to a "shopping" group.

We will follow the rise of Paul's passion for Madeleine, who is anything but tender with him.

We will see them at the Olympia, one Sunday, at the Barclay studios for the recording of Madeleine's first 45.

Midway through the film, we will see them go, one dark and rainy Parisian Sunday afternoon, to the movies.

Paul and Madeleine have gone to see a film called *With the Smile,* directed by Jean-Luc Godard (for which the credits appear on-screen). There follows a film-within-a-film that keeps to the contours of the adaptation of Maupassant's "The Signal" that Godard had originally sketched for Dauman, except that the woman is now Swedish. Paul and Madeleine leave the theater before the film ends.

> This moment comes at about one hour into the film. The last third will be devoted to the disappointment of Paul, who notices that Madeleine prefers life with her girlfriends (especially one of them, a Swedish au pair at her parents' home) to life with him.

The idea of making Madeleine a singer arose from the Maupassant story itself, in which the young woman (who, unlike Madeleine, is a prostitute) sings a popular tune that suggests to Paul the cultural gap separating them. In early November, Godard found a candidate for the role, the pop singer Chantal Goya, through a picture that he saw in a newspaper. She was nineteen years old and enjoying her first success on the record charts. Godard made contact with her through Daniel Filipacchi, the new owner of *Cahiers du cinéma,* who was also the director of artists and repertory at her record company. Goya told Godard that she was not an actress, and he responded, "That's exactly it, that's what I'm looking for: creatures who are neither film nor stage actresses." He did not audition her; as she later recalled, "He had me talk to him for more than an hour about what I liked, how I lived, what I'd read, what kind of music I admired, and so on."[14]

The story in which she would co-star covered the full range of the young couple's relationship: Paul's accidental meeting with Madeleine in a café; their flirtations during work at a teen magazine (a job that Madeleine helps him get); the stages of their affair (including the effect on their relationship of Madeleine's sudden celebrity); Paul's discovery that Madeleine is unusually attached to one of her roommates; Madeleine's discovery that she is pregnant; and the ambiguous act of self-destruction that brings about Paul's death.

Godard also expanded the young couple's story to include their relations with Madeleine's two female roommates, Elizabeth and Catherine, and with Paul's friend Robert. He cast two inexperienced actresses (Marlène Jobert and Catherine Duport) as the women;[15] to play Robert, he chose Michel Debord, a young salesman whom he had seen playing pinball in a Montparnasse café. Around these five characters Godard gave the film a simple, poignant structure infused with romantic longing: Robert loves Catherine, who loves Paul, who loves Madeleine, who loves both Paul and Elizabeth.

It was important to Godard that the actors were essentially nonprofessionals. He considered the young actors identical with their roles and said, "There is no difference between what they were doing with their days and what they were acting out in the film."[16] Their identity as people, not their ability as performers, was to be the essence of the film. It was also essential to Godard that they be young—for personal as well as artistic reasons:

> I chose young people because I no longer know where I am from the point of view of cinema. I am in search of the cinema. I have the sense of having lost it. Chatting with young people to find myself again was easier than with adults, because adults have too many personal problems and to get to the bottom of things there is an immense amount of work that one doesn't have time to do in the course of a film . . . This film is thus a need to speak with people who are more open. Who have their life before them.[17]

Masculine Feminine is a film of constant talking and is, in the truest sense, a "talking film" (which is exactly what Godard calls it in the first title card). In the casting process, Godard made clear to his actors that he expected them to be extremely verbal. As Marlène Jobert told Vianey:

> When I think . . . that he also intends to ask me questions before the camera, without any preparation, live, my armpits start to sweat . . .
> "It's very simple," he says, "I'll ask you a question through an actor and you respond very naturally. Birth control, for instance, what do you think about birth control? If you don't know what it is, say so, ask for an explanation. Really, it's very simple."[18]

Godard constructed the story to allow for such on-screen conversations. He broke the action down into fifteen discrete sequences, which he called "precise facts." The scenes were planned around simple locations (cafés, an apartment in the Grenelle neighborhood, an elevated métro line, the offices of Filipacchi's *Pariscope*)[19] with a minimum of characters, extras, and props. Each sequence was structured around simple activities—entrances and exits to and from cafés, laundromats, offices, apartments—and left ample leeway for discussions and digressions. There was little in the way of preparation or rehearsal to distract the actors from the task at hand, which was, above all, to be themselves.

On Monday, November 22, Chantal Goya came to the first day's location, a café at the Porte des Lilas: "I tried to find out where the makeup woman was: there wasn't one. I was stupefied to find neither spotlights nor floodlights. They were filming with natural light: just the light of the café."[20]

The next day, the crew moved to another café on the periphery of Paris to film the movie's first scene, which efficiently and movingly set up the fault lines of the drama: Léaud is seen sitting by himself at a table and writing a poetic and paradoxical rumination on his solitude and on "talking for twenty-four straight hours," which he slowly recites aloud as he composes it. The moment, of an intense bohemian romanticism, is first undercut by Paul's comical flip of a cigarette through the air to his lips, and then shifts when Madeleine, crisply dressed and coiffed, enters the café. Paul, who recognizes her as a friend of a friend, starts a conversation in which he admits his unemployment and asks whether she might help him find work at her magazine. (He also reads to her from his philosophical critique of his military service, a text that Godard took from a recent issue of *Les Temps Modernes*.)[21] Thus the ruminative, passionate intellectual and the practical, guarded career girl meet; the scene initiates Godard's critical view of the world of modern youth as well as his poetic rhapsody on the dreams and fears of all youth.

THE LONG DIALOGUE scenes around which Godard built *Masculine Feminine* were filmed (like those of *Vivre sa vie*) in extremely long takes. Most of the "interview" shots run over a minute or two, and one bravura shot, of an actual interview by Paul of a young woman crowned "Miss 19" for the eponymous magazine, ran more than six minutes.

Unlike *Vivre sa vie*, *Masculine Feminine* was filmed with an unadorned directness that looked the performers in the face as if in discussion with them; Godard no longer felt the need to prove his intellectual bona fides by filming the speakers from behind. Where the camera moves in *Vivre sa vie* called attention to themselves, now the style of filming emphasized the performers. If *Vivre sa vie*, with its elaborate text, was something of an oratorio, *Masculine Feminine*, with its largely improvised dialogue, was more of a work of journalism.

The film was made with an openness to chance and circumstance; Godard intended the production of *Masculine Feminine* to be both efficient and close to the reality he was filming. When an assistant suggested that the café telephone be disconnected during the shots, Godard replied that if the phone rang, the woman tending the counter should simply answer it (as indeed happened during a take that remains in the film). Godard filmed in Filipacchi's offices the same way, during business hours, with employees as extras, their telephone conversations preserved on the sound track.

THE FILM'S HIGHLY charged mood of longing and intimate engagement with daily life, its blend of realism and romanticism, are due as much to the way it looks as to what it depicts. Respect for available light was among Godard's and Raoul Coutard's standard working methods, but *Masculine Feminine* was not shot by Coutard—who, after *Pierrot le fou*, took a break from Godard and was working with Tony Richardson on *The Sailor from Gibraltar*—but by Willy Kurant.

Born in 1934, Kurant was ten years younger than Coutard. Like Coutard, Kurant was primarily a documentary cinematographer, with almost a decade of experience on newsreels and documentaries in Africa and Vietnam; unlike Coutard, Kurant had done an apprenticeship with established movie cameramen as well, and despite the extraordinary quality and inventiveness of Kurant's work, the vestiges of this apprenticeship spoiled his working relations with Godard.

The film was made with a heavy Mitchell camera, which, as in *Vivre sa vie*, enabled, indeed forced, Godard to compose his images with care. The camera was mounted on a rolling dolly, and Kurant would turn and tilt it by means of wheel-like cranks. He had never worked with such a device, but Godard told him not to worry: "We'll start slowly." Then, on the first day of the shoot, Kurant learned that he was to do what Vianey described as "a five-minute-long traveling shot with no other lighting beside the faded light of troubled waters that the steamy café windows dispense."[22] Kurant and the actors nailed the shot—in which Paul proposes marriage to Madeleine, and she defers answering—on the second take, and the day's work ended at noon, but Godard rapidly turned on him.

Kurant was more risk-averse than Coutard. Working in the mainstream industry, he was accustomed to having more time to prepare shots. When he asked for details of a scene being set up, Godard answered, "Stop whining, for God's sake, you'll find out."[23] Kurant wanted the actors to rehearse for the camera, which Godard was disinclined to do. When a question of image quality caused him to interrupt a spontaneous interview shot, Godard exploded with anger.

Godard complained to Vianey, "Willy is very good, but too fearful and that annoys me. I'd like him to be more precise in his thoughts than in his technique. . . ."[24] As the shoot went on, Godard stopped speaking to Kurant altogether, instead passing his instructions to Kurant's assistant, William Lubtchansky. The freeze-out ended, however, after Godard and

Kurant went to Stockholm together to work on the film-within-a-film based on "The Signal." Upon their return to Paris, Godard became solicitous, meeting Kurant at the airport, taking him out to dinner, extending to him all sorts of courtesies on location. Yet the damage had been done: Kurant did not have as thick a skin as Coutard (who took pride in giving as good as he got in his fights with Godard), and despite his superlative work, he and Godard never teamed up again.

As it happens, Kurant's methods were considered to be, in their way, as innovative as those of Coutard: for the little bit of lighting Godard allowed, Kurant placed lightbulbs behind tracing paper, under white umbrellas, or in front of white plastic reflectors, to raise the ambient light without harshening the shadows. The result was a muted winter effect that corresponded perfectly to the mood of the film and the days of the shoot. Kurant established a tonality of pale sun and softened shadows, a palette of grays evocative of the damp chill of the city's glass and stone.

DEVELOPING THE STORY of romantic intimacy and wordly experience with close attention to his actors' reality, Godard let them speak for themselves, except when he wanted them to get his own ideas across. In a long scene with Paul and Madeleine outside the bathroom of the magazine where they work (she succeeded in helping Paul find a job there), Godard filmed their responses to his questions and then had the actors, off-camera, repeat his questions, which were dubbed in. During their suddenly intimate talk about sex and romance, Madeleine asks Paul what he considers the center of the world; Paul (Léaud, unscripted) answers, "Love, I suppose," while Madeleine (as prompted by Godard) says, "That's funny, I would have said, 'me.'"

The film drew on Chantal Goya's pop-based rock music and the media scene surrounding it. Madeleine's new single moves up the charts, and she is sought out by print and radio journalists. But Paul is a lover of classical music; he adores the Mozart Clarinet Concerto (which Godard had put in *Breathless*) and when Madeleine brings him a record signed by the pop star Sylvie Vartan, he responds, "I'd have preferred Bach." With an antic, ridiculous rapidity, he reads aloud a breathlessly vapid piece of newspaper puffery written about Madeleine (leading her to believe that he's mocking her and not the writing). Later, Madeleine, interviewed by a radio journalist, gladly declares herself a member of the "Pepsi generation."

Saturating *Masculine Feminine* with the artifacts, trends, and moods of the moment, Godard made it both a kind of documentary on its actors and on the times in which it was made. Godard tied his characters to the concerns of the day, making current events the stuff of their private lives. He did this with form as well as content: through the skillful use of dedramatization, of having his characters talk about events taking place off-screen, he was able to stay close to his characters while conjuring the world around them.

In fact, Godard reshaped the story to admit the documentary element: Paul changes jobs midway through the film and becomes an interviewer for a polling firm. (The idea was borrowed from a notable new first novel, *Les Choses* [Things], by the twenty-nine-year-old Georges Perec, who, with a documentary audacity akin to Godard's own, subtitled his book *A Novel of the 1960s.*)[25] As part of his new job, he interviews "Miss 19" with remarkable results: she resists talking about birth control, knows nothing about politics, and speaks freely about her materialistic hopes and dreams. Godard asserts his own view of the proceedings with a title card: "Dialogue with a Consumer Product."

In filming young people, Godard was also filming representatives of a generation, and he constructed the film as a "sociological" attempt to define that generation, summing up his findings on-screen in a trio of title cards: "This film could be called / The children of Marx Coca-Cola / Understand who will." The now-famous phrase[26] is not as straightforward as it seems, because it leaves open the question whether these children are the product of Marx and Coca-Cola both, or whether there are two different groups—that is, the children of Marx and the children of Coca-Cola. Godard himself glossed it both ways:

> I no longer have any connection to my elders, who are the children of the Liberation, nor to my juniors, who are the "children of Marx and of Coca-Cola."
>
> That's the name I give them in the film. They are influenced by socialism— taken in a very modern economic sense—and by American life. The class struggle is no longer the same as we were taught in books. Formerly, "Mrs. Marx" could not be married to "Mr. Coca-Cola." Today we see lots of households like that.
>
> One can say that Jean-Pierre Léaud (the boy) and Chantal Goya (the little *yé-yé* [pop] singer) represent the left and the right, respectively.[27]

Masculine Feminine was made under the express sign of contemporary politics, with its first title card declaring the film to be "one of the 121 French talking films of which only 3 or 4 are made" (the number 121 being instantly recognizable as an allusion to the "Manifesto of 121" of 1960, in which intellectuals called for resistance to the Algerian War). In one sense, *Masculine*

Feminine is even more political than *Le Petit Soldat,* in that it refers to the specific political events that took place while the film was being shot—mainly, the presidential election of December 5, 1965, the first direct vote for a French head of state since 1848.[28]

The French staked out a remarkably short electoral season: François Mitterrand was appointed the candidate of the "unified left" (including the Communist Party) only in October, and Charles de Gaulle himself, the incumbent, did not officially declare his candidacy until November 4, thirty-one days before the election.

"Times had changed," Paul says in voice-over. "This was the era of James Bond and of Vietnam. A great wave of hope had arisen among the French left with the approach of the December elections." Paul and his friend Robert express their own hope as they travel around Paris putting up posters for Mitterrand, yet, filming young people, Godard kept their activities in an exuberantly youthful vein, with the politics coming through as well in obscene pranks, adolescent humor, and shaggy-dog stories. In the young women's apartment, Catherine and Paul play with a toy guillotine, which Godard photographs in close-up while the sound track resounds with the oratorical thunder of a speech by André Malraux at a rally for de Gaulle. Later, Paul spray-paints an election slogan in huge, slovenly letters on the blank wall behind a movie theater—"DE GAULLE = UBU" (the ludicrous despot of Alfred Jarry's play *Ubu Roi*)—but French censorship required that the shot be trimmed before *UBU* could be completely spelled out.

The results of the election, which Godard did not announce in the film, were a surprise to most observers: de Gaulle failed to receive a majority on the first round and was forced into a runoff against Mitterrand. Though de Gaulle won the December 19 runoff with 54.5 percent of the vote, his victory was hardly resounding, and many (including de Gaulle, who was seventy-five years old) wondered whether he would serve out his term. The narrow reelection, a crucial event in modern France, indicated a significant weakening of de Gaulle's authority; it was a portent of change.

Masculine Feminine is centered on one of the key issues of the presidential campaign, which appears in the film as the most pressing problem in the young people's lives: birth control. Contraception for women was illegal in France, having been banned there in 1920, and Mitterrand campaigned to rescind the ban (which, at the time, kept "the pill" off the market).[29] The young women discuss different types of contraception frequently, with each other and with Paul, specifically with regard to Madeleine's refusal to use it because she finds it "indecent."

Near the end of the film, after Paul has fallen to his death from the roof of the new building in which, with an inheritance, he has bought an apartment, Madeleine is revealed to be pregnant with his child. She tells the police that she was considering using a curtain rod on herself. (Abortion was also illegal and would remain so until 1974.) The disconnection between private beliefs and public dictates was crucial not only to the election and to radical social changes on the way but, as Godard suggested, to the young French psyche and the unending quest for love.

Indeed, one of Godard's most impressive achievements in *Masculine Feminine* is his translation of public and grand-scale politics into personal and intimate dramatic terms. The Vietnam War is frequently mentioned in the film, whether in a discussion of a newspaper clipping about the "Vietnik" Bob Dylan, or in Paul and Robert's prank of painting "Peace in Vietnam" on the side of an American military vehicle; it recurs in a shocking, somber register, in a scene where Paul describes having just seen a man immolate himself in front of the American Hospital next to a written demand for "peace in Vietnam."

The random violence that pervades *Masculine Feminine*—starting with credits accompanied not by music but by gunfire (which recurs throughout), followed by a first scene that ends with a woman shooting her estranged husband, and continuing with an evening's nightclub festivities where a stranger menaces Paul with a long knife and then stabs himself—serves as explicit political critique of the Vietnam War and American politics.

A harsh, angry scene that Godard took almost verbatim from the play *Dutchman,* by LeRoi Jones, which had opened that November in Paris,[30] is set in a moving métro car and features the play's French cast. A white woman tells a black man that all "Negroes" are "potential assassins," and he concurs, but gives her notion a radical slant:

> Take Charlie Parker . . . if you said to him, Charlie, my boy, throw away your sax and you'll have the right to shoot the first ten white people you see in the street, he'd toss his horn into the sea and never play another note in his life, not one.[31]

In response, the woman shoots him (though the event is presented off-camera, as a sound effect, because the head of French public transportation denied permission to film a killing in the métro).

Godard expressed his fundamental resistance to America, its influence and authority, in terms of the cinema. When Paul and the three young women go to the movies to watch what turns out to be a sordid Swedish sex film (the adaptation of Maupassant's "The Signal," reduced to a wordless, grunting brutality), Paul delivers a monologue in voice-over which speaks to Godard's own painful loss of allegiance to the classic American cinema.

> We often went to the cinema, the screen would light up and we would trem-
> ble, but also, increasingly often, Madeleine and I were disappointed. The im-
> ages had dated, they jittered, and Marilyn Monroe had gotten terribly old. We
> were sad, this wasn't the film we had dreamed of, this wasn't the total film that
> we all carried around inside us, this film that we would have wanted to make,
> or, more secretly, no doubt, that we would have wanted to live.

Godard clipped this monologue nearly verbatim from Georges Perec's novel *Les Choses*—but crucially added Marilyn Monroe's name to a text that had no specific American reference.

Although Godard infused the film with his critique of American society and its rising influence in France, his views focus less on his conflicts with the world at large than on his conflict with women. The young women in *Masculine Feminine* take their place in the series of women that Godard be-gan to define with *Le Nouveau Monde*, whose sexual morality, which he viewed dubiously, was correlated with their cheerful acceptance of American fashions and values.

Speaking with the young people who would be his performers during the planning of *Masculine Feminine*, Godard came to some conclusions about them, and about himself. He told Vianey, "One thought oneself to be young. For example, I thought that I was still twenty-two years old, then sud-denly, in their presence, one notices that one is old."[32] To another journalist who visited him on the set, Godard said, "At thirty-five years of age, I always say to myself that I'm twenty-two, but when I spoke with these girls, I saw that they considered me the way I myself might consider François Mauriac [who was eighty years old]. That's what ages a person."[33] His use of the phrase "these girls" is revealing, for the generation gap in *Masculine Feminine* is pri-marily a gender gap. In particular, it exists in relation to the film's young women, whom Godard depicts as self-centered, vapid, and avid only for money and comfort. In discussion after discussion—all guided by Godard— the young women are exposed as ignorant of politics and indifferent to them, enamored of the American way of life and the consumer society.

Godard summed up his view of these young women in a title card that follows a conversation between the roommates Catherine and Elizabeth: "The mole has no consciousness, but it burrows through the earth in a spe-cific direction."[34] Speaking to an interviewer about the young women's po-litical "indifference," he described it as "the lack of precision, the permanent refuge in generalities. Girls today, they aren't mean, they aren't deep, they're open. They always speak in generalities. Unless you ask them what brand of stockings they wear, or what kind of brassiere."[35]

Masculine Feminine is not the portrait of a generation but a portrait of a gender that Godard considered particularly susceptible to the political and social influences of new times—which are the same times of *Le Nouveau Monde*, *A Married Woman*, and *Alphaville*. His lack of sympathy for the young women in the film is apparent, even to Godard himself, who told Vianey that one of the film's problems was that he didn't "like the characters enough . . . at least, the girls." He continued, "They're very good, they're perfect, and yet they don't really interest me."[36]

It was rather the young men who interested him, especially Paul, who was modeled so closely on Godard. "He is in life as in his film," Godard said, "he is one of those people who walk through life seeing only the sad things. He sees them, I show them. That's how I am too."[37] Specifically, Godard said, the character of Paul is "a sort of Werther in the midst of the Rolling Stones."[38]

Far from being exemplary of his generation, Léaud is a stand-in for Godard; not only is he the third "Paul," after those of *Vivre sa vie* and *Contempt*, but he shares, most overtly, Godard's sense of life. Paul is a writer without an oeuvre, an autodidact intellectual classicist, who "talks 24 hours a day" to escape his solitude; he is hopelessly and uncalculatingly, romantically and impractically in love with a woman who guilelessly and calmly pulls him in and pushes him away, caresses him and insults him, makes love to him and betrays him, a woman whose sense of art and of life are utterly remote from his own.

As in *Pierrot le fou*, *Masculine Feminine* ends not with the death of the faithless woman but with the self-destruction of the betrayed man. Asked by the assistant Bernard Toublanc-Michel whether Paul's fall from the roof of a building under construction was an accident or a suicide, Godard responded, "Ummm . . . he falls. No. He falls. He steps back . . . One doesn't really know. He falls."[39] In the Maupassant story, Paul leaps into the river in suicidal despair; in *Masculine Feminine*, Paul and the new world he lives in are simply unsuited for each other, as unsuited as he is to the woman he loves, yet who is in perfect harmony with it. Paul's mortal fall is an even more radical version of Godard's critique of the modern city, which is built for the pleasure of Mrs. Coca-Cola, not for the well-being of Mr. Marx.

JEAN-PIERRE LÉAUD, WHO turned twenty-one in May 1965, was the most atypical young adult imaginable. He had absorbed an intensely anachronistic set of influences from Truffaut and Godard, who were his spiritual fathers. He was in life what his character Antoine Doinel represented in the cinema—the first child of the New Wave. Léaud recognized the extraordinary originality of Godard's methods in *Masculine Feminine*, asserting that Godard "was rediscovering the cinema in the course of the shoot."[40] Together with Godard's film, he inspired a new generation of filmmakers.

Godard counseled young filmmakers to imitate his simplified technique, suggesting in an interview that young aspiring filmmakers buy a roll of 16mm film and shoot: "He lives somewhere, he films his neighborhood; if he's a printer he films his print shop, if he's a cyclist he films his race."[41]

Jean Eustache, a twenty-seven-year-old cinephile in the *Cahiers du cinéma* circle,[42] picked up quickly on the example when he planned a medium-length film, to be shot in his family's town, Narbonne, in the south of France. *Le Père Noël a les yeux bleus* (Santa Claus Has Blue Eyes) concerns a young man who works as a sidewalk Santa and rapidly discovers that the role is an ideal device for picking up girls. Léaud played the lead among a cast of amateurs. The actors and the crew worked for free; the film stock came from Godard, who sent Eustache via express mail his "short ends" (the leftover, unexposed parts of rolls of film). When Eustache fell 20,000 francs (four thousand dollars) in debt, Godard agreed to cover his costs and became the film's nominal producer.[43]

The film, which went on to commercial release in France and abroad, was merely the prelude to Eustache's 1972 masterpiece, *The Mother and the Whore*—the ultimate talking film (running an epic three and a half hours) about young people desperately in love and the political critique that their intimate turmoil implies—again with Léaud in the lead role. The simplified technique of *Masculine Feminine* offered a method—one that specifically befit the director's independent film about young people, the modern cinematic Bildungsroman. It became the method that was used for more or less every first-person classic of beginning filmmakers, from *Clerks* and *Slacker* to *Go Fish* and *Judy Berlin*.

For Godard, however, *Masculine Feminine* was hardly a vehicle for a beginning filmmaker, although in a certain way he was starting over. He had fallen back on the method in the agonizing absence of former certainties. The radical simplification that Godard employed, or discovered, in *Masculine Feminine* suggests his repudiation of his complete and obsessive cinematic education. For Godard, *Masculine Feminine* was a leap into the void, and he said as much to an interviewer shortly after the film's completion.

I am in search of what it means for me [to direct a film]. And I do it because I am searching. If Sartre still writes today, I am sure that it is because he no longer knows what it means to write. He is relearning it and the only way to relearn it is indeed to begin again to write, and I have something of the same feeling with regard to the cinema. I notice that I no longer know anything at all.[44]

Masculine Feminine presented a method—but Godard was no more inclined to follow his 1965 formula than he had followed any of the others that earlier works, such as *Breathless* and *Vivre sa vie,* had suggested. The models that Godard would go on to reject included those of his own devising.

WHEN *MASCULINE FEMININE* was released in France, the rediscovery of Léaud and the emergence of the young actresses were received by Godard's particular audience with delight. In *Cahiers du cinéma,* Michel Delahaye praised the film's convergence with "life." For a laugh, the editors of *Cahiers* reprinted a review that had appeared in the teen magazine *Salut les copains:* "[Godard] has understood nothing of what constitutes the originality of a young person of today compared with a young person of his generation."[45]

It was not, however, only the cheerleaders of the *yé-yé* set who leveled such accusations. One director, Philippe Garrel, who, inspired by Godard, had started to make films at the age of sixteen in 1964, later recalled: "I remember that when I was young, the only film by Godard that I didn't like was *Masculine Feminine,* because of its mockery of young people, that way of making fun of them."[46]

Godard's harsh view of the young—or rather, of young women—provoked a minor scandal. In May 1966, the newspaper *Candide* ran an article asking, "These Horrid Little French Girls—Are They Your Daughters?"[47] In an interview several weeks later, "Miss 19," Elsa Leroy, whom Paul had interrogated at length in the film, said that Godard's efforts to expose her political ignorance left her feeling "a little bit as a woman must feel when she's invited to pose for fashion photographs and is then asked to get undressed."[48]

In the United States, *Masculine Feminine*'s intimate naturalism was better received than the extravagant symbolism of *Pierrot le fou.* Both films played at the 1966 New York Film Festival. Andrew Sarris recognized the methods of *Masculine Feminine* to be "instant classicism"[49] and understood that Godard was fusing up-to-the-minute documentary with his "wounded cry."[50] Pauline Kael also enthused about *Masculine Feminine.*

"Godard has liberated his feeling for modern youth from the American gangster-movie framework which limited his expressiveness and his relevance to the non-movie-centered world," she wrote in *The New Republic*. Having formerly praised Godard for his clever appropriation of American genre conventions, she now saw his rejection of them as a sign of maturity and worldliness rather than a sign of anguish. Kael praised Godard for joining politics and romance, and sensed that he had invented a new way of constructing a film—"Godard has, at last, created the form he needed. It is a combination of essay, journalistic sketches, news and portraiture, love lyric and satire." She claimed that Godard's view of youth had a documentary veracity, and wrote that the film contained "life," by contrast with *Vivre sa vie* and *Pierrot le fou*, which she deemed "cold and empty."[51]

AFTER FOUR MONTHS of immersion in Godard's milieu, Vianey had trouble writing his book. *En attendant Godard* (Waiting for Godard) is not a typical work of journalism. Although Vianey affirms that all of the events and quotations he provides are true, he wrote the book interpretively, attributing to the people profiled in it emotions and ideas that he deduced from his observations. In effect, he was writing nonfiction with a novelist's tools. He discussed the problem with Godard; they agreed that, rather than calling the book's main character "Jean-Luc," Vianey would call him "Edmond"—though all of the other people in the book are called by their own names. Vianey later recalled that the purpose of the shift was to scrape the received ideas of the public image off the character and to start with a fresh canvas.[52] Godard sympathized with Vianey and contributed a preface, in the form of a rebus, which graciously sought to explain to the reader the difficulty of the task that the writer had taken on. Puzzled out, it forms the sentence: "Regrettably, it's impossible to write on the subject of Godard, because he does cinema."[53]

An unnamed reviewer in *Le Monde* praised Vianey's book as "the first 'literary' transcription of [Godard's] style."[54] There were other, unfavorable, reviews of the book, however—indeed the book, with its subjective, first-person modernism, attracted vituperation akin to that which traditionalists reserved for Godard's films. Willy Kurant was furious at Vianey's revelations of Godard's displeasure with him and, fearing that his career could be damaged, even considered suing the author.[55] For several years Godard remained in intermittent contact with Vianey, but by the time of the book's release, in 1967, he was already in a remote political and cinematic universe.

Vianey himself became a screenwriter and director in the 1970s, but his career was thwarted by generational, political, and economic shifts in the industry, and he returned to writing novels. Out of print since its first edition, Vianey's book still offers the most thorough and perceptive view available of how Godard works and how his conduct on and off the set converges with his art; additionally, its stylistic and reflexive fillips have a time-capsule authenticity akin to that of Tom Wolfe's journalism. In 1993, Jacques Drillon of *Le Nouvel Observateur* acclaimed *En attendant Godard* as "a magnificent book, which one can reread every year, if one can find it . . ."[56]

One telling tribute to Godard's methods in *Masculine Feminine* came from an unlikely source. On April 13, 1966, after attending a private screening of the film, Robert Esmenard, the executor of Guy de Maupassant's literary estate and the head of the publishing house Albin Michel, wrote to Anatole Dauman, the producer, that the film bore so distant a relation to the two stories on which it was ostensibly based that "no allusion to Maupassant should be made in the screen credits for *Masculine Feminine.*" As a result, Dauman retained screen rights to the stories for an additional two years. Godard had adapted Maupassant so liberally that the connection with the adapted work had been broken and the film was transformed into an original work.

But the most important verdict rendered on *Masculine Feminine* was an intimate judgment. The arts page of *Le Figaro* for Thursday, August 12, 1965, featured a pair of photographs taken on the set of Bresson's *Au Hasard Balthazar:* one, an image of Bresson alongside a young actor and the film's eponymous protagonist, a donkey; and the other, a close-up of the young woman who played the female lead, Anne Wiazemsky, who was identified in the caption as a student and as the author François Mauriac's granddaughter. Upon seeing Wiazemsky's picture in the newspaper, Godard had called the film's coproducer, Mag Bodard, and asked to visit Bresson's set for the purpose of meeting the young woman.

Bodard invited Godard, Bresson, and Wiazemsky to lunch. Anne Wiazemsky was eighteen years old and was still in lycée. She had no prior acting experience. She was also, by her own admission, possessed of a formidable spirit of contrariness. Because of the great acclaim that Godard's films were receiving, particularly among Parisian students, Wiazemsky had assiduously avoided seeing any of them. As she later recalled, she was "very disagreeable with him" at lunch.[57]

"Then," she went on to say, "in January 1966, I saw *Pierrot le fou.* It struck me like an artistic thunderbolt.[58] Suddenly, retrospectively, the man whom I had seen at lunch fascinated me." Later that same year, Wiazemsky saw *Masculine Feminine.*

It was as if it were a letter written to me. I loved the film because I loved the man who was behind the film. That was in the month of June; until then I had been very prudent and shy; then I did one of the craziest things that I've ever done: I wrote a love letter to Godard, I told him that I loved the film because I loved him. I sent it to *Cahiers du cinéma*.[59]

fourteen

MADE IN USA, TWO OR THREE THINGS I KNOW ABOUT HER

"Living people are often already dead"

T HE POLITICAL CONFLICTS THAT PLAYED OUT IN France's 1965 elections also gave rise to a cinematic scandal in which Godard became embroiled—one that presaged far greater societal convulsions to follow. When Jacques Rivette left *Cahiers du cinéma* in May 1965, Georges de Beauregard immediately proposed that they make *La Religieuse* (*The Nun*), the film project which, under threat of censorship, Rivette had presented two years earlier as a play, financed by Godard and starring Anna Karina. Now Rivette and his screenwriter, Jean Gruault, again revised the script and submitted it for precensorship. On August 31, 1965, the commission informed Beauregard that the new version of the script contained scenes which "run the risk of being totally or partially cut." Beauregard nonetheless let Rivette start shooting the film in mid-October, with Karina in the lead role.

Even before the film was completed, it was thrust into the thick of the French presidential campaign. Days before the voting, the Paris police commissioner, Maurice Papon, together with Alain Peyrefitte, the minister of information, came under pressure from church officials who had orchestrated a letter-writing campaign against the film. The two declared their willingness to ban it. Though several journalists[1] responded with indignation to the prospect of such censorship, the issue quickly dropped out of view after the elections, while Rivette completed his work. Behind the scenes, however, Catholic institutions mobilized for a fight.

In anticipation of trouble, Rivette and Beauregard changed the title of the film from *La Religieuse* to *Suzanne Simonin, La Religieuse de Diderot*

A light moment on the balcony of a housing project
(TCD-Prod DB © Anouchka—Argos—Les Films du Carrosse—Parc Film / DR)

(Suzanne Simonin, Diderot's Nun). Rivette also added a title card in which he stated that the film "is not intended to cause a scandal on the subject of nuns in general."

When the Commission de contrôle finally screened the film, in March 1966, it voted (twice) to permit its release, but the information minister (now Yvon Bourges) overrode the recommendation and decreed that the film be banned lest it "gravely disturb the sentiments and the consciences of a very large part of the population."[2] The head of French television, a government appointee, barred news broadcasts from mentioning the ban.

Beauregard and a group of his friends, including Godard and Chabrol, immediately orchestrated a formidable outcry in the press, issuing a "Manifesto of the 1,789" (a reference, of course, to the year of the French Revolution) in defense of the film. It was signed by such writers as Jacques Prévert, Raymond Queneau, and Marguerite Duras, the leading French book publishers, and a range of public figures from the Gaullist right to the Communist left. The ban was condemned by the French film industry and by most of the press. Even many on the right who disdained the film's theme nonetheless rejected its censorship, which served, as Le Figaro editorialized, "to incite an uproar of opinion, arouse passions that a liberal attitude would have avoided."[3] Priests and nuns also spoke out to denounce the ban.

Godard personally took the fight to the media. Approached for a comment by Le Monde, he delivered a text of lofty sarcasm:

> For my part, I am grateful to [Bourges]. Because during Munich and Danzig, I was playing with marbles. During Auschwitz, le Vercors, and Hiroshima, I was putting on my first pair of long pants. During Sakiet and the Casbah,[4] I was having my first amorous adventures.
>
> As a beginning intellectual, I was all the more behind the times since I was also a beginning filmmaker. I only knew fascism from books. "They've taken Danielle." "They've arrested Pierre." "They're going to shoot Etienne." These typical phrases from the Resistance and the Gestapo struck me with ever greater force, but not in my flesh and blood, because I had the good fortune to be born late. Yesterday, suddenly, that all changed: "They've arrested Suzanne." "Yes. The police came to Georges's place and to the laboratory. They seized the prints."
>
> Thank you, Yvon Bourges, for having made me look head-on at the true face of present-day intolerance.[5]

In Le Nouvel Observateur, Godard soon went even further, publishing a "Letter to André Malraux," the minister of culture. In this searing diatribe he admits to the minister: "Since you are the only Gaullist I know, my anger will have to fall upon you."

I am sure now, dear André Malraux, that you will understand absolutely nothing of this letter in which, submerged in hatred, I address you for the last time.
Nor will you understand why from now on I will be loath to shake your hand,
even in silence . . . It's not surprising that you will not recognize my voice
when I talk of the ban on *Suzanne Simonin, Diderot's Nun* as an assassination.
No. There is nothing surprising in your deep cowardice. You are putting your
head in the sand to avoid your interior memories.[6] How could you hear me,
André Malraux, since I am calling you from the exterior, from a distant country, from free France?[7]

In both texts, Godard likened de Gaulle's government to the Vichy
regime. Although Malraux was not personally responsible for the ban, he did
not speak out against it. Yet soon thereafter, Malraux (whether despite or because of Godard's invective) took a decisive step in favor of the film: relying
on a law that exempted Cannes screenings from French censorship, he rati-
fied his handpicked commission's endorsement of *La Religieuse* as one of the
two official French entries to the festival.[8]

At Cannes *La Religieuse* received prolonged applause from the audience
and effusive praise from the critics. Meanwhile, Beauregard filed suit against
the ban on procedural grounds and won. By the time the film was sent back
to the censorship board for review, de Gaulle—who privately admitted that
the "affair" was "silly"[9]—had brought in a new minister of information,
Georges Gorce, who lifted the ban.[10] Released on July 26, 1967, the film
proved to be both a critical success and a profitable venture.

The battle over *La Religieuse,* as de Gaulle himself recognized, held the
French authorities up to ridicule and made them appear hopelessly out of
touch with modern life. It foreshadowed the open conflict between young
people with new expectations and the institutions that did not change rapidly enough to acknowledge and meet them. As Godard had understood
since 1960, the New Wave's aesthetic resistance to mainstream French culture redefined the terms of French politics, and Godard found himself in its
vanguard.

EARLY IN 1966, before receiving Anne Wiazemsky's fervent missive, Godard
had rekindled an old acquaintance. Marina Vlady, one of the younger stars of
the Old Wave of French cinema, was among the many actresses Godard had
considered for the lead role in *A Woman Is a Woman.* Born in 1938, Vlady
was one of four daughters of a Russian émigré family that provided the
French cinema with two of its leading figures (her older sister, Odile Versois,
had been an esteemed and popular actress since the 1940s). Vlady had made
her film debut at age eleven, and had been a star since age sixteen. She had

also been a tabloid sensation.", marrying, at seventeen, the actor Robert Hossein. After her divorce at twenty-five, she married Jean-Claude Brouillet, a pilot. This marriage, too, was short-lived: separated from Brouillet, Vlady moved to her parents' villa outside of Paris—both a family retreat and a Chekhovian center of Russian culture in exile—which is where she was living when she and Godard became reacquainted.

Vlady (who had three children) and Godard rapidly became friends, a couple of sorts (though, according to Vlady, a Platonic one).[11] The liaison prompted Godard to conceive a new film project: an adaptation of *Le Lys dans la vallée* (*The Lily of the Valley*) by Balzac, the story of a poor but promising young Parisian, Felix de Vandenesse, and his desperate love affair with Madame de Mortsauf, a provincial beauty who is wasting her life with an ineffectual husband with whom she stays for the sake of their children. Following her early death, Felix seeks to marry the young Natalie de Manerville, who, after hearing the story of his life, refuses, considering him still devoted to his late beloved.

The project suggested a perfect on-screen pairing of Vlady with Jean-Pierre Léaud, who would stand in for Godard in a story that again paralleled his own situation, and doubly: first, regarding his love for a mature woman like Vlady, who had retreated to the family home in devotion to her children; and second, regarding the difficulty of restoring love to his life when he was so openly bearing the wounds from the loss of his previous beloved, Anna Karina. But in the spring of 1966, Godard and Vlady discovered an interest in an entirely different kind of story, one that emerged from the news.

That April, Vlady went to Japan to star in *Atout cœur à Tokyo pour OSS 117* (Hearts Are Trumps in Tokyo for OSS Agent 117), a French James Bond–style film. Godard arranged a trip to Japan that would coincide with her shoot, on the pretext of interviewing several Japanese directors for *Cahiers du cinéma* and presenting *Masculine Feminine* to a local audience.

He arrived in Japan on April 28, bringing Vlady what she later recalled as "lavish gifts: a Picasso drawing and two notebooks containing a story that he wrote and illustrated himself."[12] He accompanied her to a Noh play and fell asleep; he bought her a record player and albums by Bob Dylan and Joan Baez as well as Bach's *Brandenburg Concerti*.[13] He spoke about making a film of the life of Jesus, in which a beggar in the modern-day French provinces would be revealed as the Christ.[14]

Official duties absorbed much of Godard's time there, such as cocktail receptions and roundtable discussions. He was observed standing at the sidelines of one gathering, staring at Vlady, and biting his fingernails while she chatted with the guests.[15] During a trip to Kyoto to visit the grave of

Mizoguchi,[16] he turned up at a dinner party with a birthday gift for Vlady—a photo album containing an image of her on one side and Godard's own drawing of a fox on the other—and explained to his hosts that the fox represented himself, since it was the "wisest and wittiest" of animals. Vlady, however, didn't show up that evening.[17]

Back in Tokyo, on the final leg of the trip, he and Vlady had the idea that changed their plans for the film, and he typed it up on his last day there.[18]

In an issue of *Le Nouvel Observateur* published several weeks earlier, an article had appeared by the journalist Catherine Vimenet called "Les 'étoiles filantes' " (" The 'Shooting Stars' ").[19] The title referred to the name professional prostitutes had given to a new breed of part-time amateurs, women who lived in the vast housing complexes springing up around Paris. Facing high rents and bills for heat, water, electricity, and the new furniture they had been forced to buy on moving in (the authorities feared vermin), the women, who had nothing left for food, trawled workingmen's cafés near the farmers' market of Les Halles to earn money they would spend on the way home to feed their families.

Godard and Vlady had read and discussed the article when it came out. What sparked the idea for a new film was a later sidebar, appended to a follow-up roundtable discussion of sociologists. This item, titled "An Atrocious Document," was a letter from an anonymous reader who told of being a single mother nearing forty, an educated but underpaid office worker who had begun to pick up male clients from a luxurious café, and who used the money to pay for twice-weekly visits to the hairdresser, to buy fine clothing, and to purchase her apartment.[20]

Godard and Vlady put aside *The Lily of the Valley* in favor of a film based on the "atrocious document" in a setting inspired by Vimenet's article on prostitution in the housing projects.[21] The story Godard outlined for the film—*Deux ou trois choses que je sais d'elle (Two or Three Things I Know About Her)*—was built around a day in the life of a young woman, Juliette, who lives in a new apartment complex with her husband and young children, and who prostitutes herself by picking up men from the sumptuous Hôtel George V in order to buy designer dresses.

Though Godard set the film in a poor milieu, his story was more concerned with poverty of imagination, specifically, of a woman caught in the same net of illusions as all of Godard's female characters since *A Married Woman*—the American-style promise of ease and pleasure, whether sexual or material, and the suppression of conscience and freedom that results from these enticements.

In Paris, Godard had producers waiting: Anatole Dauman, again joined by Mag Bodard (the coproducer of *Au Hasard Balthazar*), both of whom were joined by Godard's own production company, Anouchka, and by François Truffaut's company, Les Films du Carrosse. Together they rounded up the film's budget of nine hundred thousand francs, or $180,000, which was 50 percent higher than that of *Masculine Feminine*. The film would be shot in color and in Cinemascope, and Raoul Coutard would rejoin the crew as cameraman.

As the project advanced toward production, Godard faced a distraction that threatened to derail it. In June, he received Anne Wiazemsky's dramatic confession of love. Not knowing where to find her, he called her mother and Mag Bodard, finally learning that she was on vacation in Avignon. Godard sent Wiazemsky a telegram there, proposing that they meet the next day in front of the town hall of the village of Montfrin, near Avignon, and he took off for the south. The rendezvous took place, but the timing was awkward, due to his involvement with Vlady. Several weeks later, Godard was again in the south of France, this time visiting Vlady, when he was tracked down by Beauregard, who did succeed in shifting his focus.[22]

Beauregard was in trouble: he could not pay bills that were coming due. He was, however, eligible for loans and credits if he made a film, and so he needed to start production on something immediately. He turned to Godard, flattering him with the notion that he was the only director who could conceive and organize a film quickly enough. Godard acknowledged that this was probably true, and accepted the challenge (in part because he himself could make use of his fee to pay off back taxes); he asked Beauregard for a few hours to find a story. Godard went into a bookstore and came out with a detective novel by Richard Stark (a pseudonym for Donald Westlake), *Rien dans le coffre* (Nothing in the Trunk, the French title for *The Jugger*). In the novel, a volume in Stark's series about a hard-boiled criminal named Parker, the main character goes off on a search for an old acquaintance who knows too much.

It was out of the question for Godard to hire stars, because Beauregard couldn't afford them. As a result, Godard relied on his "stock company" of friends, character actors, and actors from his own circles—Jean-Pierre Léaud, László Szabó, Yves Afonso, Ernest Menzer, Rita Maiden (Madame Céline in *A Married Woman*), Remo Forlani, the journalist Philippe Labro, the *Cahiers du cinéma* critics Sylvain Godet and Jean-Pierre Biesse—and, in the lead role, Anna Karina.

When Godard and Karina divorced, Godard feared for her financial situation and persuaded Beauregard to give her a three-year contract. The actress would receive ten thousand francs (two thousand dollars) per month, to come out of the fees she would earn in Godard's films; her fees for films by other producers were to be split with Beauregard. Thus, Karina was an economical hire for the producer, who did not have to take additional cash from his pocket for her services.

Beauregard announced, in an ad in the trade press of July 8, 1966, that he would produce *The Secret,* directed by Jean-Luc Godard and starring Anna Karina, which was scheduled to begin shooting on July 11. Godard described the film—immediately renamed *Made in USA*—as "the conjunction in my mind of three desires: to do a favor for a friend, to highlight the Americanization of French life, and to make use of one of the episodes in the Ben Barka affair."[23]

The "Ben Barka affair" had begun almost a year earlier, on October 30, 1965, when *Le Monde* carried a brief article mentioning the mysterious arrest of Mehdi Ben Barka, the exiled leader of the left-wing Moroccan opposition and a major figure in international Marxist and anticolonialist politics. It was an arrest that the police denied making. Ben Barka had vanished, and his disappearance was at the center of the news for months, during which the French secret police was revealed to have conspired with the criminal underworld to deliver Ben Barka to Moroccan agents. Morocco's minister of the interior, General Mohamed Oufkir, was reported to have visited the hideout where Ben Barka was being held and to have tortured him to death.

The public was shocked by the conspiracy, the crime, and the cover-up. The story had been one of Godard's obsessions even before he had thought of filming it. In January 1966, on a break from editing *Masculine Feminine,* Godard told Michel Vianey that he had visited the *Le Monde* archives to catch up on the story, and said: "This morning when I woke up I wondered whether I had read that Ben Barka had been found or whether I'd dreamed it. I ended up getting lost in it."[24]

As it happened, the Ben Barka affair was not only a Cold War battleground, it also involved the cinema. The bogus arrest had taken place on the boulevard St.-Germain as Ben Barka was on his way to meet a journalist, Philippe Bernier, and the filmmaker Georges Franju.[25] Ben Barka planned to collaborate with them on a film about decolonization to be called *Basta!* He intended to use his Third World connections to open doors for Franju,[26] and to cowrite the film's commentary with Marguerite Duras.[27]

The project had originated with Bernier, who had become friendly with Ben Barka in the mid-1950s while working as a radio journalist in Morocco and who had later been imprisoned in France for aiding the Algerian struggle for independence. Bernier had brought Franju into the picture through a mutual acquaintance, Georges Figon, a singular character of the French underworld, who had promised to produce *Basta!*[28]

Born in 1926, Figon was the son of a prominent French government official. He had been a smart but troubled adolescent whose first attempts at crime resulted in three years in a mental hospital. In the 1950s, he was arrested for bank robbery and attempted murder; at trial, he unleashed an insolent tirade, declaring himself to be "a son of the bourgeoisie who had straightened himself out."[29] Upon his release from prison in 1962, he frequented the artistic cafés of St.-Germain-des-Prés, was interviewed by Duras, consulted on a TV film on prison life, tried to start a magazine, wrote for Sartre's *Les Temps Modernes,* and harbored dreams of producing films.

Figon also harbored dreams of easy money (and openly contemplated extorting it by planting bombs). When word of his indirect connection to Ben Barka (via Bernier) circulated in the underworld, a Moroccan secret agent contacted Figon and recruited him for a scheme intended to lead to the kidnapping. Figon was playing it both ways: on the one hand, he used his involvement as producer of *Basta!* to set Ben Barka up;[30] on the other, Figon really wanted to make films. If Ben Barka should become permanently unavailable to make *Basta!,* Figon had other projects to propose to Franju.

In November 1965, Figon, identified as a conspirator in Ben Barka's disappearance, also vanished (although he had been reported traveling to Belgium to visit his girlfriend). However, Figon soon made a dramatic reappearance on the public stage—not in person but through the media—with a long interview published in the January 10, 1966, issue of *L'Express,* in which he detailed his version of Ben Barka's kidnapping and death.[31]

A warrant for Figon's arrest was issued immediately. On January 17, when the police attempted to enter the Right Bank apartment where Figon was hiding, he was found dead. His death was officially deemed a suicide.[32] A tape recording was found among his affairs, and it was played in court. It featured Figon's accounts of his film scripts, one concerning an extortionist bomber and his stewardess girlfriend, and another described as the story of "a clandestine network at the heart of an imaginary country in revolution."[33]

When the Ben Barka affair took form for Godard, it was centered on Figon, an outsider and frustrated filmmaker whose situation Godard assimilated to his own. In late January, after Figon's death, the name of his girlfriend, the actress Anne-Marie Coffinet, was revealed to the press, and Godard recognized her as someone he had known from the cafés of St.-Germain-des-Prés in the 1950s. It was this personal association, Godard said, that prompted him to imagine the story of a woman who goes in search of the wanted Figon. By refashoning Westlake's novel into a film about the Ben Barka affair, Godard produced another allegory of himself:

> I imagined that Figon had not died, that he had taken refuge in the provinces, that he had written to his girlfriend to join him. She goes to the address where they had planned to meet, but when she gets there, she finds that he is dead . . . Instead of "Figon," my character is named "Politzer" . . . In the name of love, she plays detective. Then she gets tangled in a network of police and criminals and ends up wanting to write an article on the affair.[34]

Georges Politzer was a Marxist philosopher active in the wartime resistance who was arrested and executed by the Gestapo. In *Made in USA*, the character called Politzer, like Figon, leaves behind an audiotape. Paula Nelson (played by Anna Karina), a journalist who left *L'Express* because she "had come to equate advertising with fascism," is led to a copy of the tape. On it, she hears Politzer's voice intoning a series of elaborately doctrinaire Marxist incantations (taken from contemporary speeches and articles by leftist writers and politicians). The aggressively dogmatic voice is that of Godard, who thus effected a direct identification of the Figon character, whom Anna Karina is desperately seeking beyond the grave, with himself.

THE POLITICAL SUBSTANCE and historical antecedents of *Made in USA* merged with Godard's dominant story, the allegory of his romantic trials with Anna Karina. He made sure this was clear from the start: the first time she is seen in the film is in close-up, lying on a bed in a hotel room where she and Politzer are supposed to meet, with a detective novel splayed open near her face—*Adieu la vie, adieu l'amour* (Farewell Life, Farewell Love)—as she awakens and soliloquizes: "Happiness, for example. Whenever he wanted something, I wanted it too. Or fame, for him." Moments later, when a sinister character, "Mr. Typhus,"[35] arrives instead of Politzer, her character, Paula, figures out that Politzer is dead, and explains to Typhus: "We were hardly seeing each other anymore. I don't even know whether I still love him, but I owed him something because of what was between us." This line, which Godard wrote for Paula to explain what she is doing in the hotel, also sounded like Karina's explanation for what she is doing in the film.

The cartoonishly tangled intrigue concerns a conspiracy to eliminate certain political enemies and freethinkers, including Politzer—and the agents of that conspiracy are characters named Richard Nixon and Robert McNamara (played by the two young *Cahiers* critics, Godet and Biesse). The "sociological" or political aspect of the film noir allusion is contained mainly in Godard's idea itself, namely, that the structure of the American film noir is itself political, a Trojan horse for a conspiracy. The American influence seen in the fictitious France of *Made in USA* is not that of cultural epiphenomena such as Coca-Cola or the Beatles, but the crucial one of political violence. In effect, Godard's vision of a France infiltrated by Richard Nixon and Robert McNamara and terrorized by a secret police force suggests that both the Ben Barka affair and its elaborate cover-up were products of the Cold War, were "made in USA."

The film's dénouement reinforces the allegorical effect with rare psychodramatic cruelty. It involves Paula/Anna's relationship with a writer, one named David Goodis, no less—the American author of grim, scathing crime novels (including *Down There*, from which François Truffaut had adapted *Shoot the Piano Player*). In his synopsis, Godard had described the actor playing the role, Yves Afonso, as "Belmondo's double," and in the film the character wears a striped bathrobe like the one Belmondo wears in *Breathless;* he sits in bed before a small manual typewriter, pecking out what he calls "The Unfinished Novel."

At the climax of the action, the head of the secret police, a character named Richard Widmark (played by László Szabó) holds Paula at gunpoint and announces that he will shoot her, but Goodis sneaks up behind Widmark and guns him down first. Paula thanks Goodis for saving her life; the writer takes out his notebook and, reciting some phrases and jotting them down, thanks her for helping him to finish his novel. "No, David," she responds, "you must prepare to die. The truth must not be known. If you finish your novel, everyone will know it, because poetry equals truth." Paula shoots David, who, stunned, is still able to cry, "Oh Paula, you have robbed me of my youth." Sobbing, Paula / Anna is seen saying, with almost incoherent regret, "Oh, David, love, love, truth, beauty, sadness," while Godard, suggesting that the words are foreign to Karina, removes all from the sound track but *"Oh, David"* and *"sadness."* (Szabó later recalled that Karina, as she played this scene, was weeping for real).[36]

This exercise in torment and condemnation was Karina's farewell to Godard as he had constructed it, forcing her to bear responsibility, on-screen, for destroying him. Godard tied *Made in USA* together with a circular structure of hyperbolic accusations: Anna Karina goes in search of him, but he has already been killed; then she finds him again to kill him again. Since he is (in his view) a poet who will tell the truth about her, she has to kill him off.

Godard filmed *Made in USA* with an indifferent and blank flatness. The only images that Godard invested with energy in *Made in USA* are those of Anna Karina. The film's visual raison d'être is the extraordinary number and duration of close-ups of Karina. Many long scenes of dialogue are shot in extreme close-ups of her both speaking and listening. The many shots of

Karina, with their wide variety of mood—each a different pose, angle, expression—serve as a catalogue of reminiscences. These shots are less indicative of the character Paula Nelson leading her inquiry than of Anna Karina as an obsessional apparition from the past. The close-ups are the most expressive ones in color that Godard had made to date, and they are signifiers of the act of remembering. With them, the film appears to exist for the simplest of purposes, fulfilling the primal function of portraiture: to see again the face of a person who is no longer present.

ON AUGUST 29, at a month's remove from the hectic shoot of *Made in USA,* Godard filmed an epilogue that differed drastically in mood, substance, and appearance. Visually, it provides the film's only scene of landscape and light, of open space and open vistas, of a third dimension seen in depth. In content, it replaces paranoid speculation with practical politics. It features Paula escaping from the scene of the crimes and hitching a ride with an old acquaintance, the journalist Philippe Labro, playing himself.

After a close-up of a book cover that reads *Gauche année zéro* (Left, Year Zero), there follows a single long take of the pair, driver and passenger, filmed through the windshield of the car, heading down a highway in early morning, for a full two minutes and forty-five seconds. The pair engage in a rhetorical, quasi-literary dialogue about politics, which Godard treated as a platonically passionate encounter, accompanied on the sound track by a rhapsodic passage from a Schumann symphony. Labro finds Paula in a somber mood because of the failures of the left and successes of the right, and attempts to console her: "The left and the right are the same. One cannot change them. The right, because it is idiotic and brimming with nastiness; and the left because it is sentimental. Besides, right and left, it's a completely outdated question. That's not at all the way to pose the problem."

Karina responds with an open question, which ends the film: "Then how?"

Made in USA shows Godard to have been in a political crisis that was at the same time a cinematic crisis; he had no idea what to do about the things made in USA, whether the Gaullist regime or the cinema. The most politically significant moment in the film was also the simplest, most human, and most realistic. It was a scene of a calm, sincere conversation such as Godard and Labro (who had reported from the set of *Masculine Feminine* and whom Godard met occasionally thereafter) might have had on exactly these themes—and it ended with a question that Godard would seek to answer, practically, in film and in life.

POLITICS DOMINATED THE public response to the film. *Made in USA* was released on January 27, 1967, and received with a variety of critical cheers.

Claude Mauriac in *Le Figaro littéraire* wondered whether in Godard, might we "finally have an artist, a great artist, of the left?"[37] In *Les Lettres françaises,* Georges Sadoul compared the film to Picasso's *Guernica,*[38] and Michel Capdenac went so far as to claim that the film "offers the cinema after *Pierrot le fou* what *Finnegans Wake* gave to the novel after *Ulysses.*"[39]

Despite such hyperbolic praise, Godard felt that the film had been decisively rejected: "[The] first film that didn't succeed, at least in the little audience that I had formed, was *Made in USA.*"[40] Specifically, the film, as Sadoul reported, was "very badly received by a certain leftist audience when it was shown for the anniversary gala of *Le Nouvel Observateur.*"[41] This audience was the young left that had gathered at the publication, and it included the new generation at *Cahiers du cinéma,* where the response was equally reserved. Bernardo Bertolucci, writing in *Cahiers,* called *Made in USA* "a film that betrays politics, that is paralyzed in its great liberty by ideological conformism."[42]

Responding in an interview in *Le Monde,* Godard asserted that the film embodied his progressive politics in a progressive form, and reproached "the elegant left" for being insensitive to it:

> In *Made in USA,* there is a title card where one can read the cover of a book: Left, Year Zero. The last time that this card is used, one hears the beginning of a movement from Schumann's Fourth Symphony. Unless one is blind or deaf, it is impossible not to understand that this shot, that is, the mixture of an image and a sound, represents a movement of hope. One can deem it false, ridiculous, childish, provocative, but it is what it is, like a scientific object.
>
> I reproach those whom I call the elegant left for not recognizing the presence of this scientific object.[43]

Here Godard charged that the new aesthetic left—which he had long heralded and that had lately come to the fore and rallied around his films— was unable to keep up with the pace of his experiments in form (and indeed in formlessness). Insofar as his own artistic progressivism was, in his view, the touchstone for this new breed of leftists, he had traced a fault line between himself and them that would soon give way.

ON AUGUST 8, nine days after the end of principal photography on *Made in USA,* Godard began to shoot *Two or Three Things I Know About Her.* In the months that had intervened between the conception and the shoot of the film, he had intellectualized and abstracted the subject.

He planned to film the story of Juliette, the part-time prostitute, as a series of set pieces: on an unemployment line; through a case where a woman

commits suicide after prostituting herself for the first time; in an apartment where a man babysits children and rents his rooms to prostitutes in
exchange for food; in a scene with a woman getting a permanent in a hair
salon. He intended to film interviews, "real or fabricated," with such
characters as "the concierge who calls the police on a beatnik with long
hair, . . . a real prostitute, . . . a young working woman who prefers
to wear herself out in a factory rather than prostitute herself now and then,
. . . a social worker."[44]

However, Godard did not plan to organize these incidents in terms of a
story, but through a philosophical grid. His scenario set out a four-part
quasi-phenomenological analysis of the subject: "objective description" (of
objects and subjects); "subjective description" (of people and things, such as
"décor seen from the inside, where the world is outside"); the "search for
structures" revealing "laws that must be discovered and applied in order to
live in society" (a society, Godard adds, which is "too much inclined toward,
and to, consumption"); and finally, what he calls "life," or what the philosopher "Merleau-Ponty called the singular existence of a person, in the event,
that of Juliette in particular."[45]

This philosophically mediated view of the character of Juliette suggested
that Godard approached the film—and Vlady—as abstractions. With his
lead actress thus effaced, Godard would fill the film's void with his own presence, turning this philosophical and sociological project into his most direct
cinematic confessional to date.

The stakes in the partnership were high, both professionally and personally. While Godard was preparing to make *Made in USA,* Vlady went on
vacation to Romania, to visit her boyfriend at the time. Godard drove her to
the airport and, as she prepared to pass through the gate, he proposed marriage (shades of the corresponding scene in *Masculine Feminine*), asking for
her answer upon her return.[46] The news then leaked out; the day that shooting started for *Made in USA, L'Express* ran a squib: "Immediately after this
fast-track film with his ex-wife, Jean-Luc Godard will undertake another,
with Marina Vlady: *Two or Three Things I Know About Her.* There is a fourth
thing he does not know yet: will she agree to become his wife?"[47] Godard
called his friend Roland Tolmatchoff—who was also a family friend of
Vlady's—and asked him to be their witness. Upon her return from Romania,
Vlady held out hope; but not long after the start of work on *Two or Three
Things,* she turned him down, and, according to Vlady, "they never really
spoke again."[48]

During the shoot, Godard again took up his idea of a documentary
about his actors, eliciting their free responses to questions posed to them on-
screen. He wrote some dialogue at the last minute; sometimes he gave it to

Vlady just before filming so that she could memorize it; other times he dictated it to her as the camera rolled. Vlady described the method.

> I had a little speaker in my ear, and Godard would tell me right before the shot what I had to say . . . In general, he spoke a text through the little speaker, which I had to repeat at once. Often, he posed questions which I had to answer directly. These questions were often personal, so he would ask me, for instance: "Marina, how are you dressed today?" or "Marina, tell me who you are, try to discover yourself, to describe yourself." So I had to answer him, but at the same time, there was a particular prepared dialogue. The questions always took me by surprise in the middle of a text I had learned. It was actually a real gymnastics of thought and I had to react very fast.[49]

One such scene took place in a clothing shop, where Juliette was considering buying a dress. Godard spoke to Vlady through the earpiece and she answered petulantly, as if his questioning was sarcastic: "Yes, I know how to talk . . . OK, let's talk together." He then fed her lines regarding the loss of the city's "semantic richness": "The creative and formative role of the city will be confirmed by other systems of communication . . . perhaps . . . television, radio, vocabulary and syntax, scientifically and deliberately . . ." The actress found Godard's demands very difficult, and he was dissatisfied with her performance. He complained bitterly about her to his assistant director, Charles Bitsch, and to his editor, Agnès Guillemot, who later recalled watching the film's rushes: "When, during the shoot, Godard said 'Cut,' she relaxed, became more open. He was unable to get her in this state during the shot."[50] Indeed, Vlady's performance is tense yet false, whether due to her unease with Godard's "provocative" methods, or with Godard himself, or with her notion of how to act such a part.

As the shoot progressed, Godard sought to make corrections to Vlady's acting. He included on the call sheet dated August 18 a "Letter to My Friends to Learn to Do Cinema Together," which Guillemot recognized at once to be an open plea to Vlady: "I play / You play / We play / At cinema / You think there is / A rule of the game . . ." Despite the plural of "friends" in the title, the text is written in the second person singular and familiar form, *tu; jouer* (to play), in French as in English, also refers to an actor playing a role, and the word for "game," *jeu,* comes from the same root. Godard goes on to remind her that the "game" is "reserved for grown-ups" and yet that it's "a children's game."

The letter was of no practical help to Vlady, who asked Godard for more concrete recommendations. Godard gave her one. He later told interviewers from *Cahiers du cinéma* about it:

Marina Vlady said to me one day: "What should I do? You never tell me anything." I answered her (she lived in Montfort-L'Amaury): "Instead of taking a
taxi to the shoot, all you have to do is come on foot. If you really want to act
well, that's the best thing to do." She thought I was pulling her leg and she
didn't do it. I was really mad at her for that, and what's more, I still am, a
little.[51]

Godard's dissatisfaction only mounted. He complained to Charles
Bitsch, "I don't want to work with her anymore,"[52] and as he continued
working with her, he made his displeasure felt. The scenes he shot with Vlady
are bland, unenergized, affectless—and the contrast is all the more striking
with Godard's highly inflected, dynamic filming of the other objects in view,
whether cityscapes or consumer products, on which his mental and visual
interest was intensely concentrated. He composed these shots more carefully
than those featuring Vlady. The film's most famous and remarkable sequence is a series of long extreme close-ups of a cup of espresso, seen from
above, in which the bubbles (provoked by the visible addition of a cube of
sugar) and the swirling pale foam against the coffee's darkness imply a cos-
mos. The film's last shot, of a magazine ad for Hollywood chewing gum featuring a tender young couple, from which the camera zooms back to reveal
an array of gaily packaged French consumer goods spread out on a lawn and
facing the camera as if singing in chorus, simultaneously suggests the rankest
materialism as well as its charm. Godard's devotion to filming these ordinary
objects gives them a screen presence more memorable and more mysterious
than that of his lead actress.

Another actress, however, gives an extraordinary performance in her
one scene in *Two or Three Things*. In it, Robert (Juliette's husband) starts a
conversation with an unnamed young woman in a café where he is waiting
for Juliette, who, unbeknownst to him, is with an American client in a hotel
room. After the conversation starts off with banalities, Robert suggests, "Well
then, just for five minutes, why not try to talk really about what interests us
deeply?" For the subject of their conversation, Robert picks sex. The young
woman, who speaks with a fierce natural intelligence and a presence unde-
formed by theatrical mannerisms, turns the conversation around on Robert,
asking him about his attitude toward his work.

The woman, Juliet Berto, was a nineteen-year-old who had met Godard
in her native Grenoble when he went there to present *Les Carabiniers*. She
would be a regular and crucial presence in Godard's films for several years
to come.

Two other memorable young women appear in the film: the eighteen-year-old Blandine Jeanson, who does a noteworthy turn in the same café scene as a student interviewing a character presented as "the Russian Nobel Prize-winner, Ivanov"; and Isabelle Pons, Godard's assistant, who is seen standing among the gadgets and signs of a gas station. In making *Two or Three Things*, Godard surrounded himself with a trio of engaging young women who, above all, were comfortable being themselves on film. Next to them, Marina Vlady appeared as exactly what she was: an Old Wave actress who was playing the role of a star, a performer who did not know how simply to "be" on camera.

Agnès Guillemot understood the difficulty inherent in Godard's working relationship with Vlady: "She was an experienced actress, and he had difficulty making contact with people, and at the same time he was then in love with her."[53] Though Vlady was twenty-eight—only two years older than Anna Karina—she had been a star since 1953; moreover, she had first married at age seventeen, and had three children. Her wealth of life experience induced Guillemot to recall, "It was very moving, because Godard was always in love with much younger girls, and here was a woman who was almost his own age."[54]

THE SHOOT OF *Two or Three Things* found itself mixed up with additional shoot days for *Made in USA*, and when both ended, on September 8, 1966, Godard went right to the editing room—or rather, the adjoining editing rooms, where *Made in USA* was edited by his longtime editor, Guillemot, and *Two or Three Things* by her assistant, Françoise Collin.

Though Godard was no longer speaking to Marina Vlady, he certainly spoke *of* her, however, and did so promptly, in the film itself, in the form of a voice-over commentary. Guillemot recalled that at the time, "he was in a very bad mood"[55] and that he found the writing of this commentary to be "very difficult." Godard spoke it in a rushed, urgent whisper, as if he were furtively divulging secrets to each viewer personally—as indeed he was. But, as the title of the film suggests, the secrets he divulged were not only his own but also the things that he "knew about her." In his whispered voice-over, accompanying the two opening shots of Vlady on a balcony of a housing complex, Godard introduces her first as the actress—"She's Marina Vlady, she's an actress"—and then, with the second shot, as the character—"She's Juliette Janson, she lives here." With this pseudo-Brechtian device he is saying, in effect, that Juliette Janson and Marina Vlady are the same person seen from different angles.

Godard delivers the longest and most agonizingly confessional part of his monologue as the sound track to a microcosmic view into the depths of a cup of espresso. It concerns his failed relationship with Vlady. Both self-excoriating and self-pitying, Godard edges into the painful rejection from a philosophical angle.

> Since each event transforms my daily life, since I endlessly fail to communicate; I mean, to understand, to love, to make myself be loved. And since each failure makes me endure a solitude, since . . . since . . . since I can neither tear myself away from the objectivity that crushes me nor from the subjectivity that exiles me, since it is neither possible for me to raise myself to being nor to fall into nothingness, I must listen.

In another commentary, which accompanies a scene of Juliette driving to meet her husband at the garage where he works, Godard shifts the blame for his romantic failure. Over a pair of close-ups of the actress, he whispers: "Objects exist and if one accords to them a more careful attention than to people, it is because they exist more than these people do. Dead objects are always alive. Living people are often already dead."

Godard did not refer to his "characters" but to "people": it was not Juliette but Vlady whom he saw as already essentially dead—her rejection of him being proof, for him, of her inner inertness. But he nonetheless admitted the delights that she provided him in memory, as he watched images of her in the editing room (". . . to have caught in passing a reason to live, and to have held it for a few seconds"). As in *Made in USA*, his shots of a woman were romantic souvenirs viewed across the abyss of his loss.

FROM THE OUTSET of *Two or Three Things*, Godard once again blamed the moral corruption of a woman he loved on industrial modernism. To accompany the images of large-scale urban construction that begin the film, Godard whispers on the sound track a diatribe against the government's construction of housing projects, capping his charges with the claim that this policy "accentuates the distortions of the national economy, and even more, the distortions of the ordinary morality on which the economy is based."

The connection between *Two or Three Things* and Godard's earlier analytical antimodernist films, *Le Nouveau Monde* and *A Married Woman,* is emphasized by another of Godard's editing-room decisions, the use once again of Beethoven's string quartets on the sound track. But the new film added a novel element to the critique: the American cinema, which was now considered to be a part of the consumerist landscape. The film ends with the shot of a pack of Hollywood brand chewing gum and an array of packaged goods:

I listen to the advertising on my transistor radio. Thanks to Esso [spelled out "E-SS-O"] I drive at ease down the street of dreams and I forget the rest. I forget Hiroshima; I forget Auschwitz; I forget Budapest; I forget Vietnam; I forget the minimum wage; I forget the housing crisis; I forget the famine in India. I have forgotten everything, except that, since I'm being brought back to zero, it is from there that I will have to start again.

The zero to which Godard had been brought was both romantic (the loss of the glossy ideal of true love) and cinematic (the loss of Hollywood as an example to follow). In an interview, he declared the need "to flee the American cinema,"[56] but he had nothing to offer in its place. The film's principle of construction was itself a virtual cinematic zero, a simple alternation of city and object footage with narrative or anecdotal sequences. With *Two or Three Things,* Godard reached the culmination of a process of decomposition and fragmentation that had begun with *Le Nouveau Monde.* Romantic despair had corroded his attitude toward both modernity and cinema. One more short film would provide a poignant, self-lacerating coda to the series.

Suzanne Schiffman's production notes for *Made in USA* show that Godard, despite his doubts, intended to pick up the pace of production. He planned to direct a short film from September 15 or 20 to October 10; to make *La Bande à Bonnot* in December and January 1967; and in between, he would finally do *Pour Lucrèce.* The short film—like *Le Nouveau Monde,* a work of science fiction—was the only one of these projects to be realized.

Producer Joseph Bercholz[57] commissioned the film as part of a compilation, *The World's Oldest Profession,* that was to include six directors' sketches on prostitution through the ages: the prehistoric, the Roman era, the French Revolution, "la belle époque" (the 1890s), the present day, and the future. Godard's theme was announced in the film's title, *Anticipation, or the Year 2000,* and was explained in the credits as a view of prostitution in "the intergalactic era."[58] The lead role—of a prostitute—would be played by Anna Karina.

After *Vivre sa vie, Alphaville,* and *Two or Three Things,* Godard seemed to have become something of a cinematic specialist in the field of prostitution. He explained, after completing *Two or Three Things,* that the theme inspired him because it exemplified one of his "most deeply rooted ideas," that "to live in Parisian society today, one is forced, at whatever level, whatever stratum, to prostitute oneself in one way or another, or what's more, to live according to laws which resemble those of prostitution."[59]

The antithesis of prostitution was, in Godard's view, love. In *Vivre sa vie* and *Alphaville,* women were prostitutes when they did not love, and were redeemed from the bondage of prostitution by the awakening of love. In *Two or Three Things,* Juliette, who experienced no romantic revelation, ended the film as she started it, as a prostitute.

Anticipation, which Godard filmed in November 1966, took up the same theme but resolved it differently. In effect, the film dramatizes another man's happiness with Karina, and as such, it is a film of keen personal agony, mitigated only by the fact that Godard himself was already onto a new life and was closing the book on the old one with a harsh judgment of the final state of things. *Anticipation* was the last film that Godard and Karina made together, and he ensured that the experience was as humiliating as possible, both for her and for himself.

The basic visual schema of *Anticipation* is alienatingly futuristic: the film's images are tinted in red, yellow, or blue, which a mechanical voice announces as "Soviet," "Chinese," and "European," respectively. At the passport control of an airport, where disembarking passengers present inspectors the palm of their right hand, one traveler, a trim man named John Demetrios (played by Jacques Charrier) presents his *left* hand and is shunted instead to a holding area, alongside a woman. Both are presented with "catalogs"— pornographic magazines with pictures of men for the woman and of women for the man. The woman makes a "selection" and is led away. Moments later, the man does the same and is led to a hotel room by a bellhop (played by Jean-Pierre Léaud), who plugs in a light fixture and sets up a row of aerosol cans on a dresser.

Shortly thereafter, an official knocks on the man's door and greets him ("Honor to your ego!") as he presents him with his selection: a dark-haired, silent woman wearing a dress held on by thin chains bolted to a metal neckband. John invites her into his room; there, she hands him a series of wrenches to undo the bolts and remove her dress. Topless, she enters the bathroom, from which she emerges fully nude. She gets into bed, and John joins her there, asking her in a halting voice, with unnatural pauses between syllables, whether she speaks. When he finds that she does not, he calls the official and complains that she does not arouse him. The official brings him another woman: it is Anna Karina, decked out in a long, old-fashioned ruffled white dress.

Karina—who identifies herself as Eléonore Roméovitch—enters and greets him: "Honor to your ego." John asks, "You can speak?" She says, "Of course I speak" (the line from the ending of Jerry Lewis's *The Bellboy*), "that's what I'm here for." He asks her whether she is thirsty, and she requests Evian. He takes an aerosol can of Evian from the dresser and sprays her face with it. In close-up, Karina's face is being sprayed copiously wet at point-blank range: her mouth is open wide, her eyes are closed, and her tongue is agitating lasciviously to drink the fluid. It is Godard's most obscene and degrading shot to date, showing the cruel subjection of a woman, with her face sprayed as if with sperm or urine, which the actress is lapping up avidly. It is a view of Godard's readiness both to humiliate Karina and to show her in a state of carnal abasement—to a man who is not him. (He follows it with a shot of Eléonore subjecting John to the same treatment.)

John Demetrios orders her, the verbal prostitute, to undress. She responds with vehemence, "I won't get undressed"—the line with which Godard's acquaintance with Karina began, in 1959, when he offered her a part in *Breathless* that she rejected. She explains her refusal in a strange dialogue:

> ELÉONORE: Everything is specialized today . . . It may seem outdated. On Earth it's considered a very modern idea. Thousands of people have fought for it and died for it.
> JOHN: What idea?
> ELÉONORE: Integral specialization. For example, as for me, I don't get undressed. Prostitutes who get naked, that's physical love. They know all the gestures of love.
> JOHN: And you?
> ELÉONORE: I know all the words. I am sentimental love.
> JOHN: Love in language.

Godard, through Karina, condemns precisely the type of film in which he had dramatized love: there are, in effect, two cinemas, one of words, of sentimental love, in which respected actresses like Anna Karina merely talk but stay dressed and do not show the act of love, and the other of gestures, in which people get undressed and do show the act—that is, the pornographic or erotic cinema.

Eléonore strums an oversized comb like a lyre and recites fragments of the Song of Songs ("my breasts are like little gazelles") but again, John declares himself not aroused because although she speaks she does not accompany her words with gestures. She complains, "You can't have both together. It's only logical. I can't speak with my legs, my bosom, my eyes." Pensively stretched out on the bed, John comes up with an idea: "There is one part . . ." and Eléonore picks up the thread. "One part of the body which talks and moves at the same time. But which?" He points to her mouth, and she understands: "In putting the mouths one upon the other, we will speak and move together at the same time." Upon hearing this innovation, an electronic surveillance voice blares, "The prostitute in room 730 is discovering something: language and pleasure at the same time." The couple bring their lips together; in a close-up, they kiss; in an extreme close-up, they kiss again, and the loudspeaker voice emits an anguished machine-cry, "Negative! Negative! Negative!"—Godard's horrified vision of Karina kissing another man. But the image itself is positive: each time the lips touch, the harsh blue color filtration is gone, replaced by natural color and its glorious bloom on Karina's face. She faces the camera with a challenging look of demure satisfaction, a declaration of innocent pleasure, and smiles. Superimposition: the word *fin* (the end). End of film; end of filming Anna Karina.

WHEN *Two or Three Things* opened, on March 18, 1967, the reviews broke predictably, with the periodicals that served Godard's own "little audience" exalting it. The film was the cover story of *Le Nouvel Observateur,* and Jean Collet of *Télérama* recognized it as "a painful confession, a contained rage, an anguished reflection"[60]—but it didn't matter. Godard was already off in another direction, which he explained in an interview at the end of 1966.

Q: What is your new film?
A: *La Chinoise.*
Q: What will *La Chinoise* be?
A: A female student who reads Mao Zedong.
Q: French?
A: Yes.
Q: Played by whom?
A: I haven't decided yet.
Q: Have you read Mao?
A: [No response.][61]

Michel Delahaye of *Cahiers* saw where Godard was heading:

Let us note here that the year '66 (which goes from *Masculine Feminine* to *2 or 3*) is precisely the year when the world began to take notice of certain messages . . . of the demands of youth, and youth of its own demands. What they want: the death of this civilization—of which, for better or worse, the USA is the last bastion.[62]

Godard did not come to this younger generation on his own. Rather, he came to it by default. Had he married Marina Vlady, he would also have married into her family: into relations with her children and parents and siblings in and around their teeming dacha. He would have married himself into a social role of adulthood that had escaped him until then. Vlady's rejection of him also propelled him out of such a well-charted orbit and into a world of young people with new ideas, indeed of young people whose youth itself was an ideology. In effect, she pushed him into the arms of Anne Wiazemsky, and into the radically different life—and cinema—that resulted. Cinematically and romantically, Godard was starting from zero; like one dispossessed, he would make a leap of faith into an absolute and totalizing doctrine that seemed to answer with hope and with certainty his despair and his doubt.

Hundreds of Little Red Books and a toy weapon
(Pennebaker Films / Photofest)

fifteen

LA CHINOISE, WEEKEND

"You need only become Marxist-Leninist"

ANNE WIAZEMSKY HAD PASSED THE WRITTEN PART OF her baccalaureat exam in June 1966, but had failed the oral section. She asked the philosophy professor Francis Jeanson (France's leading activist for the FLN during the Algerian war) for private tutoring, which he gave her that summer—with Godard in attendance.[1] Since his proposal of marriage had been rejected by Marina Vlady, Godard started spending more time with Wiazemsky. Passing the makeup exam in September, Wiazemsky enrolled at the university at Nanterre, a working-class suburb of Paris.

The university, which had been constructed to ease overcrowding at the Sorbonne and other Paris faculties, had opened its doors in 1964. The professors who were willing to move to a new school in a poor neighborhood tended to be leftists, as were many of its students. The predominant strain of politics among students was left-wing anarchist; their ideological demands rose to open conflict over local and intimate issues. Students who lived in the dormitories were frustrated by the lack of nightlife in Nanterre and the lack of community in the university's modern, boxy dormitories and open concrete plazas. Parietal rules (which barred women from sleeping over in men's dormitories and prevented men from setting foot in women's dormitories) were viewed as anachronistic and repressive. Wilhelm Reich and Herbert Marcuse were more common intellectual references at Nanterre than Marx and Lenin.[2] Although the sociopolitical ferment was an expression of sexual tension and a rejection of sexual hypocrisy, it was expressed in more grandiose and classically political terms. Vehement meetings, protests, and fistfights between leftist and rightist students were normal occurrences, and these clashes rapidly resonated throughout French society.

Wiazemsky and Godard became a couple. When he dropped her off and picked her up at Nanterre, he met some of her left-wing activist friends and witnessed the rise of political dissent among French youth. In late 1966, Godard offered a very public yet deeply veiled tribute to her that reflected the conjunction of romance, cinema, and politics. Earlier in the year, *Cahiers du cinéma* had published François Truffaut's diary from the shoot of *Fahrenheit 451* (which, after long delays, was filmed at the beginning of 1966). This journal offered engaging anecdotes from the set but revealed nothing of his private life. Godard's response, indirect but unmistakable, appeared in the November *Cahiers:* "Three Thousand Hours of Cinema," an undated diary in which Wiazemsky is concealed under four literary names (Albertine, Gilberte, Alissa, and Chantal) but recognizable through his mention of such details as her study at Nanterre and her tutorials with Francis Jeanson—and recognizable, most importantly, to Wiazemsky herself. In this text, Godard wondered why *Cahiers* had delayed publishing long-awaited excerpts from Sergei Eisenstein's writings. Was it, he asked, due to "an echo of the Sino-Soviet conflict, and the rise to power of the [Chinese] Red Guards in the heart of those who to me were Camille Desmoulins and Saint-Just?"[3] The allusion was to the young editors of *Cahiers,* who had begun to express left-wing partisanship along with their cinephilic enthusiasm. His suspicion pointed to a political phenomenon of a growing force on the French left: Maoism, which had begun to hold sway over the foremost intellectual youth of France.

In the early 1960s, China took a strong stand in favor of third-world revolution. As the French left concerned itself increasingly with the struggle for Algerian independence and opposed the war in Vietnam, a small but growing number of local Communists realigned themselves from the French party's pro-Soviet orientation toward China and the doctrine and persona of Mao, whom they accepted as the authentic guarantor of "Marxism-Leninism."[4] In the mid-1960s, a detachment of French Communists declared themselves Maoist, founded the "Mouvement communiste français (marxiste-léniniste)," and launched a newspaper, *Humanité nouvelle.* The most dynamic of French Maoists, however, were from the student milieu. Godard was interested in meeting them. Their circles were different from Wiazemsky's at Nanterre, however, and he needed an introduction.

Godard's connection was arranged by Yvonne Baby, a young film critic at *Le Monde.* Her father, Jean Baby, a former high official in the French Communist Party, was one of the first elder French Communists to have declared himself a Maoist, for which he had been expelled from the party. Her mother, divorced from Jean Baby, had married Georges Sadoul, the film critic for *Les Lettres françaises* and also a longtime Communist. Yvonne Baby invited Godard to dinner along with her father, her mother, Sadoul, her own boyfriend (who happened to be the son of the late French actor Gérard Philipe), and one of her youngest colleagues at *Le Monde*, a literary critic named Jean-Pierre Gorin, who had gone to school with France's leading student Maoists.

Godard told the assembled company that he wanted to make a film about the young Maoists, to be called *La Chinoise* (The Chinese Woman, a familiar nickname for Maoism). As Gorin later remembered, "Jean Baby seemed to have a precise idea of what a film called *La Chinoise* should be. It was classic socialist realism." Gorin had other thoughts and, "talking about what political cinema could be or might be," he "stole the show," as he recalled—at least as far as Godard was concerned. "Afterward, on the way out, Godard said, 'It would be great to see each other again,' and we started to meet on an increasingly regular basis."[5]

FRANCE'S MOST INTELLECTUALLY vibrant group of Maoists attended the Ecole normale supérieure. The Ecole normale, founded in 1794, is, even now, France's most prestigious liberal-arts educational institution. Until recently, admission required thorough mastery of Greek and Latin, and most applicants spent one or more years of study in a specialized lycée, or *khâgne*, to prepare for the entrance exam. In the 1960s, only forty students were admitted per year, and they—the presumptive future professors of France—received a stipend as civil servants as well as a dormitory room in the school's building, on the rue d'Ulm, in the Latin Quarter.

A group of Gorin's friends from his *khâgne*, having entered the Ecole normale (Gorin did not), had come under the influence and personal tutelage of one of the school's best-known professors of political theory, Louis Althusser. Living in the school as a sort of house master, Althusser had an unusual amount of contact with the students. Althusser was a Marxist who had the idea, surprisingly original at the time, of reading Marx closely and freeing his texts from a century of traditional interpretations. His approach to Marx was similar to the psychoanalyst Jacques Lacan's work on Freud. In effect, Althusser and Lacan set in motion a pair of intellectual Reformations, complete with a return to the orders' founding texts and a quest for doctrinal purity. Both of these masters founded groups that functioned with the intensity and the exclusiveness of cults, of substitute religions.

Althusser's leading disciple was a "normalien" named Robert Linhart, a friend of Gorin's. In 1964, Linhart, joining a group of students in a left-wing summer program in Algeria, was influenced by a Spanish emigrant who had taken up Maoism in the name of third-world Marxism. Upon his return to Paris, Linhart began to proselytize in favor of Maoist thought as the authentic modern application of Marx and extension of Lenin.

In 1965, Althusser published two books of political theory that would inspire the new radical left: *Pour Marx* (*For Marx*) and *Lire le Capital* (*Reading Capital*). That year, Linhart and the others in his Althusserian circle at the Ecole normale (who had followed him in adopting Maoism) founded an austere intellectual journal called the *Cahiers Marxistes-Léninistes*. The title, of course, recalls the other influential *Cahiers* that had launched a small band of enthusiasts on a mercurial path from theory to practice. Linhart's doctrinal rigor had an enormous appeal for his cohorts. His approach to Mao, taking even further Althusser's stringent fidelity to the texts of Marx, exemplified the intellectual perfection of France's most perfect students: they no longer consumed ideas, they were consumed by them. They were in effect France's political New Wave.

In the summer of 1966, Mao launched the Cultural Revolution, ostensibly to extirpate the vestiges of feudal and bourgeois culture and to reinfuse the country with revolutionary zeal. But the young shock troops mobilized on behalf of Mao and his allies in the government, the Red Guard, were also deployed as part of an internal power struggle. The violence of the Red Guard was reminiscent of that of Italy's Fascists and Germany's Nazis, as hundreds of thousands, or even millions, were killed in public attacks or in government custody. In the eyes of their foreign admirers, the Red Guard had the idealism of youth without American hedonism or European aestheticism, a Marxism cleansed of heterogeneous notions and put immediately into practice. The Althusserian Maoists of the Ecole normale revered the Red Guard: these highly theoretical French youths similarly dreamed of converting their intellectual authority into actual authority, of incarnating their force of mind in the actual use of force, of confirming their physical and social existence in flesh and blood—the blood of others. According to the philosopher Bernard-Henri Lévy, who was then a high school student preparing for his own entry into the Ecole normale, the leading Maoists there were "the secret kings of France at that time";[6] their charismatic fervor was matched by their desire to rule.

Gorin introduced Godard to the Maoist group at the Ecole normale, which had now formally constituted itself as the "Union des jeunesses communistes (marxistes-léninistes)" (Communist [Marxist-Leninist] Youth League). Gorin understood that for the Maoists, he served as "a conduit to a certain press" and afforded them "the possibility of being talked about."[7] Gorin himself was not an active Maoist—*Le Monde* discouraged its writers from political activity—but his friendship with the movement's leaders marked him as a fellow traveler. His influence on Godard was evident in the concrete form that the film *La Chinoise* began to take: Godard now planned to do a "reportage akin to a television news documentary," bringing editors from the orthodox French Communist Party publications, *Humanité-Dimanche* and *L'Humanité,* together with those from the Maoist *Humanité nouvelle* and the *Cahiers marxistes-léninistes* and filming their discussions. Godard claimed to have one motive in making the film: "to reunite Moscow and Peking against the common enemy: the Americans."[8] All of the groups he approached, however, refused to participate.[9]

Nonetheless, Gorin, as Godard's connection to the intellectual Maoists, remained crucial to his thoughts on a new film. It was of no small importance that Gorin was also an informed and engaged cinephile. He had been the sole person to show up at a screening of *Les Carabiniers* shortly after the film opened disastrously in 1963.[10] Gorin considered Godard's films to be the only modern aesthetically revolutionary cinema, and the two talked about films endlessly. "We started to discuss movies," Gorin recalled, "which is also to discuss all sorts of problems about movies and which, in turn, produce the kind of movies we have. And we started to discuss politics and aesthetics and aesthetics as a kind of politics."[11] Godard had long considered his cinematic aesthetic to be a touchstone of the new left, but in its ideological orientation and zealotry the new left had been redefined in a few short years, and now Godard, in the company of Gorin, similarly introduced a new ideological element to his aesthetic. Gorin had become, for Godard, not merely a collaborator but the embodiment of a new idea of filmmaking. Godard explained to an interviewer the nature of his involvement with Gorin: "I don't have a screenwriter, but I have perhaps an extra guy, who Preminger doesn't have, and who I need. A kind of assistant with whom I can speak, who is at the same time my friend, who doesn't help me with the film, but simply helps me because I have someone to live the film with me while I am creating it."[12] Ultimately, the mere fact of their collaboration proved to be of a more enduring importance to Godard's career than the ideology they shared. But at the time, Godard's work and thought were more overtly marked by a radical ideological turn, a leftism dominated by his opposition to the Vietnam War, to American influence in politics, economics, and culture, and, above all, to the Hollywood cinema.

In late January and early February 1967, Godard visited Algiers and presented his films at the Cinémathèque algérienne. On Sunday, February 5, 1967, after a screening of *Le Grand Escroc,* he answered questions from the audience for two hours. Asked about his view of the American cinema, Godard responded:

It wouldn't be bad to ban the American cinema for a while. Three-quarters of the planet considers cinema from the angle and according to the criteria of the American cinema . . . People must become aware that there are other ways to make films than the American way. Moreover this would force filmmakers of the United States to revise their conceptions. It would be a good thing.[13]

Godard continued with this theme as it pertained to him personally: "I am distancing myself from the entire cinema that formed me, I am distancing myself from thirty years of talking pictures. And as for silent film, I don't really know what it was. So I'm working in foggy terrain." While in Algiers, Godard sought out different kinds of films, going to the Chinese embassy to view several Chinese-made documentaries. He explained to an interviewer there that the film he was about to make would be "the story of a group of Communists in Paris who break up into two tendencies, pro-Soviet and pro-Chinese."[14]

In late February, the foggy terrain onto which Godard advanced, together with Anne Wiazemsky, was centered on an apartment in the rue Miromesnil, near the Champs-Elysées, that Godard's friend, the theater director Antoine Bourseiller, and his wife, the actress Chantal Darget, rented. They lent the apartment to Godard as the location for his next film, and he and Wiazemsky moved in there together.

Despite the cinematic passions (Godard's for the image of Wiazemsky in Bresson's film, Wiazemsky for *Masculine Feminine*) that had brought the couple together, Godard (in an echo of his earliest relations with Anna Karina) had not wanted Wiazemsky to act in movies.[15] But as his plans for *La Chinoise* advanced, they inevitably involved Wiazemsky and her role in his initiation in student politics. She would play a student at Nanterre University named Véronique—a reprise of the character Godard had filmed in *All the Boys Are Called Patrick* and of the name he had assigned Karina's character in her first role, in *Le Petit Soldat*.

The project was inchoate, even by Godard's own standards: as in *Masculine Feminine,* he brought together five young people, each of whom played a role derived from their own lives. In addition to Wiazemsky as Véronique, Jean-Pierre Léaud played Véronique's boyfriend, a young bourgeois actor named Guillaume (as in Goethe's *Wilhelm Meister*); Juliet Berto, who had appeared as a café dialectician in *Two or Three Things I Know About Her,* played Yvonne, a young woman from the countryside. They were joined by two others: Michel Semeniako, a science student at the University of Grenoble, as Henri, a science student (and Yvonne's boyfriend); and a Dutch painter, Lex de Bruijn, as a painter by the name of Kirilov (a character from Dostoyevsky's *The Devils*).[16]

Though four of the five actors closely resembled the characters they were playing, Léaud, who was living a threadbare existence in a tiny apartment, was hardly a member of the bourgeoisie. To prepare him for his role, Godard gave Léaud money to eat: "I forbade him to spend it chez Langlois [at the Cinémathèque], so that he could eat calmly, for an hour and a half, every day, without reading the paper and without doing anything beside having a normal meal in a normal restaurant."[17]

In *La Chinoise*, the five call themselves the "Aden-Arabie" cell (a name taken from the title of the first novel by the late Paul Nizan, Sartre's close friend who had migrated politically from the right wing to Communism in the 1930s while Sartre was still apolitical). They are staying together in a comfortable apartment that Véronique has borrowed from friends' parents during the summer between university terms. These young people are in effect on summer vacation and not so much forming a cell as playing at one. Holed up together, they study political texts, deliver lectures to each other, invite guest speakers, and dream of revolution.

The story concerns the group's passage from theory to practice. After reading a series of texts advocating violence in the name of revolution, the group—with the exception of Henri—decides to assassinate the loyal Soviet novelist Mikhail Sholokhov, who is in Paris as a cultural ambassador representing the Soviet government.[18] The painter, Kirilov, who had been planning his own suicide, volunteers for the murder, but the group decides to draw lots to determine who will commit the crime. Véronique is chosen. To facilitate her task, Kirilov writes a letter falsely confessing to the crime that she will commit, then kills himself.

Véronique is driven by a young sympathizer from outside the cell to Sholokhov's hotel. She goes inside and reads Sholokhov's name on the guest register. The driver waits in the street for Véronique to reappear (Godard punctuates the scene with a comic-strip panel of a gunshot blast). Véronique re-enters the car, tells the driver that she's done the deed, then exclaims: "Shit, shit, shit, shit! Stop!"; she realizes that she read the hotel register upside down, took Sholokhov's room number, 23, for 32, and shot the wrong man. She now returns to the building, as the driver waits again until Véronique signals from the balcony of room 23 that the deed has really been done this time.

Henri, in a kind of on-camera exit interview, explains that he left the group because he found the others "too fanatical." Guillaume—as announced in a series of title cards heralding "The Theatrical Vocation of Guillaume Meister"—enters the ruins of a building labeled "Theater, Year Zero." Among the ruins, two women, one young and slender in a bikini, the other aging and plump in a one-piece bathing suit, face each other from behind matching panels of glass and knock loudly on them. The actor then stands in a barren industrial zone selling fruits and vegetables for "ten centimes" each;

he exhorts his customers, "Try your luck!" and they pelt him with his merchandise; leeks, tomatoes, eggs, and zucchini come raining down on his head. Guillaume's last "work" is to knock on the door of a woman in an apartment building. She tells him tearfully that her boyfriend has left her, and he responds in slightly altered verses from Racine's *Andromaque:* "Fear not, madame. A god is on your side. The fatal sacrifice is still in abeyance, you need only become Marxist-Leninist!"

The children of the apartment's tenants (including Blandine Jeanson, who had appeared so memorably in *Two or Three Things*) return from their vacation and are appalled to see copies of the Little Red Book and agit-prop posters strewn about their home. On the balcony, the young women, who learn what Véronique has done, ask what in the world she will tell her family. She says, "Yes, OK, it's a fiction, but it brought me closer to reality," and declares, "I thought I had made a great leap forward, and now I realize that I have only made the first timid steps of a very long march." Going inside the apartment, she closes the shutters, ending her summer interlude, as a title card declares, "The End of a Beginning."

THE FILM WAS shot with a wildness unusual even for Godard: he had prepared a number of scenes that he intended to shoot, but had little sense of how he was going to organize them into a film. He joked with an interviewer that he "shot the film in the order of shooting"[19]—in other words, without regard to the order of the story's events, which he had left vague even as the camera rolled. Michel Semeniako had come to Paris with little idea of what he would be doing. Indeed, he expected to work with Godard behind the camera—and found out differently. As he later recalled: "The very day of my arrival, after hours of train travel, completely exhausted, he had me start work at once. Godard thrust a typewritten two-page synopsis in my hands and a little red book (which I wasn't at all obliged to read) and I had to speak the text which is at the beginning of the film."[20]

There are also long scenes of the group's teach-in meetings, where the others listen to Guillaume's report on newsreels or to Omar, an African student from Nanterre who presents a text on the effort "to give a little existence and theoretical consistency to Marxist philosophy."

The continuity notebooks of the script supervisor, Suzanne Schiffman, reveal the shoot's randomness and improvisation. Many scenes were reshot, others went unused. Godard not only did a great many takes (Semeniako, an untrained actor, remembered doing up to twenty of one scene) but also printed many of them in order to leave himself a wide range of choices in the editing room. Godard explained in an interview that *La Chinoise* was "exclusively a film of montage," and added, "I shot autonomous sequences, without any order, and I organized them later."[21] Cobbling together scenes from different takes shot on different days with different backgrounds, Godard used inserts and music to paper over the differences.

This element of improvisation, together with the lively spontaneity of the performers, gives the film the exuberant simplicity of Judy Garland and Mickey Rooney putting on a show in a Maoist garage. The film is comprised largely of bizarre, tendentious skits: a man in a tiger mask pretends to speak amicably on the phone with the Soviet leader Aleksei Kosygin; Yvonne plays a Vietnamese peasant (using a conical lampshade as a hat) who fends off toy American fighter planes dangling from strings while crying out, "Help, Mister Kosygin!" or plays the same peasant, camped behind a barricade of piled-up Little Red Books.

The poet and critic Alain Jouffroy met Godard often during the shoot of *La Chinoise* and the two spoke about modern painting. Jouffroy believes that the subject of their talks is reflected in the film,[22] which is highly decorative, a painter's film. Godard smeared the shutters and the apartment walls in red. He took particular care daubing the actors with blood-red makeup. Throughout the film, graphic images—of Brecht, Shakespeare, Sartre, of young Mao and young Marx, an engraving of Alice in Wonderland, a detail from a painting by Bonnard and another by Klimt, a poster of Chinese theater, and a picture of a newborn baby red with blood—appear in the midst of the live action. The walls of the apartment are a canvas for Godard's graphic sense: on them, we see a poster of Malcolm X, the covers of magazines (*Peking News, Cahiers Marxistes-Léninistes, Red Guard*), and Godard's own designs, including a large-size slogan done in rectilinear letters ("One Must Combat Vague Ideas With Precise Images"). There is also a wall of shame that serves as a target for the group's sport, archery with a suction-tipped toy arrow, and is adorned with a collage of images of Descartes, Sartre's book on Descartes, Himmler (inscribed "Emmanuel Kant"), the poet Novalis, Lyndon Johnson, Kosygin, and Leonid Brezhnev. Other walls in the apartment feature blackboards filled with Godard's recognizable scrawl ("anarchism, ultra-democracy, subjectivism, individualism") and the last work of the painter Kirilov, a series of polychrome parallel stripes meandering the length of a bedroom.

After the shoot, Antoine Bourseiller returned to his apartment to find it covered with the film's graphic decorations, including a huge poster in Godard's own handwriting. On one side, in red, was a doctrinaire decree: "It is the rich who create languages and who endlessly renovate them from top to bottom . . . A school that selects, destroys culture. It removes the means of expression from the poor. It removes the knowledge of things from the rich."[23] The other side of the poster listed the exemplary agents of this oppression: the world's film producers, on both sides of the Iron Curtain.

In effect, *La Chinoise* is less a document of Maoist thought, action, or organization than a collage of Maoist graffiti and paraphernalia. The Red Book itself is featured, on bookshelves, in endless rows of uniform authority. Even the sound track contains a sign of the moment's political effluvia, a bouncy but aggressively intoned song, "Mao Mao." Godard had wanted a rock song for the film, and Gérard Guégan, a Marxist who wrote for *Cahiers du cinéma* and also had a foot in the world of French pop music, quickly patched the song together from Maoist catchphrases that were in the air.

In *La Chinoise*, Godard breaks the fourth wall more overtly than he had done in any film to date. Dialogue between Godard and his actors is included, as in *Masculine Feminine*, though in *La Chinoise* he often left his voice on the sound track, if faintly, coming to the actors from off-camera as they acknowledge the director's presence by responding to him directly, without pretending to remain in character. He leaves the slate in many shots, uses a second camera to film Raoul Coutard at the eyepiece of the large studio camera and the small bank of lights behind him, and shows the sound technician at his tape recorder. The proceedings are nominally Brechtian: in his first scene, Léaud as Guillaume defines his theatrical mission with a political parable of a Chinese student protesting in Moscow. After the student's protest was broken up by Russian police, he appeared before the press with his face bandaged, crying, "Look what they've done to me!" While telling this story directly to the camera, Léaud mimes it, putting a bandage on his own face and then unwrapping it to reveal his face, unharmed:

> So naturally, the journalists started yelling, "What kind of jokers are these Chinese, what's this all about?" but they didn't . . . they didn't understand at all. No, they didn't understand what theater, real theater, is: a reflection on reality, I mean, something like Brecht, or else . . . or else, Shakespeare, of course.

The Brechtian aspect persists as Guillaume continues his interview and tells the camera, "You think that I'm pulling your leg, you think that I'm playing the clown because I'm being filmed, or because there are technicians around me, but not at all. It's because there's a camera in front of me that I'm being sincere." He then refers to a text by Althusser on a play by Brecht; at the end of the monologue, Godard says, "Cut. Very good," and a technician is heard saying, "*La Chinoise*, R-seven, take five."

The set piece that speaks most clearly from and to Godard is one that takes place at a blackboard: as Kirilov delivers a lecture, off-camera, on the history of art (praising Mayakovsky and Eisenstein, who was "stabbed in the back by Trotsky"), Guillaume stands at a blackboard covered with the names of several dozen playwrights including Sartre, Giraudoux, Racine, Cocteau,

Goethe, Sophocles, Chekhov, and Shakespeare. One by one, Guillaume takes a sponge and effaces the names. The first to go is Sartre. In the end, all are erased except one: Brecht. The effect is that of an intellectual purge—a purge largely of Godard himself, who was wiping out his own ample literary culture in favor of the sole writer he could rescue in the name of his narrow new political doctrine—indeed, something of an intellectual suicide.

Most of *La Chinoise* takes place in the comfortable apartment that Bourseiller had lent for the shoot. During that time, Godard lived there with Anne Wiazemsky, who found it odd to share his bed at night and then to share it on-camera with Léaud the next day. The experience was all the more odd in that Godard often had Wiazemsky and Léaud speak in the film the dialogue that she and Godard had had the night before. They also spent much time watching movies: despite Godard's declaration that he needed to return to life after having immured himself in the cinema, he saw to what Anne Wiazemsky called her "cinematographic education," taking her to see two films a day when they weren't shooting.[24]

Their evolving relationship is echoed in the romantic aspect of *La Chinoise,* involving Guillaume and Véronique, although this is significantly underplayed in the couple's three important scenes. In the first, which begins the film, only their hands are visible. In the second, they sit face-to-face at a table, studying and attempting "to speak to each other as if words were detached from sounds and from matter," speaking as if in ideograms: "Beside a river," "Green and blue," "Tenderness," "A bit of despair," "The day after tomorrow," "Oh, maybe," "Theory of literature," "A film by Nicholas . . . Ray." In the third scene—which Godard admitted he derived from Max Ophüls's *Le Plaisir*—Véronique attempts to teach Guillaume how to do two things at once ("to fight the battle on two fronts," citing Mao) by playing a record of Schubert while explaining to him (falsely, just to get his attention) that she doesn't love him. Wiazemsky later recalled, "There is a great deal of me in this scene," a great deal of her own personal life with Godard: in a fight, she had told him in anger that she didn't like the color of his sweaters, and this appears verbatim in that scene.

Godard presents a spare and unemotional, formalized, politicized, abstracted view of love, a solely intellectual intimacy, as if, unsubordinated to ideology, romance itself was suspect. At the end of the film the couple's story is unresolved; it is unclear whether it continues or ends. Godard told an audience, "About *La Chinoise,* it's clear that I don't want to talk about human emotions . . . There's no interest in relating a story of two young Marxist-Leninists in terms of a love story. What's important is to try to know what Marxist-Leninism is and how it helps them in their love."[25]

Masculine Feminine and *La Chinoise* share Léaud as a lead actor in a love story, and both films feature five young people. But in the earlier movie, the young people are not a group, whereas the group in *La Chinoise* takes precedence over its individuals. (When Henri leaves the group, he is also excluded from his relationship with Yvonne.) In both films, a young man fails to fit into a woman's ideology—in *Masculine Feminine,* the romantic and consumerist notions of prefabricated pleasure, a stereotypical woman's world; in *La Chinoise,* the political fanaticism and paramilitary violence that reach an apex as voiced by Véronique in the film's longest, most important, and most audacious set piece: her dialogue on board a train with Wiazemsky's philosophy tutor, Francis Jeanson.

Throughout the film, Véronique expresses a desire for violent, revolutionary action, at one point declaring, "But seriously, what I mean is that if I had the courage, well, I would go and blow up the Sorbonne, the Louvre and the Comédie-Française." Now, on a train ride from Paris to Nanterre, Véronique faces Jeanson, who reveals his plans for "cultural action" with a theater company in Dijon; she, in turn, reveals her own plans: "To shut down the university." He asks her how she intends to do it, and she answers, "With bombs," justifying her plans by likening herself to Algerian insurgents and "the young Russian nihilists." After hearing Jeanson's diverse arguments against her methods, she asks bluntly whether he thinks she is making a mistake. "Yes, I think that it's an error," he says. "Yes, I think that you are heading into a perfect dead end." His reasoning and his judgment do not at all dissuade her, and, immediately thereafter the group decides to kill Sholokhov.

Years later, Godard discussed the scene and recalled that when he made *La Chinoise,* he thought that Wiazemsky—that is, himself, speaking into her earpiece the lines she repeats in the scene—had won the debate about shutting down the university by acts of terror. In retrospect, however, it seemed clear to him that in the film, Jeanson's argument is the more persuasive. Godard attributed these results to the difference between his conscious sympathies at the time, with Wiazemsky's terrorist position, and his unconscious ones, with peaceful forms of political action.[26] His inner conflict would only be exacerbated in the years that followed.

DESPITE THE IDEOLOGICAL rigors of *La Chinoise,* its exhilarating cinematic style, with its collage-like assemblage of disparate scenes and allusive fragments, is as provocative and enticing as any in Godard's films. And yet from the beginning, the film conveys a frenetic sense of self-destruction in the name of the enthusiasms of youth. It is as if Leonard Bernstein had thrown down his baton for an electric guitar in a three-chord garage band: the momentary surge of joy, the shock of incongruity and aesthetic invigoration, quickly give way to a view of pathetic self-abnegation. The dogmatic rhetoric that dominates the film has an incantatory appeal, a self-enclosed and circular religious certainty that shuns the ambiguities of critical thought and introspection for the energizing simplicity of exhortation and advocacy. To reach such naive ecstasies, Godard had to film his own brainwashing.

In *Masculine Feminine*, Léaud was assigned Godard's intellectual qualities and interests in order to contrast them with those of the young women, who are satirized and criticized. In *La Chinoise*, despite the dazzlingly spontaneous and daring technique, Godard filmed an altogether more somber spectacle: he applied his own attributes to Guillaume and then filmed the young man's private chastisement (by Véronique) and public self-humiliation (the pelting of vegetables) in an attempt to purge himself of them. If the Aden-Arabie cell stood for Godard's notion of an aspiring group of French Red Guards— something simultaneously absurd and touchingly romantic—he himself was the first of the bourgeois intellectuals to face its derision and wrath.

Godard had intended to use new filmmaking techniques to build the Marxist concept of self-criticism into *La Chinoise*. Amateur video cameras had just come on the market, and Godard acquired one, with the intention of including scenes of the characters videotaping, then watching and discussing their political conversations. However, he had trouble with the new equipment and so eliminated it from the film. The self-criticism that was applied to Guillaume, who represents Godard, was implemented by means of the traditional movie camera.

The mockery and abuse that Guillaume endures joyfully at the end suggest Godard's position: he is willing to submit to ridicule in the name of his absolute political doctrine, and there is masochistic pleasure in his humiliation, which seems to define the art announced by the title card, "Cinema, year zero."

La Chinoise is widely understood to be prophetic: 1967 was a year of political confrontation, and 1968 a year of legendary upheaval, especially in France. The film expressed the latent proclivity for violence among the highly politicized youth of France and suggested that their opposition went far beyond the local concerns of the university, extending to revolution in the literal sense—a sudden, radical, and violent change that would affect all of society and culture.

The coming transformation that Godard both foresaw and helped to foster was one of art as well as of politics. In *La Chinoise*, Godard was doing more than exploding the conventions of the cinema: he was expressing despair that the radical politics of the time had surpassed the radicalism of his cinema. There, the contortions to which he would have to subject himself to press the cinema into the confining mold of those politics began to come into view.

THE FILM WAS completed in the spring of 1967. On July 21, in Begnins, in the canton of Vaud in Switzerland, Jean-Luc Godard, thirty-six years old, and

Anne Wiazemsky, who was not quite twenty, were married. Wiazemsky was thin and angular, with wide cheekbones, large, soft eyes, and an easy grin. Her manner was a blend of quiet, blunt sincerity and ethereal contemplation. She was something of an aristocrat, being descended on her father's side from Polish nobility and on her mother's from the Nobel-Prize–winning novelist François Mauriac. Like Godard, she was the scion of a notable family; like Godard, she enjoyed the cultural advantages—and the freedom from conventional expectations—it afforded. She was, in effect, a bourgeois bohemian of a similar stripe, less of an omnivorous intellectual, perhaps, but emotionally more spontaneous and less guarded.

Godard and Wiazemsky got a cocker spaniel and were photographed washing it in their bathtub and walking it together on the rue de Miromesnil. Mauriac, Wiazemsky's grandfather, was interviewed, and he declared Godard to be "nice." The newlyweds (and their dog) spent three days in the country at Jeanne Moreau's estate.[27] Two weeks after the marriage, on August 3, *La Chinoise* was shown publicly for the first time, at the Avignon theater festival. Antoine Bourseiller had persuaded Jean Vilar, the festival's august director, to show *La Chinoise* in the unusual setting of the courtyard of the Palace of Popes, which he recalled as a "mythical place for the theater."[28] Many of the spectators, according to Nicole Zand of *Le Monde*, were unpleasantly surprised by the film, which they expected to be "a report on the Chinese Cultural Revolution and the Sino-Soviet ideological conflict," but she herself recognized it as an attempt "to capture a certain youth as one captures a radio frequency."[29]

The film was released commercially in Paris on September 1 and shown at the Venice festival on September 4. (Godard and Wiazemsky went to Venice to present the film; there, on a vaporetto, she met by chance the director Pier Paolo Pasolini, who asked her to play a leading role in his upcoming film, *Teorema*. She didn't know who Pasolini was; Godard explained, and she accepted.)[30] Pierre Daix, of *Les Lettres françaises*, wrote: "The power of Godard's fable does not come from the *way* that these young people pose the question of revolution, but from the *fact* that they pose the question seriously in France in 1967." He concluded that what would be most important about the film was "what young people will make of *La Chinoise*."[31]

What they made of it soon became clear. Those who had inspired it, the Marxist-Leninist Maoists of the Ecole normale, were furious with Godard for having, they thought, made them look ridiculous, and with Gorin for having transmitted what they assumed to be false or misleading information to Godard for that purpose. One member of the group was calmly derisive: "He exploited a need for romanticism. He described a fanatical little group that has nothing Marxist-Leninist about it, which could be anarchist or fascist . . . It's a film about bourgeois youth who have adopted a new disguise."[32] Another young Maoist called the film "a provocation. A police provocation," because it showed Maoists to be "irresponsible terrorists."[33] Others threatened Godard with a people's tribunal.[34]

Older critics, however, readily embraced both the film's message and its characters. Claude Mauriac, Anne Wiazemsky's uncle, declared Godard's "condemnations of the ongoing American barbarity" to be "sublime and terrifying."[35] Jean de Baroncelli wrote in *Le Monde* that the film's story is "an avatar—vintage 1967—of the eternal revolt of youth, of that irresistible élan for an ideal of purity, propriety, and nobility, that is the trait of all the adolescents of the world (at least, of those who have some soul and some heart)."[36] Baroncelli hoped that the film would win the Golden Lion at the Venice festival. It did not; Luis Buñuel's *Belle de Jour* did.

La Chinoise indeed showed that Maoist groups existed and made clear their charismatic force. Yet the film's "documentary" view of sweet-tempered revolutionaries and naive terrorists, joined with Godard's anarchically exuberant method of construction, got in the way of a view of Godard himself in the picture. Where his previous films had all appeared as self-portraits, as entries in a journal, *La Chinoise*, the work of a self-abasing and self-excoriating filmmaker on the verge of a political and aesthetic breakdown, was less a portrait of him than the attempt to efface one.

WHILE GODARD WAS making *La Chinoise*, Chris Marker—whose politically engaged documentaries included *Le Joli mai* (a portrait of life in France at the end of the Algerian war) and whose fictions included *La Jetée* (a dystopian yet romantic science fiction constructed of still photos with a voice-over)— organized a project called *Far from Vietnam*, a compilation film involving volunteer work from dozens of technicians, actors, and suppliers of motion picture goods and services. He invited Godard, along with Joris Ivens, William Klein, Claude Lelouch, Alain Resnais, and Agnès Varda, to contribute a short film to the ensemble. Godard's initial contribution, however, which he described as a shot of a naked woman accompanied by a description on the sound track of what a fragmentation bomb would do to her body, was rejected by the group. As the project's deadline was nearing, Godard delivered, at the last minute, a short film called *Caméra-Oeil* (*Camera-Eye*, a title taken from the Soviet agit-prop newsreels *Kino-Glaz*, made mainly by Dziga Vertov in the 1920s). Although it, too, as William Klein later recalled, disappointed others in the group, this short film was included in the compilation.[37]

In *Camera-Eye*, Godard himself, seen at the eyepiece of a massive 35mm Mitchell camera, meditates on the title of the film and on his situation— namely, that of a Frenchman wanting to do something for the Vietnamese people despite being "far from Vietnam." Godard refers to his first, rejected film, and admits that he had wanted to go to North Vietnam but was denied a visa by its government. He intercuts his own image with documentary news images from Vietnam, of battlefields and urban defenses. Most of all, the sequence is a twin self-portrait of Godard and a professional movie camera, a double identity that suggested a double identity crisis. *Camera-Eye,* a film of wit and agony, promised political cinema that would be both aesthetically sophisticated and intensely personal. But Godard did not fulfill that promise; he was seeking to erase himself, and his contribution to *Far from Vietnam* would be the last time for many years that he would face the camera.

In another short film, made in Paris at the same time, Godard expressed even more clearly his political sentiments—together with their romantic implications. He was commissioned to make a short film for a compilation called *Vangelo 70* (Gospel 70, ultimately released under the title of *Amore e Rabbia,* Love and Rage), a French-Italian coproduction. (Other commissioned directors included Bernardo Bertolucci, who filmed a production by the Living Theater with Julian Beck, and Pasolini, who filmed his waifish alter ego, Ninetto Davoli, romping through the streets of Rome bearing a giant flower.) Godard's contribution, credited simply as "Love," was given a bilingual title: *L'Aller et retour andate e ritorno des enfants prodigues dei figli prodighi* (The Departure and Return of the Prodigal Children). As the title suggests, Godard took the bilingual premise of the French-Italian coproduction to its ultimate extreme: the film features a couple in which the man speaks Italian and the woman French.

The setting is the same rooftop garden where *Camera-Eye* was filmed—Michèle Rozier's garden in the sixth arrondissement. The bilingual couple contemplates and discusses another young couple, as if the second pair were in a movie.

The young woman in the "observed" couple speaks (in French) of aesthetics, nature, psychology, and love, while her lover speaks (in Italian) of a new era of world revolution. He tells her that they are at odds because he is a revolutionary and she is not, and adds that he is planning to leave for Cuba later that day. The woman in the "watching" couple declares that the other pair is destined to break up because the young woman is Jewish and the man is an Arab (the film was made immediately after the end of the Six-Day War); her partner explains that it is their parents whose ethnicity is so clearly determined, not theirs.

This dialogue of lovers destined to separate because of political differences suggests that love between ideological opponents would be realized only in a future Arcadian utopia, as the "watched" man says: "When the world is returned to a single black forest to our four astonished eyes, and to a beach for two loyal children, we'll meet again." And the herald of that dream of idyllic love is the age of revolution: "The war that China, and the rest of humanity, will wage, will lead the world to a new age." As in the series of films that he had begun with *Le Nouveau Monde,* Godard put the blame for his earlier failed romantic relations on the hostile conditions of the world; it was as if Godard was explaining his past to Wiazemsky, with whom things would be different because, as an ideological comrade, she shared his point of view.

Godard's dreadful and fantastic vision in *L'Aller et retour* is at odds with the elegant formal games that framed it. His next feature film would depict an age of ideological apocalypse with a wild, scattershot fervor more appropriate to his political hysteria and aesthetic revulsion.

IN INTERVIEWS AT the time of the release of *La Chinoise,* Godard mentioned his plans for a new film, *Weekend* (the English-language word). Its subject was "the God of leisure" and he described his idea: "By following a young managerial couple on the road, I will attempt to show all the perversions which flow from that state of affairs. The journey, begun in apotheoses, will end in tragi-comedy (having left in a new car, our heroes will come home on foot . . .)."[38] The film was produced by a consortium of French and Italian companies that demanded the casting of two stars: Mireille Darc and Jean Yanne. Both were in the commercial mainstream of the French film industry, neither had any New Wave associations, and, though Godard described them as "a very plausible couple,"[39] he was unhappy about working with Darc, an actress known for films of vapid eroticism.

Godard had left little time to prepare for the film and had to leave the Venice festival before the screening of *La Chinoise* on September 4 because the shoot of *Weekend* was scheduled to begin the next day.[40] He told a journalist that the film would be about "a couple . . . who go driving on the highways for a weekend" and described the sort of things that would happen. As the journalist reported:

> One will see accidents. Hippies with flowers in their hair, led by [the avant-garde theater actor] Jean-Pierre Kalfon. And also Jean-Pierre Léaud, who will sing into a telephone. And Juliet Berto, who will make speeches on the street. And a Christ, who will change a flock of sheep into a junkyard full of cars.[41]

The overriding structure of the film, unlike that of *La Chinoise,* was simple, and Godard recognized the difference: "In *La Chinoise* I had nothing but details to assemble, lots of details. For *Weekend,* on the contrary, I have the structure, but not the details."[42] The pretext for the couple's trip was grotesquely mercenary: they were rushing to her family home before her mother died to make sure they would not be disinherited by her stepfather. Their trip and its purpose fit squarely within Godard's own moral mythology: the film's first scene, of the couple in comfort and at leisure in a modern suburban house, features the woman (Darc) whispering on the phone to her lover, telling him that she will leave her husband as soon as she gets the money. Once again, Godard associated the political and social immorality of the bourgeois and consumerist way of life with sexual immorality and marital infidelity.

To make his point, Godard created an extraordinary array of set pieces of a bourgeois world desperately out of joint. After the woman's telephonic tryst, she confesses an erotic incident to her husband in great detail (including, among other things, an egg placed between her legs), during a scene shot in a single long take, with a text derived from Georges Bataille's *Story of the Eye*. Godard films the scene with a remarkable series of slow zooms in and out, on both husband and wife. (He claimed to have gotten the idea from the scene in Bergman's *Persona* in which Bibi Andersson describes a sexual encounter.)[43]

Then the couple sets out from their apartment, chased by the child of a neighbor whose car bumper they have dented while pulling out: the child (Christophe Bourseiller) is dressed in an American Indian headdress and fires toy arrows at the departing couple. His parents emerge from their own modern apartment building, and his father fires a shotgun at the couple as they drive away.

The most famous set piece in the film, and one of the greatest conceptual gags in the history of cinema, is the traffic jam that the husband and wife encounter on their way out of town. The sequence lasts for nine minutes; it is a series of three tracking shots, cut together by intertitles to simulate the impression of a single take. In this sequence, the camera simply follows a line of cars inching forward—often entirely stopped—on one lane of a two-lane highway. Some people have left their cars, others picnic at the roadside, children throw a beachball from one sunroof to another as horns honk, tempers rise, drivers attempt to cut in on the line and are rebuffed by other drivers, until, at the head of the traffic jam, the cause of the bottleneck is revealed: drivers have stopped to stare at an accident which has strewn wrecked cars around trees and left blood-spattered bodies dispersed on the road. The sequence connects the two scourges of automotive life—traffic jams and car crashes—in a single comic idea and a single image. Despite the very long takes and the very few cuts, the scene is, above all, a masterwork of montage, as Godard had primordially conceived it.

After a series of sardonic calamities in which they lose their car and money, the couple find themselves stranded on a country road. They meet a group of men sitting by the roadside and ask them who they are. The answer: "We're the Italian extras"—whom Godard had hired to fulfill the requirements of the Italian coproducers. The couple sit by the roadside like Beckett's Vladimir and Estragon, each blaming the other for their misfortune and their bilious marriage. Two passersby drag the woman into a ditch; the man doesn't lift a finger as, off-camera, they rape her (a bitterly serious moment that is played, by way of the passivity of the husband and the matching passivity of the camera, as dark, absurd comedy).

The couple then hitches a ride on a truck carrying a group of workers, who soon stop to eat. The couple asks to share the food; the response (from a worker played by Godard's friend László Szabó): "If this sandwich represents the gross national product of the West, this"—offering the woman a crumb—"represents aid to Africa." He then delivers a lengthy lecture on revolution in Africa and the Arab world—the only sincere, noncartoonish, nonexaggerated moment in the film, the only dialogue Godard could bear to hear spoken straight and performed without histrionics.

The couple is next abducted by a band of revolutionary "hippies," the FLSO (Front de Libération de la Seine-et-Oise, a suburban region of Paris), who turn out to be cannibals. To save herself, the woman joins them; they butcher and roast her husband, whom, in the film's last shot, she eats. The point is clear: the bourgeois woman does whatever she must to save herself, including joining a band of cannibals and becoming its leader's lover. The betrayals dramatized by Godard since the start of his career here took on their most bitter and evil form. As for the cannibals (led by Jean-Pierre Kalfon), Godard seemed ready to pardon them on the grounds of their revolutionary principles. Mao had famously declared (a citation spoken by Wiazemsky in *La Chinoise*) that a revolution is not a dinner party. Godard begged to differ: why not a dinner party, at which the enemy would be served?

IN WEEKEND, GODARD offers a wide range of cultural references, including the apparition of the fictional revolutionary and sorcerer Joseph Balsamo, the title character of a novel by Alexandre Dumas; the dual role of Jean-Pierre Léaud as the revolutionary Saint-Just and as a desperate lover singing a pop love song in an isolated phone booth; a philosophical Tom Thumb and a philosophical Emily Brontë (dressed as Alice in Wonderland); the appearance of Godard's friend Paul Gégauff as an itinerant pianist whose truck brings a concert grand to a desolate barnyard where he performs a Mozart piano sonata, with spoken commentary (filmed in a colossal series of circular tracking shots); and the declamation of Lautréamont by the revolutionary cannibals (whose radio code names are Battleship Potemkin, Johnny Guitar, and Gösta Berling, the defrocked priest and title character of Mauritz Stiller's 1923 film). The references are ironic and mocking; in a world gone cartoonish, culture does the same.

Godard called his film "closer to a cry" than to a movie, and he was right. His characters are lost in a landscape of pain.[44] France is depicted as an automotive inferno in which people beat and shoot each other over right of way or a dented bumper; where a mile-long traffic jam is caused by compulsive rubbernecking at a corpse-strewn flaming wreck; where overturned and burned-out blood-doused cars and their victims are as common as trees in the landscape; where emotionally dissociated monsters remain as unaffected by the farmers in a barnyard as by the Mozart incongruously played there, and who set afire a poet (Emily Brontë) when she will not interrupt her musings to give them directions. *Weekend* is a prolonged howl of rage at the perceived vanities and cruelties of bourgeois life.

Imagining that the world as it was had to be destroyed, and knowing that his cinematic instincts and thought processes were a part of that world, Godard decided to leave both behind. Even before the last title cards reading "end of story" and "end of cinema," it was apparent that a chapter in Godard's films and life had come to an end. As it happened, a chapter in the life of France—of the world—was coming to an end as well.

Interviewed as the shoot of *Weekend* was getting under way, Godard expressed despair: "I know that my films don't do well. *Made in USA* was a total flop. *Two or Three Things* isn't doing well. If nobody goes to see my films, I'll have to stop. Or to find another way of making them. Or do something else."[45] He told Charles Bitsch, "If only I knew a way to make as much money doing something else, I'd do it."[46] Bitsch thought the remark was just "a provocation," and was shocked by what happened at the end of the shoot: Godard convened his crew, among them his regulars—Coutard, Schiffman, Guillemot[47]—and told them they should look for other work, because he was going to stop making films for a while.

HE DID, HOWEVER, make a television program.

Years of negotiations and contacts had finally paid off: as early as 1964, Godard had sought commissions from French television to do a documentary on American women, an adaptation of Racine's *Bérénice,* and even a multipart series on American mystery writers. Now, in mid-1967, he announced that his next project would be a television film, based on Jean-Jacques Rousseau's *Emile* (published in 1762), which concerns a young man who finds his education outside the academy, in life itself. The film, Godard said, would deal with the same theme: "the story of a young boy who refuses to go to high school because his class is always full, and who starts to learn outside, who watches people, goes to the movies, listens to the radio or watches television."[48]

The film, which Godard gave the Nietzschean title *Le Gai Savoir* (The

Joyful Wisdom), was conceived as a reprise of the central couple from *La Chinoise*, Jean-Pierre Léaud and Anne Wiazemsky. She, however, was interested in working on still photography—she had shot stills for *Weekend* and appeared in the film only as an extra—and, having previously agreed to shoot stills on the set of critic Michel Cournot's first feature film, *Les Gauloises bleues*, which coincided with Godard's shoot of *Le Gai Savoir*, she turned down the part in her husband's project.[49]

Léaud played Emile Rousseau, and the role of his friend, Patricia Lumumba, was played instead by Juliet Berto. The film concerns their meetings at a dark television studio, where they discuss the making and viewing of images and the political activities that they plan to undertake. The pair come up with a three-year program of study and action: in the first year, to make some basic images and sounds; in the second, to analyze those images and sounds; in the third year, to begin to recompose them into some more complex images and sounds. Patricia and Emile are filmed in a void, sitting on the floor, illuminated only in silhouette or in partial view: their images matter little and are expressive mainly in the absence of surroundings, the absence of context, the absence of visual reality, in favor of what they are saying, in favor of their voices.

Once again Godard makes use of his graphic skills, tearing still photographs from magazines and inscribing words and diagrams on them (as, for instance, a quote from Che Guevara, "At the risk of seeming absurd, I would like to say that the actions of a revolutionary are akin to the act of love") as part of the process of analysis, and then editing these visual inserts as collage-like material that illustrates the ideas under discussion. The film was shot in December 1967 and January 1968, at a television studio near Paris, but he did not finish it until later in the year, after May 1968, by which time it was an artifact of a bygone day.

And yet the film was, in its way, even more prophetic than *La Chinoise*. The most painful aspect of *Le Gai Savoir* is the comparison of the natural education that Rousseau's Emile receives and the one that Godard considers ideal for his own Emile. For Godard, experience was a dark room infused with images and sounds—an editing room—and the "joyful wisdom" was the leftist ideology that determined and overdetermined the interpretation of them. The reeducation that Léaud's Emile undergoes is surprisingly close to what Godard would inflict upon himself, soon thereafter—and his editing room would offer him a similar self-imposed imprisonment in doctrinal orientation.

Godard and Jean-Pierre Gorin
(New Yorker Films / Photofest)

sixteen

REVOLUTION (1968–1972)

"I stopped doing lots of things"

T
HE STORY OF JEAN-LUC GODARD AND 1968 IS BOTH SIM-
ple and painful. Godard had lost his moorings in the cinema
before adopting a fidelity to a nominally Maoist ideology. The
political events in France in May 1968 led him to associate with a new set of
young activists and to adopt views and methods that were influenced by
their activities. He made films in dogmatic service to his new politics, the
best of them in close collaboration with an inspired and inspiring companion: Jean-Pierre Gorin. Their time together was full, energized, and turbulent; it was a time of breakups and couplings, of practical militancy and
theoretical study, of constant work and shared purpose.

Yet the films that resulted, petrified by ideology, by doctrine, suggest hardly
a glimmer of the brilliance and the vital energy that went into them. Despite
Godard's seeming withdrawal from the cinema after *Weekend,* he in fact went
on making films, and at an even faster pace than before. Godard's obsessive ideological devotion generated a remarkable yield of political rhetoric, a repetitive
series of variations on the same theme, a language which filled sound track after
sound track of films that served as relatively indifferent and interchangeable
platforms from which to deliver it. Nonetheless, Godard's own experience in
those years, and in particular, the effort that went into the making of those
films, can be understood as a set of counterscripts, of alternate scenarios for
films that he did not make, that no one made—and this experience is of greater
artistic importance than the films that derived from it.

THE PARADOX OF Godard's withdrawal from the cinema in late 1967 was that
it coincided with the resuscitation of the New Wave, which came back stronger

than ever. Though the New Wave had come to seem like an obsolete concept, the filmmakers who launched it were only now coming into their own. François Truffaut, who had endured quiet years when he struggled with his own production company, with his Hitchcock book, and with his obsession to make *Fahrenheit 451*, again became prolific: in 1966 he signed a contract with United Artists to make *La Mariée était en noir* (*The Bride Wore Black*), with Jeanne Moreau, and signed again with them in mid-1967 for *Baisers volés* (*Stolen Kisses*), a new film in the Antoine Doinel series starring Jean-Pierre Léaud. He averaged a film a year for a long time to come. Claude Chabrol, who followed years of box office failures with some blatantly commercial projects, returned in 1967, with *Les Biches* (*The Does*), to the bilious bourgeois melodramas that he had set out to make and then directed a memorable series of noirish films, including *La Femme infidèle*, *Que la bête meure* (*This Man Must Die*), and *Le Boucher*. Jacques Rivette and Eric Rohmer, whose careers as filmmakers seemed to have died a quiet death after the unsuccessful releases of their first features, were now working again. In the wake of the critical and commercial success of *La Religieuse*, Rivette was soon able to make another film, the epic psychodrama *L'Amour fou*. Rohmer made a low-budget feature in 1966, *La Collectionneuse*, with funding from Beauregard and the cinephile heiress Sylvina de Boissonas. Its acclaim enabled him to make *My Night at Maud's* in 1967, followed soon thereafter by *Claire's Knee* and *Chloé in the Afternoon*. In short, four of the five core figures of the New Wave were definitively launched between 1966 and 1968, at exactly the time that Godard left his orbit and, without ceasing to make films, dropped out of the cinema.

Godard's relations with Truffaut had remained vigorous—he visited Truffaut in England on the first day of the shoot of *Fahrenheit 451* in January 1966 and received financial assistance from Truffaut's company on *Two or Three Things*, and Anne Wiazemsky joined Truffaut on the set of *The Bride Wore Black* as an apprentice photographer.[1] Godard continued to see Rivette regularly and, as Wiazemsky recalled, their meetings were a crucial part of her cinematic education: "Rivette is quite a scholar. They had great discussions about the cinema. Then Jean-Luc began to harden."[2] The controversy over *La Religieuse* brought the group together to link arms in a public battle, reviving the spirit of *politique* that they had honed while asserting the *politique des auteurs*, but in 1967 Godard began to take his politics in the literal sense and they got in the way of his cinematic relationships.

Yet when practical politics once again intruded on the heritage of the New Wave, Godard was in the front lines of its defenders.

THE CENSORSHIP OF such films as *La Religieuse* and *A Married Woman* suggested the distance between the government's version of France and real life. Then a decision made secretly by government representatives in late 1967 and put into effect the following February rallied the French cinema with a remarkable—and militant—unanimity. In a meeting held at 10:00 AM on Friday, February 9, 1968, the executive council of the Cinémathèque Française, which had been packed with government appointees, voted to remove Henri Langlois as the head of the Cinémathèque.[3] The ostensible reason for Langlois's ouster was his indifference to administrative norms, which, his detractors charged, resulted in deficits, unexplained expenses, and chaotic warehousing of films. The government's real motives seemed to lie elsewhere. The Cinémathèque had become a world-renowned institution, a cinematic Louvre, but one which, despite his government subsidy, Langlois ran with utter disregard for the interests of the politicians he nominally served and their narrowly defined notions of the glory of France. Moreover, the government, which also controlled television, seemed eager to lay hold of Langlois's collection in order to gain free and permanent access to a rich and ready source of programming.

Within hours of Langlois's removal from office, the French film community mobilized, uniting the major New Wave and "Old Wave" directors, leftists and rightists, as signatories to an indignant petition "to forbid the screening of their films at the Cinémathèque Française, both at the screening room of the rue d'Ulm and that of the palais de Chaillot," which had opened in 1963. The petitioners included Godard, Truffaut, Chabrol, and such elder luminaries as Jean Renoir and Abel Gance.[4] In official circles, François Mitterrand, an opposition member in the National Assembly, demanded that the government explain the "particularly shocking circumstances" of its "eviction" of Langlois from the Cinémathèque, "to which the cinema owes, for a quarter-century, the safeguarding of its creations, and to which our country owes the possession of an artistic patrimony of an inestimable value."[5]

Within days, foreign film directors, including Charlie Chaplin, Carl Theodor Dreyer, Orson Welles, Michelangelo Antonioni, Nicholas Ray, John Ford, Howard Hawks, Roberto Rossellini, Pier Paolo Pasolini, Fritz Lang, Raoul Walsh, Vincente Minnelli, Joseph Losey, Elia Kazan, and Samuel Fuller, signed on to forbid screenings of their films at a Cinémathèque without Langlois. On Monday, February 12, Godard, Chabrol, Rohmer, and Jean Rouch led a demonstration outside the rue d'Ulm screening room. On February 14, at the palais de Chaillot, 2,500 people protested the removal of Langlois, with Godard, Wiazemsky, and Truffaut in the front lines. Baton-wielding police officers clubbed Truffaut on the head and, in a scuffle, broke Godard's glasses. After forty-five minutes of confrontation, Godard himself gave the order to end the demonstration. "But now, there is only one imperative: as soon as the Cinémathèque opens and is no longer protected by the police, each spectator must find his own means of sabotaging the screenings."[6]

The new administrator of the Cinémathèque, Pierre Barbin, expected trouble and immediately closed both screening rooms. At a press conference led by Godard on February 16, it became clear exactly what kind of trouble Barbin could expect. Godard suggested that, if the new administrators dared to reopen the Cinémathèque, audience members should engage in "perpetual sabotage: discreetly slash the seats with a razor blade, throw inkpots at the screen." It was Jacques Doniol-Valcroze, however, who suggested a more bureaucratic form of sabotage—"We can paralyze the functioning of the Cinémathèque by forbidding the projection of films"[7]—all films, not just those by Langlois's supporters—and his suggestion hit the government where it was vulnerable.

The following week, Barbin, seeking to contain the potential damage of such threats, proposed to require the mandatory deposit with the Cinémathèque of a print of any film *shown* in France—meaning, of course, Hollywood films. (The new American films he would thereby acquire for the quasi-nationalized Cinémathèque would compensate for the classics being withdrawn from it.) In response, S. Frederick Gronich, of the Motion Picture Association of America, resisted this coercive measure and demanded directly of Minister of Culture André Malraux the return of all U.S. prints that had ever been submitted to the Cinémathèque by the major studios.[8] In the face of this potentially catastrophic depletion of the Cinémathèque's holdings, the government was forced to reinstate Langlois and announced that a meeting of the Cinémathèque council would be held on April 22.

In a joint communiqué, Truffaut and Henri-Georges Clouzot promised that if Langlois were not reinstated at that meeting, they would bring the fight to the Cannes festival in May. Finally, Langlois was restored to his position, but the Cinémathèque was stripped of its government funding—and Langlois lost his government salary. Nonetheless, the Cannes festival turned out to be a battleground and the fight, albeit of a different nature, was fought by many of the same cinematic activists, and again Godard was among the leading combatants.

MEANWHILE, LEACOCK-PENNEBAKER, the company run by the documentary filmmakers Richard Leacock and D. A. Pennebaker, acquired American distribution rights to La Chinoise. Godard's recent films had not been commercially successful in the United States, but Leacock-Pennebaker decided to release the film mainly to a university market, where Godard was a celebrity, and to bring Godard to meet with students on American and Canadian campuses. This was no benevolent educational mission: Godard was paid from $1,000 to $1,500 for an evening's talk, which equaled the highest lecture fee of anyone on the university circuit at the time. Louise Crest of Leacock-Pennebaker confirmed that Godard, who would be traveling, all expenses paid, with Anne Wiazemsky, was also guaranteed "50% of the take where admission is charged," and that Godard could make "more than $30,000 for his month's work."[9]

But before fulfilling his obligations in America and prior to the battles over the Cinémathèque, Godard went to Cuba, in response to an invitation by the government to participate in a cultural conference there in January, which, in the event, attracted hundreds of intellectuals and artists from around the world. Godard told the Cuban authorities that he would gladly come to Cuba, but after the conference ended, and at his own expense. He and Wiazemsky visited from February 3 to 11, 1968, and while in Havana, he told a journalist: "It was important for me to come here, because I am planning a trip to the United States to give talks at several universities and I couldn't do it before getting to know Cuba."[10]

In fact, Godard was planning to make a two-part film—"one part in America, one part in Cuba"[11]—and he started work on the Cuban part. Photographs from the trip show him filming a group of children lined up side by side and a man crouching in the bush.[12] No film resulted, however; as Wiazemsky later recalled: "We were both very enthusiastic about what we saw there. Jean-Luc was looking for what to do, but he didn't find it."[13]

FOR GODARD, AMERICA was the right place at the right time. In France, he could have found financing for any quasi-commercial project he chose, but his celebrity itself was of no value. In America, he was paid merely to show up.

In February, a retrospective of Godard's films at the Museum of Modern Art in New York was received, one journalist wrote, "like a Beatles concert."[14] The comparison was apt: the filmmaker was the cinematic idol of American university students and young intellectuals. Francis Ford Coppola, interviewed in 1968, declared, "There are kids at UCLA and USC who are incredible Godard addicts."[15] Brian De Palma, fresh from his first feature film (*Greetings*), declared, "If I could be the American Godard, that would be great."[16] George Lucas, a prizewinning student filmmaker at age twenty-three, said to a *Newsweek* correspondent about Godard, "When you find someone who's going the same direction as you, you don't feel so alone."[17] As one enthusiastic reporter declared, "For me and for an increasing number of serious young people, Jean-Luc Godard is as important as Sartre, Hesse, and Dostoyevski."[18]

Godard stayed at the Algonquin Hotel in New York for several days in late February (together with Wiazemsky, who would soon leave for Rome to appear in Pasolini's *Teorema*). After speaking at New York University, he went to the West Coast for four nights of panel discussions at the University of Southern California, including one with Agnès Varda and another with Samuel Fuller, King Vidor, Roger Corman, and Peter Bogdanovich. Godard spent four days at Berkeley, where he was hosted by Tom Luddy, a young political activist who worked for Pacific Film Archives. Godard went with Luddy and Mark Woodcock, Godard's translator, to the courthouse in Oakland to observe the murder trial of Black Panther leader Huey Newton, but, lacking a press pass, they could not get in.

The tour included screenings of *La Chinoise*, which played to twelve sold-out houses in Berkeley.[19] The student audiences who came to hear Godard speak were not only cinematic but political, and Godard gave them what they came for. Asked in Berkeley whether, after failing to get a visa to go to North Vietnam, he would try again, he answered, "No, because I think that the North Vietnamese will have won the war before I get it," and received a huge ovation.[20] Godard explained to a reporter from *Newsweek*, "Every film is the result of the society that produced it; that's why the American cinema is so bad now. It reflects an unhealthy society."[21] He divulged his thoughts on a "revolutionary cinema": "I think that the future for a revolutionary cinema is an amateur cinema. And television is the only true possibility we have of making a popular cinema, the true possibility for the people to express themselves on a screen."[22] Students invited him to film their activities that summer at the Democratic National Convention in Chicago, where, they said, they intended to bring about nothing less than "the destruction of the United States as we know it."[23] Godard demurred, recommending newsreel cameramen instead.

On Friday, March 8, Godard spoke at the University of Texas at Austin.[24] On Saturday night, at St. Thomas University in Houston, students dove for shards of the print of *La Chinoise* that were scattered by a broken projector.[25] On Sunday afternoon, Godard arrived in Kansas, where a local journalist captured the scene: "Almost immediately he was thrust into a cocktail party, which was followed by a dinner, a screening of *La Chinoise*, a public question-and-answer session and another party at the ultra avant-garde digs of a group of theater students."[26] The pace was wearying, and, on Thursday, March 14, Godard went to visit Wiazemsky in Rome for his days "off"—and did not return for the last twelve stops of his nineteen-city tour.

GODARD HAD TOLD Louise Crest of Leacock-Pennebaker that he needed the money from his lecture tour "to get started on a picture he wanted very much to make. Something planned for early spring."[27] It was a massive project; it would also be hugely expensive. He wanted to produce a film that was less the work of a director than of an impresario: a twenty-four-hour-long film, *Communications*, which would be made in many parts by many filmmakers. The new project's utopian tone made it hard for Godard to find funding; without financing, the film could not go into production and Godard was deprived of both his director's and producer's fees. Seed money for the project had been put up by the actors Yves Robert and Danièle Delorme, but it proved to be unrealizably vast, and Godard had no cash flowing to his production company, no immediate source of income.[28]

Meanwhile, Jean-Pierre Gorin had also gone to Cuba—in January, to report for *Le Monde* on the country's cultural conference—and what he saw there disheartened him. He recognized that the event "had nothing to do with the dreams and the hopes attached to Cuba," that the country "was obviously repressed, undemocratic," and, moreover, that "all the foreign intellectuals came and ate up a whole month of the people's food." This posed a problem for Gorin, who, as a left-wing journalist, "became aphasic"; as he later recalled, he "neither wanted to lie nor to hurt the cause."[29] Gorin left *Le Monde* and asked Godard for a job. Godard invited him to make an hour of *Communications*.

Holed up in his apartment, Gorin wrote a script, something he had never done before. He called his segment *Un film français* (A French Film);[30] but by the time he completed it, Godard had already spent the money earmarked for the project and was being sued by Robert and Delorme. According to Gorin, Godard "pretended he hadn't read it."[31] It was, in any case, an impossible project, far out of line with any budget that could plausibly be found, and nothing was done to realize it. Godard and Gorin fell out of touch for several months.

GODARD WENT BACK to New York on April 4, 1968, for a discussion with NYU film students which was filmed by Leacock and Pennebaker and later released as *Two American Audiences*. The session took place the day after the opening of *La Chinoise* in a mainstream theater in the residential Kips Bay neighborhood of Manhattan. Neither Leacock-Pennebaker nor the exhibitors had high hopes. As Pennebaker later recalled:

> Even the films of his that were famous, like *Breathless*, really didn't do that well here, so we really didn't have any expectations for the film; we didn't run any ads or anything. The day the thing opened, we get a call from the guy who ran the theater—it was the day we were shooting at NYU—he asks us what we were doing for publicity; there was a line around the block. We were astonished.

Pennebaker later came up with what seemed to him a plausible explanation: "Turns out, it was within a day or two of the Columbia riots, and people were coming down to get their politics straight."[32]

It was actually twenty days before the "riots" at Columbia University, which were sparked by the university's plan to build a gymnasium on land in the public Morningside Park in a predominantly black neighborhood. The building would contain two separate facilities, one for the students and one for the community. The uprising against the implication of official segregation led to the student takeover of several buildings. But at the time of the release of *La Chinoise*, that construction program, as well as recent changes in the draft law, had already sparked protests; the campus was in a state of political tension. As the writer and film critic Jonathan Rosenbaum later recalled, "I went to see *La Chinoise* with friends at Columbia, before the students took over the administration building, and I think that it actually had an effect."[33] In any case, the effect was mutual: if Godard had, to some small extent, inspired the Columbia takeover, the political ferment in American universities gave Godard cause for hope regarding student activism in France.

IN THE SPRING of 1968, another youth-oriented project came to Godard from an unlikely source. In Paris, he met a Greek film producer, Eleni Collard, who wanted him to make a film in London about abortion, but then, according to Richard Roud (then the director of the London and New York film festivals), Britain's newly liberalized abortion laws obviated the film.[34] However, soon thereafter, at a Paris nightclub, Godard met a young British talent agent, Mim Scala, who told him about the London rock scene and, upon returning home, sent Godard some records. Soon Collard called Scala on Godard's behalf to inquire about the possibility of making a film in London with either the Beatles or with the Rolling Stones.

Scala spoke with John Lennon and with the Rolling Stones's agent; both were interested in working with Godard. Scala advised him to choose the Stones, who, unlike the Beatles, had not yet appeared in a film.[35] Godard preferred the Beatles and met with Lennon in London, offering him at the same time the lead role in another project—a film about the assassination of Trotsky, from a script by Robert Benton and David Newman—but Lennon was not interested. While in London, Godard and Wiazemsky spoke more frequently with Paul McCartney, who was ready to work with Godard, but now Lennon refused to let the Beatles be filmed in the recording studio.[36]

The Stones, however, agreed to have Godard film them in a London studio, but the project's producers, Collard and her partners, Iain Quarrier and Michael Pearson, got nervous: consistent with his view of revolutionary cinema as amateur cinema, Godard planned to shoot with 8mm home-movie equipment. The producers talked Godard out of it; Godard, for his part, prepared to go to London in May to film the Rolling Stones.

But events would intervene. As *La Chinoise* had shown, the engine of radical political change in France was its student population, and in early 1968, protests persisted in Paris and throughout France. Universities were on edge, especially the campus at Nanterre.[37] In January 1968, student protesters attacked busloads of policemen and chased them away from the school grounds. In Paris, on the night of March 17–18, two American banks and the offices of TWA were attacked, as was American Express on March 19. A protester from Nanterre, Xavier Langlade, was arrested, an event that led to a new round of demonstrations at the university. On March 22, Daniel Cohn-Bendit, the most prominent of Nanterre's left-wing anarchists, led a takeover of the Nanterre administration building,[38] which he declared the founding act of the "Movement of March 22," named in tribute to Fidel Castro's Movement of July 26.

Student anarchists now took control of Nanterre's classrooms, disrupting lectures at will. The newsletter of the Movement of March 22 contained an authentic recipe for making Molotov cocktails. Several days later, the dean of Nanterre, Pierre Grappin, told Minister of Education Alain Peyrefitte, "We have gone far beyond the stage of protest. We have reached the stage of pre-revolution."[39] The dean added that many of the professors were siding with the student militants, whose goals were nothing less than utopian: they demanded a reorganization of academic life for the purpose of producing "revolutionaries" and a change in the political order to align with the plans of Ho Chi Minh and Che Guevara, whose names they chanted with enthusiasm.

In Nanterre and in Paris, Cohn-Bendit's allies physically assaulted right-wing student groups, which counterattacked. Protests and poster-pasting were occasions for fistfights, ambushes, and serious bloodshed. Parisian high school students organized their own coordinated revolutionary annex, the Comités d'action lycéens, or CAL (High School Students' Action Committees); as one of their leaders, Romain Goupil (who would later work closely with Godard as an assistant), recalled: "There was an unbelievable political ferment; those who didn't see anything coming were really very cut off from reality. We considered ourselves the heirs to 1789, the Commune, 1917: we carried the torch."[40]

The hard-line intellectual Maoists of the Ecole normale supérieure were dubious of the ideologically vague, temperamentally libertarian, joyfully nihilistic anarchists of Nanterre, but recognized their usefulness, their ability to attract large numbers of committed, militant, and fearless protesters on short notice, as well as their effective control over their university.

The Maoists saw the anarchists as an important link between theory and practice and hoped eventually to infuse the fervent freethinkers with a strong dose of theory. On April 28, Maoists and anarchists together destroyed an exhibit on the rue de Rennes that presented a favorable view of the South Vietnamese government. Cohn-Bendit answered a journalist's question regarding the violence: "We demand freedom of expression in the school but we deny it to the partisans of the Americans. Nobody would allow a meeting on the theme, 'Hitler was right to massacre six million Jews.' Why tolerate a pro-American meeting, organized by fascists on an entirely similar theme?"[41]

On May 2, reports of a right-wing counterattack on a two-day "anti-imperialist" teach-in at Nanterre brought out Robert Linhart and his Maoist shock troops, who had studied the tactics and techniques of the Red Guards. The police turned up and closed down the meetings. Word got around that Cohn-Bendit, together with other student leaders, was threatened with expulsion and would have to appear before a university tribunal at the Sorbonne the following week. In anticipation of massive protests, the dean of Nanterre suspended all classes until further notice and closed the university.

On May 3, students from Nanterre took the fight to the heart of Paris, and together with students from the city's universities occupied the Sorbonne. Shortly before 5:00 PM, busloads of police came to dislodge them. Cohn-Bendit later recalled,

> The entry of the police into the university sufficed to outrage thousands of students. Although all the militants were imprisoned, the student rebellion began spontaneously. The police were surprised by the aggression and mobility of the protesters. It took them several hours to restore order.
>
> During the weekend, several protesters were sentenced to prison. Solidarity with the imprisoned was a motive as strong as liberating the Sorbonne in the expansion of the movement.[42]

For several hours, students and police fought in the streets. Officers not only blocked streets with tear gas grenades but indiscriminately beat passersby who were in their path. Student organizations called for a general strike. On May 6, while Cohn-Bendit and others were attending their disciplinary hearings, an even more violent protest began. Five thousand students headed toward the Sorbonne, which was blocked by police. Ten thousand students filled the streets of nearby St.-Germain-des-Prés. When the police began making arrests en masse, the violence rapidly spread. As Goupil recounted:

The [university] students, our leaders, were there from ten in the morning with their two-by-fours. We high school students said, "No, we can't be there before 4:30, when school lets out." That's when things got wild. The students were loaded onto buses [by the police], and we threw rocks at the cops. To be fifteen years old and be pelting the cops and protected by the crowd, perfect bliss! The cops were dumbfounded. The student leaders too. They were in the buses and said to themselves, "Unbelievable, it's catching on."[43]

Police threw tear gas canisters into movie theaters and used water cannons to beat back crowds; students smashed and overturned cars and hurled paving stones. Police arrested people in large numbers, often beating them. One of the people in the streets that day was Godard, with a handheld camera, filming the events from atop a bench and from the street, accompanied by Wiazemsky.

The next day, May 7, thirty thousand students marched in Paris. That week, left-wing unions called for solidarity strikes. On the night of May 10, unable to dislodge the massive police presence from the Latin Quarter, students barricaded themselves in the streets with overturned cars, refrigerators, construction debris, and chopped-down trees, and enjoyed the support and assistance of many of the residents of the buildings they had blocked off. Police pressure broke the blockades; injuries and arrests numbered in the thousands, and central Paris, the next morning, resembled a desolate wartime landscape.

ALAIN JOUFFROY, THE writer whom Godard had met during the making of *Pierrot le fou* and frequented thereafter, had become increasingly engaged on the left. As the demonstrations gathered momentum, he brought together at his home Godard, the critic and filmmaker Michel Cournot, and the filmmakers Philippe Garrel, Jackie Raynal, and Patrick Deval. Jouffroy remembered:

It was May 4 or 5, right after the first demonstrations. "So, what are we going to do?" Someone said, "We must destroy the archives of the Centre du cinéma," and Philippe Garrel said, "No—in the Center for Research, there are cameras—we must go there, take the cameras, and give them to the students." So Godard, Garrel, Cournot, and I went there—and we went into [Center director] Pierre Schaeffer's office and we told him to give us the cameras. "What?" We said, "The students are outside." And Godard said, "Call the police, if you want." Schaeffer said, "That's blackmail!" and Godard said, "No, it's advice." He gave us the cameras, and Garrel and I took one. At the time, I had a convertible sports car, a Lancia that I'd bought cheaply because it had been in an accident. With me at the steering wheel, we filmed the demonstrations. We called it *Actua One*. We printed about twenty minutes. We did the editing together. Then Philippe Garrel said, "We need a commentary." I said, "The Marquis de Sade." I chose some political texts of de Sade. Then we showed it. Godard said, "It's a masterpiece, I would like to have done such a thing. Look after it." And he was right. A young man came, he said, "We need your film for a screening." He took off with it and he never came back.[44]

Godard recalled *Actua One* as "the best film made about May '68," and regretted that it had all been lost.[45]

ON MAY 13, the day of a march of almost a million people denouncing the government of de Gaulle, students again occupied the Sorbonne and turned it into an ongoing seminar and festival (the "Université autonome populaire," the People's Autonomous University), covering walls with a proliferation of one-liners that remain, to this day, catchwords exemplifying the exuberant sense of freedom and limitless possibility the young participants felt: from "Under the paving-stones, the beach," "Prohibiting is prohibited," and "Don't ever work!" to "Art is not coming back, and there's nothing Godard can do about it."[46] (Also, one that read, "Godard: the biggest jerk of the pro-Chinese Swiss.") On May 15, the Odéon theater was occupied and became a sort of public forum, where round-the-clock audiences were present to hear speakers from any walk of life address themes of their choice. On the same day, a Renault factory was taken over by its workers, and the next day, strikes were widespread throughout France.

Meanwhile, film technicians and professionals met at the Vaugirard film school in Paris and, on May 17, declared themselves the "Etats généraux du cinéma" (General Estates[47] of Cinema). Godard attended these meetings and described them in derisive terms: "For two or three days there were meetings with several thousand people from film who had never seen each other before and never saw each other again."[48] They debated and voted on many motions of no lasting value (such as the demand that admission to movie theaters be free of charge) and on one of immediate effect: to shut down the Cannes Film Festival, which had gotten under way on May 10. The festival had already taken a one-day hiatus on May 13, in sympathy with strikers. On May 17, Truffaut, who did not participate in the protests or the Etats généraux, arrived at Cannes for a planned public conference regarding the Cinémathèque and found at his hotel a bunch of messages from Jacques Rivette in Paris. Calling back, Truffaut learned that the Etats généraux had voted to stop the festival.[49]

Godard himself arrived at Cannes at about 11:00 AM on Saturday. As Truffaut later recalled, "Jean-Luc, who had just come from Paris, where he lived through the whole affair much more closely than I had, said, 'Let's go into the big hall to deliberate.' That was the Sorbonne-like part of the story. It was 11:30 AM. We occupied the hall."[50]

The festival, as Truffaut recognized, was in effect closing down anyway: Alain Resnais, Claude Lelouch, and Michel Cournot had withdrawn their films; Louis Malle, Roman Polanski, Monica Vitti, and Terence Young resigned from the jury. Nonetheless, some debating took place onstage, with most calling for the simple and complete termination of the festival. Truffaut thought it absurd to continue the event when the rest of France, and especially Paris, was for all intents and purposes shut down. Godard, however, argued that instead of showing festival films, the forum should be used to screen militant films and documentary footage of the events taking place; otherwise, he too called for shutting the festival down. Godard was a vocal and impassioned leader of the debate, shouting,

> There isn't a single film showing the problems of workers or students today. Not one, whether by Forman, by me, by Polanski, by François, not one! We're late! Our student comrades have set an example when they got their heads bashed in a week ago. There's no point to showing films here . . . It's a question of showing solidarity, at a week and a half's remove, of the cinema with the students' and workers' movements that are happening in France, and the only practical way to do that is to stop all screenings immediately.[51]

Truffaut stood beside Godard looking uneasy. He seemed to wish to be anywhere else as Godard cried with the voice of one possessed, in response to a festival defender, "I'm talking to you about solidarity with the students and the workers, and you're talking to me about tracking shots and close-ups!"

The festival administration decided that the 2:30 screening of Carlos Saura's *Peppermint Frappé* would take place as scheduled: the public, largely Cannes locals, began to fill the hall, but the protesting filmmakers—including Godard, Truffaut, and Saura himself—kept to the stage and held on to the curtain to prevent it from opening. The lights went down and the screening began, but the loudspeakers had been cut off; as Truffaut later recalled, the beginning of the film was projected onto the bodies of the protesters standing in front of the screen. Finally the film stopped, and the house lights came back on. Viewers stormed the stage to force it clear and to continue the projection, and a brawl erupted.[52] Freddy Buache of the Cinémathèque Suisse was at the festival; arriving at the hall for the screening, he found a demonstration in progress: "I climbed up on stage, and a guy said, 'Who are all these people?'

and he spread his arms wide and knocked Jean-Luc Godard's glasses to the floor. I picked them up for him. Godard said, 'Oh, it's you!' "[53]

The next day, the festival was canceled.

THAT SAME WEEKEND of May 11–12, the country was nearly paralyzed: gasoline was not getting through to the capital; stores were closed; food was running short. Strikes multiplied throughout the country. In Paris, people walked from place to place in the absence of métro service. Godard recalled that his memory of May 1968 in Paris was "a moment where one heard the sound of pedestrians in the street simply because there was no more gasoline."[54] (Godard had lent his own sports car to militants who wanted to rally support in the provinces.)[55]

Many people remember that time as a moment when people were constantly talking to each other, trying to get a sense of what was happening, and more important, of what was yet to happen. The film industry had stopped working, but the need to make images of the surprising, spectacular events was irrepressible, as Claude Mauriac (the novelist's son and Wiazemsky's uncle), wrote:

> Perhaps there has never been as much film shot in France as during these weeks of a total shutdown of the film industry. In 16mm or 35mm, in black and white or in color, with whatever film they could find, young cameramen undertook a collective anonymous work that the times have not yet managed to make use of and that will serve as a common fund for filmmakers of the future.[56]

Godard was among them. He joined Chris Marker in the production of a series of political films made on rolls of 16mm film, each of which cost a mere fifty francs (ten dollars). They were edited in-camera, done, at first, only with still images taken from photographs and from the press, and intercut with brief texts. They were called *Cinétracts* and were meant to serve as education and exhortation at political meetings. Those made by Godard are easily recognizable by the use of his own handwriting on and between images. He concludes his third *Cinétract,* number nine in the series overall, with a magazine clipping of an article called "Hollywood-on-the-Seine," featuring a picture of Truffaut: the prior image read, "Obvious truths belong . . ."—and on the image of Truffaut, Godard inscribed, "to bourgeois philosophy."

As it happened, while bourgeois philosophy yielded to the revolutionary spirit, bourgeois life proved more resilient and resistant, and the truths of the revolution seemed to be anything but obvious or enduring—even to the instigators. Early in the morning of May 11, with the Latin Quarter barricaded and under police siege, Robert Linhart, the leader of the Maoists of the Ecole normale supérieure, had a crisis. He had stayed outside the fray even as his school served as a sanctuary for protesters fleeing the police, because he considered the May militancy to be an unguided, tactically dubious, and ideologically unprincipled free-for-all. Now he had come to believe that the lack of ideological guidance from above—his own guidance, that is—would result in catastrophe. He was in a state of delusion. As Jean-Pierre Gorin explained, "Linhart panicked—he thought that what he had created would lead to massive cruelty, to a massive repression. At 4:00 AM, he banged on the door of Communist Party headquarters, crying and apologizing for what was about to take place."[57] Unable to find any officials to talk to, he took a train out of Paris and leaped from it, believing himself followed. He survived but was immediately hospitalized, given tranquilizers, and treated for mental illness.[58]

On May 23 and 24, there were two more nights of flaming barricades and police violence in the Latin Quarter. The second of those nights was the crisis point of the uprising, when the students set fire to the Paris stock market, and other students, blocking the streets, delayed the fire department's response. "There was talk of occupying a ministry," Gorin recalled, "which would have radicalized [the protests] because it would have required a response of maximal force."[59] But in the early hours of the morning, he said, the police began to take control of the area, and the students decided not to press the fight against the government but to return to the Latin Quarter.[60]

On May 29, Charles de Gaulle suddenly disappeared from Paris. He went in secret to a French military base in West Germany to consult with his trusted officer, General Jacques Massu. The next day, de Gaulle returned and made a speech. Yves Afonso, an actor from *Masculine Feminine* and *Made in USA,* was at the Etats généraux du cinéma that day: "We had transistor radios pressed up against our ears, we were all glued to our little radios. De Gaulle said, 'I'm not resigning, I'm not changing prime ministers, I'm dissolving the National Assembly'—there was silence, then we left."[61]

The speech was followed by a rally in defense of de Gaulle and the French government. Hundreds of thousands of marchers showed up in the Champs-Elysées. Though many of France's businesses remained on strike (including French television, which functioned only minimally), the turning point had been reached because the students had refrained from intensifying their violent conflict with the government, and because an overwhelming number of workers did not stay on strike and did not rebel against de Gaulle's presidency or the Fifth Republic. De Gaulle successfully negotiated with the large labor unions and, in exchange for raises and other legislated improvements in working conditions, gained their accord. As the journalist

Claude Roy noted in late May, when students were still parked behind burning barricades,

> The students had managed to restore to the workers the forgotten idea of the recourse to force. But if they provided the idea, they also aroused distrust. To the workers' leaders, they are anarchistic libertarians. To the mass of workers, they are the angry sons of the bourgeoisie. To militant workers, the "entrenched camp" of the Latin Quarter is a fight between the sons of the ruling class and their fathers, which is, in general, true.[62]

Indeed, one student occupier of the Sorbonne recalled, "On Sundays, nobody was there: everyone went home to lunch with their family; it was a bourgeois revolution. I proposed that since Lenin was born on a Tuesday, we take Tuesdays off."[63] By mid-June, the occupiers had faded away, abandoning their redoubt to the government authorities.

Over the next weeks in June, strikes continued, factories were occupied, protests ensued, and there was even another night of Latin Quarter barricades, but the numbers and the enthusiasm had diminished. The June elections that de Gaulle had called for turned out to be his trump card: choosing him over the perceived threat of anarchy, the voters overwhelmingly voted in his party's favor and gave him, in the two rounds of voting (June 23 and 30), a vast majority (358 out of 465 seats) in the legislature.

The failure of the predominantly anarchist-led revolt to destroy the government, indeed its contribution to the government's strengthened position, led to something of a revolution within the ranks of the revolution. The days of May had been wrought by the anarchists. The Maoists had stayed on the sidelines at first, deploring the ideological vagueness that motivated the festivities, or else they had merely gone along, followers more than leaders. As Gorin recalled, "The Maoists were involved on an individual basis in the streets, but not as an organization."[64] It was only at the moment that the revolution did not happen—when the workers by and large threw in their lot with reform of the existing order rather than with its overthrow, when strikes abated, when de Gaulle won an overwhelming majority in the National Assembly—that the Maoists, rejecting both the modest reforms that the government offered and the vast psychic, moral, and aesthetic change that had taken place in French society, continued down the road toward real political revolution.

The militants who created the days of May had the virtue of being one with their historical moment, and their leaders had exhibited spontaneous tactical genius; the Maoists' coming journey toward cataclysm and utopia was, by contrast, an act of faith. It was a faith that Godard shared, and to which he tied his fate.

ONE SIGN OF the hardening of positions and the deepening of differences was a painful scene witnessed by Wiazemsky:

> In June '68, Jean-Luc had a fight with Truffaut, in front of me. Jean-Luc wanted to stop the Avignon festival . . . Truffaut took up the position of Pasolini, who had said, "I can't be for the bourgeois students against the working-class National Guardsmen." Truffaut said, "I will never be on the side of the sons of the bourgeoisie," which is how he saw the students. This was in the offices of Les Films du Carrosse [Truffaut's company]. Jean-Luc really got angry: "I thought you were a brother, you are a traitor." That was their breakup.[65]

There had always been political differences at the heart of the Hitchcocko-Hawksian cabal. Rivette was never a rightist, and the younger members teased Rohmer for his support for de Gaulle, but at the time, the cinema was what counted, whereas now, for Godard, in the wake of what happened in May, politics took precedence over the cinema and personal relations.

Truffaut was not the only person with whom Godard broke up in June 1968. Antoine Bourseiller, whose theater Godard had financed and who had supplied the apartment for *La Chinoise*, recalled:

> In June 1968, he saw my wife in the rue de Miromesnil and told her, "We will never see each other again. I am saying adieu to you, and to Antoine. I don't want to see you anymore, because you are actually still in the capitalist system. I will not see you again." When I got back to Paris, I met him and said, "You're the one who made this decision, and I respect your decision. But I must tell you one thing: there will always be soup for you at my home; if ever you need something to eat, come to our house, you will always be welcome."[66]

At that time, Suzanne Schiffman, who had worked closely with Godard for eight years, ran into him on the Champs-Elysées: "We saw each other, he smiled, then he turned his back."[67] The filmmaker and critic Luc Moullet, who had known Godard since the mid-1950s, said, "In June 1968, we saw that Godard's views were different than from before May."[68]

Godard sought a cinematic outlet for these views. The kind of project he had in mind—and the extreme break that the days of May represented to him—were suggested by remarks he made at a press conference, which indicated what he owed, or thought he owed, to the militants and the effect they would have on his life and work. A questioner asked whether Godard's withdrawal from the film industry was part of an attempt to become "invisible"; Godard agreed, and explained that this impulse was the result of his inescapable sense of humility before the students:

> A lot of people, younger than I, were discovering a lot of things I had maybe not yet discovered. Things I was discovering at the same time but which I had been working on for twenty years . . . they discovered it very easily and, I mean, the good in their movements was not coming from us, it was coming from them. So, we were speaking of culture, art, and a lot of things, and they, they found things apart from us. So we have to learn from them instead of pretending to teach them. That's why we cannot speak of being . . . an artist or making a piece of art. This has to be completely destroyed.[69]

He also phrased the conflict in impersonal terms: "Culture is an alibi of imperialism, so we have to destroy culture."[70]

Godard had long foreseen that a new left would be principally an aesthetic phenomenon. May 1968 did not achieve a real political revolution, but it did bring about what Gorin recalled as "the collapse of the pillars of the intellectual temples."[71] This created the impression of radical change having taken place, with little bloodshed and very little practical political change. Alain Jouffroy recalled the days of frenzied activity: "Everywhere, unreality seemed to take fictive revenge on reality."[72]

The students stopped short of total revolution in part because they lacked a political program, and in part because the revolution of which they dreamed had, at a cultural level, already been achieved. The political program articulated most clearly by the students was one of intellectual and aesthetic politics. The revolution, according to Gorin, was effected by radicals who were "steeped in the classical tradition," yet who experienced that tradition "as oppression." The revolt was the work of "a generation of people who fantasized [the tradition] had a solidity that it didn't have. They felt free to shake the edifice, and to their surprise, it collapsed."[73]

In practical terms, countercultures high and low came to the fore: whether through the deconstructionist philosophy of Jacques Derrida, the anti-psychology of Gilles Deleuze and Félix Guattari, or Nietzschean analyses of power by Michel Foucault, or through rock music, urban communes, and psychotropic drugs, the young people of France were clearing the ground of traditional thought and morality. As old and artificial distinctions were swept away by new modes of cultural critique, a more inclusive, more tolerant, and freer society would result—in the long run. However, in the short term, there was no shortage of utopian dreaming that found its way into practice, often with disturbing results, whether in the emotional burnout of communal or libertine living, mental damage due to drug use, or the delusions of violent political confrontation.

Godard knew that he was now living in a changed world. One of the changes that had taken place had to do with his own reduced status among the would-be revolutionaries. With his high-culture and Hollywood references, Godard had long been a target of the Situationists, the anticultural anarchists whose provocations had inspired student revolt (notably at the University of Strasbourg). Now that the student rebellion had broadly rejected official culture, Godard, despite his engagement alongside the students, came in for insult (as seen on the slogans in the Sorbonne and on the walls of Paris, many of Situationist inspiration.) Later recalling the insults, he also cited their effect on him: "I felt myself to be opposed; it did me good. I felt . . . concerning myself, I was also a little afraid; I said to myself, 'Look, maybe it's the end.' "[74] Godard was not the only recognized intellectual hero to cast his lot with the revolutionary students. Intellectual France was largely in thrall to its youthful rebels, whose expression of total discontent seemed to embody its own efforts at radical social critique. Sartre joined Maurice Blanchot, Pierre Klossowski, Jacques Lacan, and others in signing a joint manifesto in support of the students, published on May 9, in the heat of the action.[75] He spoke in praise of the movement in *Le Nouvel Observateur* and then, still in May, published a dialogue there with Cohn-Bendit.

In the wake of the rebellion, Godard sought to make films differently, and in the summer of 1968, he told interviewers from a German film cooperative what this would mean: "One must give everything up. One must change one's life . . . One must completely change oneself, and that is very difficult."[76] The specific change that Godard had in mind: "For someone who is known to quickly become unknown, which is much better anyway."[77] Godard told Wiazemsky that he wanted them to leave Paris and move to the provinces. "I said that I absolutely didn't want to leave Paris," she recalled. "I think he sensed that he had gotten to the end of a certain cinema and that he had to go away in order to find another one."[78] They stayed in Paris, but Godard and his cinema changed nonetheless.

GODARD INDEED RESUMED WORK. Earlier in 1968, he had abandoned *Le Gai Savoir*, the collage-like film based on Rousseau's *Emile*, but now, in the summer, he finished editing it (adding several images of the combat in the streets). French television, which had commissioned it, refused to broadcast the film, so Godard sought authorization for its release as a feature film. On January 2, 1969, Wiazemsky (whom Godard had installed, for financial reasons, as the chief executive of Anouchka Films, the production company he had started in 1964) wrote to the CNC—under the name "Anne Godard"—to request a visa to permit the film's distribution. The commission took exception to several insults aimed at de Gaulle and Pompidou and another aimed at French television itself, and demanded that various shots—including ones showing how to make a Molotov cocktail—be cut. The film was authorized for export for noncommercial, that is, festival, screenings and, in May 1969, by which time Godard had made the required cuts, it received a "green light without restriction" for theatrical release.[79] Nonetheless, though it was shown at the Berlin Film Festival in July of that year and the New York Film Festival in September, and was released theatrically in New York in May 1970, it was not released theatrically in France until 1977. (In 1969, in the absence of the film's availability in France, Godard arranged for a small press to publish a transcript of the film's sound track as a book).[80]

Le Gai Savoir, a film of intricate analysis and sophisticated montage, had been made prior to the May protests, and was completely different from what Godard sought to do in their wake. His film of the Rolling Stones—a mix of documentary footage and staged agitprop—demonstrated what he had in mind. He told the *Sunday Times* of London, "I'm trying to make it as simple as possible, almost like an amateur film." He repudiated editing, declaring, "The length of the takes are decided by Kodak—I've four or five choices of lengths of film available from them and I'm quite happy with that."[81] He arrived in London on May 30[82] and filmed the Rolling Stones at the Olympic Studio in London on the first four nights of June 1968. He was reluctant to do the film, Wiazemsky recalled, because he did not want to leave Paris just at that time, but the English producers insisted that he fulfill his contract.[83] According to Mick Jagger, it was "very fortuitous" that the song on which the group was working should be "Sympathy for the Devil," a song which revealed the secrets of its composition on-camera.[84]

Godard had the crew lay down tracking rails that ran in a figure-eight throughout the studio. The 35mm movie camera was outfitted with a special film magazine that could take exceptionally long loads of film. In ten-minute takes, Godard followed the song's metamorphosis from a straight-ahead rocker to a pantheistic samba. Drummer Charlie Watts put down his drumsticks in favor of Algerian hand drums, and the four backup singers (including Marianne Faithfull) congregated around a microphone for gospel exhortations. The last night of the shoot ended prematurely as the studio caught fire when a gel filter on an overhead light ignited. Godard returned to Paris with the intention of adding to the film later; he disclosed to a London journalist his plan to intercut the footage of the Rolling Stones with a drama, described as "a tragic triangle: a French girl in London is picked up by a Right-wing Texan but then falls for a Left-wing Negro militant."[85] Godard explained that the black man leaves the white woman (who would be played by Wiazemsky) for the

Black Power movement, and she commits suicide. But in the end he filmed something else altogether to intercut with the Rolling Stones footage.

First, however, in Paris, in July and August, Godard made *Un Film comme les autres* (*A Film Like the Others*), a rapid-response reflection on the May events, which consists largely of a discussion on a lawn among three students from Nanterre and two workers at the Renault factory in Flins. Godard had wanted Wiazemsky to appear in it as a radical student, but she had refused, because, as she recalled, "I did not share the ideology."[86]

However, *A Film Like the Others* also revealed Godard's own divergence from the student revolutionaries. The discussions that comprised the film, as its cameraman, William Lubtchansky, later recalled, were shot with direct sound, in a single day. The participants are seen from the neck down, their heads outside the frame. Color images—from one fixed angle—are intercut with hallucinatory images, in black and white, shot by the Etats généraux of events from the streets during May: cars burning, barricades, students armed with metal gratings, tear gas attacks, blocked-off factories. These images are accompanied by a sound track of practical discussions about revolutionary tactics and how to unite students and workers. Over the live discussion, Godard recites political texts derived from Mao and French militants, literary citations, and his own reflections.

The differences between the students and Godard emerge when he attempts to instruct them in revolutionary methods: "If cars interest you," he tells them, "you can go to work at Renault; if airplanes interest you, you can go to work" at an airplane factory. But the students do not agree; they do not see how anything might interest them within a big company; it was one thing to take a job in a factory to endure the workers' misery and perhaps imbue them with Marxist theory, another to take an interest in the work being done there. *A Film Like the Others* is in two parts, each a fifty-four-minute reel of 16mm film in which the images are identical and only the narration is different. When it was shown on December 29, 1969, in a special screening at Lincoln Center, Godard requested that the order in which the reels were shown be determined by a coin toss. Many of the approximately 1,000 viewers loudly complained that the sound track, which featured a dubbed English commentary over the French dialogue, was incomprehensible, and they not only demanded their money back but, as D. A. Pennebaker, whose company distributed the film, recalled, "they began to tear up the seats."[87] The few viewers who remained in the hall frequently booed (though, notably, they kept quiet during the clips of documentary footage from May).[88]

RETURNING TO LONDON in August 1968, Godard shot another series of ten-minute takes for his film with the Rolling Stones, which he now called

One Plus One; the title was derived from a May 1968 graffito and suggested the simple alternation of the film's two disparate elements: the Rolling Stones plus the new footage, a series of political masques. One sequence in a junk-yard featured the English militant Frankie Dymon Jr. as the leader of a group of black revolutionaries who declaimed texts by Eldridge Cleaver and LeRoi Jones as well as the Black Panther manifesto, while receiving captive white women wearing white shrouds.[89] A scene in a pornography-filled bookstore featured long recitations from *Mein Kampf.*

But the movie's most important footage are the scenes featuring Wiazemsky, and the personal significance of those sequences is as telling as her rejection of the doctrinaire premise of *A Film Like the Others.* Godard had changed her role in *One Plus One:* no longer a "French girl in London," she now played Eve Democracy, who wandered through fields and forests in a delicate gown, taking elaborate political questions (in English) from a tele-vision journalist while being filmed by a documentary news crew. Being the personal representative of democracy, she could only answer "Yes" or "No" to the ever more complex questions—many of which Godard took from an interview with Norman Mailer in the January 1968 issue of *Playboy.*[90] (Wiazemsky spoke no English, so Godard cued her when to say "Yes" by wav-ing his hat at her from offscreen.)[91] In bringing Wiazemsky to London and casting her as the absurd and naive Eve Democracy, he mocked not only democracy but Wiazemsky's nonrevolutionary commitment to it.

These hectoring, bewildering sequences were crowned by a closing shot, which, almost against Godard's will, turned out to be majestic. Eve Democ-racy is led to a camera crane while acting a scene in a movie about guerrilla warfare that is being filmed at a beach. She is positioned on the crane, where her body is splayed out on the seat, alongside a large studio camera. The crane, with the actress's limbs dangling from it, glides aloft with two flags waving from it: the black flag of anarchism and the red flag of communism. Wiazemsky's character meets an untimely end. In this bloody ending, Godard suggested not only that democracy was doomed in an age of armed conflict, but that Wiazemsky's political views, which he characterized visually as a sort of oblivious docility, would prove calamitous. Seek as he might an un-remittingly political subject, a neutral camera style, and a thought-free method of editing that was determined by Kodak, Godard was nonetheless unable to avoid filming an allegory of his days and his life: Wiazemsky's non-revolutionary sympathies, he charged, would be her downfall.

Godard introduced *One Plus One* at the London Film Festival. The pre-miere, which was scheduled for November 29, proved complicated. Michael Pearson and Iain Quarrier, the producers, were displeased that Godard had included in the final cut neither the finished version of "Sympathy for the

Devil" nor the song in its entirety. In his absence, they reedited the ending to include the whole song over the closing shot of the Stones in the studio and the sequence of the body of Eve Democracy on the camera crane (which they held in a freeze-frame to let the song play out). They called Godard in Paris to tell him so,[92] and he was very unhappy, telling a journalist that the change "would alter the whole spirit of the thing." The producers responded, "We have to consider ten million teeny boppers in the United States alone. The film cost us £250,000." A long day of negotiations mediated by the London festival director, Richard Roud, yielded a compromise: the producer's cut would be shown, followed by Godard's original ending, and then Godard and Quarrier would debate the two versions' merits onstage. However, before his film was screened, Godard urged the audience to refuse to watch it, demand their money back with an additional ten shillings, and send the money to "black power" leaders; then he punched Quarrier in the face and stomach and was physically ejected from the hall.[93]

One Plus One—Godard's version—finally opened on May 7, 1969, at a single Left Bank movie house. It was the first film by Godard to come out in Paris since *Weekend*, more than a year earlier. The film was not seen in the United States until screenings at Hunter College in March 1970[94] after which it was released theatrically, with Godard's and Quarrier's versions shown on alternating days.[95]

GODARD SEEMED TO be flailing in various directions. He had gotten to know the artist Gérard Fromanger, whose paintings of French tricolor flags with the red dripping down them like blood had been one of the defining graphic images of the open street battles. Fromanger came to Godard's apartment, where Godard sought to extract from him the secret to these pictures. Fromanger agreed to teach him how to make such paintings, while Godard recorded on film the dripping of paint on the flag in a short called *Rouge* (Red). In October, the two collaborated on a stunt. Fromanger brought trucks to deliver to a sidewalk plaza outside a church in the fourteenth arrondissement a series of enormous red and blue plastic half-spheres; Godard filmed the responses of passersby, who, as Alain Jouffroy recalled, put their heads inside the half-spheres to use their reflective inner surfaces as mirrors.[96] Godard and Fromanger were arrested, and Godard—who claimed that he represented a government ministry—was additionally charged with impersonating a public official. The police used Godard's sound equipment to listen to the filmmaker's remarks upon arrest,[97] but nothing came of the charges.

As the revolution lost steam in France, Godard returned to the United States, where it seemed to be heating up. A new project brought him back together with the American documentary filmmakers Leacock and Pennebaker.

Executives at the Public Broadcasting Laboratory (New York's WNET, channel 13, and the precursor to PBS), were eager to produce a film by Godard, and Leacock and Pennebaker were able to package the project. On October 15, 1968, the Public Broadcasting Laboratory issued a press release for Godard's film, *One American Movie,* which he would begin to shoot on October 30, "using actors and actual figures in fictional and factual situations. Tentative locations include New York, Chicago and San Francisco."

Leacock and Pennebaker would be the cameramen on the project, with their documentary orientation determining its course. Godard's idea was to film people expressing views that interested him and then to refilm those discussions as fictionalized recitations and performances by actors.

In New York, Godard had Rip Torn, dressed first in a Civil War–era uniform, then a contemporary army uniform, speak with students in an elementary school classroom in Ocean Hill–Brownsville, a predominantly African-American neighborhood in Brooklyn. Leacock also had the idea to film Rip Torn in the cramped and rickety construction elevator of an unfinished skyscraper reciting a text along with the actor's own prerecorded performance of it that blared from a portable cassette player. (Godard, who was afraid of heights, spent the entire ride clinging to Leacock's waist.) The crew also went to the headquarters of Chase Manhattan Bank to interview Carol Bellamy, a young lawyer who worked there. In Newark, Godard arranged for LeRoi Jones (later Imamu Amiri Baraka) to recite a text in the street. But all of this work was, for Godard, merely a preliminary for the main event: he was impatient to get to the West Coast. "We've got to get to California before it's over," Pennebaker later recalled Godard saying. "Before what's over?" Pennebaker asked. Godard responded, "The revolution: the students are going to rise up and take over."[98]

Once in Berkeley, Godard had Leacock and Pennebaker film Tom Hayden, the national leader of the Students for a Democratic Society. Then he interviewed Black Panther Eldridge Cleaver. Godard later described the scene: "He received us in his house in Oakland. We were searched more than at the airports here. They all had berets, submachine guns . . . and then, he agreed to be interviewed because Tom [Hayden] . . . gave him five hundred dollars and he desperately needed money because two days later he fled to Algiers . . . or I don't know where."[99]

The crew returned to New York, where, on November 19, Godard filmed the Jefferson Airplane. He took over from the specialists and operated the camera from the window of Leacock-Pennebaker's office on West Forty-fifth Street, shooting the band on the roof of the Schuyler Hotel across the street. (Pennebaker recalled him to be an amateurish cameraman who could not avoid the beginner's pitfall of frequent zooming in and out.)[100] The performance took place without a permit, at standard rock volume: as singer Grace Slick later wrote, "We did it, deciding that the cost of getting out of jail would be less than hiring a publicist . . ."[101] Eventually, as the band expected, the police came to the hotel roof to stop the music, all to the loud protests of the audience that had spontaneously formed in the street.[102]

GODARD, WHO HAD arrived in California a little early for the revolution, did not finish *One American Movie*. He abandoned the United States for several days in November, traveling to Montreal with Wiazemsky and the French producer Claude Nedjar (whom they had met by chance in New York) for the Festival of Political Cinema. Wiazemsky later recalled that both she and Godard were "seduced" by the Canadian landscape and wanted to return to Quebec. When they got back to Paris, she suggested that Godard make a film in Canada.[103] Nedjar, who had a connection with media executives in Rouyn-Noranda in rural Quebec, proposed an ambitious scheme: that Godard put together a ten-part television series there in collaboration with a group of leftist filmmakers whom the director had met at the Montreal festival.

The ten-part project was to begin with documentary material: Godard intended to film discussions with local workers and students and to develop a fiction film from that research. Working with a group of politically active video-makers from the area, Godard recorded a large amount of video footage, but, according to Anne Wiazemsky, he was unclear about what he wanted to do. "There was a blizzard," she recalled. "He said to me, 'It would be nice if you would climb on the roof, like that, in your underwear.' I was wearing woolen underwear. I said, 'No, it's too cold.'"[105] Godard quickly lost interest in the project and told her simply, "We're going home."[106] Which they did, without informing the local group or the television station of their departure.[107]

Thus Godard and Wiazemsky soon returned to Rouyn-Noranda, where, on December 16, Godard appeared on television and declared that he wanted to open the medium up to people who, he said, were usually "prevented" from appearing there, meaning, workers, students, and political militants, who might be unaware of being prevented "because in the United States, television belongs to the rich, and elsewhere it belongs to the governments." Godard took on not only the executives of the airwaves but also the conventions of the medium: he pointed to the cameraman who was filming him head-on and said, "There is a man who is filming me but who is not listening to what I am saying." Godard rose from his seat beside the host, crossed the stage, approached the cameraman, and asked him, "Why don't you ask me questions too?"[104]

It was a fittingly inconclusive end to a year of frenzied, unfocused activity, which was only to escalate.

ISABELLE PONS, WHO had been Godard's assistant since the shoot of *Two or Three Things* and who was now keeping his books, realized, at the end of 1968, that Godard was in desperate financial straits. She suspected that the aborted project in Canada might well have been a matter not of politics or art but of money.[108] In late 1968, Godard wrote to Truffaut asking for financial help. He claimed that seven hundred thousand francs (about $120,000) were due him from *Two or Three Things,* which Truffaut had coproduced. He said that the money would "increase the rate of production of anti-boss films" and concluded, "I have nothing to add, either about you, or about myself, and the others, we no longer agree about anything."[109] Truffaut considered the request outrageous but sent funds anyway. Godard eventually wrote to thank him: the money, he said, "greatly helped us pay for our editing room-office." The plural, *us,* is no accident. The collective life Godard had once shared with Truffaut and "the others," in the early days of cinematic fanaticism, was undergoing a sort of resurrection, in the name of another totalizing ideal.

In September 1968, Godard had invited the twenty-year-old Jean-Henri Roger, from the militant newspaper *Action,* to work with him. As Roger recalled, Godard intended "to break with his practice as a filmmaker—never to do things as he had done them before—and to join politics and aesthetics."[110] Wiazemsky had less faith in Roger's contribution. Of his "arrival" she said: "Jean-Luc was in awe of him, whereas in my opinion his discourse was prefabricated. He crashed at our house; he took us for his mother and father."[111]

Godard and Roger had coffee together almost every morning at the café La Favorite on the boulevard St.-Michel, close to Godard and Wiazemsky's apartment on the rue St.-Jacques. Up to that point, Wiazemsky recalled, Godard, despite his increasing distance from conventional cinematic practice, frequently went with her to the movies, listened to music, and read books, but then "politics took the place of literature, of music, thanks to Jean-Henri Roger."[112] When, in early 1969, Godard started work on another film—one even more aridly doctrinaire than the fictional scenes of *One Plus One* or the narration of *A Film Like the Others*—Roger joined Godard on location.

A BRITISH PRODUCTION COMPANY, Kestrel Productions, had commissioned Godard to make a television film about Great Britain. Godard decided that rather than make a film of "British Images," it should be called *British Sounds.* The innocuous title could not have been more apt. The opening ten-minute sequence is a sterile series of long tracking shots of an assembly line in a British car factory together with the factory noise on the sound track.

(Speaking to interviewers, Godard warded off criticism with an analogy: "The workers have to listen to that sound all day, every day, for weeks, months, and years, but bourgeois audiences can't stand to listen to it for more than a few seconds.")[113] The screech of metal on metal is indeed terrible, as is the cadence of heavy labor; but more terrible still, indeed unbearable, are the hectoring pronouncements that accompany it, a monotonous description of surplus value and class conflict, drawn from the *Communist Manifesto* with particulars altered to refer to the automotive industry.

The sounds indeed took precedence over the images. A sequence of a nude woman descending and reascending a staircase (the allusion to Duchamp's painting is both obvious and undeveloped) followed by a medium close-up, not titillating but simply leering, of the woman's pubic zone, is accompanied by a feminist tract; a workers' meeting in a cramped office is paired with a recitation of more political dogma; a bad imitation of a television news reporter spews leaden phrases that Godard claimed were taken from speeches by such politicians as Harold Wilson, Edward Heath, Georges Pompidou, and Richard Nixon;[114] students in a lounge rewrite the Beatles' "Hello, Goodbye" to read, "You say U.S. and I say Mao"; the film ends with a bloodstained hand struggling to emerge from a covering of earth. Along with the doctrinal badgering is a series of political lessons, recitations of dates and events, spoken by a father and repeated by a child. Godard was the self-appointed child learning his basics; he was the elder taking dictation from his juniors.

The film has the stiff and self-punishing feel of a cinematic hair shirt. And yet the activity that went into its making—from the producer's wife, Mo Teitelbaum, finding Godard the feminist text by Sheila Rowbotham, to Godard attempting to persuade the writer to perform the nude scenes herself ("Don't you think I am able to make a cunt boring?" he told her),[115] to his sarcastic doctrinal discussions with the producers and their associates, to his rejection of stage blood in favor of cutting his own arm to provide the prop for the final sequence—suggests the intensity of Godard's devotion to the absurd and failed project. The making of *British Sounds* was far from dull, but the actual images (except for the opening and closing ones, the fist through the Union Jack and the bloodied hand, which are potent living posters) range from neutral to vacant.

The flaws of *British Sounds* could have been predicted, not only from the attenuated work Godard had done after May but also from remarks he made in January 1969.

A better film would result from taking a film by de Funès and redoing the dialogue, as the Situationists redo the dialogue balloons of comic strips. Whenever I go to the Third World, that's what I tell them: don't refuse films you don't like, redo them; an image is so simple; a film is nothing at all; it is what you make of it.[116]

It was the sound, not the image, that mattered, because the sound carried the lecture, the doctrine, or rather, the indoctrination. Godard's own doctrine, as concerned himself and his world, had become rather chilling. In London, he told the journalist Jonathan Cott:

> You have to burn the opera. Not British Motor Corporation or General Motors, because that's not so clear. You do have to build some cars. But Covent Garden, Lincoln Center, the San Francisco Opera House, yes, we can burn them . . . We've tried other ways, but it's no use. If we don't burn them we'll always be absorbed by going into them.[117]

He then corrected himself, suggesting, "No, not burn them, just forget about them a bit. As Mao said, if we burn books, we would not know how to criticize them." But when the interviewer praised Bresson's film *Au Hasard Balthazar* as an "extraordinary emotional spiritual height," Godard responded, "Then it has to be destroyed. Catholic! It's disgusting." He defined the cinema as being not a gun but "a light which helps you check your gun."[118]

As for the film *British Sounds,* it was rejected by British television, as *Le Gai Savoir* had been rejected by French television.

IN THE MEANTIME, Claude Nedjar's production company was able to secure agreement from a documentary film unit in Czechoslovakia to finance a shoot by Godard. In August 1968, Czechoslovakia had endured the Soviet invasion which crushed the relatively liberal government of Alexander Dubček and reimposed Soviet orthodoxy. Godard, Jean-Henri Roger, and the cameraman Paul Burron went to Prague in April 1969. They filmed trucks and trains, the inside of factories and the outside of government buildings; they tried to speak with people, but as Roger later recalled, nobody was willing to speak with them and they were quickly expelled from the country.

Once again, the voice-over text was revolutionary boilerplate, though this time it had a particular edge of acerbity. Although Czechoslovakia was suffering through a murderous and repressive Soviet occupation, Godard was obsessed with what he considered the "revisionism" corrupting communism there; he took pictures there of logos for Western products (there were not many), and commented in voice-over, "Yes, we're in the Occident: in the fields, there are billboards for the big American trusts. The young workers like the Beatles and the government lets them wear their hair long: we must be in Yugoslavia. No, we're in Czechoslovakia."

Speaking of the film the following year to Andrew Sarris of the *Village Voice*, Godard let loose a sordid remark that revealed how dogmatic blinkers had left him oblivious of the reality of Czech life (and also betrayed his lack of personal experience of an actual occupying army): "Anyway, Czechoslovakia had been invaded by American tanks from United Artists long before the Russians came in."[119]

Godard's increasing ideological rigidity isolated him even from political comrades. Soon after the Prague adventure, Daniel Cohn-Bendit, who had moved to Germany after having been expelled from France, offered Godard an idea for a film: he proposed that they go to Italy and make a leftist spaghetti western. Cohn-Bendit, it turned out, had an ulterior motive: wanting to see his old colleagues from the March 22 group, he knew that the project would deliver him and his friends to Italy in style.[120] Godard and Wiazemsky went to Frankfurt to meet with Cohn-Bendit and to discuss the film. "It was all very vague," Wiazemsky recalled, adding that Cohn-Bendit "was too joyful for Jean-Luc."[121]

Nonetheless, Godard worked out a story about the kidnapping of the head of Alcoa Aluminum by striking workers in the American West. He found funding from the film production arm of the Rizzoli publishing house, Cineriz, and recruited the mainstream actor (and leftist activist) Gian Maria Volonte to play the lead role (Wiazemsky would also appear in the film). Godard expected to work with Cohn-Bendit to turn the nominal leftist spaghetti western into doctrinaire hardtack; however, when he met the exuberant militant and other members of the March 22 group on location near Rome, he rapidly discovered that Cohn-Bendit, though a political revolutionary, really meant to convey his message by means of a traditional movie. As Cohn-Bendit admitted, "We were a group who had nothing to say about the cinema. We wanted to have fun. It was a little unfair to Godard. He really expected us to have a discussion, an exchange; we were incapable of it."[122] Godard, who wanted to make a film that bore no resemblance to the commercial cinema, became desperate.

At the time, his political interlocutor, Gorin, was in the hospital, recuperating from a motorcycle accident. Godard contacted him. "I've got a ticket for you. Either you come or I stop the film," he said.[123] Gorin lifted himself from his sickbed and went to Rome. The ongoing conversations between the two had to that point only begun to inform Godard's work; now Gorin was going to become a co-filmmaker with Godard, exactly as he had long hoped.

When Gorin arrived in Rome, he found a shambles. Godard and Wiazemsky were not getting along. Production money that Godard was channeling to local revolutionaries had been used to open a transvestite bar. During the production, Godard and Gorin called a meeting with the crew and the political activists to debate the underlying problem of the project. This general assembly was filmed and footage of it is included in the finished product. Gorin walks about with his cane, Cohn-Bendit lounges serenely in the grass, smiling and waving impishly at the camera, and Godard, in a sharp and hectoring tone of voice, denounces the way the shoot was going: "There is, in the film, something that dates from Stalin and which we are in up to our necks, the—what's it called—Socialist Realism."

According to Wiazemsky, Gorin's arrival was taken by others working on the film as something of "a putsch"; soon after, "there were no more assemblies, there were just two people who gave orders." Cohn-Bendit left, saying, as Wiazemsky recalled, "I'm ready to work as two, as three I'm off."[124]

Gorin had been waiting for just this chance, and he had come with a clear idea of what to do with *Wind from the East,* as the film had come to be called: to pit the sound track against the image, revolutionary verbiage against the visual beauty of nature. Gorin considered the film a work of citation: while the outdoor images referred to D. W. Griffith's films, the fulsomely doctrinaire dialogue on the sound track replicated the rhetoric heard throughout Paris at the time. *Wind from the East* may well have been a film of citation for Gorin and Godard; but, unlike the intertextual webs in Godard's earlier films—which were cued both by journalistic remarks and by specific, pointed, and aesthetically highlighted allusions—the references here were general and vague. With no guidance to tie the images and texts to their sources, the film is an unmediated experience; its images lack the dramatic logic and emotional power of Griffith's work and the sound track simply sounds numbingly, un-ironically dogmatic.

Godard and Gorin returned to Paris and edited *Wind from the East.* As Gorin recalled, "We did nothing but work. We were 24/7 in the editing room. That's what we thought about."[125] Through the discussions in the editing room, Gorin reoriented the film—and, in the process, reoriented Godard. First, instead of assembling the film as a narrative, or for that matter, as a fractured narrative, Gorin structured it on the basis of political doctrine. He divided the film into a series of practical sections labeled "The Strike," "The Delegate," "The Mobilizing Minority," "The General Assembly," "Repression," "The Active Strike," and "The Police State," followed by analytical sections called "Theory," "Self-Management," "Armed Struggle," and "Civil Violence." Godard praised Gorin's conceptual contribution to *Wind from the East* as "work that consists in overturning the traditional notion of editing, of no longer making a simple assemblage or collage of shots but an *organization* of shots."[126] Godard was right. His last great advance in film form was the associative blend of fiction and documentary of *A Married Woman.* By contrast, he edited *Two or Three Things, Le Gai Savoir,* and *One Plus One* by simply alternating their two categories of footage, and *Made in USA* and *La Chinoise* were free collages of fragmented elements. Godard's work in the editing room with Gorin was his first step toward a great and distant goal of new cinematic composition—which would take him a decade of work to realize.

Wind from the East, however, in Gorin's "organization," was raised from fiction to manifesto, laying all the more bare his and Godard's doctrinal presumptions, which ranged from catechistic to repugnant. The film's culminating section, labeled "Civil Violence," features additional footage that Godard and Gorin shot in Paris, which teaches militants how to buy weapons and assemble the materials needed to make homemade bombs. In footage of shoppers in an outdoor market and of children congregating after school, voice-over commentators repudiate "bourgeois humanism" and redefine terrorism as the moment "when the exploited provides itself with the means to grab the exploiter by the throat."

Then, after joining Godard in the editing room, Gorin also applied his new ideas to the footage from Czechoslovakia, which Godard had put aside. Like Godard's other recent films, these two were not released in France; *Wind from the East* was screened at Cannes in 1970 but received little notice.

ABOVE ALL, GORIN brought Godard a new philosophical perspective. Through their discussions, Godard was prompted to reconsider the cinema from a historical point of view. Prior to his partnership with Gorin, Godard's historicism was aestheticized: drawing on Langlois's synoptic approach at the Cinémathèque, Godard drew freely on moments from films he loved to make his current preoccupations converge with his cinematic passions. Gorin, however, brought theoretical rigor to Godard's absorption in the history of cinema, working with him to correlate aesthetics with politics. Thus, not long after their collaboration had begun, Godard explained that "producing films at this moment means nothing else than studying the changes undergone by the cinema from Lumière and Eisenstein to the present, and studying them in practice; that is to say, by making films about the world of today."[127]

In keeping with this idea, Godard and Gorin engaged in a series of experiments. The first concerned Eisenstein's unfinished 1937 *Bezhin Meadow.* The film displeased Soviet officials, who forced Eisenstein to make a horrific public self-criticism for having made it, and destroyed the film. However, at the time of Godard and Gorin's collaboration, still photographs of the film had recently resurfaced. As Gorin later recalled, they filmed every still image and re-edited the resulting footage in two different versions.[128]

Godard and Gorin also joined with Gorin's friend Raphaël Sorin, an editor, to create a book, *À Bas le cinéma* (Down with the Cinema), a collage of images and texts, to which Godard wrote the introduction. (It remains unpublished.)[129]

Another project that Godard and Gorin worked on together was what Gorin called "the daily news in video," in which the two of them played the role of news anchormen, videotaping themselves as they sat behind a table in Godard and Wiazemsky's apartment and discussed the day's events. The work was "shown in the radical bookstore of François Maspero. We did it for a few weeks or months. The bookstore was completely packed," Gorin said. Their performances included what Gorin termed "skits" and "so-called secret messages."[130] Despite the interest they aroused, these exploits brought in no money. Godard needed to make films with real producers.

One possibility that presented itself was a film based on the play *Little Murders,* by Jules Feiffer. Elliott Gould had bought film rights to the play and Feiffer, after seeing *Weekend,* suggested to Gould that Godard was the right person to direct a film version.[131] Gould then sent Godard a copy of the play. While filming in California in late 1968, Godard met Gould—and demanded fifteen thousand dollars just to consider the project, which Gould's production company paid.[132] Godard had insisted that if he were to direct, the script be written by Robert Benton and David Newman, who had written *Bonnie and Clyde.* Gould agreed. Their script was completed in May 1969. However, Godard never planned to use it: "My intention was not to shoot that picture, but to take the money and make a picture on a subject I chose."[133] As Benton remembered, "Godard told us that what he wanted to do was a film about a French director coming to New York to do a film of *Little Murders* and who is unable to make it."[134] But United Artists, which financed the film, would not accept Godard as director and the job was ultimately given to Alan Arkin.

Finally, in December 1969, Godard and Gorin received financing from Italian television for a film called *Luttes en Italie (Struggles in Italy),* which they filmed almost entirely in Godard and Wiazemsky's apartment (and one day in Milan).[135] "There was a pizzaiolo downstairs," Gorin recalled, "We were ordering a lot of pizza because we called him up every time we needed a shot of him."[136] (The young woman is played by Christiana Tullio Altan; Wiazemsky has a small role, as a saleswoman in a clothing store.) The film, based on a text by Louis Althusser, concerns a young woman's realization that her political commitment is less revolutionary than she had believed. The film is in three parts, with each part almost identical, while the sound track in each differs, though less than the filmmakers seemed to think. The images, of the young woman at home, are of a crushing banality: she eats soup, reads a book, makes love, tries on clothing. An occasional angle suggests a sad vestige of aesthetic inspiration. Once again, the theoretical justifications that Godard and Gorin elaborated for the film are far more substantial than the film itself, which is stultifyingly dull. It was not broadcast on Italian television.

At this point, Godard and Gorin began to call their circle the Dziga

Vertov Group, named for the Soviet filmmaker of *Man with a Movie Camera*. Gorin recalled, "The name of the group was originally a joke, but at the same time it was, of course, a political act in aesthetics." He explained that they chose the name because Vertov's aesthetics, they thought, were more revolutionary than Eisenstein's: "Vertov—more explicitly than Eisenstein—was dissolving his individuality into the forces of the revolution."[137] According to Jean-Henri Roger, the group considered narrative, character development, and dramatic realism ideologically suspect: "We adopted the name of Vertov after careful thought. We didn't want the vulgarity of narrative. If there are characters, it's bourgeois."[138]

Godard's next project hardly ran the risk of identification with bourgeois narrative: it was a commission from the Arab League to make a film about the Palestinian struggle for independence, and would be called *Jusqu'à la victoire* (*Until Victory*), from a Fatah slogan. (The Arab League put six thousand dollars into the project, the actor and producer Jacques Perrin added three thousand dollars.) Godard, Gorin, and the cameraman Armand Marco (who had been a camera assistant on Godard's *L'Aller et retour* in 1967), traveled to Jordan, the West Bank, and Lebanon, making several trips throughout 1970. They were not there to make a documentary film but a doctrinal one. Marco recalled, with unintended irony, the trio's working conditions: "There was a certain liberty, but it was totally controlled," though, as he understood, "one does not drop three 'tourists' into situations of war—we weren't there for that, we weren't war reporters." The cameraman also recalled the theoretical questions he and the filmmakers discussed as they worked:

> What does it mean to film a literacy class for women, the assembly and disassembly of arms, to film a woman? How should we ask a woman to let us film her? Should we film her in close-up or not in close-up? We were trying at the same time to escape, to change, to try to understand a little bit better what was going on there—and how to film it.[139]

The filmmakers were submitting their assumptions about movie aesthetics to the challenge of political problems, or rather, rephrasing their cinematic questions in terms of political ones in the hope of finding new answers. Yet the theoretical discussions served a predetermined end. Before traveling to the Middle East, Godard had put together an elaborate storyboard of the action to be filmed. He and Gorin approached the project like advertising: they had a message that they wanted to expound, and they decided in advance what they wanted to show in order to exemplify it. "There were drawings and shots" already worked out, Marco recalled. "We went to verify that structure. We laid the structure on top of a situation that we did not know."[140]

Elias Sanbar, a Palestinian activist who had been called from Paris by Fatah to serve as translator and guide, took note of Godard's carefully constructed scenario: "Throughout the trip, Godard did not stop looking at his notes, adding remarks, crossing out passages with three markers of different colors . . . Godard wrote a lot, with a certain jubilation which seemed to leave him during the shoot, giving way to an apparent detachment."[141] This could have been foreseen: Godard's commitment to shooting had always been correlated with its spontaneity, of which this project offered little. As Sanbar said, "The film was very prepared, very scripted. So when something was going on and we said, 'Come film it,' he said, 'I don't need it for the film.' "[142]

Between November 1969 and August 1970, Godard traveled to the Middle East six times, not always with Gorin and Marco.[143] Though the project was shot on film, Godard also brought video equipment, which he used to make preliminary versions of the film. Much to the surprise of the Palestinian participants, Godard, after viewing his tapes, often rewrote scenes and asked for immediate reshoots. (He later left his video equipment behind for a Palestinian fighter who used home movies to restore his troops' morale.)[144]

Much of the footage consisted of military parades, children reciting propaganda, and soldiers receiving instructions. One difficult shoot involved a group of Palestinian commandos returning from a night mission against Israel after having suffered losses. Godard, following his scenario, called one of the fighters forward and had him recite, in front of the others, a text about self-criticism. Godard also wanted to interview Yasser Arafat on-camera, and later described his meeting with the Fatah leader:

> I prepared all the equipment, the camera, the Nagra, we started shooting, and I asked Arafat, "What is the future of the Palestinian revolution?" He said, "I have to think about it, come back tomorrow." And he didn't come back. At least he was honest.[145]

In his discussion with Arafat, Godard had also brought up a subject that seems so strange as to be unworthy of serious discussion, but which nonetheless informed his ideas on the subject of Israel to a surprisingly great extent. The notion would find its way into the film, as well as into his later works that refer to the Middle East. The idea, such as it is, was a metaphor drawn from historical sources, and one which, to Godard, seemed to exemplify the essence of the problem in a theoretically minimal schema, as if in a mathematical equation. He recalled his conversation with Arafat:

> I told him that the origin of the Palestinian difficulties had to do with the concentration camps, and he said, "No, that's their story, the Germans and the

Jews," and I said, "No, you know that in the camps, when a prisoner was very weak, close to death, they called him 'Musulman' [Muslim]." And he said, "So what?" And I said, "You see, they could have called him 'black' or any other name, but no, they said 'Muslim.' And that shows that there's a relationship, it's a direct relationship."[146]

While working on the film back in Paris, Godard and Gorin began to fear that they would be targeted for assassination by Israel; they worked in an unmarked editing room and barricaded themselves in. Gorin later recalled that he and Godard knew "everyone"—all the Palestinian agents—"from *Munich*," Steven Spielberg's 2005 film about Israel's attempts to kill the European-based Palestinian militants responsible for the massacre of Israeli athletes at the 1972 Olympics.

The filming was interrupted by Black September, the Jordanian army's attack in September 1970 on Palestinian fighters. For the next two years, Godard and Gorin spent endless hours in the editing room working on the footage. Gorin later announced their plan "to make four or five films, each lasting one and one-half hours, out of the ten hours of material [they] have."[147] But the project, like so many that they undertook, was never completed—at least not in that form.

BLACK SEPTEMBER WAS not the only reason for the project's interruption. Godard did not have enough money to complete the film, or even to live. To generate income as well as funds to finish *On Victory*, he signed on for another university tour of the United States, in April and May 1970; this time, he traveled with Gorin and saw the monthlong trip through to the end. But by now, the magic of his celebrity had somewhat worn off. American students, who were more motivated by politics than by cinema, were far more confrontational than they had been; Godard was coming as a political figure, showing political films (*British Sounds* and *Pravda*), and he attracted political audiences. In Berkeley, where the films were denounced for their abstraction, he and Gorin were pelted with tomatoes. "Throwing tomatoes in Berkeley was absolutely normal because [the students] are more involved in the mass struggle than Harvard. So it was in the more progressive areas that we got a violent response," Godard said.[148] In Minnesota, the local organizers thought the pair looked so threadbare that they gave them an additional hundred dollars in cash.

While in New York, however, Godard and Gorin did important business. They went together to the Leacock-Pennebaker studio to watch the rushes of *One A.M.*; Godard was welcomed despite his failure to deliver the film in April 1969, which had forced the company into bankruptcy. He now hoped to be inspired to complete the film together with Gorin, but Gorin declared it a "corpse" and they did nothing more with it. (D. A. Pennebaker had already edited his own version of the footage and called it One P.M.—One Pennebaker Movie.)

During this tour, Godard also said of his own earlier political-themed movies, particularly La Chinoise, "They are just Hollywood films because I was a bourgeois artist. They are my dead corpses,"[149] though Gorin reported that Godard "has been noting—putting in a notebook—every student insurrection just after a showing of La Chinoise, and coming to me and saying, 'Look! You see, it works!'"[150]

In any case, Godard found a new American source of financing: in the summer of 1969, Grove Press and its publisher, Barney Rosset, had paid six thousand dollars for distribution rights to Pravda and British Sounds (retitled See You at Mao); now he gave Godard a five-picture deal for an investment of twenty-five thousand dollars per film. The first in the series, for which the publisher issued an advance in March 1970, was to be a film of The 18th Brumaire of Louis Napoleon, by Karl Marx—an account of the restoration of imperial rule which followed the failed French revolution of 1848.[151]

Instead, Godard and Gorin performed a by-now-familiar bait-and-switch move, making Vladimir and Rosa, a film inspired by their American sojourn, which, despite its title's allusion to Lenin and Rosa Luxemburg, was about the trial of the Chicago Eight, which had gotten under way in the spring. In New York, Godard told an interviewer, "With Vladimir and Rosa we'll try to begin again with fiction, but it will be very difficult."[152] Godard and Gorin's experiments aimed at a reconstruction of storytelling in an ideologically determined form.

The difficulty that Godard foresaw proved to be worth the struggle. A study in political psychology, Vladimir and Rosa is by far the most impressive of the projects that Godard and Gorin did together. Filmed mostly in the pair's new editing room on the rue de Rennes, it features actors declaiming their texts against blank walls in a series of crudely Brechtian skits resembling the trial of the American radicals. (For instance, Bobby Seale, a Black Panther activist, is portrayed as being held in the courtroom with two guns pointed at his head.) The sound track features Godard and Gorin analyzing, in alternation, the behavior and motives of the "radical attorney" William Kunstler and his clients.

Despite framing devices that remove the characters from any realistic context and despite the actors' antic recitation and gesticulation, Vladimir and Rosa represents a first step toward the depiction of people who are not mere ideological abstractions but bundles of complex and mixed motives. The "courtroom" images are crudely functional, but several scenes featuring

Godard and Gorin as performers suggest new forms of political cinema: the two men walk side by side on a tennis court, on opposite sides of the net, and talk to each other in a constant stammer. They are wearing headphones, which are connected to the tape recorder that Gorin is carrying as Godard points a microphone at whichever one is speaking: the momentary tape delay with which they hear themselves, a sort of feedback, impedes their ability to speak clearly. The image, along with the metaphor it conveys, is the most powerful moment of cinema that the pair produced.

Nonetheless, Barney Rosset was dismayed by the film, particularly by Godard and Gorin's alternately satirical and critical views of the Chicago Eight defendants, whom he considered heroes. The publisher thought that the film's young and politicized audience would be put off by the filmmakers' judgments, and so he modified the film. He brought two of the real-life defendants, Abbie Hoffman and Jerry Rubin, to the Grove Press screening room and filmed them watching and mocking the film, then cut that footage into *Vladimir and Rosa*. The movie's coproducer, a Munich television station, refused to broadcast it.[153]

The film was unreleased in France; upon its brief American release, a year later, *Vladimir and Rosa* was poorly received.[154]

ALTHOUGH GODARD HAD reached new prominence in the United States following his tour in the spring of 1970, his recent films were almost impossible to see in France. *Pravda* was screened, unannounced except through word of mouth, three times in February at the Musée d'Art moderne, where, taking questions from the audience, Godard all but apologized—"The film is 99 percent a failure but I think that it's going 1 percent in the right direction." But then, slipping back into character, he added, "For me, this film is a minuscule, tiny turn of the screw in the vise that will crush the bourgeoisie and its culture."[155]

He was essentially off the French map, both cinematically and journalistically. Interviews appeared in such small-circulation journals as *Cinéthique*, an expressly far-left alternative to *Cahiers du cinéma* (which quickly caught up and politicized to the extreme), and in other radical journals. In the mainstream press, occasional reports detailed Godard's activities, generally with the sort of ironic yet incredulous admiration inspired by a rich man who joins a religious order and fulfills a vow of poverty. In June 1970, Michel Cournot wrote with pathos in *Le Nouvel Observateur* about "Jean-Luc ex-Godard,"[156] and the next month, Claude Mauriac wrote that Godard's "body and effects disappeared" into the Dziga Vertov Group.[157]

While Godard had done a good job of disappearing in France, he was uninterruptedly visible in the United States. Indeed, from an American perspective, he hadn't really left, in part, as a result of the vagaries of American film distribution, which kept his earlier work in the limelight. *Weekend,* shown at the New York Film Festival in September 1968, was released immediately thereafter, and the short film *Anticipation* (part of the compilation *The World's Oldest Profession*) came out in November; *Pierrot le fou* was released to enthusiastic reviews in January 1969, *Montparnasse and Levallois* (in *Paris vu par . . .*, released as *Six in Paris*) in March; *Le Gai Savoir* played at the New York Film Festival to great acclaim (particularly from Vincent Canby in the *New York Times*) in September 1969, and *Two or Three Things I Know About Her* was hailed when it opened in April 1970, coinciding with Godard's tour.

Godard's most recent work (with and without Gorin) also received wide exposure and respectful attention. Indeed, in New York, Godard seemed to be everywhere, with *One Plus One* opening in April 1970 to praise in the *New York Times* and *Newsweek* (though in the *Village Voice,* David Ehrenstein hedged his admiration by addressing Godard as "you old charlatan, you faker," and suggested that the film was "a 'put-on'"). *British Sounds* and *Pravda* opened commercially in May, to an extended and enthusiastic study by Penelope Gilliatt in *The New Yorker;* in the *Village Voice,* Jonas Mekas exulted that "*Pravda* is Godard's best film to date" and piled it on, saying that it also "may be his most romantic film." *Le Gai savoir* opened in June; *Wind from the East* played at the 1970 New York Film Festival and was received with rapt attention by Canby in the *Times.*[158]

Godard's American tours had done much to maintain his celebrity, and the haphazard releases of his films led many critics to overlook the break in his career and his life. The interest American critics and viewers took in the Dziga Vertov Group and its films was sustained in part by nostalgia and the willful assertion of continuity with Godard's earlier work, and partly by political exoticism. Despite the ideological insistence of those works, the political worlds they addressed were remote from America's own concerns. The critic who took Godard's change the hardest, who most clearly perceived its political imposture and cinematic aridity, and who publicly challenged him, was Andrew Sarris.

During the 1970 tour, Sarris profiled and interviewed Godard. Summarizing Godard's recent career path (and incidentally dismissing Gorin, whom he called an "assistant"), Sarris had little good to say about the recent films. He quoted with astonishment Godard's dismissal of the realities of the Soviet occupation of Czechoslovakia, and he attacked what he perceived as implications of anti-Semitism in Godard's lengthy diatribe in favor of Fatah. His questioning elicited Godard's quasi-totalitarian defense of his new methods: "Hollywood provides many images and not enough sound . . . It's better to have no images than too many. The Chinese don't have millions of books like us. They have only one, and that's all they need."

Nonetheless, Sarris attempted to extract some aesthetic sense from Godard's response, explaining it as a resistance to "the current craze with image quantification for its own sake," an idea that transcended Godard's anti-aesthetic purpose. Sarris presciently perceived the long-term application of the ideas latent in Godard's numbingly rigid films of those years, claiming that he remained "in the vanguard of expressing the almost inexpressible logic of artistic evolution." Still, summarizing his discussion with Godard, the critic eulogized the director: "The death of an artist is too high a price to pay for the birth of a revolutionary, even when the revolution seems to make more sense than ever before."[159]

FRENCH LEFTISM AFTER 1968 had hardened into a fearsome dogmatic rigor, and Godard had gone along with it. In 1969, after the confused response of the Maoist leadership to the events of May 1968 and the restoration of a tense, reformist calm, a new hard-core Maoist group, the Gauche proletarienne (the GP, or Proletarian Left), was formed. The group saw May and June 1968 as a "dress rehearsal," a bourgeois show that failed due to its lack of contact with French workers. The GP wanted to infiltrate and organize factories and labor unions, with the purpose of creating an authentically proletarian group of Maoists and the expectation that revolution would inevitably follow. But the government now responded to threats of unrest with overwhelming force. Successful strikes and factory takeovers led by the GP caused the government to ban its newspaper, *La Cause du peuple*, and to arrest its editor, Jean-Pierre Le Dantec. Prominent intellectuals, including many who had no particular sympathy for the GP cause (such as Truffaut), took to the streets to sell *La Cause du peuple*. Sartre became its titular editor. In October 1969, alongside Sartre, Godard sold the magazine in the street and visited the journal's offices and presses. On October 21, Sartre addressed the workers outside the gates of the Renault factory in Boulogne-Billancourt, and Godard videotaped the event.[160]

With *La Cause du peuple* banned, the GP founded, with financing from Godard's friend Jean-Pierre Bamberger, a new journal, *J'accuse*, edited by Robert Linhart. For its first issue, on January 15, 1971, Godard wrote a critique of Jean-Pierre Melville's recently released *Le Cercle rouge*, a crime drama, which he had gone to see in the company of "two or three" factory workers, transcribing and including their discussion of the film with his own review. He equated Melville with the minister of the interior Raymond Marcellin.

He signed the review under a self-dramatizing pseudonym, "Michel Servet," a Protestant burned for heresy in Geneva by Calvin's followers in 1553.

In January 1971, jailed Maoists began a hunger strike, and supporters undertook a hunger strike in sympathy, assembling in the chapelle Saint-Bernard (beneath the Montparnasse railway station). As one of the celebrity activists who visited the strikers, Godard suggested that the group needed to found its own press agency, which he dubbed the APL (Agence Presse Libération). The agency that resulted (founded soon thereafter by younger militants) turned into a daily newspaper in 1973, *Libération*, which ultimately became (and remains) the leading newspaper of the French mainstream left.

The depth and totality of Godard's involvement in Maoist politics ultimately put an end to his relationship with Wiazemsky, completing the break that had begun with the arrival of Gorin on the set of *Wind from the East*. "Gorin brought out the worst in him, dragged him toward a cinema that was not his own," Wiazemsky claimed. "He created a void around him. I left because of [Gorin], because of living with him. He was like the political commissar. All of my problems with Jean-Luc date from his arrival."[161] The problem that Wiazemsky had with Gorin's influence on Godard was not necessarily personal but cinematic: "[Godard] asked me to become a partner in his work, but it didn't interest me. If it hadn't been for politics, Gorin, yes. It would have been a classic actress-director relationship." Although Wiazemsky did appear in *Wind from the East, Struggles in Italy,* and *Vladimir and Rosa* (where she plays a feminist T-shirt maker), her roles were schematic and her involvement in them merely formal. (In the meantime, she had acted in several films by Pasolini, pursued her interest in photography, and even acted—shades of Anna Karina—in a film directed by Michel Deville, starring Maurice Ronet, *Raphaël ou le débauché*.)

Wiazemsky's view of Gorin's negative influence on Godard echoed that of many French cinephiles, who viewed Gorin with great suspicion as a sort of Maoist guru who held Godard under his sway. Gorin recalled, "People hated my guts in Europe because of what I had done, which they thought was so sacrilegious in nature."[162] What he "had done," of course, was simply to work closely with Godard at a time when Godard withdrew from his quasi-popular way of working. But Gorin was blamed for luring Godard, like a cinematic Yoko Ono, toward work of arid hermeticism. Godard's own behavior during this period did not help. He remained out of the public eye, surfacing only rarely on the occasion of a trip to the Middle East or a Parisian museum screening of his recent films.

Godard's marriage to Wiazemsky broke up when he moved out of their apartment in the Latin Quarter and slept in his editing room. Then, Wiazemsky left and Godard moved back in—but not alone.

Some months earlier, in 1970, Godard had been invited to the Cinémathèque Suisse in Lausanne to show *Struggles in Italy*. Freddy Buache, the director of the Cinémathèque Suisse, was a leftist who addressed his audience as "comrades" and was sympathetic to local radical groups and the radical political cinema. It was there that Godard met the person who would play a crucial role in his life and his work for the next three decades and beyond. "Anne-Marie Miéville often came to the Cinémathèque Suisse," Buache recounted. "That's where they met."[163]

Anne-Marie Miéville, born in 1945, was active with the local Swiss group, Rupture pour le communisme, connected to the French GP.[164] Her family, like Godard's, was from the canton of Vaud in Switzerland, and, also like him, she had moved to Paris. There she briefly sang pop music, then took up photography. She worked at a pro-Palestinian bookstore in Paris and helped Godard make contact with Palestinians and sympathizers there while he worked on *Until Victory*.

Miéville had a young daughter and also had family in Switzerland, and was in the habit of shuttling between the two countries. Godard wrote to Miéville every day in her absence (and continued to do so for more than a decade).[165] Isabelle Pons, who kept the production company's books (and who was living with Gorin), recalled that Godard had a calendar on which he marked the days that he made love to Miéville.[166]

With Miéville's arrival in Godard's Paris apartment, his domestic life stabilized, but his financial state became ever more precarious. Pons recalled that by 1971, Godard was in desperate need of money. She said that Godard thought nothing of living on a large sack of rice as his diet for the entire week. In early 1971, Pons brought Godard together with a young and ambitious producer, Jean-Pierre Rassam, "who needed to produce something to gain some credibility."

For Rassam, Godard and Gorin conceived a project that they first called *Love Story* and then changed to *Tout va bien* (All's Well). It was intended to be an imitation of a Hollywood film but with a heavy infusion of ideology. At first, the project was to be produced by Max Palevsky, of the Xerox Corporation. Then, it was slated to be coproduced by Paramount and the distributor Donald S. Rugoff.[167] It featured singer-actor Yves Montand, an engaged leftist, as a filmmaker who had withdrawn from the movies after 1968 and who was getting by making commercials, and Jane Fonda as his girlfriend, an American journalist in Paris. The story concerned a strike at a factory where the workers sequester the boss in his office. The journalist and the filmmaker, coming to interview the boss, witness the strike and are themselves briefly detained. The woman journalist begins to question her professional practice and her relationship with the filmmaker.

In sympathy with the film's political message, the actors agreed to accept a percentage of the film's earnings in lieu of a fee, and the shoot was scheduled to begin in late 1971. For Godard, the project signified something of a return to the film industry, if only pro forma, and he began to participate again in industry-related activities. In Rome, he took part in a panel discussion with five other directors (including Louis Malle and Alain Tanner) about the distribution of art films.[168]

There on June 7, Godard was preparing to fly to New York to meet with Frank Yablans of Paramount. Before his flight, Godard wanted to buy a book, and his film editor, Christine Aya, offered to give him a lift on her motorcycle. For some reason, Gorin foresaw trouble and warned Godard that he would have an accident.[169] Moments later, the motorcycle slid under the wheels of a bus. Aya was thrown clear, but Godard suffered a skull fracture, a broken pelvis, and numerous internal injuries. Doctors feared that his femoral artery was irreparably severed. Godard was in a coma for almost a month. As Gorin recalled, Godard "lost so much skin from his buttocks that you could touch the bone." He also lost a testicle.[170] Anne Wiazemsky, who was still his legal spouse, was the only person legally empowered to deal with his doctors. She came at once from Rome and arranged with the doctors and hospital staff to keep Godard's condition secret. It seemed clear that Godard would be unable to direct *Tout va bien,* but, as Gorin remembered:

> I found myself having to maintain the fiction that the film would be made. Otherwise the insurance that was keeping Jean-Luc alive and was paying for his hospitalization would collapse. So I work like crazy on it, and I'm pleading with the stars that they maintain the illusion that the film will be done. There's no problem with Montand, despite the fact that he's very wary of us. Simone Signoret was afraid that we were going to make her husband look like an idiot. I was berated by her on the phone at 3:00 AM. In the middle of this, Jane Fonda calls . . . She says, "I have decided not to work with men any more." I tell her, "I think you should come to Paris and tell that to the man who is between life and death on a hospital bed."

Gorin resolved the situation by confronting Fonda in person. The actress was in the south of France, where her ex-husband, Roger Vadim, lived:

> I got my girlfriend's car—I had no license—and drove to meet her. I surprised her. I told her, "At least have the guts to tell [Godard] face to face." I was constantly arguing with her. Her people were afraid—they thought I was connected to two billion Chinese. The next day, I heard from the lawyer that she would do the film.[171]

After coming out of the coma, Godard was in need of intensive physical therapy and was admitted to another hospital. Though his initial hospitalization was frightful, Wiazemsky remembered him being in excellent form in the second round, "with the piles of Red Books and the joking around . . . First of all, he was a survivor, he was fairly cheerful. Then on top of that, he played the clown a little."[172] Yet Godard was in terrible shape. He came to the set but was hardly able to do much work. He used a crutch and needed a catheter.

Tout va bien was largely directed by Gorin. He had arranged for the factory set to be built as a cutaway, like the house in Jerry Lewis's *The Ladies Man*, with all the rooms exposed. The riotous goings-on, with the boss as the buffoon, betrayed their origin in popular comedy. Gorin directed scenes that were intended to mime scenes and styles from Godard's earlier films, such as a long tracking shot which ran the entire length of a supermarket.

The work that Godard did on the film was largely of a theoretical nature. He elaborated the idea that the two stars not in fact be the main characters, so although Fonda and Montand do get the bulk of the screen time, they were not filmed in a glamorous or glorifying way. This led to conflict. Both actors had political advisers on hand—Fonda's from feminist circles and Montand's from the French left—to whom they complained because they felt "disarmed" by the experience.[173] There was talk of revolt, but Godard adroitly convinced the intermediaries of his worthy intentions. He conceived a sequence in which Montand would be filmed from behind, his head concealing half of Fonda's face, and he initiated a long discussion on-set as to whether Montand's ear should have a light on it. Montand, upset by the perceived diminution of his role, argued and at one point raised his hand as if to strike Godard, who replied, "You wouldn't hit a cripple!"[174]

Despite Godard's separation from Wiazemsky, he wanted her to act in the film, writing three different parts for her, two of which would be dubbed. When Gorin balked, Godard proposed that she do the still photography from the set instead, but, as Wiazemsky recalled, "Anne-Marie Miéville got upset, and said, 'My brother is a photographer, I can do the photography too.'" Miéville did the photography; Wiazemsky had a small part in one scene. "I spent the whole week doing nothing," she recalled.[175]

Despite its tendentious politics and ample speechifying, *Tout va bien* nonetheless suggests, in a quasi-documentary way, a new world of relations between men and women: Jane Fonda's feminist discourse in the film presages a coming world of politics that has little to do with strikes and marches, with bourgeois bosses and the proletariat. *Tout va bien* suggests a requiem for years of a one-dimensional engagement that it couldn't entirely shake off.

After completing *Tout va bien*, Godard and Gorin made a 16mm film to accompany it at the New York Film Festival in the fall of 1972 called *Letter to Jane,* a fifty-two-minute-long analysis of a still photograph of Jane Fonda in Hanoi, published in *L'Express* on July 31, 1972. This film features Godard and Gorin talking to each other on the sound track about the picture. Their insistent, incantatory analysis, centered on Fonda appearing as the star of a political image in lieu of allowing her North Vietnamese interlocutors to take the lead role, and comparing her image to others, including Richard Nixon's, is a clever and enlightening work of journalistic semiology. In the literal sense, the film is documentary in its relentless investigation of the political psychology implicit in a single image. Yet Godard and Gorin approach it as an immediate experience, not through a scrim of doctrine; in speaking about the image, they speak in their own voices, without the deflecting burlesque of *Vladimir and Rosa.* The work is personal, sincere, and spontaneous; the direct discourse suggests a will to restore their personal presence to their films. The effect is that of a verbal jam session; for all of its analytical intensity, *Letter to Jane* marked a return to aesthetics. The exchange also points to its origins in the kind of vigorous discussion Godard and Gorin had been sharing privately for half a decade. It is the closest thing to a documentary of their behind-the-scenes laboratory work.

Again, Godard and Gorin undertook an American university tour to raise some cash; it was less festive than Godard's first, in 1968, less contentious than the one with Gorin in 1970. They planned to come back again in the spring of 1973, but by then, their relationship had undergone a change.

After *Tout va bien,* Gorin was ready to make a film on his own. Godard implored him to remain in their partnership, but Gorin was desperate for his own well-deserved identity. Gorin recalled bitterly a derisive review of *Tout va bien* in the satirical *Charlie-Hebdo* that was just a few words: "Quite a guy, this Gorin"—implying that the younger man had managed to hijack Godard's fame to generate his own. When *Le Monde* wanted to interview Godard and Gorin upon the release of *Tout va bien,* Godard, in an act of support for Gorin, stipulated that they be interviewed separately and that the two interviews be exactly the same length. Godard measured the columns to make sure of it.[176] In October 1972, while in New York to show *Tout va bien* and *Letter to Jane,* Gorin told an interviewer, "Now I know what it's like to be a woman. I am the Yoko Ono of the cinema."[177]

But Gorin's reputation as the artist responsible for coming between Jean-Luc Godard and the cinema was undeserved. Though Gorin and Godard went on to do better, greater, and more important work separately, their partnership was, in effect, the crucible from which that subsequent work arose.

The crucial ideas they explored were hardly in evidence in the films Godard and Gorin actually made together, but they shaped Godard's work for decades to come. When Godard fled the movie industry in 1967, he was escaping not just a set of narrative conventions or even his own public image; he was also fleeing the entrenched industrial schema of movie production. If Godard's post-1968 ideological straitjacket inhibited his actual filmmaking, the underlying ideas behind the ideology—the notion of workers' control of the means of production to reduce the emotional distance between the worker and his product; the notion of collaborative work as part of a collective—provided the foundation for a new, cooperative form of filmmaking. It is what Godard began to realize with Gorin, and what he would bring to fruition with Anne-Marie Miéville.

Godard now began to rethink the system of production, distribution, and consumption of films from a material point of view; he would become a producer, in the Marxist rather than the Hollywood sense: he would own the means of production and apply the labor of his own hands to those tools. He turned to the fledgling technology of videotape in order to localize the entire chain of production under his own roof. Several years later, Godard explained:

> I prefer to consider myself a producer, but in the sense of the Internationale: "Producers, rely on yourselves,"[178] because if you count on others to produce, you are lost . . . And the word "producer" is especially interesting in the cinema, where it means "boss," it doesn't mean "worker." The cinema has the same terms as Marxism: "production," "distribution," "exploitation."[179]

In 1975, Godard declared, "The only original filmmaker I ever encountered in my life was Jean-Pierre Gorin, whose originality was not that he wanted to make shots like Hitchcock or Eisenstein, but that he wanted to make his mark on film together with somebody else."[180] In another interview he remarked that "just to do something I need to be more than one . . . the only aim of a self is to be two."[181]

Gorin went on to direct a film which he called *L'Ailleurs immédiat* (The Immediate Elsewhere). It was an extremely personal film, in which he starred and which took as a central subject his own sex life. The arrest on drug charges[182] of the lead actress had a disastrous effect on the film. Gorin abandoned the project and left Paris for Morocco, Mexico, and ultimately California. He soon began work there on *Poto and Cabengo,* a documentary about twins who seemed to be speaking a private language and who, when separated in school, began to speak comprehensibly. It is an extraordinarily touching allegory for his years of work with Godard.

Gorin was the nominal administrator of his company with Godard, Tout Va assez Bien Films, and so, was financially responsible for it, although Godard and Rassam actually handled the money matters. After Gorin left France, Godard encouraged him to return to take care of the business. Gorin did not want to return to France, and Godard arranged matters to suit himself. He removed the equipment—which had been bought with funds set aside for that purpose—to his new studio and from there to Grenoble, and left behind rent due on their joint editing room. Gorin, out of touch and officially owing the back rent on the editing room, was held to be in "fraudulent bankruptcy."

While in California, making *Poto and Cabengo* with little money to work with and little to live on, Gorin had gotten word that *Tout va bien* was scheduled for broadcast on French television and called Godard about getting the fifty percent share of the deal to which he was entitled. Godard's response was, first, that there was nothing left after Montand and Fonda got paid; and then, as Gorin recalled, Godard told him, "Ah, it's always the same thing, the Jews come calling when they hear the cash register."[183] Gorin hung up on him. The two did not speak again for years—until *Poto and Cabengo* was completed and shown at the Rotterdam Film Festival. Godard saw it there and paid it fitting tribute—albeit not in public.

MAOISM WAS A peculiar foible of French intellectuals in the wake of the student-led revolts of 1968. Those who yielded to its allure—they were legion, and included Sartre and Philippe Sollers, as well as countless lesser figures—did so with a peculiar form of cognitive dissonance. They defended as humane and enlightened the government of Communist China even as, at home, they called for the necessity, even desirability, of a cleansing political violence exercised in the name of the dictatorship of the proletariat. Their blindness to the firsthand meaning of dictatorship was all too evident, and when, in 1973, Simon Leys, among others, began to issue reports of the brutal realities of Mao's China, French Maoists began to grow scarce.

With any perspective, the undesirability of the utopia that French Maoists dreamed of seems self-evident; but, unlike other intellectuals, Godard suffered deeply for his engagement on its behalf. Where others simply continued their careers under a new banner, Godard had profoundly, even recklessly and enduringly, altered his way of working. Where others drew from their political enthusiasms a newfound currency, a newfound identity, or simply shed them with no ill effects, Godard suffered something like nonexistence, having risked and to some extent lost his art for his political commitment. Describing his life in that doctrinaire time, Godard later explained, "I think that in those years, I stopped doing lots of things without even realizing it: reading, going to the movies. Music must have been a forbidden pleasure but I had already listened to so much of it that I had stocked up."[184] Referring to that era in terms of Eric Rohmer's famous description of the abstemious years of ciné-fanaticism during the 1950s, Godard said, "I would say, like Rohmer: in those years, one did not live."[185]

seventeen

RESTORATION (1973–1977)

"A film about myself"

IN JANUARY 1973, WITH NO OTHER PROJECTS BEFORE HIM,
Godard submitted to the CNC a written outline for a film, in the
hope of receiving an advance on receipts.[1] He called it *Moi je*—
the same title as the recently published political memoir by the ex-rightist
and ex-Communist Claude Roy.[2] In that book, Roy, born in 1915, studied his
personal development through his political engagements; he had been a
right-wing anarchist in the 1930s before signing up with the Communist
Party during wartime and leaving it after the Soviet invasion of Hungary in
1956. Roy's political path was, with several decades' head start, similar to
Godard's, and Godard sought to accomplish in his cinematic *Moi je* a political self-investigation similar to Roy's in literature. In his proposal, he made
clear his intention of shooting his project on videotape, and sought at length
to justify doing so. Indeed, rather than an outline of an autobiography, the
application was largely an essay on the need to use video technology to create a new kind of cinema.

Godard contended that video was a superior medium because editing on
film was limited to placing the images sequentially, whereas video permitted
superimposition of multiple images, or the incrusting of one image within
another, directly in the editing room, without the cumbersome, inexact,
time-consuming, and expensive intermediary of a special-effects studio. He
considered the ability to see two images at once, by means of video editing,
to be a crucial tool of visual analysis, since it permits "thinking two aspects
together, to think montage, to think mixing." Since the 1950s, Godard had
conceived of montage not principally as a succession of images but as the simultaneous appearance of distinct ideas in a single image ("At the same

Anne-Marie Miéville
(Jean-Luc Godard and Anne-Marie Miéville. "Soft and Hard [A Soft Conversation on Hard Subjects]," 1985. Courtesy of Electronic Arts Intermix [EAI], New York)

time, the weather is nice and the train enters the station").[3] But now, Godard hoped to use video to render such simultaneities explicit and to study them.

In dense philosophical language, Godard introduced a series of examples drawn from the history of cinema, with references to Griffith, Eisenstein, and Vertov, and the social history of their times. He argued that by means of video superimpositions, he could prove visually that these directors' aesthetics, their style, were inseparable from the political contexts in which they worked. For Godard, whose cinematic ideas were imbued with impressions from the history of cinema, the ability to extract the politics latent in his predecessors' work was essential to understanding his own personal and political journey.

The mere fact that Godard acknowledged his dependence on the history of cinema was a sign that, after his years of self-imposed exile in the dogmatic wilderness, he was indeed returning to himself (thanks to a new approach to the classic cinema that Gorin had inspired). But the proposal also included a new metaphorical element which suggested that, instead of going back, he was moving ahead, both intellectually and artistically, into uncharted waters.

In his CNC proposal, Godard argued that superimpositions are important not only for the cinema but also for *biology*. As an example, he reproduced in the proposal a one-line telegram, which featured seven lines of Western Union code at the top of the message. He compared the message to the genetics and the phenomenon of reverse transcription, the form of genetic transmission specific to a retrovirus. In Godard's analysis, it is not the telegram's code that conveys the message, but the message that surreptitiously conveys the code, which is replicated and transmitted by the recipient. In effect, Godard was arguing that the aesthetics of cinema were inherently political, that movies passed along to their viewers a secret ideological code that viewers then, in their own communications, also passed along; he was refashioning his ideological advocacy as a theory of communication.

This analysis was a radically dialectical version of Godard's early insight that "at the cinema, we do not think, we are thought": his idea was to use the technique of video editing to reveal, analyze, and, ultimately, counteract the formal codes with which viewers like himself were unconsciously afflicted.

Although Godard would subject these abstract notions to a variety of modifications in the years to come, they would remain at the heart of his most important projects, which would be made on videotape and rely on the special effects of video editing. These ideas and the work that resulted would ultimately provide Godard with the creative impetus that would return him to the mainstream of the French film industry—and help him make films about himself that were even more direct and self-revealing than those of the

1960s. But the CNC was evidently bewildered by Godard's application for *Moi je;* the project won no financing,[4] and, as he had done so often at critical moments in his career, Godard took his troubles public.

In the July–August 1973 issue of *Cinéma Pratique,* the principal French magazine devoted to amateur and Super-8 filmmaking,[5] Godard expressly redefined his aims away from the political back toward the personal: "I have noticed, after fifteen years of cinema, that the true 'political' film that I would like to accomplish would be a film about myself to show my wife and my daughter what I am—in other words, a family film." (Godard was referring to Miéville and her daughter, Anne, despite his still being married to Wiazemsky—whom he would not divorce until 1979.)

Godard saw that the obstacle to his "home movies" was financial. He believed that he would have no choice but to create and distribute them on his own, outside the prevailing system, and that he would have to make them in video because it was cheaper: tapes are cheaper per minute than film, require no processing, and can be reused. He imagined that his videos could be rented by small groups of people to watch together, and he understood that this was not likely to be much of a business. "That is why I clearly envision taking a part-time job," he noted, although doing so was never a serious option.

More than ever, Godard felt isolated from other filmmakers and from the industry. He expressed his frustrated desire to "talk about cinema in a way that's a little bit different" and, sensing that his connection with the public was cut, knew that he would have to "seek a way to talk, individual to individual." To break his isolation, Godard sought out a favorite old companion in cinema, albeit in a way that was so peculiarly aggressive and self-serving that it seemed almost solipsistic.

François Truffaut's new film, *La nuit américaine* (*Day for Night*), about the life lived by a crew while making a film, opened in Paris on May 24, 1973. Godard saw it and, on June 1, he sent Truffaut a three-page letter about it (also enclosing a note for Jean-Pierre Léaud, the film's star). Calling Truffaut a "liar" for what he had chosen to leave out of *Day for Night,* Godard demanded that his old friend, in effect, make amends by giving him money to make a film in response. Instead of an extended hand, Godard preferred both a slap and an outstretched palm. Truffaut responded in kind, giving vent to fifteen years of pent-up grudges in a twenty-page letter of venomous fury. The two men never spoke amicably again.

So, at least, the exchange appears on a cursory reading. But the letter to which Truffaut responded so vehemently was, from different angles, several different kinds of communication. It was, certainly, a reproach and a demand; but it was also a plea and a nostalgic wink of complicity, an extended hand as well as, plainly and simply, a sketch for a film. Truffaut saw only the reprimand and answered accordingly. Although Godard's approach to Truffaut was insensitive, Truffaut's response was no less so: Godard poorly read the man, but perhaps Truffaut poorly read the letter.

Lacking the customarily ingratiating tone of a request for financial help, Godard's letter also had none of the warmth of a proposed reunion. Instead, it was a provocation, even an insult: Truffaut is "a liar," Godard wrote: "because the shot of you and of Jacqueline Bisset the other night chez Francis [a restaurant] is not in your film, and one wonders why the director is the only one who doesn't fuck in *Day for Night.*" Godard then describes the counter-film that he had in mind:

> At the moment I am in the process of shooting a thing called *A Simple Film*, it shows in a simple way (in your way, Verneuil's, Chabrol's, etc.) the other people who make movies, and how these "others" do it. How your intern dials the phone, how the guy from Eclair carries bags, how the old man from Publidecor paints the ass [in the ad] for [*Last*] *Tango* [on a billboard], how Rassam's receptionist dials numbers, how Malle's accountant lines up the numbers, and each time, we compare the sound and the image, the sound of the messenger and the sound of Deneuve that he carries [when he transports a film], Léaud's numbers for his linked images, and the welfare numbers of the unpaid intern, the sexual output of the old man from Publidecor and that of Brando, the accountant's daily budget and that of *La Grosse Bouffe* [by director Marco Ferreri], etc.

Godard complained that money "reserved" for him went into big-budget films by Truffaut, Malle, Ferreri, Rassam, and others, and thus asked Truffaut to enter into coproduction with him ("The film costs about $40,000 and is produced by Anouchka and TVAB Films (my company with Gorin). Can you enter into coproduction for $20,000? for $10,000?[6] Given *Day for Night*, you should help me, so that viewers don't think that films are only made your way." Godard offered in exchange his own rights in *La Chinoise*, *Le Gai Savoir*, and *Masculine Feminine*, and concluded, "If you want to talk it over, fine."

Truffaut's twenty-page answer, accusatory and rebarbative, was filled with large, scratchily formed handwriting, as if it had been put together in great haste. It began:

> Jean-Luc.
>
> So as not to oblige you to read this disagreeable letter to the end, I begin with the essential: I will not enter into coproduction in your film.
>
> Second, I am returning your letter to Jean-Pierre Léaud: I have read it and

find it disgusting. It is because of this that I feel that the time has come to tell you, at length, that in my view you behave like a shit.

Godard's letter for Léaud had been enclosed in an unsealed envelope. It was also a request for money, and this, in particular, outraged Truffaut, who considered it indecent for Godard to ask a poorer, younger man for help, particularly one who had both worked for Godard and greatly admired him. It is unclear what prevented Godard from contacting Léaud directly, though the association of the actor with Truffaut was incontrovertible and significant.

Truffaut admitted, in his angry letter, to retaining some vestigial affection for Godard; he had stayed in his office one Saturday several years earlier to hear a new radio interview with Godard, and he brought up a few fond moments from their earlier days ("I've never forgotten how you used to get rid of centimes by slipping them down the backs of chairs in cafés"). Despite what he called Godard's "posturing," Truffaut thought that he had genuinely "changed quite a bit" recently, and confessed that had it not been for the enclosed note to Léaud, he would have been inclined to welcome the letter.

Instead, Truffaut dredged up a litany of accusations, professional and personal, that had been silently brewing for years. He repeatedly called Godard a "shit"; he brought up offhanded remarks from long ago that had stung him as well as charges of attempted seductions by Godard from more than a decade earlier—of bit player Liliane David from *Breathless* and of Catherine Ribeiro from *Les Carabiniers* ("I am enumerating all this to remind you not to forget anything in your truthful film about cinema and sex"). He reproached Godard for not showing up at film festivals he had promised to attend ("you don't go, to surprise people, to astonish them, like Sinatra, like Brando, you're nothing but a piece of shit on a pedestal"), for calling the producer Pierre Braunberger a "dirty Jew," for leaving crew members feeling useless on the set when Godard ran off without shooting, for having given the instructions for Molotov cocktails in *Wind from the East*, for chickening out of selling *La Cause du peuple* when there was danger of arrest.

In the letter, Truffaut reproached Godard not for his politics but for the behavior that went with it: "Anyone who has a different opinion from yours is a creep, even if the opinion you hold in June is not the same one you held in April. In 1973, your prestige is intact, which is to say, when you walk into an office, everyone studies your face to see if you are in a good mood."

Truffaut criticized what he saw as Godard's political publicity-seeking: "You have never succeeded in loving anyone or in helping anyone," he charged, "other than by shoving a few banknotes at them," whereas he himself, he asserted, helped people in need by offering private assistance rather than public agitations ("Between your interest in the masses and your own narcissism there's no room for anything or anyone else"). Truffaut cited numerous instances where he had come to Godard's aid, even without Godard's knowledge, as when the writer Alberto Moravia wanted Truffaut to take over as the director of *Contempt*. Truffaut called Godard "both jealous and envious" of him, despite his own desire "to remain friends." He reproached Godard for the 1968 letter in which Godard wrote demanding money due from the production of *Two or Three Things,* and concluded, "In any case, we no longer agree about anything." Truffaut said he had taken Godard at his word and had closed the book on him ("I've felt nothing but contempt for you ever since.")

Yet Truffaut admitted that he remained interested: "For a while, following May 68, no more was heard of you or else it was all very mysterious: it seems he's working in a factory, he's formed a group, etc., and then, one Saturday, there's an announcement that you're going to speak on the radio with Monod. I stay in the office to listen to it, in a sense just to know what you've been doing; your voice trembles, you seem very nervous, you declare that you're going to make a film called *La Mort de mon frère*" (The Death of My Brother). Truffaut then lambasts Godard as a "poseur" and a "phony" for mentioning this humanistic project, which he had no intention of making.

Truffaut also offered an unsparing critique of *Tout va bien,* which he compared to *Breathless* and found "disheartened and cautious." He closed with a pointedly chosen quote to criticize Godard's politicized work with the Dziga Vertov Group. The line came from *The Diary of a Country Priest,* the novel by Georges Bernanos and the film by Robert Bresson: "If, like you, I had forsaken the vows of my ordination, I would rather it had been for the love of a woman than for what you call your intellectual development."[7]

What Truffaut failed to notice about Godard's letter was that in an oblique and backhanded way, Godard was crediting him with having found a fruitful subject in *Day for Night*—a film contrasting the private lives and public image of people in the film industry—and was in effect proposing to do with it what he had done fourteen years earlier with Truffaut's sketch for *Breathless*: to use its naturalistic drama as a framework for his own preoccupations.

Just as Godard appeared, haltingly but determinedly, to be returning to the cinema and to himself, he was also attempting to return—with an aggressive pride as if concealing shame and penitence—to Truffaut. Despite his financial demands and his peremptory, insulting tone, what Godard seems to have wanted was simply "to talk it over." The clearest sign of his intentions was found not in the letter but outside it, on the back of the envelope, which Godard marked with a return address of subtle tenderness: "Sender: a former admirer of J. Daniel-Norman."[8] Jacques Daniel-Norman was a popular

French director of the 1940s and 1950s whose films Truffaut and Godard had often seen together.[9] When Godard reminisced in *Cahiers* several years earlier about his New Wave youth, he called it "the period when François loved the films of Jacques Daniel-Norman." In a preface to the published screenplay of Truffaut's *The Soft Skin*, Godard had mentioned their adolescent passion for the actress Tilda Thamar in *The Red Angel*, from 1948, directed by Daniel-Norman. The director's name was a sort of code between the two men, signifying the first years of their friendship, and in 1973, Godard used it to send his letter. The message conveyed the code, but Truffaut had become immune to it.

Although Godard had sought to talk with Truffaut, his effort at communication did not signal a desire to resume his old place in the French film industry or among his peers of the New Wave. He had left the New Wave, had gotten out of the film industry that he and his associates had so defiantly entered, and had now also left the ideological enclosure for which he forsook the cinema. He was not about to go back; he was going still further ahead, working in new collaboration with Anne-Marie Miéville. However, he thought that he could learn from Truffaut—not necessarily about how to direct, but about how to produce. Truffaut had kept his production company, Les Films du Carrosse, afloat since the late 1950s, even through hard times, and had just made a film, *Day for Night*, in which he attempted something that Godard had in mind to do (even if Godard would do it differently): a film about himself and his work as a filmmaker.

Stymied by Truffaut's response, Godard nonetheless kept the dialogue going (his side of it, at least)—through sniping in public. Although the angry exchange of letters was at the time unknown to the world (it was first published in 1988, in a volume of Truffaut's correspondence), Godard put his criticisms of Truffaut's filmmaking on the record at every chance he got. Truffaut, for his part, kept his views to himself, until he made use of an interview in *Cahiers du cinéma* in 1980—his first there since 1967—to vent publicly about Godard: "Even at the time of the New Wave, friendship with him was a one-way street . . . One had to help him out all the time, to do him a favor and wait for a low blow in return."

In 1980, Godard invited Truffaut (along with Chabrol and Rivette) to join him in a roundtable discussion on the occasion of their new works; Truffaut refused, writing Godard another angry, derisive letter in which he again brought up Godard's slur against Braunberger and declared that Godard should next make a film called "A Shit Is a Shit."[10] The two men crossed paths in New York, but Truffaut refused to shake Godard's hand. Yet until the end of his life, in 1984, Truffaut collected press clips about any project of Godard's (albeit highlighting the mean remarks made about their old cohorts). Godard, for his part, kept the tacit dialogue going in the way that, then as always, meant the most to him—in his films. Truffaut became, in his absence, as crucial a reference for Godard as he had been when the two were close, in the early 1960s.

TRUFFAUT WAS RIGHT that Godard had changed greatly; indeed, Godard had changed even more than Truffaut believed. Video technology, and the new methods it suggested, were now at the heart of Godard's campaign to re-approach the cinema; in fact, for the moment, the accumulation of new equipment took priority over the actual creation of films or videos with it. But Godard had had little experience with equipment; he had not gone to film school, he had not come up through the ranks of technicians, and, as his machinery grew far more complex than consumer electronics, it began to outstrip his ability to handle it. He needed to study; he needed to practice; he needed lessons.

In mid-1973, Godard attended a meeting of Marxist-Leninist film technicians on the Île de la Cité in Paris. After the meeting ended, he talked to a younger man from Grenoble, Jean-Pierre Beauviala, about his attempts at "kinéscopage," the transfer of images from videotape to film. He asked Beauviala to come up to his studio on the rue Rochechouart to lend him a hand.

Beauviala was—and still is—something of a cinematic utopian. In the wake of 1968, he planned to make a film about street life in Grenoble (which was being menaced, he thought, by monumental modernization). To film with direct sound in the street, he wanted a 16mm movie camera and a professional-quality tape recorder that would be synchronized without a connecting cable running between them. No such equipment existed, so Beauviala set out to invent it. He did so, with great success. In 1971, Beauviala formed his own company, called Aäton,[11] to produce the camera, and installed the company in a Grenoble storefront.

After meeting Beauviala, Godard remained in contact with him, learned of his camera project, and took an interest in it. Godard asked Beauviala to move to Paris; Beauviala refused. The next logical step was for Godard to follow him to Grenoble. This suited Godard in several ways. To film himself and the life of people in and around the cinema and television, Godard needed to hear again the sound of his own voice, to recover his own identity. He needed a quiet place away from the clamor of protest, away from the closed circuit of sympathizers and allies, away from the hum of intellectual currents and those who plugged into them. Godard needed to leave Paris, the capital of ideology. Anne-Marie Miéville also wanted to leave Paris to be closer to her family in Switzerland, so they departed for Grenoble in late 1974, taking with them the equipment they had acquired.[12]

For Godard, leaving Paris also meant turning his back on the capital of the French film industry. Godard had traveled to Cuba, England, Czechoslovakia, Quebec, the United States, and the Middle East, but each of these other places was, in its own way, the capital of something—of revolution, of rock, of "revisionism," of populism, of empire, of resistance. In going to Grenoble, he was moving to the capital of nothing.

But since his motorcycle accident, Godard had become agoraphobic and easily panicked: he had limited tolerance for contact with others. The move was as much the refuge of a convalescent as a withdrawal from the turbulence of ideological exhortation. This exile was a sign of political remorse, a search for personal understanding, far from the city's stimulations and currents and trends. With regard to the cinema, Godard described his move to Grenoble as "an auto-expatriation"[13]; during his time there, he deliberately ignored contemporary films, except when he actively dismissed them. He later described that time as "coming attractions"[14] for his next change of venue, of cinema, and of life—his move to Switzerland in 1977—and even recalled his years in Grenoble as "nothing."[15]

However, his activities there were of far greater importance than he allowed. Godard was putting into practice the video techniques and methods that would inform his work in the future. There he learned to make films in a newly collaborative way, and to integrate behind-the-camera social relationships even more openly into the film's substance. There he began to make images in a daily notebook-like process, working like a writer or an artist in his own studio, and joined that process to the compositional demands of a feature film. Most importantly, he established the groundwork for a colossal history of the cinema which would become both the pathway that led him back to the center of the French film industry and the great obsession of his later years. No matter how far Godard went from the movie business, he never abandoned the cinema. Whether from the ideological enclosure of post-1968 Paris or his physical and mental recuperation in the provincial isolation of Grenoble, he worked with an undiminished fervor and achieved ever-more-copious results. But by exploring the history of cinema—the intellectual cornerstone of his identity—with a newfound depth, he would effect both an artistic and a personal renewal. And by the time Godard did make his return to the film industry, it was with a more developed sense of craft, a replenished and novel idea of film form, and a reinvigorated personal commitment to the medium. The preceding disjunctive years had led so decisively to his return that they seem to have followed a plausible, purposeful plan.

ALTHOUGH BEAUVIALA HAD refused Godard's invitation to move to Paris, he was delighted for Godard to join him in Grenoble. He offered Godard and Miéville his own apartment in an old building in the center of town, around the corner from the workshop of his company, Aäton, in exchange for use of Godard's apartment in Paris. But Miéville refused Beauviala's home, calling it "dirty," and she and Godard rented a recently built apartment outside the city limits, in the Olympic Village (which had been constructed to house athletes when the Winter Olympics were played there in 1968).[16] Godard also rented a storefront that would serve as an office and a studio, at 2 rue de Belgrade, just across the street from the river's south bank. Further down the street, Godard also rented a garage in which he installed his bulkier equipment.

The first project Godard planned there was a film about Aäton itself, which he intended to call *L'Instant fatal* (The Fatal Instant). He was interested in filming the moment of industrial creation, the moment at which an idea becomes a material reality. Aäton was to be the model for Godard and Miéville's new company, Sonimage (Sound Image, or His/Her Image); Beauviala was in business to make money, but to do so by producing a highly technical product (in Aäton's case, cameras; in Sonimage's, films) to serve an aesthetic end.[17] But just as Godard began to prepare the shoot, Aäton lost its two main clients, the BBC and Swedish television, and was at risk of bankruptcy. There was little patience in the desperate, panicked workshop for Godard's inquisitive presence, and he was quickly forced to abandon the idea.

At the same time, Godard and Miéville had been spending long hours in the editing room watching the abandoned footage from the Middle East that he had shot with Gorin. They tried to figure out what to do with it. The first thing they needed was a good translation of the recorded Arabic discussions. The former translators, Palestinians living in Paris, had refused to translate literally what was being said, reducing the exchanges to generic sloganeering. When Godard and Miéville brought in a United Nations translator, they were shocked to discover that the Palestinian fighters who had been filmed in the heated wake of failed battle were talking about their inability to resist the superior Israeli forces and accusing their officers of sending them to their doom in hopeless combat.

As he and Miéville worked on the footage, Godard was contacted by Nourdine Saïl, a journalist from a Moroccan newspaper, *El-Moudjahid*, to whom he granted, on April 5, the only interview he would give in 1974, and with whom he discussed at length his return to the long-dormant project. Speaking with Saïl, Godard criticized the cinema of pure militant exhortation that he and Gorin had set out to make, and suggested that the film he and Miéville were making was to be a self-critique: "All we want to say about Palestine, four years later, is that we didn't look at these shots. We didn't listen to them." He blamed himself and Gorin for having attempted to make a film that was not about what the Palestinians were in fact saying and doing, but about what he and Gorin had wanted to say and to do (as was of course apparent from their storyboard and script). Godard and Miéville took a problem of principle underlying the shoot—the idea that French people in France wanted to make a film in the Middle East about Palestinians, which would then be shown in France—as the subject for their film. They called it *Ici et ailleurs* (Here and Elsewhere).

They organized *Ici et ailleurs* around the "and" of the film's title, the thing that mediates between France and Palestine, between French people and Palestinians. Godard and Miéville considered that mediating thing, that medium, to be the cinema; but in their film, they suggest that the relevant medium for ordinary French people was not cinema but television.

The Palestinian footage—of guerrillas training and talking strategy in the brush, speechmaking, chanting, a little girl's furious declamation of a poem by Mahmoud Darwish, children in military formation learning martial arts, gunmen firing rounds at unseen targets—is revolutionary boilerplate, heavy with the weight of obligation, and is also aesthetically meager, as if filmed without enthusiasm. Godard suggests as much on the sound track of *Ici et ailleurs*.

He and Miéville added to the material an array of supplemental 16mm footage, largely of three sorts. One was the "here"—a French family (a mother, a father, and their two young daughters), filmed from the point of view of the television set on which they view the kind of images from "there" that Godard and Gorin had brought back from the Middle East; another was symbolic material, including wooden letters spelling out the "ET" of the title and extras holding photographs up to a video camera; the third was analytical—a videotaped series of photographs from newspapers and magazines, which Godard then deconstructed with such editing effects as superimpositions, wipes, fades, and text graphics.

The resulting video collages reveal Godard's point of view on the media politics of the Palestinian struggle. Through these video techniques he expresses the film's principal historical idea: that, in a relay from Lenin to Hitler to Israel to Palestine, each element is derived from that which preceded it. Thus Hitler is a reaction to communism, Israel a result of the Holocaust, and Palestinian sufferings a rebounded result of the Holocaust. The principle is illustrated by the pairing of images of dead Palestinian fighters with a sound track of a cantorial voice intoning the words "Auschwitz, Maidanek, Treblinka." (Indeed, Godard told an audience in 1977 that he and Miéville "use the sound of Hitler" in *Ici et ailleurs* "to show what's going on in Israel.")[18]

In his interview with Nourdine Saïl, Godard maintained that he could no longer "sit at a table and say, 'The Vietnamese were right to do this, they did what had to be done. The Palestinians are right.'" Yet in the film that is exactly what Godard and Miéville did. The self-critical motive that Godard asserted as the basis for *Ici et ailleurs* nonetheless resulted in a work of doctrinaire exhortation. *Ici et ailleurs*, despite its critique of the original footage for its dubious relation to its target audience, expresses the same unquestioned advocacy of the Palestinian cause and hostility to Israel that motivated the original shoot. For instance, in voice-over, Miéville criticizes the Palestinian guerrillas who took hostage and killed eleven Israeli athletes at the 1972 Olympics in Munich—not for their actions but for their tactics: rather than demanding the release of Palestinian prisoners held by Israel, she said, they should have demanded that the television networks broadcasting the games transmit during each championship finale an image of Black September, and should have killed the hostages only if that demand was not met. Her 1974 words were no less tendentious than Godard and Gorin's 1970 images.

Nonetheless, *Ici et ailleurs* departs significantly from the original hortatory venture in one significant regard: it dramatizes the personal relationship on the basis of which the film was made, that of Godard and Miéville. The film is a sharp and political lovers' dialogue: Godard speaks at length on the sound track to apologize for having shot the original footage in the Middle East without regard to the reality of the participants and the audience, and Miéville intervenes midway through to debate with him both his earlier approach to the subject and his attempt to make good on it now. In this regard, the film is something of a return for Godard, in its explicit enactment of his off-camera relationship with Miéville. And, unlike his films of the 1960s, here both he and his partner speak their own words in their own voices rather than through the symbolic mediation of fictional characters.

As an awkward but inventive cinematic expression of philosophical and historical ideas, the film explores fundamental problems of television, of the way things are watched at home, and of the social and psychological significance of the family context. In general, it establishes the notion of the medium as mediating between two distant and remote realities. In *Ici et ailleurs*, Godard and Miéville were aware that they were working for television (even if television had not commissioned the film)—that television had taken over for the cinema as the principal mode of audiovisual communication and for the press as the prime source of information. As a first document of Godard and Miéville speaking together in the first person and representing their personal and artistic relationship, the film is an important step in

Godard's artistic reconstruction. As a political film, it is a work of propaganda, not inquiry.

ICI ET AILLEURS was, however, shown in cinemas. Its first screenings, at small festivals, were unexceptional, but its commercial release, on September 15, 1976, was eventful. A militant Zionist group called Talion (An Eye for an Eye) planted a bomb in one of the two Paris theaters where it was showing. The bomb did not go off, but the theater owner canceled the booking. The other theater where it was being shown belonged to Godard's former assistant, Marin Karmitz, who had become a distributor and exhibitor of political films. Karmitz steadfastly kept the film playing and organized a public discussion with Godard on September 20. On the evening of October 12, a showing was interrupted by members of the same Zionist group, who broke a window, released mice in the theater, and left behind a gas canister with Hebrew printing on it.[19] Again, Karmitz resolutely kept the film on view.

Louis Marcorelles, writing in Le Monde, praised Godard's "very dense reflection on the play of information, on the faking of information, on the lies of information," but avoided mention of the film's political content. In Libération, Ali Akika, who had codirected a film about the Palestinian cause, enthusiastically endorsed Godard and Miéville's views. Writing in Le Quotidien de Paris, Henry Chapier called the film a "cry of hatred" and a moral atrocity: "an attack by bomb is the same as an attack by film."[20]

Godard, for his part, expressed indignation and a remarkable egotism as he denied that the film could have been considered in any way harmful to Israel and the well-being of Jews. He failed to see the content and the significance of the images that he had filmed: his immersion in video equipment and theory had brought him unwittingly back to the sort of unworldly aestheticism with which he had charged himself and the rest of the New Wave. Now, Godard was in thrall not to the myths and forms of the American cinema, but to advanced video editing techniques. Although he believed that he was learning to think in images rather than in words, his theoretical eye did not see clearly the actual content of these images. This failure would recur in several of the works that followed in the mid-1970s, and would be most apparent in works where his use of video technology was at its most sophisticated.

IN NOVEMBER 1974, the producer Georges de Beauregard went to Grenoble to visit Godard and satisfy his curiosity about the filmmaker's life there. Beauregard had produced few films since 1968. Now he suggested to Godard the one project that seemed to be surefire for both of them: a remake of Breathless (though not with the same actors). Godard accepted. As with the original, Beauregard raised the money from the distributor René Pignières (who had financed the original *Breathless*) and Pignières's associate, Gérard Beytout. Predictably, however, Godard had no actual interest in filming a remake.

In March 1975, Godard said as much when he broke his silence in the French press to discuss this new venture: "To the contrary of what has been announced, the film will not be called *Breathless Number Two* but rather *Number Two (Breathless)*. I am not doing a remake, but I am posing a reflection on the basis of *Breathless*."[21] There were only two things he was sure would remain from the earlier film: Beauregard's participation and the budget (600,000 francs; $120,000). But the budget was not exactly the same: "The originality consists in saying that the cost of living has increased by a factor of four, but we are making a film with . . . the same budget." In other words, due to inflation, the budget was worth only one-fourth of its 1959 value—and this fact was what Godard called the actual subject of the film.

Godard spent much of the money on the purchase of additional equipment, and put some of it into the completion of *Ici et ailleurs*. It was only after finishing *Ici et ailleurs*, in the spring of 1975, that Godard and Miéville turned to *Numéro Deux* and fulfilled the commission.

Numéro Deux is a film, but only in the most literal sense: almost every frame of the movie has one or more video monitors in it. The movie begins and ends in a video studio in which Godard is working alone; the rest of the "action" takes place on two monitors in a dark space. Thus the viewer is watching a movie in which he is either watching television, or watching television being made. As in *Ici et ailleurs*, this is the real story of *Numéro Deux*: a family awaits the images of a remake of *Breathless*, while a director is commissioned to provide them. Between the opening and closing shots, of Godard himself, a representative family—two parents, two grandparents, two young children—appears, for the most part, on other video monitors. In an interview at the time of its release, Godard said that it was an "ethnological film" that could be called "The Sexual Economy of the Inhabitants of Lower Grenoble."[22]

Three generations of inhabitants of "Lower Grenoble"—a young couple, the man working in a modest job in a local television studio, the woman home with the two young children (a boy and a girl), one grandmother, and one grandfather—express, in long monologues and dialogue, their frustrations with each other and with society. The couple's sexual problems are related to their problems with work or the lack of it; the grandfather is lost in tall political tales of erstwhile activism, the grandmother weighed down by her years of domestic suffering.

And where is *Breathless* in all this? The two children sit at the breakfast table and recite uncomprehendingly to each other a hackneyed pulp fiction story of violence and betrayal. Thus Godard disposes of his decades of devotion to Hollywood genres. Godard would no longer tell the story of *Breathless,* but he tried to tell the story of where such a story comes from. *Numéro Deux* would be the first in a new kind of film about the "sexual economy" within the family, about the stories that are told to compensate for unexpressed needs: in this meta-fiction Godard would attempt to conceive—and to tell—the kind of story that would reflect the undistorted reality of those unsatisfied desires.

Desire is presented literally in *Numéro Deux,* which is sexually explicit in word and in image. The old man delivers his monologue—about his adventures as a veteran Communist international militant—while seated at a table, naked from the waist down ("Instead of watching movies, I watch my prick"). The old woman recites a text from Germaine Greer about the servitude of women as she, naked, washes herself in a bathtub. The daughter takes a bath with her mother and asks about her own body, "Is that the hole where memory comes out?" The mother is seen naked while doing housework, speaking about weeks of constipation, explaining it as an inability to express herself verbally: "It comes in one end but does not go out the other."

The film's sexual images are, to say the least, unarousing, but they are disturbingly manipulative, particularly in their use of children, as with the girl in the bath, her genitals exposed. Elsewhere, the two children are brought into their parents' bedroom to observe a lesson in love, as the naked parents fondle each other and describe their genitals as lips and a mouth that engage in a conversation of love. To the extent that the film comprises a story, one of its turns involves the little girl accidentally espying her parents having anal sex, an image of which is shown, with the little girl superimposed in close-up. The implications of bringing two such images together in a single frame go past the trauma of the primal scene; the sequence becomes almost a surrealist vision of dangerous sexual suggestiveness.

Miéville is credited as the film's producer, but Godard considered the title intentionally ambiguous. Godard explained in an interview, "This film was produced by Anne-Marie and by me. She worked on it as a technician, but she also 'produced' the film, in the sense of 'producing crude oil.' "[23] In other words, Godard drew much of the dialogue from his life with Miéville. He further explained that Miéville was "at the same time the earth and an oil well" and that he himself was "a refinery." But in *Numéro Deux,* Godard did not do much refining: he presents his raw material in a fairly raw and undeveloped way. *Numéro Deux* has the unpleasant aspect of a medical document, a revelation of sordid woes that reduced such extraordinary people as himself and Miéville to clinical cases.

But the extreme exposure is precisely the point of the film. In *Numéro Deux,* Godard took the first step toward realizing the idea behind the unmade *Moi je,* a film about himself: *Numéro Deux* begins and ends with Godard on camera. At the beginning, in a single eight-minute-long fixed-frame shot, he stands in shadows next to his "kinescoping" equipment and beside a large TV screen on which his own talking head is transmitted live on closed-circuit video, and delivers a monologue about how he came to make the film—specifically, about Beauregard's visit ("He saw all these machines and then he said, 'Look, Johnny,[24] you've got to make something with all these machines' ").

At the end of *Numéro Deux* Godard is seated at a console of video equipment, not speaking but listening to the voice of the woman in the film, whose dialogue was largely "produced" by Miéville, as she discusses her burgeoning desire to become an artist too: "To be able to do that, and to want that ability." He is listening to the future filmmaker whose untapped creativity is the new source of Godard's own reawakening artistry. Though Godard had previously taken dialogue from Karina and Wiazemsky as he now took it from Miéville, the latter's main contribution was something new: her presence in and around the shoot, her input in the editing room—in general, the fact that she talked cinema with Godard, indeed was willing to criticize his cinematic practice. And, though *Numéro Deux* heralded Godard's newfound cinematic ambition, his actual appearance in the film conveyed not triumph or breakthrough, but anxiety, self-doubt, and reticence.

GODARD KNEW THAT his fame was the commodity that would enable him to continue to make films, but he did not want to make the films that would nourish his fame. Still, he was deeply adept at the process he and Beauregard were setting in motion, and he participated in it as far as necessary: despite his harsh indictment of the information industries, Godard once again played them like a virtuoso.

Even prior to its release, *Numéro Deux* gained Godard a great deal of publicity in the general press, the first he had received since the release in 1972 of *Tout va bien.* Godard complained to an interviewer that his move to Grenoble had deepened his isolation: "Leaving Paris at a given moment consists of burying yourself, of no longer seeing anyone, because no one wants to see you anymore."[25] And yet, when he went to the Cannes Film Festival the following week, he found that everyone wanted to see him.

A press conference held at the Carlton Hotel was packed with journalists, and Godard expressed his surprise that they should bother to hear him plug the film ("I'm just here to do my job"). But he made use of this bully pulpit to explain his new methods of production, which, he claimed, distinguished him from every other filmmaker in the business. In the process, he slammed his former colleagues in the New Wave:

> I am amazed that people who lack ideas for new films (including some old friends like Truffaut, Rivette, who don't have any more ideas than the guys whom they denounced twenty years ago), continue to adhere to the one and self-same system of filmmaking, which is easy to describe: a sum of so many million, multiplied by so many weeks, multiplied by a certain number of people.[26]

Godard considered himself, like them, to be inescapably trapped in old ways of thinking about movies, but described his studio as a way of "seeing [his] prison." He summed up his new way of working: "I'm remaking my life from zero."[27] It was quite a performance; a journalist from *Libération* called the press conference "the best film of the festival."[28]

When the film was released in September 1975, Godard went to Paris to do a series of interviews. Asked in *Le Monde* about his return, Godard answered, "I was never away." In *Le Nouvel Observateur*, Jean-Louis Bory declared, "Finally Godard returns. Better: he is reborn."[29] The talk of a return was wishful thinking. And the film was not the commercial success that it would take to relaunch him in the industry.

GODARD DID NOT wait for the verdict on *Numéro Deux*. As he had done at the time of *Breathless* (with *Le Petit Soldat*), he got Beauregard to finance a second film before the first was completed. The initial point of departure of this new film, *Comment ça va*, was another tawdry affair, about a woman on a Club-Med-like vacation who has an affair with one of the employees: "The two, who are fucking together, are fucked by the system which draws them toward each other . . ."[30] The project was impractical—it demanded travel—but the idea behind it proved fertile.

Comment ça va would, on the basis of that outline, borrow from *Ici et ailleurs* the problem of a trip to "elsewhere" that served only to reproduce the discontents of "here." But the outline was revised later in 1975 to address the question of journalism, particularly the journalism in which Godard was most implicated, the new daily newspaper *Libération*.

Godard knew many of the editors and writers who worked at *Libération*, and they, in turn, took an interest in his new ventures. On September 12, days before the release of *Numéro Deux*, several writers from the paper received Godard in their offices for an interview that would be published along with coverage of the film. In the interview, Godard suggested that *Libération* itself might be the subject of his next film: "My next film will be called *Comment ça va*. It's the story of a guy who gets hired as a compositor and who says to an editor: 'You are dictating too fast for my hands.' That's all. *'How's it going?'* [Comment ça va?] 'Well, it's going too fast!' "³¹

Several days later, Godard picked up *Libération* and saw a photograph that accompanied a report by the editor-in-chief, Serge July, on a protest by leftist Portuguese soldiers against Portugal's new, non-Communist government.³² He wrote a letter to the editor in which he criticized as uninformative the coupling of the photo and the text. He thought that the photograph of the Portuguese conflict should have been paired with another photograph, one that showed a young worker confronting a policeman during a strike at the Joint Français gasket company in Saint-Brieuc, Brittany, in 1972: "And I would have tried to 'speak' starting out from this montage, that is, to start out listening to these two comrade photos taken two years apart."³³ He did not say "photos of comrades" but "comrade photos": it was the images themselves that were the militant subjects he wanted to "listen to."

Godard seemed to be planning a kind of *Ici et ailleurs* analysis of leftist militancy, in which two images that were distant in time and space informed and interrogated each other. Soon thereafter, he went to the offices of *Libération* to film the hands of typists and compositors at their keyboards. Then he returned to Grenoble and made *Comment ça va,* which would have as its centerpiece the analysis, through video superimposition, of the two photographs from Portugal and Saint-Brieuc—the journalistic work that he charged *Libération* with not having undertaken.

Comment ça va can be summarized as a film about the writing of a letter about a series of meetings regarding a failed attempt to make a videotape about the workings of a left-wing newspaper. And yet, these nested forms of communication are coiled tightly with stories that build and resolve their tension as surely as a political thriller. Like *Le Petit Soldat* in relation to *Breathless,* *Comment ça va* is more sincere, more naturalistic, and more classical than *Numéro Deux.*

From the very first scene, *Comment ça va* exudes nostalgia for the possibility of filming a fictional love story. In a moody, romantic shot from inside a car, a young man with long hair and a gentle voice drives and talks with an unseen young woman; the city at night is seen through the rainstreaked windshield, as a gruff male voice-over describes a letter "from one guy to another guy; and this guy is the other guy's father." The young man and young woman hesitantly discuss the beginning of their relationship. The voice-over, which turns out to be that of the young man's father, mentions a woman he met, Odette,³⁴ at the Paris newspaper where he works. The father says that his

relations with Odette, who has proposed videotaping the newspaper's operations, are "relations of production," but the two have argued.

The son has taken up factory work in the provinces, and Godard's images of the younger man's life in a smaller city suggest the glimmer of newfound aesthetic ambition, a yearning for beauty. He films the young man at
a café in a wistful image in which a glass of beer and a notebook are seen
on the table in the foreground while through the window behind it, street
life unfolds. A recurring shot of the young man walking in the street at twilight has a nostalgic, melodramatic aura. Yet politics are never far from intimate relations: as he and his girlfriend sit in their kitchen and listen to
radio reports on strikes in Portugal and the death of the Spanish dictator
Franco (November 20, 1975), they quarrel, exactly as do the father and
Odette. Ultimately the newspaper union's central committee rejects
Odette's videotape project, and the father-journalist never sees Odette
again.

Godard does not appear in the film (though his voice is briefly heard on
the sound track). Odette, whose voice and silhouette dominate the film but
whose face is never shown, is played by Anne-Marie Miéville.

If *Comment ça va* suggested Godard's desire to return to the cinema, it
was not the only return in the air at the time. In 1976, critics Serge Daney
and Serge Toubiana took control of *Cahiers du cinéma,* purged it of the most
rigid ideologues of its Maoist years, and adopted a catholic, open-minded
view of the cinema, based on a revived but wary cinephilia, in an effort to articulate an auteurism that would be politically aware and self-questioning.
They saw Godard's new films as a touchstone of their critical line.[35] In May
1976 they sought to put this new line into action by presenting a weeklong
series of films at a Paris theater, the Artistic-Voltaire, under the magazine's
aegis. The centerpiece was Godard and Miéville's three recent films. *Comment ça va*, labeled as a premiere, and with Godard in attendance, played to
a full house. Godard used the occasion to lament his solitude in Grenoble
and admitted that he came to the screening "to get a sense of the boys and
girls who would want to see [his] films."[36] Two weeks later, "the film was
shown at a sidebar to the Cannes festival. It was eventually released in May
1978. In *Cahiers,* Alain Bergala recognized the film as "narration rediscovered," as Godard's incipient return to fiction.[37]

THE DECEIT OF *Numéro Deux*—the failure to deliver anything that resembled a remake of *Breathless*—had left Godard stranded in the industry. After
Comment ça va, Beauregard's support came to an end, and other movie producers (at least, those with the money to finance a film) kept their distance.

Godard announced plans to make a film in Mexico, financed locally, in which he would revive his idea about tourism, specifically, the story of a French travel agent who has a relationship with a Mexican woman.[38] However, before he could go to Mexico, French television stepped in.

Manette Bertin, an executive at the newly formed INA (Institut National de l'Audiovisuel), went to see *Numéro Deux* and thought that such a film was well-suited to television. (The film's explicit sexual elements were no impediment to her appreciation of its aesthetic originality.) In late 1975, INA, courtesy of Bertin, made a small financial contribution to *Ici et ailleurs* and *Comment ça va.* Then Bertin approached the office's new general director, Michel Roux, about coproducing a film by Godard; Roux was enthusiastic.

Soon thereafter, in early 1976, Bertin and Roux went to Grenoble to visit Godard and see his studio. They signed with Sonimage for a series of four one-hour television essays to be made over a two-year span. Two of these projects were derived from notions left over from the unmade *Moi je:* one offered Godard's speculations regarding retroviruses as the cause of cancer, and another concerned the history of cinema. But in June, Bertin and Roux turned to him with another more pressing commission.

The third, noncommercial French channel, FR3, had six 100-minute Sunday night prime-time slots to fill in late July and August and an unfulfilled quota of programs from INA. Bertin asked Godard to make a feature-length film to fill one of those slots. He responded with a paradox:

> A program of one hour forty in three months, we can't do it, it usually takes us a year to do one hour. On the other hand, six times one hour forty—that makes almost ten hours[39]—that isn't the same thing. If one considers ten hours altogether, one has the time to think, one has the time to start over, to correct oneself, not to be panicked.[40]

Bertin told Godard, "You're crazy! You'll never finish, because even a half of that is already a lot." But unable to find another filmmaker who was willing to make even one program on such short notice, she gave his and Miéville's Sonimage the full commission. When Bertin shared this news over lunch with Roux's retired predecessor, Pierre Schaeffer—whose cameras Godard had "liberated" in May 1968—he told her, "My dear girl, you are screwed."[41]

Godard's initial idea was to do six live 100-minute interviews and discussions, but he was told that his programs had to be recorded. So he divided each time slot into two parts, the first "a little more composed," the second "simply someone talking," and he called the whole series simply *Six fois deux*

(Six Times Two).[42] Godard had set up his video studio to permit him to work copiously and rapidly with a small crew, and *Six fois deux* gave him the chance to prove it. The budget was low, less than half the typical cost of a television documentary of that length, and his crew featured only three people—the cameraman William Lubtchansky, the camera assistant Dominique Chapuis, and the production assistant Philippe Rony.

Miéville and Godard were cocredited as the project's directors. Miéville's role was as Godard's constant interlocutor. Because of her lack of technical knowledge and on-set experience, she exerted her creative authority largely through her relations with him. She was aware of how she was likely to be perceived as a result: as an "unknown cow" benefiting from her association with "a famous filmmaker," similar to the way that Gorin had been misperceived; and she defined her role in the production as "trying to collide gently with people from behind the images."[43]

Godard described his partnership with Miéville as "one and a half because we are only half of three."[44] He was in search of the third party who would, so to speak, complete the artistic duo. Jean-Pierre Beauviala's involvement was proving less useful than he had hoped. The distance between his workshop and Godard's office was small, but sufficient to get in the way of spontaneous and continuous collaboration.

Throughout the making of *Six fois deux,* Godard had felt the need for a full-time technical collaborator. As with *Numéro Deux,* there was no sound recordist, and Godard recorded the sound himself. But Godard also sought a manual mastery over his equipment that surpassed his actual competence, as the cameraman William Lubtchansky recalled:

> When there was a problem with a cable, it was he who soldered it. And he didn't know how to solder.... He tried to use tape, which doesn't hold, so he tried to use solder, which does. But his didn't hold, he redid them, he spent all his time soldering, the cables were covered with solder.[45]

Godard had hoped that Lubtchansky would move to Grenoble to work constantly with him. Lubtchansky had been Willy Kurant's assistant on *Masculine Feminine;* he had helped Godard film his *Ciné-tracts* and *Un Film comme les autres* in 1968; and when Godard was setting up his studio in Paris, Lubtchansky responded to his call and gave him a lesson in lighting. Lubtchansky subsequently shot *Numéro Deux* and the supplementary footage for *Ici et ailleurs.* Godard admired Lubtchansky's inventiveness: for *Six fois deux,* Lubtchansky got a small van and turned it into a "camera car" that carried videotape recorders and an independent electrical system—a miniature and homemade version of the sort of mobile video studio used by television stations. Lubtchansky, however, was unwilling to relocate, so his visits to Godard in Grenoble were limited to two weeks at a time.

THE SHOWS WERE to air every Sunday from July 25 to August 29, and Godard worked on a last-minute schedule, with episodes being shot three weeks or less before their broadcast. This put terrible pressure on Godard, who was, throughout the series, in a bitter mood.

He was both liberated and exasperated by the video equipment that he used. It was relatively light and portable, but its simplicity entailed other inconveniences. Editing was very difficult, because it had to be done strictly sequentially: to change an image at the beginning of a tape meant to begin editing the entire tape from scratch. The demands of the process forced him to work rapidly and decisively. Also, his equipment was not considered broadcast-quality, and Godard spent time and energy debating with technicians from the television station over their smoothing-out of his visual concepts in the transfer of the footage to a professional-format master tape.

Also, Godard, who was still convalescent, hesitated to film out of doors and was still withdrawn in company—odd and trying conditions under which to produce interviews. Indeed, like almost all the scenes in Godard's three films of 1975, most of *Six fois deux* was shot indoors, and for exterior shots where he was not interviewing, Godard often stayed behind and sent his crew out alone ("Go film the river," Lubtchansky recalled him saying). These difficulties almost derailed the first day of shooting: Godard had posted a notice at a state employment agency seeking unemployed people willing to be interviewed for a small fee, but on the day of the shoot, he tried to avoid meeting them. He didn't want to come to the office that day, telling Lubtchansky, "I have nothing to say to them." Lubtchansky recalled, "At the moment of the shoot, he disappeared," and Godard had to be persuaded to come in and do the interviews.[46]

Each of the six two-part programs of *Six fois deux* is based on a different theme—unemployment, montage, journalism, photography, childhood, love. These ideas, taken together, would dominate Godard's work for decades to come in their relevance to his own situation as a filmmaker, specifically regarding the possibility of joining work and love. The first part of each pair treats the subject in the form of a video essay, and the second reflects the idea in interviews with unemployed people, a farmer, an amateur filmmaker, a mathematician, a war photographer, a journalist, several women, two psychiatric patients, and Godard himself. The series would also involve theoretical issues regarding communication—and would draw the two problems, of communication and personal relations, together, as Godard had anticipated doing in the unrealized *Moi je*.

One long interview features "Marcel," an elderly watchmaker in a small Swiss workshop and an amateur filmmaker who records only scenes of nature. Godard shows Marcel's naive but majestic images of mountains and rivers, and when he asks the craftsman why he doesn't add a commentary ("to record what is going on inside you"), Marcel answers, "The images show what is going on inside me." Within several years, Godard too would start to film nature, and would do so more insistently, and with more originality, in order to show what was going on inside himself. Marcel opened up to Godard the possibilities of filming nature spontaneously and simply, yet grandly. The amateur movies of Marcel Reymond would prove to be a more direct inspiration to Godard's later work than even Bresson or Rossellini had been to his earlier films.

One installment features Godard at a café in discussion with a man identified only as "Paulo" (and whom Godard later identified as Dominique Chapuis, the camera assistant); only their hands, cigarettes, and espresso cups on a café table are visible. The exchange begins with word games, as a picture of a bed appears on-screen. Godard identifies it as a bed, while Paulo calls it a table: "It's a special kind of a table, it's an editing table [une table de montage]": he explains that "montage" means "mounting," that editing a film is like a man mounting a woman, and likens the creation of a film to the creation of a family, the making of a film to the making of a child.

The series is full of children, including a little red-haired child whom Godard films at length in a park, and a photograph that appears on the cover of a manual for pregnant women, an image that recurs passingly in many of the episodes but which becomes here the object of a lengthy meditation: a woman and a baby, face to face but upside-down, the woman kissing the baby's head and the baby reaching up to the mother's. With a device called the Telestrator, permitting Godard to "write" with a magnetic pen directly onto the video image, he sketches on the picture to analyze the mother-child relationship: in voice-over, he likens their contours to the banks of the river, and explains, "What makes possible the love between a man and a woman, in this case an adult woman and a baby, is work." Godard's use of a popular journalistic image to exemplify the bond of mother and child suggested precisely where he thought that breakdowns in personal understanding derive from: the failure to understand the codes embedded in messages.

The series is also full of women, and one woman in particular—Anne-Marie Miéville, who watches Godard film other women in an episode called "Nanas" (Chicks) and then intervenes to criticize his method: "One hour of interview after centuries of silence is either too much or too little." (The interview was originally to have been with Miéville herself, who instead preferred to be heard from behind the scenes.) In another episode, Godard writes, directly onto the screen, a love letter to Miéville, in the form of a man in prison writing to his beloved explaining that the thoughts of her and of their daughter make him able to endure his imprisonment and withstand his jailers' blows.

When an elderly woman complains in an interview that her great-granddaughter rarely visits her, Godard asks her why she thinks that the child is hers, and why the child is different from a neighbor's child. "Are they a part of you?" he asks. The woman answers that they are, in a way, a part of her, and changes the subject. But the question lingers, especially for Godard, who was living with Anne-Marie Miéville and her daughter from a prior relationship.

In Godard's view, being with Miéville put him into a relationship not with one woman but with two. As he explained to Manette Bertin, in his life with Miéville and her daughter, "There are two couples": Miéville and Godard, and Miéville and her daughter.[47] The issue would come up, explicitly, in the strangest of the episodes, 5A, an interview with René Thom, the mathematician who invented "catastrophe theory," the theory of discontinuities. Godard challenges the mathematician's notions by questioning him about the making of children, considered numerically. Thom calls the creation of children the conversion of two into one; Godard thinks it should be called the turning of one into two. An especially disturbing sequence at the program's conclusion suggests the emotional ambiguities that such a redoubled relationship entailed for him. It features pictures of a child—Miéville's daughter, who was approximately ten years old—growing up, from infancy to pre-adolescence. The girl is shown next to Miéville in a photograph, and then in a long clip of a fuzzy black-and-white video, taken in a bare modern apartment: the prepubescent girl, naked except for toe shoes, does an antic and exaggerated ballet to orchestral music coming from a tinny cassette or record player. The dance is as odd, as innocent, and as funny as the filming of it is unseemly. The sequence appears to be a home video by Godard or Miéville. The strange decision to film the girl this way is surpassed by the indiscretion of Godard and Miéville's inclusion of it in a television program. It is hard to watch, and it is astonishing that it was shown on French television. (It aired at 8:30 PM on August 22, 1976.) And it was all the more astonishing that nobody cared.

MANETTE BERTIN AND officials at INA and FR3 were pleased with *Six fois deux*. The series gained the new station a great deal of publicity and respect. Despite the bewilderment of the popular press—and a viewership so low that it did not register with the French rating service—the programs received extraordinary coverage. *Le Monde* published a long interview with Godard; *Le Nouvel Observateur* devoted a full page to a journalist's account of a day of videotaping that he had witnessed;[48] *Cahiers du cinéma* interviewed the philosopher Gilles Deleuze for his views on the series; *Libération* featured news of the programs on its front page and ran full-page spreads with interviews with Godard, a text by Miéville, and discussions of the broadcasts each week for the duration of the series.

And yet, Godard sensed that the series was just a beginning, indeed hardly even a beginning, telling an interviewer, "These films, they're from before the work, not after. The elements of the salad, not the salad . . . It isn't even a sketch. It's the eraser, the paper to make the sketch."[49] He had produced tools and material—but for what? The series ordered by INA marked a short break in a long commissionless stretch. The brief flurry of attention and activity provided by the release of *Ici et ailleurs* in mid-September that year was a further distraction from Godard's isolation. But the absence of work was not a crisis that he alone endured.

In the mid-1970s, the French film industry seemed to go out of its way to leave its premier artists out in the cold. The disappointment of the left after the 1974 presidential elections, which put conservative Valéry Giscard d'Estaing into power, was magnified by France's overall mood at the time, famously described as "morose."[50] The oil crisis of 1973–1974 had struck France's prosperity at the root; the "trente glorieuses"—the "thirty glorious years" of postwar economic growth—had come to an end, unemployment was dramatically on the rise, and France turned not only sour but vindictive. Those in power sought excuses and turned to culture wars; they offered nostalgia for the pre-1968 verities, viewed the activists of 1968 as enemies, and put the New Wave high on the list of cultural scapegoats. The centralized film industry, which derived financing from the government and depended on the good graces of state administrators, choked off funding to the New Wave and its acolytes.

Despite the success of *Day for Night*, Truffaut had to finance his films mainly with American money. Rohmer made only one film between 1972 and 1979 (and with German financing); Rivette filmed on minuscule budgets cobbled together with great difficulty. Younger directors who were close to and inspired by the New Wave, such as Philippe Garrel and Jean Eustache, had it even worse, and found the doors of the industry closed to them.

As for Godard, he had sought to make himself a forgotten man, and he now had to work to be remembered. The industry distrusted and repudiated him; producers seemed to fear that Godard was a political propagandist, so now he was worse than forgotten; he was rejected. He did, however, have one self-provided advantage that his former associates from *Cahiers* lacked: because he had video equipment, he could always produce, edit, and show some new work, even without funding. But he was not a part of the cinema, and his work had little to do with the cinema, whether its current state or its history, of which he had absorbed such vast amounts.

Television, this time the second channel, Antenne 2, tossed Godard a small gift: he was asked to make a short film—in effect, a music video *avant la lettre*—of a song, "Faut pas rêver" (Mustn't Dream) by the pop singer Patrick Juvet, to be broadcast on January 1, 1977. Godard tested the station's new political independence: he gave them a three-minute-long shot of Miéville's now almost-adolescent daughter eating an apple at the kitchen table as her mother questions her off-camera about whether all of her things are packed for school. As the saccharine ballad plays in the background, electronic text crawls up a black screen: "When the left takes power, will television still have so little relation to people?"

But Godard was looking for something more substantial—and more lucrative—to do. He did not delude himself about the motive behind his next venture: it was commercial. Godard's idea was for a million-dollar cash cow: he would make a series of videotapes on the history of cinema that he would sell to American universities, where, as he had seen in his trips to American campuses in the late 1960s and early 1970s, cinema studies were growing and thriving. He intended to use videotape to combine his knowledge of the cinema with his vestiges of fame to derive a source of income. Yet for all the mercenary considerations, no product could have had a more personal origin: outer and inner necessity happily coincided in Godard's project. He had proposed a one-hour video on the history of cinema to the INA in 1976, but the program never got made. His plans were now far greater, more ambitious, and wider in scope than that one-hour commission. The project would unleash a terrific burst of mental energy, one from which Godard would continue to draw for decades.

AT CANNES IN 1975, Godard said, "The cinema can only interest us to the extent that we succeed in destroying it. Just as one splits an atom or a biologist opens a cell, in order to examine it."[51] He did not hesitate to share his jaundiced view with the living prophet of the history of the cinema, Henri Langlois. Discussing with him the future of the Cinémathèque, Godard suggested that Langlois sell off the entire collection and use the money to produce films, and that, if the collection should find no buyers, Langlois should just burn it all, so that the history of cinema, which had, in Godard's view, strayed so far off course due to the influences of commerce and politics, could start again. Langlois, who of course rejected this modest proposal, was nonetheless to be the heart, the engine, of Godard's new project concerning the history of cinema.

The plan was to analyze cinema and television by way of video, and in particular, by way of the video editing effects (such as the incrustation of one image in another) which he considered essential to the project. The intended result was ten hourlong videocassettes, "Studies in art, economics, technics [*sic*], people," to be sold at a price of "between 250 and 500 dollars" per cassette, a figure arrived at on the basis of Godard's calculation that each episode would require a budget of between sixty thousand and one hundred thousand dollars.

Godard stated that the project would take two years to complete. The first year's cassettes would be devoted to the silent cinema, the second year's to sound, with both series featuring, in order, the cinema of the United States, Europe, Russia, and "others," with the fifth and tenth "both a sum up [*sic*] and an introduction." "Silent U.S.A." would concern Griffith's discovery of the close-up. In "Talking U.S.A." a picture of Franklin D. Roosevelt would indicate "a new deal between image and sound." In "Silent Russia," Godard said, "Eisenstein discovers the angle." "Talking Europe" would show a shot of Hitler with "Albert Speer, director of photography" and another of Marlene Dietrich with "Joseph von Sternberg, director of photography." Speaking with a West German journalist, he used the "Talking Europe" episode to explain the allusive, associative method he had in mind:

[Dietrich] was the *femme fatale*. Hitler was an *homme fatal*. If there was a *femme fatale*, there was also the German people who had the same fatality. Thus one could say, that's how they used lighting. This story is fairly curious. For if one looks deeper into it, one sees that Sternberg, Marlene, like all German intellectuals, fled to America . . . Sternberg, who was Jewish, met another Jew, who was American. Of European descent. Ben Hecht, a playwright. And it was they who made the prototype for the American crime film. First Sternberg with *Underworld* and *The Docks of New York*. Then *Scarface*, and then Sternberg's other films. It was German-American Jews who after the existence of Nazism came up with the prototype of gangster films.[52]

Just as Godard had relied on Miéville as the "raw material" for *Numéro Deux*, he intended to turn to Langlois to supply the raw material for *Histoire(s) du cinéma et de la télévision*. Langlois would both gush ideas that Godard could refine, and supply films that Godard would excerpt in the series.

But circumstances intervened to reorient the project and to hasten it into reality.

In late 1976, Godard accepted an invitation from Serge Losique, a professor of French literature at Sir George Williams University in Montreal, to spend a week there in March 1977 and present a retrospective of his films. Losique had known Langlois since the 1950s, and when Langlois was fired from the Cinémathèque in 1968, Losique immediately invited him to come to Montreal to teach cinema history. Though Langlois was restored to the Cinémathèque, he honored his commitment, flying to Montreal twice a month in the academic years 1968–1969, 1969–1970, and 1970–1971, but the travel put a strain on his already poor health, and, on his doctors' advice, he gave up his Montreal classes.[53]

When Godard approached Langlois for help regarding the set of video courses, Langlois contacted Losique about resuming his classes in the 1977–1978 academic year. Langlois's lecture-discussion would be videotaped and Godard would use the tapes as a prime source for the series. Losique accepted the proposal, but on January 12, 1977, Langlois died, at age 62.

When Losique came to Paris shortly thereafter, Godard offered to take over Langlois's classes. Losique enthusiastically agreed, but Godard put a peculiar spin on their agreement: having proposed to teach in Langlois's place, Godard not only wanted the classes to be videotaped for use in the *Histoire(s)*, but told Losique that the videotapes themselves would be the raison d'être of the journeys. Instead of being a visiting professor who would arrange to have his lectures taped for his own use, Godard wanted Losique to sign on as "coproducer" of the videotapes themselves. The difference was partly psychological, partly economic, in that Losique would not pay Godard a fee, but would deposit money into the Sonimage account toward production costs. In any case, their agreement launched the series with a momentum that carried it through to completion—twenty years later.

GODARD'S VISIT, from March 9 to 13, 1977, was a major event in Montreal. One journalist noted, "Never has a press conference been so widely covered. There was a little bit of everything, television, radio, the press naturally, and even several Anglophones. Everyone was there."[54] But more important, the weeklong film retrospective was a major event in Godard's life and work: in the course of five days, Godard watched, contemplated, and discussed his own personal *histoire(s) du cinéma*.

Godard also spent five days with Losique's students, answering their questions about his films. These conferences were videotaped, showing

Godard sitting on the floor of the low stage alongside Losique and responding with some hesitation and diffidence. He reviewed his career, expressing relief that his films after *Breathless* were financial failures, which, he said, kept him from becoming what he thought Truffaut had become: someone who "talks to nobody, except to Polanski."[55] He mentioned having gone to see *Rocky,* and said that he preferred such "honestly commercial" films to films that are "dishonest in their principle, like films by Polanski or Altman, for example, which seem to me to pretend to be intellectual when it's pure merchandise." He took stock of his years of absorption in his video studio, and enumerated its virtues, including the ability to have the equipment at home for immediate and daily use ("It's like a blank page for the writer, he says, 'I have to fill it' ").[56]

Above all, he talked of his own films, of his experiences and intentions while making them, of his methods and the reasons behind them. For the first time since he had begun to conceive his project regarding the history of cinema—indeed, since he had left the cinema in 1967—Godard approached the subject not merely as a form of propaganda or as a diseased cell, but as an aspect of himself, and considered himself as an aspect of that history. This is what Losique had prompted: until that point, Godard's view of the history of cinema had been one thing and his own films another; from now on, they would be one—and it was in Montreal again, several months later, that Godard said as much.

As a favor to Losique, Godard agreed to go to Montreal in the summer of 1977 to help inaugurate the first World Film Festival, which Losique founded. During the festival, Godard spoke with a journalist about the decisive shift in his conception of the *Histoire(s)* project:

> I will soon be fifty years old, and it's the moment when in general people write their memoirs, recount what they've done. But rather than write those memoirs, rather than saying where I come from and how I happened to have followed this trajectory in this profession of mine, which is the cinema; instead of doing that, I would like to tell my stories, a little like tales of the cinema. And that's what I propose to do.[57]

The project had decisively shifted from the standpoint of a quasi-detached professor to that of an autobiographer in relation to his cinematic life, and had reawakened Godard's desire to consider his work, and his life, in relation to the classical cinema. It was now called *Histoire(s) du cinéma;* television had dropped out of it.

Nonetheless, while at the festival, Godard spoke with Losique about postponing his cinema history course at the university until 1978 because of

a new project for which there was a deadline. The reason for the postponement came up in this exchange with a student who asked Godard what he
planned to do next.

"A TV series for Antenne 2, *Le Tour de France,* based on the book."

"You're going to do what?"

"We're going to do *Le Tour de la France.*"

"Bicycles?"

Not bicycles.

Camille Virolleaud
(Jean-Luc Godard and Anne-Marie Miéville. "France / tour / détour / deux / enfants,"
1978. Courtesy of Electronic Arts Intermix [EAI], New York)

eighteen

FRANCE TOUR DÉTOUR DEUX ENFANTS, ET AL., 1978–1979

"Men's problems"

*L*E *TOUR DE LA FRANCE AVEC DEUX ENFANTS* (ALL AROUND France with Two Children), by G. Bruno (a pseudonym for Madame Augustine Tuillerie or Thuillerie), a children's book, was first published in 1877. Written in the wake of the Franco-Prussian War, it depicts two young orphan brothers leaving German-occupied Alsace and traveling through France in search of their uncle, who will assure their French citizenship. The book, with its patriotic affirmation of civic virtues, was an instant national success and remained familiar school and family fare well into the twentieth century. Marcel Jullian, the chief executive of the second television channel, Antenne 2, wanted to commission an adaptation of the book for broadcast in the Christmas season of 1977, but the directors he approached rejected the subject as too old-fashioned. Jullian, who was impressed by *Six fois deux,* was considering asking Godard to do something for the station. When Manette Bertin of INA suggested that Antenne 2 commission a fiction film from Godard, Jullian responded, "As long as it's *Le Tour de la France avec deux enfants.*"[1]

The commission was an important one: loosely modeled on the book's sections (each corresponding to a region of France that the boys visit), the adaptation was to comprise twelve broadcasts of twenty-six minutes each, which would be shown each evening during the 1977 Christmas season at 7:30 PM—early enough for children to watch it. Unlike *Six fois deux,* which Godard had to get on the air in a hurry, he had nine months of lead time for *Le Tour de la France*—not a lot for other filmmakers but plenty for him.

Toward the end of the school year, in the spring of 1977, Godard asked his assistant, Philippe Rony, who lived in Paris, to look for children to play the lead roles in the series. Rather than placing an ad in newspapers or going to casting agents, Rony and his girlfriend at the time, the theater actress Betty Berr, videotaped approximately fifteen children from their neighborhood. In July, after reviewing the tapes, Godard selected two, Camille Virolleaud and Arnaud Martin, who were neighbors and schoolmates. Godard's choice of a boy and a girl, both nine years old, represented a departure from the children of G. Bruno's novel, who were two brothers of fourteen and seven, but this would prove to be the least of his departures from the book. Yet Godard was slow in getting to work; having so much time before him, he pursued the project only intermittently, and instead attempted to launch his *Histoire(s) du cinéma* and other projects, in a newfound flurry of activity that was intended—in contrast to this new television commission—to bring him back, or closer, to the cinema.

GODARD'S FIRST UNDERTAKING, however, was to leave Grenoble. He and Miéville had chosen the town as a compromise between Paris and Switzerland, but the place itself left Godard cold: "In Grenoble, there is a center. It's hell. There are little cameras everywhere, there are accordion players everywhere, in all the stores. All this in concrete, in plastic, in chrome. This is the France of today. This is what they call neighborhood renewal."[2] Grenoble had a local cable TV station, but Godard claimed to have nothing to do with it: "Since I have no product to bring them, I don't want to see them. In any case I live in a neighborhood where you can't get cable."[3]

In mid-1977, Godard and Miéville moved to the town of Rolle, Switzerland, midway between Geneva and Lausanne, at the foot of a sweeping hillside that runs down to the strand of the lake. The small town boasts a medieval castle on the east shore and farms on the west hills, and it is only a short walk from one to the other. Rolle, which is more like a village than a city, is a few miles from Godard's childhood home, and a brief drive from Geneva and Lausanne, the two cities of his youth. Godard and Miéville had been contemplating the change for a while. For both of them, it was a sort of homecoming, but they also had a practical motive: Miéville's daughter, Anne, had been accepted to a nearby "collège," or middle school.

The relocation also had consequences for Godard's cinematic reconstruction: he left behind his video and 16mm film equipment for university film students in Grenoble, because he intended to reconstruct a more advanced studio in Geneva.[4] He was thinking of a return to the professional cinema, and began to make contact with new notables of the French film business. He told Marin Karmitz that he now wanted to make a film within the norms of the industry. Karmitz, whose production of *Padre Padrone,* directed by Paolo and Vittorio Taviani, won the grand prize at the Cannes festival in May 1977, suggested that Godard write a script treatment and submit it to the CNC for an advance on receipts. Godard, for the time being, demurred.

Godard also met with a new star of the French cinema, Gérard Depardieu, who had been discovered by Marguerite Duras to play a door-to-door salesman in her *Nathalie Granger* in 1972, rose to prominence in Bertrand Blier's *Les Valseuses* (*Going Places*) in 1974, and had recently appeared in Duras's *Le Camion* (*The Truck*) alongside the writer herself. Depardieu told a journalist of two projects he discussed with Godard: *On va voir* (We'll See) and *Machin-Machine*,[5] a takeoff on the recent French hit film *Cousin Cousine:* "It's Machin who meets Machine, there is a male connection and a female connection, as in *Numéro Deux*."[6]

Meanwhile, in mid-1977, Godard pursued yet another thread of opportunity, which suggests how frenetically he was seeking to relaunch himself. The German independent filmmaker Hellmuth Costard, derisively called by a German critic "the little Godard," decided to make a film about his own attempt to find funding to construct a system of four synchronized Super-8 cameras. At the same time, the Cultural Committee for the city of Hamburg, of which Costard was a member, invited Godard to present a retrospective of his films. Godard was willing to attend the Hamburg retrospective on the condition that the local television station finance a film for him: either an episode of *Histoire(s) du cinéma* or something to be called *Is It Possible to Make a Film Today in Germany?* Costard decided to record Godard's negotiations with the Hamburg officials and to include the footage in his own film. In September, Godard went to Hamburg to meet with the Cultural Committee, which turned down his request. Costard's film, *Der kleine Godard* (*The Little Godard*), resulted; Godard's did not, and the time was lost.

On October 26, 1977, Bertin traveled to Rolle to hear of his plans for *Le Tour de la France avec deux enfants*. Upon her arrival, Godard insisted that she first watch a short video that Miéville had made, in which a young orphaned girl talks about her mother. Telling Bertin, "She must be independent in relation to me," Godard tried—unsuccessfully—to elicit a television commission for Miéville, for fifty episodes of twenty-six minutes each.[7]

Then Godard turned to the matter at hand. He told Bertin that he had personal reasons for having accepted the commission: because he wanted to have his own child with Miéville,[8] and because of his relationship with the young Anne, he wanted to make the television series in the hope that it would help him to understand children better.

Although the commission was for a dramatic film based on a fictional period piece, Godard explained that the series—which he renamed *France tour détour deux enfants* (France Tour Detour Two Children)—would feature only "a moment of fiction, which would deal with the father and the mother" (another departure from the orphaned brothers of the book). He told Bertin that it would mostly be a documentary about the two children, who would not be traveling around France, but rather, living in one particular place, namely, Paris. Bertin warned Godard, "Bear in mind that Jullian expects a work of fiction," and Godard responded, "I had thought about doing a *Tour de la France* but with Daniel Cohn-Bendit and Arlette Laguiller"—a left-wing activist—and added, "You can tell him that it was you who stopped me."

Godard gave Bertin a poster with a grid that represented the shooting script. He made a postcard-sized version of the same grid and gave it to his crew (Lubtchansky, Chapuis, and Rony), and it was the only "script" that they received. It showed sketches of a girl and a boy in Godard's own hand, with days of the week and brief notes: "power (snack, music)"; "reality (dinner + family)"; "violence (punishment)"; "light (street)." The peculiar implications of this work plan soon became clear: although Godard was making a documentary about two children, he already had a clear idea of what his film would document. He had not chosen child actors, but children with whom he felt he could speak. But this was not quite clear to the children themselves, who had been recruited to appear in a "film"; they were expecting a conventional movie in which they would play roles. As the girl in the film, Camille Virolleaud, later recalled, she anticipated impersonating a character and performing a text and action provided by Godard. On the first night of shooting, in the fall of 1977, she discovered otherwise; she found herself to be taking part in a documentary about herself, but one in which Godard swung her reality around to match his preconceptions.

> Godard asked me, "What do you do before going to bed?" I said, "Nothing, I go to bed." He persisted; he asked me questions—"and before that?" "And before that?" I avoided saying, "I change out of my clothes," because I didn't want him to film me doing it; he must have understood and that's why he was questioning me. He wanted to have access to my intimacy. I didn't even have the word to say it.
>
> My mother said to me, "You aren't usually shy." True, but first of all, not in front of the camera, it was as if all of France was going to see me; and also, Mr. Godard is not part of the family.
>
> When I resisted doing it [undressing], my mother said that I was supposed to do what Mr. Godard asked me to do. And as for him, he blackmailed me— he said that, if I didn't do what he asked, he was going to stop the shoot.[9]

Camille's mother, Martine Virolleaud, confirmed that she indeed urged Camille to comply with Godard's direction.[10] Camille was horrified at having to undress on camera, but did so and put on her nightgown, as rapidly as possible.

After that initial trauma, Camille feared what might come next: "I was afraid that this was only the beginning, that he was going to ask me to do more and more unpleasant things." Thus many other activities related to the taping, which might under other circumstances have been fleetingly annoying or mildly embarrassing—such as a family dinner which Godard videotaped—became instead, for the nine-year-old girl, an ordeal. She was a documentary subject, but, as his gridlike chart had foretold, the reality of her life and her character was manipulated by Godard to fit into his script.

Shooting with Camille and Arnaud took place on Wednesdays (which in France, then as now, is a day off from school), on Saturdays (a half-day), and Sundays. Only three scenes were filmed in the Virolleaud household, where Godard told the family, "Above all, the shoot must not disturb your way of life; do everything as if we weren't here, or else the film won't be good."[11] But that was not, in fact, how the film was made.

Despite the documentary appearance of much of the children's action, much of it was carefully arranged. One scene filmed in school showed Camille's teacher keeping her late for the age-old punishment of copying a sentence fifty times ("I must not talk during class"). Godard had asked the teacher to give Camille this punishment, though the teacher affirmed that Camille had not done anything wrong and indeed had never been punished in school. Camille experienced her fictional punishment as real and undeserved, and later recalled: "I was ashamed to be shown as punished when I was not. He made me do it, it was not the truth, it was his truth, but in relation to me, it was a lie."

Outdoors, Godard instructed Camille to run through the street and to leap on a bench, run the length of it, and jump off—which she was not at all inclined to do, and did only reluctantly. He filmed her in her bedroom, listening to a record of classical music that he had chosen, though ordinarily, Camille never listened to classical music. He pulled her aside in the school's courtyard during recess and interviewed her when in fact she wanted to play with her friends. After the filming ended, she endured the taunts of classmates who wondered why she had been chosen and not they. In fact Camille did not at all feel chosen, she felt singled out, and would gladly have resumed her former unremarkable life.

The filmmaker who had never wanted to acknowledge the distinction between cinema and life, who denied any difference between an actor and a nonactor, unfairly effaced this distinction regarding children. Although Camille, like any actress, was paid, she did not appear in the guise of a fictional character. Although Godard had, in his fictional works, implicated his actors personally in the construction of their nominal characters, their fictional identities always gave them an out. Not only did Camille have no out; she had never wanted to be in.

GODARD'S MAIN ACTIVITY with the children was to question them, at length, in his own voice. Initially, as he had told Bertin, he had intended to create fictional scenes with a mother and a father, to be played by actors. But he decided to dispense with these scenes and instead hired the actors Betty Berr and Albert Dray to take on other fictional roles. At first, Dray was to be Godard's stand-in. On the first night that Godard wanted to interview Camille, the director put an earphone in Dray's ear and relayed the questions to him. The process, however, proved slow, and Godard took over the questioning himself.

Godard's intention was to speak to children about subjects not usually considered appropriate for them, in a way that was not condescending. As he admitted, he wanted to talk to them about the things that concerned him personally.

> G: The last time we talked about it, you said that when you get undressed, or
>   right before you undress, you often look at yourself in the mirror.
> C: Yes.
> G: And who did you see then?
> C: An image of me.
> G: Your image. And your image, is it you or someone else?
> C: It's me.
> G: And this "me" that you see, does it too have an existence?
> C: Yes, because I'm the one who is looking at it in the mirror.
> G: Yes, but the image, does it too have an existence?
> C: Yes.
> G: So it is as if you had two existences?
> C: Maybe.

Godard's approach did not work as intended. Though Camille started out voluble, she grew more and more inhibited as the filming went on, and finally she clammed up.

> At the beginning I was freer, I spoke more freely. In the French educational system, when one is asked a question in class there is just one right answer, and when Godard asked me questions, I looked for the right answer, I didn't want to make a mistake. But the questions he asked were often very complicated, very abstract, I didn't really understand them, so I tried to give the minimal responses where I was least at risk of making an error.

If the educational system was responsible for Camille's increasingly in-hibited responses, if the system had disciplined Camille into internalizing shame when punished even unjustly, if it compelled childhood into a regime of quasi-martial training—as Godard says over images of students marching during gym class—then, by capturing Camille's frustration and inhibition on videotape, he did render the effect of that miseducation visible on-screen. But Godard provoked this response by preventing her from speaking and be-having as she normally did. Although his unwillingness to approach the chil-dren on their own terms reeked of self-centeredness, there was a deeper theoretical and political principle at work. Godard treated the children like little adults because he considered them to be copies of adults (as he says to Arnaud in one scene where the boy is cranking out copies of an assignment on a mimeograph machine). His approach to the children in adult terms was his way of approaching, in microcosm, the world that is made by adults.

Christmas came and went, and the series was still being filmed. In Janu-ary, the shoot continued, in Rolle, with what Godard had called, for Bertin's benefit, the "moment of fiction," in which Betty Berr and Albert Dray play a pair of television commentators named Betty and Albert.

Throughout the series, the commentary spoken by Dray and Berr refers to "the monsters," the adults who do the things that constitute daily life and which, seen as regimentations imposed on the children, come off as mon-strous. Their recorded commentaries relate the life of the schoolchild to training for servitude in the military-industrial complex. As Camille leaves the teacher's desk and heads to her seat, Godard superimposes the word "vi-olence," then truncates it to "viol" (in French, "rape"). There follows news footage of tanks, gunships, and warplanes, and then, again with the word "violence," a line of students in gym class being ordered to march in step, as Dray's voice explains, "From birth, the monsters are taken in charge by mili-tary organizations in the aim of providing cheap and docile labor to the large industrial companies."

Godard and Miéville, who collaborated on much of the series, albeit largely behind the scenes, depict children in a state of class subjugation in a factory-like environment, and view homes as replicas of society's political maladies—women not paid for their housework, money matters kept con-cealed, cultural inadequacies resulting from noxiously deceptive television broadcasts, a stultifying ordinariness of routine that is the equivalent to col-laboration with tyranny. The conclusions that they draw from these analo-gies are disturbing. During a sequence showing rush-hour commuters in the underground passageway of a métro station while a busking cellist plays Bach, Betty accuses them of complicity in the making of a monstrous world.

In voice-over, she declares that terrorists are people who "would rather die standing up than live lying down," but advises them to change their methods: rather than kidnapping the famous, they should take ordinary people hostage "to make the people who believe in the goals agree to change the program." The image freezes on individual passersby as she asks: "Guilty or not?" Betty declares each person guilty: "of having slapped a child . . . of having refused to go out for a drink with friends . . . of not having complained about the low quality of sweaters or the price of medicine." Her suggestion is that the terrorist-kidnappers declare, "We'll kill them unless fifty thousand employees of Volkswagen give ten percent of their salary. If it's too much, they should ask for a raise. If they don't, he'll be executed and it will be your fault."

The advocacy of terrorism—such as Miéville had already undertaken in *Ici et ailleurs,* where she defended the methods of the Palestinian attackers at the 1972 Olympics in Munich but criticized their demands—takes off from the extreme means pursued by radical leftist groups in Europe at the time, after the mass mobilizations of 1968 failed to bring about revolutionary change. The rhetorical call to murder, however, was at odds with the contemplative tone of the images it accompanied. Godard's calm, even tender, images of daily reality belied the call—notably made in Betty's voice—for its destruction. Despite the vestiges of revolutionary cant, the sheer profusion of thought—in image and sound—in the six hours of *France tour détour* is exhilarating; the series conveys the impression of an artist emerging from a chrysalis of his own making. Godard was struggling to be able to represent and to create beauty without sacrificing his newfound powers of cinematic analysis. The music from Camille's record player, the Bach in the subway corridor, the Handel aria that accompanies the scene of a waitress in a café, suggested that he was, with the help of Miéville, coming back to himself and to what he loved.

FRANCE TOUR DÉTOUR is a vigorously political work that silently but constantly poses one fundamental question: what, then, is left of 1968?

The question is asked through the fictional use of one real name that dominates the series. Godard, who is questioning the children, is not called in the voice-over commentary by his actual name. He is called Robert Linhart, the most charismatic intellectual behind the revolution of 1968—and the one who, like Godard, fled (in his case, to a clinic) and returned, unbroken but more realistic.

In the wake of his personal debacle, Linhart, like many devoted Marxists of the time, became a factory worker to identify more closely with workers' struggles and to raise the workers' political consciousness. In the mid-1970s, he became a professor of economics and wrote a book that pertained to the cinema and contributed a crucial concept to *France tour détour*. This book, *Lénine, Les Paysans, Taylor* (Lenin, Peasants, Taylor), published in 1976, analyzes the rationalization of labor by the Soviet leadership. Its cover is a still from Dziga Vertov's 1930 film, *Enthusiasm*, and a key chapter relates Vertov's films to industrial modernization. In particular, Linhart emphasizes Vertov's efforts to use the movie camera "to decompose work into *simple elements.*" Taking Linhart at his word, Godard used new video technology to analyze the gestures of his subjects with a quasi-scientific precision. Moreover, in the role of Linhart, Godard provided both the visual study of action and the verbal commentary on it.

The footage of the children and of the action in Paris was filmed with Godard's new equipment, one of the first Betacam packages to come on the market. It featured a time code, which made it possible to capture and to manipulate individual frames of video. Godard used this device to break the action down via slow motion. He invented his own type of slow motion, repeating each image in freeze-frame a number of times, with the result being not a continuous flow but a sequence of staggered stop-action images. This breaking-up of the moving images into their constituent moments is the principal visual trope, and discovery, of the series. To distinguish it from ordinary slow motion, and to make sure that its significance was understood, Godard gave it a special name—borrowed from Linhart: "Slow motion is a falsely poetic movement; I chose the decomposition of movement."[12]

The series starts with Godard "decomposing" the first shot of the first episode: Camille getting undressed for bed. When Camille saw the scene in Paris, at the offices of INA, she was shocked at the exposure of her body, all the more so because what she had tried to do as quickly as she could was slowed down to play out on-screen at length. "I was terribly ashamed, I didn't want anyone to see it. When the film was shown on television, the next day in school the other children said that they had seen me on TV, and I said, 'That wasn't me.'" Her denial went even further: for more than two decades, she never spoke about the series with anybody, not even with her parents. In retrospect, she considers the effect of the film on her to have been "hyperviolent."

Is THE FILM's shock effect on Camille emblematic of what was left of 1968?

Camille said in jest that she considered herself to be a "soixante-huitarde," a veteran of '68, because that was the year she was born. This self-identification conveyed a truth that Camille perhaps did not intend. In *France tour détour*, Godard brought together those who made 1968 and those who were made by it—philosophically as much as biologically. He made clear that what was left of 1968 was not the expressly ideological side, but the desire to change personal relations and to reform the education of children in order to bring about a true revolution. But the liberating currents of 1968, which were reflected in the easing of laws regarding abortion and censorship, offered children a far more ambiguous legacy. Camille Virolleaud suggested that if, on the first evening of the shoot, Godard didn't hesitate to film her undressing and her mother didn't intervene to prevent him from doing so, it was perhaps due to the fact that at the time there was less inclination to hear the voice of the child in distress—precisely as a consequence of the permissive forces of 1968. As Virolleaud observed, "It was a time of liberation, of openness to sensuality, the rejection of inhibition."

But there was also something more aggressive and more troubling at work: an active, respected, and influential movement in favor of sexual relations between adults and children.

Le Grand Bazar, Daniel Cohn-Bendit's book of interviews concerning his course of action and thought after 1968, features a discussion of his work as a teacher at a nursery school in Germany in the early 1970s:

> It happened to me many times that certain children opened my fly and began to tickle me. I reacted differently according to the circumstances, but their desire posed a problem for me. I asked them: "Why don't you play together, why have you chosen me, and not the other children?" But if they insisted, I caressed them anyway. Then I was accused of "perversion."[13]

This passage, which elicited no particular attention in 1975, when the book was published (and sold well), was exhumed in 2001 in an attempt to embarrass Cohn-Bendit, and it worked. Though parents of children who had attended Cohn-Bendit's school immediately came to his defense, a media frenzy nonetheless ensued in France. Cohn-Bendit defended himself against the charges, claiming to have based his ostensible first-person account on the deeds of another teacher. He said, "Knowing what I now know about sexual abuse, I regret having written all that."[14] However, crucially, he added: "Without seeking to justify myself, it was the debate of the era." At the time of the book's publication, he explained, this passage "did not arouse any reaction,"[15] because "we thought that an anti-authoritarian education should permit a child to grow up without sexual 'forbiddens.' "[16]

In 1976, *Libération* published an article in defense of a confessed pedophile and in favor of "a society of tolerance which will recognize children's liberty to enjoy their bodies and adults' right to all differences." Alongside the article, the philosopher René Schérer (Eric Rohmer's brother) defended the "inalienable right" of children to have sexual relations. In 1977, the same journal published a petition seeking to lower to age thirteen the legal right to consent to sex with adults. Among the eighty petitioners were Sartre, Simone de Beauvoir, Louis Aragon, Roland Barthes, Gilles Deleuze, Félix Guattari, André Glucksmann, Dr. Bernard Kouchner, Philippe Sollers, and Jack Lang. At the time of the 2001 controversy, one of the signatories, the psychiatrist Bernard Muldworf, explained: "It would have seemed dishonest to me not to sign it because there were ideological stakes: to be on the side of the challengers rather than of the cops."[17] The writer Pascal Bruckner, also a signatory, described the mood of the times: "Every notion of authority was synonymous with abuse. Every allusion to rules, to regulations, to norms was intolerable."[18]

However, the intellectuals—who by and large signed petitions freely (Sollers noted that "there were so many petitions at that time that one didn't pay close attention to what they said")[19]—were mainly pro-pedophile in the same way that some among them had been pro-Maoist, advocates in theory of a perversion that they would not have put into practice. Yet their extreme and impractical positions nonetheless had psychological and aesthetic effects. In the name of ideology, Cohn-Bendit did not hesitate to depict himself (albeit fictitiously) as participating in sexual relations with children. Under the influence of the times, Godard, through his film, explored tense relationships of power with children, especially with Camille; and he implicated himself personally through images in a nexus of curiosity and anxiety that was, for him, as emotionally self-revealing as it was revealing of Camille's body. Godard did nothing physically inappropriate with Camille, but his representation of her, and his use of his directorial authority, were themselves powerful signifiers of the highly charged and hazardous emotional relationship between adults and young people, between parents and children, between fathers and daughters. This relationship had made an earlier appearance in Godard's work, in *Six fois deux,* and, because of his quasi-paternal relation to Miéville's daughter, Anne, it would remain in evidence for years to come.

The twelfth and last episode of *France tour détour* ends with a music video-like sequence of a song by Léo Ferré,[20] "Richard," about a man alone in a bar at night, one of many who are there, "near a pinball machine, simply with their men's problems, problems of melancholy." Godard filmed a single shot, for the length of the song, of a crowded bar at night and a lonely man, uneasy in a three-piece suit, at the center of it. It was as if Godard was saying that he, too, had his "men's problems," and the video series that the long musical take concluded had focused on one of them. This man's problem, and the real story of *France tour détour,* was that, in addition to the "two couples" in his home—Godard and Miéville, Anne and Miéville—he had the problem of the third couple, that of Godard and Anne, the daughter—which Godard did not hide under sentimentality but filmed as a nexus of power and desire, of inevitable intimacy and fear.

THE SERIES, WHICH was supposed to be shown during the 1977 Christmas season, was not completed until early spring 1978; but in January, Marcel Jullian was replaced as head of Antenne 2 by Maurice Ulrich, who had little interest in Godard or in the project. The new management required that the tapes be transferred and retransferred to so-called broadcast-quality tape, and used that technical issue as a pretext to avoid airing them. According to Manette Bertin of INA, the series was considered difficult, even impossible, to broadcast.[21]

Instead, the series premiered at the Rotterdam Film Festival in January 1979 and then ran for a week at the Action-République movie theater in Paris in April. (Alain Bergala, a critic at *Cahiers* who helped organize the screenings, later recalled that Godard "came every night to the République by taxi, gave us the Beta copy of the episode to be shown that night, and picked up the one from the preceding night. He never came into the theater.")[22] Then, on May 3, they were shown at the Pompidou Center in Paris in a single six-hour session, followed by a public discussion on "seduction, utilization, manipulation of the child." The series attracted enthusiastic notice in *Cahiers du cinéma, Le Nouvel Observateur,* and *Le Monde,* where the critic Louis Marcorelles reported that "Godard accomplishes for the art of video the same return to the origins, to Lumière, to Méliès, as he had done twenty years earlier with his first great film."[23] Television broadcast waited until 1980.

Godard proposed many other projects to INA—including eight hours of *Histoire(s) du cinéma* and nine 26-minute episodes called *Work,* to feature Robert Linhart himself—but none of them was produced. Manette Bertin, of INA, explained why: "After *France tour détour deux enfants* . . . no one wanted to finance him."[24] Upon completing *France tour détour,* Godard went to Montreal to fulfill his commitment to Serge Losique. He had explained to Bertin that he simply had nothing better to do: at least, in going to Montreal, he would be given "$50,000 overall and a first-class ticket once a month, and what's more, it will yield videos for the series on the history of cinema."[25]

What Godard wanted most of all was a return to the cinema itself. He told Bertin that he would "no longer blend finished work and essay," as he had done in his three films of the mid-1970s, *Ici et ailleurs, Numéro Deux,* and *Comment ça va;* he wanted, "with video, to make a film, for the cinema." His history project in Montreal would provide a bridge to this goal.

ALTHOUGH THE ostensible point of Godard's visits to Montreal was to generate videocassettes of his discussions about the history of cinema, he now proposed a crucial addendum: to show his own films alongside other films, classic or recent, that related to them. Linking the history of cinema to his own cinema, he discussed the cinematic past in terms of himself and his work, a process that had begun the previous year in Montreal. This decisive shift was the spark for his return to feature films.

Godard traveled to Montreal seven times between April and October 1978. Losique presented the talks in a lecture hall seating 840 people, and later recalled that there were never fewer than eight hundred students on hand.[26] As moderator of the question-and-answer sessions, Losique asked many of the questions himself, occasionally opening the floor to the audience.

On April 14, Godard began the first session, concerning *Breathless,* with an admission of his nervousness. He likened the occasion to "a psychoanalysis of myself and of the place where I'm at in the cinema." He showed Otto Preminger's *Fallen Angel* along with *Breathless,* and then described the experience: "It was as if I were flipping through a family album and felt a little embarrassed, especially in front of other people."

Godard was usually voluble in interviews, but now the remarks that followed Losique's questions were positively eruptive. He did not shy away from discussing his own past; when the conversation on *Le Petit Soldat* turned to the overall problem of history in cinema, he unhesitatingly brought up his family's own political history as wartime "collaborators" and described his grandfather as "ferociously not even anti-Zionist, he was anti-Jew; whereas I am anti-Zionist, he was anti-Semitic."[27] In relation to *Vivre sa vie,* he declared,

> I was above all preoccupied by my problems with women, or with one woman, or with two women, or with three women . . . Or my problems in going to see prostitutes, or . . . And at times the shame that I could have had, given my past or my moralism or things like that . . . I found the cinema useful since one could, say, expose it without embarrassment.[28]

Godard asserted that the problem with the French New Wave, as well as with his own earlier films, was the inability to present personal problems with even greater frankness; he charged that he and his cohorts had made their films "too much . . . in relation to the history of cinema" and that each of them had "completely mixed up his subjectivity of personal desires coming from [his] own story, trying to situate it solely in relation to the history of cinema."[29] He complained that "if one wants to tell stories, there is only the American way to tell them, at least in the cinema,"[30] yet said that he was going to try, anyway, to go back to making films with stories.

THE FIRST NEW project that he developed under the influence of the Montreal courses was similarly self-psychoanalytical. At an airport bookshop in 1978, Godard found the newly published *Bugsy Siegel*, by the investigative journalist Henry Sergg. The book's subtitle: *The Crime Syndicate in Las Vegas and Hollywood.*

Godard brought the story to the attention of Georges de Beauregard, who had recently restored his finances with the success in 1977 of *Le Crabe tambour (The Drummer Crab)*, directed by Pierre Schoendoerffer. Beauregard seemed to bear no grudge following *Numéro deux,* since *Le Cinéma français* reported that he would produce Godard's film, *Bugsy Siegel,* starring Vittorio Gassman. The report suggested Godard's more elaborate plans: he had "expressed his intention of integrating into his tale some excerpts of films from the great era of Hollywood."[31] A project on the connections of Hollywood and Las Vegas opened the doors to a meditation on the history of the American cinema. Yet Godard knew that he would have to generate some kind of story to be able to make a full-length film, and he resorted to a traditional solution: he called a screenwriter.

Jean-Claude Carrière, screenwriter for Luis Buñuel, Louis Malle, Milos Forman, and Patrice Chéreau, among many others,[32] knew Godard since the early 1960s, and met him for lunch. Godard explained his project of making a film "about Hollywood and the Mafia."[33] Carrière and Godard bounced ideas back and forth and, in mid-1978, Godard explained that the fruit of their collaboration would not be "a traditional fiction film" but "a documented film."

> Against a backdrop that will include certain facts illustrated by the high era of Hollywood, I will inscribe a fairly simple story: a critic (Gassman) and his ex-wife (Charlotte Rampling) will investigate the disappearance of a star. A certain Johnny G. was killed when he was about to make a film about Bugsy. Coincidence or a crime by the Mafia?

The journalist to whom Godard spoke added this summary:

> Jean-Luc Godard is not interested in Bugsy (he won't even appear in the film) but in the investigating couple, who represent for him the essential relations which

make up the equation of love and work, and above all, in the cinema . . . The filmmaker intends to mix fiction and reality. He would like to integrate into his tale some excerpts from old gangster films and comments from people as different as Franck [sic] Coppola, Jack Nicholson, Wim Wenders, Lillian Hellman.[34]

Of course, "Johnny G." suggests Godard's own name; he wanted to make a film about a man and a woman investigating the death of Jean-Luc Godard in the process of making a film. The "investigating couple" suggests Godard and Miéville. The story behind the old cinema, the classic cinema born of the connection between Hollywood and the mafia, was to be overlaid by the palimpsest of the new cinema, that of the "investigating couple," who, joining love and work, create something new on the basis of their personal story. The film would, at the same time, tell the old story of the money, desire, crime, and will that went into the founding of Hollywood, the story that Hollywood embodied, transmuted, and concealed in the creations of its golden age. The new Godard would make a film out of the attempt, with Miéville, to study the old Godard and the Hollywood cinema of which he had been born and to which he was all too tempted to return. Godard decided to call the film *The Story*, since its subject was the origins of the story as such—the story of stories.

Seeking financing in the United States (he even met with Charles Bluhdorn of Gulf and Western),[35] Godard was told that he'd need to have a script. Beauregard paid for the creation of a script—but Godard channeled much of that money to Jean-Pierre Beauviala for the creation of a lightweight 35mm camera that he thought essential to the project, to his return to the cinema. Godard wanted a movie camera with which he could shoot film as independently, spontaneously, and casually as video.

The story of *The Story* advanced, but the project did not: Vittorio Gassman couldn't commit to it; Charlotte Rampling simply refused. Godard contacted a new pair of lead actors: through Tom Luddy, whom Godard had met on his California tour of 1968 and who was now working at the Pacific Film Archives, he spoke with Robert De Niro; with the help of Catherine Verret of the French Film Office in New York, he contacted Diane Keaton (he wanted, he later explained, to reveal on film "another Diane Keaton than the one she pretends she is").[36] While he was waiting for Keaton in Verret's office, Godard put on the table a large piece of music paper. Verret asked him what it was. He answered, "The script." He also carried a briefcase everywhere: it contained the cash he was prepared to offer Keaton for the role.[37] Keaton refused.

Godard had prepared a new synopsis that included collage-like images of Keaton, De Niro, Bugsy Siegel, and Las Vegas, and others taken from Kenneth

Anger's book *Hollywood Babylon*. The plot involved the exile of a star—now called Frankie—during the McCarthy era, and the self-imposed refuge of Diana, the ex-wife of a critic, Roberto, at a teaching job at the University of San Diego (where Jean-Pierre Gorin now taught), along with their daughter. The synopsis was a collage of motifs, in which Frankie is run over by a truck (in what seems to be no accident), the nonaccident is captured in a Zapruder-like Super-8 film by Roberto, and Johnny Weissmuller, Rita Hayworth, Wim Wenders, and Elia Kazan play small roles.

Through Tom Luddy, Godard received some financing from Francis Ford Coppola to make *The Story* and got an office at Coppola's studio. Godard asked Luddy to find him an oceanfront apartment in Malibu. But then, despite having produced his elaborate illustrated synopsis, Godard decided not to go ahead with the project; as Luddy later recalled, "He seemed to lose interest or confidence, and he backed off."[38] Yet this synopsis, which is as readable as a graphic novel,[39] is, in Godard's account, precisely the reason why he demurred. In an interview, he explained, "As Anne-Marie [Miéville] told me, I've already shot the film three times. Each time I photocopied the photographs, my pleasure in making images was satisfied."[40]

Nonetheless, the creation of the synopsis of *The Story* was a big step for Godard toward the reconception of a classical film. Although the film was not produced, its themes' nexus remained important to Godard, and would dominate his *King Lear*, on which he would work from 1985 to 1987. As for Coppola's seed money, it was spent; in exchange, Godard promised to grant Coppola American distribution rights to his next two films, whatever they might be.

Godard knew that he needed stars in order to find financing for a film that would have a place in the French film industry. In mid-1978, he contacted Jean-Paul Belmondo on the pretext of offering him a role in *The Story*. During their conversation, however, Godard came around to his real point: Belmondo had purchased rights to a recent book, *L'Instinct de Mort* (The Death Instinct), by Jacques Mesrine, France's new public enemy number one, famous for his ruthless crimes and for his daring jailbreaks, and Godard proposed to direct Belmondo in a film based on that book.

Godard was in effect asking to be hired. Belmondo was hesitant; he was ready to bring Godard in to direct, provided that Godard wanted, as the actor said, "to make a film in the style of *Pierrot le fou*." But Godard had no such thing in mind. He proposed a film in which Belmondo would play an actor who wanted to play the role of Mesrine, and in which Godard himself would play a director seeking to make that film. Belmondo turned the proposal down. Godard later took his frustration public, claiming in an interview in May 1980 that Belmondo was "scared" of him and adding some choice insults about the actor's recent work. Belmondo responded in kind, writing an angry full-page retort: "There's no doubt that the person I saw who called himself Godard, with his lies and his little tricks, has nothing to do with the auteur of *Breathless, Pierrot le fou,* or *Band of Outsiders.* The Godard of the 1960s is dead forever."[41]

Still stymied in finding a film to direct, Godard attempted to advance his cause through publicity. He granted the request of two journalists from *Télérama* magazine for an in-depth interview covering his entire career—for which he demanded to be paid four thousand francs.[42] The interview, which took place in early June, ran in July and August 1978. The magazine's banner declaration, "Godard Tells All," was a natural lure: his name was more valuable to the magazine than was his new work to France's producers.

Godard fulfilled his end of the bargain: he spoke with flair about his family of "collaborators" with Vichy, his postwar years in Paris, his first attempts at making films. He discussed the early days of *Cahiers*—and he settled scores: "I think that François absolutely doesn't know how to make films. He made one that truly corresponded to him, and then it stopped there: afterwards, he only told stories . . . Chabrol is honest like a thief. Truffaut is a thief who passes himself off as an honest man, which is the worst thing." As for Rivette and Rohmer, he called them "believers. Super-Catholics. People who belong to a sect and who are faithful to those who keep the rites of that sect," and he added: "I should rather have called them little fetishists. They brought the plague, and everyone caught it." The journalists asked, "You too?" "Yes, me too. But it's over. It was long. The essential thing is to recognize that one is living with the plague. As for the others, they don't know it."

GEOGRAPHICALLY AND CONCEPTUALLY, Godard was obliged to go very far to find financial backing. When the *Télérama* interview ran, he himself was in Mozambique, with Miéville, working under the auspices of Mozambique's national film program, run by the Brazilian filmmaker Ruy Guerra (who had been born in the former Portuguese colony). The project's roots dated back to 1977, when Godard attended a conference in Geneva on the subject of Mozambique. There, he spoke with a representative of the government. The newly independent country, ruled by its socialist revolutionary leader, Samora Machel, had no television station yet, and on December 9, 1977, Godard signed a contract with the government to help it develop a broadcast system unsullied by Western bourgeois and capitalist influences. He was also contracted to make a film about the project.[43]

Carlos Gambo, a cameraman who owned the only video camera in the country (prior to Godard's arrival) and who worked with him there, later recalled Godard's lengthy meetings with "engineers from the university, with technicians from radio, and with filmmakers from the National Institute of Cinema, to discuss the future television of Mozambique." The issues under discussion were practical—whether to choose the PAL or SECAM broadcast standards, how to set up a local repair service for the video equipment.[44] Gambo explained the group's preliminary fieldwork: "We filmed and captured the image of a countrywoman, then we showed her the image to see the reaction of this person who couldn't read or write. This way, we saw who we needed to make television for. For the peasant or for the intellectual? And if it was to be for everyone, how would we do it?"[45] The minister of information at the time, José L. Cabaço, later described Godard's plan to "go to the villages, train the peasants to use the equipment, and leave the equipment in their hands, so they could produce whatever they wanted."[46]

What emerged from Godard's Mozambique visits appeared in *Cahiers du cinéma*. He was asked to guest-edit the ceremonial issue number 300, to be published in May 1979. One section of the issue, "The Last Dream of a Producer," devoted to Godard's work in Mozambique, was a photographic essay, similar to the pictorial synopsis for *The Story*. Godard planned to make a film about his ongoing project in Mozambique, to be called *North Against South, or Birth (of the Image) of a Nation*. It would in fact comprise five films: two centered on a couple, a man who is a producer and a "woman commentator/photographer" traveling to and from Mozambique—fictional stand-ins for Godard and Miéville—who would be played by an actor and an actress; and three collections of visual sketches, drawings, and notes regarding Mozambique.

The essay-outline incorporated a snapshot travelogue of Godard and Miéville's trip. The photographic evidence, which showed meetings with local and international officials, and views of local inhabitants, suggested little of the locale or the project's promise. In a separate text published in the same issue of *Cahiers*, Godard wondered "why people of the cinema have such a desire to film other people with so much frenzy." He answered his own question: "In fact, they tend to hide behind the image of the other, and the image then serves to erase."[47] The interest in Mozambique was unfortunately close to this category: despite Godard's plan to film fictionalized surrogates of himself and Miéville there, the country's significance for him was unclear. He was not connected to it by language, history, or culture. He did not know Mozambique, and his outsider's view of the illiterate and visually inexperienced villagers was no different from that of any travel journalist. The photographs were neither analytical nor ethnographic, no more revealing than souvenir snapshots.

The unrealized project was, however, significant in one regard: it suggested the extent to which Godard had become, in a sense, the outcast of the Western cinema world. *The Story* was blocked for lack of stars, Belmondo had rejected him, and Godard was traveling wildly, from Mozambique to Paris to Montreal to San Francisco to Los Angeles to Grenoble to get something going. Though he lived in Rolle, his home there might as well have been a hotel. He was desperate and constantly on the road—but it was in his peregrinations that he would soon find the key to his return.

IN OCTOBER 1978, Godard returned to Montreal to fulfill his remaining commitments to Serge Losique. There, Godard decided that the story he wanted to film was not one taken from the Hollywood story machine but his own—the story of his wanderings. Again he called upon Jean-Claude Carrière to help him shape it. Once again, the two met for lunch. According to Carrière, Godard said, "I have an idea for a film." The idea: "A man leaves Paris, a horrible city, he goes to Switzerland or someplace else, he meets a woman or two, and he stays there or he comes back."[48]

The return of nature
(New Yorker Films / Photofest)

nineteen

SAUVE QUI PEUT (LA VIE)

"To return to my homeland in the cinema"

ODARD HAD THE IDEA; THE MEANS WERE, AS ALWAYS, elusive. But his new project about his travels went forward when Marin Karmitz, who urged Godard to apply for an advance on receipts, bought advance distribution rights to the film and a young producer, Alain Sarde, decided to produce it. Sarde, a cinephile who loved Godard's films, had met Godard in the early 1970s while working as an assistant to Jean-Pierre Rassam. A fledgling producer, he had a bright new approach: he knew that French television had a new mandate to coproduce films for the cinema, and he became an expert in such coproductions. For Godard's new film, Sarde lined up financing from television stations from France, West Germany, and Switzerland.

Godard called the film *Sauve qui peut (la vie)*; it was released as *Every Man for Himself* in the United States and as *Slow Motion* in the United Kingdom, though Godard said that the best translation was really "Save Your Ass."[1] He referred to it as his "second first film," suggesting its great significance for him. As with *Breathless, Sauve qui peut* was marked by its unusual and personalized ways of production. Godard was intent on making the film on the basis of an ongoing dialogue with its participants. The production would create a set of personal relationships that the film would reflect. *Sauve qui peut* was even more permeable than Godard's previous films to the people who worked on it and to his life while making it; the film would embody a new era of intimate politics. *Sauve qui peut* would be an intensely personal film, about Godard's years of not making films, and, in particular, about his relationship with Anne-Marie Miéville.

In Montreal, when Godard discussed his plans for a return to what he called "cinema cinema"—movies with stories and stars—he said, "Relying on what I learned from audiovisual journalism, [I want] to do fiction but in a somewhat different way . . . it will take lots of time, to compose as if for an orchestra, or instead alone, like a painter."[2] He was right: it did take lots of time. To create a "screenplay," Godard used videotape instead of paper: as a result, he needed to have a cast and crew on hand from the project's conception.

Godard treated video as a sketch pad with which he stayed in constant practice making images. Moreover, he used his "sketch pad" as a painter does: by referring to preparatory images of the actors and locations, he gave the film a more finished quality. While Godard's work of the 1960s was impressionistic, recording his thoughts and caprices of the moment, his later movies, beginning with *Sauve qui peut,* emerged as more classical, more composed. The new means of visual notetaking, or sketching, allowed him to achieve a kind of plastic, formal perfection with limited crew and equipment. That small group of actors got to work early on, holding meetings, researching locations, practicing gestures, shooting tests.

Godard's work methods were not all that had changed. The world of French cinema to which he had returned was quite different from the one he had left. New producers, actors, new technicians, and even new equipment had made their presence felt. Godard could not help but work with the people of these times, citizens of a post-1968 world. Like Alain Sarde and Marin Karmitz, who came of age in the film industry at a time when Godard was already an established and central artistic figure, the other participants in *Sauve qui peut* recognized him as an artistic hero; unlike many elders, they did not hold Godard's years of political extremism and artistic experimentation against him.

Early in 1979, Godard called on three young actors: Isabelle Huppert, who was about to travel to Wyoming for a major role in Michael Cimino's *Heaven's Gate* (Godard visited her on location for a single day); Miou-Miou, an actress who had started doing guerrilla theater in Paris in the late 1960s and had made her name in the Swiss director Alain Tanner's film *Jonah Who Will Be 25 in the Year 2000;* and Jacques Dutronc, a French rock star of the 1960s who had moved into acting.

Dutronc would play an idled filmmaker shuttling between a large Swiss city and a smaller one; Miou-Miou would be his ex-lover, who moved from the small city to the countryside, and Huppert would play a prostitute in the big city who is also looking to change her life.

The "script" of this vague plot, which Godard submitted to the CNC on April 12, 1979, for an advance on receipts, was composed on videotape.

Accompanying still photographs of his actors, Godard explained, in a voice-over commentary, that he was not trying "to show the images of the film, how they will be," but instead to show "how I see." He said that his way of seeing was derived from his planned use of effects in editing, "For example, superimpositions, dissolves. And then slowing down, slowing down in order to see." He wanted to construct the film around the technique of "decomposition" devised for *France tour détour* and intended to use this technique to analyze his characters' travels from place to place.

The videotape also served as the springboard for the film's action and the story's particulars. But it was not Godard who came up with those details: for that, he again called on the screenwriter Jean-Claude Carrière and asked him to come to Rolle to view the videotape. As Carrière recalled, Godard showed him images and asked him, "Is there a scene there?" The screenwriter knew that he had to say "Yes"—"or else there's no movie"—so he associated freely and improvised story lines as he watched the tape.[3] But *Sauve qui peut* also depended on another corpus of preexisting images—the vast stock of images that Godard had in mind, if not at hand, from the history of cinema. While working on *Sauve qui peut*, Godard was also planning his video series, *Histoire(s) du cinéma*, which he related directly to his return to the film industry and to the making of this film in particular. At a symposium at the Cinémathèque Suisse in June 1979, Godard spoke candidly of his effort to "attempt to live again":

> Sooner or later, one returns to one's homeland. I wanted to return to my homeland in the cinema, in other words, in the fact that I need images in order to live and need to show them to others . . . Because at a given moment, I myself belonged to the history of cinema, little by little I became interested in the history of cinema . . . and finally started to wonder how the forms that I was using had been created, and how this knowledge could help me.[4]

The *Histoire(s) du cinéma* series was conceived with an expressly political purpose: to relate the forms and subjects of film history to events in political history. Thus, by combining his return to the cinema with his return to the history of cinema, he associated *Sauve qui peut* with the politics of the day—not directly through the filming of political subjects, but through the use of formal elements which corresponded to contemporary life. As implied by the ambiguity of the French word "histoire," which means both "history" and "story," Godard connected his ideas on film form and political history to his new effort to tell his own story.

As *Sauve qui peut* developed, the casting changed: when Miou-Miou found out that she would be playing opposite Huppert, she left the production.[5]

To replace her, Godard contacted Nathalie Baye, whose first important film role was in François Truffaut's *Day for Night,* and who had also played significant parts in his *The Man Who Loved Women* and *The Green Room.* Godard took unusual steps to integrate his prospective actress into the production: he asked whether he could spend several days with her in her country home. As Baye later recalled, "He was with me when I lived my daily life, when I was cooking. He observed me. He said very little to me about the film." She sensed that, in order to work with her, he "needed to imbue himself with each of [her] gestures."[6]

Despite the commercial allure of his three young stars, and despite the involvement of Karmitz and Sarde, Godard still had difficulty getting full financing. Sarde's efforts at cobbling together international coproduction money resulted in long and enervating negotiations. Godard turned to his cousin Jérôme Monod, the politically connected CEO of the French water company and (through industrial conglomeration) of a television station, but Monod refused to see him,[7] and Godard had no choice but to turn to the mainstream of the industry. Suddenly the exiled artist of Rolle found himself entangled in a new web of personal and professional obligations. These stresses and uncertainties, combined with Godard's own trepidations over returning to the regular milieu and recognized norms of the commercial cinema, made for an exceptionally tense mood during the planning and the shoot of *Sauve qui peut.*

Early in pre-production, Godard hired Romain Goupil as his assistant, even though the backing for the film was not yet guaranteed. Goupil, a teenage student activist in the revolts of May 1968,[8] had recently worked as an assistant director (an administrative position) to Chantal Akerman and Roman Polanski, and was beginning work on a documentary film about a militant friend who had disappeared. As Goupil later recalled, Godard asked him, "Are you ready, even if the film doesn't get made, to spend a year with me, at a small salary, to see whether we can do something?"[9] (And indeed, when funding came in, Godard offered him the industry-scale rate for an assistant director.) In addition to helping organize the shoot, Goupil served as something of a paid companion, an interlocutor with a great dedication to the cinema as well as to Godard's own work.

Godard went even further to personalize his relations with the crew: in his letter to the CNC of April 12, he explained his plan to hire "two or three" directors of photography so that during the shoot, he "could listen calmly, ask them some questions, and even see them each give a different answer, like doctors to a sick person."[10] He wanted William Lubtchansky, who had worked on all of his productions since *Ici et ailleurs,* to be joined by Renato Berta, a Swiss cameraman, and by Vilmos Zsigmond, who was shooting

Heaven's Gate. Zsigmond, however, priced himself out of the running, leaving Berta and Lubtchansky to work together. Both were skeptical of the plan, but accepted in deference to Godard. The pair joined Goupil, Pierre Binggeli (Godard's video technician), and Jean-Bernard Menoud (the assistant cameraman) in a sort of managerial committee, and Godard organized pre-production meetings with them in order to generate conversation.

The meetings were tense. Godard claimed that he didn't know what he wanted to film or how to proceed; at times he cried in the presence of his team. Then, as his ideas for the project became clearer, he became increasingly desperate about the possibility of realizing them. He could not decide whether to shoot *Sauve qui peut* on videotape or film. Initially, he wanted to work in video to take full advantage of the special effects of video editing, particularly the "decompositional" slow-motion technique that he had used in *France tour détour.* But knowing that the finished product would have to be released on 35mm film for theatrical distribution, he shot video tests and sent the tapes to four different laboratories in order to compare the quality of their transfers to 35mm film. Though the tests proved to be unsatisfactory, Godard was nonetheless unwilling to rule video out.

At one such meeting Godard brought in every kind of 35mm camera available, so that his technicians could examine them and discuss their pros and cons. He met Lubtchansky and Jean-Pierre Beauviala in Paris and filmed several images with the prototype of the lightweight 35mm camera, the "35-8," that Beauviala had made to his specifications. Godard wanted a camera light enough for him to carry easily at arm's length, small enough to fit into a car's glove compartment, and simple enough that he could shoot 35mm film images as spontaneously and casually as with a Super-8 camera—or a video camera. He had channeled a large chunk of the budget of *Sauve qui peut* to Beauviala for its production. But the prototype did not work as Godard had hoped—the images were not, according to Lubtchansky, as sharp as those of a full-sized 35mm camera—and it did not fulfill a specification that Godard had not foreseen: it was too noisy for filming indoor dialogue scenes. Within weeks of the shoot, which was scheduled to begin in October 1979, the crew still did not know whether *Sauve qui peut* would be shot on film or on video. Godard himself claimed not to have decided, and he put the matter up for a vote among his crew. Video won out. Then Godard decreed that the film would be shot on 35mm film.

A crucial aspect of the project's modernity was the presence—so to speak—of a new literary model for Godard, the novelist Marguerite Duras. The sixty-five-year-old author of such books as *The Ravishing of Lol V. Stein* and *Moderato Cantabile* (she was still several years from writing *The Lover*) and the director of such films as *India Song* and *Le Camion* (The Truck) had developed a style that could be called postexistential: her stark, incantatory sentences seemed to be wrenched from a cosmic silence. The writing and the struggle to write were one, and she worked herself into her books as a writer trying to write them. She began to direct films in 1966, claiming, "My films are the same as my novels," and she made them so, involving her writing overtly and explicitly in the process of her filmmaking. *Le Camion,* from 1977—in which she and Gérard Depardieu sit at a table in her house and read passages from the script and discuss them, thus conjuring and analyzing a fictional story but without staging it—was an impressive and intimidating example for any self-implicating filmmaker, and for a filmmaker of literary inspiration, like Godard.

Duras herself recognized that "the film was made at the same time as it was filmed; the film was written in step with its unspooling,"[11] and criticized directors who did not understand "that the making of the film is aready the film."[12] *Le Camion* was something of a template for Godard's *Sauve qui peut,* and he wanted Duras to participate in it. Specifically, Godard recalled a recent incident in which Duras, invited to present her work at a film festival, showed up at the festival but refused to appear in public. Godard wanted to re-enact that scene in his film, with his stand-in, Dutronc, inviting Duras to a class where she would refuse to appear. On the set, Duras replicated the scene beyond Godard's expectations: she also refused to appear in his film, but allowed him to tape-record several conversations with her. Godard then filmed a scene in which Dutronc was supposed to be driving Duras, unseen in the passenger seat, back to the airport. Although she was not actually there, her voice, clipped from the interviews onto the film's sound track, created the illusion of her presence.

For Godard, Duras represented a model for integrating his own private experience with the work of art without sacrificing any of its political or vatic power. He had criticized Sartre, in the wake of 1968, for having distinguished his writing of the time (his biography of Flaubert, *The Idiot of the Family*) from his political activism—for having two separate "drawers": a "Flaubert drawer" and a " 'class struggle' drawer."[13] Duras made no such distinction: *Le Camion,* a story of a woman who hitches a ride with a pair of truck drivers, is dominated by the political delusions of the twentieth century, fascism and communism, without yielding to dogma or diluting the film's artistic immediacy—and Duras told that story herself, on-screen. Adapting Duras's strategies, Godard, beginning with *Sauve qui peut,* would approach politics by other means, creating feature films that reflected his first-person implication in their subjects, however great or abstract.

THE INTIMATE VIEW of political events that Godard would present in *Sauve qui peut* was inseparable from the film's personal aspect. He explained that the film represented the beginning of his "real life," namely, "the cinema": "Godard returns to civilian life after having made many voyages. He returns, he settles down, he seeks a profession. He no longer tries so much to change the world, but to change what he can change, himself."[14]

The film's main character, played by Dutronc, is called Paul Godard, a filmmaker who is not making films. Paul Godard goes back and forth between the big Swiss city where he now lives and the small one where he used to live with Denise, his lover. Denise works in television and is about to quit her job for a local newspaper in rural Switzerland. She has left Paul and wants to find someone to sublet the apartment they shared. Paul attempts to remain involved in the cinema through teaching, but his inactivity weighs on him. He also tries to maintain contact with his pubescent daughter and her mother, his ex-wife. In the city, Paul meets Isabelle, a prostitute who is being pursued by some pimps she refuses to work with and who wants to leave the large communal apartment where she lives and move elsewhere. Isabelle answers an ad for an apartment, which happens to be Denise's. Paul meets up with his ex-wife and his daughter, and tries to restore relations. His ex-wife is hesitant to do so. Paul walks away, looks back at them, and is hit by a car.

Sauve qui peut tells a story of multiple conflicting relationships, and conflict was at the heart of its production—of the experiences that informed its story. In the film, Godard presents yet another "Paul," the name of his cinematic surrogates since 1962, giving his actor his own last name (and his father's first name), as well as his sport jacket to wear.[15] Dutronc knew that he was playing someone closely modeled on Godard. Nathalie Baye similarly understood that her role was closely related to the character of Miéville.

Anne-Marie Miéville was often present on the set, taking still photographs and discussing with Godard the work at hand. Their tensions were in the open—according to William Lubtchansky, "They argued all the time"—and affected Godard's relations with his colleagues. On the set, he had become extremely difficult with his crew and permitted himself violent transports of anger. It was a familiar pattern for Godard, reminiscent of many of his shoots in the 1960s, but now the people were different and the times had changed. In the old days, Godard and Coutard might have had a shouting match, Anna Karina may have avoided Godard, Beauregard and Godard might have come to blows, but they were all of a hard-nosed generation. Now, social relations had advanced; society itself was growing more civil, and the turmoil that Godard sowed was considered, by the younger, more idealistic actors and crew, a needless and troubling aggression that did not serve the creative process but disturbed and poisoned it.

Godard often spoke very sharply to Nathalie Baye, who was sometimes reduced to tears. Relations with his two cameramen, particularly with Lubtchansky, were also troubled. Godard had expected Lubtchansky and Berta to talk together during the shoot, so that he could make images on the basis of their discussions. The two cameramen, however, quickly realized that they had different styles of lighting (Lubtchansky preferred high contrast; Berta tended toward softer illumination); since neither planned to adopt the other's style, they took turns deferring to each other and becoming, in effect, the other's assistant, depending on the scene—and, as Lubtchansky said, "depending on who didn't want to talk with Jean-Luc."

Lubtchansky often found himself in that position, he said, and their tensions rose to fury during the shoot of a scene that took place in a television studio:

> It was a close-up on [Baye], and she was wearing an earphone. [Godard] was asking her questions. It wasn't written. We were filming her with short magazines of 35mm film which lasted four minutes. While we were doing the shot, I noticed that the film had run out. I was above, Godard was below, under the table. I wondered, what to do? I let it go; then after a minute without film, I leaned over and said to him under the table, "Jean-Luc, there's no film." He comes out, insults me, "Imbecile, what kind of jerk, you don't know that the cinema is also sound!" He kept on insulting me, and I got angry. We came close to having a fistfight.[16]

The scene is not in the film. When the filming was over, Lubtchansky vowed never to work with Godard again.

A further source of stress was the sexual minefield of incestuous implications which Godard's work of the 1970s had approached. In *Sauve qui peut*, Paul Godard was divorced, with an adolescent daughter. The child's role was played by Cécile Tanner, the twelve-year-old daughter of Godard's Swiss colleague Alain Tanner.

In January 1979, Godard had met Cécile by chance at Orly Airport in Paris, as they both were to board a flight to Geneva. (She was traveling alone and, to spare her from having to wear a pinney and to sit near the flight attendants, he volunteered to sit with her.) Godard asked her what she liked to do, and Cécile said that she liked to play soccer. A few weeks later, he sent Cécile a present: a new soccer ball. Shortly thereafter he called to ask her whether she would appear in a film about soccer that he planned to make. She agreed, but he made no such film. Instead, later in the year, he asked her to play a role in *Sauve qui peut*, for which she would play soccer. She again agreed. To prepare her for the role, he sent her to practice in Geneva with a girls' team.

Cécile's first appearance in *Sauve qui peut* is on a school soccer field, where Paul has come to meet her. Godard filmed her in close-up as she prepared an inbound throw. In the editing room, he slowed the close-up down with his stop-action "decomposition," while, on the sound track, Paul talked with the soccer coach, a man:

PAUL: Do you have a daughter?
COACH: Yes.
PAUL: How old?
COACH: Same as Cécile.
PAUL: Does she have breasts?
COACH: Same as Cécile.
PAUL: Have you ever wanted to fuck her in the ass?
COACH: No.

During the shoot, Cécile had no idea what the men had discussed. Then she saw the film. "When I saw it, at the private screening for the crew, I crawled under my seat, I was dying of shame," Tanner recalled.[17] She had been unaware that her face would be studied in slow motion; but most of all, she was shocked to find herself portrayed as an object of incestuous pedophilic lust. Although it is of course the character Paul Godard's self-abasing confession that is presented on-screen, the object of the character's illicit curiosity was publicly displayed under her own name—and Cécile felt humiliated.

This would not be the film's only scene of sexual debasement. After Paul Godard encounters Isabelle the prostitute, played by Huppert—she approaches him as he waits on line at a movie theater showing Chaplin's *City Lights*[18]—the film veers into a section called "Work," regarding the prostitute's experiences. These experiences are harrowing: in a hotel room, a paunchy older man tells her to strip from the waist down so that he can stare at her while he talks business on the phone, then he orders her to pretend to be his daughter. Later she shows up for a call at an office; a harsh, adamantine executive orders her, another prostitute, and a young male employee to create a sexual "assembly line." The pair of scenes represents the two polar extremes of the sex industry—a false identification of role-playing and a dehumanizing mechanization—which resemble the two poles of performance and subjection which actors endure in the cinema.

While visiting Huppert in Wyoming during the shoot of *Heaven's Gate*, Godard had explained her role in a sentence: "I want it to be the face of suffering." But, though he intended the character of Isabelle to suffer, Godard did not permit the actress to express it: Huppert recalled that he wanted his

actors to be "neutral": "He had us speak like oracles . . . He doesn't want
an interpretation, he wants the affirmation of a thought." She considered
that, though he sought "to remove all psychology," he revealed the character
all the more. The result, she sensed, rightly, was that he made a film "on" or
"about" her, personally, as an actress: "He showed my fragility and my dependence, as a beginning actress, with respect to the world of men, of power,
of money," and also what she called her "indifference to [her] own body."[19]
She spoke of Godard's control of her diction and of her gestures, of his sense
that "one must imprison the actor so that his true soul can emerge." She felt
that Godard's methods brought her closer to herself and, paradoxically, to the
character she was embodying, and she found the experience artistically gratifying.

THE FILM BEGINS with a flourish—shots of wispy cirrus clouds in a bright
blue sky, accompanied by electronic new-age music by Gabriel Yared. These
shots announce what is to come: some of the most serene, exalted images of
nature yet put on film. These are also images of Switzerland, which Godard
considered his "studio of exteriors," with "forests, lakes, snow, mountains,
and wind."[20]

The presence of nature in the film is associated with Paul Godard's
withdrawing lover, Denise, played by Nathalie Baye. As Denise pedals her
three-speed bicycle along a tree-lined road bordering Lake Geneva, a traveling shot shows the lake, the grassy banks, and the mountains, suffused with
golden sunlight. Later, alone in her apartment, Denise reads aloud from her
notebook. The text forms part of what she calls her "project," which is not a
novel but "may be part of one." The passage is drawn verbatim from Robert
Linhart's 1978 book about his years as a factory worker, *L'Etabli*:[21]

> The temptation of death. But life rebels and resists. The organism resists. The
> muscles resist. The nerves resist. There is something in the body and the head
> that buttresses itself against the repetition and the nothingness. Life: a more
> rapid gesture, an arm that falls back out of rhythm, a slower step, a gust of ir-
> regularity, a false movement . . . Everything that, in each of the men of the
> assembly line, silently shouts: "I am not a machine!"

Godard's new editing methods—the "decomposition" of motion into
successive freeze-frames—were a visual equivalent of Linhart's attempt to
recover and to analyze the human element of work. In *Sauve qui peut*, Godard "decomposed" such motions as Denise's solitary bicycling, the beating of a woman at a train station, and Paul tackling Denise in a passionate
embrace; he studied these intimate moments as if they too were work.

Paul and Denise's problems are centered on work, or rather, on their inability to work together. Like Godard in recent times, Paul is in a state of flux. Paul Godard is making nothing, doing nothing, suffering from an uncreative confusion. Denise is in flux too, but working toward a positive change: she is a producer at a television station but is leaving it to join the staff of a rural village newspaper that a former urban revolutionary friend of hers inherited from his father. Denise is leaving the city to return to nature, and to seek the calm that she needs for her "project."

The conflict that separates them in their quest—Godard's quest, shared with Anne-Marie Miéville, to unify life and work—is expressed with an unusual clarity in a scene in which the two, seated at the bar of a café, try to talk out their practical difficulties:

> PAUL: Have you really put in an ad for the apartment? . . . That's really nasty. Give me a little time. I'm getting sick of living in this big city too.
> DENISE: I don't believe you anymore. And I'm beginning to get fed up even in a small city like Nyon. It would have helped me if you'd moved in. But you said you needed quiet for your new projects.
> PAUL: I still have these projects.
> DENISE: No. They depend on me staying put. You want a guardian angel, and I'm sick of it . . . You always wanted love to come from work, from the things we could do together, not just at night. You wanted the nights to come from the days, not vice versa.
> PAUL: It's not me, it's how people arrange things. We agreed that love isn't possible without a little work, or else it's just explosions, nothing that lasts.

The scene continues outside the café, where Paul tries to get Denise to follow him, and Denise yells at him, slaps and wrestles him, and leaves him behind, anguished and humiliated, in the street. Later, when he visits her, he leaps across the table to embrace her, and both crash to the floor in pain, in a shot that Godard "decomposed," increasing the ambiguity of the blend of romance and violence. Isabelle happens to walk in on their rough scene, and Paul says, "We can't seem to touch each other without giving each other bruises." It is a line that Godard, in interviews, admitted to having gotten from Miéville.

At the film's end, Paul Godard, who runs across a street to chase after his ex-wife and daughter, is struck by a car and is lying in the street, bewildered by his own oncoming death: "I can't be dying, my life isn't flashing before my eyes." He closes his own eyes with his hands, like Belmondo at the end of *Breathless,* as his ex-wife leads his daughter away, saying, "It has nothing to do with us." The music on the sound track swells with a phrase of violins, and as they walk away, they pass an orchestra standing in a passageway, playing the music heard on the sound track.

Technically, the sequence, comprising a long pan shot from Paul in the street to the ex-wife and daughter walking through a dark tunnel, was difficult to execute—and also very expensive to shoot, due to the string orchestra in the tunnel. At the time, Godard was still somewhat agoraphobic and uneasy working in public. As Romain Goupil recalled, "He was afraid of being in the street, of stopping traffic, of the people who were watching, so he did things too fast."[22] As a result, Lubtchansky recalled, Godard ignored his advice and the shot was ruined; the crew returned to film it again a week later—without the director.

The self-pitying ending, of a man being hit by a car as he turns to follow a woman, is taken from Truffaut's 1977 film, *The Man Who Loved Women*. With this ending, *Sauve qui peut* presents the specter of a world without Godard as a filmmaker: only the existence of the film itself brings the world back from the edge of that precipice. Godard depicts the mythic self-sacrifice of the artist so that his art—and his myth—may live on.

GODARD HAD DESCRIBED his situation lucidly, months earlier, at the Cinémathèque Suisse, when he spoke of wanting to return to his "homeland in the cinema."[23] Where Paul Godard failed, Jean-Luc Godard succeeded. The sentiment is evident in *Sauve qui peut*: despite the film's casual depictions of despair and brutality, the overall mood, strangely, is that of a newfound equilibrium. It was a sentiment that Godard retrospectively confirmed.[24] The equilibrium is that of Godard who, despite all conflicts on the set and in life, despite his years of doubt, frustration, and wandering, was now, again, where he belonged. In the credits, he noted that the film was "composed by Jean-Luc Godard." It was a role that suggested a calmer, more serene, and more classically artistic method.

Godard attributed his new compositional precision and his attention to nature to his preliminary work on *Histoire(s) du cinema*. He explained to a German interviewer that, while composing his shots for *Sauve qui peut,* he "was constantly seeking a grammar which used to be manifestly present and which has since been lost, such as is seen for example in the films of Griffith."[25]

The film's equilibrium is also a reflection of the times, in which the great ideological wars of western Europe seemed now to be a thing of the past and personal matters and conflicts were moderated in serene and modern infrastructure nations. (In this regard, the film was as predictive of coming changes—the social-democratic consensus that derived from the election of François Mitterrand in May 1981—as *La Chinoise* had been of the political and cultural crises of 1968.)

The images themselves also contributed greatly to the film's surprising serenity. *Sauve qui peut* was the first film that Godard filmed in color with the same freedom with which he had filmed in black and white in the 1960s. Godard used Zeiss "super-speed" (ultra-wide aperture) lenses, which eliminated much of the need for added lighting, and allowed him to capture in the film the painterly, quasi-impressionistic textures of ambient and natural light. However, the wider the aperture, the shallower the depth of field, making it very difficult for a camera operator to keep in focus anything in motion. The lenses thus influenced Godard's aesthetic in a second way, by encouraging static shots of static people.

Godard spoke of his new style: "With *Breathless*, I rebelled against all those tired shots with the camera anchored on a tripod, and now I made a film full of what I used to think were those awful steady shots."[26] A certain type of image resulted, suggesting a poised, receptive neutrality: "I did not express [*exprimé*] much, but I impressed [*imprimé*—"printed" or "registered"] quite a lot of things."[27] He used many wide-angle shots which allowed lots of action to take place at the edges of the frame, conveying a sense of teeming and nuanced reality.

Yet at the same time, Godard's restrained, inclusive framings fulfilled another more personal, documentary ambition: to show the making of the film in the film itself. He said that the significance of living and filming in his "studio of exteriors" in the canton of Vaud in Switzerland was that, unlike in a Hollywood studio, "here everything"—life and work—"happens in the same place. So, in addition, one sees how the film was shot!"[28] Godard's idea was that, by showing the sights and activities of the place where he lived and worked, he included in the film the elements of his own behind-the-scenes reality. A loose frame of the streets of Lausanne was the equivalent, for Godard, of filming what took place in a studio beyond the edges of the set; his shots of the lake and the sky were not only a paean to the natural beauty of the Swiss landscape, but also a report on his own daily experience.

IF GODARD'S LIFE was implicated with what he filmed, he also bore the burden of responsibility for what his film's subject suggested about his life. At its premiere at Cannes on May 21, 1980, *Sauve qui peut* was booed; after the screening, Godard faced the anger of spectators who, responding to the film's sexually provocative scenes, flung at him such epithets as, "Filth!" and "Degenerate!"[29] One journalist called Godard's post-screening press conference "the closing argument in a criminal trial."[30] The festival, which was supposed to have been Godard's triumphant return home, quickly turned into a disaster.

Marin Karmitz, as coproducer and the executive in charge of distribution, stepped in and saved the day. Karmitz had originally planned to release
the film in France immediately after the festival, but now he postponed it, declaring that *Sauve qui peut* had been screened as a work in progress and was
not really finished. During the summer, he organized screenings for journalists as well as for such cultural luminaries as Duras and Michel Foucault, and
let them know that "in the meantime, Godard had changed and finished the
film." The producer later recalled what happened when *Sauve qui peut* was released in October: "The same journalists who had demolished the film at
Cannes now declared it a masterpiece. Of course, [Godard] hadn't changed a
thing."[31]

The French critics did indeed declare *Sauve qui peut* a masterpiece; to
herald its release, *Le Monde* featured no fewer than three rave reviews on the
same day, including Yvonne Baby's: "Thanks to Jean-Luc Godard, 'painter in
letters,' the cinema recovers the risks of art, comes back to life."[32] As Godard's
"second first film," it was also a great financial success, rivaling that of
Breathless. Having returned to the institutions of the mainstream French
cinema, Godard had also succeeded in recovering the kind of good graces
that its potentates best recognized: commercial viability.

In the United States, *Sauve qui peut* was similarly restorative to Godard's
commercial fortunes and popular recognition. Vincent Canby of the *New
York Times* called it "funny and surprising . . . by far the most stimulating
and encouraging film at Cannes."[33] Andrew Sarris of the *Village Voice* recognized the film's importance:

> No Godard film since *Pierrot le fou* has excited me as much as *Sauve qui peut
> (la vie)* . . . *Sauve qui peut* is perhaps more like a piece of music than a
> movie. Every image is suffused with such elegant and exquisite insights into
> what makes the medium interact with its material that the total effect is intox-
> icating . . . Somewhere on the screen he has captured the subtle reality of
> what it is to be a thinking, feeling being in these ridiculously convulsive
> times.[34]

Sauve qui peut played in the New York Film Festival on October 8 and
11, and started its commercial run as *Every Man for Himself* on October 12.
Godard promoted the film feverishly, in the press, on television (including
on *The Dick Cavett Show*), and in person. Despite criticism of his depiction
of brutality toward women (in Los Angeles, according to theater owner Max
Laemmle, "Our audiences were personally offended, personally insulted, that
we should expose them to such a film which shows in detail how men abuse
women"),[35] the film was reported to be a greater success in the United States

than, again, even *Breathless* had been; yet the American enthusiasm was to be short-lived.

In a sign of trouble to come, Pauline Kael of *The New Yorker* rejected the film with the vindictive cruelty of a disappointed lover.

> More than the fat has been burned out of "Every Man for Himself": the juice is gone, too . . . If it were possible to have lyricism without emotion, that might describe the film's style . . . I got the feeling that Godard doesn't believe in anything anymore; he wants to make movies, but maybe he doesn't really believe in movies anymore, either.[36]

At a time when she exhibited an increasingly passionate devotion to popular, even simplistic, cinematic sensations, Kael was unable to appreciate Godard's first successful new effort to create images on a newly ideal basis, and she took his rejection of her anointed popular models as an affront.

Kael's insensitivity to the film heralded obstacles to Godard's new manner. Over time, many of Godard's leading critical supporters in the American press would drop off, one by one, and his audiences, out of sync with his increasingly intellectualized range of concerns and abstract connections to Hollywood's moods and models, would drift away. Godard was heading in the direction of high art at a moment when even serious viewers were, more than ever, in thrall to the popular. The New Wave's claim to have found art disguised as Hollywood's commercial fare had worked too well: now many took it preeminently as movie art and turned away from more demanding films.

IN FRANCE, by contrast, a remarkable confluence of politics and culture was to make Godard's position particularly secure. Godard's assistant, Romain Goupil, was a friend of Coluche, a provocative comedian whose radio broadcasts won him a great public following and the bitter enmity of those politicians he mocked on the government-controlled airwaves. Goupil put Godard in touch with Coluche; the two got along famously, and Godard sought to have Coluche play the lead in a film that seemed to have little to do with the comedian's public persona: an adaptation of Jim Thompson's classic noir novel, *Pop. 1280*. Despite Karmitz's efforts, however, he could not get rights to the novel, which had been purchased by the director Bertrand Tavernier. (Godard suggested to him that they both make films based on the book, but Tavernier demurred.)[37] Instead, Godard developed another project involving himself, Goupil, and Coluche.

Coluche was hired by Radio Monte-Carlo in February 1980, and was removed from the airwaves (under orders from Prince Rainier) within weeks because of his sharp-edged political humor. Goupil at once conceived a scheme of high comedy: the only way for the comic to assure himself of access to the airwaves was to get himself elected president of France in the May 1981 elections.[38] Coluche liked the idea, and spent months laying the groundwork for what proved to be a salutary jolt to the French political system and foreshadowed the cultural turn that French politics would take.

In October 1980, Coluche began to float the plan publicly; on October 30, he convened journalists at the theater where he performed nightly and officially declared his candidacy.[39] On November 2, a list was published of the first 150 signatories in support of Coluche for president; the names included Godard and Goupil, along with other luminaries of the arts: Gérard Depardieu, Jacques Dutronc, Léo Ferré, Johnny Hallyday, Serge July (the editor of *Libération*), Miou-Miou, Roman Polanski, and many others of popular music and the cinema. Within days, such intellectuals as Gilles Deleuze, Félix Guattari, and Pierre Bourdieu came to the support of Coluche. Jean-Paul Belmondo and Daniel Cohn-Bendit joined in. *Libération* officially endorsed him. Television and radio, still under state control, largely barred him from the airwaves; nonetheless, in a poll taken in December 1980, he was preferred by 16.1% of the electorate.[40]

Coluche's popularity threatened the presidential aspirations of the leading left-wing candidate, the Socialist Mitterrand, whose campaign depended on uniting the left against the two conservative candidates, Valéry Giscard d'Estaing and Jacques Chirac. Mitterrand, however, was careful not to alienate Coluche, and, though the performer had had little good to say publicly about his rival, behind-the-scenes contacts between representatives of the two campaigns helped Coluche to acknowledge the relative proximity of their political and cultural preoccupations. On March 15, 1981, seven weeks before the election, Coluche withdrew from the race, and soon thereafter endorsed Mitterrand.[41]

Coluche's candidacy, and the support he attracted from avatars of the post-1968 generation, proved the extent to which the new French left was different; it was a joyful and culturally oriented left, a left in which the comedian's antics and the ironic derision of institutions and their seriousness went together with the work of intellectuals and artists. The aesthetic left that Godard had foretold in 1960, that had brought its anti-authoritarian attitudes to bear on the revolts of May 1968, was on the verge of pushing its way into the halls of power and becoming part of France's cultural authority.

twenty

PASSION AND *FIRST NAME: CARMEN*

"The world and its metaphor"

DESPITE THE CRITICAL RECOGNITION AND COMMERCIAL success of *Sauve qui peut,* Godard did not have another project awaiting him. A recurring motif in the film features the word "passion," with characters reproaching others for misusing it: "That's not passion." Huppert asked Godard what, in fact, he thought passion was; his response was that she should make another film with him to find out,[1] but did not specify what the project would be.[2] Marin Karmitz hoped to incite a film by bringing Godard and Marguerite Duras together for a meeting in the Normandy seaside town of Trouville, where both filmmakers had apartments. Godard wanted to work with her on something "having to do with incest,"[3] but they could not come to an agreement about what it should be. On her own, Duras converted the subject of their talks into her next feature film, *Agatha et les lectures illimitées* (Agatha and the Unlimited Readings), a story of incestuous siblings. For his part, Godard told the audience at the New York Film Festival in October 1980 that his next film would be about "fathers and daughters," but took no concrete steps toward making it.

Some months earlier, after the success of *Apocalypse Now,* Francis Ford Coppola had bought the former Hollywood General studio and renamed it Zoetrope. He planned to bring together filmmakers, actors, and technicians as in a traditional Hollywood studio, but to run a "civilized, pro-artistic" enterprise.[4] He included Godard in his creative program and anticipated producing the video "script" for *The Story,* as well as Godard's adaptation of Jack Kerouac's *On the Road.* Godard likened Coppola's activities to his own, saying that Coppola "tries to make a home out of his studio, and I have a home and I would like to make a studio out of it."[5]

The return of culture
(United Artists / Photofest)

In January 1981, the actress Hanna Schygulla was visiting Zoetrope. Godard met her there by chance and asked her to appear in his next film. She had never been in a film by a director other than Rainer Werner Fassbinder, but she agreed at once—on the condition that Godard give her a written story. Shortly after getting back to Rolle, he typed up a three-page synopsis for *Passion: Work and Love,* addressed to Schygulla. Godard's idea was to remake Jean Renoir's 1934 film *Toni,* about immigrant workers and their conflicts over work and love. He was unable to obtain the rights to do so, but he transformed the general idea into the basis for his next film.

The story outline had little to do with fathers and daughters; it was the story of a German-speaking woman, or a German woman, a French-speaking woman, and a foreign man, "neither refugee nor immigrant, or both,"[6] and another unspecified man. The vaguely described action, which Godard likened to the classic American film noirs *Fallen Angel* and *Criss Cross,* was set around a small factory behind a train station, and ended with the male foreigner killed by a stray police bullet. (Godard planned to use a special scientific camera to capture in slow motion a bullet crossing space, and intended to film a troupe of clowns miming the motion of that bullet.)

The synopsis was enough to convince Schygulla to put her name to the project. The success of *Sauve qui peut,* plus the illustrious international names associated with *Passion,* brought Godard what he called a "magnificent" budget, announced as twelve million francs (more than two million dollars). But instead of organizing the shoot, he got to work on what he called the "production of the visual screenplay."[7] Godard estimated that he spent 60 percent of it before the shoot began in December 1981. To do the copious preliminary shooting, Godard needed a cameraman on hand, and he went far to find him.

Godard called Ed Lachman, a cameraman from New York, who had shot *Lightning over Water* for Wim Wenders and Nicholas Ray, and met him in New York at the Hotel St. Moritz. As Lachman later recalled, "He told me that he wanted to have a director of photography who would work with him in a different way, who would be with him not just when the film was being shot, but all the time."[8] One of the places where Lachman joined Godard was on the set of Coppola's new film, *One from the Heart,* a technical extravaganza in which sophisticated new video technology was used to create a fantasy version of Las Vegas. Coppola had involved Godard in the project early on, inviting him to come along on a scouting trip to Las Vegas (which he did) and to film some of the images of the city that would be used as video backdrops (which he refused to do).

The troubled eight-week shoot of *One from the Heart* began on February 2, 1981.[9] Before it started, Coppola had lost his European financing and had to come up with $1 million a week to keep it going. The difficulties had little impact on Godard, however, who came to the set with Ed Lachman and sound recordist Mitch Dubin to do some filming. Godard used a Super-8 camera, and Lachman shot both 35mm and 16mm film, surreptitiously; although Coppola himself had authorized their presence, their covert shoot was against union regulations. The idea, as Lachman recalled, was to make an essaylike film that Godard would call *Anatomy of a Shot*: "While Francis was shooting, Godard would say to me, 'Pick out that extra': I'd follow her for the whole length of the shot. Then, 'Pick out that dolly grip,' and so it would go for all the takes." The intended visual study of the crew's activities derived from the longtime project, born with *France tour détour*, to analyze the gestures of work, which became a basic element of *Passion*.

Then Godard oversaw a second shoot on Coppola's set—and this one added a crucial new element to the new film, and indeed, to his work for years to come. At a cost of $30,000 for one day of shooting, he used Coppola's studio, sets, and crew to film several *tableaux vivants*—including one of a painting by Rubens, *The Fall of the Damned*, and another of *The Newborn*, by Georges de la Tour. Hanna Schygulla recalled the staging of *The Newborn* as "a sort of holy image of a woman holding a baby, and in the background you would see these actresses going through all kinds of neurotic [gestures] with their bodies and shaking their heads. It had that mix of being funny, grotesque and beautiful, with this glorious music in the background."[10] Fifty babies were present as extras on the set, but, as Martine Marignac, Godard's associate producer, recalled, Godard sent them away and replaced them with dolls "so that it would make less noise."[11]

The quiet that Godard required was central to the day's work—which found its origins in the "glorious music" that accompanied the shoot. Godard explained:

> The film more or less began with my listening 450 times to the Mozart Requiem, thanks to a Sony Walkman, and then Anne-Marie Miéville made me listen, one day, to the Fauré Requiem, and I thought that there were also other musicians, Czech and French, and that one should try for once to create almost a scrupulous kind of democracy on and in a film . . . As much painting as music, neither one without the other, and no more reality than metaphor. That was a bit of the subject of the film; one could say, as a subtitle, "Passion, the world and its metaphor," or, the social element and its metaphor.[12]

Passion would bring together work and love, politics and personal relations, reality and symbolic life and art. It would be a film of dualities and it would suggest a more radical overcoming of them than it would actually effect.

The story that emerged from the preliminary shoot would be centered on three hives of activity in a provincial town: a small factory that a worker

(Isabelle Huppert) attempts to unionize; a motel and bar, owned by a former factory worker (Hanna Schygulla) who is married to the factory's owner; and the set of a "gigantic superproduction" for film or television that is shooting nearby, involving a Polish actor (Jerzy Radziwilowicz). The woman who owns the motel would fall in love with the Polish actor, who would be in love with the young striker.

The film-within-a-film involving the Polish actor would be derived from Godard's day at Zoetrope: it would incorporate the staging of vast historical or mythological scenes from classic paintings which related metaphorically to the lives of the characters, joined by "an orchestra that plays movements from great symphonies of the past."

In July 1981, Godard put together a more elaborate version of the story, full of possibilities and digressions.[13] Hanna Schygulla's character was now named Bruna, short for Brunnhilde. The factory worker played by Isabelle Huppert, modeled on the philosopher of sainthood, Simone Weil, was called Odile and was a virgin. The specific elaborations made to the project within a mere few months could not conceal the fact that Godard did not know what to do. He was "wandering, in both senses of the word," as Huppert observed, both in body and in mind.[15] The increased demand for Godard's personal appearances after the success of *Sauve qui peut* turned him into even more of a wanderer. Lachman recalled following him "around Europe and across the States for a year."

> He'd pull out a first-class Swissair ticket from his pocket and give it to me and say, "Can you meet me next week?" I'd fly to Paris, he'd pick me up at the airport—he always picked me up himself—drop me off at my hotel. We'd have breakfast the next day, we'd talk a little bit, he'd say he wasn't ready yet, then he'd give me another ticket and say, "Meet me in Berlin."

Lachman depicted crazed, frantic activity: "He'd always have a first-class ticket with him. He'd tell me, 'I won't be here for lunch tomorrow.' He'd fly to Paris from L.A., meet with somebody, then get back on the plane after lunch and fly back to L.A. the same day. That's how I see him at that time, always in motion."[15]

But these peregrinations and indirections were not only an essential part of Godard's process of discovery, they had become—once again—the subject of his planned film. While presenting *Sauve qui peut* at the New York Film Festival on October 3, 1980, Godard had shocked his audience by declaring to film lovers brought up on the auteurist gospel that the producer was more important to a film than the director.[16] Later, when editing *Passion*, Godard permitted a television crew to videotape and interview him: he described himself as a "small businessman" and, holding up his ledger book, declared, "This is a script."[17] He now considered the financial risk of a producer, of a businessman, to be the most concrete form of jeopardy, and thought that a director could not be serious about creating personal stories if he did not share in that risk.[18] Godard's jet-propelled wanderings to talk business were, in effect, the production of an enormous backstory; through this frenetic activity, he experienced and embodied the dangers and demands of high-level filmmaking.

Despite producing backstory, Godard was still having trouble coming up with the story, and he put off plans to start shooting *Passion* in the summer of 1981. Instead, he called again on the screenwriter Jean-Claude Carrière to help him come up with something and had Huppert, Schygulla, and the Swiss actor Jean-Luc Bideau (as the factory owner) improvise in the presence of Carrière, in sessions that were videotaped by Goupil.[19] Afterward, Godard and Carrière spent long hours together talking "about *Passion,* about painting," as Carrière recalled, "in the street, in a restaurant"—and Romain Goupil recorded all that, too.[20]

Then, in the fall of 1981, Godard summoned his actors to Rolle to begin shooting, but he was still not ready. He simply did not know what to film, and with Carrière away in Mexico helping with Luis Buñuel's autobiography, Godard was on his own. He gave his actors specific tasks relating to their roles. Huppert spent days in a button factory; Schygulla worked as a waitress in a roadside café; and Radziwilowicz had the most exacting assignment of all: Godard changed the role from a Polish actor to a Polish director, and had the actor follow him around all day to see what sorts of things a director did.

To prepare for the shoot, Godard interviewed Schygulla, Huppert, and Radziwilowicz on video. He told Schygulla that the roles were not yet definitively assigned, and that she might play a foreign actress and Radziwilowicz might play the union organizer. He told Radziwilowicz that he wanted to "do things a little differently" concerning love in the film, and he brought Schygulla and Radziwilowicz together for guided improvisations toward that end. He put on a cassette of a movement from Mozart's C-minor Mass, "Incarnatus Est," and told Schygulla, "I want you to direct with your head like a musical conductor." He wanted the physical connection between the actors to be mechanical, not expressive. As Schygulla later recalled, "He said, 'I'm not asking you to be in love. You should do it like with a chair.' He thought that things you have inside you come out anyhow—you shouldn't express them."[21]

Godard sent the actors into a separate room where they could rehearse by themselves, but as Radziwilowicz and Schygulla worked together on their musical number, Schygulla noticed Godard hiding behind a column. He revealed himself and, declaring his satisfaction with their work, decided to shoot it on video.[22]

In this videotape, Schygulla and Radziwilowicz are seen sitting face to face, in medium close-up, as the aria plays. First Godard himself comes around behind her and, taking hold of her head, runs his hand over her face and caresses her lips lasciviously. Then he leaves the frame and restarts the music as Radziwilowicz assumes Godard's role. The actor takes Schygulla's head in his hands, and she allows him to move it together with the music, until she lets herself go, singing and swooning beatifically to the aria.

This taped sequence, which Godard would include in the film—indeed, its most powerful scene—dramatizes the inseparability of art from love, and of love from the act of artistic creation.

WHEN GODARD FINALLY planned to shoot the film in December 1981, Ed Lachman was no longer available: he had left to work on another project. Before leaving, however, he had recommended that Godard replace him with Raoul Coutard (like many who had been associated with the New Wave, Coutard had not worked much in the late 1970s). But Godard demurred, citing his political differences with Coutard. Instead, he brought in other cameramen—Vittorio Storaro, Ricardo Aranowicz, Henri Decaë, Henri Alekan—who all refused to yield to Godard's insistence on natural light. So he returned to Coutard, who had not worked with Godard since 1967. Coutard found him a changed man. Though their relations in the 1960s had often been turbulent, Godard now, according to Coutard, "looked for relations of conflict—more than before. Now he can say some very unpleasant things to you. It stimulates his ideas."[23]

Conflict dominated the shoot even before it began. After months of preparatory work with Jean-Luc Bideau, who was to play the factory owner, Godard fired him—over the telephone—and replaced him with Michel Piccoli. Marin Karmitz was also treated in a way that he found "very aggressive," and he quit the film, leaving its production to Alain Sarde.[24]

IN *PASSION*, AS it was shot, Jerzy is a Polish film director trying to make a film in a studio in a small roadside town in Switzerland. The production is going badly. Although he has a large crew and an army of extras working on setting up scenes—*tableaux vivants* of classic paintings—he films very little and merely erects and dismantles sets, stages and restages *tableaux*, and rides the crane that holds a heavy television camera, but hardly shoots at all.

Isabelle, a worker in a small nearby factory, is trying to organize a strike. Having been fired for her militancy, she goes to the factory to demand that the boss, Michel (Piccoli), reinstate her. Following him to the motel that Hanna (Schygulla), his wife, owns, Isabelle finds the film crew gathered there, and meets Jerzy. They become lovers.

Meanwhile, Hanna—who was one of Michel's former employees at the factory—meets the members of the crew and becomes interested in Jerzy, who persuades her to do a screen test with him. The videotape of her audition is the one that Godard had made prior to filming, of Schygulla singing while Radziwilowicz guides her head with his hands. The scene in which they watch the audition tape together is the emotional center of the film, the critical moment where work and love intersect.

Passion concludes with Jerzy's film unfinished. He decides that he needs to return to Poland; both women, as well as a third woman from the hotel, accompany him. Life takes precedence over the film, but the conclusion is nonetheless calmly confident: Jerzy's departure does not suggest his artistic impotence, despair, or collapse, but rather, his hope that a more appropriate film will arise from his new relationships, his departure, his new journey, and his imminent homecoming.

Just as the ending OF *Sauve qui peut* refers to the ending of Truffaut's *The Man Who Loved Women,* so the ending of *Passion* alludes to that of Truffaut's *Day for Night,* in which the members of the film crew hitch rides to leave the set at the end of the shoot. For Truffaut, the film was finished and the crew returns to life; for Godard, the film is unfinished and cannot be finished until Jerzy returns to life—to home, to Poland, where he has a family—and incorporates his life into the film.

THE ENDING OF *Passion,* in which Jerzy abandons the "superproduction" and the studio enclosure, suggests Godard's own dissatisfaction with his production of the film. His frustrations with the producers, with money problems, with the apparatus of the large crew, resembled Jerzy's; yet Godard also bore the small businessman's practical burdens, akin to Michel's. Jerzy's film studio, supposedly located in the same Swiss border town as the motel and the factory, was in fact a film studio in the suburbs of Paris. As a result, Godard could not shoot the story sequentially, and had to engage in the sort of narrative engineering that had always been inimical to him: he had to film in Switzerland with an eye toward the later studio shoot, which in turn had to cohere with what had already been completed.

Coutard found Godard "more indecisive" than before: "He no longer had the certainty he had before that things should be made in this or that way . . . It is a film that he could have made in six weeks and he needed four months."[25] Huppert was aware of Godard's unhappiness and uncertainty with his production of *Passion,* and recognized that Godard found the shoot "painful": "The film was very complicated for him, and he held us quite responsible for his difficulties."[26]

When *Passion* was shown at Cannes on May 25, 1982—and went into commercial release the next day—the critic for *Le Monde,* Louis Marcorelles, called it "the profoundly discouraging film of a solitary man, jealously closed in on himself, whom unconditional praise risks pressing further ahead into his solitude."[27] Despite copious and favorable attention from Godard's familiar outlets, *Cahiers du cinéma* and *Libération,* the film did poorly in relation to its high budget and to the expectations aroused by its stars. Shortly after its release, Godard, speaking on television, blamed the cast and crew for its failure, ascribing it to their detachment while it was being made: "Since my film isn't doing well, I sometimes say to myself, 'Nobody talked to me about it, about this film' . . . I asked people: 'This one or that one?' Silence. 'It's up to you to decide, Jean-Luc.' "[28]

Godard wanted his cast and crew to offer their views and help him make decisions. But in this film, the decisions that he was making were atypical for them: his quandaries concerned the substance of the film, Delacroix and Dvořák, Rembrandt's *Night Watch* and Mozart's Requiem. He thought that even those who had no particular artistic education could offer useful ideas on such subjects, if only they would speak thoughtfully and honestly—indeed, if only they would speak.

His wishes were not ridiculous, harsh, unreasonable, or for that matter insincere, but they were unusual, and the people who worked with him hesitated to voice judgments on such matters in the presence of such an intellectually gifted—and critically peremptory—man, nor were they prepared to face his ridicule or his wrath in case of his dissatisfaction with their remarks. Huppert, however, had sufficient fortitude to respond to his requests, and the results showed up in the film. Godard asked her to write him a text each night and was "furious" with her when she copied out a passage from a book by Samuel Beckett. In response to his fury, she produced a line about the film's central theme—"One must work at loving or else love to work"—which Godard put into the film through the voice of her character.[29]

As Huppert understood, Godard was unaware of the effect that he had on the participants in his film: "He depends on others, but he doesn't take into account that the people with whom he works and on whom he depends are under the influence of a power relationship" with him.[30] But Godard claimed, in a radio discussion with Piccoli the night of the film's premiere, that this submission was the fault of the actors and the crew: "I always ask people to want to make the films that they want to make. And instead of that, it was: 'We'll do what you want, Daddy,' or 'We'll do what you want, Master.' " In the face of this submission, he admitted that his only "recourse" was "to put the actors into a state of disequilibrium and of catastrophe," but he understood the gravity of the method: "One does not play around with such catastrophes."[31]

Godard knew that his artistic methods were risky, both practically and morally. He had undertaken what he called the search for "the grandeur of the ordinary," for "the arts, and that which it transmits,"[32] but sensed that this new quest for traditional notions of beauty was fraught with moral danger: "One must run the risk of sin as one approaches it."[33] The sacred and the profane, as they came into play in the personal relations which were, in his view, a prerequisite for creating a filmed story of personal relations, were the grand themes of Godard's new approach to human reality in *Passion*. He promptly made another film, about *Passion* itself, in which to say so—in which to make these themes explicit and to explain what he had tried to do, had done, and had not been able to do.

On May 5, 1982, several weeks before the premiere of *Passion* at the Cannes festival, French television broadcast *Passion: l'amour et le travail, introduction à un scénario* (Passion: Love and Work, Introduction to a Screenplay), Godard's own assemblage of video material that he had shot prior to the making of the film.[34] Programmers at Swiss television, however, found the compilation too scrappy and disconnected, and commissioned from him a video "screenplay" of *Passion*, after the fact, which would be shown on television following the film's Swiss commercial release.

The commission for this video, *Scénario du film Passion*, inspired Godard to return to his underlying motives for the film; without the massive industrial mechanism of the full-scale shoot, he was able to lay his ideas bare. From within his own video studio, Godard addresses the audience ("Good evening, friends and enemies"), using the monitors before him on which to project the images of *Passion* (as well as one large white blank screen) as he describes the series of associations and considerations that link them. Superimpositions done in the editing room put Godard in front of the film's images. He raises his hands as a sort of orchestral conductor or magus and invokes the divine power that brought the film to life:

And there was light and there were soldiers, there were bosses, there were children, and there was light, and there was joy, there was war, there was the angel, and there was fear, and there was light, there was the universal wound, there was night, there was the virgin, there was grace, and there was light, and there was light, and there was light, and there was fog, and there was adventure, and there was fiction, and there was reality, and there was the documentary, and there was movement, and there was cinema, and there was the image, and there was sound, and there was cinema, there was cinema, there was cinema. Here is work.

The central idea of this invocation—the religious essence of the birth of cinema, and of a single film, in a process akin to Genesis—would inspire

Godard's next decade of work. While *Passion* merely hinted at the transcendent aspect of the creation of cinema, the *Scénario* made for Swiss television put the hieratic and suffering figure of the creator himself at the center of the cinema. In its clarity, inventiveness, and intimacy, the *Scénario du film Passion* is superior to the feature film *Passion*.

The *Scénario* brings to light an important shift in Godard's career that two other short films from that time hinted at—*Lettre à Freddy Buache* (Letter to Freddy Buache), a promotional short commissioned by the city of Lausanne made in the summer of 1981, and *Changer d'image* (A Change of Image), commissioned by INA for broadcast in May 1982 to commemorate the first anniversary of the election of François Mitterrand.

In *Lettre à Freddy Buache*, a commission that Godard had elicited more than a year earlier but did not fulfill until he was deep at work on *Passion*, he evoked the subject of Lausanne by emphasizing his personal relation to the city, starting out by filming himself in close-up behind his record player as he puts on the turntable a recording of Ravel's *Boléro*. He speaks the film's voice-over commentary throughout as he attempts to decide which images best capture the city's essence. In *Changer d'image*, broadcast on French television in May 1982, Godard discusses the concept of change by showing himself in front of a blank film screen and a microphone, and uses the occasion to dramatize his own role in political change—through the failure of his Mozambique project—as he stages a scene of himself being beaten and left for dead by an official of an unnamed country where he had gone to make a film.

In both films, as in *Scénario du film Passion*, Godard made his own physical presence the principal subject and the pretext of the work; he did so again, to more decisive and self-revealing effect, in the feature film that followed *Passion*.

While presenting *Passion* at the Cannes festival, Godard was already pessimistic about the film's commercial prospects. He wanted to get another project under way immediately, fearing that if he waited, the anticipated failure would make it harder to raise money. He again sought the allure of a star—this time, Isabelle Adjani, with whom Godard's producer, Alain Sarde, had previously made two films.[35] Godard was frank about his motives: he wanted to work with Adjani because he knew that, on the basis of her name, he could get financing.

As it turned out, he needn't have worried.

MITTERRAND'S PRESIDENCY and his Socialist Party's resounding victory in the parliamentary elections in June 1981 brought about a new attitude and a new policy regarding the arts in France. After his victory, Mitterrand declared that "the Socialist enterprise is first of all a cultural project,"[36] and he named as his minister of culture Jack Lang, who rivalled in ambition his famous predecessor, André Malraux. Lang was trained as a lawyer, but his first love was theater, in which he had long been a prominent administrator.[37] He had big plans and Mitterrand had given him formidable means to realize them: in their first year in power, the Socialists doubled arts funding in France.

Lang, born in 1939, was a member of the 1968 generation that had carried Mitterrand into office, the generation whose artistic values and cinematic tastes had been formed by the French New Wave, and for whom Godard was a prime cultural hero. One of the first things that Lang did after taking office was to bestow upon him the French Order of Merit. (Godard, however, refused the honor, claiming that as a Swiss citizen he would have to receive special dispensation from his home canton of Vaud).[38] But Lang's administration offered Godard more concrete benefits as well.

Lang's cultural intentions were openly political. In one controversial speech, he called for "a real crusade" against what he termed the "financial and intellectual imperialism that no longer grabs territory, or rarely, but grabs consciousness, ways of thinking, ways of living."[39] The imperialism he had in mind was, of course, American, and in seeking to limit the American influence in France, he saw the French cinema as a crucial rampart against it. In September 1981, four months after his appointment, Lang clearly drew the lines of battle with his pointed refusal to attend the Deauville festival of American cinema. He crafted policies intended to favor and to foster the French cinema, as art and as industry, increasing government aid more than sevenfold, giving tax breaks to capital investments in films, expanding the advance on receipts, and introducing aid for script development and for exhibition.[40] Lang also tripled government aid to the Cinémathèque and in 1984, inaugurated classes in cinema history for high school students.

Because of the esteem in which Godard and the French New Wave were held by the new cultural authorities, producers and television executives now understood that in dealing with Godard, the New Wave, and its cinematic tributaries, they were, in effect, dealing with friends of Mitterrand and of the government. And in a system in which the government played such a large role in industry in general and in the media business in particular, this was an important advantage. Godard was soon invited to edit and report the noontime news on the French television channel Antenne 2 for a week in August 1982. (He refused.)[41] He was approached by the Ministry of Culture about a "research project" which, Godard said, "concerns the way a film is made," and he also lectured about filmmaking at the leading film school, IDHEC.[42]

Godard and his erstwhile New Wave colleagues were now able to film copiously. Eric Rohmer, who was no leftist but was a de facto ally of the government's cultural program, had made only three films from 1972 to 1981; under Mitterrand, he unleashed a torrent of films, making six between 1982 and 1987. Jacques Rivette, who had worked under extraordinary financial constraints in the 1970s, suddenly found himself able to realize large-scale productions with substantial budgets.[43] Truffaut, who had managed to keep busy through the 1970s with financing from American producers and had had great success in France in 1980 with *The Last Metro,* was honored by the new regime: having campaigned actively for Mitterrand, Truffaut was awarded the French Legion of Honor in 1981 but refused it, wanting to retain his sense of independence from authority. Lang also offered him the director-ship of the Cinémathèque. Truffaut refused again, recommending Rivette.[44] (The job ultimately went to the director Constantin Costa-Gavras.)

As for Godard, his status was definitively transformed by Lang's policies: a high-culture figure, his value was henceforth measured not in ticket sales or short-term profits but in prestige. He had been relaunched by his own ef-forts; through Lang's vision he was now canonized. His pace of filmmaking accelerated suddenly and drastically. Having dramatized himself as the pro-ducer and the director in *Passion,* Godard chose a fitting moment for a new role: he began to film himself as an actor, and imbue his work with his own quasi-mythic persona.

AT CANNES IN May 1982, Godard offered Adjani the lead role in the story of Carmen, because, he said, he expected her to agree "at once" to play "a leg-endary figure."[45] The story had regained currency in France for the odd and simple reason that Bizet's opera had recently fallen into the public domain.[46] Other films of *Carmen* (by Carlos Saura, Francesco Rosi, and Peter Brook) were also in the works and would be released in 1983. Unlike the others, however, Godard's version was inspired, he said, by Otto Preminger's film *Carmen Jones,* an adaptation of the opera featuring an African-American cast that included Harry Belafonte and Dorothy Dandridge; it had recently been rereleased in France after having been unavailable there since the 1950s due to legal challenges by Bizet's heirs. (In particular, Godard was inspired by the Preminger film's translation of a line from the famous "Habanera": for the sentence, "Si je t'aime, prends garde à toi" (If I love you, watch out), Pre-minger's film had "If I love you, that's the end of you."

Like Preminger, Godard would make the story a contemporary one, and he imagined Adjani as Carmen "Dupont," the equivalent French Every-name.[47] But no sooner did Godard recruit the actress to his project—for which Sarde quickly found financing—than he also began to complain in a radio interview about the restrictions entailed by working with a busy star:

> In my next film, the one with Adjani, I'd like there to be a female basketball player. But to resemble a professional basketball player, she has to practice a

minimum amount. And because actors go from one film to the next, they can't do it. So I have to say bye-bye to the basketball. So, what can we do? Subway conductor? Same thing. Lover? That's not a profession.[48]

The training and preparation of actors for their roles had become very important to Godard: the films with which he had returned to the cinema, *Sauve qui peut* and *Passion,* had had long periods of gestation that involved his cast and crew. He wanted to work at length with Adjani as he had worked with Goupil, Lachman, and even Schygulla. But, unable to secure the services of an established star for such a duration, Godard would have to create his own.

During the shoot of *Passion,* Godard had selected Myriem Roussel, a young female extra who had been hired for her background as a classical dancer, as a last-minute replacement in a small role. He asked her to play a deaf and mute young woman, working in the factory, who was chosen by the production manager in the Polish director's film to be an extra on that superproduction—a nude extra, whose "performance" was mainly to disrobe on camera, beside a swimming pool.[49]

After completing *Passion,* Godard stayed in contact with Roussel. He planned to film her in the project he had begun to discuss several years earlier, *Fathers and Daughters.*[50] To prepare Roussel, he began to train her in cinema, taking her to see many movies and videotaping her. Now, to extend his working relationship with Roussel, he wrote her into his film of Carmen as well.

The first version of the project, which Godard called *Prénom: Carmen* (*First Name: Carmen*), was a twelve-page script treatment.[51] It specified that the film would start with Godard himself: "Assorted shots of JLG arriving from distant voyages, ill and tired from carrying suitcases, ideas, and money, and yet jovial." This character, JLG, checks into a hospital in Paris, where he lives among "the sick (mentally handicapped)," and there "exchanges a few words with the young female nurse of an old man (Mr. Lear and Miss Cordelia)."[52] Then Carmen comes to visit him at the hospital. She had been married to JLG, and had starred in his early films, but "political events and art" had separated them. She had wandered through Germany and Italy, and came back to France "without hope and without money." JLG proposes a role for her in a new film, as Electra. In this version, Carmen suggested Anna Karina in disguise. Godard's choice of Germany and Italy was not random: there the Baader-Meinhof gang and the Red Brigade had been active, and his Carmen was to carry out a bank robbery as an act of political terrorism (a nod to *La Chinoise* and Anne Wiazemsky). However, Godard ultimately left this side story out because, he later said, "too many things would be brought to it from the outside by critics and the audience"—he didn't want the political story to detract attention from the erotic one, the obsession that grips and, finally, dooms Carmen's lover, Joseph.[53]

Early on, Godard also included a character named Myriem, Joseph's girlfriend, who refuses to sleep with him until he gets a steady job. To please her, he becomes a bank guard, which displeases her: she calls him a "pathetic cop" and is dismayed that he works "to protect rich people's money." Carmen is one of a band of robbers who descend on the bank where Joseph works. During the robbery, Joseph captures Carmen, but instead of arresting her, they escape together.

Godard's second version of the story proved decisive: it was not a script in the usual sense but an audiocassette. The story of *Carmen*, according to Godard, required music, but he had no intention of using Bizet's opera. Instead, he wanted to develop the film from "fundamental music. Music that marked the history of music. Music that is at the same time the practice and the theory of music": Beethoven's quartets.[54] The cassette comprised Godard's descriptions of the action, sequence by sequence, along with excerpts from the quartets as interludes and accompaniments to his narration.

On the tape, Godard states his intention of using Beethoven's later quartets, in the order in which Beethoven composed them, so that the film would "follow the story of his music, and his music is a part of the story." These compositions would appear in the film in chronological order; the film and the action would begin with the Ninth Quartet and end with the Sixteenth, Beethoven's last.

For the cassette, Godard relied on existing recordings of the quartets, but for the film, he hired the Prat Quartet, based in Paris, to perform them—on-camera. Myriem Roussel, who had never played a string instrument in her life, was to appear as a member of the chamber music group. For four months, through the summer and fall of 1982, Roussel studied for the role: she listened to music under Godard's guidance, and she practiced the violin, on her own and with members of the quartet, to learn to replicate the gestures of playing the instrument and of playing the Beethoven quartets in particular,[55] because Godard intended to correlate images of the musicians at work with the film's dramatic action. For example, he envisioned matching what he called the "rounded" gesture of an arm bowing a violin with the gesture of Joseph or Carmen putting an arm around the other's shoulder, as well as with the arm of a driver turning a steering wheel. On the audiocassette, Godard described the music as being "on" or "off"—performed on- or off-camera—and so, he knew exactly which passages in the Ninth, Fifteenth, and Sixteenth quartets Roussel would have to learn to play.

The audio script also features the character of JLG, who was now integrated into the film's dénouement. He is shooting a film in the lobby of a grand hotel, and the Prat Quartet, including Roussel, is playing salon music at teatime for "the big businessmen and the old American women." As Godard describes his own appearance, "There is JLG who is doing his shoot in his sick person's bathrobe, with the technicians of the film and the nurses who are taking care of him." The criminal gang, including Carmen—and a seller of videos played by Alain Sarde—then attacks the lobby. The police arrive, and, after a shoot-out, Carmen's last words are a dialogue with JLG, derived from Giraudoux's play, *Electra*: she says, "What is it called when everyone is dead but something remains?" and he answers, "It is called dawn."

> Then it's over, the end of the shoot. We say, "See you tomorrow at such and such a place and time." They put things away, Myriem too. We'll have to see about Joseph, maybe he died from a bullet fired by the police. Myriem thanks JLG for having hired her for his film, "Goodbye, Monsieur." "Goodbye, Mademoiselle." And Raoul says, as he watches her leave, "My God, is she beautiful," and JLG says, "You know what beauty is? You know what it is? It's the beginning of the terror we are able to bear."

Thus *First Name: Carmen* was, in Godard's conception, to be the film of two couples: Carmen and Joseph, and JLG and Myriem. But in a written sketch that followed, in December 1982, Godard made clear that the film was also primally based in a third relationship, that of JLG and Carmen, which is shown in a sort of prelude to be an essential precondition to the drama:

> Carmen comes to ask JLG, her uncle, whether she can use his seaside apartment to shoot a documentary film with her friends. What's more, they are looking for an inexpensive director, and wouldn't JLG want to take this opportunity to make his return to the cinema? Carmen would play a role in it and the film would bear her name. Her explanations are a bit confused.[56]

Godard would film himself in the melancholic guise of a sick and confused man returning to work as an unwitting front for bandits. It was a self-dramatizing lament for his own sense of isolation, a sarcastic view of the film industry as a den of thieves—and a presentation of himself as the enabler of a scam enacted by Adjani. This accusatory definition of a movie star and pathetic view of a director were soon reflected in the eventful first days of the shoot.

THE "RAOUL" WHOM Godard mentioned in his outline was Raoul Coutard, who again worked with Godard, albeit in a modified role. Where *Sauve qui peut* had featured two directors of photography, *First Name: Carmen* was to have none: Coutard was hired as the film's "lighting consultant," Jean-Bernard

Menoud was brought in as the camera assistant, and Godard himself planned to compose and shoot the film—principally with the lightweight Aäton camera that Jean-Pierre Beauviala had manufactured to his specifications. Godard told the twenty-year-old actor cast as Joseph, Jacques Bonnaffé, that the project was "an amateur film."[57]

Adjani, however, was not an amateur actress. Godard's difficulties with her began before the camera rolled in January 1983. He wanted her to appear without makeup. Adjani not only refused, she brought her own personal makeup artist to work with her. She insisted that Godard shoot copious test footage, and she also placed many restrictions on what could be shot—in particular, concerning nude scenes, of which Godard had planned many.

The first sequence to be shot was that of the bank robbery, when Carmen and Joseph meet. During the shoot, all the brewing sources of tension came out into the open. Adjani complained to one journalist that Godard wouldn't let her wear makeup; to another, about the small camera that reminded her of home movies; according to Anne-Marie Miéville, who was present, Adjani said that Coutard "was a misogynist and didn't know how to photograph women."[58] The Saturday after the first week of the shoot, in which little real work was done, Adjani called Alain Sarde in tears to tell him that she would not continue.

The recasting started at once. The agent Myriam Bru sent Godard an inexperienced twenty-year-old actress from the Netherlands who had arrived in France just two years earlier and was working as an au pair. The young woman, Maruschka Detmers, came for an audition and left a head shot. Godard asked her to come to his office again to do a screen test on videotape. She played a scene with Jacques Bonnaffé in which she had to grab him by the arm and speak sharply to him. Her instinctive reaction, she said, was very violent, and, she said, "I yelled at him anything that came into my head."[59] Godard told her point-blank that he didn't think that she could do the part, to which she responded by calling him "mean."[60] That night, he called and asked her to sign a contract. He later said that Detmers was the only actress beside Adjani "who corresponded with the idea that we had of the character. Brunette, wild. She seemed to have a vigor, a natural autonomy in the scenes that we rehearsed. She didn't interpret."[61]

Yet no sooner did he cast Detmers than he was, as usual, disappointed: "And then afterwards, you discover the perversity: immediately, interpretation."[62] Godard continued to work with and against actors in order to keep them from identifying psychologically with their characters. He favored precise physical behavior, exact recitation of texts, and a relation to action that was based on knowledge and experience rather than emotional extrapolation.

Time was limited, however. Detmers had been called in to step into Adjani's role on short notice, and she could not go through the kind of complex training that Myriem Roussel had had. Instead, Godard told Detmers and Bonnaffé to listen to the Beethoven quartet recordings that he gave them, and to visit the Rodin Museum in Paris. Detmers (according to Godard) did not go to the museum and did not bother to listen to the music, either. Bonnaffé—to whom Godard had said, "Don't obey, I detest that"—obeyed, and paid the price, as he later recalled:

> Once I had listened to the Beethoven, he was able to come yell at me because I didn't know how to listen and it hadn't served any purpose. He said: "But it's completely crazy, we've been shooting together for three weeks and you haven't yet figured out that you are the viola, not the solo, the viola. Don't listen, listen to nothing, don't listen anymore."[63]

For Detmers the shoot went worse: "Godard told us, 'If you listen to the music, you will understand what you have to do, let yourself get carried away.' When we didn't understand, he said that he had made a mistake, that he shouldn't have made the film."[64] Godard's instructions to her had nothing to do with what she had learned in acting class. "For example, for the scene in the bank, I had asked him whether Carmen was angry, or vulnerable or something else. He was shocked. He answered, 'What kind of words are these, I don't know them, maybe she is vulnerable, I wouldn't know, you have to follow the movements of the music, that's all.' " In the end, Detmers found herself unsure of what he wanted: "The only fixed point of reference I had," she said, "was my contract."[65]

Miéville, however, noticed that Godard directed his actors more specifically and more precisely than before, and attributed this to their inexperience and their theatrical training—which his meticulous instructions were intended to counteract. As Bonnaffé, a skilled theater actor, remembered: "If we tried to understand, to analyze our character's psychology, Godard got angry, he stopped us at once. He said that destroyed expression, which should remain intuitive and free. We lived in a climate of tension. Wanting us to share his concerns, his creative anxieties, he left us on the tightrope."[66]

In the film, though, Godard joined his actors on their tightrope. After making the film, he recalled, "Making a film, for me, is nebulous. It's painful. Each time it's like the creation of the world."[67] Now Godard conveyed his anxieties directly: he played them out on-screen, in performance. He compared his performance to that of the string quartet in terms of the layer of behind-the-scenes reality that it added to the film: "Just as we see the musicians, so the one who is inventing the story takes part in the story."[68]

The film begins with Godard—"Uncle Jean"—in a hospital; he is not sick, but is using it as a sort of nonwriter's retreat during his enforced exile from the cinema. In his role, Godard comically elevates his suffering to tragic proportions, as, for instance, in a parody of his struggles with Jean-Pierre Beauviala to produce a camera of his own. Uncle Jean sits in his hospital bed, holding on his shoulder a boom box that he calls his new "camera," which he claims to have built together with the kitchen staff. This "camera" emits a few tinny notes pecked out from all registers of a frail old piano, a haphazard rendition of the children's song "Au Clair de la Lune"—the first line of which continues, "mon ami Pierrot." The song, with its reference to Godard's film from 1965, invokes the buried notion of Carmen as a surrogate for Anna Karina.

Hired by the criminals to make a film that will serve as a front for their robbery scheme, Uncle Jean wanders through the story in anticipation of his return to glory. But his was not the only self-abasement that Godard filmed; if, in general, he was hard on his actors, he required of Detmers a sacrificial degree of self-abnegation. When he had put Isabelle Huppert into sexually demanding situations in *Sauve qui peut,* she was an experienced young actress consciously taking on the sort of challenge that would define her career. Detmers, however, was appearing in her first film and was hardly in a position to defend herself. She was called upon to expose her body and to unleash a carnal energy, a physical rage, and an emotional cruelty that Godard took to be in her nature. Detmers and Bonnaffé were remarkably pliant and uninhibited in the face of Godard's difficult demands—as when, while handcuffed to Joseph, Carmen is pulled by him into the men's room of a roadside gas station/convenience store, and has to urinate, while still captive, by sitting on a men's urinal, or when Joseph attempts to rape Carmen in the shower.

Detmers performed several intense nude scenes with Bonnaffé, including a close-up of her pubic area that is reminiscent, in its directness, of Courbet's painting *The Creation of the World.* Godard made Carmen's carnality the focus of the character, and throughout the film, both her erotic power and her vulnerability govern the action. Indeed, despite the sexual degradation to which Detmers submitted during the shoot, the character of Carmen is in subjection not to men but to sex itself, a blind destructive force which brings down the men under her influence—exactly as suggested by the line that inspired Godard, "If I love you, that's the end of you." Ultimately, it does her in as well.

Even Carmen's dealings with her Uncle Jean are rife with lust. In the film's first scene, Carmen visits him in the hospital to ask whether he would lend her his seaside apartment so that she and some friends could make a film there. He demands a kiss from her, then walks behind her and—as Godard had done with

Schygulla in the video sketch for *Passion*—lasciviously caresses her lips with his fingers, which she disgustedly rebuffs.

Indeed, *First Name: Carmen* deepens the psychodrama of incest Godard had been staging since the mid-1970s and paves the way for his next film, the long-delayed story about fathers and daughters. While Carmen and Joseph hide out in Uncle Jean's empty seaside apartment—Godard's own apartment in Trouville—she indicates the nature of her relations with her uncle. Reminiscing about the time she spent there when she was young, she gestures in one direction and tells Joseph, "That was his room," then after a pause, repeats, more softly, "His room."

Godard acknowledged that he could not have made such an eroticized film if the role of Carmen had been played by Adjani rather than Detmers, "because with Adjani we wouldn't have been able to do anything, she would have refused to do three-quarters of there things. They're nothing extraordinary, but stars are like heads of state, they do certain things, they don't do others."[69] Detmers was not a star; she did things on-camera that more established performers might have resisted; and as a result, she endured, in the course of the shoot, "vulnerability, shame, paralysis."[70]

Cavalier treatment of the actors and the crew was not uncommon during the shoot. Christophe Odent, who played the head of the band of criminals, described Godard's behavior toward him: "He constantly calls meetings where he asks you to say why you are bad."[71] Bonnaffé recalled that, during the shoot, Godard took refuge in a neighboring café and wrote "a tract, which he distributed, in the style of *J'accuse:* 'the technicians do what I ask them but bring nothing of their own, the actors act, but like cabinet ministers, the producer criticizes but doesn't have a word to say about how things could be made better.' "[72]

Godard also complained about Coutard much as he complained about Detmers: "I had asked him to go see Rodin's sculptures . . . I thought it was good for the film, for the body, and then I thought that if you're being paid nine thousand francs per week, maybe you could . . . He didn't go."[73] For his part, Coutard found Godard disturbingly vague about his wishes: "On *First Name: Carmen* we only worked with natural light, but that wasn't something Jean-Luc expressed clearly from the outset. He wasn't very conscious of what he wanted. We only understood as we made the film."[74] This was the last film the two made together.

Even the camera Godard wanted to use for the film, the small Aäton that he had commissioned, was a source of conflict. Though Godard had originally meant it to be no quieter than is needed to film dialogue scenes in the street, he had Beauviala modify it to run still more quietly to film intimate conversations in interior spaces. It was a tall order on a short schedule, and despite Beauviala's efforts, the camera did not work as Godard or Coutard had hoped. Godard reacted angrily,[75] used Beauviala's camera for only a few shots, and then switched to a conventional-sized Arriflex.

Godard later accepted an invitation from *Cahiers du cinéma* to join Beauviala and several other film professionals to talk out the problem in a roundtable discussion published as "Genesis of a Camera." The discussion was heated.[76] The two protagonists vigorously debated the terms of the commission for the camera, the uses for which it was designed, the handling of it by Godard and his crew. Throughout, Godard repeatedly lamented his inability to bring about the desired relations with his associates—"the phenomenon of the troupe, of the family."[77] Beauviala recalled the roundtable discussion as cathartic: "We were like an old couple who needed to have a good shouting match."[78] This dénouement seemed, to him, typical of his years of working with Godard. "He needs drama; he needs discord; he needs provocation; he needs conflict; he needs difficulties; he needs to yell at people—he needs to be unhappy."[79]

The shoot ended on a sour note. As Bonnaffé recalled, "One day, [Godard] said, 'You're doing something other than making the film, and the technicians don't understand it. We're not managing to do anything. Goodbye.' That's how he announced the end of the shoot to us."[80] Yet the bitterness, the disillusionment, the regret, the self-loathing, self-revelation, and self-pity that had burst forth in Godard's conduct on the set were no mere caprice; they were the scathing emotional center of *First Name: Carmen*, and as such they were the stuff of art.

GUIDED BY THE film's two dramatic axes—the director's self-pitying view as a rejected filmmaker and a debilitated sinner, and the destructive power of a woman unleashed on the unfortunate man who loves her—Godard filmed nature and art, the ocean from the Normandy coast and the string quartet in rehearsal, with daring and originality. In particular, his filming of the string quartet, materializing the music and evoking its creation as a blend of emotion, sport, and labor, arguably comprise the most revelatory depiction of musical performance in the history of cinema.

As he had done in his preliminary audio script, Godard films musical phrases as if they were literary phrases: he takes the music at its word, and he was explicitly aware of this effect: "Here, it's Beethoven, he's telling me something . . . Everything depends on the story that he's telling me, finally."[81] The blend of high and low cultural elements, classical music and the gangster story, renews the tale of Carmen as did none of the other versions made at the same time.

Befitting a film in which music played such a decisive part, Godard edited with a newfound attention to sound. Though he had always made distinctive use of the sound track, he had started, since his return with *Sauve qui peut,* to do his own sound editing using only two tracks. As he knew, twelve tracks were the industry standard at the time, and some Hollywood directors even used sixty. But where such elaborate sound mixes were used to create artificially natural ambiance, Godard used his two tracks to achieve what he described as "sculpting with sound."[82] In *First Name: Carmen,* Godard's quick sonic cutting and intricate interweaving of dialogue, sound effects, and music created an extraordinarily complex sound world that is itself musical.

The film's qualities were recognized at once. *First Name: Carmen* premiered at the Venice Film Festival in September 1983 and was awarded the Golden Lion, the festival's top prize, as well as "a special prize for the technical value of the image and the sound."

First Name: Carmen opened on January 11, 1984, in Paris, shown together with a short film that was screened as a prelude, *How Can I Love (A Man When I Know He Don't Want Me)*—Anne-Marie Miéville's entry into filmmaking. Miéville, who was also credited with the adaptation and screenplay of *First Name: Carmen,* took the title of her film from a line in Preminger's *Carmen Jones.* Unlike Godard's work, *How Can I Love* is simple and naturalistic in form. The film is a series of brief sketches in which a woman faces four men who successively pose a drily comic array of obstacles to their relationship. A fifth man, her daughter's teenage friend, propositions the woman, but she rejects him. Miéville audaciously placed her scenes in blunt succession without any transitional devices, thereby gracefully invoking a greater sweep of life than the film's modest scope suggested.

Godard had originally planned to release *First Name: Carmen* by personally presenting it in provincial theaters, in order to break the hold that Parisian audiences and critics had on a film's destiny. These plans fell through, but Godard need not have worried: the critical reception was exultant. In *Le Monde,* Louis Marcorelles declared, "The cinema has never been so futile nor so noble."[83] In *Libération,* Serge Daney wrote that "after the film's first press screening in Venice, everyone (including Godardians) came out like sleepwalkers who had been given a series of uppercuts in their sleep."[84] The film was both a popular and a commercial success.[85]

However, the paradox of the canonization of the New Wave in general and of Godard in particular during the first years of Mitterrand's presidency is that—despite such apparently good results as those of *First Name: Carmen*—this artistically progressive strain of cinema was out of step with the mood in France. The men and women of 1968 who had come to power were the artistic children of the New Wave, but they were also the children of rock music, television, comic books, and other popular forms of a commercial culture that they accepted with equanimity, even enthusiasm. Indeed, Jack

Lang also sought to canonize other mass-media creations, hiring an adviser from the pop music world who was widely known as the "minister of rock."

Godard's work was becoming ever more intellectual at a time when French society, high and low, was increasingly turning toward a quasi-universal American vernacular mass culture. Lang may have turned his back on the Deauville festival and inveighed against the pervasiveness of American pop culture, but he would have come off as reactionary had he rejected local adaptations of that culture by members of generations, including his own, who were raised on it. If he was using his office to reinforce, financially and pedagogically, the artistic heritage of the New Wave, it was largely because the phenomenon, left to the marketplace, would not have survived on its own. As a living symbol of France's highest tradition, Godard was invulnerable; as a player in the industry, his place was shakier than ever.

Godard's response to the changing trends was to express his displeasure with them in diatribes that grew increasingly heated; he also became openly, publicly nostalgic for the era before television, before mass media. In an interview in the first week of 1984, he sharply criticized the French media—"It's true that, today, I can't find information, my information, in the newspapers"—and cited this failure as the reason for his switch to classical subject matters: "That is to say, one can't find material [for a film] in the local news. So one has to copy, and since one has to copy, I prefer to copy Antigone than the life of Raymond Barre," a French politician.[86] Contemporary life, Godard suggested, had become so impoverished that it no longer inspired his films; belonging to the age of living myths, he needed to resuscitate the great artistic legends as a way of telling his own story. His next project, which he announced while presenting *First Name: Carmen* at the Venice festival, promised to do so with an even more grandiose and radical flourish:

> What interested us [in adapting *Carmen*]was to show what a man and a woman said to each other . . . What did they say when they were in the kitchen? What did they say when they were in the car? We don't know what they said. In my next film, by chance, I keep the male character Joseph: his Carmen will be called Mary. Well then, what did Joseph and Mary say to each other before they had the baby?[87]

A woman named Mary, played by Myriem Roussel
(New Yorker Films / Photofest)

twenty-one

HAIL MARY

"The extraordinary in an ordinary way"

A FTER MEETING MYRIEM ROUSSEL DURING THE SHOOT of *Passion,* Godard returned to the long-planned project called *Fathers and Daughters.* At first, he announced that it would take the form of an adaptation of *King Lear;*[1] he also considered calling it *The Man of My Life.* He stated explicitly that *Fathers and Daughters* would be "about incest,"[2] and to prepare for it, he started to read Freud's accounts of his early psychoanalyses. He then decided to make a film about Freud and Dora (Freud's first patient) in which the analyst's countertransference would converge with the father's taboo desire. Roussel was hesitant to appear in such a film. As Godard later admitted: "The actress with whom I was also hoping to have mixed relations, personal and work, naturally became afraid."[3] He looked for a way of approaching the subject that might allay Roussel's fears of uneasy personal implications:

> I came upon a book by [psychoanalyst] Françoise Dolto called *The Gospel at Risk of Psychoanalysis* and in her introduction—I didn't really read the rest of the book—she spoke of Mary and Joseph in a way that I never heard before. It seemed very cinematic: the story of a couple. And I'm very traditional. I've always made love stories and stories of couples. So that's how I got to the story of "God and his Daughter."[4]

Godard explained further:

> Since I have no daughter, I've wanted to have a daughter. I thought for a while that I would make a film about Freud and his first patient: on the problem of

the father. Then, I looked at it with regard to God the Father. And I came upon the story of Mary.[5]

Godard was to play the role of God the Father; he would remain both invisible and ubiquitous, but his universal presence would be especially felt in one particular place: Mary's body. Godard imposed on Mary—on Roussel—his "shadow," his "spirit," and his "power," and in his absence from the screen he in fact dominated the film more forcefully than he had in *First Name: Carmen* with his living, breathing presence.

He was no less intrigued by the part played by Joseph in this drama:

> We have few documents on the life of Joseph and Mary. A few sentences, that's all, but they convey an extremely powerful situation. Joseph's place in it is, however, a little forgotten. What happened? How did he take Mary's secret? How did he cope with this violence? I wanted to present the two of them as an ordinary couple, an archetype of a couple, who accept the extraordinary in an ordinary way.[6]

By approaching the story of Mary in terms of her relations with Joseph and with God—with the one she does not take physically, and with the other who takes her, spiritually—Godard had found his project of fathers and daughters, with all its sexual implications.[7]

Originally, Godard intended to cast in the role of Joseph an actor who was close to his own age and mythical resonance: the grizzled and elegant Jean Marais, who was born in 1913, the star of Jean Cocteau's *Beauty and the Beast* and *Orpheus,* and Cocteau's lover, friend, privileged interpreter, and literary executor. Marais was surprised at being considered for the role of Joseph, since, as he said, "there was no reason for Joseph to be an old man with a white beard!"[8] But Godard too came to the same conclusion: on three different occasions, he made appointments to meet Marais; all three times, Godard canceled on the pretext of illness. The two men never met.

Then Godard offered the role to the philosopher Bernard-Henri Lévy, who was then thirty-five years old and the most prominent young thinker in France; Lévy was known especially for *Barbarism with a Human Face,* which in the wake of the 1974 publication of Solzhenitsyn's *Gulag Archipelago* repudiated communism and helped launch the movement of the *nouveaux philosophes,* a group of young French intellectuals who had come to recognize (and sought to theorize) the abuses and cruelty of the Soviet and Chinese systems. Godard told Lévy the idea for the film and gave him a copy of the brief outline. Lévy finally refused the part. "I was afraid," Lévy said. "Afraid he was going to hijack my image . . . I was very afraid. Not only of his extraordinary intelligence but also of his perversity. Was I up to avoiding the trap he would eventually set for me?"[9]

Instead, Godard cast as Joseph a young and inexperienced actor whom Myriem Roussel knew from Paris, Thierry Rode, who, like her, had few in-grained professional habits and was not established enough to contest Go-dard's unusual methods. Rode is physically imposing yet inexpressive, stocky yet impassive, stolid, with a sort of frustrated forcefulness, and thus all the more moving as an ordinary man with ordinary desires who is forced to make an extraordinary sacrifice and to learn extraordinary love.

THE EXPERIENCE OF *First Name: Carmen* had inspired Roussel to become a professional actress. She auditioned for an acting class in Paris and was ac-cepted. In advance of the film, now called *Je vous salue, Marie (Hail Mary)*, Godard had a different kind of preparation in mind: he had Roussel keep video equipment in her Paris apartment, and he shot copious footage of her there—particularly when she was doing nothing in particular, simply living daily life. He also asked her to videotape herself in his absence. Meanwhile, he had her read the Bible and Françoise Dolto's book about it. He also had her watch many films, including Carl Theodor Dreyer's *The Passion of Joan of Arc*, Martin Scorsese's *The King of Comedy* and *New York, New York*, Eric Rohmer's *Pauline at the Beach*, as well as several of his own.

Committed to developing the film on the basis of their personal relations, Godard wrote to Roussel constantly—between three and five letters each day, as she recalled—and, she added, "When we didn't see each other, we were always on the telephone." He also gave her collage-like dossiers of images and text, all of which left her feeling both "flooded with information and affection" and nurtured "like a baby."[10] Roussel accompanied Godard to New York in October 1983 when he presented *Passion* at the New York Film Festival; speaking to a journalist there, he said, "Myriem is my beautiful link to the outside world."[11] Yet the blend of personal and professional relations proved to be trouble.

"Through working, rehearsing scenes, and rigorously questioning our-selves about these relationships, it ended up resembling an authentic psycho-analysis," Roussel recalled. "It was exhilarating and exhausting."[12] But it was also extremely uncomfortable and difficult for Roussel. The situation in-volved her in a virtual triangle with Godard and Miéville, who was making her own film at the time. "There was him and her, him and me; the three of us, it wasn't working," Roussel said.[13] And when the shoot began, in January 1984, Godard withdrew his nurturing protection.

As usual, Godard had trouble getting started. This time he was also in-hibited by the subject matter, by its grandeur and its depth, and he was unsure of how to approach it.

What I'd like is for the people at IBM—I could tell them: "Look, I've got a book by Françoise Dolto on religion and psychoanalysis, I've got two characters, Joseph and Mary, I've got three Bach cantatas, a book by Heidegger. Make me a program which will arrange all that for me." But they can't, and so I've got to do it myself and I don't want to spend twenty years on it![14]

By now, it was a given that Godard's shoots would be difficult and burdened by conflict. He sought such conflict and seemed to find it productive. But in this case, he was struggling less with the individuals than with, so to speak, the angel, with the sanctity and significance of the story.

Again Godard sought to involve his cast and crew in discussions about the film's subject—which for him was virginity, the intimate relationship between a man and a woman, the birth of a child. He assumed that he could talk at least about lust with his male collaborators and about birth with his female collaborators. But he failed to elicit a dialogue that he found satisfactory and he blamed this failure for his difficulties in making the film—he shot everything repeatedly, doing many more takes than usual, refilming the entire story "four or five times,"[15] so that it took seven months to shoot a film that runs only seventy minutes. "I'm messed up by not being able to talk about the soup that we're making," Godard said, "not being able to talk about virginity to a boy or a girl, or to a cameraman, implicating him a little . . . I go back over things twenty times."[16]

The crew of four included the cameraman Jean-Bernard Menoud, the sound recordist François Musy, a production manager, and an assistant. Godard frequently convened the crew and actors and then sent them home without having done anything at all. One day, to avoid shooting a scene that had already been set up, by the shore of Lake Geneva, Godard jumped into the water fully clothed. It was a winter day and the crew rescued him at once and hustled him indoors to keep him from freezing. The day's shoot had come to an end before it started.[17]

Godard thought that the film's subject imposed technical requirements that were different in kind, even metaphysically so, from other films, including his own. In recent years he had become careful about composition, but for *Hail Mary* he was singularly meticulous. He replaced framings with "centers," places in the frame on which to focus: "The only thing I succeeded at doing—which the crew didn't understand at all, even technically—is that there is no frame . . . I can't manage to explain to a camera operator that there's no frame, that there's a point to find . . ."[18] He came to feel that the film offered him no "margin of error"—that with a difference of even one millimeter, in camera placement or focus, "the shot was ruined." He had no patience for the technical talk of technicians. During one daytime shoot, when the sun was bright, the cameraman, Menoud, talked of requiring an aperture of f/22. Godard recalled telling him: "Listen, you're 1m70 tall, the sun is much bigger than you, and you want to measure yourself against the sun? All you can do is get down on your knees and wait! But you can't measure yourself against the sun!"[19] This quasi-mystical quest for an image worthy of the subject made Godard even less confident of what he was doing. Roussel remembered:

> I'd see him arrive and say, "OK, we're not shooting, I don't know what we can do . . ." We'd rehearsed the dialogue the night before, so we had the dialogue, we knew it, but he didn't know what to film. That might happen three or four times in a row . . . The dialogue was rehearsed, but he simply didn't see the frame that he wanted, or what he wanted to show, or why this sequence now and not another.[20]

Godard's hesitation and reshooting upset the actors. He kept Roussel in a sort of supervised isolation in Nyon, between Rolle and Geneva, where the film was shot. "He picked me up every day by car, and would talk to me," she later recalled. "He put me in the state of mind for the scene we were going to shoot. It might be gentle, it might be violent. He did not like actors who . . . had training. He wanted to put me back to the state of acting for the first time."[21] Roussel sensed that Godard not only was trying to inform and condition her for the day's work but was also trying to strip her of what she had learned in her previous training and experience.

With Roussel, Godard achieved the effect that he desired, which was similar to the effect achieved by Robert Bresson through compelling his nonprofessional actors to retake shots dozens of times. As Roussel understood, Godard removed any trace of theatrical expression from her performance.

> This is what Godard wanted. I, on the contrary, wanted to act. It's because of this film that our relations began to deteriorate. He doesn't ask. He steals. Twenty times, at the moment of the shoot, he sent us home to bed. As a result, I was so exhausted that I ended up doing what he wanted—which is to say, nothing. When I saw the film, I finally understood what he had been looking for. Without my realizing it, Godard had filmed me exactly as I had seemed to him two years earlier.[22]

By "stealing," Godard had transformed her back into what she was at the time of *Passion:* a dancer who had never acted, a virgin before the camera.

IN ITS OUTLINE, *Hail Mary* consisted largely, at least for its first half, of a fairly literal modernization of the New Testament story of Mary and

Joseph—though with a comic tone that seems inimical to the intense earnestness that Godard brought to its visual aspect. Mary Magdalen, played by Juliette Binoche (a newcomer who, when Godard cast her, was working as a package wrapper in a home furnishings store), confronts Joseph in a café over a beer and suggests that they get married; Joseph refuses, claiming, "People say that a man enters into a woman . . ."—suggesting, with his powerful ellipsis, that he has been entered, albeit spiritually, by Mary, the Madonna. Mary works in her father's gas station and plays basketball for a local women's team. Joseph, a taxi driver, has been with Mary for two years; in this time she has not let him touch or even kiss her.

The angel Gabriel arrives with his news via airplane, in a majestic evening shot of high-contrast shadows, accompanied by the soaring strains of Dvořák's Cello Concerto. He is accompanied at the Annunciation by a cherubic yet solemn little girl who defends him against crabby businessmen at the airport and makes sure that he gets his lines right. A dark-jawed man with a glowering gaze and a hulking mien, Gabriel hails Joseph's cab and gives him five hundred dollars to take him to Mary's father's service station. There, the angel makes his stunning declaration: Mary comes over to the cab, and Gabriel tells her that she will have a child. Joseph asks who the father is; Gabriel tells him, "Not you."

Mary goes to her elderly family doctor, who ridicules her assertion that she is a pregnant virgin. But when he examines her he is compelled to accept the evidence: "It's true that it's true."

The story of Mary and Joseph is intercut with another religious story, that of a young professor who has been exiled from his native Czechoslovakia for his religious teachings. The man, who remains unnamed, propounds a theory of intelligent design to his students, suggesting that it is highly improbable that life evolved naturally, and far more likely that "it was willed." He declares (in a text from the English scientist Sir Fred Hoyle) that life did not develop spontaneously on Earth but came from outer space, and tells his students: "You want to know what an extraterrestrial looks like? Look in the mirror." (He has an affair with a woman in his class before leaving her to return home to see his wife and child.)

To this point, the story of Mary and Joseph updates the classic theme with enough wit to place the events at human scale and avoid the bathos of devotional kitsch. But after Mary's virgin pregnancy is revealed to Joseph, the story takes a profound, disturbing turn that bears the mark of Godard's deepest, most intimate concerns.

Joseph assumes that while Mary has been rejecting his approaches, she has been sleeping with another man. He nonetheless agrees to marry Mary but asks that she at least let him see her body before the marriage, once, even if he cannot touch it. Mary accepts Joseph's request and, in a tense, solemn scene, undresses from the waist down and stands before him to teach him how to say and to gesture "I love you." Joseph must learn to say this serenely and without insistence, to give love, a special, holy love, without demands; his outstretched hand does not touch Mary. When Joseph's gesture is, at first, too aggressive, the angel Gabriel appears in the room to grab him by the throat, hold him down, and compel his submission: "Because! Because it's the law! Get it?" Joseph submits—"Yes, I will sacrifice myself"—but Gabriel will not hear of sacrifice: "What kind of asshole are you? Taboo eliminates sacrifice!" Godard mocks Joseph's common, self-centered, utterly normal lust, if not the lesson that he will learn in its stead: Joseph will not be sacrificed but rather saved by love.

It is Mary, however, who is sacrificed: later, when she is alone, Godard depicts her writhing naked on her bed, tormented by forbidden sexuality— and by God's possession of her, a possession that, though not physical, is utterly sexual. She convulses in a ferocious agony which joins orgasmic ecstasy to violent resistance. Godard filmed these scenes with Roussel by himself, with no crew present. In the editing, he added to the scene Mary's voice-over recitation of a text by Antonin Artaud: "God is a jerk and a coward who doesn't want to fight, and who counts only on sex, that is, on the calm of the heart, to exist . . . God is a vampire . . . he profited from my pain."[23] The text, joined to the images, alludes with a perverse exaltation to the identification of Godard with God: Godard filmed Mary's erotic battle under the power of God by means of filming Roussel herself enduring a similar agony under Godard's influence.

The film concludes with the young Jesus, a dark, impish, and brilliantly inventive child, dashing off to take care of "his father's affairs." Mary, greeted by Gabriel's gruffly sardonic "Hail, Mary," responds, "I am of the Virgin, and I wanted nothing to do with this being. I marked the soul that helped me, that's all"—Godard's moving tribute to the enduring mark left by Roussel on the soul who helped her, himself.

IN KEEPING WITH Godard's intentions, the images of nature and the quality of light in *Hail Mary* have an appropriately metaphysical splendor, which reflects the difficulty of their creation. Yet the price in personal struggle and cinematic doubt was very high, and Godard acknowledged that he had been tempted to stop the shoot and reimburse Alain Sarde, his coproducer. He claimed that kept going only for the sake of Anne-Marie Miéville, who was making a short film, *Le Livre de Marie (The Book of Mary)*, that would be released together with *Hail Mary*.[24]

Miéville's film is a graceful yet painful melodrama of a girl's effort to cope with her parents' separation. As in her first short film, *How Can I Love*, Miéville deftly condenses a long period of time into a brief and efficient narrative framework. *The Book of Mary* covers the period from the parents' decision to divorce, through Mary's comings and goings between her home and her father's new apartment, to the first time she faces the reality of her mother (Auroré Clement, whose wavy blonde hair and angular features resemble Miéville's own) going out on a date with another man. Mary, a serious yet whimsical girl, travels with a doll yet is learning geometry in school—her father, Paul (Bruno Crémer), who wears Godard-like sunglasses indoors, helps her with it. She speaks to her school friends of her parents' divorce. Then, returning home, she listens to music very loudly—Mahler—and dances with an intensely sincere exuberance that ends with her mimed collapse. (The dance is reminiscent of the naked antic ballet of Miéville's daughter in *Six fois deux*.)

Miéville's film has the ring of intimate confession. She films the characters with a naturalistic simplicity that avoids the grandiosity of myth. Their dialogue is heartfelt, direct, true. *The Book of Mary* presents the material and emotional reality of a modern family, in sharp contrast to Godard's film, which subjects the family to mythopoetic and philosophical abstraction—and to a tragic pain expressed with an exaltation approaching that of the greatest classical art.

IN MAY 1984, Godard took a break from the shoot of *Hail Mary*, which had begun in January, to attend the Cannes festival. The shoot was already over-long and over budget, and Godard, who was coproducing the film, bore financial responsibility for the overages. Even before the filming of *Hail Mary* had started, Alain Sarde had proposed to Godard an avowedly commercial project on a neo-noir theme, to be called *Détective (Detective)*.[25] Now, Godard needed it, and at Cannes he helped Sarde to get it under way and to recruit its stars, Claude Brasseur and Nathalie Baye.[26]

In the summer, after completing the shoot of *Hail Mary*, Roussel, who still wanted to become a professional actress, took the next step: she accepted a role in another director's film.[27] Godard put the footage of *Hail Mary* aside and devoted himself to the production of *Detective*. During the shoot of that film, which took place in Paris in September and October 1984, Godard met Roussel again and felt motivated to complete postproduction work on *Hail Mary*.

A pre-release screening of *Hail Mary* was held at a ciné-club in Versailles on January 22, 1985. Members of a group called the "Association familiale et catholique" were there and, as soon as Mary's naked body appeared on-screen, they disrupted the showing, shouting and throwing stink bombs. The police intervened and the screening continued, but so did the disturbances. One group sang a prayer in the theater. A reel of the film was stolen from the projection booth. The next day, when *Hail Mary* opened, a conservative local official banned the film, ostensibly not as an act of censorship but in an attempt to ward off trouble. Catholic groups insisted that the government either outlaw the film completely or require the suppression of scenes purporting to show Mary's body. Minister of Culture Jack Lang defended the film's release, but the groups still filed suit to ban it. Finally, on January 28, the courts ruled that the film was free to be shown, without cuts.

The protests, however, continued—and intensified. Catholic groups demonstrated in the streets of Paris and Versailles, and conservatives interrupted a mass by Archbishop Jean-Marie Lustiger to protest his unwillingness to speak against the film. Throughout France, from Nantes to Toulouse, conservative Catholics disrupted screenings and protested outside theaters.

In April, Pope John Paul II, who had long expressed a singular devotion to Mary,[28] denounced *Hail Mary*, saying that it "distorts and offends the spiritual meaning and historical value of the fundamental themes of Christian faith," and in May he led prayers in condemnation of the film.[29] In response, Godard wrote to his Italian distributors to ask that the film be withdrawn from theaters in Rome,[30] offering a mischievous explanation: "It's the house of the church, and if the Pope doesn't want a bad boy running around in his house, the least I can do is respect his wishes. The Pope has a special relationship to Mary. He considers her a daughter, almost."[31]

Controversy over the film had by then spread worldwide: there were violent protests against it in Germany, Spain, Greece, and Australia.

In the United States, the film was scheduled to be premiered on October 7 at the New York Film Festival. When the screening was announced in September, New York's Archbishop John O'Connor spoke out against it and many Catholics mobilized for a show of force. The night of the screening, angry crowds, many brought into town on chartered buses, lined the streets around Lincoln Center; Broadway was filled with an estimated eight thousand protesters. They encircled the theater and attempted to prevent viewers from entering. The police parted the crowd, creating a narrow path for ticket-holders to enter the theater, albeit through a gauntlet of jeering protesters. Godard himself had been present at Lincoln Center for the film's press screening on October 4 and fielded questions from journalists, but, despite the pleas of festival officials, he left town before the public screening.

The film's original American distributor, Triumph, a subsidiary of Columbia Pictures, owned by the Coca-Cola Company, soon abandoned its long-standing plans to distribute *Hail Mary.* Instead, the American release was undertaken by New Yorker Films in conjunction with Gaumont.[32]

BY THIS TIME, in the fall of 1985, Godard had moved on to a new stage of cinematic life. The availability of favorable sources of financing from the French film industry and European coproducers, together with his new and well-defined set of methods and themes, had launched him on another round of rapid and copious production. With *Hail Mary,* Godard's legendary artistic status only grew, and yet his contemplative isolation in his "studio of exteriors" in Rolle and his perceived distance from the contemporary world—both physical and intellectual—rendered his prominence largely virtual.

Yet in his isolation, Godard was developing a radically new way of filmmaking, one that was based on a practical state of affairs—the long period of gestation. Ever since his return to the industry with *Sauve qui peut,* he had taken a long time to get his films under way. Unlike his work of the 1960s, which derived their tone from the rapidity of their production, his later films replicated on his own small scale the Hollywood development process. Instead of passing through the hands of diverse producers and screenwriters, his projects metamorphosed through long meditation, changes in his own life, the happenstance of readings or breaking news, and contact with different actors and producers (whether or not they ultimately participated in the film). He took the quasi-industrial methods of the movie industry, abstracted them, and rendered them personal; he made high-concept films that had truly high concepts.

The cost in personal relationships was also high, however. After the shoot of *Hail Mary,* Godard and Roussel fell out of touch. She had found the intensity of her conjoined personal and professional relations with Godard to be very difficult; she was exhausted by the conflicts engendered by the long shoot and by her awareness that the work depended on them. In general, this way of working was difficult for the film's participants because the extended relations, involving plenty of time spent not shooting, inevitably became personal. The blending of work and life, the blurring of boundaries between the professional and the personal, was immensely nourishing for Godard's films. His work thrived on the resulting tensions, even as he seemed to suffer from them as greatly as his associates did. This ordinary, intimate, human pain left its mark on the films, infusing with firsthand emotion (and a touch of irony) Godard's grand, tragic, classical aspirations.

In the wake of *Hail Mary,* his inclinations were metaphysical, supernatural, even religious—and yet, utterly unorthodox. Godard linked his spiritual quest with a search for a worldview derived from the classics of Western culture, and set them in opposition to a narrowly materialist and materialistic way of life. He was filming miracles and mysteries, and the first among them were those of art itself.

The link between the long gestation of Godard's new series of works and their deep classical origins is suggested in a remark that he made to a journalist the week of *Hail Mary*'s opening: "A long time is needed to go searching far."[33] Godard would now make the time of his search a part of his films. For the next decade to come, they would touch on transcendent matters— and the cinema itself, and his own work in it, would be presented as the ultimate form of metaphysical striving.

"Martyr" means "witness."
(TCD-Prod DB © Gaumont / DR)

twenty-two

DETECTIVE AND SOIGNE TA DROITE

"It is always a little sad to leave the earth"

F ROM THE CONCEPTION OF *DÉTECTIVE* (*DETECTIVE*), Go-dard had little emotional attachment to the project, which Sarde had cooked up with an eye toward the box office and Godard pursued in a hurry in order to pay for *Hail Mary*. Yet, Godard claimed, this aspect of detachment appealed to him, explaining to an interviewer, "I'm a Renaissance painter looking for commissions. Michelangelo didn't come up with the idea all by himself to paint the ceiling of the Sistine Chapel. The Pope went looking for him."[1] After getting the commission for *Detective*, Godard worked hard to turn it into a personal work of art. He succeeded, to some extent; but as a result, the film did not.

Even the title turned out to be a subtle joke. In classic detective films, the detective is the main character, and is played by the star. In *Detective*, the detective is played by a supporting actor in a secondary role, and it is not even obvious which character the title designates. The film begins with a woman and two men engaged in surveillance of a Paris street from the terrace of a hotel room by means of a video camera. A title card lists the three—Aurèle Doazan, Jean-Pierre Léaud, and Laurent Terzieff—as "actors." As the presence of video equipment, the tools of Godard's trade, suggests, these are the characters in whom he is interested. The slender, romantic Terzieff (whom Godard had considered for the lead in *Breathless*) plays Uncle William Prospero, the former house detective at the hotel where the film is set, the Hôtel Concorde-St.-Lazare. He lost his job there two years earlier when he was unable to find the assassin who killed "the Prince" in the same room where the surveillance stake-out takes place. The ex-detective's nephew, Isidore (played by Léaud, now forty-one years old and a bit stocky), is a specialist in the analysis of images, and the young woman, Ariel (Doazan), who is operating the camera, is Isidore's fiancée; she has joined him on the assignment in the hope that it will bring them closer together. By making and studying their videos together, the filmmaker-detectives will solve the mystery, i.e., discover and tell the film's story. Isidore and Ariel, who make and interpret images as the basis for their work and love, are analogous to Godard and Miéville.

Their inquiry and the story that emerges from it are centered on three characters played by Nathalie Baye, Claude Brasseur, and Johnny Hallyday (the French rock musician who was also married to Baye at the time), who are introduced in the next scene. As they appear on-screen, their credits appear: they are billed as "stars." In their story, Jim Fox Warner (Hallyday), who manages the boxer Tiger Jones (played by the boxer Stéphane Ferrara), is heavily in debt to two people: a pilot, Emile Chenal (Brasseur, who had starred in *Band of Outsiders*), whose wife, Françoise (Baye), is Jim's former lover; and a mob boss, also called "the Prince" (the elderly, leonine actor Alain Cuny). Both of these creditors have threatened Jim's life if they don't get their money by Friday, the day before Tiger Jones's big fight, which promises Jim a big payout. Meanwhile, Françoise meets Jim at the hotel and reveals that the money he owes Emile is really hers; she pairs up again with Jim, but with unclear motives—either from true desire or to make sure that she, and not her husband, gets the money.

Meanwhile, Ariel and Uncle William make love while Isidore is out of the room, and Ariel now doubts whether she will marry Isidore. When Isidore takes on another woman, Anne (Ann-Gisel Glass), as his associate, Ariel becomes jealous and rejoins him in the quest and ultimately in life.

In a final, rapid, and absurd shoot-out, both Jim and Emile are killed, and Uncle William is accidentally gunned down by Isidore, who was aiming at Emile. The two characters played by the male "stars" are in effect brought down by the predatory Françoise and the Mafia together—two different versions of "family." The story that they were living—the story that was discovered by the three observers with their camera—was pointless; the real narrative and emotional force behind the fiction is not the vain agitation and forced destinies of the stars, but the experience of the three observers with their camera: as Isidore tells Ariel in the film's last scene, when they leave the hotel after the bloodbath, "Witness means martyr."[2] As for Uncle William Prospero—the patron-saint of the theater, the witness without a camera—he is sacrificed for the creation of a story which would live on in Ariel and Isidore's conjoined life and work.

Godard admitted to his lack of interest in the story; he had fulfilled his obligation to Sarde in making a film with stars, but he did not make much of their situation. To fill out his ninety minutes of film, he stuffed it with literary citations. He had been reading the poet René Char, and took lines from his poetry for the film. He referred to Joseph Conrad's *Lord Jim,* Shakespeare, Rimbaud, and André Breton, explaining, "In this film, there are only quotations, not a word of my own. In times of emergency, one empties one's storehouse."[3]

Since the project was conceived with a "retro" air, in response to an ambient nostalgia for a lost age of cinema (the '80s in France were a time of taking stock of the cultural heritage), Godard filled the film with allusions to the pulp fiction of years past and to many other forgotten artifacts of a former world. One scene involving the "stars" stands out as particularly heartfelt and emotionally charged: as Jim and Emile await Françoise in the cramped, overdecorated hotel bar, Jim brings up memories of the Orient Express of his youth, the motorman who hammered on the axles and the vendor who walked the train selling ice cream with an incomprehensible cry. Françoise arrives and asks the men what they are discussing: "Men's problems," Jim says, "problems of melancholy"—a line from the song by Léo Ferré, "Richard," with which Godard had concluded the television series *France tour détour deux enfants.* Jim brings up *Lord Jim,* the book his mother had given him when he left home, and Emile apostrophizes that for him "the only real book is *Parti de Liverpool* and also *Le Voyage d'Edgar*"—two adventures, published in the 1930s, by the sailor-turned-writer Edouard Peisson, boyhood fantasies that Godard loved in his own youth. To underscore the point, Jim immediately asks the waiter, "What is Salade Vaudoise?"—salad from the canton of Vaud, Godard's homeland.

With its false air of a traditional police story—and of Godard's earlier work—*Detective* was calculated to evoke nostalgia. Even the casting, with its stars of the 1960s (Léaud, Brasseur, Terzieff, and Hallyday), and earlier eras (Cuny), alludes to a glorious cinematic past. To emphasize the story's pseudo-classical origins, the detectives' hotel room is filled with piles of instantly recognizable yellow and black *Série noire* paperback crime novels. Emile and Françoise's family name, Chenal, is that of a French director of popular films from the 1930s through the 1950s whose police drama *Rafles sur la ville* Godard had praised in *Cahiers* in 1958.

Detective comprises a peculiarly rich lode of retrospective elements for Godard personally, as the central twist in the detectives' investigation depends on the discovery, by Isidore, that the murder in the hotel two years earlier was the result of a hit man's error in reading the hotel register upside down—an echo of Véronique's crucial mistake in *La Chinoise.* The film's opening image, a video surveillance shot of the sculpted entrance of an arcade, features a pair of young lovers in a passionate kiss, an image that resembles a scene that Bruno Forestier photographs in *Le Petit Soldat.*

Detective's retrospective aspect also depended on a new technology that was central to Godard's historical preoccupations as well as to the fashion for nostalgia: the VCR. With the commercial release of videotapes of classic movies as well as the ability to tape television broadcasts, Godard finally had access to films from the history of cinema that he could excerpt and "quote" in his own work. While planning *Detective,* Godard was also laying the groundwork for his long-delayed video series, *Histoire(s) du cinéma,* and, in *Detective,* he puts his newfound archive on display, placing televisions in the hotel rooms that show such classic films as Cocteau's *Beauty and the Beast* (featuring Alain Cuny) and the 1932 *The Lost Squadron* (a scene of Erich von Stroheim as a tyrannical director barking orders on a set).

BUT DETECTIVE ITSELF was not a contemplative editing-room essay. For all his efforts to personalize the film, Godard was working with actors who brought star habits to the set, a genre story that left him indifferent, and a large crew, as his agreement with Sarde had stipulated. The director of photography, Bruno Nuytten, had been chosen by Sarde despite Godard's expressed wish to work with Raoul Coutard again. Godard was frustrated, and he took his frustration out on others. Witnesses observed that Godard exceeded his prior excesses in trying to elicit responses through provocative thrusts of anger.

Godard was particularly hard on Claude Brasseur, whom he considered unprepared for the role. Nathalie Baye was aware that Godard disliked the presence of "the makeup artists, the hairdressers," and described the director as "a little like a lion in a cage."[4] Laurent Terzieff remarked that working with Godard put him in a state of "insecurity" and made him feel like "an ingredient in dough that may or may not rise."[5] Baye considered herself and the other actors to be Godard's "tubes of paint."[6] Emmanuelle Seigner, eighteen years old, who played the girlfriend of the boxer Tiger Jones, was topless in most of her scenes, and recalled years later: "From the first day of the shoot, Godard asked me to show my breasts. On the third day, he asked me to remove my panties. I refused and he said, 'But I only hired you because you had a nice ass.' With that, I left the set at once."[7] The fourteen-year-old Julie Delpy, playing another member of the boxer's entourage (in her first feature film role), was subjected to lascivious implication when Jim Fox Warner's assistant, a young man, holds her clarinet upright in his fist for her to blow.

Johnny Hallyday remembered, "On the shoot of *Detective,* I was the only one he treated humanely."[8] Hallyday was not principally an actor and brought the physical discipline of singing and performance to the film without the psychological techniques of acting; on the set, Godard told him,

"When you act, do what you do when you sing."[9] Godard considered that Hallyday, with his way of being that derived from outside the cinema, "brought a great deal" to the film, namely, his own character: Godard wanted actors "who have a certain value in themselves, who have their own existence"[10]—and this was how he saw Hallyday.

Hallyday delivers a crucial soliloquy in a revealing scene, in which he stands before a window in a hotel room and delivers a line that sums up Godard's disdain for the subject of the film and the place where it was being filmed: "For all the time that we've been dragging from one city to another, there is never any light, there is only hard lighting. Because big cities, Lord, are accursed."[11] The shoot of this scene, in which daylight striking a facing building contrasted sharply with the dark interior and Nuytten asked about putting in some added lighting, resulted in a provocative outburst by Godard that was extraordinary even by his pugnacious standards (this tirade was caught on videotape by a crew engaged by Sarde to do a "making-of " for *Detective* and was broadcast). Godard doubted whether Nuytten had read the script and understood the point of Hallyday's text, then went so far as to challenge whether Nuytten knew that the camera they were using, the Arriflex, had been invented in Germany to film German soldiers on the battlefield during the Second World War. In his wrathful exaggerations, Godard was in effect calling Nuytten's preference for an extra lightbulb an unwitting complicity with genocide.

The tirade may have been outrageous and unfair, but the scene that provoked it expressed an idea that was central to the film—and to Godard's life. His own move from Paris to Grenoble to Switzerland had been a flight from the accursed city. Even the films he had made since then that took place in Paris, whether *First Name: Carmen* or *Detective,* looked at the street only from a safe remove. His rejection of the city was a rejection of modernity, modern people, and modern mores. In the 1960s Godard's social politics had been peculiarly conservative, even puritanical, but his move to the small town of Rolle in the late 1970s represented a different form of conservatism. He now embraced nature and the local as a response to, a rejection of, the tumult of urban life; he also embraced his record collection, his books, and his art reproductions as a way of recovering a cultural heritage, he thought, that was lost in the aggressiveness of modern media life. Nature and culture were peculiarly joined as a source of Godard's inspiration; art and nature were one, and the business of modern life was inimical to both.

The celebrity of the stars in *Detective* was not merely a gimmick to collect needed financing; their celebrity was the enemy. Godard's ending to the film, with the two male stars dead and Baye carted off in an ambulance, was a symbolic purge of the accursed city. Under its whimsical and nostalgic airs,

Detective is a hiss of anger and self-pity from one pair of witnesses, Godard and Miéville, who were martyring themselves to their duty to bear witness to the degradations of modern life.

THE PRESENTATION OF *Detective* at the 1985 Cannes Film Festival began inauspiciously. After the film's second screening, on May 10, Godard, while advancing through a hallway toward the podium for a press conference, was nailed in the face with a cream pie by Noël Godin, a philosophical provocateur who calls himself "Georges le Gloupier" (George the Glopper). Godin targets cultural luminaries whom he considers "worthless celebrities."[12] Among his chosen were Marguerite Duras (one of his first targets, in 1969) and Bernard-Henri Lévy (who was victimized no fewer than seven times at last count). After the initial shock, Godard wiped himself off and did his press conference, addressing the assault good-humoredly as "an homage to silent film." He even intervened to prevent Godin from being banned from Cannes, though later admitted he was "glad it was not like John Lennon, a bullet" and confessed that he felt "ashamed afterwards. Very strange."[13]

The film was booed by viewers expecting a more traditional reprise of film noir, and the critical reception was generally unfavorable. Michel Mardore of *Le Nouvel Observateur* reported from Cannes that Godard "got a Belgian cream pie in the face that he didn't deserve. There's no provocation in *Detective,* which he made as if wearing his slippers."[14] The film's release, after the festival premiere, did not fare well. *Detective,* undertaken as a commercial venture, even a mercenary one, did not fulfill its purpose: the publicity generated by the pairing of Godard and Hallyday did not attract a wider audience. Despite the film's personal implications and innovative touches, its compromises were all too evident.

From a practical perspective, however, the visit to Cannes was useful to Godard: he contacted the producer and director Menahem Golan at the festival and asked whether he would produce a film for him. (Cannon Films, the company that Golan owned together with Yoram Globus, had made its money with such films as *Death Wish II* and *The Happy Hooker Goes Hollywood* but had recently made a splash in the industry by producing films by such notable directors as John Cassavetes, Robert Altman, and Andrei Konchalovsky.) Within minutes, the two concluded a deal—signed on a napkin taken from the bar of the Majestic Hotel, where they met—for Godard to direct an adaptation of *King Lear,* based on a screenplay to be written by Norman Mailer.

ONE FURTHER OBLIGATION remained from the financial rescue of *Hail Mary:* Channel Four, based in London, had invested one hundred thousand dollars toward the film's completion and had added sixty thousand dollars for the production by Godard and Miéville of a video that the channel's programming associate, Colin MacCabe,[15] proposed calling *British Images,* a successor to Godard's 1969 *British Sounds.* To fulfill that commission, Godard and Miéville now made a video, but it had nothing to do with Great Britain: rather, working at home in Rolle, Godard and Miéville produced a fifty-two-minute-long video called *Soft and Hard (A Soft Conversation between Friends on a Hard Subject).* Though a minor effort, it nonetheless suggested an important new aspect to Godard's effort to fuse work and life: the "friends" it shows in conversation are Godard and Miéville, and the hard subject they discuss is the cinema.

From the start of his career, Godard had made his working methods a crucial part of his films—and had also provided access to journalists who could watch him work, in order to make his methods public. Since Godard now worked, in effect, at home, and sought to derive his films from the life that he lived while making them, he began to make his private life even more strikingly public than before.

Soft and Hard shows Godard and Miéville in an apartment, Miéville ironing and Godard miming tennis with his racquet, Godard getting into bed and writing in a notebook, Miéville at an editing table reviewing footage from *Detective,* Godard sitting at his desk, talking on the phone with Menahem Golan. The longest sequence is a discussion between Godard and Miéville about her attempt to make a film. Their exchange turns on Miéville's admission that the cinema does not have the mythical status for her that it does for Godard, and Godard's recollection of her criticism of him for not having written convincing lovers' dialogue for the actors in his recent films.

Miéville, who was not devoted to the history or the mythology of the cinema, sought to make films that reflected her experience, and the originality of her work derived from her intense attention to the subject and its personal significance to her. Godard sought to develop his work from his experience, too, but also aspired to reconstruct film forms from a historical standpoint—and to understand his own life in terms of the cinematic elements with which he was imbued; for him, the ability to tell a personal story was inseparable from the history of the cinema. And *Soft and Hard* offers a singular visual metaphor to depict their shared efforts and differing views.

The video ends with Godard and Miéville showing taped images on a video monitor: these include the credit sequence from *Contempt,* in which Raoul Coutard manipulates a heavy studio camera on tracking rails and ultimately turns the camera to point it directly at the viewer. This image from *Contempt* is superimposed on a white wall, toward which Godard and

Miéville stretch their bare arms; that image then disappears, leaving only the two friends' arms reaching out together in the same direction, before a blank white wall. This ingenious and moving conclusion posed the question of working together against the background (as for Godard) of the mystical, mythical mechanism of the history of cinema or (as for Miéville) against the tabula rasa of experience.

SOFT AND HARD was the first in a series of explicitly biographical projects that Godard embarked on. Godard granted MacCabe, who was listed in the credits of *Soft and Hard* as "Friend," authorization to write his biography and spoke with him at length about his personal life.[16] Godard also cooperated with the critic Alain Bergala, who had written some of the most trenchant and insightful criticism of his later films, on the editing of an updated and amplified edition of *Jean-Luc Godard par Jean-Luc Godard,* a book of Godard's criticism, interviews, and documents that had first been issued in 1968. Bergala collected published interviews, culled images from photographic archives, and was granted access to work materials that Godard and Miéville had saved.

The augmented *Jean-Luc Godard par Jean-Luc Godard* was released to favorable notices in November 1985. But Bergala then sought to take the project a step further, proposing to direct a biographical film about Godard that would be produced by *Cahiers du cinéma* and Marin Karmitz. Godard agreed, and planned to take an active role in its preparation. As Bergala recalled:

> I wanted us to revisit all the places of his life; so I wrote a structure, I scouted locations *with* him, we went to see his father's house in Switzerland, his apartment in Trouville . . . I even chose the clothing. But I made a big mistake: I had hired Raymond Depardon as director of photography, and that was the beginning of an immediate hatred. They were like cats and dogs . . . Before the shoot we had lunch together. Depardon was totally overwhelmed in Godard's presence, he didn't say a word, not a single word, so I spoke for two. Godard said to me, "What's with him? He's not saying anything to me." I should have known that it wouldn't work. And it didn't.[17]

As Bergala noted, Depardon had signed on as an integral partner in the project and could not be fired. "We shot a little bit. Godard couldn't stand it any more and he left."[18]

Godard may have gone along energetically with Bergala's and MacCabe's projects but, for all of his self-dramatization and self-presentation, for all of the exposure to which he submitted his working methods and his private life, and despite the rapidly increasing productivity that resulted from his unimpeachable celebrity, he was ambivalent about this display of himself and claimed to regret the turn of affairs that had prompted it:

> People pronounce the name "Godard," which paralyzes me, alienates me, and even prevents me from reaching my true public, the public to which I have the right . . . I have the impression that with the New Wave, I participated in my own misfortune. Since then, people name things without wanting to know them. So when we said, for the first time in the history of the cinema, that we were "auteurs," we found ourselves trapped. The name "auteur" stuck to us, and we became our own name. Today, talking about me does me harm. I feel more solitary than ever. I feel like a nothing, a non-being, nonexistent. People say "Godard" but they don't go see my films.[19]

Godard's fame, his iconic status as the living face of modern art, had become both the source of his continual artistic renewal and of his sense of public martyrdom. This sense of martyrdom would itself become a central subject of his art and a principal mode of his self-representation.

HAIL MARY HAD brought not only obligations, but also some financial stability. When the film was menaced by censorship, the production and distribution company Gaumont had come to the rescue, deciding to throw its weight and prestige behind the film. The chairman of Gaumont, Nicolas Seydoux, who had known Godard since the early 1970s and had helped to finance *Tout va bien,* now stepped in again and signed a four-year contract that paid Godard not by the film but by the month, like an employee, in exchange for distribution rights to his films made in this period.

As a result, Godard could now put together a team to work with him steadily. In September 1985, he called Caroline Champetier, William Lubtchansky's former assistant, who had recently begun to work as a director of photography, and told her, "I'm looking for someone who knows a little but not too much."[20] She accepted, despite having witnessed vehement arguments between Godard and Nuytten (on the set of *Detective,* where she took still photos), which left her feeling like "a child watching her parents argue."[21] With Champetier, Godard inaugurated the sort of working relationship with a technician that he had long sought: she was hired not to work on one particular film but to work with him over a period of time on whichever projects might come up. He also hired an assistant, Hervé Duhamel, to work with him full-time. And he bought a 35mm Arriflex camera and a set of Zeiss lenses so that he and Miéville, who was preparing to make her first feature film, would not have to rent equipment and could shoot on their own schedule.

Godard's studio was now, Champetier said, "like a small business,"[22] and like any small business, Godard found himself being audited by France's fiscal authorities. As Duhamel recalled:

> Godard had an appointment with Jack Lang. He called him and said, "I can't come, because your colleague from the Ministry of Finance here is being a pain in the ass." So Lang calls Claude Davy, our press agent, to find out what's going on. There was an audit but it was done quickly; he had to pay a small tax penalty, that's all, because of his apartment in Paris which was paid for by the production company. The inspector said, "You live here, it's not like an office." Godard said, "I shoot here."[23]

For two weeks, the auditors occupied the office and went through Godard's records on site (as is standard practice in France). The inquest was all the more stressful for Godard because of his financial practices. As Duhamel explained: "With him, all the accounts are combined. He takes money from someone to make the film that he wants to make"—not necessarily the film that he has been commissioned to make—"then he has to find some elsewhere."[24]

In Godard's next work, in early 1986, a television film that he shot on video, he documented this state of affairs and its implications, both cinematic and personal. In the process, he turned his commission into a study of the burdens that he faced, artistically and financially, in attempting to fulfill it.

The production company Hamster Productions, which had a contract with the French television station TF1 to provide a monthly film based on a *Série noire* story, asked Godard for a film in the series based on a novel by James Hadley Chase, *The Soft Centre,* called, in French, *Chantons en chœur* (Let's Sing in Unison).[25] To put his patrons at ease, Godard stated in advance that he planned to make a standard film noir adaptation of a classic pulp fiction novel. Despite these assurances, his film is minimally related to the Chase novel. It is, instead, based mainly on his own life and crises, on his financial worries as a producer and his creative worries as a director, and on the role of women in his working life. With this project, *Grandeur et décadence d'une petite entreprise de cinéma* (Rise and Fall of a Small Film Company), Godard again managed to convert a conventional *Série noire* story into an extraordinarily personal, painful, and revealing work—into a film noir, of sorts, about the making of a film.

The casting, and the names given to the lead roles, suggested Godard's emotional investment in the small-scale piece. Jean-Pierre Léaud played a film director, Gaspard Bazin, whose creative crisis stems from a television commission for a film based on a *Série noire* novel by James Hadley Chase; Jean-Pierre Mocky, a director whom Godard had known since the 1950s,[26] played Jean Almereyda (the real name of the director Jean Vigo), a film producer with a small and troubled production company.

The film was constructed in three parallel stories, involving a classic Godard triangle: Gaspard's frantic quest for actors and for a story; Almereyda's struggle to keep his company afloat by juggling the books, siphoning off cash, and seeking to fend off tax inspectors; and Almereyda's conflict with his wife, Eurydice, who wants to become an actress and tries to get Gaspard to cast her in his film.

In Bazin's story, the director observes a depressing parade of unemployed actors marching through his studio in a line and auditioning for a video camera (each declaiming one word from a phrase by Faulkner), and he labors deep into the night to try to find something interesting to do with what he calls the "bad novel" that he is compelled to adapt—none other than *Chantons en choeur,* by James Hadley Chase. Meanwhile, Almereyda struggles to make films, meet a payroll, and make a living while contending with a tax audit. In Almereyda's company, Albatross Films, the production manager is exhorting the producer to find original receipts for everything, but Almereyda's main worry is an outstanding question over a bundle of missing deutschmarks.

The two men are brought together when Eurydice comes to see Bazin late one night to beg him for a screen test. When Almereyda finds out, he counsels her against it: "Look at Gaspard, the cinema has killed him." She complains, "Albatross Films is your life. I don't have a life. At least let me share it."

Godard himself makes a comic appearance near the film's end, meeting Almereyda by chance and hitching a ride with him (the gag is that Godard now lives in Reykjavik); he and the producer get nostalgic, tossing each other names of classic-era French actresses Eurydice reminds them of, and Godard offers the struggling producer a word of advice that also serves as a touching credo: "Everything is going backwards today—fashion, politics, and whatnot. The cinema is going backwards too . . . So maybe since she's old-fashioned, she has a chance. To each his freedom, after all. But you have to land in the right place. It's not a question of time or of era, it's a question of tempo."

But Almereyda never finds his way out of his crisis: he attempts to sneak away from his office (disguised, with poignant ineptitude, as a woman) but is caught by intruders; when Eurydice turns around, she finds his body lying beside his Mercedes.[27] Having lost his producer, Bazin—a director who is not also a producer—is reduced to auditioning, in vain, for the hip new company that has taken over the offices of Albatross Films, where stylish young people lounge about in stylish indolence.

The title, which appears as "The Rise and Fall of a Small Film Company as Revealed by the Search for Actors for a Film for Public Television Based on an Old Novel by J. H. Chase," is Godard's elegant way of biting the hand that was feeding him: the state. To make sure that his message was understood—or rather, to make sure that it was misunderstood—the final title card is a dedication as well as a jibe: "To Jack Lang." The left had lost the legislative elections in March, François Mitterrand had to share power with a center-right legislature, and so by the time the film was broadcast, on May 24, 1986, Lang was no longer minister of culture. Godard's next film, *Soigne ta droite* (Watch Your Right), drew its title from this state of affairs.

MORE THAN ANY project that Godard had realized to date, *Soigne ta droite* took its inspiration from practical, electoral politics, to which, as Godard recognized, his cinematic fortunes were peculiarly bound. In taking on politics, he was, therefore, also taking on his own prominence and his own persona: accordingly, in *Soigne ta droite*, Godard gave himself his first lead role as an actor.

It was a film that Godard had planned as early as April 1983, when he outlined for an interviewer a project "which will be an homage to what [Jacques] Tati did" and which he planned to call either *Soir de fête*, a play on *Jour de fête*, Tati's first feature film, or *Soigne ta droite*, referring to a short film from 1936, *Soigne ton gauche* (Watch Your Left), in which Tati stars.[28] Godard's idea was to act alongside the popular comic actor Jacques Villeret (who had appeared in a small role in *First Name: Carmen*) in a comedy about two policemen, one a leftist, the other a rightist. He intended the film to serve as a prelude to the March 1986 legislative elections, but when it clearly could not be completed (or even begun) by that date, he changed the theme drastically.

"Witness means martyr," Godard had Jean-Pierre Léaud say in *Detective;* in *Grandeur et décadence*, Godard had another stand-in, Jean-Pierre Mocky, suffer a filmmaker's martyrdom after he declares that the cinema is an art that kills. Following that train of thought, Godard reconfigured *Soigne ta droite* as a confrontation with death; the film was to define the cinema itself and his own cinema in terms of that confrontation. *Soigne ta droite* became a grandly philosophical film based on the classic existential definition of life in terms of death. Yet Godard kept its political aspect and indeed amplified it. The retrospective view of the cinema and of his own life that he planned in *Histoire(s) du cinéma* also entailed a growing obsession with political and social history; and *Soigne ta droite*—as the title hinted at in its allusions to Tati's 1936 film about the French left-wing Popular Front government as well as to the right-wing victory in the elections of 1986—reflected, with a new fullness and directness, Godard's meditations on modern history, and also confronted its deadly toll.

DEATH HAD PASSED close to Godard in the recent past. In 1984, Georges de Beauregard, who was ill with cancer, won an honorary César for his contributions to the French cinema. In his acceptance speech, Beauregard first acknowledged Godard for "his natural talent, his constant solicitude, always seeking what will happen next in the new audio-visual world and in life itself."[29] On September 10, 1984, Beauregard died. Godard wrote a memorial and published it as an advertisement in the trade magazine Le Film Français, praising him, in brief phrases separated by ellipses, for his "soul of Faust . . . under his airs of a shopkeeper," and credited him with producing "Belmondo's first smile and Bardot's last."[30]

Then, on October 21, 1984, another old ally, François Truffaut, died. Truffaut had been suffering from a brain tumor. He and Godard had never reconciled. Cahiers du cinéma published a special issue in December 1984, Le Roman de François Truffaut (The Novel of François Truffaut), for which Godard wrote a text, "Tout seul" (All Alone), in the same elliptical style as the memorial for Beauregard. Even now, Godard could not bring himself to honor Truffaut the filmmaker. He hailed the critic: "There was Diderot . . . Baudelaire . . . Elie Faure . . . Malraux . . . then François . . . there was never any other art critic." He praised the critic's audacity if not his consistency: "He didn't hesitate to cast the first stone . . . I don't know whether he continued . . . one can't do everything . . . taking on other people's sins before his own." But then, Godard derided the filmmaker: "We knew that a film had to be made alone . . . but we were four . . . so it took us some time to admit it . . . then some of us recanted . . . in our case, the screen was the judge." The screen, Godard hinted, had judged Truffaut guilty of a kind of perjury. Godard lamented Truffaut's obsession with books, suggesting that it killed him ("too much information . . . it went to his head") and wrote that when Truffaut went to "Father Alfred"—meaning Hitchcock—to be "absolved," the unfortunate result was yet another book (meaning Truffaut's famous volume of interviews with Hitchcock). Ending with a note regarding both departed filmmakers (Hitchcock had died in 1980), Godard wrote, "we'll surely meet them again."

Yet the specific inspiration for the death-saturated story of Soigne ta droite came to Godard by chance. In the summer of 1985, the song "Marcia Baïla"—Portuguese for "Marcia Dances"—by the French rock duo Les Rita Mitsouko, became a national hit as a result of its music video. The rock critic of *Le Monde*, Alain Wais, advised Godard to watch it.[31] After seeing it, Godard contacted the duo about the possibility of filming them at work.

The two musicians, Catherine Ringer and Fred Chichin, operated in a way that mattered to Godard: the two were a couple, and they worked at home. Their "studio" was a small two-room apartment in the twentieth arrondissement of Paris where they lived. They were tinkerers who filled their apartment with audio equipment, much of it nonprofessional, and they recorded their music themselves. "Marcia Baïla" was acknowledged to be the first "homemade" French pop hit.[32] (With its success, the couple moved to another nearby apartment and used the first as a recording studio.)

Despite the song's exuberance, its subject is death. The "Marcia" of the title is Marcia Moretto, Ringer's former dance teacher, who died of cancer.[33] Chichin had composed the soaring melody and the bouncy Brazilian rhythm, to which Ringer put the lyrics: *"But it's death that has killed you, Marcia/It's death that has consumed you, Marcia."*

When Godard approached Chichin and Ringer, Les Rita Mitsouko were about to record an album, *The No Comprendo,* but, as the musicians discovered, they had another thing in common with Godard: they no more knew what they were going to record than Godard knew what he was going to film. Their songs took shape in the studio, and—over a two-month span at the end of 1985 and beginning of 1986—Godard filmed the duo in the various stages of composition, creating an electronic rhythm track, searching for a guitar or keyboard riff, composing lyrics, laying down vocals.

The duo gave Godard the key to the apartment where they worked. He sometimes arrived in the morning before they did, and generally came by in the late afternoon with Caroline Champetier and a gaffer (electrician), though sometimes Champetier shot footage in Godard's absence.[34] When he was there, Godard usually recorded the sound himself, and his methods surprised Ringer: instead of keeping a microphone solely on the musicians, she explained, he had three microphones in three different places: "He had a boom [on the musicians], a microphone outside at the window for the ambient sounds, and he himself wore his little clip-on microphone."[35]

The Zeiss superspeed lenses that Godard had purchased allowed him to shoot in extreme low-light situations without adding ordinary movie lighting. The setup in the band's studio was spare, with daylight coming in from windows and a few added incandescent bulbs which he redirected with mirrors. In a procedure that would mark Godard's work from that time forth, he filmed in the direction of the source of light—with the small spotlights shining directly into the lens. This technique, which greatly surprised Champetier at the time, was more than a style. It would ultimately become the film's dominant metaphor—for the confrontation with death.

During the shoot, Godard said that he was unsure of what he would do with the footage of the musicians: "Depending on the results, we will keep the images as they are, in a documentary . . . Or else, we will create a fiction as a setting for the strongest images."[36] Ultimately, he kept the documentary images but also elaborated a linked group of fictional sketches inspired by the song that had drawn his attention to Les Rita Mitsouko in the first place. "Marcia Baïla" had helped Godard find the subject for his film: like the catchy song, *Soigne ta droite* would be a comedy about death.

THE FILM BEGINS with images of the French landscape viewed in low overflight as a deep male voice-over sets forth the film's main premise:

> Near the end of the 20th century, the telephone rings at the Idiot's home. He has finished his work and is about to spend one of those quiet evenings that one can still have in certain out-of-the-way parts of Europe, halfway between the forests of southern Germany and the lakes of northern Italy. That's when the telephone rings: the voice is unfamiliar and polite, but commanding. In high places, they are prepared to forgive the Idiot his many sins, but he has to act fast: to invent a story, to film it, and to deliver the print that very afternoon to the capital. The film must be in distribution that very evening. A car will be waiting for him at the garage in the valley and a plane ticket at the local airport. On those terms, and only on those terms, will the Idiot be forgiven.

The opening credits end with what Godard called the film's "real title"[37]—*Une Place sur la terre* (A Place on Earth)—and then the Idiot appears: Godard himself, in a garage, wearing a three-piece suit of an old-fashioned cut and a short-brimmed felt hat, sitting in front of a Rolls-Royce. Godard the Idiot, as his opulent display suggests, turns out to be a Prince too (and to make sure that the point is not missed, he shows himself reading a copy of Dostoyevsky's *The Idiot*). In the garage, he launches into a riff of cultural nostalgia: reminiscing about the decline of tennis at Wimbledon, he mimes the rhythmic head-turning and polite applause of tennis of an earlier era and then the violent smashes and snarling bravado of contemporary champions.

Godard attempted to model his own performance not on Jacques Tati or Jerry Lewis but the mild-mannered silent-era comedian Harry Langdon, whose persona embodied innocent sweetness in a coarse world. The pairing was apt: filming himself as the living representative of a lost age of refinement, of culture and art, Godard played the Idiot and Prince with a similarly belea-guered dignity.

Yet he also suggested the moral burden and personal price of his civi-lized and artistic anachronism, setting the tone for the film's grave import in the first scene that includes Jacques Villeret. The scene, which delivers high literary drama from an antic conceit, builds to one of the most moving mo-ments Godard has ever filmed. The pudgy, soft-eyed Villeret plays the Indi-vidual, a lost soul and an object of ridicule. He pays a visit to an imperious, elegant man in a lavish apartment: the Man (the stately, bluff veteran François Périer). The Individual's visit to the Man resembles the visit of an artist to a patron, a child to a father, or a clown to a king. The Man demands of him, "Have you invented something?" After a series of charades which the Man rejects, the Individual sits beside the Man at his table, pulls out a book, and an-nounces, "The most striking example of fraternity that I know—and which I have invented." The Man takes the book from him and reads aloud:

> In a hotel in Peïra-Cava, I am in the midst of writing the scene where the wounded revolutionaries from Shanghai are going to be thrown into the boiler of the locomotive. Katov managed to conserve his cyanide. In the night, his hand meets that of Souen, beside him, who presses his. I then divine that Katov will place the cyanide in the hand that has just embraced his own.

The Man asks the Individual, "What is this called?" The Individual an-swers, "La condition humaine"—"the human condition," which is also, of course, the title of a novel (in English, *Man's Fate*) by André Malraux.[38] In the human condition depicted by Malraux and crystallized by Godard, the ultimate state of freedom is the possibility of suicide, and the greatest act of fraternity, of love, is to make the suicide possible. In one scene, one shot, one sentence, Godard unfolds the inseparability of love and death, of life and death.

In the Idiot's breakneck quest to deliver the film, he boards an airplane—a comic set piece, with jostling and yelling and roughhousing, as a pilot calmly reads "Suicide: A User's Manual." In the middle of it all, the Id-iot sits beside an old woman whose skein of red wool he holds on his out-stretched hands as she winds it. When she comments that he seems sad, he explains, "It is always a little sad to leave the earth."

The airplane, a vehicle leaving earth, is also heading toward death: the passengers and crew ardently scoop and consume soup from an industrial-sized pot reminiscent of the large soup pot of cyanide-laced Kool-Aid that the followers of Jim Jones used to kill themselves and their children in Jonestown in Guyana in 1978.[39] Godard said that he conceived the airplane scene in homage to two Jerry Lewis films, *The Family Jewels,* from 1966, which features a comical airplane scene, and *Smorgasbord,* from 1983, in which Lewis's character repeatedly tries to commit suicide but comically fails.

Godard had originally wanted to develop *Soigne ta droite* in close collaboration with Villeret. The actor later recalled that the project arose from his and Godard's shared interest in the work of Samuel Beckett,[40] and that Godard had wanted him to play an essentially Beckettian role, "the solitary man, on the stage of the world."[41] The collaboration went poorly—Villeret was afraid of Godard, who in turn found the actor inhibited—but Villeret composed his own physical gags for the character of the Individual. Godard filmed that character staying alone in a nearly bare seaside apartment and crawling toward a massive dining-room table to start a cassette player emitting lines from Beckett ("That's how he talks, how he talks to himself, that afternoon, here on earth, there's only me, and a voice that can't be heard through the noise, because it's headed toward nobody"). Also in Trouville, filming the sky through an old-fashioned set of swinging doors, Godard added a voice-over to explain the image: "Westerners, among others, think that there's one room, Life, and another, the Beyond, and that Death is the door by which one passes from one to the other, is that not so? But why do they dramatize the door? Man is born for Death."

In another extraordinarily poignant sketch, the Individual plays a Belgian being deported by train. A secret police agent keeps him handcuffed to the curtain rod above the train window. The result is a pair of images, among the most beautiful that Godard ever filmed, first with the handcuffed hand in focus and the landscape rushing by in the background as a vague greenness, and then with the hand out of focus, an ominous and chilling presence before the inhabited landscape that is seen clearly behind it. The Individual plays this scene with a comically broad Belgian accent (jokes about Belgians being the French equivalent of Polish jokes in American humor) and hears from his captor the list of people killed because they could not learn to speak French properly, including "little Odile with a name like a town in Switzerland"—the town being Versoix, the woman being Odile Versois (the actress Marina Vlady's sister, who died in 1980) and an allusion to Godard's mother Odile, also from a town in Switzerland.

The Individual is transported to a sports stadium, where he enters a section filled with people strewn about, barely alive and barely speaking, like concentration camp victims in a mass grave. The incident is a double reminiscence, bringing together the recent catastrophe at a soccer match at the Heysel Stadium in Brussels on May 29, 1985, when rowdy fans pushed on a wall that gave way and killed thirty-nine spectators, and the use during wartime of the Vélodrome d'Hiver (the winter bicycle racetrack, the "Vel' d'Hiv") in Paris as an internment point for Jews prior to their deportation to Auschwitz. To reinforce the suggestion, one deportee on the stadium floor says he lives in the "Hotel Terminus" (the title of Marcel Ophüls's documentary about the Nazi war criminal Klaus Barbie), and the narrator refers to a dream that became "a second immensity, it became the law that presides over the development of crystal"—Kristallnacht.

Meanwhile, the Prince, rushing to deliver the cans containing his finished film, descends from the airplane. In this climactic moment of the film, Godard falls from the staircase to the tarmac, beside the film cans. As he lies dying, a woman banker from the airplane negotiates with him to purchase the film, and pays him with a party-noisemaker rattle, which he twirls in the air with his last breath. The film that he completed under the deadline has been finished at the cost of his life.

The voice-over commentator makes clear the implicit metaphorical point: "Death is the path toward the light." Thus the views into the lightbulbs that were filmed in the musicians' studio and the shots through the swinging doors at the beach apartment in Trouville toward the sky and directly into the sun take on their full meaning. Indeed, as Champetier reported, in scenes where no source of light was available, Godard gave characters hand mirrors to reflect it into the frame: as she described it, "We had to find something to pierce the shot, to pierce it with light."[42] When Godard filmed directly into an incandescent light that illuminates the faces of Catherine Ringer and Fred Chichin, or into the sun illuminating Villeret, or into the overhead fluorescent lights in the airport illuminating the Prince, he was filming the view toward death.

Soigne ta droite concludes with a screening of the Prince's film. However, it is not something that can be viewed in a theater; rather, the airplane pilot and his wife take up places alongside the river Seine and gaze upon Paris. The Prince's final work is the whole of reality, as it appears to them after returning to earth after their brush with death in the airplane. The grand cinematic embrace of all existence demands the ultimate sacrifice of its creator. The "solitary man on the stage of the world," the artist, working alone, works at the cost of his life. The self-martyrdom to art that the Prince endures is the same one that Godard, behind the camera, suggests he endures as the burden of his solitary work.

Soigne ta droite features a love story, that of Ringer and Chichin. They offer the example of how love and work together can bring about a kind of art that keeps its back toward death and faces life. From this perspective, *Soigne ta droite* is an open letter to Miéville, whose collaboration with Godard was the slender thread holding him on earth. As Hervé Duhamel later recalled, Godard and Miéville now had separate apartments in Rolle, directly across the hall from each other, yet they continued to live in close proximity and complicity, indeed intimacy: Duhamel often stayed in Godard's apartment, and he noticed that whatever went on in one apartment was audible in the other.[43] At the same time, Miéville was preparing to make her own first feature film, *Mon Cher Sujet* (My Dear Subject),[44] which the new commercial television channel La Cinq agreed, in the spring of 1986, to cofinance. She was setting out on her own lonely and perilous path, and putting at risk her own place on Earth. *Soigne ta droite*, in its cautionary hints to the woman with whom he was sharing work and life, as well as its self-pitying intimations regarding his own solitude, recalls the strategies of Godard's works from the 1960s. His public allusion to artistic and personal distance from Miéville is one of the most poignant and painful aspects of the film.

THE FIRST SKETCH scenes of *Soigne ta droite* were shot in May and June 1986, in Paris and Trouville. Then, in July and August, Godard added the airport and airplane sequences, which he realized under remarkable conditions: he insisted that the airplane scenes actually be filmed in flight. Each morning, the cast and crew met at Orly Airport in Paris and flew to the airport at Nantes (a brief trip, taking less than an hour), which is the airport seen in the film. But then, as Duhamel later recalled, "Afterwards, we took off again from Nantes in order to shoot in the airplane. An airplane is very noisy, so we had to fly at low speeds around Nantes. We would film one shot, then land."[45] At a cost of ten thousand francs (at the time, seventeen hundred dollars) per hour, he filmed in the air for thirty hours.

The two musicians of Les Rita Mitsouko were originally slated to participate in the sketches, but Godard could not figure out roles for them. He kept them waiting as they prepared to go to London for additional production and mixing of their album. When he met them to talk it over, as Ringer recalled, they ended up in a fistfight—"He spilled his coffee on me, and I spilled my beer on his head, and then we punched each other"—because the musicians refused to repay the money Godard had given them ("he stood us up many times and we lost lots of time waiting for him").[46]

Godard shot some added footage in January 1987 (in the corridors of LTC, a film processing laboratory near Paris),[47] but then had to put *Soigne ta droite* aside: he had to fulfill his outstanding commitment to Menahem Golan to have *King Lear* ready in time for the Cannes festival in May 1987 and so did not complete the film until later that year.

Soigne ta droite was released commercially in France on December 30, 1987. It had been more than two years since the release of Godard's previous film, *Detective,* in May 1985. Godard promoted *Soigne ta droite* vigorously. One French journalist remarked that the publicity campaign was unprecedented in his career,[48] another remarked that "Jean-Luc Godard is everywhere."[49] Godard even went so far as to allow a televised reunion with Anna Karina on a talk show. The sentimental occasion, however, soon broke down over Godard's unsentimental response to the host's softball question about their great youthful romance:

> INTERVIEWER: Can one ever be as happy afterwards? Did this great love that was given . . .
> KARINA: One can, but differently.
> INTERVIEWER: I see.
> GODARD: I think that one can be much happier . . .

Karina responded with a gasp of shock, and Godard continued, "And that tomorrow, and day after day . . ." but before he could complete his sentence, she got up and went off in tears, leaving Godard behind looking bewildered and humbled, as if he had been slapped.

If Godard's other public appearances on behalf of *Soigne ta droite* were less dramatic, they were nonetheless rich in what Danièle Heymann of *Le Monde* called "aphorisms and maxims on the state of the world, which he adorns with digressions about tennis."[50] His frank revelations, his prodigality with his thoughts, and his playful yet intensely committed, quasi-oracular presence generated a sort of metacritique that amplified their usefulness as advertising for the film.

The critical response to *Soigne ta droite* was enthusiastic. Michel Boujut of *L'Evènement du jeudi* said that the film was "rather a filmed poem, a soft electroshock, a Dadaist collage where what remains on the retina is nothing but light, movement, and emotion."[51] Michel Perez devoted his entire column in *Le Nouvel Observateur* to the study of a single image from the film, the view from the swinging doors of the Trouville apartment to the ocean.[52] In its opening week, *Soigne ta droite* was number-one at the Paris box office, and it shared the prix Louis Delluc, the most prestigious French film award, with Louis Malle's *Au Revoir les enfants.*

The warm readmittance of Godard that took place in France with the release of *Soigne ta droite* was not replicated in the United States, where the film remained unreleased until 2000. Yet in an English-language film intended primarily for the American market, *King Lear,* which Godard had already shot, he took up the principal themes outlined in *Soigne ta droite:* his burlesque yet tragic view of history; the terminal corruption of the cinema and his sufferings at the hands of the indifferent businesspeople who had laid hold of it; and his metaphysical view toward a mythical world beyond. In *King Lear,* he evoked these themes even more explicitly, and with a boldness regarding the power of cinema that is unprecedented, in or outside the work of Godard. *King Lear* would show artistic martyrdom at an unsurpassable level.

The first image
(Cannon / Photofest)

twenty-three

KING LEAR

"The dawn of our first image"

THE ADAPTATION OF *KING LEAR* WAS THE CULMINATION of Godard's effort to make a film about fathers and daughters, which he had been discussing publicly since 1980. In July 1982, shortly after completing *Passion* and while preparing to work with Myriem Roussel on their joint project, Godard expressed his desire to film Shakespeare's play, but he took no practical steps to fulfill it. However, in the wake of *Hail Mary*, he felt he had found a new approach to the subject, through *The Lover*, Marguerite Duras's 1984 novel about an adolescent girl's affair with an older man.

Godard asked Marin Karmitz to call Duras on his behalf and tell her that he wanted to make a film of the book. Duras told Karmitz, "It's too personal, it's really me, the only way to detach me from it would be with lots of money." Karmitz replied, "Very well, I'll tell him, he won't want to make the film anymore."[1] In the end, Duras sold her novel to the producer Claude Berri, and the resulting glossy costume production, directed by Jean-Jacques Annaud, resembled neither a film by Duras nor one by Godard.

Instead, Godard made *King Lear,* which came into being through a tortuous process resembling a comedy of errors. Every early effort on Godard's part to advance the project was in vain, and his relationships with most of the participants sooner or later turned bitter. Yet power plays and clashes of will were singularly appropriate to *King Lear;* since Godard wove the making of the film into the film itself, the behind-the-scenes conflicts coalesced with the substance of the drama.

King Lear gathers in one film all of Godard's preoccupations from this period, and does so in an extremely original, albeit elusive, form. It culminated a cycle of work that began with *Sauve qui peut* and was centered on Godard's self-mythologizing in and through cinema and his recuperation and redefinition of the grand tradition of art by way of the cinema. As such, *King Lear* is something of a personal manifesto—and yet the conditions of its production were so troubled and so pressured, so comically disastrous, as to invite wonder that anything at all, let alone one of Godard's greatest artistic achievements, should have resulted.

At the Cannes festival in 1985, when Godard signed with Menahem Golan to make the film, he told the producer that his idea was "to do King Lear as King Leone, as a sort of a patriarch-gangster . . . like a godfather."[2] Golan approved the project, with the proviso that Godard have a screenwriter who would meet with Golan's approval. Godard suggested Norman Mailer, and Golan approved.

Mailer was contacted on Golan and Godard's behalf by Tom Luddy, who worked with Francis Ford Coppola and was also an independent producer whom Godard had hired to be his "go-between," as Luddy put it, with the American participants and with Golan.[3] From Cannes, Luddy called Mailer to ask whether he would write the script. Mailer was deeply reluctant.

> At that time I had a great deal of respect for Godard, but I also knew that he was hell on writers, so I said, "Well, thank you Tom, but no thanks." And he said, "What if you could also direct *Tough Guys Don't Dance*"? . . . And I said, "In that case, Paris is worth a Mass."[4]

Golan then took the phone from Luddy and told Mailer, "Mr. Mailer, I welcome you to a two-movie contract."

Mailer, who had directed three feature films in the 1960s that were mainly improvised, was sympathetic to Godard's own rejection of the traditional film script. Nonetheless, he had forebodings: "My feeling was precisely, this is going to be a tough job and it probably won't be too agreeable, and certainly what I write is not going to be of much moment in this. But it's the only way I can get to make *Tough Guys Don't Dance*." In the event, Mailer's misgivings were justified.

GOLAN HAD AGREED that his company, Cannon, would pay Godard one million dollars in twelve monthly installments, at the end of which period the director would deliver a negative. The napkin contract called for Godard to keep rights in Switzerland and half the gross in France, and to have final cut only for the Swiss and French releases.[5] The film—his first English-language feature—was supposed to be filmed in the U.S. Virgin Islands and be ready for the 1986 Cannes festival. Soon after signing with Golan, Godard got to work. His first step was to turn to Orson Welles to be his "guide" to Shakespeare, but Welles died soon after, in October 1985. Godard worked on *Soigne ta droite* and *Grandeur et décadence* instead; as the Cannes festival of May 1986 approached, he had hardly begun *King Lear*.

Nonetheless, Luddy had remained active behind the scenes and contacted Woody Allen, getting him to agree to appear in the film with the promise that Godard would come to New York to meet with him, to discuss the role, and to shoot "for a day or two." However, Godard did not come to New York, did not meet with Allen, and was not ready to shoot anything. Luddy was concerned that Allen, if ignored, would drop out of the project, so he came up with another idea.

> I heard that Woody's film *Hannah and Her Sisters* would be at Cannes in '86 and I knew [Allen] never goes to Cannes, and unlike all other major films there is no press conference with the auteur . . . so I suggested to Godard as a way to keep Woody engaged that he ask Gilles Jacob [the festival director] if Cannes would fund him to do a filmed interview with Woody about *Hannah*.[6]

Godard liked the idea, and with the additional backing of Swiss television, he came to New York in the spring of 1986 to film Woody Allen.

Godard has one crucial affinity with Allen: both artists film themselves and stories derived from their own lives in their own milieus. In the videotaped discussion, however, Godard makes a distinction between them that he considered crucial: he criticized Allen's way of filming New York buildings in *Hannah and Her Sisters*, stating that some of those images conveyed the unfortunate impression of having been made "under the influence of television." Allen, looking dismayed, said that television affected him like "radioactivity." When Godard edited the tape, he rendered his inquisitorial stance comically explicit, repeatedly intercutting the images of Allen with a shot of himself surrounded with cigar smoke and lighted from below like an ogre in a horror film. Another inserted element was a photograph of Fred Astaire in full swing, superimposed on an image of Orson Welles, as if to suggest Allen's redoubled career in comedy and tragedy as graceful performer and solitary director. The interview had the desired effect on the fortunes of *King Lear*: Allen agreed to remain involved.

While in New York, Godard finally met with Norman Mailer (along with Tom Luddy). As Mailer later recalled:

> We had our first set of talks—we had probably four or five talks before the shooting of the movie began. Each time he took the Concorde to New York

and we'd meet for an hour or two and make plans and then he would leave, and go back to France. Each time, we were supposed to go off on a trip, because he was thinking of shooting it up in Maine or in Provincetown or in places that I knew . . . The assumption was this: he wanted me to play King Lear. I had done a little bit of acting. I was more than a little uneasy about the idea, because we didn't even have a script yet, and he also wanted . . . my daughters to play Goneril and Regan and Cordelia. One of them was an accomplished actress, Kate Mailer. She was going to play Cordelia.[7]

Mailer found the discussions with Godard unsatisfyingly vague and Godard himself "taciturn and heavily depressed." Though Mailer and Luddy came to their lunches prepared to leave at once with Godard to go location scouting in New England, they instead always went back home. "He would just sit there in this depression that was so heavy you could almost reach out and touch it," Mailer recounted, "and then at the end of the lunch he'd say, 'I think I'm going back to France again, I will see you all in another month or so, and then we will go look for a place to shoot the film.' "[8]

At the time of the first meeting, Mailer had not yet written the script. Luddy warned him that Golan would want to see it very soon, and Mailer got to work. He recalled asking Godard for a clue to his intentions and getting none. This lack of direction spurred Mailer, as he later maintained, to imagine a modernized Lear as a Mafia don—although both Golan and Godard claim that this idea originated with the director himself.

Each time I saw him I'd ask him if he had read King Lear yet but he hadn't, he'd shrug and look away, and seemed totally disinterested in the thought, and I finally decided the only way to do a modern King Lear, because that was what Menahem Golan wanted, was to make him a Mafia godfather. I couldn't conceive of anyone else in my range of understanding who would disown a daughter for refusing to compliment him. So I turned it into a script I called Don Learo [lay-AH-ro], which had its merits but generally speaking it had one terrible loss in it, which is, you couldn't use any of Shakespeare's best language. I was working with Mafia equivalents, and I didn't try to stay too close to Shakespeare with it. However, I ended up with a shootable script, which to my knowledge Godard never looked at.[9]

Godard admitted that he did not read Mailer's script (telling Hervé Duhamel, "I didn't ask for a script").[10] Godard didn't need Mailer's interpretation of the play. His interest in it was the relationship between Lear and Cordelia, which, he noted, was "the smallest part of King Lear." He had already found an essay that now served as his guide, "Le Silence de Cordelia" (Cordelia's Silence), by the French writer Viviane Forrester, in which she describes "a violent silence. Cordelia's silence. To the question of the king, her father, to the question of Lear, she answers, 'Nothing.' No thing."[11] Godard said that this idea sufficed for him as "the first route on the 'Shakespeare map.' "[12] Regardless of who initiated the project's Mafia angle, it was not the film's dominant aspect; for Godard, it was less context than pretext.

As the film inched forward, Godard thought of recruiting Richard Nixon for a " 'distancing operation,' a sequence of about twenty minutes during which Nixon and Mailer would discuss 'power and the loss of power.' "[13] Godard offered Nixon $500,000 for one day of shooting.[14] Not surprisingly, Nixon did not respond.[15]

One firm decision was made, however: Godard decided to shoot the film in Switzerland. Money was a factor: the million-dollar budget was worth far less to Godard, as the dollar had dropped precipitously against the French franc between 1985 and 1986. Golan had offered to deposit production funds directly into his Swiss account, but Godard instead regularly took the Concorde to California in order to pick up the checks. According to Golan, Godard's travel expenses consumed a significant portion of the production budget; by his own accounting, Godard made seventy trips by Concorde during the making of the film. To avoid additional foreign exchange costs, Godard brought suitcases of cash back and forth between Paris and Switzerland.

Golan was getting impatient. Tom Luddy would stall him by saying, "The bad news is, we've got delays. The good news is, we've got Woody Allen—and by the way, if we get Woody Allen, we'd like another hundred thousand."[16] On this basis, Golan paid several hundred thousand dollars beyond the original million—and yet claimed at Cannes in 1986, "We already have one million dollars profit on the Godard film,"[17] on the basis of presales to distributors.

In September 1986, without a script or even a synopsis and with very few indications of Godard's plans, Norman Mailer and his daughter Kate went to Nyon to begin the shoot. Godard, Mailer, and Golan have differing memories of these few days of shooting, but they all recall constant conflict. The differences would have been irrelevant if the shoot had gone well for the two artists, but it did not, and their relationship ended in recriminations: Mailer's remain the subject of his illuminating and detailed recollections; Godard's went into the film.

Mailer recalled that immediately on his arrival in Nyon, Switzerland, in September 1986, Godard wanted to begin shooting.[18]

> I was hardly playing *King Lear*. He said, "You will be Norman Mailer in this." And then he gave me some lines and they were really, by any comfortable measure, dreadful . . . I'd pick up the phone and I'd say, "Kate, Kate, you must

come down immediately, I have just finished the script, it is superb"—stuff like that. He was shooting, and we were getting some dreadful stuff. I said to him, "Look, I really can't say these lines. If you give me another name than Norman Mailer, I'll say anything you write for me, but if I'm going to be speaking in my own name, then I've got to write the lines, or at least I've got to be consulted on the lines." So he was very annoyed and he said, "That's the end of shooting for the day." We'd only shot for about three hours at that point.[19]

Godard felt that the breakdown was caused by other factors. First, he said, "The film was supposed to be made among his family, like reportage, and *King Lear* would be him with his daughters, especially with his one daughter." According to Godard, when Mailer "saw that he was going to have to talk about himself and his family, it was all over in a quarter-hour."[20] Moreover, "he saw that, above all, I wasn't very . . . that I don't know very well what I want to do, so he couldn't really have a discussion about it, he had nothing to do but obey, to have confidence in me."[21]

Duhamel offered another perspective:

> [Godard] had just begun and he didn't really know what he wanted to do. He had to do something quickly, to calm Golan and Globus . . . A guy like Mailer asks a lot of questions. They had a long discussion, which Godard doesn't like. Godard started out in a very bad mood. Then there was a moment when Godard told [Mailer] to mention "King Lear," and Mailer said, "Why King Lear? I'm King Lear," and Godard said, "Be quiet and do as you're told."[22]

The next morning, at breakfast, Godard and Mailer had what the writer called a "terrible row." After they calmed down, Mailer offered to withdraw: "Look, if you want me to go home, I'll go home." He added, "I will only go if you want me to go." Godard reportedly replied, "Well, yes, under the circumstances perhaps it's best that you do go back, and I will make the movie in another fashion."[23]

In Godard's telling, Mailer "still asked for $500,000, and he got it. It was in the contract, that we'd pay his lawyer. They said, 'Oh, that's very nice of you.' That's all there was to it. We made the film afterwards. We made it with what was left, with nothing."[24]

Mailer contended that he was paid directly by Golan,[25] although Golan himself maintained that Godard "had the budget and the money and he paid the actors." Golan made a more pertinent observation, however: that Mailer "left because he refused the insinuation—you know his daughter was in the movie, too—so he refused the insinuation that King Lear had a kind of sexual attraction to his daughter."[26]

Danièle Heymann, from *Le Monde,* who visited Godard during the shoot, concurred. Godard told her that Mailer "left, being unable, he said, 'to see himself represented in a situation of incest.' "[27]

Mailer readily confirmed this:

My wife always felt that that was his secret kicker, and that that was why he wanted Kate to play Cordelia. But the thought of that was just anathema to me. To begin with, to play it in my own name would have been absolutely absurd. Is it a reasonable demand to ask someone to, in their own name, play that they have an incestuous relationship to their daughter? . . . He never put it that way directly. There may have been a few small directions like, "Put your arm around her," or stuff like that . . . And of course there was this dialogue he was giving me, you know, "Oh, Kate, darling, I have finished the script and it's wonderful, please come down," you know. But it wasn't overt. I think that may well have been the underside, the subtext that he had in mind.[28]

Of course, it was.

WORK ON *KING Lear,* which had gotten under way so laboriously, now stopped cold. Tom Luddy had the impression that Godard would gladly have abandoned the project had he been able to do so without financial penalty. But Godard had to deliver a film to Cannon or else face the possibility of legal action.

To please Golan, Godard reportedly paid sixty thousand dollars to the Actors Studio in New York so that two actors—Al Pacino and Paul Newman—would read several lines of Shakespeare in order for their names to appear in the credits.[29] He also wanted to add two pop stars, Prince and Sting, to the cast; Sting was willing, but Godard couldn't figure out anything for him to do.[30] On the producers' insistence, Godard met with Tony Curtis and found him "charming" but did not offer him the role of Don Learo.[31] He did offer it to Lee Marvin, who accepted but then backed out. He offered the role to Rod Steiger, who accepted—with the proviso that the scenes be shot in Malibu.

The project remained stuck until, on a hunch, Tom Luddy brought Godard together with the theater director Peter Sellars. "I somehow knew," Luddy said, that he "would be the catalyst to jumpstart the film."[32] Sellars, a prodigious director in both the opera and theater, served as Godard's "guide" to Shakespeare, someone who, as Godard said, "knows Shakespeare as . . . as I know *Cahiers du cinéma,* say . . ."[33]

As befit what Godard considered Sellars's privileged relation to the works of Shakespeare, he created a new character for him, one that would reproduce within the film his behind-the-scenes work on *King Lear.* Sellars's

involvement spurred Godard to make the project even more oblique and potentially comical in its approach to Shakespeare's work. Sellars was to play
"William Shakespeare Junior the Fifth," who had been commissioned by the
Queen of England and the so-called Cannon Cultural Group to attempt to
rediscover the works of his ancestor, which had been lost in the catastrophe
of Chernobyl. Godard avoided making a naturalistic drama adapted directly
from a familiar object of high culture, instead presenting *King Lear* in a
metaphorical frame, as if to find out which aspects of that classic work were
relevant to the modern age.

Sellars's arrival prompted a renewed start to the shoot. In January 1987,
Godard traveled to New York to film Woody Allen in his editing room at the
Brill Building, at Forty-ninth Street and Broadway. The shoot was inauspi-
cious. The terms of Allen's contract were satisfactory for Godard but quite
unfavorable for Golan: Godard later recalled that Allen was paid "ten thousand dollars—in exchange, we don't use his name."[34] Allen maintained that
he did the part as "a favor," and that "there was no money involved."[35] During
the shoot, Allen asked Godard to permit him to leave earlier than planned
and before they had completed the filming. Godard agreed.[36]

The work they did consisted of Allen reciting Shakespeare's sixtieth sonnet and editing film with safety pins and a needle and thread, like a tailor. "It
didn't make sense to me when I did it," Allen said, "but I knew I was in good
hands."[37] To the critic Roger Ebert, however, Allen reportedly said, "I had the
impression that I was being directed by Rufus T. Firefly"—Groucho Marx's
character in *Duck Soup*.[38]

Godard then added a new cast member as Cordelia, Molly Ringwald,
who was a major star of American teen comedies and dramas. She met him
and Sellars at the Sherry-Netherland Hotel in New York, where, as Ringwald
later recalled, Godard "basically just sort of puttered around the room and
explained the whole concept"—the idea of making Lear a mafioso and filming the attempt to rediscover the play—"and it just seemed really interesting,
so I asked him why he wanted to use me . . . and he said, because Cordelia
was a princess and I was the closest thing at the time to what a princess is in
America, which is an actress, a teen actress."[39]

Godard finally found his King Lear, or Don Learo, in Burgess Meredith
(after Rod Steiger withdrew from the project, which ruled out Malibu), as
the 1987 Cannes festival loomed and Golan insisted that he had to have the
film in time to be shown there in May.

THE MAIN PART of the shoot began in Nyon in March 1987; by this time,
Godard knew that the project would have to be completed with twelve days
of filming, twelve of editing, and twelve of laboratory work. And yet this

headlong production went far more smoothly than many others, partly because of Godard's respect for his performers and partly because Sellars proved to be tremendously helpful in assembling the film's text (which was not exactly a script—among the elements were index cards issued daily, many from Sellars).

The cast included several additional participants whose roles were not to be found in Shakespeare. Shortly before the shoot, Juliette Binoche, whose first important role had been in *Hail Mary,* called Godard. She had recently starred alongside Julie Delpy in *Mauvais Sang* (Bad Blood), the second film by the young filmmaker Leos Carax, with whom she was living. Binoche told Godard that Carax was "desperate," and asked whether he could come to the shoot of *King Lear* to do "anything, chauffeur, or whatever."[40] Godard, who admired *Mauvais Sang* and recalled fondly Carax's visit to the set of *Sauve qui peut* with Alain Bergala for *Cahiers du cinéma,* invented a role for him: Edgar (as in Poe). He also invited Delpy, for whom he created a part to be played alongside Carax: Virginia (as in Woolf). To ensure the associations, the film shows a copy of Woolf's *The Waves* and includes a citation from it, as well as one line from Poe: "Nevermore."

Godard himself plays Professor Pluggy, a solitary inventor housed in a raw, blasted barrack—actually Anne-Marie Miéville's new house in Rolle, which was still under construction—where he conducts experiments toward the invention of something he calls the "image." Pluggy wears a headdress made of jingling ornaments and video cables, which Godard explained in a brief synopsis prepared just before the shoot: "His hair is made of hi-fi cables so that he is able to plug his head directly into the unknown."[41] From the play itself, only Lear—Don Learo—played by Meredith, and Cordelia, played by Ringwald, remained.

As usual, Godard did not provide his actors with their lines until the moment of the shoot. For Burgess Meredith, who was seventy-nine years old, this posed memory problems, and he asked Godard to give him his dialogue the night before he needed it. Godard ignored his request. Molly Ringwald observed that this discomfort seemed to be the effect that Godard was trying to achieve; as she put it, Lear turned into a "rattled old guy." As for the actress herself, she admitted, "I didn't know at all what I was doing. I just did everything he told me to do, basically." Meredith's stalwart acceptance of Godard's method, Ringwald's respectful obedience, and Sellars's intellectual contributions helped to smooth the film's hasty path to completion.

Godard was observed to be in a peculiarly good humor, but aspects of his genial mood played startling tricks on the substance of the film itself. Ringwald reported that Godard "short-sheeted" Meredith's bed and also put fake blood on it, and that this "completely perplexed Burgess. He just didn't know what to make of him."[42] Yet Godard's pranks with stage blood were no joke; they were, instead, a surprising fulcrum of the film.

Meredith's bed, in the hotel Beau-Rivage in Nyon, was actually used on-camera as Don Learo's bed. Danièle Heymann of *Le Monde* described a scene in which several goblins, played by young models, were supposed to enter Learo's room. There, she noticed, "His bed was unmade. An atrocious pool of blood stains the sheets." She further described the shoot of that scene: "Godard speaks to the tall Swiss 'spirit': 'OK, you come in and you lean over the bed and say, "Abracadabra Mao Zedong Che Guevara." ' A discreet laugh is heard." Godard reportedly responded with anger: "What's that? Did someone say something funny?" After the scene was shot, Heymann asked Duhamel whether the blood was "what's left of Lear." He responded, "Yes . . . and of Cordelia's virginity."[43] The "kicker" of incest that Norman Mailer had suspected was indeed revealed on-screen.

THE GRAND METAPHORICAL conceit of Godard's *King Lear,* albeit arch and puckish, is a project of vast aesthetic, quasi-cosmic ambition, in which Godard's own comic role as an artistic shaman is central. On the one hand, the film's metaphysical speculations exceed even those of *Hail Mary;* on the other, its concrete incorporation of the specific conditions of its creation are greater than in any of Godard's other films. If, in *Passion,* Godard sought to film reality and its metaphors, in *King Lear* he rendered the symbolic and the concrete inseparable, even indistinguishable. In this film more than in any other, he brought together the material and the transcendent, life and art.

The first voices in the film are those of Godard answering the telephone and Menahem Golan—in an authentic conversation surreptitiously taped by Godard—demanding that the film be finished in time for the 1987 festival. Tom Luddy's voice comes on the line and asks Godard to answer. The response is a voice from the set: "Action."

The action begins with two successive takes of Norman Mailer in his hotel room in Nyon, writing a line of dialogue for a character he named "Mailer." He calls his daughter Kate on the phone just as she comes in and looks with dismay at his finished script, asking why he's so interested in the Mafia. Mailer answers, "I think the Mafia is the only way to do *King Lear.*" Meanwhile, on the sound track, Godard states his case against Mailer, complaining about the writer's "ceremony of star behavior." Godard concludes, "After the fifth take of the first shot, the great writer left the set. He took off for America, he said. He and his daughter, first class. His daughter's boyfriend, economy. Anyway, I was fired."

From the beginning, the sound track is elaborate: using Dolby stereo, Godard had conflicting sounds and voices come contrapuntally from the two sides of the screen. He used slowed-down and electronically manipulated versions of Beethoven's last string quartet, as well as sea sounds, bird cries, and Shakespearean recitations in voice-over, to create a complex sonic texture. The film's images are equally rich, with soft natural light from Lake Geneva leaving the actors in deep, detailed shadows. The film is replete with reproductions of classic paintings, from Giotto to Rembrandt to Watteau, Doré to Renoir and van Gogh; like a visual music, they set the mood.

Engrossed in his ongoing research for *Histoire(s) du cinéma,* Godard also anchored the search for *King Lear* in the history of cinema. Shakespeare Jr. the Fifth contemplates an album of photographs of Luchino Visconti, Jean Renoir, and Orson Welles, and wonders which other directors might have taken on the job of recovering *King Lear.* As more black-and-white stills of directors—Marcel Pagnol, Jacques Rivette, Georges Franju, Robert Bresson, Pier Paolo Pasolini, Fritz Lang, Joseph Losey, Jacques Becker, Jean Cocteau—come on the screen, Shakespeare Jr. the Fifth announces each of the filmmakers by their first names, enthusiastically adding "Yes" after each. But when an image of François Truffaut appears, he says, "No, no, no. François, I'm not sure"—a reprise of Godard's blunt funerary judgment of Truffaut.

The quest by William Shakespeare Jr. the Fifth to rediscover his ancestor's plays after their destruction along with all of culture, particularly "movies and art," is of course an absurdist futurist comedy, but its tone and import are parodies of classic film noirs and detective stories. Before getting to the particulars of *King Lear,* Godard inscribed the film firmly within the cinematic tradition.

The effort to rediscover *King Lear* begins at an elegant table in the Nyon hotel dining room, where Shakespeare Jr. the Fifth is slurping soup as he listens to dialogue being spoken off-screen: a man's gravelly voice pronounces lines that capture his attention; as he hears them, he writes frantically in a notebook:

Meantime we shall express our darker purpose.
Give me the map there. Know, that we have divided
In three our Kingdom: and 'tis our fast intent,
To shake all cares and business from our age,
Conferring them on younger strengths, while we
Unburthen'd crawl toward death.

The voice is that of Burgess Meredith as Don Learo, who adds, with a Brooklyn-tinged snarl, "Are ya listening?" and issues the command to his "joy," to his "last and least," that she speak. A young woman's voice—Molly Ringwald's—speaks: "What shall Cordelia speak? Love, and be silent."

Learo and Cordelia are now seen sitting at a nearby table, and Shakespeare Jr. the Fifth continues to take notes as Learo launches into a disquisition for Cordelia on the subject of Bugsy Siegel and Meyer Lansky. Siegel was "a real killer, not like this Richard Nixon" and Lansky, "a little guy, he was a philosopher." Shakespeare rises to thank Cordelia for her contribution to his quest, but Learo angrily sends him away—"Are you making a play for my daughter?"

King Lear is infused with Godard's unmade film *The Story,* a tale of Jewish gangsters and their ties to Las Vegas and Hollywood. In his hotel room, Learo dictates to Cordelia, who types at a manual typewriter, from a book about Siegel and Lansky. She reads back to him: "By the late '60s, the whole country was Las Vegas-ized. Entertainment conglomerates like MGM today own the largest establishments in Vegas . . . All of these vice and leisure centers are linked together by my Learo Jet company. All of America is now embracing our vision, and Bugsy Siegel's death"—he changes the word to *martyrdom*—"was not in vain." Referring back to the long-dormant outline for *The Story,* about the connections between Bugsy Siegel and modern Hollywood, Godard brings together Learo's "royal" and paternal authority with the origins of cinema in the violent power of the criminal underworld. In his quest for a single story, Shakespeare Jr. the Fifth finds himself plunged into the story of stories, at least, as Godard saw it: the material reality of gangsterism and high finance that gave rise to the classical cinema, and which, in its stories, the cinema reflects.

Meanwhile, Godard introduces five Shakespearean goblins—"the secret agents of human memory," Shakespeare Jr. the Fifth says—and they show up on the balcony of Learo's room. Learo stands on the balcony with a goblin beside him, as a voice speaks: "Does Lear walk thus, speak thus? Where are his eyes? . . . Who is it that can tell me who I am?" As one goblin dances before Learo's bed, another intones "Abracadabra Mao Zedong Che Guevara." A chambermaid comes in, turns down the bed, and finds bloodstained sheets; so does Shakespeare Jr. the Fifth. The goblin's lines, spoken of Lear, allude to Oedipus, who is first blind to his own identity and then, after discovering it, dashes out his eyes. The implication of Cordelia's virginity sacrificed to her father is clear, though achieved without any overt declaration on the set. Molly Ringwald was unaware during the shoot that the scene had any such erotic implication.

The film then moves to Shakespeare's quest for Professor Pluggy, whose research was said to be moving in a "direction parallel to [his] own." He finds the reclusive sorcerer. It is Godard himself, speaking sepulchral English from one side of his mouth—in his bare house, surrounded by acolytes (including Leos Carax as Edgar). He then goes to witness the professor perform an experiment in his "laboratory," a darkened video studio. The two face a bank of video monitors on which Pluggy has intertwined images from cartoons, classic paintings, advertising, and silent films. As Edgar stands beside the screens, Professor Pluggy intones lines from the French surrealist poet Pierre Reverdy (lines which Godard had previously cited in *Passion*), a definition of "the image" that stands as Godard's own manifesto for the complex and highly constructed images of his later work:

> The image is a pure creation of the soul. It cannot be born of a comparison, but of a reconciliation of two realities that are more or less far apart. The more the connection between these two realities are [*sic*] distant and true, the more it will have emotive power . . . An image is not strong because it is brutal or fantastic, but because the association of ideas is distant and true . . . What is great is not the image but the emotion that it provokes.

To observe Pluggy's next experiment, Shakespeare goes to a movie theater. There, the professor is interviewed by Michèle Halberstadt, a journalist for the *New York Times,* to whom he explains that the room is his invention: all the seats face the same way, so that the audience will know which way to look when they hear voices. Now "Professor Kozintsev" (the director of the Russian film of *King Lear,* impersonated by Freddy Buache of the Cinémathèque Suisse) arrives—"from Siberia"—and shows the assembled guests his work. Halberstadt asks Kozintsev what he calls it; Kozintsev answers, "I was thinking of calling it 'image.'" Shakespeare takes out his notebook and writes, exclaiming, "'Image,' that's a good word." What Pluggy and Kozintsev—Godard and Buache—have reinvented is the cinema itself.

In the brief synopsis that Godard showed a journalist on the set, the experiment was a failure, and Pluggy and Kozintsev "kill themselves from shame and despair."[44] But in the actual film, the experiment is a great success—and the cinema is reborn, but at shockingly high cost, as Shakespeare discovers. After having seen Kozintsev's film, he declares his ancestor's play rediscovered, and goes to thank Pluggy for his help. Shakespeare finds him gathering flower petals strewn in the grass, and watches furtively as Pluggy, through the miracle of reverse photography, puts the petals back on the flowers (an homage to Jean Cocteau's similar gesture in *The Testament of Orpheus*). Through his cinematic learning and artistry, Pluggy has singlehandedly brought nature back to life—and then expires from the exertion, as church bells peal.

Pluggy's last words, whispered into Shakespeare's ear, are "Mister Alien! Mister Alien!" In voice-over, Shakespeare explains, "Yes, they were Easter bells. The images were there as new: innocent, shy, strong. Now I understand that Pluggy's sacrifice was not in vain. Now I understand, through his work, Saint Paul's words: that the image will appear in the time of resurrection." As in *Soigne ta droite*, Godard here depicted the rebirth of the cinema as the result of his sacrifice. He presents himself in *King Lear* as a Christ-like figure who gives his life to redeem the world.

The possibility of a new cinema, one that would follow on his own demise, is raised in an epilogue. Shakespeare, Edgar, and Virginia are sitting on rocks beside the lake as they watch Learo walk through the underbrush with Cordelia. She is wearing a shroudlike white dress and leading a white horse. Learo takes Shakespeare's notebook and reads aloud: "I might have saved her, now she's gone forever." Learo exchanges his butterfly net for Edgar's shotgun, and follows Cordelia. Watching Learo and Cordelia, Edgar wants to invent a word, which Shakespeare says will "accompany the dawn of our first image."

This "first image," a majestic tableau, shows Cordelia dead, her corpse stretched out on a rock by the side of the lake as, with his back to her, Learo stands, the shotgun in hand, facing the water, the mountains, and the sky. With this, the primal image of the incestuous father enduring the death of his daughter—the scenario at the basis of Godard's work throughout the decade—Pluggy's project is realized: the cinema is reborn, albeit in darkest sin.

Declaring that the motion picture industry is again growing fast, Shakespeare Jr. the Fifth announces, "I was finishing the picture in a small editing place they had hired for me. The man in charge was Mister Alien." In the editing room, Mister Alien, Woody Allen, is wearing a T-shirt inscribed "Picasso" and editing film with safety pins and needle and thread, as Shakespeare Jr. the Fifth recalls a remark by Professor Pluggy about "handling in both hands the present, the future, and the past." As film runs through the editing table, Mister Alien recites aloud from Shakespeare's sixtieth sonnet:

> Like as the waves make towards the pebbled shore,
> So do our minutes hasten to their end;
> Each changing place with that which goes before,
> In sequent toil all forwards do contend.

The genesis of the film is present: Mailer, Welles, Sellars's knowledge of Shakespeare, the pressure from Golan, the trip to New York to film Woody Allen, the absorption in the history of cinema to which Godard sought to link his *King Lear*, the origin of the cinema in the story of stories, the criminal underworld's violent power, and the suggestion of incest, so subtle as to defy both vulgarity and horror. And, crucially, Godard himself is also there as the self-sacrificing demiurge who brings these elements to life.

In Godard's preceding films he had stormed the bastions of high art: in *Passion*, he took on the history of painting; in *First Name: Carmen*, he approached music as such, through the rarefied summit of Beethoven's quartets; in *Hail Mary*, he assumed the challenge of the founding Christian myth. With *King Lear* he went further still: he raises his claims for the power of the cinema—of his own films—to the level of divine power.

REQUIRED TO FINISH the film in time for Cannes, Godard claimed he stayed awake for sixty-two consecutive hours making sure that the rough cut was ready for its May 17 screening. He declared that the film was "ninety percent" complete.[45] At the festival, *King Lear* was admired by the happy few critics who were particularly sensitive to Godard's work, but was generally viewed by others as a very expensive practical joke, or even as simply "incomprehensible."[46] At his press conference, Godard claimed never to have read the play *King Lear* and asserted, "Shakespeare is untranslatable, and I don't understand half of what is said in the film."[47] Golan, who was outraged by the inclusion of his private telephone conversation, complained that Godard had "spit in his own soup,"[48] and said that the director should make press conferences rather than films.

Mailer, whose film *Tough Guys Don't Dance* also played at the festival, out of competition, was present as a juror. In advance of the screening of *King Lear*, the writer magnanimously told a journalist, "We separated amicably . . . I'm sure that he has made a good film."[49] Mailer had not seen it; in private, he was seething. In June 2000, Mailer said, "Working for Godard on *King Lear* was probably the most disagreeable single experience I've had in all these years as a writer."[50]

After Cannes, Godard finished the film, which was shown in July at the Avignon theater festival, again to acclaim from the best critics but to little note in the movie business.[51] Being an English-language film, it did not open promptly in France; its "untranslatability" was taken quite seriously in the industry, as was its generally harsh reception at Cannes: no French distributor bought rights to release it there. It thus went unreleased in France despite Godard's artistic reputation and widespread recognition.

Instead, *King Lear* had its commercial premiere in New York on January 22, 1988, at the Quad Theater, its elaborately contrapuntal stereo sound track mixed down to a garbled mono. The famous actors in the cast had signed contracts with Godard that prohibited their names from being used in advertising. Reviewers generally abhorred Godard's approach to an English-language classic: Vincent Canby, in the *New York Times,* called the film "lifeless";[52] in *Time* magazine, Richard Corliss called it "cynical" but also "Godard's most infuriating, entertaining pastiche in two decades."[53] At three evening screenings in the film's brief first run, the viewing audience was never more than twenty people.

King Lear did not open in France until 2002—with Godard's revelatory stereo sound track—where it received great attention from the press, but mainly for the curious stories of its genesis rather than for what was on the screen. Moreover, the writer Viviane Forrester, whose essay on Cordelia's silence was quoted on the sound track, sued the filmmaker for copyright infringement and won. The French distributor, Bodega Films, now was obligated to mention Forrester's book in the credits, and Godard and the distributor were both required to pay Forrester and her publisher damages in the amount of five thousand euros.[54]

The reception of the film, at home and abroad, was grotesquely anticlimactic; its minimal impact at the time of its completion was absurdly disproportionate to its vast artistic significance. *King Lear* is one of Godard's artistic summits; it is also a dead end of sorts. In it, he combined the themes, tones, moods, and methods that had dominated his work since his return to the film industry in 1979. Immediately after completing it, he embarked on a massive project that had been gestating for years, *Histoire(s) du cinéma*, which would occupy his attention for a long time to come and which would prove to be his most subjective and personal cinematic essay.

MEANWHILE, IN LATE 1987, Anne-Marie Miéville finally got the opportunity to make her first feature film when a Swiss production company added funds to those already committed by Gaumont and the CNC.[55] She started with a well-defined and carefully elaborated story (though she, like Godard, preferred not to write dialogue until the time of the shoot). Miéville did not, however, know what to call her film and claimed that from being asked for years about her progress on "her dear subject," she decided to call the film *Mon cher sujet.*

The film is a modern melodrama, a worthy successor to the work of Douglas Sirk. Miéville filmed three generations of women: an elderly grandmother, still working (in the office of a garage); a woman in her early forties, a writer of some renown but whose love life was unsatisfyingly distributed between two men, one crude and tender, the other intellectual and cold; and a young opera singer whose boyfriend, a saxophonist with a rock band, tries to persuade her to sing pop music. The young woman becomes pregnant, and the arrival of the child, a boy, becomes the focus of the three women's lives, taking the place of the men who are absent.

Miéville's film is also a noteworthy attempt to capture the mental and physical discipline of an artist's apprenticeship. The daughter's singing lesson with an older male teacher is among the most powerful moments in the film. Miéville's own daughter, Anne, was a singer and writer of popular songs, and she performed one of her compositions on-screen. Several months after the film was completed, Anne gave birth to a child. Miéville admitted the correlations of the film's substance to her own experience, likening her family situation to that of the woman writer, as a daughter, a mother, and a new grandmother.[56]

Miéville, as she confessed, was not a person of the cinema; as such, like a young first-time novelist, she was able to work in the first person, without references to movie genres or other cinematic antecedents. Her first feature film was spontaneous and alert to her actors as well as to her own emotions. She fully justified the confidence that Godard had expressed in her ability when they had discussed the question two years earlier in *Soft and Hard*. *Mon cher sujet* premiered in the Critics' Fortnight at the Cannes festival in 1988 and was released commercially in Paris on January 18, 1989. Despite generally favorable reviews, Miéville was not immediately able to launch another project.

THE TIME THAT followed the completion of *King Lear* was suddenly busy for Godard. Shortly before the 1987 Cannes festival, Godard had asked René Bonnell, the historian of cinema economics who had become the head of the film production department at Canal Plus, France's pay-television channel, to approve that company's investment in *Histoire(s) du cinéma,* which the station had been planning to broadcast since its inception in 1984.[57] Bonnell agreed, and at the festival announced the joint venture with Godard. Soon thereafter, Godard immersed himself more deeply than ever in the project, nurtured for years, that concerned his own "cher sujet"—the cinema itself.

Godard presents the first draft of *Histoire(s) du cinema* at the Cannes festival, May 21, 1988.
(AP Images)

twenty-four

HISTOIRE(S) DU CINÉMA, PART 1

"I'd like to make a film on the concentration camps"

THOUGH GODARD HAD BEEN TALKING ABOUT MAKING HIS personal history of cinema since the mid-1970s and had announced plans for it in 1983, he did not start work on it until signing a contract with Gaumont in 1985. At that time, after hiring a full-time cameraperson, Caroline Champetier, and an assistant, Hervé Duhamel, he asked Champetier to buy the entire series of videocassettes of classic films, *Les Films de ma vie* (The Films of My Life). According to Champetier, when the tapes arrived, "he spent lots of time organizing them, and he wouldn't let anybody else touch them. Then he watched them—and he thought that he had to watch the entire film to find one shot." As he explained to her, "Nobody takes into account the screening time";[1] he knew that the project would take a long time to complete.

The original impetus for the series had been his and Gorin's meditations on the political implications of cinematic form. In the 1970s, as Godard set out on his slow return to the cinema, he thought he could make money with his knowledge of film history, but then the project turned into an autobiographical tour through his own experience of that history. But in 1985, Godard landed on a third principle to orient the entire project, the passage from the history of cinema to history as such. Godard's view of political history rapidly came to dominate the series—which, as it turned out, took him more than a decade to complete—and all of his subsequent work.

ON APRIL 24, 1985, Claude Lanzmann's epochal film *Shoah* opened in Paris. The film—the Hebrew title means "catastrophic upheaval"—provided the French with a new word to designate the Holocaust.[2] It also provided the French with a new frame of reference for the devastation wrought upon the Jews of Europe, a view derived from Lanzmann's method for studying it. *Shoah* features no archival footage; it is made entirely of images filmed by Lanzmann in the 1970s and 1980s, mainly featuring the people he interviewed: Jews who survived the concentration camps, Germans who participated in the camps' functioning, and Poles who lived near the camps. Starting from the principle of the moral primacy of testimony, Lanzmann recovered the events of history from their enduring (if subordinated) presence in the current world. *Shoah* is a film of history that takes place entirely in the present tense.

Years before Lanzmann's film was released, the Holocaust was already on Godard's mind as a potential subject. As early as 1963, he had imagined what he called "the only true film about the concentration camps," which he thought could never be made because "it would be intolerable." Such a film would concentrate on the practical problems that the "torturers" faced:

> How to get a two-meter body into a fifty-centimeter coffin? How to dispose of ten tons of arms and legs in a three-ton truck? How to burn a hundred women with only gasoline enough for ten? One would also have to show the typists typing out lists of everything. What would be unbearable would not be the horror aroused by such scenes, but, on the contrary, their perfectly normal and human aspect.[3]

During the 1980 Cannes festival, where he was presenting *Sauve qui peut*, Godard offered a different view of the subject: "I'd like to make a film on the concentration camps. But one must have the means. How to find twenty thousand extras who weigh thirty kilos? What's more, one would have to really beat them. But what assistant would be willing to beat up a skeletal extra?"[4] Behind the flip remark, Godard implied the serious notion that no fiction film about the concentration camps could adequately convey their horror. But he added, cryptically, "The camps—nobody has ever shown them."[5] In the years that followed, Godard repeated this remark and unpacked its meaning: he made many references to his certainty that the Germans had produced images of the concentration camps and that these images had not been seen for the simple reason that nobody had done the archival research to find them. For instance, in 1985, he asserted:

> The camps were surely filmed in every which way by the Germans, so the archives must exist somewhere. They were filmed by the Americans, by the

French, but it wasn't shown because if it had been shown, it would change something. And things mustn't change. People prefer to say: never again.[6]

Godard was, at the time, unimpressed by *Shoah.* In a televised discussion with Marguerite Duras in December 1987 (one of the many broadcasts that served as advance publicity for the release of *Soigne ta droite*), Godard deprecated Lanzmann's film, complaining that it did not show what had happened: "But it suffices to show; there still exists such a thing as vision." Duras defended *Shoah,* claiming that "it showed the roads, the deep pits, the survivors."

> GODARD: Lanzmann didn't show anything—he showed the Germans.
> DURAS: One is invaded by the images.
> GODARD: It isn't broadcast every Monday.
> DURAS: But that's something else.
> GODARD: But that's the thing I'm talking about. If it had been seen, people wouldn't judge [Klaus] Barbie as he's been judged.

Godard seemed to suggest that the widespread responsibility for the camps adduced in *Shoah* would have prevented the quasi-expiatory demonization of Klaus Barbie, the head of the Gestapo in Lyon as of May 1942, who was arrested in Bolivia in 1983, tried in France in 1987, and convicted of crimes against humanity.[7]

Then, regarding *Shoah,* Godard added, "The film wasn't shown in '45." In response to his critiques, Duras gets visibly and audibly angry; her tone rises as she declares, "It's an absolute reference. Let's not talk about it, we won't talk about all this, it's a horror." While she scolds Godard for his critical detachment from Lanzmann's film, he looks chastened and lowers his eyes.

For Godard, the crucial aspect of a cinematic approach to the Holocaust was the presence or absence of footage of the camps themselves, of the actual killing of inmates. This idea determined his response to *Shoah*—and ultimately his creation of *Histoire(s) du cinéma.* Indeed, that series of videos, on which Godard began work in 1985, is most clearly understood as Godard's response to *Shoah,* his counter-*Shoah.*

During an interview from 1989, as he was completing the first two of the eight episodes of *Histoire(s),* Godard emphasized the centrality of World War II to his series, "because that's where everything"—the cinema—"came to a halt." This historic break in the history of cinema occurred, in his view, because "nobody filmed the concentration camps, no one wanted to show them or to see them."[8] The world's (though primarily Europe's and America's) film industries were responsible for two crucial failures—to make fictional films about the camps at the time that they existed, and to find the German footage Godard believed existed. He argued that the result of this failure was "the death of the European cinema and the triumph of the American cinema."[9]

Godard's thesis reflected his view of the power of the cinema and his assumption that the medium's overwhelming popularity would have compelled a worldwide public outcry against the Holocaust, had it only been shown in movies. He took for granted the power of images—whether authentic documentary ones or fictional ones that offered irresistible, psychologically rich and subtle simulacra of reality—to inspire viewers' confidence, compel their belief, and arouse their outrage.

This failure, according to Godard, signified the abandonment of cinema's documentary essence in favor of its spectacular side, which he took to be Hollywood's specialty. And the postwar success of the American cinema (which in fact captured a large share of the European market) meant, to him, that the intrinsically historiographic aspect of the cinema was also destroyed—because, in his view, the essence of America was its lack of history (an assertion that he would elaborate in interviews and films). He considered the renunciation of documentary and history to represent nothing less than the end of the cinema.

The end of the cinema, as Godard understands it, is the thesis he expresses in the opening episodes of *Histoire(s) du cinéma*. The series is the embodiment of a single, dominant, coherent argument, which Godard himself voices with the clarion directness of a lecturer—often on-screen. Completed in 1998, the series is not widely recognized as the clear statement that it is because the form in which Godard couches his argument is the most complex that he had realized to date. The video series is also demanding in its length, which is just over six hours.

In *Histoire(s) du cinéma*, Godard assembled a vast number of film clips, still photographs, on-screen texts, and images of himself and other performers in recitation and discussion, as well as music, film sound tracks, and voices, including his own. He joined these disparate elements in an allusive collage featuring a wide array of editing devices and optical effects, such as superimpositions, flashing alternations, and slow dissolves, and the sudden clash of contrasting elements, whether color and black-and-white, light and dark, or quiet and loud. Godard drew the strands of thought related to his thesis into an amazingly intricate web of guided visual and audio associations. But ultimately, the most remarkable aspect of *Histoire(s) du cinéma* is not its complexity but its simplicity. The text of Godard's own remarks, mainly in voice-over, would—if transcribed—comprise a concise exposition of a powerful set of arguments.[10]

The first section, 1A, *Toutes les histoires* (*All the Stories*), asserts, in Godard's voice, that the fall of the cinema came about not through the transition from silent to sound films but as a result of the absence of images made during World War II, in fictional films—especially from Hollywood—of the concentration camps. The second part of the thesis, expounded in section 1B, *Une histoire seule* (*One Story Alone*), is personal, an attempt to trace the effect on Godard himself of his lifelong devotion to that decadent cinema—a devotion that began in the early postwar years.

The *Histoire(s)*, with their rapid superimpositions and blinking alternations of images, convey an associative intensity of experience that defies description or explication from a single regular-speed viewing. Godard uses video analytically, in a particular sense of the word: the freedom of association of images and sounds is reminiscent of the work to which an analysand is subjected by a psychoanalyst. In fact, Freud is a major reference in the series, and its central consciousness, its thinking subject, is Godard's own cinematic self.

The result is a sort of cinematic confessional, as Godard defines his own work and life in the cinema in terms of his faith in this fallen art form—and ultimately, its personal and moral price. *Histoire(s) du cinéma* can be understood as an intellectual autobiography, in which the subject (Godard's own story) and the object (the history of cinema) converge in a single circuit of thought. This subjective element of the series, a kind of working-through on screen of the network of associations that formed in Godard's movie-colonized unconscious—the logical extension of his notion that "at the cinema, we do not think, we are thought"—becomes a kind of cinematic self-psychoanalysis, in which the profusion of night thoughts and daydreams is oddly, decisively dominated by a single idée fixe: the cinematic nonrepresentation of the Holocaust.

GODARD'S *HISTOIRE(S)* ARE stories in yet another sense: his notion of history is comprised of stories, anecdotal history, and the opening episodes consist of clusters of good yarns that relate to his central themes. In section 1A, *All the Stories* (dedicated to Mary Meerson, Henri Langlois's longtime companion), he recounts "the story of the last tycoon, Irving Thalberg," who imagined "fifty-two films a day," and of whom Godard said, "it"—this fertile imagination—"had to pass through a beautiful and fragile body" (the handsome Thalberg died of pneumonia at age thirty-seven, in 1936) "so that, as Fitzgerald put it, 'this' could come to pass—this, the power of Hollywood." He tells of Max Ophüls's failed attempt to film Molière's *School for Wives* in Geneva in 1940, with the actress Madeleine Ozeray, and crudely correlated the German director's affair with the French actress with the invasion of France by Germany: "He falls on Madeleine Ozeray's ass just as the German army was taking France from behind." Godard tells the story with which he had harangued the cameraman Bruno Nuytten on the set of *Detective,* concerning the camera manufacturer Arriflex, "which Arnold and Richter invented to keep up with the German army." He suggests, hauntingly, that the cinema foretold the coming of war and the concentration camps, in such scenes as the death of Boieldieu in Renoir's *The Grand Illusion,* the shooting of rabbits in the same director's *The Rules of the Game,* the skeleton dance in the same film, or the death of the hero in Fritz Lang's *Siegfried.* And Godard summarizes the cinematic tragedy in wartime: that before the war, spectators in movie theaters "burned the imaginary to warm the real," and that afterward, "reality takes its revenge and demands real tears and real blood."

> From Vienna to Madrid, from Siodmak to Capra, from Los Angeles to Moscow, from Renoir to Malraux and Dovzhenko, the great directors of fiction were unable to control a revenge that they had staged twenty times.

This "revenge," that of reality on the imaginary, was the Second World War. Though Godard was obsessed with the Holocaust as an unparalleled horror, he relativized the monstrosity of the political force that brought it about. As Godard asserted in *All the Stories,* the war resulted in not one but two attempts at world dominion—Germany's unsuccessful military conquest, and America's successful cultural one: just as "after the First World War, Hollywood destroyed French cinema, after the Second World War Hollywood destroyed all the cinemas of Europe with television and money."

On-screen, Godard flashes the word *Endlösung* (final solution), suggesting that, while Hitler had used the cover of war to try to exterminate the Jews of Europe, the United States had used it to wipe out the national movie industries of Europe. He shockingly presented these two deeds as parallel, as motivated by a similar sense of national self-righteousness and drive for hegemony. Thus, rather than considering Germany alone to have been the invaders and the United States the liberators, Godard saw wartime France and the other European nations as innocent victims caught between these two behemoths (a notion that he would develop more deeply later in the series and in other works to come). If his view remained abstracted from the practicalities of life under occupation (the adolescent Godard spent the war years in Switzerland), it nonetheless implied a harshly self-deprecating judgment on his own cinephilic devotion to the American cinema, an avowal of something like a mental collaboration.

THE SECOND SECTION, 1B, *One Story Alone,* is dedicated to John Cassavetes. With the flashing title "Cogito ergo video" (a play on Descartes's

"Cogito ergo sum"—I think, therefore I am), Godard asks, "What about me, my *histoire*? Where do I come into it?" He describes the cinema as "a world without history but a world that tells stories," claiming that, thanks to cinema, "men saw that there was a world there, a world of stories." He asserts that the cinema is "the only place where memory is a slave," and that "cinema, like Christianity, is not based on historical truth; it gives us a story and says, 'Believe it.'" And Godard, who had been, in his youth, blissful in that faith, was now repentant, because the stories in which he had put his faith had been corrupted: "Later one or two world wars will suffice to pervert this state of childhood." The cinema had been born "with the colors of mourning, in black and white," but the postwar decades of oblivion, through television, did their best to distract viewers from mournful reality by means of "infantilisms."

Like the other New Wave filmmakers who were true believers in the cinema, he had put his faith in a simulated world, one shorn of political and historical consciousness. As a consequence, he had been doomed to create work that made inadequate contact with politics and to devote himself to the attempt to redeem that original artistic sin.

Here Godard echoes the theme he had been repeating since his midsixties' repudiation of the pure cinephile heritage of the New Wave: he and his friends knew nothing of life and had learned what they know from the movies. He was suggesting that, having identified with the stories he saw onscreen in the years after World War II, he had sworn fealty to this postwar cinema of historical ignorance and was, even now, even against his will, in its thrall. The completed version of episode 1B, first shown in 1989, ends with Godard as seen in *Soigne ta droite,* the Prince/Idiot, carrying film cans down an airplane stairway moments before he tumbles and falls to his death. He depicts himself as a martyr to his faith in the cinema.

Godard suggests that he was thus the unwitting yet all too eager victim of a delusion and a snare: if, at the cinema, he did not think but was thought, if his mind had been colonized by a cinema of concealment and of distraction rather than of revelation and of accusation, then he had been an acolyte of a false faith. Now, living the life of the damned, in a contemplative redoubt which seemed penitent or monastic, he was enduring an all too fitting punishment for his peculiar sin, that of having believed, with a profound faith, what the fallen postwar cinema had told him.

DESPITE THE SOLITUDE of the enterprise, Godard did not work entirely alone. As Hervé Duhamel later recalled, Godard "found his bearings by talking," and would say, "Let's go see some people." To start out, Godard invited the film critic and historian Jacques Siclier to Rolle for an open-ended conversation that he videotaped. Duhamel, who took notes, found Godard to be "typically brilliant" and Siclier to be "intimidated"; Godard was dissatisfied with the results and threw away the cassettes."[11]

He brought in others who represented for him a diverse set of personal associations and memories: he called upon Julie Delpy, Alain Cuny, the actress Maria Casarès (who had starred in Robert Bresson's *Les Dames du Bois de Boulogne,* in 1945), the actress Sabine Azéma (the star of Alain Resnais's *Mélo,* from 1986), and others, to read texts that he selected. He invited Isabelle Huppert to his studio, sharply criticized her way of reading a text by Schopenhauer, and decided not to record her. He videotaped an extended discussion about film history with the critic Serge Daney, of *Cahiers du cinéma* and *Libération.*

The project did not progress rapidly. Though René Bonnell of Canal Plus, who often visited Godard at his studio in Rolle to observe and to discuss the work-in-progress, had announced, in May 1987, at the Cannes festival, that the station would broadcast the first installments of the series in the fall of that year,[12] Godard did not have anything to show until the 1988 Cannes festival, where he presented forty minutes of rough video sketches.

The presentation was received with great enthusiasm and interest by critics in attendance. It also piqued the curiosity of journalists, who wondered how Godard was able to get the rights to the innumerable clips of films and music, still photos and texts, of which the videos were comprised. Danièle Heymann reported in *Le Monde* that Godard was "fighting to obtain excerpts from films, and swears that, if he is refused them, he will go to court."[13] When first conceiving the series, in 1979, Godard had suggested that the cinémathèques and film museums of the world install equipment to create video transfers of their collections in order to make them available for researchers—for Godard himself. Now that videotapes of films were readily obtainable, Godard simply took the clips he needed, on the self-proclaimed basis that he was using "citations," which were not being utilized for their commercial value but as the subject of study and analysis. As he told Nicolas Seydoux, the head of Gaumont, he considered himself to be not a filmmaker but "a philosopher who uses a camera,"[14] and asserted that his citations were not the domain of media or even of art, but of science and scholarship. With the approval of his producers, Godard simply forged ahead, assuming that the legal right of citation would suffice.[15] (René Bonnell of Canal Plus later claimed that Gaumont, which coproduced the series, gave its rights for free, and that "for the others, we knew that no one would do anything to Godard."[16])

These citations served a dual function. In the series, Godard expressed his view that the cinema—as a medium that is essentially both popular and artistic, fictional and documentary, grand and intimate, spectacular and personal, of its times and enduring, pulp and philosophy—had come to an end. The *Histoire(s) du cinéma* was thus a memorial, a personal remembrance of the cinema and a public commemoration of it, a reminiscence and a monument. But it was also the repository of shards of cinema that Godard rescued from oblivion—the oblivion that ultimately resulted from the modern cinema's original sin, overlooking the Holocaust.

Episodes 1A and 1B were broadcast on Canal Plus on May 7 and May 14, 1989, and were received with great admiration if little comprehension, generating a profusion of reports and interviews. According to the programming executive René Bonnell, "We had great press, but nobody watched. It was practically a grant—the films hardly had an audience, they had an audience too small to be measured—but we had extraordinary press, and Canal Plus doesn't live on viewership alone, but also on its image."[17] In *Le Monde,* Jacques Siclier wrote that Godard "remade, according to his dreams, a lost paradise" of cinema: "So strong is his love of the cinema that Godard communicates it to us like a trance."[18] The journalist and novelist Noël Simsolo conducted ten half-hour interviews with Godard about the series for broadcast later in the year on the France Culture radio station.

Most important, because of the favorable interest in the first two episodes, its producers, together with the television channel FR3 and the new seventh, cultural channel, La Sept, commissioned a continuation of the series. In the later episodes of the *Histoire(s)* and in the other works that developed concurrently with them, Godard's approach to questions of history and memory—particularly the Second World War, Germany and America, and the Jews—remained constant. The *Histoire(s) du cinéma,* with their collection of clips, anecdotes, and allusions, were a funeral oration in the grand tradition, a rescuing of fragments from the great library after its sacking. And the political orientation of the series left little doubt as to who had sacked it.

Alain Delon flees the cruel world and finds a refuge.
(TCD-Prod DB © Peripheria / DR)

twenty-five

NOUVELLE VAGUE

"I have lived two dreams in my life"

O N MARCH 7, 1987, GODARD WAS AWARDED AN HON-
orary César, an official sign of his now-canonical status in
the French film industry. He attended the ceremony and,
carrying a trenchcoat over his arm, came to the podium, where, not without
irony, he thanked "the professionals of the profession." He also offered "thanks
to the girls of the negative cutting department at the LTC laboratory, thanks
to the switchboard operator at Gaumont, because without her I wouldn't
know Nicolas [Seydoux]." Godard was asked by the master of ceremonies,
the talk-show host Jean-Pierre Elkabbach, whether it was important for his
films to be successful at the time of their release; in response, Godard referred to a van Gogh exhibit taking place in Paris at the time: "There are two
million people waiting outside in the rain a hundred years later."[1]

Yet in a way, the evening's festivities were an anticlimax to the afternoon's
events: Godard had met Marin Karmitz for lunch to discuss a new project.
Godard had recently called Karmitz claiming to need money (since he was in
the process of completing *King Lear* under pressure), in exchange for which
he had offered video rights to some of his older films. Karmitz told him on
the phone, "I'm not an antiques dealer, make me something new," and Godard
responded, "OK, you're the producer, give me an idea of what I should do."
On the spot, the producer made two suggestions: either a film with no story
whatsoever, comprised of images set to music, which would be called *La
Musique*, or a film with a well-defined story. Godard asked, "What story?"

At the time Karmitz had no answer, but when they met for lunch on
March 7, as Karmitz later recalled, he offered Godard a more concrete
suggestion:

I told him, "Do something about an actor." He said, "Now you've really said something; but which actor?" I had no idea, I just said it like that, now I had to come up with something; and all of a sudden, I said, "Mastroianni." He said, "That's brilliant, I've never worked with him." So I arranged a meeting. Mastroianni did nothing but talk about his romantic troubles. In his superb accent, he said, "Oh, she cuckolded me," etc. Godard was delighted, they got on famously.

The actor asked Godard for a story; Godard came up with something that pleased Mastroianni and Karmitz, in which Mastroianni would play two roles, a man and his double. Then, Mastroianni said he was going away for two months and asked Godard to write the idea up in "two pages." Godard agreed. Yet then, as Karmitz recalled:

Two months later Godard calls me. He talks in a small voice when he has screwed up. He said, "Listen, I made a mistake. Another producer offered me more money to do it. I need the money, so I'm doing it with him." I said, "OK, as you wish." He said, "But you came up with the idea, so I'll pay you the percentage that you would get as screenwriter."

Shortly thereafter, Karmitz recalled, Godard called him again and said, "I made a mistake, I should have made it with you," in response to which Karmitz, angered, hung up on him. The two never spoke again.[2]

Godard announced plans for this film in December 1987, but with Karmitz out of the picture and no mention of Mastroianni. He knew, in any case, that he would not be able to get to it before completing the first installments of *Histoire(s) du cinéma* and several other commissioned videos. He expected the delay to last two years and he called it his "vacation from fiction." The project's title, *Nouvelle Vague* (New Wave), aroused anticipation: Godard said that the film would "have to do with the sea,"[3] and, though the gag on "wave" was obvious, the real question was whether he planned to film an autobiographical account of the adventures of the group from *Cahiers*. He deliberately left the question open to speculation; in fact, the project was the one intended for Mastroianni.[4]

THIS "VACATION FROM fiction" was tied to Godard's difficulty getting approval from Gaumont for his fiction projects, which included *Conversations with Dmitri* and a film based on Beethoven's Ninth Symphony. *Conversations with Dmitri* (which had been in development with the television channel La Cinq since 1986) concerned the last four years of a hypothetical occupation of France by the Soviet Union. Dmitri, the Russian commissar of the French film commission, wanted to delegate filmmaking to French directors, but they were unwilling to collaborate with the Russians, except for one older filmmaker. The film would feature four conversations, one for each season, over four years, between the willing filmmaker and the commissar, and it would end with the departure of the Russians and the reinauguration of the Deauville festival of American films (which, Godard said, was "what's left of the Normandy landing").[5] *The Ninth Symphony* would feature the singer-songwriter Léo Ferré as Beethoven. But Nicolas Seydoux was not ready to finance these projects solely on the basis of a title and an idea; he wanted to see "a real script,"[6] which Godard was unwilling to provide.

Instead, Godard fulfilled commissions for promotional videos from the fashion designers Marithé and François Girbaud, the appliance store chain Darty, France Télécom, and *Le Figaro*, the first three of which were related to the *Histoire(s) du cinéma* by technique, the fourth by theme. These works were no mere commercials; ranging from thirteen to fifty minutes in length, they were cinematic essays that honored their patrons only glancingly. Yet because of Godard's celebrity and cultural status, the executives who commissioned them could justifiably expect these videos to get far more attention in the general press than standard-issue promotional or industrial films.

The first three were principally works of editing. For the Girbauds, Godard made *On s'est tous défilé* (We All Marched—"défilé" being the word for a parade, a political march, and a runway show). He sent Caroline Champetier to shoot footage by herself, and then he took her shots of models at work and passersby in the street and, in the editing room, applied to them the slow-motion "decomposition" technique that was so important to *Sauve qui peut*. Adding a text by Mallarmé that he read on the sound track, he likened the models' movements to the grace of daily gestures latent in street life. In the process, he flattered the Girbauds with the suggestion that fashion, like the cinema, is an art of fiction nourished by documentary, and is, as such, an art akin to Godard's own.

Darty commissioned Godard in late 1987 to make a videotape about the company itself.[7] Hervé Duhamel did the camerawork on his own, having been instructed by Godard to "show that there are people who go into the store, who buy things and who go home with them."[8] In 1989, Godard and Miéville belatedly completed the film with their own voice-over duet, reciting philosophical texts selected by Duhamel and his wife. The film's techniques of superimpositions and juxtapositions of text and image resemble exercises for the *Histoire(s)*; nonetheless, *Le Rapport Darty* (The Darty Report or The Darty Revenue) generates a distinctive emotional current through the joint self-portraiture of Godard and Miéville. They conclude the video with a moving and audacious stroke, likening themselves to one of the most exalted of cinematic pairs, Charlie Chaplin and Paulette Goddard, by way of a visual citation from the end of *Modern Times*, in which the little tramp and his beloved walk the lonely road together.

France Télécom, the French telephone company, commissioned a promotional film, *Puissance de la parole* (The Power of the Word). Godard drew on a text by Edgar Allan Poe, "The Power of Words," in which Poe suggests that each word has the power to change the course of history. Godard excerpts a lovers' dialogue from James M. Cain's *The Postman Always Rings Twice* to convey the practical force of language. He again employed the editing techniques of *Histoire(s) du cinéma*, superimpositions and rapid-fire alternation, to create the film's strongest visual metaphors, linking the sky and the sea to suggest the quasi-supernatural link that makes conversation at a distance—telephone service—possible.

The fourth commission, *Le Dernier Mot* (The Last Word), a promotional film for *Le Figaro*, is a remarkably condensed account of a powerful story concerning France during the Second World War. A man who is doing research visits a house in order to ask its inhabitants about a nearby place that he is seeking. He is trying to find the exact spot in a nearby forest where a man who had once lived in that house was killed by the occupying Germans in 1942. The current resident is a violinist, and he brings his instrument along as he accompanies the researcher on a walk into the forest. There, the violinist plays the Chaconne from Bach's D-minor Partita, as Godard conjures on-screen the execution of a young philosopher, Valentin Feldman, on July 27, 1942. While preparing Feldman for execution, a German soldier asks him if he has anything to say, and then sardonically jokes, "Everyone knows that the French always want to have the last word." Feldman's response, his last words, are: "Imbecile, it's for you that I die"—an anecdote cited in Claude Roy's *Moi je*, the book that lent its title to the self-examination that Godard had intended to film in 1973.[9] The substance of *Le Dernier Mot* was connected with *Histoire(s) du cinéma* (the philosopher Feldman and his fate are mentioned in episode 1A), but the thesis of the short video, the embodiment of history in the artistic classics, formed the starting point for the film with which Godard ended his "vacation from fiction," *Nouvelle Vague*.

DISAPPOINTING THOSE WHO hoped Godard would tell the story of his formative years alongside his *Cahiers* comrades, *Nouvelle Vague* was set not in the world of filmmaking but in the world of big business, not in Paris of the 1950s but on a rural French estate in an indeterminate timeless era which blended the 1930s and the present day. Yet Godard's film nonetheless fulfilled the audacious promise of its title: he reconceived the history of cinema, and his place in it, as a biblical allegory.

Godard's two-page synopsis for *Nouvelle Vague*, from 1988, starts, "A woman. Rich, beautiful, authoritarian, active. At the wheel of her BMW, she knocks over a guy in the street."[10] She takes him in, cares for him, and they become lovers. She neglects her business for him, and he remains passive and dependent. When she teaches him to water ski, he falls in the lake and calls for help, but she lets him drown. "She returns to Paris, takes up her work again, her business," but one day there's a knock on her door: "A man who resembles the other like a brother," and who claims to have seen the drowning. This man is "enterprising and a charmer." He becomes her lover; she becomes passive, and he takes control of her affairs. The next summer, she falls in the water but he saves her from drowning. "Several days later, at breakfast on the terrace, she looks at him pensively. In the second man, she recognizes the first."

The tale's allegorical aspect is unambiguous: the first man is the Old Wave, the second is the New Wave; and the woman is the producer, the industry. In a subsequent draft of the synopsis, Godard made the biblical analogy explicit, calling the story's two parts the Old Testament and the New Testament. The Old Testament depicts the classic era of cinema in its industrial-age dynamism. The first coming is that of the classical director, who is raised to unexpected dignity by the cinema and disposed of by the cinema (such as Griffith, Stroheim, Welles, and other great directors who were made and destroyed by the system). The New Testament is the story of the New Wave, Godard's own story. Though the cinema itself is weakened (as it was, economically, by television) at the time of the second coming, the dynamic newcomer is endowed with knowledge of his predecessor's experience and fate. Taking the torpid cinema in hand, he reinfuses it with his energy, nearly doing away with it in the process, but ultimately bringing it back from the brink of disaster.

The idea had its origins in the heyday of the New Wave itself: Godard first proposed it to the producer Mag Bodard in 1964 as a project for Anna Karina and Jean-Paul Belmondo. At the time, it came to naught when Bodard insisted that the female lead be played instead by Catherine Deneuve. Now the project was being coproduced by Alain Sarde's Sara Films and by Vega Films, the company of the Swiss producer Ruth Waldburger. For them, Godard amplified his synopsis with evocative details: the first man and the woman spend the summer at "the splendid estate she inherited," where he becomes even more passive "upon contact with astonishing nature, the devastating green and blue beauty of the waves, the tranquil severity of the immense trees, the grace and innocence of horses, etc."; the second man persuades the woman to take him to "the beautiful prewar estate which she had told him about, to brighten her cheeks with the caress of foliage."[11] This milieu of material opulence, of natural splendor as an attribute of wealth, is that of Godard's own childhood.

Godard's assistant Hervé Duhamel recognized the subject's literary implications and was inspired by them. Duhamel offered to do research to find texts from the history of literature that could go into the film. Godard accepted the offer. Working full-time as assistant on *Histoire(s) du cinéma* and on other video commissions, Duhamel—who, Godard said, "knows a good deal of literature"[12]—also spent his weekends, together with his wife, rummaging through his library to locate quotations he thought would be apt for each scene. He gave Godard a collage of photocopies—from Hemingway, Faulkner, Georges Bataille, and René Char, among others—that ran to more than a hundred pages. Months passed with no response from Godard. Duhamel, somewhat disheartened, asked him whether he had looked at it; the director answered, "Later, later."

"Later" came in May 1989, when, after the Cannes festival, Godard asked the renowned actor Alain Delon to play the double lead role in *Nouvelle Vague.* Delon immediately accepted.[13] Delon expected that Godard's film would get him to the Cannes festival, where he had not been since 1963, with *The Leopard,* by Luchino Visconti; moreover, he told Godard that he was getting bored with the run of police stories in which he usually starred. But when, soon thereafter, Delon met Godard at the bar of the Plaza-Athénée Hotel in Paris, he laid down one condition: that there be a screenplay with dialogue.[14] Godard was in luck: he took Duhamel's file of citations and turned it into a screenplay for Delon; though prior to the shoot Godard rearranged, tore apart, and (literally) threw out the file (which he then asked Duhamel to reconstitute), almost all of the dialogue in the film is composed of literary citations from Duhamel's research.

During the summer of 1989, Delon met with Godard only twice more: once when Godard introduced him to the lead actress, Domiziana Giordano (who had played the lead in Andrei Tarkovsky's *Nostalgia*), and again, to discuss Delon's wardrobe for the double role.

THE SHOOT BEGAN on September 4, mainly at a majestic old house on the Swiss side of Lake Geneva. The shoot was unusually long—two months—the crew was large, the equipment was burdensome, the action was complex, and Delon's demands for written dialogue were stringent: though Godard prepared text in advance, he kept changing it at the last minute. Delon, who had never worked that way before and whose last-minute memory was not good, became very frustrated. For some scenes, strips of paper with his lines were pasted on walls or doors out of camera view. Moreover, Delon found Godard's instructions, or lack of them, confusing. The two had bitter arguments, and Delon later admitted, "If I had yielded to my inclination, the film would never have been completed."[15]

In what was by now a familiar pattern, Godard's relations with the film's other participants were not much better. For a part as a governess, he called the young actress Laurence Côte, who had been in his video *Puissance de la parole*. In her audition, he told her, "Since the video, Laurence, your soul has gotten thinner."[16] She reacted with outrage, but he mollified her and then cast her in the role—which, during the shoot, he reduced to a few lines.

With his principal associate, the director of photography William Lubtchansky, things were worse. Not long before the shoot of *Nouvelle vague*, Lubtchansky, who had finished *Sauve qui peut* in bitterness and had had no contact with Godard since 1980, happened to be in Geneva, called Godard "just to say hello," and invited him and Miéville to dinner. As Lubtchansky later recalled, "It was marvelous, we really talked, and he asked me to do *Nouvelle Vague*—and it was the same hell."[17] The cinematographer found Godard unbearably aggressive and nasty and vowed, yet again, never to work with him—a vow he has kept, to date.

IN AN INTERMEDIATE draft of the plot, Godard framed the legend-like theme of the two identical men as a flashback from the point of view of a woman, Clio, the muse of history. In her telling, the story of the two men took place during her childhood, and the woman who gets involved with them is Clio's mother, who would be played by the same actress as Clio herself. In Godard's allegorical scheme, the cinema was both the mother of Clio and her double—the source and the image of history. Although Godard did not in fact film this framing device, he nonetheless channeled its import, regarding the conjunction of history and legend, into the film.

Nouvelle Vague unfolds in a mythical place in a mythical time, an isolated world of a lost refinement and formality, sheltered from the outer world. For the film's setting, Godard chose a château that reminded him of the estate on the French side of Lake Geneva that belonged to his maternal grandparents; this was the cloistered environment where he spent his childhood in prosperous ease.

Godard's visual schema was somewhat abstract: "It isn't the dialogue that should be broken up into spaces, but space into blocks and series of dialogue," he said. In practice, this meant that he planned to do long traveling shots "in the style of Ophüls," in which he would emphasize "the comings and goings of various and sundry—servants, passers-by, technicians, waiters." He modeled the estate on the château in Jean Renoir's *The Rules of the Game*: "The fluid aspect of social and worldly movements, transmitted by the motion of the camera, would bring out the love relationship as a solid entity, a little as if music brought forth sculpture." To accomplish this, Godard planned to use "the large crane of Hollywood films."[18] Sweeping, majestic camera movements would link characters from the two worlds of the château, those of master and servant, and a very large cast would represent a wide array of characters. Elaborate physical setups, such as coordinated entrances and exits of cars, would convey an old-fashioned order and splendor.

The rural estate, in its grace, grandeur, and self-possessed isolation—and its industry—recalls the classic movie studio, a closed-off fantasy land which made myths in its own image. Unlike the real Hollywood studio, this "studio" resembled the one Godard found in Switzerland: a distillation of natural splendors, the water, the sky, the land and the light.

DISCUSSING NOUVELLE VAGUE, Godard likened his family background to his formative years in the cinema:

> I have lived two dreams in my life. I lived my childhood in an extremely rich family, like the one we filmed here, at the same place, in these chalets, on the other side of the lake. They educated me and they left me alone. There was so much money that we didn't notice it. That was during the war. I knew nothing of the war at that time, which has brought me lots of remorse. The result is that today, as even Sarde knows well, I don't feel the need for a film to make money. And then, there was the New Wave: a team . . . It disappeared, it couldn't last long. So after having known that, one begins to know the real and to move forward.[19]

In *Nouvelle Vague,* Godard faced up to the aspect of reality that linked his comfortable family life to his cinematic fancies: these worlds of his personal mythology ran on money and, to emphasize the connection, he drew on references to money from American literature. The drowning man who is rescued by the woman industrialist says to her, "Your dirty money" (from Hemingway's "The Snows of Kilimanjaro"), and when Cécile, the governess, asks her mother whether the rich are really so different from them, her mother gives her a version of the famous answer: "Yes, they have more money."[20] This line conveys Godard's revisionist view of the Fitzgerald/Hemingway repartee, as shown in the film: the money of the rich indeed makes them different, insofar as it gives them access to power, beauty, experience, and freedom that are unavailable to the poor.

Yet Godard concludes the film with the end of the sheltered idyll: when the second man is revealed to be not the first man's brother but the same person (a metaphysical conceit with Christian implications), he and the woman dismiss the household entourage and, leaving the estate, drive off together in search of the wider world. Their departure is the end of the film, but it suggests the beginning of an intimate and contemplative adventure similar to Godard's own in response to the cinema's industrial tumult.

As befits a film that presents a grand allegorical schema of the history of cinema—and a filmmaker in the midst of making his *Histoire(s) du cinéma—Nouvelle Vague* is replete not only with literary allusions but also with cinematic references to anchor its story: the rich and mighty woman at the story's center is Countess Elena Torlato-Favrini—the first name from Jean Renoir's *Eléna et les hommes,* the title and family name from Joseph Mankiewicz's *The Barefoot Contessa.* The two characters played by Delon are Roger Lennox and Richard Lennox—the family name of a character from Raymond Chandler's *The Long Goodbye* (filmed by Robert Altman). The drowning, on which the story turns, recalls René Clément's *Plein Soleil (Purple Noon)* (1960), in which Delon had his first major role, as well as George Stevens's *A Place in the Sun* (1951), to which Godard made pointed mention in the first episode of *Histoire(s) du cinéma.*

The references proliferate: a recurring line, from Howard Hawks's *To Have and Have Not,* is that of the servant who asks, "Was you ever bit by a dead bee?" One character is called Schpountz, after Marcel Pagnol's 1938 satire of a country boy's dream of movie stardom, and others are called Robert Aldrich, Dorothy Parker, and Della Street (from *Perry Mason*); one of the Countess's lawyers is named Dorfman, like the French distributor Robert Dorfman, and one character in her entourage bears the name of the actor who plays the part, Joseph Lisbona, who directed two films in the early days of the French New Wave.

Godard himself does not appear in *Nouvelle Vague*—and would not appear in any of his feature films for the next fourteen years—and this, too, is a result of *Histoire(s) du cinéma,* which now siphoned off from his features the role of the subjective essay and the personal voice, and became Godard's mode of self-identification and self-revelation. His feature films, as a result, became objects of Olympian contemplation and mythic universality. Indeed, the grandeur and solidity of the images in *Nouvelle Vague* are conceived as if in opposition to the frenetic subjectivity, the proliferating associations, the hysteria of semiological profusion of *Histoire(s) du cinéma. Nouvelle Vague* bears the imprint of Godard's own story through its embodiment of history, of the story of the New Wave, rather than through Godard's own mediation or self-presentation.

THE TEXT OF *Nouvelle Vague* is especially rich, even for Godard, thanks to Duhamel's generous supply of quotes, and these literary citations are also used differently from the way that language figured in such films as *Soigne ta droite* and *King Lear.* In *Nouvelle Vague,* Godard sets these texts with a higher level of style. In part, this is due to the film's setting and milieu, which lent itself to a lofty diction, a declamatory style of speech which would fill the vast halls and the open spaces with resonant words—a rhetorical manner that he also associated with his childhood lessons, which involved the mandatory recitation of poetry. But *Nouvelle Vague* presents another crucial difference which determined the way that literary texts were used: the music is unlike any in Godard's previous films. This, too, was the result of an unexpected collaboration.

Manfred Eicher, who had founded ECM Records in 1969 with the intention of seeking a distinctively clear and natural sound in his recordings—and who was, he claimed, inspired to do so by the sound track to *Vivre sa vie*—sent Godard some CDs of music by Arvo Pärt and David Darling in the hope that he might find it useful for a film. Godard was intrigued by the music, saying, "I had the feeling, the way he was producing sound, that we were more or less in the same country: he with sounds, me with images,"[21] and he wrote to Eicher to ask him for more.

Godard later recalled that, when he listened to the recordings Eicher sent him, it was "like hearing music from films that didn't exist."[22] Intended as praise, Godard's remark was, however, also on-target in an invidious way, which explained why the music appealed to him: it is reminiscent of movie scores, in that for the most part it neither requires nor bears up under repeated and concentrated listening. At a higher level of modernistic style, much of the music that Eicher recorded at ECM and sent to Godard has the same status for the cinema as the music by Paul Misraki or Georges Delerue in Godard's earlier films.[23]

Nouvelle Vague and almost every film Godard subsequently made features recordings of music produced by Eicher. As a result, Godard's sound tracks—which, from *Passion* through *King Lear,* had featured samplings of classical music, along with some jazz and popular music—changed definitively. The Beethoven quartets, last featured in *King Lear,* were gone. Excerpts from Beethoven's quartets are the musical equivalent of literary quotations: they bring with them their own history and context. The music produced by Eicher, however, is, for the most part, mood music, a set of sonic icons that induce an emotion or a sentiment rather than a specific idea or history. Eicher's recordings shifted Godard's attention from the music itself to its function in the film. While Beethoven was a part of Godard's life and experience, Eicher's productions were pure sound, free to acquire a new set of associations by way of their place in the film. Godard's preference for these contemporary recordings rather than classical music was another mark of his return to a cinematic classicism of sorts, with "movie music" which he used to reinforce emotions rather than classical music to comment on them.

In the sound editing, the many literary texts Godard worked into *Nouvelle Vague* were set against music and ambient sounds to create a dense stereophonic soundscape. Godard claimed to have been particularly inspired by the music of David Darling, which, with its brief, emphatic phrases and dramatic silences, resembles punctuation awaiting a text. The composer and audio researcher Jean Schwarz, whose music Godard had also included in *Nouvelle Vague*, was invited to sit in on the sound mix. Schwarz later described what he saw: "For him, everything was music—voices, sounds. He had a way of making it come alive like a symphony." He likened Godard's work on the film's sound track to "sculpture."[24] Godard was still working on this "sculpture" three days before the film's first screening.

Nouvelle Vague was shown at the Cannes festival on May 18, 1990. Its presentation was a triumph: the film's monumentality, timeless poise, and overt sensuous beauty were widely praised, with Serge Toubiana in *Cahiers du cinéma* declaring it "from the outset a great classic."[25] The film, which went into commercial release in France on May 23, was generally acknowledged to be the complex masterpiece that it is.

During his press conference at Cannes, Godard said, "If one only took the images from *Nouvelle Vague,* the film would be better. And if one only listened to the sound track it would be better still."[26] Eicher took Godard up on the suggestion: ECM released the sound track to *Nouvelle Vague* as a set of audio CDs. The liner notes were a reprint of an article by Claire Bartoli about the experience of watching *Nouvelle Vague* as a blind woman.

On September 29, 1990, *Nouvelle Vague* had its American premiere at the New York Film Festival. After the undeserved neglect of the teeming, fragmented, subjective *King Lear, Nouvelle Vague* could reasonably have been expected to win favor with art-house viewers. Indeed, it received serious attention from a wide range of writers, who welcomed it as a major addition to Godard's oeuvre. Gilberto Perez, writing in *The Nation,* called attention to Godard's correlation of natural splendor with the dubious business that buys access to it, arguing that the film is "a thing of beauty and at the same time a critique of that beauty, of the conditions of that beauty" and that it calls attention to "a contradiction between stirring beauty and the ugly privilege enabling that beauty."[27]

But the widespread critical enthusiasm was in vain, because Vincent Canby's review in the *New York Times,* which appeared at the time of its festival screening, was the equivalent of an assassination. He called the film "featherweight," likened its visual beauty to "a feature-length lipstick commercial," and declared that there was little beside this beauty "to occupy either the mind or the eye." He asserted, "Mr. Godard's passion for Cinema now seems perfunctory," and concluded with a murderous judgment: "Only people who despise the great Godard films, everything from *Breathless (A Bout de Souffle)* (1959) through *Every Man for Himself (Sauve Qui Peut la Vie* [*sic*]) (1979) could be anything but saddened by this one. The party's over."[28] *Nouvelle Vague* was never released commercially in the United States. After this hatchet job, no film by Godard played at the New York Film Festival until 2001.

WHILE GODARD WAS shooting *Nouvelle Vague,* the Berlin Wall fell, and, with it, the Soviet satellite states of Central Europe began their inevitable collapse. The United States seemed poised to increase its political and cultural influence in Europe, a turn of events that Godard viewed as ominous. For him, the fate of the film only confirmed his recent invidious statements regarding the United States and its cinema. For instance, a principal and recurring theme of a series of interviews that Godard had done with the critic and novelist Noël Simsolo in June 1989[29] was the American "hegemony of the spectacular" and the American plot to dominate the world through mass culture in general and the audiovisual in particular:

> For the moment, it's their problem and their drama—Americans have no History . . . They have perhaps chosen not to have one, they suffer from this greatly, and for this reason they need to take over the History of others, who usually accept being the valets, because that's how they get some savings and a pension.

In these interviews, Godard repeated his position, which he had expressed in the first of the *Histoire(s) du cinéma*, that the cinema's definitive fall resulted from the American domination of it that followed the Second World War. He said that America's entry into both world wars served "to impose, by way of images, their economy, which permits them to re-impose their images. That's all." He considered the Second World War from the same revisionist perspective: "If one does a historical summary of the events, America has always been a sort of big sister to Germany. The brother rebelled for a moment, but after the second war, the situation became the same as it had been before." Godard cited the German film production company UFA, which continued to function under Hitler, as "the only company that wanted to struggle knowingly against the American hegemony that Fox, Paramount-France, etc., installed before the war."

In a subsequent interview, he went further: "The German cinema under Nazism is the only cinema that wanted to be European . . . The German cinema is the only one that fought against America, that did what Jack Lang would like to do."[30]

At Cannes in 1988, discussing his *Histoire(s) du cinéma*, Godard set forth an underlying principle: "I have always detested America and adored the American cinema. I do not understand the French political obsession which results, if not in outright genuflection, in always turning toward the West rather than toward the East."[31]

And so now Godard turned his attention toward the East.

twenty-six

GERMANY YEAR 90 NINE ZERO

"One week after the fall of the Wall"

IN MID-1989, THE PRODUCER NICOLE RUELLÉ ASKED FOUR directors—Jean-Luc Godard, Wim Wenders, Stanley Kubrick, and Ingmar Bergman—to make a film for television on the subject of solitude.[1] Godard accepted, but with a catch. "I didn't want to make a film on a lover's or a drug addict's solitude," he explained. "I rather wanted to concern myself with the solitude of a country, of a state, of a group. I said to myself: why not East Germany?"[2] Then after the Berlin Wall fell in October 1989 and East Germany itself collapsed, Godard decided that the film would instead be simply about "the Eastern part of Germany,"[3] or, more invidiously, "on the east and the west of Germany, on a landscape of the east that was about to be retaken by its former owner."[4] The project had its political agenda built into it. But after formulating the idea, Godard did little to realize it until late 1990 when, acknowledging that he had to deliver the film in 1991 or reimburse his advance, he got to work.

For Godard, contemporary Germany was a triple palimpsest. First, for him, it meant German cinema, the "haunted screen"[5] of Murnau and Lang, of *Nosferatu* and *M*, of *The Last Laugh* and *Siegfried*. Second, it stood for his own youth in the late 1940s and early 1950s, when he first saw those films at the Cinémathèque and the CCQL. Third, it had a personal significance, in relation to his father, who, Godard said, had been a Germanophile and who had introduced him to the literary classics of German romanticism, especially the poetry of Novalis and the novels of Goethe.[6]

Godard was teeming with ideas and references, allusions, and associations, but had no organizing principle for a film. He also had another, greater, problem: unlike *Nouvelle Vague, King Lear,* or Godard's other recent

Lemmy Caution meets Freud's Dora in Berlin and Lotte in Weimar.
(TCD-Prod DB © Gaumont / Peripheria / DR)

works, a film about the eastern part of Germany could hardly be shot where Godard lived, whether in Rolle, Paris, or his Trouville apartment. He would have to go to Germany; he would have to scout locations and organize a cast, a crew, and equipment far from home. He was not up to doing either job alone; he sought an experienced film companion who could help him develop his ideas into a synopsis for a film and could also manage the practicalities of a shoot on the road.

After *Nouvelle Vague* was completed, Hervé Duhamel left his job as Godard's assistant and Godard asked Romain Goupil, now an important filmmaker in his own right, to work with him for a year to help him pull together the film about solitude. One of Goupil's first responsibilities was to join Godard on a location-scouting trip through Germany. Before they left, in the fall of 1990, Godard typed out a list of preliminary ideas. Many of them ended up in the film, including a Don Quixote character (defined as "in search of: Dulcinea, History, mise en scène, the cinema"), and a female character, Lotte in Weimar (from the Thomas Mann novel about Goethe's later years), who would "come back to see the old man in his house." Other plans involved the violist Kim Kashkashian (who recorded for ECM) playing "the last notes (b-a-c-h) of the Musical Offering," and a Russian soldier or officer who "comes to say goodbye to his fiancée who is teaching or rehearsing a violin sonata in a house by the North Sea"—the last sonata of Shostakovich (actually for viola).

Godard wrote that if he chose to appear in the film, it would be under a name made from the acronym for "Gulf Oscar Delta Alfa Romeo Delta." He noted that there might be an appearance in the film by "Lemmy Caution, American federal ex-agent," and suggested that the film might make reference to "the camps," specifically, Oranienburg, Buchenwald, Auschwitz, and Ravensbrück (the latter, as "the supreme stage of capitalism: not to provide sustenance to the workers' bodies").[7]

Once in Germany, Godard, Goupil, and the actor Hanns Zischler—who was very well read in German literature and philosophy and had appeared in Anne-Marie Miéville's *Mon cher sujet*—drove around together to search for locations. As Goupil later recalled, "We didn't talk in the car, [Godard] doesn't like that." When Goupil and Godard got back to Rolle, on November 18, 1990, Godard preferred that they not talk about the trip: "If we say it, it just spills out."[8] Instead, Godard asked Goupil to type up his impressions in one room while Godard did the same thing in another; then they exchanged documents and discussed what they had written.

The trip through Germany left Goupil with an impression "contrary to the thought behind the project": instead of finding the solitude that was at the core of the commission, he saw "traffic, passers-by, street-sweepers, markets, cars. In all this incredible activity, there's the feeling of an overturned anthill which seeks nothing but its place, its brands, its path, but this all exists, the goal is there: THE WEST."[9] In his impressionistic jottings, Goupil seemed to have difficulty finding the fall of the Berlin Wall as unequivocally dispiriting as Godard did; what Goupil saw made him want "to talk about the future." He proposed to Godard a main idea for the film: "You as Don Quixote, your horse straining to drag my Trabant on the sands of the beaches of Rostock, and we head toward the two Berlins, and we seek, without finding, the traces of one of your thoughts."

Godard had no intention of playing Don Quixote; he preferred not to appear at all, and thought of having Eddie Constantine reprise the role of Lemmy Caution. (At the time, Constantine, the star of *Alphaville,* was seventy-three years old and had not appeared in a film since 1987.)

To this embryonic story Godard appended a list of references, two of which left no doubt as to his intentions: "the hope of Europe: the death of Communism (find the speech or text by Goebbels)," likening American post–Cold War triumphalism to Nazism; and "one week after the fall of the Wall, the porn cassettes come through the Brandenburg Gate," suggesting that the end of communism means the start of capitalist debasement and vulgarity.

Godard now put together a simple framework for the film: "I had this idea of an old spy from the West who finds himself all alone in the East after the fall of the Wall, and who tries to return to the Occident."[10] Offered the role of the old spy, Eddie Constantine accepted at once. Godard's choice of a mythical actor as his own questing surrogate, as well as the decision to shoot the story on 35mm film stock, indicates that although the project was commissioned for television he considered it cinema. Even the choice of title made clear that its model was cinematic: Godard rejected the producer's recommended *Solitudes* in favor of *Allemagne Année 90 neuf zéro* (*Germany Year 90 Nine Zero*), an allusion to Roberto Rossellini's film *Germany Year Zero,* filmed in West Germany in 1947, which dramatized the failure of the postwar reconstruction to suppress Nazi ideas and sympathies.

Germany Year 90 Nine Zero (or, as Godard nicknamed it, *Germany Nine Zero*) would embody history—or, rather, Godard's view of it. A work of a tendentious grandeur, a diatribe with Olympian airs, *Germany Nine Zero* took on a monumental aspect akin to that of *Nouvelle Vague.* Unlike *Histoire(s) du cinéma,* which offered a historical thesis in terms of Godard's personal experience, *Germany Nine Zero* does the opposite: it presents a strong historical thesis—one crucially related to that of the

Histoire(s)—but suppresses Godard's speaking voice and on-screen presence.

AFTER WORKING OUT the story, Godard sent Goupil back to Germany to arrange the practical aspects of the shoot. In early 1991, Godard joined him there and brought a crew along, including the director of photography Christophe Pollock, who had been William Lubtchansky's assistant on *Nouvelle Vague*. The crew, which traveled through Germany in two cars, was never more than eight people, according to Goupil. Because of the complex logistics, involving many shoot locations throughout Germany, Godard was agitated and indecisive. "There were lots of discussions about everything," Goupil recalled, "about clothing, shoes, cars, locations."[11]

Despite Godard's elaborately sketched shooting notebook that, with his thick-lined cartoons, resembled a storyboard, very little was decided in advance. Instead, the two cars would reach a given location and Godard then tried to figure out what to do. He described the process: "When we saw things, we filmed them. I told Eddie Constantine, 'Walk a bit in this setting and then we'll see.'"[12] He wanted Constantine to walk across a frozen lake, and first sent Goupil to test whether the ice would hold. Another day, according to Goupil, "He did a shot of Eddie Constantine reading. He watched it the next night . . . he looks at the shot and says, 'It's empty.' But there's a moment when Constantine gets up, and he says, 'Voilà'—and we went back to the same place and redid it."[13]

Goupil found the process difficult: "We go to a place that has been reserved, we look around, he searches, we look around, then when nobody expects it, he says, 'Let's shoot.' It's very hard. There was a great deal of tension." Often, Godard went to the location but chose not to shoot. Sometimes, he sent crew members off on their own, telling them, "Go try." Goupil and the crew brought back footage of the stadium where the 1936 Berlin Olympics were played, to invoke its having been filmed by Leni Riefenstahl. "Afterward, [Godard] looked at the shots and we had a violent argument," Goupil recounted. "'You say you're anti-Fascist,'" Godard told him, "'but you were unable to retransmit the past with these images.'" In other words, Godard thought that in Goupil's shots, the stadium looked merely like a stadium, not like Hitler's stadium; these shots are not in the film.

On another such occasion, Godard accused Goupil of working "too much by illustration"—of making images that merely illustrated an idea from the script—and Goupil responded, "If you don't show up, we run that risk." Yet Godard was just as harsh in his criticism of his own rushes. He shot an enormous amount of footage of a Russian character (played by Anton Mossine), a sailor who was making his way East, through a Germany where he was no longer at home. Dissatisfied with the material, Godard edited the sailor's role down to a bit part. He considered his indecision and divagations to be a consequence of the conditions of the shoot—namely, working in a foreign country where he had never lived and which he did not know well ("When one knows nothing, why go here rather than there?"). The migratory shoot was truncated when Godard became sick, for which he sarcastically declared himself grateful because otherwise he "would never have stopped."[14] He completed the film with the footage on hand.

GOUPIL OBSERVED THAT in the diverse aspects of the film, "music, sound, cinema, text—each image arouses references." The organizing principle of the shooting and editing was to construct a web of references that were at once historical and personal. Goupil described Godard's creative process on the film: "We discussed a lot, he wrote a lot, he had all of his ideas, and the images came afterwards to concretize them—it's almost a film that was dreamed into existence." Asked whether he had chosen to film in "sites of memory," Godard answered, "Everything is a site of memory," and explained his chain of associations.

> I wanted to go up north, that's the Baltic, the sailors of the Baltic. I remembered the story of the [German] revolutionary unions [of 1920], and we added Russia into the film. And then we certainly had to go see Weimar, the tree of Goethe. So we filmed the tree, it's at the center of Buchenwald. There's the sign which says "Buchenwald," I didn't make it up. That's how we did it. Then we ended up in Berlin.[15]

The travels of Lemmy Caution through a recently liberated East Germany—where "corpses," played by extras, were theatrically scattered at the base of the Berlin Wall's remaining sections—featured such artifacts and events as a philosopher working on a French translation of Hegel's *Reason in History;* a young woman transformed into Freud's Dora; the statue of Schiller in Leipzig; the statue of Pushkin in Weimar; Goethe's oak in Buchenwald; a knight on horseback, reminiscent of Don Quixote; a man pushing a Trabant; and the crumbling remains of Germany's legendary Babelsberg studios, with Marlene Dietrich's voice on the sound track reminiscing about its past glories.

What Godard added of Russia was the brief remaining footage of the young sailor, Dmitri, who comes to say good-bye to a violist (Kim Kashkashian) while she is rehearsing the last composition, the Viola Sonata, of another Dmitri—Shostakovich.

As a sort of visual punctuation, he used clips of classic German films; for instance, as a doorman helps people out of a hotel with his umbrella, the voice-over commentary makes reference to "the last man" (the German title of the 1925 film by F. W. Murnau, *The Last Laugh*); then a clip from that film is seen, in which a doorman, played by Emil Jannings, similarly helps two women into a car. The clips offered Godard a kind of visual shorthand by which to condense his scenes into brief clusters of few but highly composed images, to break the continuity of shots without breaking the flow of ideas and emotions.

THE DIALOGUE AND voice-over commentary, which was spoken by the critic and television director André S. Labarthe (who had played the abandoned husband in *Vivre sa vie*), was comprised of literary references, mainly from German literature and from writings about Germany (Tacitus, Christopher Isherwood). But the film's principal literary reference was to an author whose work had haunted Godard since the 1950s, and whose example had haunted France since 1939: Jean Giraudoux.

Though opposed to German occupation and an unreproachable antifascist, Giraudoux offered, shortly before the German invasion of France, a scathing indictment of the French national situation, in a book called *Pleins Pouvoirs* (Full Authority). He decried the growing influence of America and the increasing presence of Jewish refugees from Eastern Europe. Though he expressed no love for Nazi Germany, the principal targets of his diatribe were the same as those of the Nazis. Giraudoux was not a collaborator in deed, but by sharing enemies with the German ideology, he implied that Nazi Germany might hold valuable political lessons for France.

In his earlier novel *Siegfried et le Limousin* (published in 1922), Giraudoux had expressed similar views; this novel, which had loomed in the background of *Le Petit Soldat*, was central to *Germany Nine Zero*. The novel's plot—about a French soldier named Jacques Forestier who, suffering from amnesia, recuperates in Germany and considers himself German—was of secondary significance to the film (though a character from the book, Count von Zelten, played by Hanns Zischler, turns up as Lemmy Caution's occasional fellow traveler). Rather, *Germany Nine Zero* is centered on a pair of lengthy quotes taken from Giraudoux's novel that convey the film's governing ideas. The first is cited verbatim:

The United States imagines no other war besides a civil war. In each war it is always fighting against itself and against those faults of its own that the enemy nation embodies. It calls war a moral crisis. When it was English, it fought against the English; as soon as it became American, Americans fought among themselves; as soon as it had become sufficiently Germanized in its morés and culture, it tilted at the Germans. The first American taken prisoner in 1917 was named Meyer, and so was his captor.

The second quotation, carved sentence by sentence from a longer passage, is spoken in the film in voice-over by Labarthe:

I do not want to die before having seen Europe happy, without having seen the two words that an invincible force spreads further and further apart each day, the word "Russia" and the word "happiness," come together on my lips once again. To be happy—I say this for those who are younger than twenty-five years old, since they aren't aware of it—is, at the borders, not to hear people multiply by 100 or by 1,000 the contents of their wallets, like children. It is not to have the impression, when seeing someone repatriated from starving regions, that he once fought over food with a child . . . And so, the day when I see the world, once again robust, place side by side like two warriors' bucklers[16] the word "Russia" and the word "happiness," I will gladly die.[17]

As these citations suggest, the real subject of *Germany Nine Zero* was Godard's view of three countries, plus a fourth: Germany, the embodiment of the ultimate political sin, the greatest historical transgression, which rendered it taboo among the nations; the United States, which, under its guise of angelic innocence, is guilty of similarly great misdeeds; Russia, which, accused of other grave political crimes, must, as the common enemy of Nazi Germany and the United States, have been doing something right (as, for instance, shielding East Germany from American influence); and, in the shadows, France, which, caught between Germany and the United States, would do better to turn its attention to Russia.

The film concludes with Lemmy Caution's return to the West: as he walks through woods, the first sign that he has indeed reached the West is a woman jogger in a track suit. Next, in what was West Berlin, he faces the consumerist trappings of modern life: "Well, Christmas, with all its ancient horrors, is on us again. The stores are full of useless junk, but what we really need, we can't find."[18] Lemmy Caution comments on "the assault of money against spiritual power," and asserts that money "invents Auschwitz and Hiroshima." To reinforce Godard's implied equation of German and American wartime deeds—and, even more decisively, Germany's wartime dominion and America's present-day hegemony—Lemmy Caution takes a room in a modern hotel, where he comments sardonically to the chambermaid who is preparing his bed, "So you too have chosen freedom," and she responds, "Arbeit macht frei."

GODARD'S DESIRE TO make *Germany Nine Zero* a work of cinema rather than television is evident in the way it looks. The precisely composed static shots are carefully textured with natural light that sculpturally integrates the actors into the locations and the decor: the characters are not set in the landscape, they are a part of it. Like *Nouvelle Vague, Germany Nine Zero* is poised and monumental, yet at sixty-two minutes in length, it is a feature film condensed into epigrams, an odyssey in fragments. This odyssey, however, is missing a basic element of the classic homeward trip after wartime: a love story. Lemmy Caution plays an Odysseus without a Penelope. This lack turns *Germany Nine Zero* into a condensation of a possible feature film rather than a fully realized feature: its brevity is due in part to its lack of inner motive, of romantic adventure. The lived experience to which it bore testimony was not intimate, but purely historical, cinematic, literary, and political. *Germany Nine Zero* is less a film than the idea for a film that Godard might have made were its subject more completely derived from his own experience.

To emphasize his view of *Germany Nine Zero* as a work of cinema, Godard insisted on showing it at the Venice Film Festival in September 1991. The movie was awarded a gold medal from the presidency of the Senate, and was hailed by *Cahiers du cinéma* and *Le Monde* as an important addition to Godard's body of work. Jean-Michel Frodon, in *Le Monde,* praised him for including "all the memory which not one journalist, not one 'leftist' politician, uttered in the month that followed the liquefaction of the Soviet mummies."[19] The film's television broadcast, on November 8, 1991, was heralded as an event not to be missed—all the more so since, despite Godard's intentions, the film was not scheduled to open theatrically. The series to which it was supposed to belong had never been made: *Germany Nine Zero* was its only production.

The project's extended and open-ended development had come at a price: Godard admitted to having gone over budget by 1.5 million francs and accepted personal responsibility for that sum. To pay off his debts, he announced, at the time of the Venice festival, that he had accepted "a very burdensome project, of filmed memories, for the cinema's centenary in 1995."[20] He also pushed ahead with *Histoire(s) du cinéma,* which continued in the same political vein as *Germany Nine Zero*. He drew inspiration for that series from his newfound devotion to Russia—an intellectual devotion, which soon became a practical one.

THE CULTURAL SERVICES of the French government had long been planning a retrospective of Godard's films in the Soviet Union and had hoped that he would accompany it. While working on *Germany Nine Zero*, Godard received an offer to go to the Soviet Union, and he accepted. The retrospective was planned for February 1992, but it took the French and Swiss governments more than a year of negotiations with the Soviet authorities to organize the trip, and by the time it took place, the Soviet Union no longer existed.

For the retrospective, which was to take place at the Moscow Kino-Center, or cinémathèque, Godard had selected the fifteen films to be shown, including his first, *Breathless*, and his most recent, *Germany Nine Zero*. To verify that the films which featured a stereo sound track would be shown under appropriate conditions, Godard dispatched his sound engineer, François Musy, to Moscow to test the equipment. Musy returned with an unfavorable report. Godard then declared that the films could not be shown if the projection and the sound were not adequate. The Swiss government agreed to finance the installation of new equipment, but its commitment was insufficient, and Godard decided to pay for the sound system himself—with money, he said, that he made from TV commercials.

While working with Goupil on *Germany Nine Zero*, Godard was commissioned to create two commercials for Nike sneakers. One featured young people in a field, successfully fleeing the Grim Reaper thanks to their Nikes. (For this, Godard asked Goupil to do iconographic research on the changing image of the figure of Death, from medieval to modern art.)[21] Godard also filmed a variation on this theme, in which a wolf chases Little Red Riding Hood and catches her because he was wearing Nikes.[22] The sneaker company paid Godard for these spots but never showed them.

Soon after, the Swiss tobacco company F. J. Burrus, based in Lausanne, approached Godard to make a commercial for its Parisienne brand of cigarette. Its marketing director was undaunted by Godard's cinematic provocations and was confident that his name would suffice to give the commercials, and the cigarette company, favorable publicity. In January 1992, Godard and Anne-Marie Miéville worked together to shoot, in a shopping mall in the Zurich train station, scenes of a skateboarder slaloming between packages of cigarettes, a tracking shot of bare feet trampling through piles of cigarette packages, and a person kneeling before a woman reading a novel called *Parisienne People*. On the sound track, Godard recited passages from Racine.[23]

The marketing director was right: the commercials tested favorably in a focus group, and Burrus's hiring of Godard attracted a great deal of attention in the local press.

Then, Godard went to Moscow. His arrival there in early February made the Russian national news. Not only had he paid for the sound installation, but he also sent a truck full of his own video equipment for the students of Naum Kleiman, the director of the Kino-Center. The screenings and the question-and-answer sessions were crowded with enthusiastic and appreciative audiences. With a group of film students, Godard discussed the political implications of film technique, describing stereo as "democratic" and mono as "totalitarian"—but then continued, "We often forget that in Fascist countries the Fascist governments were in the beginning elected democratically." The students, for whom democracy was still a new enthusiasm, were surprised by what seemed to them Godard's hinted preference for mono over stereo; one asked, incredulously, whether Godard still thought of himself as "a radical."[24]

Godard praised Naum Kleiman as "a Kutuzov of Russian culture"—a clear parallel between the resistance of the great Russian general to Napoleon's army and that of Russian cinema to American media—and told assembled film students of his devotion to Russia.

I have visited Russia many times, but they were not physical voyages. I visited your country in books, through music. The Swiss Ministry of Foreign Affairs didn't have enough money to pay for the renovation of the film center. That's why my assistant and I shot a commercial for cigarettes. It's a way of paying my debt to Chekhov, Dostoyevsky, Tchaikovsky, Eisenstein, Solzhenitsyn.[25]

Le Monde reported on one cinematic consequence of the trip.

In Moscow, Godard declared that he had come up with the subject of a new film . . . It would involve recounting a meeting, in a Swiss airport, of a filmmaker (himself) and several key elements of Russian literature (*The Seagull, Anna Karenina, The Idiot, Crime and Punishment*), that was prompted by an American producer who is waiting for the departure of the last Aeroflot flight to Moscow.[26]

This notion was no pipe dream. There was in fact an American producer behind Godard's next project. WorldVision, a home-video distribution company owned by the producer Aaron Spelling, which also distributed such series as *Twin Peaks, Beverly Hills 90210,* and *The Fugitive,* commissioned a series of direct-to-video programs called *Momentous Events: Russia in the '90s.* Among the directors approached were Godard, Peter Bogdanovich, Werner Herzog, and Ken Russell.[27] Herzog went to Russia to film *Bells from the Deep: Faith and Superstition in Russia;* Godard accepted the commission but this time, he did not go to Russia.[28] Instead, he made his unwillingness to go to Russia the subject of the video, *Les Enfants jouent à la Russie* (The Children Play Russia). He sent Caroline Champetier to Moscow in his place and he directed her by telephone, as she later recalled:

> I made a tremendous number of images, in a chess club that seemed right out of the nineteenth century, in a market where people were selling their possessions to live. Then [Godard] called me; he said, "Today this is what you're going to do: you're going to film the death of Anna Karenina." I was very scared; I said, "I can't do it." He said, "It's simple, you dress her in a big dress, you go to the station, you film the crossing, then the arrival of the train in the station, that's death."[29]

Meanwhile, in Switzerland, Godard himself videotaped scenes with actors: László Szabó played Jack Valenti (in real life, Hollywood's main Washington lobbyist, but portrayed in the film as a producer); André S. Labarthe and the film historian Bernard Eisenschitz were Alcide Jolivet and Harry Blount (the pair of journalists from Jules Verne's novel *Michael Strogoff,* about a Tartar uprising in Siberia); Godard played himself, in an echo of *Soigne ta droite,* as a filmmaker who is both the Prince and the Idiot (as Valenti says, "If the film is good, he's an idiot, if it's bad, he's a prince"); and the actress Aude Amiot played Valenti's secretary, Mademoiselle Amiel.

The story concerns Valenti's offer to Blount and Jolivet to make a film in Russia. The Prince is invited to join them but refuses:

> Do what you want, but I won't go. After Hitler and Napoleon, all the intelligent people have been taking advantage of poor Russia by invading it. Today it's happening again. I am not intelligent, therefore I will not go. Why does the West want to invade this country again? It's simple: because it is the homeland of fiction, and the West no longer knows what to invent.

Godard called *Les Enfants jouent à la Russie* an "annex" to *Histoire(s) du cinéma,* and the connection is proven in a scene in which he, as the Prince, explains the birth of cinema. The anecdote is one that Godard claimed to have read en route to Moscow in February 1992, in a popular history of mathematics he had brought along for the flight; and the conclusion that he draws from it is consistent with the political and historical theses that he had been working out in *Histoire(s) du cinéma* and *Germany Nine Zero.*

> In a Moscow prison, Jean-Victor Poncelet, a member of the engineering corps of Napoleon's army, reconstructs without consulting any notes all the geometry he had learned from his lessons with Monge and Carnot, a treatise on the projection of figures, published in 1822 . . . It took a French prisoner pacing before a Russian wall for the mechanical application of the idea and the desire to project figures onto a screen to take off in practice, with the invention of cinema . . . One might say that this marked the first Franco-Russian alliance. I am one of the last survivors.

In a subsequent scene, Godard illuminates the implications of his eastward orientation, when Harry Blount (the film historian Bernard Eisenschitz) expounds his idea that in the Russian cinema there is no shot-countershot. Instead, according to Blount/Eisenschitz, there are only images akin to icons, whereas shot-countershot, the standard Western pattern of filming dialogue, was invented in the United States by 1910, because, as Eisenschitz says, Americans found an advantage "in teaching people to look stupidly at things rather than to see." Godard via Eisenschitz thus ridicules the idea of seeing events from two different perspectives and praises the one truth of one religion, the icon, as the authentic model of cinematic representation.

If Godard's aesthetic methods were, so to speak, to the left of the commercial cinema, in that they embodied critical judgments of conventional narrative form, their political undercurrent was radically conservative, celebrating and preserving notions of national character derived from static, pre-republican societies. Though Godard praised the Soviet Union over the United States, the political entity and anecdotal history that he chose to celebrate was not that of the post-revolutionary U.S.S.R. but of czarist Russia. The teeming household of the rural estate of *Nouvelle Vague,* though maintained with a modern industrialist's fortune, is a vestigial feudal manor.

The United States, Godard suggests in *Les Enfants jouent à la Russie,* seeks to conquer Russia in order to supplement its own failed imagination, an imagination that failed because of freedom and secularism. Better, Godard suggested, a prisoner in Russia than free in America.

As the god, Gérard Depardieu walks in water but not on it.
(TCD-Prod DB © Alain Sarde / Peripheria / DR)

twenty-seven

HÉLAS POUR MOI, JLG/JLG, HISTOIRE(S) DU CINÉMA, PARTS 2 AND 3

"We still know how to tell the story"

*H*ISTOIRE(S) *DU CINÉMA*, A LONG-TERM RESEARCH PRO-ject, had developed from Godard's first official academic af-filiation, the Montreal seminars of the 1970s. Godard had long likened his use of a camera to scientists' use of microscopes and tele-scopes and considered his work to belong to the realm of research. Indeed, he thought that the cinema made him a sort of super-scientist because, he said, "Scientists aren't trained to see. I must be one of the few who want the cin-ema to go deeper toward philosophy and the sciences, things for which it is made."[1] He thought that his investigations should be supported, like a scien-tist's, by a research or academic institution.[2]

Jack Lang, France's minister of culture in the mid-1980s, agreed. He re-cruited Godard to lecture at the CNC and, after the legislative elections of 1988 returned Lang to office, came up with a new plan for him.

The national film school, IDHEC (L'Institut des hautes études cinématographiques—the Institute for Advanced Cinematographic Study), was mainly a technical school, and it had not recently produced many direc-tors of note. (Alain Resnais, Jacques Rozier, and Louis Malle were its most exceptional graduates.) The school was generally not greatly respected by the artists of the French cinema, who had little contact with it.

The truly important French film school, which had produced the New Wave, was the Cinémathèque, which held its exams in the pages of *Cahiers du cinéma*. In 1986, under Lang's influence, IDHEC's name and mission were changed to acknowledge this heritage: it was now called La fémis (Fondation Européenne des métiers de l'image et du son—the European Foundation for Image and Sound Trades). The new school was highly selective (accepting approximately thirty students each year), and it was meant to teach not only the trade but the art. Working directors and technicians were encouraged to spend time there and, because the reorganization took place under the aegis of Jack Lang, the school was reoriented toward the New Wave.

Lang had recruited Godard for occasional involvement with La fémis, including a preliminary seminar in Toulon on screenwriting (at which he sarcastically asked the students, "What do you really think you can learn? . . . Does Gallimard offer novel-writing courses?"[3]). He gave a lecture on the subject of montage and also invited a pair of students to assist him in the editing of *Nouvelle Vague*.[4] In 1989, Lang sought to formalize Godard's connection to the school, ultimately brokering a five-year deal for Godard and Miéville, under cosponsorship of La fémis and the CNC, to establish a studio on the school's premises in Paris for the purpose of producing films in which students would participate, including additional chapters of *Histoire(s) du cinéma*. Their company was to receive three million francs over the course of the contract.

Lang sponsored Godard's appointment in the hope that the filmmaker would create what Alain Bergala described as "a sort of studio for experimentation where students would come."[5] Godard's plan, according to Bergala, was "to install himself on the periphery of La fémis." He even changed the name of his company, JLG Films, to Peripheria, because, now that Miéville had directed her first feature, JLG was no longer the company's only filmmaker.

Godard conceived two new projects to be realized at the school in addition to *Histoire(s)*. The first, *Science sans conscience* (Science Without Conscience), was to be a four-part series involving the Nobel Prize winner Ilya Prigogine, a philosophically inclined physicist who cowrote a book applying relativity to traffic patterns. Godard planned to use consumer-format Hi-8 video, with its ability to record one-hour-long shots, to analyze Prigogine's ideas and to stage a comic pageant of scientists and their discoveries.[6] The second project was a high-definition video adaptation of Racine's *Bérénice*—a play in which King Titus is compelled for reasons of state to renounce his love for Bérénice, the Jewish queen. (It is also the play that Godard had hoped to direct for television in the 1960s and with which he had concluded *A Married Woman*.)

La fémis was located in the Palais de Tokyo, near the Cinémathèque; Godard had plans to install a studio-like facility there that would, he said, include an editing room, an office, and a library that would feature both a laser copier and a wall against which to hit tennis balls.[7] He decided to call his new studio the Palais des images (the Palace of Images), and it was scheduled to open in the fall of 1991.

The studio never materialized. Jack Lang had envisioned a grand renovation of the Palais de Tokyo that would involve the relocation there of other

French film institutions, including the Cinémathèque, but this ambitious project was stalled by a combination of high costs and institutional resistance.[8] The delay entailed a postponement of the construction of Peripheria's space, and Godard bitterly declared, in a diatribe in *Le Monde* on October 8, 1991, that since his studio would not be completed at the specified times, he considered that La fémis had abrogated the agreement. He therefore deemed the agreement annulled, and he enumerated and mourned the projects that he considered "canceled" as a result, including *Histoire(s) du cinéma* itself.[9] But, most significantly, he charged that the failure of La fémis to meet its obligations was, above all, political :

> The United States feeds a more-or-less good part of the world with its agriculture. It does the same with its culture. It is the right of this more-or-less good part of the world to make this choice, but it certainly is not its duty.
>
> The day that every television station in Europe regularly broadcasts a Greek, Portuguese, or Slovakian film, whether insipid or not, Europe will be made. Otherwise, it will remain American.

Principally, Godard was suggesting that his project with La fémis had fallen through because the school did not live up to the word "European" in its title—that the school could not fulfill its obligations to Godard because it did not distance and distinguish itself from the American cinema, as its name implied it must. Broadening the scope of his rant, Godard complained about the cultural implications of high-definition video, which was to have played a role in his production of *Bérénice:* "This term, 'high'—fidelity, definition—doesn't it come by way of the Germanization of the United States that Siegfried describes to his woman friend in Giraudoux's novel, from 'Herr Oberst' or 'Ober Kommando'?"

If Godard was infuriated by what he considered America's dominance of the television and movie industries—and, by implication, its quasi-Nazi dominance of modern audiovisual technology—he was equally furious at what he considered the resulting Americanization of aesthetics, which he considered inflicted on him by the unnamed producers who expect him to "tell a story": "But which story do they mean? That of the battle of Borodino and of the end of French domination that Tolstoy told? That of the battle of Baghdad, told by CNN, that of the triumph of American television and its servants?"[10]

THE CNC RESPONDED in *Le Monde* three days later, ignoring the charges and stating that the contract had merely been "prolonged," but Godard treated it as null and void. Although construction work at the Palais de Tokyo began in October 1992, it did not involve a tennis wall; Godard continued to work with La fémis, but only as an occasional visitor.

According to Alain Bergala, however, Godard's complaint in *Le Monde* was a means of breaking the engagement while shifting responsibility for the break onto the school.[11] Godard had been dissatisfied with the people he was meeting at La fémis, telling him, "They're zeroes, I can't work with them." Although Godard's desire for collaborative work was strong, and the notion of a studio-like atmosphere was appealing, the burden of founding an institution-within-an-institution and of committing himself to working long-term with students of varying ability and temperament did not correspond to his desires, and he got out of the arrangement. Godard told a journalist what he really wanted instead: "What I'd like is to teach cinema at the Collège de France or elsewhere and get paid for my films as for laboratory work."[12] The Collège de France, a research institution, offers public lectures by its professors but has no classes or students.

Godard's informal connection with La fémis did allow him to help younger filmmakers in diverse ways. For example, after seeing a short film by Noémie Lvovsky, he advised Alain Sarde to help her launch a feature film project, which became *Oublie-moi* (Forget Me), an extraordinarily intense and intimate melodrama that was released in 1995; he also lent a camera to Xavier Beauvois for the film *N'oublie pas que tu vas mourir* (Don't Forget That You're Going to Die), released the next year. But his help came without any direct involvement in their work or personal mentoring (indeed, Lvovsky, who owes her career to Godard, has never met him).

The didactic impulse had guided Godard's recent work, including *Histoire(s) du cinéma,* in which he rescued, preserved, and transmitted the remains of the cinema, and which was originally conceived for use in classrooms. Though Godard's teaching mission remained unfulfilled, the question of youth and the transmissibility of his thought became the central question of his next film. And where, in *Nouvelle Vague,* Godard had imagined the problem in terms of an Old and New Testament, his new film would make explicit the religious implications of that schema.

AFTER SEEING MAURICE Pialat's 1987 film *Under the Sun of Satan,* Godard had contacted its lead actor, Gérard Depardieu, to praise his performance.[13] The two met again soon thereafter, and Depardieu said that he would like to work with Godard. Although they had discussed projects in the 1970s, Godard now admitted to having doubts. But with *Germany Nine Zero* completed and Godard having no feature film project awaiting him, Alain Sarde suggested that the time had come to make a film with Depardieu.[14] Godard knew that the actor's involvement would "put bread on his plate,"[15] and when Depardieu accepted, financing indeed came rapidly. Now Godard had to find a subject.

When Godard read the poem "To the Patriarch; or, on the Origins of the Human Race," by the Italian poet Giacomo Leopardi (1798–1837), he got an idea for a film. The poem describes, in Godard's words, "the slow and difficult journey of humanity, the anguish, the constant worries and the permanent disturbance of its creator before the numerous misadventures of man."[16] He envisioned a film about life on Earth as seen by God. Godard then brought in a classic story that was in the air due to a much-discussed Paris stage production of Kleist's play *Amphitryon*. In the Greek myth, Amphitryon is betrothed to Alcmene, who refuses to marry him unless he avenges her brothers' death. Amphitryon goes to war to fulfill this duty. While he is away, Zeus comes to Alcmene's bed in the form of Amphitryon, and she becomes pregnant (she will bear Zeus's son Heracles). The same night, Amphitryon himself returns to Alcmene and consummates the marriage, making her pregnant a second time (with Heracles's fraternal twin, Iphicles).

Godard read three plays that told this story: Kleist's *Amphitryon*, Molière's comedy of the same name, and one that was closer to him in time and sensibility: Jean Giraudoux's *Amphitryon 38*, from 1929. Joining Leopardi's notion of God observing humanity from above and the myth of Amphitryon concerning the lusting Zeus come to Earth, Godard put together a story, and then, in a departure from his usual practice, he wrote a full-length screenplay.

He also began to assemble his cast and crew. At the Venice Film Festival in 1991, where Godard presented *Germany Nine Zero*, he saw Philippe Garrel's latest film, *J'entends plus la guitare* (I No Longer Hear the Guitar). Godard, who had known Garrel since the 1960s and admired his films, was greatly impressed. He asked Garrel's director of photography—his own former associate, Caroline Champetier—to rejoin him. He also hired Garrel's lead actress, Johanna Ter Steege, from the Netherlands, to play Alcmene opposite Depardieu's Amphitryon.

The legend of Amphitryon comprises three stories: a man leaves home and his place is taken by another; a woman, thinking herself faithful to the man she loves, is unfaithful to him; a god, in love with a woman who is otherwise unapproachable, uses his godlike powers to possess her. The story of a man and his double revisits the plot of *Nouvelle Vague*. The story of the god's lust for a human woman reprises the key element of *Hail Mary*, God's sexual possession of Mary, and Godard thought about it in those terms, speaking of the new film with reference to the book that had inspired *Hail Mary*, *The Gospel at Risk of Psychoanalysis:* "Man especially needs to feel himself a god.

Woman is different: she needs a god. Françoise Dolto said, 'Doesn't every woman seek in her man the shadow of God?' "[17]

In the new film, *Hélas pour moi* (Woe Is Me), Godard would depict God's appearance on Earth, reinventing the myth of Amphitryon in terms of Christian theology. But his approach to the New Testament differed now from that which marked *Hail Mary:* it was inflected by Godard's work on the subject of testaments in *Nouvelle Vague* as well as his recent, failed efforts at passing along his knowledge as a teacher. The subject of *Hélas pour moi* became the very nature of a testament, whether in words or in the cinema. Godard's speculations regarding testaments led him to wonder what was new about the New Testament; in harking back to the Old Testament, he would make *Hélas pour moi* his first expressly Jewish film—and not his last.

IN LATE 1991 and early 1992, the French press was making much of the critical theoretician Walter Benjamin (the centennial of his birth was in 1992) as well as of his lifelong friend, the scholar of Jewish mysticism Gershom Scholem. Godard drew on a newfound familiarity with these thinkers' work to nourish *Hélas pour moi:* Benjamin, Scholem, and mystical Judaism became central elements of the film.

Champetier recalled that the screenplay for *Hélas pour moi* had eighteen sequences (eighteen being the Hebrew number signifying "life," a key number in Jewish mysticism), and that its bravura centerpiece would show God's wanderings on Earth, where "he was supposed to see all the battles of history." She and Godard worked together on video tests of special effects that would produce such spectacular moments as Depardieu, playing God in the guise of Amphitryon, walking on water.

The shoot was scheduled to take place in June and July 1992. But right before it began, Godard made two major changes. First, he dismissed Johanna Ter Steege. He had chosen her, he said, because she had what he called "a Dutch nature, similar to Dutch painting." But, recalling the decision humorously, he added: "There was something like blindness on my part. Nobody noticed that she didn't speak French . . . I couldn't get her to speak a text by Claudel, nor have her play the role of a mute, which would have been uselessly meaningless for the story."[18] But Champetier observed the problem from another point of view: "In my opinion, she fell in love with him, and Anne-Marie Miéville intervened, and he fired her. He took the other actress . . . but he wasn't happy."[19] Laurence Masliah, "the other actress," had played a small role in *Soigne ta droite;* with her traditional theater training, speaking a text by Claudel was precisely what she was prepared to do. (Other theater actors, whom Godard had seen in a Geneva production of Botho Strauss's play *Time and the Room,* directed by Patrice

Chéreau, had been cast as well, including Roland Blanche, a friend of Depardieu's.)

The second change concerned the script. Godard had written a long and detailed one because, he felt, the exalted subject matter demanded it: "I didn't want to have a shot of the god just arriving and starting to talk."[20] But he was not satisfied with what he had written, and—in what had become a familiar pattern—still had no clear idea of what he wanted to do. He told his producers that the production was heading toward "a sure catastrophe"[21] and that he wanted to delay the shoot by a year in order to rework the material.[22] Depardieu, however, would not be available then, so Godard was told to make the film that summer, as planned.

Nonetheless, before the shoot started, Godard undid his script. As Champetier later recalled, he was "afraid" of the practical and technical complexity of the elaborate project he was about to undertake, and he "withdrew from everything. He removed eight or nine of the eighteen sequences. He systematically destroyed his screenplay."[23]

Once the shoot started, Godard lost confidence in Depardieu as well, who, he said, "could not stay in one place. He makes phone calls, he moves around, he can't work."[24] In what was by now a predictable response, Godard was dissatisfied, too, with his crew: they did not take seriously his advice that the only way for them to do good work on a film about a god on Earth was to go to church. He told them, " 'Listen to the silence, think about yourself or don't think about it . . .' Nobody in the crew did it."[25] He seemed to reach new levels of irritation while directing Roland Blanche, who played a supporting role. Blanche described their conflict:

> During the shoot of *Hélas pour moi,* he said to me: "You are so bad that I can't even call you by your name, I'll say 'it.' When I say 'it,' you'll know that it's you." Obviously, I got rather upset, and Gérard intervened. He got hold of him and said, "If you talk like that again to Roland, I'll hang you up on that tree." I told him, "Lay off, I'll do it myself."[26]

According to Godard, Depardieu left the film before the end of his contract, approximately halfway through the planned six-week shoot. For his part, Depardieu refused to promote *Hélas pour moi* and would not speak of it publicly, except to joke that in 1992 he had appeared in two commercials: one for Barilla pasta, and Godard's film.[27]

At the end of the shoot, Godard was so displeased with the footage that, after editing it, he was left with just an hourlong film. To fill it out, he decided to shoot additional scenes for a framing story, about a book publisher named Abraham Klimt, who, after receiving an unfinished manuscript concerning an appearance of God on Earth, goes to the village where the event was said to have occurred and conducts an investigation into the incident. This material turned the Amphitryon story into long flashbacks depicting the events about which Klimt inquires. To play the publisher, Godard cast, from the Strauss production in Geneva, the veteran actor Bernard Verley, who understood that the character was actually a stand-in for Godard as a filmmaker "who seeks to understand the reasons for the non-completion of the film."[28]

This second shoot, at the end of the summer, was the latest of Godard's artistic afterthoughts, from the LP version of *A Woman Is a Woman* to the cinematic cosmogony of *Scénario du film Passion:* when he had problems with the shoot of a film, Godard made a new work in which he commented on the project and reworked its main ideas more explicitly and personally. But with *Hélas pour moi,* the analysis became an essential part of the film itself. As a result, *Hélas pour moi* is simultaneously a film and a reflection on a film—and the second, late-summer shoot of the investigative publisher Abraham Klimt provided the cinematic material that made the whole film both a testament and a meditation on the nature of artistic transmission.

HÉLAS POUR MOI is set in a legendary village of craftsmen and merchants, a small town of Protestant piety and petty venality. The couple at the story's center, played by Depardieu and Masliah, are called Simon and Rachel, both biblical names, and, like the apostle whom Jesus renamed Peter, Simon rowed a small boat. (Rachel was also the name of Godard's older sister, who had died in 1991.) Unlike Amphitryon and Alcmene, they are already married, and their family name is Donnadieu (Give to God), which also happened to be Marguerite Duras's actual name. The great event for which Simon will spend his first night away from Rachel is a voyage to Italy to buy a small hotel from a man named Paul (the name of Godard's father). There is a pastor and a schoolteacher in the village, who are also married; their name is Monod, that of Godard's mother. And, in homage to the crucial role that Godard's mother played in his literary awakening, Madame Anne Monod's adolescent students visit her during summer vacation to ask, "What is the novelistic [le romanesque]?"

The story dramatizes nothing less than humanity's rise from paganism to Christian monotheism. Several of the old, diverse, humanoid gods (including one who speaks with a croak like that of the computer Alpha 60 in *Alphaville*) come to town in order to find a woman for the one God. It is this invisible God who lusts after the faithful Rachel and who comes in the form of Simon in order to sleep with her. This God identifies himself as the Christian God, the lusting God who did not come to Earth in *Hail Mary* but nonetheless took carnal possession of Mary. As this God, speaking in Simon's voice, says to Rachel, "I had a little boy once. He died for all of you." God the Father has taken Simon's place in bed with Rachel.

The material that Godard added in the reshoot, however—the story of Abraham Klimt—turns *Hélas pour moi* into a Jewish story. The film begins with Klimt on a country road, as, in a long voice-over narration, he recites the parable that concludes Gershom Scholem's *Major Trends in Jewish Mysticism*. Godard removed its many references to the Baal Shem Tov, other rabbis, and Judaism:

> When my father's father's father had a difficult task to accomplish, he went to a certain place in the forest, lit a fire, and immersed himself in silent prayer. And what he had to do came to pass. When, later, my father's father was faced with the same task, he went to the same place in the forest and said: "We no longer know how to light the fire, but we still know how to say the prayer," and what he had to accomplish came to pass. Later, my father too went into the forest and said, "We no longer know how to light the fire, we no longer know the mysteries of prayer, but we still know the exact place in the forest where it happened, and that must suffice." And it was sufficient. But when, in turn, I had to confront the same task, I stayed home and said, "We no longer know how to light the fire, we no longer know how to say the prayers, we don't even know the place in the forest, but we still know how to tell the story."

Thus from the beginning, Godard frames the film in terms of transmission, the handing-down of knowledge, by a man named Abraham. The publisher's investigation later leads him to a video store, the owner of which is named Benjamin, who rents out mechanically reproduced works of art.

The central scene in Klimt's inquiry regarding the events behind the report of an appearance of God on Earth is a long discussion with a young woman, Aude (played by the young actress Aude Amiot), who turns out to be his best source of information. She tells him that she is very good friends with Benjamin (of the video store) and then mentions Scholem: "Sir, do you know the ten historical propositions about the Old Testament?" she asks. Abraham does not. She continues: "Scholem's text affirms that there exists a tradition regarding the truth, and that this tradition can be transmissible. I laugh, because the truth in question between us has all sorts of properties, but certainly not that of being transmissible."

Klimt responds, "I don't see what you're talking about," and Aude counters, "You said it just right: 'I don't see'; and yet I saw it. Or rather, heard it. That's how I'd say it." She begins to describe what she heard—the story of Simon and Rachel, which is seen in flashback. And after it is seen, on-screen, Aude rests her head on Abraham's shoulder and says—in a line that confirms the proximity of Godard's film to mystical theology—"Seeing the invisible is tiring."

To show the invisible, Godard relies on an array of visual effects: an assistant to the gods walking toward the camera and putting his hand on the lens; a shot of one young townswoman in the water which starts brightly overexposed, but then, as the aperture is slowly stopped down, the image turns dark and the woman falls into silhouette against a darkly luminous sea; a close-up of the red-haired Rachel's pubic zone superimposed on the orange reflections of the lake in sunset and followed by rapid flashes of a knife, in black-and-white. These low-tech optical effects, which have nothing of the elaborate technical inventions that Godard had foreseen in the script, nonetheless suggest his sense of the inadequacy of regular photography for the transcendent tasks at hand, and his frustration—expressed directly in the film—with what could and could not be achieved by realistic means.

In *Hélas pour moi,* the possibility of knowledge is its transmission through the words of a prophet—a young Cassandra-like acolyte of Jewish mysticism—as seen in the images of another prophet, Godard, whose borrowings from mystical Judaism are connected to the film's element of visual striving, of straining against the conventions of naturalism in order to achieve a metaphysical cinema. The subject of Aude's prophecy is living history, the news of the day, which—as in Benjamin's philosophy of history—Godard presented as a metaphysical disaster. In *Hélas pour moi,* he raises to a new level the devotion to history through and as cinema that had characterized, in a variety of ways, all of his work since *Sauve qui peut.*

In June 1991, Slovenia and Croatia declared their independence from Yugoslavia, and the nominally Yugoslav but predominantly Serbian army attacked both of those breakaway republics. The war on Slovenia ended after just nine days, but Croatia was subjected to fierce and prolonged attack. In March 1992, the republic of Bosnia and Herzegovina declared its independence. Bosnian Serbs who did not want to become a minority in an independent Bosnia attacked police stations and other government offices in Sarajevo. The Yugoslav army joined them in attacking towns throughout Bosnia and, in April, began bombarding Sarajevo. This new European war quickly devolved into a massacre; the Soviet Union was collapsing, the so-called New World Order was settling into place, and the first major event of this new era was one of persecution, destruction, and murder. Godard was outraged by the horrific spectacle, which prompted his renewed political engagement, as evinced in *Hélas pour moi.*

During a conversation in the film, one local tells another, "Communism fell: other things fell with it." Aude explains to Abraham, "In the word 'Yugoslavie' [French for Yugoslavia] there is 'vie' [life] and 'gosse' [child, kid]." One of the young men from the video store, Ludovic, goes off to war in the former Yugoslavia, marching down a country road as a fiddler plays and a voice-over cites the opening line from the naive yet rueful text of Stravin-sky's *L'Histoire du soldat* by Charles Ferdinand Ramuz.[29] Later, Aude reports to Abraham that Ludovic was killed in Dubrovnik.

By film's end, Simon is brought back to Rachel, and he reclaims her for himself by lifting her skyward in the same gesture with which John Wayne lifts Natalie Wood in *The Searchers*. Abraham Klimt leaves town after having seen, through the words of Aude, what could not be seen in the manuscript: that God had indeed come to Earth and that he had departed, leaving it no better than he found it.

BUT WHY JEWS? Why Abraham, Benjamin, and Scholem? Because their tra-dition had indeed been transmitted, whereas in Godard's view, the tradition of the image—of seeing the invisible—had failed to be transmitted. The cin-ema, as Godard understood it, had ended with its failures during World War II, and specifically, with its failures in relation to Jews and the genocide to which they were subjected. The tradition of the image that Godard had in-herited could not be transmitted, because of the insurmountable obstacles of television and material comfort, the psychic oblivion of mass culture or cul-turelessness, the broken thread of artistic and cultural achievement that had run from Homer to Godard himself (a lineage that Godard himself as-serted). And yet Godard felt compelled to transmit it. *Hélas pour moi* is a re-statement of Godard's own cinematic testament: he had taken on the cinema as a personal responsibility and burden, and was also taking on the impossi-ble task of transmitting it by means of his films, his *Histoire(s) du cinéma*, his attempt at teaching, and his own media presence as a representative and an embodiment of the lost tradition.

Hélas pour moi was released in September 1993 to appreciative, even over-awed, reviews. In *Libération*, a pair of writers, Gérard Lefort and Olivier Séguret, expressly sought to avoid the "rave or pan?" dialectic and "to evaluate it from the point of view of the scientific disciplines that it invokes."[30] The phi-losopher Régis Debray enthused in *Le Monde*: "A collage of naïve mosaic, with rays of light between the facets . . . With the sense of history collapsed, there emerges from the ruins a nostalgia for the origins."[31] *Le Monde*'s critic Jean-Michel Frodon also wrote rhapsodically about the film and its philosophical and literary speculations, praising its "beauty," "happiness," and "innocence," but also mentioning a "sadness" that "pervades the film which, with its strange chemistry of fragments, manages to produce melancholy by means of energy. Melancholy it is to know that all this won't be of interest to many people . . ."[32]

Frodon's intuition was right; though Godard did extensive publicity for the film, traveling to the southwest of France to present it in an art house there, appearing on television (including Bernard Pivot's popular talk show

Apostrophes), and doing a wide range of interviews in the press, the film did poorly, drawing approximately 80,000 viewers in first run. Depardieu did not promote it and his usual audience stayed away.

Godard's philosophical and theological meditations were cast into a marketplace where patience for them was short. In interviews at the time of the release of *Hélas pour moi*, in September 1993, he discussed his sense of isolation. Little had come of his plans to teach at La fémis. He saw few films by others, whether by young filmmakers or by his peers.[33] He admitted to having little contact with his former associates.[34] Godard was working in a painful solitude, exacerbated by the demands of the project that he was far from completing, *Histoire(s) du cinéma,* for which he had to deliver eight episodes in all, in four groups of two—work which took place largely in the isolation of the editing room.

In the United States, *Hélas pour moi* did not attract the interest of the major film distributors, and was released by Cinema Parallel, a small company founded and run by the filmmaker Rob Tregenza. The New York opening, on March 18, 1994, was at a small nonprofit screening room at Joseph Papp's Public Theatre. The admiring reviews focused less on the film than on Godard himself (Caryn James of *The New York Times* called him "warm and cerebral, and more quietly provocative than he has been in years").[35]

IF GODARD'S PRESENCE and persona had become more valuable in the film marketplace than his actual work, he proceeded with a project that was calculated to take advantage of that state of affairs—and that he turned into a study of his own solitude. In conjunction with a centenary retrospective of Gaumont's productions at the Museum of Modern Art in New York that opened in January 1994, the company commissioned Godard to make a film about himself to premiere there. Godard came to New York to present it, on May 6, 1994, and to answer questions afterward. The sixty-two-minute film, *JLG/JLG,* is an extraordinarily moving document that fulfills Godard's ambition to make not an autobiography but a self-portrait, in keeping with the classic genre of painting. Godard shows himself—or rather, stages scenes of himself—at work, at home, at thought, playing tennis—and also creates several fictional sketches that exemplify his thought in action.

A small video camera with a pivoting lens is set on a table in a night-dark room and used for a stunning self-depiction by firelight: Godard strikes a match and brings it to the cigar in his mouth, the match providing the sole light on the extreme close-up of his face on the tiny video screen in the film frame. He shows himself walking on a strand in Lake Geneva, tramping through the shallows, and approaching the camera while, comically mimick-

ing the gesture of a waiter in his *King Lear,* he points across the water and declares with a smile, "The kingdom of France"—a double reminiscence of his
recent film and his childhood, which was divided between the two countries.

But the key view of himself that the film features is a black-and-white
photograph of Godard as a child. Contemplating his own childhood image,
Godard wonders why that unsmiling face has such a somber aspect: "I was
already in mourning for myself, my sole companion, and I suspected that the
soul had stumbled on the body and that it had left again without offering its
hand." He poignantly suggests that the basis of the problem is "the unconscious," specifically, "the two forms of existence between which living matter
navigates. Crystal and smoke also designate the tragic element of the deaths
which, in my parents' generation, struck down those individuals carrying on
that tradition"—i.e., Jews—"the night of crystal and the fog of smoke." His
mourning for himself, for his lost soul, was, he suggests, an unconscious
mourning for others, for those lost in the concentration camps.

World War II, its shocks and aftershocks, provide the crucial historical
theme of Godard's self-portrait. A jolting notebook inter-title—preceding
shots of a tennis game played in prewar costume, with women wearing long
dresses and Godard wearing first a striped shirt and then an old-fashioned
V-necked ivory-colored tennis sweater—introduces a writer and a thread of
references that persisted in Godard's work for the rest of the decade. The title,
in Godard's handwriting, is "notre avant-guerre" (our prewar)—the name of
a memoir written by the rightist collaborator, Robert Brasillach, in the first
months of the German invasion and occupation of France in 1939 and 1940.

Godard's films were now motivated by a single philosophy of political
aesthetics: nostalgia for a cultural aristocracy. That nostalgia extended, peculiarly, not only to ideas that equivocated with race prejudice, such as Jean
Giraudoux's, but also to the right-wing politics of Godard's childhood and
even to the German occupation and French collaboration—a period which
he seemed to consider immensely fertile for the arts. A leftist, Godard now
openly adopted a rightist style.

The peculiarity and ambiguity of the reference to Brasillach are shown
in another sequence, which Godard calls "the true legend of stereo" and
places soon after the comment about "night" and "fog," itself a reference to
Alain Resnais's documentary about Auschwitz. Showing a close-up of
white paper on a desk, Godard draws a triangle, then superimposes another triangle on it, making a Star of David, which he calls "the mystic
hexagram," and then, taking another piece of white paper, redraws the
same figure, saying, "But in history, the history of history, there was Germany, which projected Israel, Israel which reflected that projection, and

Israel found its cross, and the law of stereo continues. Israel projected the Palestinian people, and the Palestinian people, in turn, bore its cross. This is the true legend of stereo."

The "legend of stereo"—the modern recording industry—was that of Jews who, having suffered, inflict suffering. This was, for Godard, not merely a law of history but one that was uniquely inscribed in Jewish identity. In his way, Godard was inveighing not only against Israel but against the Jewish media. Godard's self-portrait was ultimately dominated by his reflections on Jews and Judaism—indeed, by his inability to stop thinking about Jews, negatively—by what can fairly be called his anti-Semitism.

As obsessed as Godard may have been with Claude Lanzmann's film *Shoah,* and, for that matter, with the horrors of the Holocaust which the cinema could neither prevent nor, on his view, properly document, many of his remarks recalled the genteel anti-Semitism of the prewar period, when the terrible consequences of such prejudices were largely unanticipated. While discussing *Histoire(s) du cinéma* on radio in 1989, Godard spoke of the inevitable association of Germans with Jews.

> The Germans . . . took themselves for a chosen people. That ended up putting them in conflict with another chosen people, who said: "No, pardon us, we're the chosen people, and for a lot longer than you." This virus—taking oneself for the chosen people of Europe—Germany transmitted it to America. Those are the two countries that understood both the image of industry and the industry of the image, the cultural and economic role that this represents.[36]

In the same interview:

> For a long time, certain Jewish producers who had to emigrate were working with money from UFA, mounting French-German coproductions in which they hired technicians like Eugen Schüfftan, director of photography, or Robert Siodmak, director, who were also expatriates. And these producers profited by underpaying these anti-Nazis, who cost them less than the French Republicans. One should draw lessons from that too.[37]

The suggestion of Jewish miserliness and crass disregard for political morality—as well as the hint of French protectionism against the refugees who were undercutting French natives—could be dismissed as an aberration if Godard hadn't found so many different contexts in which to recycle and repeat it. In 1994, he explained the point of his Bugsy Siegel project, which had filtered into *King Lear:* he wanted to show, he said, "How, in fact, Hollywood was invented. How all the gangsters from New York"—Jewish "gangsters," since, as Godard well knew, the producers who created Hollywood were predominantly Jewish—"came to California and took over the film business."[38] It was the cinema of this Hollywood, which Jews had created, that betrayed its own birthright and corrupted the cinema, by failing to depict the Holocaust in its time.

Some years earlier, in 1985, Godard discussed the founding of Hollywood by Jews in terms of the familiar slander of the Jewish usurer.

> What I find interesting in the cinema is that, from the beginning, there is the idea of debt. The real producer is, all the same, the image of the Central European Jew. They're the ones who invented the cinema, they brought it to Hollywood . . . Making a film is visibly producing debts.[39]

But the problem with the Jews, Godard said on television in 1981, went back even further: "Moses is my principal enemy . . . Moses, when he received the commandments, he saw images and translated them. Then he brought the texts, he didn't show what he had seen. That's why the Jewish people are accursed."[40] In Godard's obsessive view of the Jews, they are to blame for the fundamental cultural flaw of society, its preference for text over images, its anti-cinematic prejudice.

In Godard's formulation, Jewish people, who were crucial to the development of the cinema, were also fundamentally responsible for its downfall—its repudiation of the image, specifically, its failure to prevent the Holocaust.[41] His argument, such as it was, depended on a reformulation of age-old prejudice. His expressions of sympathy for the Jews killed in the Holocaust were interwoven with expressions of disdain for the Jews not killed in the Holocaust. In 1980, in a context of personal aesthetics, Godard let slip a disturbingly detached and indifferent view of the perpetrators and victims of the Holocaust:

> When I began making films, I started with fiction, or what my parents thought was fiction—whether my real parents or John Ford. But as I worked, I felt the need for documentary. Society told me I must choose between the two. But I don't like to choose. I don't like to choose between Cain and Abel, between the Nazis or the Jews—one too dreadful torturers, the other too dreadful martyrs.[42]

Godard's view of Jews has been conditioned by many factors: the milieu of his childhood; ambient French prejudices; the pro-Palestinian politics of post-1968 radicalism; the turn against Hollywood; the renewed interest in Christian theology; the perverse fascination with the German occupation and the art produced under it; a speculative historiography of the conflict between image and iconoclasm. All contributed to the hardening and sharpening of Godard's anti-Semitic attitudes; but the unifying premise of these factors is his obsessive, all-consuming devotion to the cinema. By viewing all of human history as a precursor to or tributary of the history of cinema, Godard stood on its head the stereotypical question of clannish self-interest, "Is it good for the Jews?" and interpreted all events, from Biblical times through the Nazi era to the current day, from the perspective of the question, "Is it good for the cinema?" And whether it was good for the Jews, the French, the Russians, or society as a whole, was utterly irrelevant.

SEATED AT A desk in *JLG/JLG,* Godard is visited by "inspectors from the Centre du cinéma" who include André S. Labarthe and the film historian Bernard Eisenschitz. As they inspect his shelves of videotapes and books (and register sixteen rows of American films, two of German, two of Russian, one of Italian films, and two devoted to films by Jean Renoir), a young, scantily-clad cleaning woman declares, "Europe has memories, America has T-shirts." She states that "in 1914, Senator McBridge declares to Congress, 'Trade follows films,'" and repeats Godard's remark from *Histoire(s) du cinéma,* 1A, that Georges Méliès's New York offices were "stolen by Paramount during the offensive of Verdun."

The concluding encounter of *JLG/JLG* shows Godard walking on a snowy country road and finding an old woman bundled in an old coat, resting on a log and reciting Virgil in Latin—with some modifications, as becomes clear when Godard sits beside her and translates: "Whatever the extent of America's power over conquered lands, its people will read me, and, once famous, for all the duration of eternity, if I believe that there is some truth in the mouth of poets, I shall live."

IN NEW YORK, Godard presented, along with *JLG/JLG,* two new episodes of *Histoire(s) du cinéma,* 2A and 2B, *Seul le cinéma* (Only the Cinema) and *Fatale beauté* (Fatal Beauty), both of which extend the themes of the first two episodes, the cinema's failure to document the concentration camps and the irreparable deception that the fallen cinema inflicted on Godard.

Seul le cinéma is dominated by two long sections: Godard's videotaped discussion from 1988 with the late critic Serge Daney (who had died in 1992) concerning the New Wave and its historical approach to the cinema, and a reading by Julie Delpy, also filmed years earlier, of Baudelaire's poem "The Voyage."

Daney suggested that what made the New Wave new was its approach to film history, and specifically its understanding of the succession over time of film styles and forms. Godard disagreed, claiming rather that he and the others of the New Wave had a novel understanding of their personal relation to cinema; for him, the cinema "was the only way to do, to tell, to recognize, myself, that I have an 'histoire' in and of myself . . . if there had been no cinema I would not have known that I have an 'histoire.'" Godard meant at once a history and a story, and the overwhelming power of the cinema compelled him to identify his history and story with the ones it told. As he explained to Daney, "For me, the big history is that of cinema; it is bigger than the others because it is projected, whereas in a book, it is reduced."

After again citing the discovery of projection by Poncelet, "a French prisoner pacing before a Russian wall," Godard turns to the reading by Julie Delpy of Baudelaire's poem "The Voyage," which he remarkably excerpts to turn it into an allegory for his own youthful discovery of the cinema:

"We want to travel without steam and without sail! To brighten the boredom of our prisons, make your memories, which are framed by the horizon, pass over our minds which are as taut as a canvas"—a movie screen.

"We saluted idols of trumpery, starry thrones of luminous baubles, elaborate palaces the fairy-tale pomp of which would be a ruinous dream for your bankers, costumes which intoxicate the eye, women with painted teeth and nails, and clever jugglers caressed by snakes." And yet, the memory of such deceptions is still, late in life, a wonder: "Oh, Death, let us set sail! If the sky and the sea are as black as ink, our hearts, which you know, are filled with beams of light!" Godard still had sixteen rows of American films in his library; he had been deceived, but the illusions were beautiful ones, beautiful to believe in, even after their fraud was revealed.

In New York, Godard was a model guest: he calmly answered questions from the MOMA audience, telling a spectator who had asked about his use of video that the medium was more like music because it allowed the contrapuntal layering of images in the editing. He reacted with disdain only when another viewer asked whether he had ever made a film without the right to final cut. He was interviewed by the young director Hal Hartley for *Filmmaker* magazine and by a wide range of journalists from other publications, including Andrew Sarris of the *Village Voice.*

Godard's enthusiastic reception in New York had been primed by MOMA's major retrospective in late 1993 of his video work. The retrospective had received a great deal of favorable attention, had been well attended, and generated a catalogue, *Son + Image,* which was the most important English-language publication about Godard since the 1972 translation of his critical writings and early interviews, *Godard on Godard.*[43]

However, in January 1995, Godard refused an invitation from the New York Film Critics Circle to attend an awards ceremony. The group had voted Godard a special prize, which he declined by fax. The first of his many "incomplete reasons" was that "JLG was never able through his whole movie-maker/goer career to: Prevent M. Spielberg from rebuilding Auschwitz."[44]

STEVEN SPIELBERG'S SCHINDLER'S List (released in December 1993) had gotten under Godard's skin: it had entered the public arena in the guise of the legitimate fictional successor to Shoah. Godard did not immediately expand, cinematically, on his specific charges against Spielberg's film, but he, together with Miéville, soon returned to the theme of the cinema's representation of the Holocaust. They were commissioned by the British Film Institute to make a film about the centennial of the French cinema, which was officially set for 1995, the one-hundredth anniversary of the first public display of the Lumière brothers' films. Godard and Miéville decided to make a quasi-documentary sketch, and invited Michel Piccoli, the head of France's own commission for the centennial, to Rolle, where he was filmed in conversation with Godard in the dining room of a hotel, the Hostellerie du château.

Godard asks Piccoli why they should bother to commemorate the cinema, since nobody remembers it anyway, and challenges the actor to interview people at the hotel about what they remember of the cinema. Piccoli goes to his room and, as chambermaids, bellhops, and other staff (actually, actors) come in, he puts them to the test. One does not know Albert Préjean but knows Arnold Schwarzenegger, not La Grande Illusion but Madonna; another doesn't know Jacques Becker but knows Boris Becker ("He serves well, and so do I"). The centerpiece of the scene, and of the film, is an extreme close-up of a young chambermaid at whom Piccoli recites dozens of names of classic French actors that she does not recognize—Odile Versois, Jules Berry, Marcel Dalio, Tilda Thamar, Jean Servais, Jany Holt, Danielle Darrieux, Catherine Hessling, Eddie Constantine, Julien Carette, Gaston Modot, Simone Simon, among others—while she listens with a quiet, blank calm. With her face framed in a luminous intimacy, this unnamed actress, as she listens to the parade of notables, instantly takes her place as the newest among them. This shot is Godard's lesson, a tenacious act of faith: even now, a filmmaker can use an ordinary video camera to extend the history of cinema by a few heartbeats.

But the film's crucial idea, the one that exemplifies Godard's overarching historical thesis, is contained in its title. He and Miéville did not call the film, as per the commission, "One Hundred Years of French Cinema," but rather, 2×50 ans de cinéma français (2×50 Years of French Cinema). The first fifty years ran from 1895 to 1945. The dividing line set down was the same one defined in Histoire(s) du cinéma, the line between the innocent prewar cinema and tainted postwar cinema.

That year, Godard found two more ways to extend this argument through cinema and art, in episodes 3A and 3B of Histoire(s) du cinéma, La

Monnaie de l'absolu (The Coin of the Absolute), and *Une Vague nouvelle* (A New Wave, or A Vague Piece of News).

La Monnaie de l'absolu is principally a paean to Italian postwar, "neorealist" cinema—and thus about the war. The episode begins with a condemnation of contemporary European governments for allowing the massacres in the former Yugoslavia to take place without intervention. Godard asserts that the cinema is capable of recording such events, and thus, of doing "something."[45] He adds that this is the crucial and historic role of the cinema, which is, "to begin with, made for thinking. This is forgotten immediately, but that's another story. The flame will go out definitively at Auschwitz." Citing the readiness of the French cinema to collaborate with the occupying Germans during World War II, Godard says that there was no cinema of resistance, except for one film—but he redefines "resistance" in terms that elide the actual German occupation and turn the argument against his real nemesis: "The only film, in the sense of cinema, which resisted the occupation of the cinema by America, which resisted a certain uniform way of doing cinema, was the Italian cinema"—specifically, Rossellini's *Open City,* made in 1945.

Episode 3B, *Une Vague nouvelle,* is Godard's summation of the New Wave. It begins with Aude Amiot's voice from *Hélas pour moi* citing Gershom Scholem's assertion of the transmissibility of tradition, as intertitles state, "What we wanted was to have the right to film boys and girls in a real world and who, in seeing the film, are themselves astonished to be themselves and in the world." Godard added, in voice-over, "One night we showed up chez Henri Langlois, and there was light." Yet in his voice there is accusation and regret: "We were without a past, and the man from the avenue de Messine [Langlois] made us a gift of this past, metamorphosed into the present, in the midst of the wars in Indochina and Algeria, and when he projected *L'espoir* for the first time, it was not the Spanish war that astonished us, but the fraternity of metaphors." The New Wave directors saw metaphors instead of wars, he argued, because the fallen postwar cinema was, for them, an art that had lost the ability to project history and instead concealed it.

Godard concludes the episode sentimentally, with clips from his own films, including *Alphaville, King Lear, Germany Nine Zero, Passion,* and *Nouvelle Vague,* images of Marguerite Duras (who had died in February 1995), and his own discussion with a young man and woman who are leaving a house that is, she says, a "museum of T-shirts" (the young man corrects her: "New Wave"). She complains that it shows pictures of works but not of people, and the young man explains to her, "That's what the New Wave was: *la politique des auteurs,* not the *auteurs* but the works." Godard agrees with him: "First the works, then the men." She then asks Godard directly, "And yet, Becker, Rossellini, Melville, Franju, Jacques Demy, Truffaut, you knew them?" With images of these men and their films on-screen, Godard answers, "Yes, they were my friends."

"FIRST THE WORKS, then the men," Godard exhorted, and yet, as ever, he put himself in the fore of his *Histoire(s) du cinéma* and, as he had long understood, got attention for his work through his personal involvement in its public presentation, through his skillful reliance on his celebrity. His New York junket to present new work at MOMA in May 1994 was major film news in France, as was his presentation, in August 1995, of the first six episodes, 1A through 3B, of *Histoire(s)* at the Locarno Film Festival. There, he received an award, the Golden Leopard, with its prize of twenty thousand Swiss francs (which, he declared, he would donate to Amnesty International), and participated in a public roundtable discussion about the *Histoire(s)*. Godard displayed his displeasure with the proceedings, casting doubt on whether anything true and useful was being said by anyone: "If we were doctors, we would have already operated on five thousand sick people in an hour. But would they be cured? I don't know."[46]

Although Godard's films were on the margin of the European movie business, the man himself came in for more honors. In September 1995, Godard went to Frankfurt to accept the city's philosophy prize, named for Theodor Adorno and offered only every three years. In his acceptance speech, he reprised his theses from the *Histoire(s) du cinéma*: "The concentration camps have never been shown. Basically, they have been talked about, but nothing has been shown . . . No one wanted to show them. They preferred talking, saying: 'Never again.' And it started again, so to speak, Vietnam, Algeria—it's not finished—Biafra, Afghanistan, Palestine." At the end of the Second World War, as a result of not showing the concentration camps, the cinema—or what Godard called the *cinématographe,* Robert Bresson's term for the art of the cinema—"disappeared at that moment."[47]

Godard may have won the Adorno prize, but unlike Adorno, he did not think it impossible to write poetry after Auschwitz. For Godard, the cinema after Auschwitz would be a funerary art, an art of the ever-too-late which, as he said of himself in *JLG/JLG,* is in mourning for itself. It remained nonetheless necessary to recover what could be recovered, to reclaim what could be reclaimed—of what had existed before the war. This, however, also entailed the reclamation of writers and artists who had led the way to Auschwitz, such as Brasillach. For Godard, the cinema had retained the ability to tell the story, but the story that he chose to tell, the story of the cinema itself, was far more ambiguous than that of the history it had ostensibly failed to reflect. His funerary art was, in human terms, a lament at arm's length. For the time being, Godard was obsessively telling a Jewish story from which Jews were kept out.

twenty-eight

FOR EVER MOZART, HISTOIRE(S) DU CINÉMA, PART 4

"How can you do this to me?"

THE FIFTIETH ANNIVERSARY OF D-DAY, IN 1994, WAS commemorated in France with countless reports, broadcasts, and diverse audiovisual memorabilia. The occasion inspired Godard to plan a film that would be about the war, in its way, but also about Manfred Eicher and his company, ECM Records, and music itself. The story concerned the present-day return to Vienna of an American soldier who "on a day of drunkenness in 1945 had killed Anton Webern," the composer.[1] Godard decided to call the film *For Ever Mozart,* because the aging American veteran would "be recognized by a critic at a given moment during the performance of a piece by Mozart."[2]

The film would ultimately be hijacked by Godard's consuming obsession with an actress forty-five years his junior, Bérangère Allaux. For well over a year, Godard's filmmaking would be driven by the frantic efforts to give cinematic expression and remain in proximity to the object of his longing. But even as *For Ever Mozart* gravitated around her presence, it nonetheless bore the conspicuous imprint of Godard's philosophical, political, and cinematic concerns.

Through the story of Webern's death, Godard wanted to bring together Germany and the United States, classical music, the persistence of history in the present, and the year 1945, which he had defined as the great divide in the history of cinema. Before he could get to work on it, however, the Portuguese producer Paulo Branco offered him the chance to make a low-budget film in Portugal. Godard proposed a film called *The Return of Columbus,* featuring a boat arriving in port and a very long tracking shot ("maybe three or four kilometers") that would show "hands setting down everything that has come

The actress agonizes; the director broods.
(TCD-Prod DB © Peripheria / DR)

from America from Columbus to today, to T-shirts, to McDonald's." With Portugal in mind, Godard read *The Book of Disquiet*, the philosophical, diary-like novel by the Portuguese writer Fernando Pessoa, which was posthumously published in 1982 and appeared in French ten years later as *Le Livre de l'intranquillité*. Godard then abandoned his first proposal for Branco in favor of *Le Film de l'intranquillité*, an analytical project that would concern "the basic gestures of cinematographic creation, not the shooting of a film." For this outline, Godard received an advance on receipts from the CNC but subsequently decided that he did not have enough ideas for a feature film and put the project aside.

Soon after, Godard happened to read an article in *Le Monde* by Philippe Sollers in which he criticized Susan Sontag for her 1993 voyage to besieged Sarajevo to mount a production of Samuel Beckett's *Waiting for Godot*. Sollers's argument was, in Godard's words, that "they're already miserable enough. She shouldn't put on Beckett over there. She should do Marivaux."[3] This gave Godard the idea to make a film about a production in Sarajevo of *The Game of Love and Chance*, a play by Marivaux; the film would be called *The Game of Love and Chance in Sarajevo*. Then, as Godard later recalled,

> I went to buy a copy of Marivaux at the little bookstore in Rolle . . . But, of course, they didn't have any Marivaux. On the other hand, they had a Musset, which was *One Doesn't Trifle with Love*. So the film became *One Doesn't Trifle with Love in Sarajevo*, which sounds much better, I think. I imagined that in the film there would be two or three young people who would go off to put on this play in Sarajevo. It would be about their adventures on the road and the places where they would stop along the way. And they wouldn't get where they were going.[4]

Godard decided to put all three elements—the trip to Sarajevo, the study of filmmaking, the essence of music—into one film. The project was built around a familiar pair: a young woman and her father, an old movie director who would be something of a stand-in for Godard. The young woman would organize the trip to Sarajevo to put on Musset's play and would bring along a young man, her cousin, and another young woman, her parents' maid; the old director, who was frustrated in his effort to make a movie—in particular, to find actors for his movie—would join them but chicken out en route. His daughter and her cohorts would be killed by Serb paramilitaries, and the mourning director would make his film with great difficulty. Music would be the closest thing to consolation and redemption that he finds.

The filming was supposed to begin in January 1996, but Godard's troubles mimicked those of the director in the film: he had difficulty finding actors. To play the role of the young man, Godard had his assistant, Gilbert Guichardière, videotape actors reading from Musset's play. He offered the role to Frédéric Pierrot but then took it back because he didn't like the actor's long hair (which he had grown for a World War I movie he was acting in at the time). By chance, Anne-Marie Miéville saw an actor in a TV movie and told Godard she had found the man for the part: it turned out to be Pierrot, and Godard called him back within hours to offer him the role again.

Godard also had great trouble finding someone to play the actress in the film that would be made following the young people's death en route to Sarajevo. After long searches, he happened to notice a picture on a casting agent's desk and called the actress in. Bérangère Allaux was a first-year student at the Ecole nationale de l'art dramatique (National School of Dramatic Art) in Strasbourg, one of the eleven young performers in her class who had been culled from two thousand applicants. Godard met her at his office in mid-December 1995, six weeks before the shoot, and offered her the role—of the actress who, in the film, remains nameless. He gave her no screenplay. As Allaux later recalled, "I had no idea what I was going to do in the film. Neither did he. What I knew was that I was the Actress—that I represent all the actresses with whom he had filmed."[5]

To prepare Allaux, Godard had her watch Ava Gardner in *The Barefoot Contessa* and *Pandora and the Flying Dutchman*. Soon thereafter, he told her that she was not really his kind of actress, because she was too "carnal." She responded, "If I'm not your kind of actress, too bad," and got up to leave, but Godard, surprised, called her back. Allaux admitted that she behaved impulsively and temperamentally; the dark-haired, dramatic young woman with a "carnal" presence and impulsive temperament had a great effect on Godard. He was in the grip of a terrible crush, which exerted a powerful influence on his behavior and on his creative activity after the film was completed. Bérangère Allaux became the main character in his life, and his primary effort in that time was to find a way to represent that relationship on film and to use the cinema to keep it going in life.

IN THE FILM, the daughter, Camille (Madeleine Assas), an out-of-work professor of philosophy (as well as Albert Camus's granddaughter), recruits her cousin, Jérôme (Frédéric Pierrot), who is in love with her, and her family's maid, Djamila (Ghalia Lacroix), to accompany her to Sarajevo. Her father, Vicky Vitalis (Vicky Messica) a taciturn, elderly director who is frustrated with the slow and uncertain course of pre-production on a film, decides to join them.

In midcourse, at a border crossing, after exhorting his companions to grand deeds, Vitalis abandons the three young people and goes home. They continue on foot into Bosnia and are captured by Serb paramilitaries. Djamila is separated from the others and vanishes. Camille and Jérôme are raped by their captors, then, during an outbreak of fighting, die in a ditch they had been forced to dig.

Vitalis resumes work on his film and completes it, with tragicomic difficulty. When it is finished and rejected by the public he retreats to a concert hall where a seraphic young man is playing a Mozart piano concerto with a youth orchestra.

In January 1996, the shoot began with the most physically demanding action, the young people's trip to Sarajevo and their doomed captivity; but Godard and the crew did not go to Sarajevo. Rather, the war scenes were filmed in forests on the French side of Lake Geneva. For the Serb paramilitary base, Godard rented a dilapidated old manse—the ruins of his maternal grandparents' house, which now belonged to a Saudi prince and had been abandoned to the elements and left without windows, doors, and in some places, walls. The derelict palace of civilized treasures was itself a sign of a Europe gone to ruin. At a moment during the shoot in the blasted house, Jérôme and Camille point to markings on a wall and read them aloud: the record of dates and heights of Jean-Luc Godard and his siblings as they grew up. (Although Godard put the shot in the film, he removed the voices from the sound track.)

The filming took place in very cold weather; the ground was dusted with snow, but the actors playing Camille and Jérôme were stripped to their underwear in the unheated, wind-blown house. They had to walk, barefoot, on the cold ground and in icy mud. The shoot was gruelling, and it required careful practical organization on the part of Godard and the technical crew. For the battle, Godard rented tanks and sent them barreling down the long, unpaved driveway toward the house and brought in pyrotechnicians to create realistic explosions disturbingly near the actors. One mortar on a strand in the lake was manned by Godard himself (his face is not visible but his silhouette is familiar), who dropped a shell into its barrel and quickly turned and covered his ears as it shot its charge.

The action involved highly technical choreography integrating much equipment and many extras; Godard knew he needed to film the sequence but had little desire to do so. He called Romain Goupil for help with the scene, confiding his lack of interest in it.[6] Goupil was not available, however, and Godard oversaw the shoot himself; his reluctance is evident in the results. The rote, dull violence is de-aestheticized, a theatrical replica of war that presents neither the range of its horrors nor its vicarious thrills.

In the face of the hardships of the shoot, Godard was particularly tender with his long-suffering young actors. On the first day, he showed an actor playing a paramilitary how to strike Pierrot on the hand with a rifle butt, and accidentally drew blood. To Pierrot's astonishment, the director took Pierrot's hand in his, wiped the blood, and licked the wound clean, which Pierrot recalled as "the gesture of a father."[7]

Godard's stringent preparatory work with the actors was unusually calm. He slipped dialogue for Pierrot and Madeleine Assas under the door of their hotel rooms without specifying which lines were meant for which role and asked them to learn the texts by rewriting them in their own handwriting, which, as Pierrot later recalled, he explained as the way to internalize the lines: "For him it is very important that, for the writer, the work passes from the head to the arm to the hand to the paper. He says that to learn a text, to really understand it, the relationship must be reversed: the text must pass from the paper to the hand up to the head."

As ever, Godard wanted his actors to overcome their inhibition in his presence and to speak to him about the substance of the film, complaining to Pierrot the evening before the shoot started, "I sent you the text but you haven't said anything to me. I should have made you pay me for the text; if you had paid 3,000 or 5,000 francs, you would have said something—you would have felt you had the right to say something, to say that the text doesn't work." When Pierrot took Godard up on the challenge, approaching him in the hotel restaurant to point out a shift in subject, the director responded with warm gratitude.

Godard's solicitude reflected the subject of the film, the relationship of an older filmmaker to young people close to his heart: where *Hélas pour moi* treated the issue of transmission theoretically and philosophically, *For Ever Mozart* treated it dramatically and intimately. The center of the film, both formally and morally, is the dividing line between the young people's ordeal and the beginning of Vitalis's shoot of his own work. Not only does Vitalis, with his hortatory rhetoric, press the young people onward to their destruction, but he is unable to make his film until after their death: his mourning for them, together with his self-loathing, are the stuff of his art.

In *For Ever Mozart*, Godard self-revealingly dramatizes the tragedy of transmission after the end of the cinema. If he was to be the last of the line, then those who presumed to follow him were merely passing him on the way to the abyss. Not only was there nobody to whom to pass the torch, but those who would accept it from him were being lured to their doom—and only in mourning for them could his own work find its true meaning.

THE SHOOT OF the film-within-a-film, which Godard had originally called *The Film of Disquiet* and now called *The Fatal Bolero*, took place at the end of January 1996 on a beach near Bordeaux. It depicts the pathetic comedy of the cinema, the attempt to make art in the context of pimplike producers and the self-important underlings they employ. The producer, an arrogant old man signing checks at a table in a deserted casino, supervises his overripe and no-longer-young daughter, who is studying for her "baccalaureate exam in cinema" by taking dictation from a tape recorder emitting grotesque pornographic phrases. The production manager comes in to announce that he has found "really cheap actors"—meaning the newcomer Bérangère Allaux—for Vicky Vitalis's project.

Allaux's first scene is one of utter passivity and vulnerability: playing a corpse in Vitalis's film, she is dragged, nude and inert, onto the sand by one of Vitalis's assistants and placed alongside a naked young man. They lie side by side and exposed on the frigid shore of the wintry beach; another assistant then covers her with a red gown and the young man with a coat. The two are the cinematic representations of Vitalis's dead daughter and her cousin, but Vitalis decides not to film the scene, and merely contemplates it in search of inspiration.

Allaux was thus introduced to the cinema limp and naked, a subject of violence and an object of desire. She understood that the moment was, for Godard, an unconcealed form of personal gratification and emotional compensation. "He shows in his films what he doesn't have in his life," she later said. "He likes vulnerable young girls."[8] As they worked, Godard told her, "I have gotten you to enter into the house of the cinema,"[9] and he made sure that she knew it to resemble a whorehouse.

When Vitalis begins to shoot his film, he does so with an ancient movie camera, a boxlike device on a wooden-legged tripod, which he sets up behind a large glass sliding door inside a beachfront house. Allaux's role in it is undefined; she wears a vast, old-fashioned gown and, standing outside on the beach, is buffeted by a terrible winter wind. She attempts to recite her text on-camera—"Since I am unemployed, in these slow and empty hours a sadness comes to mind from the depths of my soul . . ."—but the wind forces her to shout the words in order to be heard, and she stumbles over her lines. Vitalis says, contemptuously, "Don't worry, we'll simplify it," and reduces her text to a single word, *Oui*, which, as the camera rolls, she attempts to speak to suit Vitalis's pleasure. They reach take fifty-nine. After each pronouncement of "Oui," Vitalis calmly says, "Non," calling for another take. Now, Allaux howls and shrieks the single word, as Vitalis himself murmurs the number of the takes—115, 217, 303, 445, 517, 608 (for Godard, a recollection of Charlie Chaplin's reported 900 takes of a single shot in *City Lights*)—until she yells "Oui!" at him and, exhausted from the effort, stretches out on the cold sand. Meanwhile, Vitalis, seen from behind in his stolid immobility, hunched heavily in his coat and beneath his hat, remains impassive, mutely bearing the dreadful burden of grief and guilt that concentrates his formerly dispersed and slackened powers of creation into her single word, which she delivers at the price of her agony.

Allaux's role in *For Ever Mozart* is an unusual one: though central to the film and to Godard's work, she hardly had anything to do in it. She found Godard's emphasis on the spoken text, to the exclusion of an actor's identification with character, antithetical to acting: "In acting, there must be pleasure," she said, and considered Godard's comportment on the set an obstacle to any such physical pleasure in performance. "Godard did not even dare speak too loudly," she later recalled, "he whispered, 'Is everyone ready? Let's shoot.' For him, it was a cathedral, the shoot. That's why the bodies don't come into play; one doesn't let bodies exult in a cathedral."[10] Indeed, her body does not exult; it rages and rises in revolt—if apparently against the wind, in reality against Godard and his methods.

In the concluding section of *For Ever Mozart,* Vitalis has finished his film, *The Fatal Bolero,* and is presenting it at a provincial movie theater where a number of patrons are waiting in line. One hopes the film will have no "poetry," another asks whether it has "tits," or "titties," or even "bazooms,"[11] and some young people in line decide to go elsewhere to see *Terminator 4. The Fatal Bolero* is a flop; while the public is mocking it, Vitalis wanders into a concert hall where an orchestra and a young pianist with long, flowing hair, a ruffled shirt, and a frock coat are playing a Mozart piano concerto.

Why Mozart?

Because Mozart, who died poor and unappreciated, labored under the demands of his patrons and suffered the accusation of composing with "too many notes"—an accusation spoken in the concert hall by a member of the audience—to which Vitalis responded disdainfully, "So they think." *For Ever Mozart* ends with Vitalis sinking down into a crouch in the shadows on a staircase in the concert hall. The gesture is the same as that of the ill and weary theater director Julian Marsh (played by Warner Baxter), at the end of *Forty-Second Street:* Vitalis, like Marsh, has given his last measure of strength and health for his show, yet the crowd dismisses his achievement.

AFTER THE SHOOT, Godard spent a week with Allaux at her family home. There he talked at length with Allaux's father (a veteran of the Algerian War) and her grandmother (who was Jewish and had survived deportation to a concentration camp during the Second World War). He played tennis and rode horses. Yet the ambiguities of their friendship were troubling both to Godard and to Allaux. As she later recalled, "I did not need either a father or a grandfather or a boyfriend, and he wanted to be all three."[12] When the film was completed, in late spring of 1996, the confusion worsened. According to Allaux, "I went to see *For Ever Mozart* in the sound studio at Joinville [a suburb of Paris] . . . I arrived with my best friend, a man, by motorcycle. We got there and Godard wept, saying, 'How can you do this to me?' He insulted me, called me a whore. I had gone from Ava Gardner, the Barefoot Contessa, to a whore."[13]

Godard nonetheless involved Allaux in the presentation of *For Ever Mozart*. It was scheduled for a fall release, but he offered the premiere to the city of Sarajevo, where, in June, it would be the opening-night screening in a series of recent French films under the auspices of the French Cultural Services. He intended to go to Sarajevo, along with Allaux and others from the cast, to present it. But before the trip could take place, Anne-Marie Miéville asked Godard to take over, "at a moment's notice,"[14] the male lead in her new feature film, *Nous sommes tous encore ici* (We Are All Still Here), and he accepted. (Allaux did in fact accompany it, and read a note from him to the Sarajevo audience.)

The next screenings, several days later, were also arranged around the presence of Allaux: Godard introduced *For Ever Mozart* at another pre-release premiere—this time, in Strasbourg, where Allaux lived and studied. The event was of major local interest, and Godard threw himself into it energetically, offering the new film for the opening night of a three-week series of his rarer films, including *King Lear* (which was yet unreleased in France), which he provided. He also held a related public discussion with Daniel Cohn-Bendit, who was now a member of the European Parliament, located in Strasbourg. Yet the festivities took a melodramatic turn. Jean-Louis Martinelli, the director of the Théâtre National de Strasbourg (TNS), with which the Ecole nationale de l'art dramatique was affiliated, observed the pathetic conclusion to the night of the premiere, when Godard, who had brought his car to drive Allaux back to her parents' house, could not find her after the screening. Martinelli saw Godard wandering desperately through the streets in search of the young woman, and, struck by the pathos of the moment, likened him to King Lear.[15]

MIÉVILLE, IN HER new film, also presented Godard in a diminished, beleaguered aspect, though there he is diminished, rather, to a brilliant but unsocialized child. Her second feature film, *Lou n'a pas dit non* (Lou did not say no), from 1993, dramatized the difficult relationship between a crabby, narrow, hyper-literary man and a woman artist who strikes out on her own as a photographer without wanting to detach herself completely from him. In the new film, *Nous sommes tous encore ici,* Miéville had a similar idea for the lead male role, an older actor, Robert, with sedentary habits and set ways.

Nous sommes tous encore ici is in three parts. The first section features a woman, played by Aurore Clément (a slight but commanding actress with wavy blond hair like Miéville's) discussing with her friend (played by Bernadette Lafont) the definition of the "good man," in a text derived from Plato's *Gorgias*. The second part features Robert, the actor, who climbs up to an empty stage to rehearse his performance of a monologue taken from a text by Hannah Arendt. The third and longest part shows the life of this "good man" with the woman who chose him, the one played by Clément. The couple agonize over taking a long-deferred trip to visit museums in Italy. She criticizes his habits, his hat, his jacket, his sexism, his driving, his selfishness, his moods, his silences, and then adds, "Would you say that you've learned to keep quiet? I'd say rather that you permit me to speak, isn't that already a lot?" After a dinner (in a hotel dining room) replete with such criticism, Robert looks like a chastised little boy. She wants to take a walk; he refuses, and returns to their room to read. She takes her walk and lets herself be accompanied by a man, the hotel pianist, whom she embraces. When she returns home with Robert, she accuses him with coldness, throwing at him lines that Godard spoke in *Histoire(s) du cinéma*—"In any case you're interested in the work, not in the man or his heart, you said so yourself "—and admits the pain that his closed-off nature causes her. She finally persuades him to join her for a walk, and he speaks the film's last words: "Oh, I'm suffocating."

Miéville's film is a touching yet unsparing portrait of a difficult yet deeply dedicated couple. Miéville did not hesitate to dramatize the stresses of her relationship with Godard and to suggest what each of them put up with from the other (Clément's inconsequential dalliance with the hotel pianist mirroring Godard's own infatuations). *Nous sommes tous encore ici* is not indulgent of either of them, and Miéville's intimately fictionalized yet meticulously naturalistic view of a private life so close to her own—and Godard's willingness to participate in its public revelation—is as much a tribute to their mutual devotion as to their devotion to the cinema.

MEANWHILE, GODARD PURSUED his relationship with Allaux and tried to make a film that would keep them closely connected through work. After the Strasbourg screening, Allaux went to New York. There, she stayed with Gill Holland, an assistant in the French Film Office as well as a freelance publicist who was also beginning his career as an independent producer. Godard called her at Holland's apartment every day. As a result, the two men spoke often by phone and with increasing familiarity.[16] Holland did some work for Cinema Parallel, the distribution company founded by the filmmaker Rob Tregenza, which had released *Hélas pour moi* and *JLG/JLG* in the United States, and to which Godard now offered American distribution rights to *For Ever Mozart*.

In July, Godard flew Tregenza to Paris to see the film along with Piers Handling of the Toronto Film Festival. Handling immediately offered to premiere
the film at Toronto, but Godard and Tregenza would not commit before hearing from the New York Film Festival. However, when the New York festival
committee turned For Ever Mozart down, Godard settled for Toronto.[17]

Handling invited Allaux to Toronto as well, on Holland's advice, in order
to ensure that Godard would show up at the festival along with the film.
Handling also asked Godard to program for the festival a North American
independent film of his choice. Having heard Handling and Allaux praise
Tregenza's first film, Talking to Strangers, from 1988, Godard watched a tape
of it and decided to present it in Toronto. Moreover, when Allaux expressed
the wish to act in Tregenza's forthcoming film, Godard agreed to coproduce
it with Holland.

The Toronto festival, which was held in September 1996, proved quite
eventful. In addition to presenting For Ever Mozart and Talking to Strangers,
Godard showed the next, penultimate, installment of Histoire(s) du cinéma.
His written agreement with the festival management stipulated that he be
provided with a tennis court and a tennis "professor" to play with him.[18] A
dinner was held in Godard's honor, during which he got up claiming to go to
the bathroom and never returned. Later that night, he joined Holland at the
hotel bar, where they drank beer and played pool until 1:00 AM.

At the festival, he discussed with Holland the practical side of producing
Tregenza's next film (called Springfield): officially, Godard considered his
$100,000 investment a "pre-buy"—a purchase of distribution rights prior to
production—but he did not want his name attached to the production of the
project, saying, as Holland later recalled: "Anne-Marie would kill me."[19] But
to raise the project's profile, Godard agreed to play a role. He also discussed
an idea for the end of the last episode of Histoire(s) du cinéma in New York
City, in which Tregenza would operate the video camera for a single long
take in which he would film Godard meeting Allaux and Holland in a bar.

Tregenza, Allaux, and Holland were Godard's closest connection to a
younger generation of filmmakers; though he invested a great deal of time,
money, and emotion in them, these relations foundered on the most unyield-
ing of obstacles: an unreciprocated obsession and the increasingly frantic attempts to gratify it.

After the Toronto festival, Allaux and Holland returned to New York and
Godard to Rolle. He frequently faxed the three, referring to Allaux as "our-
son" (bear-cub) or punningly as the "bear foot contessa." (Her American
friends called her "Bér," pronounced, New York-style, "Bear.") Godard
planned to come to New York on September 21 for lunch with Holland and
Allaux, but postponed it due to illness. He also cancelled a second New York

lunch date, because he and Miéville left for a Greek island on September 25. On October 7, back in Rolle, Godard invited Tregenza to visit him and finalize the plans for the coproduction of *Springfield*. Meanwhile, he was nurturing plans for another film with Allaux.

In mid-1996, the book publisher Paul Otchakovsky-Laurens, who also published the film magazine *Trafic* (founded by Serge Daney), sent Godard an advance copy of a yet-unpublished first novel by a twenty-nine-year-old author, Marie Darrieussecq, that his publishing company, P.O.L., would be bringing out. The novel, *Truismes* (a play on words: *truism*, and *truie*, a sow), is the story of a young woman who works in the perfume industry and occasionally turns tricks, and who is transformed into a sow.[20] In September, Godard bought film rights to *Truismes*.[21] When Darrieussecq spoke with Godard about the book, she sensed that he was interested in it because he "was in a period, visibly, where his cinematographic ideas revolved around the body, in particular around the female body."[22] Intending the part for Allaux, he wrote to Gill Holland for help finding a "comic/strip artist for numerised [i.e., digital] shots,"[23] and asked Tregenza for information about high-definition computer animation. He abandoned the film, however, because it seemed too expensive to make. *Truismes* unexpectedly became one of the major publishing events and bestsellers of 1996 in France; Godard tried to resell the rights but without success, and his option expired.

His connection with Otchakovsky-Laurens, however, continued. Their relationship dated back to 1993 when Godard had called him and expressed a desire to make a book based on *Hélas pour moi*. The publisher was willing, but Godard did not pursue the project. But after making *For Ever Mozart*, he contacted Otchakovsky-Laurens again to say that he now wanted to create a book of "sentences" from that film and to do the same for other works of his.[24] The publisher prepared a transcript of *For Ever Mozart*, and Godard removed all descriptions and stage directions, "everything except what is said in the film." Then he rearranged the spoken text in a process which Otchakovsky-Laurens described as "an authentic work of versification." The result did not resemble a published script; the sentences, broken into short, unpunctuated lines, without attribution to characters, indeed resemble poetry. Godard expressed his satisfaction with the result, declaring, "These are sounds and phrases which correspond to a type of diction, my own."[25] The genre under which the book is listed is also Godard's own—"phrases," that is, sentences—although many of the book's phrases, or sentences, were not his own: the book features a list of sixteen cited authors, including Georges Bernanos, Marguerite Duras, James Agee, and André Bazin.

The book of *For Ever Mozart* was issued in November 1996, concurrent with the film's theatrical release, making it available as a souvenir or libretto of the film.[26] Godard managed the film's theatrical release, in October 1996, with his usual flair for publicity. He offered a typically generous range of interviews to the media and appeared on the cultural talk show *Le Cercle de minuit* (The Midnight Circle), to which he invited an imposing list of co-panelists: the writer Alain Finkielkraut, the philosopher Jean-François Lyotard, the novelist and essayist Philippe Sollers, and the film critic Jean-Claude Biette. During the broadcast discussion, Godard repeated his notion of the villainy of Moses in the "great conflict between the seen and the said":

> I think that Moses cheated; that he saw, then translated—since he wrote—the tables of the law, and then, at that moment, everything got fucked up, because what he had seen, even the burning bush, was finished. It always went through a translation, by an anchorman or an anchorwoman, by a writer or something.

The reviews of *For Ever Mozart* were respectful if uncomprehending. Many critics limited themselves to describing the film, as if in fear of appearing not to understand its intellectual intricacies. Its blend of melodrama and melancholy, its call for the self-sacrifice of the idealistic young, its depiction of disdain for the wisdom of the elders—for the wisdom of Godard's directorial stand-in, Vicky Vitalis, and its mockery of youthful ignorance induced by pop culture—offered younger viewers little but despair and self-loathing. Lacking stars, the film had no hook but Godard himself; the public stayed away. The film's rapid disappearance meant that it did not succeed in turning Allaux into a popular actress. Godard himself attributed the film's failure to its composite nature, his inability to get the four disparate elements from which he had composed it to coalesce into a dramatic unity. This was a less painful thing to believe than that he was unable to endow Allaux with a star-like allure—or perhaps that she herself was unable to attain it.

The failure of *For Ever Mozart* heralded a breakdown of relations with Allaux. In December, Godard withdrew from his role in Tregenza's film, which had been retitled *Inside/Out*. On January 7, 1997, with the shoot already under way, Godard declared that Tregenza could not use his name or that of the company Peripheria in connection with the film. Several days later, Godard came to Maryland, where Tregenza was shooting, to watch dailies. He also discussed with Tregenza a plan for the ending of *Histoire(s) du cinéma*, where he and Allaux and the crew of *Inside/Out* would be filmed "in Maryland with a 35mm Steenbeck table in the middle of a muddy cow field," the younger filmmaker recalled. But Godard returned to Rolle and did not come back. After Allaux's own return to France, Tregenza sensed that Godard's attitude toward him had changed.[27]

Now, only two outstanding projects with Allaux remained. The actress had spoken glowingly to Godard of her classmates at the Ecole nationale de l'art dramatique in Strasbourg and had suggested that he make a film there, at the school, with her and them.[28] In the fall of 1996, Godard had invited them to work with him on a film about the theater, which, Allaux said, was "his way of being together" with her. Jean-Louis Martinelli, the school's director, welcomed the idea. First, Godard brought the students to Rolle and showed them *JLG/JLG* and *Les Enfants jouent à la Russie.* As one student, Delphine Chuillot, later recalled, he told them, "I don't know the theater, it's up to you to show me what it is," and expressed his willingness to take up a three-month residence at the school to work with the actors at length on a film, but he first wanted their input.[29] Godard sent them copies of *Wilhelm Meister's Apprenticeship,* by Goethe, and asked them to write to him about it; he sent them a video camera and requested that they tape their rehearsals for him.

Yet most of the students seemed uninterested in the project. According to Martinelli, they said, in effect, "Jean-Luc Godard may be important for your generation, but we don't give a shit about him."[30] Martinelli implored them not to pass up this opportunity, but he also suspected the students understood that the project did not truly belong to them collectively but was centered on Allaux. For her part, Allaux sensed the resentment of her peers at her status as first-among-equals. She heard excuses from her classmates for their indifference to Godard's film: some claimed to want to do theater and not cinema; "others said that they didn't want to do a film by Godard but a film by Tarantino." Godard urged her to "break away from the group" and told her "that they were jealous."[31] However, Allaux remained in school, the students did not videotape their acting classes for Godard, and the film was never made.

Godard's final project with Allaux was called *Eloge de l'amour* (In Praise of Love). He described the first version of the script as a film in which "an older man leaves a younger woman for an older one and is happier."[32] The story would take place over the course of seven or eight years, and its action was recursive, working backward in time. The man drives a taxi, and both women are prostitutes. The story featured explicit sex scenes and scenes of horrific sexual violence.

For the role of the man, Godard thought of Jacques Bonnaffé, who had played Joseph in *First Name: Carmen,* and who was now thirty-five years old. As the actor later recalled, Godard told him, "It's good to see you having aged a bit, you can really do something now." Godard described the film to him as "something different. Others call it hard core; I call it hardy."[33] In early 1997, he asked Bonnaffé and Allaux to come to the Peripheria office in

Paris to read scenes together from the synopsis. After the two had read, Godard told them, as Allaux reported, "I need to see your skin, to see whether your skins go together." Both performers were uncomfortable with Godard's request, but they exchanged uneasy glances and complied with it, completely undressing in the office. Allaux remembered: "We said nothing, we stood still, side by side, for a moment, then we got dressed again." Allaux decided then and there not to participate in *Eloge de l'amour*. "I went to have a coffee with Jacques in the café next door, and we agreed that we wouldn't do the film."[34]

Bonnaffé was particularly shocked by a scripted scene in which his character is tortured by a Russian mafioso who rams his hand high into his rectum, takes out a handful of feces, and smears them on the young woman. He let Godard know that he could not do the role; he had children now and did not want to appear in anything that "hard."

When Allaux told Godard that she too refused to do the film, they argued. The two did not see each other again. And yet she continued to inspire his work: after much rethinking, rewriting, and recasting, Godard went on to make *Eloge de l'amour,* which bore even stronger and more personal traces of the relationship than those on display in *For Ever Mozart*. So did a short film that he made immediately after the connection was severed.

IN THE MID-1990S, a young Parisian writer, Philippe Loyrette, made a film in which a friend videotaped him chanting, in psalmodic incantation, the poetic "testament" written by the fanatically anti-Semitic and pro-Nazi French writer Robert Brasillach in 1945 while awaiting execution, for collaboration, in a prison cell near Paris. Loyrette sent a copy of the tape to Godard.

The performance made a strong impression on Godard and he used it as the basis for a videotaped recitation of his own, in 1997, after Allaux ended their personal and working relationship. He called it *Adieu au TNS*. Like Loyrette, Godard used accordion music as the background to his chant. Like Loyrette, Godard intoned a text by himself, standing alone in a bare room. He filmed alone, setting up his camera and beginning each shot by walking to it, turning it on, and then taking his place before the lens. Godard, however, composed his own text, a poem in a classical form of twelve five-line stanzas, in which he lamented having "pursued a princess into a theatre— heavens, what misfortune!"[35]

He never showed the tape publicly. The critic Alain Bergala, to whom he did show it, asked him why not, and, as he later recalled, Godard explained, "I made it on the basis of this other actor and his music, I lost the cassette, so I can't cite the source, it would bother me."[36] Bergala considered this to be a ruse: several years later, Godard found Loyrette's tape, but he still did not show his film.

THE FINAL TWO episodes of *Histoire(s) du cinéma*—4A, *Le Contrôle de l'univers* (The Control of the Universe), which Godard had shown in Toronto in 1996, and 4B, *Les Signes parmi nous* (The Signs Among Us), which was shown at the Cannes festival in May 1997—completed Godard's theoretical reflections on the fallen cinema and on his personal identification with it, while also expressing his undiminished faith in the cinema and submission to its power. Both films are even more intensely personal than the prior episodes.

Le Contrôle de l'univers is focused on Alfred Hitchcock, the exemplary figure of the New Wave's devotion to the American cinema. Godard overlays his voice and Hitchcock's on the sound track: as the classical director is heard describing his conception of montage, Godard explains his principal thesis regarding Hitchcock:

> We have forgotten why Joan Fontaine leans over the edge of a cliff and why Joel McCrea went to Holland. We have forgotten what Montgomery Clift swore to be eternally silent about and why Janet Leigh stops at the Bates Motel and why Teresa Wright is still in love with Uncle Charlie. We forgot what Henry Fonda is not completely guilty of and exactly why the American government hired Ingrid Bergman. But we remember a handbag. But we remember a bus in the desert. But we remember a glass of milk, the blades of a windmill, a hairbrush. But we remember a row of bottles, a pair of glasses, a music score, a clutch of keys. Because, through them, and with them, Alfred Hitchcock succeeded where Alexander, Julius Caesar, Hitler, Napoleon failed: he took control of the universe.

Hitchcock's genius, in Godard's view, was not the ability to sustain narrative suspense but to make images that imprint themselves on the mind. Godard calls him simply "the greatest creator of forms of the twentieth century," and explains that his own devotion to—or seduction by—these forms was the source of inspiration and infatuation in his own artistic youth, when he was first drawn to the cinema. He makes clear that the essence of this artistic faith, and of the power of Hitchcock's and the cinema's forms, is connected to the most deeply intimate of experiences, as indicated in the episode's grand paean to the cinema, recited in the grave and gravelly diction of Alain Cuny:

> The cinema does not weep for us, does not weep over us, because it is with us, because it is us. It is there when the cradle brightens, it is there when the young girl appears to us at the window with her unknowing eyes and a pearl

between her breasts, it is there when we have undressed her, when her naked body trembles with the flutter of our fever, it is there when the woman opens her legs to us with the same maternal emotion with which she opens her arms to a child . . . and it is there when we are dead and our corpse offers the shroud to the arms of our children.

Godard concludes with a tribute to the irresistible power that the cinema, the American cinema, the cinema of Hitchcock, held over him in his youth, the site of his primal possession. On the sound track Godard includes Bérangère Allaux's voice (reading from Jean Genet's text *Le Funambule*) and shows a clip of her crucial scene from *For Ever Mozart*, where she shrieks into the wind. The video breaks the words *Histoire(s) du cinéma* down to the two words *toi né* (you born) and then just *né*. It was from Hitchcock's control of the universe that Godard was born, and with the cinema that he continued, even to doom: among its last images is one of Allaux, in her flouncy red dress from *For Ever Mozart*, running away on the sand dunes, as the title says, "à suivre"—"continued" or "to be followed." By joining images of Allaux (and the need to follow her) to an episode about Hitchcock, Godard likened his own unguarded attachment to the actress to Hitchcock's famously pathetic infatuations with his own actresses. His own possession by the forms of the American cinema, of Hitchcock's cinema, led him, he suggested, down the same path of vain obsession.

The deeply personal aspect of the episode that followed, 4B, is suggested already in its title, *Les Signes parmi nous* (the name of a novel by the Swiss writer Charles Ferdinand Ramuz that Godard had considered filming in 1962) and confirmed by Godard's dedication, "To Anne-Marie Miéville and to myself." It begins with Godard's praise of love—"I now well know which voice I would want to precede my own, to carry me, to invite me to speak, to inhabit my own discourse." It is Miéville's voice, echoing Godard's on the sound track as if they were speaking together from the beyond. Godard then tells the story from the Ramuz novel:

One day a peddler came to a village by the Rhône and he became friends with everyone because he knew how to tell a thousand and one stories, and then a storm broke out and lasted for days and days and the peddler told them that it's the end of the world, but the sun finally came out again and the residents of the village chased the peddler away. This peddler was the cinema. Was the cinema. Was, was, was.

It was and is no more. Godard's ambivalence—toward the beauty of art to which the cinema opened his eyes and to the agonies of the world to which the cinema closed them—is evident when he shows stills of Sartre along with the superimposed text of his famous dismissal of *Citizen Kane:* "Citizen Kane is not an example for us to follow. Orson Welles cares nothing about history." To show exactly which history it was that Godard had in mind, he inserts the following titles: "Israel / Ismael / If I'm not wrong, it's German Jew, Jew Muslim." The invidious and repugnant parallel had also become, for Godard, an indispensable part of his identity, inseparable from his cinematic faith.

The episode, and the colossal series, concludes with a self-portrait in images and words: a still close-up of Godard, in black-and-white, with a rose superimposed over it, as Godard himself recounts a parable by Jorge Luis Borges: "If a man passed through heaven in a dream and received a flower as proof of his passage, and if, on awaking, he found that flower in his hands— what to say then? I was that man."

THE *HISTOIRE(S) DU CINÉMA* were done, but Godard was not done with the series. When he got to the end, he went back to the beginning and re-edited all the parts to make the video effects and the overall tone of the earlier episodes consistent with the later ones. Freddy Buache saw Godard frequently and expressed some concern to Miéville.

> I told Anne-Marie that it seemed to me that with the editing of *Histoire(s) du cinéma,* he was on the brink of madness—he adds an image, then another image on top of it, then a sound, then he changes the first image—I told her that it was a kind of madness. She agreed. He'd get up in the middle of the night to change an image. He could go on doing that for the rest of his life.[37]

Godard knew that he had to stop, but he also knew that he could have gone on—"I would have added, to the six hours, two hundred hours of annexes, like little footnotes"[38]—and actually imagined doing such a job for a DVD release. Though the work was complete, he was unwilling to let go, re-editing it for home video release (to his dismay, on videocassette rather than DVD) by Gaumont. He delivered the sound track to Manfred Eicher of ECM Records, who released it in 1999 as a lavish black box of four audio CDs slipped inside four books of "libretti" featuring the entire text of each episode in French, German, and English, along with stills and a concluding essay by the critic Jonathan Rosenbaum. Godard even considered mounting *Histoire(s) du cinéma* as a stage production in a theater (but never actually did so). The *Histoire(s) du cinéma* did allow him to achieve his lifelong goal of having a book published by the august publishing firm of Gallimard in Paris.

In conjunction with the public presentation and discussion of the first three episodes of *Histoire(s)* at Locarno in August 1995, Godard printed 150 copies of a luxury edition with images and text from the series and, the following month, contacted Gallimard about producing it as a book. Work on the project lasted more than two years; Godard was deeply involved in the layout and tirelessly reviewed the color photos that were printed from his videos.

Gallimard's production supervisor, Jacques Maillot, later recalled, "At first he wanted a very elegant, large format. Then he preferred that it come out in a pocket edition to make it affordable for students."[39] Ultimately Godard chose a large format because, Maillot said, "the small format made it impossible to leave enough white space," but he still worried that the books, which would cost approximately six hundred francs, would be far too expensive for students and young people. At that point, a surprise phone call altered the state of things: the CNC called Godard to ask for reimbursement of the 500,000 francs he had been paid to work with La fémis in 1990. Godard suggested that he instead deliver the money to Gallimard to subsidize the cost of the book. The CNC agreed; as a result, the four sumptuous volumes of image and text cost 490 francs at the time of their release in August 1998.[40]

With the Histoire(s), Godard diversified his fields of creation; he yearned to be accepted as an intellectual among intellectuals, and pinned fond hopes on an appointment to the Collège de France. He had been nominated for a chair at the Collège by the sociologist Pierre Bourdieu, and Jack Lang had also pressed for his admission, but to no avail: reportedly, other members, fearing that Godard would expose the institution to ridicule with his flair for provocation and destabilization, refused to admit him.[41]

Upon completing Histoire(s) du cinéma, he invited the historians François Furet and Pierre Vidal-Naquet (separately) to view the series and discuss it privately with him. They did so, but Godard was dismayed by their curtly complimentary yet condescending responses: "I was expecting [Vidal-Naquet] to debate me, to contradict me on one point or another, some historical choice. Instead, he said to me, 'You're a poet.' " Furet too, as he later said, called him either a poet[42] or a "great painter."[43] Godard had a fierce desire for intellectual discussion. He was the model of an intellectual filmmaker in the eyes of moviegoers and critics, but for professional intellectuals, he remained an aesthete.

The end of Histoire(s) du cinéma found Godard at a plateau of accomplishment—and alone on a high point of Olympian contemplation. He produced three more books of "phrases" published by P.O.L., for Germany Year 90 Nine Zero, Les Enfants jouent à la Russie, and 2 × 50 Years of French Cinema. He worked with Alain Bergala on the second volume of Jean-Luc Godard by Jean-Luc Godard, a collection of interviews, texts, images, and work materials relating to films from *Detective* to unrealized projects to the preliminary synopses for the yet-unrealized *Eloge de l'amour.*

Godard was archiving himself; he was extending his brand name, but he was also extending the reach of the cinema, leaving traces of it in the many art forms and media that it encompassed. Insofar as the cinema—his cinema—was also a project to reclaim the other arts in its name, he was also dispersing the cinema, and his thoughts about it, to those other domains. Reflecting and preserving all culture, the cinema would be reflected and preserved in it as well.

twenty-nine

ELOGE DE L'AMOUR

"I am left only with images"

IN AN OCTOBER 1998 INTERVIEW, GODARD AGAIN INSISTED that a photographic record of the Holocaust must surely exist:

I have no proof of what I'm saying, but I think that if I got to work on it with a good investigative journalist, within twenty years I would find images of the gas chambers. We would see the deportees arriving and we would see in what state they left.[1]

Pursuing the issue further in this discusion, Godard rejected Claude Lanzmann's claim that, if he found an image of the gas chambers, he would "destroy it,"[2] and also Theodor Adorno's declaration that poetry was impossible after Auschwitz.

There's no point to issuing prohibitions like Lanzmann or Adorno, who exaggerate, because then we find ourselves caught up in endless discussions over formulas such as, "It's unfilmable"—one must not prevent people from filming, one must not burn books, or else one can no longer criticize them.[3]

In asserting the importance of such images and such art, Godard made no distinction between archival and newly produced material, between documentary records and fictional reconstructions. As the writer Gérard Wajcman noted in a seminal article in *Le Monde* in December 1998, " 'Saint Paul' Godard versus 'Moses' Lanzmann?" Godard was obsessed with Lanzmann's *Shoah*: "For J.-L. G., it is as if *Shoah*, by its mere presence, 'looked at' the entire cinema,

Godard interviews the historian Jean Lacouture at a hotel in Brittany.
(Courtesy of Hugues Le Paige)

like a sort of Hugolian eye in the tomb of a cinema guilty for fifty years of being a traitor to the real."[4] Wajcman rightly recognized that Lanzmann, in rejecting dramatizations and archival images, posed a formidable challenge to Godard's aesthetic principles and artistic practice. In Wajcman's view, if *Shoah* was a successful act of cinematic redemption through the filmed word, then Godard's condemnation of the cinema as irredeemably fallen was cast in doubt.

The article made an impression on Godard, who agreed to participate in a public discussion with Wajcman at La fémis. The event took place, but Godard was, according to Alain Bergala, a reticent and detached interlocutor: "Godard didn't say a thing. He said, 'I don't understand,' and that was it."[5] Nonetheless, the dialogue was just a warm-up: afterwards, Godard approached Bernard-Henri Lévy (to whom he had recently sent a note of consolation after the troubled release of Lévy's 1997 film *Le Jour et la nuit*)[6] and asked him to arrange a meeting with Lanzmann. Lévy invited Godard and Lanzmann to his home for dinner, along with several other guests (including Alain Sarde and the Canal Plus executive Nathalie Bloch-Laîné).[7] There, Lanzmann told Godard: "Let's not talk about it here, let's have a one-on-one, just you and me. And if you want it to be filmed and shown on television, like with Duras, that's OK."[8]

Just at that time, the producers of a television series on political themes, *Gauche-droite* (Left-Right), invited Godard to make an episode.[9] He proposed filming his discussion with Lanzmann, with Lévy as both moderator and director. Lévy later recalled:

> I was to be the auteur in this film of the three of us. I was like a piece or a card in [Godard's] game. I think that he wanted to make the film because he is an anti-Semite who is trying to be cured. Lanzmann and I were part of the cure. That's fine; I'd like to help an anti-Semite be cured. Like epileptics who feel a seizure coming on, he felt one coming on—a seizure of anti-Semitism. He called on us so he could administer some preventive self-medication. I was ready to play this game.[10]

But then the plan changed once again. Godard now proposed that he have dinner with Lanzmann and Lévy and that each of the three bring a cameraman to film the event. Each of them could then finish his own film and, after watching the others' films, add a five- or ten-minute afterthought. All three works would be shown together as a single program called *Pas un dîner de gala* (Not a Dinner Party), a reference to Mao's line about revolution ("Revolution is not a dinner party"), or else *Le Fameux Débat* (The Great Debate).[11] Godard modeled the idea on televised electoral debates: he would represent the Party of Images and Lanzmann the Party of Words.[12]

To prepare for the great debate at the non-gala dinner, the three men had four preliminary dinners at a location chosen by Godard, the Hôtel Crillon (a place charged with historical significance, as the German occupation headquarters during World War II and then the American headquarters after the Liberation). They ate together, and the project's coproducer Gilles Sandoz ate at another table. "At the four dinners, none of us said a word," Lévy recounted. "Each of us was afraid to be the idiot."[13] After these nondiscussions, Lanzmann withdrew from the project. According to Lévy, Lanzmann was afraid of being "caught in a trap."[14] For his part, Lanzmann was wary of the setup; he recalled that he was willing to do a televised debate, but not a "competition" of films with Godard and Lévy.[15]

YET THE GREAT debate nonetheless continued, if one-sidedly, in *Eloge de l'amour*, the film that Godard had been planning since late 1996. Its main characters are Jewish, and the film is imbued with the memory of the Holocaust—a memory which Godard renders mainly in images and which does not depend on testimony. As such, it is Godard's response to Lanzmann and to *Shoah*. But at the same time, in its dramatization of the Holocaust from the standpoint of the present day, without recourse to fictionalized reconstructions of wartime events, *Eloge de l'amour* is also Godard's response to Steven Spielberg's *Schindler's List*. And, finally, Godard also joins the memory of the Holocaust to that of the French Resistance, and, as such, responds to the French film *Lucie Aubrac*, the 1997 biopic of the famous resister, directed by Claude Berri.

With *Eloge de l'amour*, Godard turned the unquenchable flow of meditations and associations that he had channeled into *Histoire(s) du cinéma*—and specifically, those concerning history—toward his feature filmmaking, but to an entirely different end. Having completed the *Histoire(s)*—the product of a twenty-five-year quest to realize, on film, a fifty-year identification of himself and the cinema—he made *Eloge de l'amour* as radically different from his recent work as those films were from his work of the 1960s.

In *Eloge de l'amour*, Godard fulfilled in fiction the project of uniting his personal history and the history of cinema with political and social history. He used classical cinematographic means and modern video technology to join audiovisual history with the traces of his own earlier self. The film's dramatic narrative would reach back to his earlier experiences while looking ahead to a world of diminished cinematic possibilities in which fragments of cinematic history would nonetheless persist and endure—albeit in other spheres. *Eloge de l'amour* is a film of history in which the past is revealed to live in the present, as in *Shoah*. Godard depicts the attempt to live with a full consciousness of the presence of ambient history, and this effort becomes a motor of fiction more powerful than the nonreflexive fiction of *Schindler's List*. Moreover, honor is paid to a living heroine, Lucie Aubrac, of the French Resistance, by a much greater intellectual and emotional fidelity to her complex and ambiguous experience than in Berri's naturalistic hagiography—as well as by the attempt to draw out the present-day implications of her life and struggle.

The thematic and formal originality of *Eloge de l'amour* was reflected in the practical aspects of its production. *Eloge de l'amour* was constructed with greater forethought than any other film Godard had made. The draft scripts evolved drastically, indeed unrecognizably, from the original impulse that gave rise to the story; the shoot stretched out over the longest period of any in Godard's career; and, taking great care with casting, Godard found actors, and in particular, a young lead actor, with whom he could finally do extensive preparatory work regarding the film's intellectual substance as well as diction and performance.

After *Breathless* and *Sauve qui peut*, *Eloge de l'amour* would be Godard's third first film. It fulfilled the promise of the title: its love story is Godard's least inhibited and most ardent. And the sinuous, exacting processes by which it developed, from version to version of the script and from conception to realization, indicated his extraordinary care and devotion to the film, as if it ran the risk of being also his last.

In the earliest version of the scenario for *Eloge de l'amour*, Godard described a story in which "an older man leaves a younger woman for an older one and is happier."[16] There, the plot is centered on the young woman, who shoots the man when he leaves her. The second version, the one rejected by Bérangère Allaux and Jacques Bonnaffé, involved a book editor who wants to publish a first novel by a young woman, Katyusha, a Russian ex-prostitute who is in jail for the shooting. In a notably self-pitying self-reference by Godard to himself and Miéville, the older man, Franck, ends up with the older woman, Yvonne, homeless but happy.[17] (Regarding that version, with its sex and violence, Godard said, "It's very bad, it's horrible; fortunately I didn't make it.")[18]

For the third version, composed after the departure of Allaux and Bonnaffé, Godard extracted and distilled several essential elements of the original story, primarily the problem of age difference. It was extremely schematic, with twelve sequences about three couples, young, adult, and elderly, who separate and then get back together again. This version, too, was abandoned, though traces of it remain in the final film, including the story of a young couple, Perceval and Eglantine, who meet at a political protest and reunite while volunteering at a homeless shelter.

The names are taken from Godard's reading: Perceval is from Robert Walser's novel *La Rose,* from which Godard cites that character's declarations of love ("I love you so much, you are so much there all the time, you exist so strongly for me, forever, that it is from now on pointless for me to see you again; since you will always be there, whatever happens"). Eglantine, from the eponymous novel by Jean Giraudoux, is a servant girl who turns into a woman of the world, first becoming the lover of Moïse, a Jewish banker, and then leaving him for Fontranges, a landed French aristocrat.

Eglantine's Jewish connection is evident in the first scene of Godard's synopsis: she is attending a protest while wearing a yellow star sewn on her jacket, and Perceval meets her in the grocery store where she seeks refuge after she has been beaten by counter-demonstrators. (The pairing of the two names is itself an act of historical montage: both books were published at approximately the same time—*La Rose* in 1925; *Eglantine* in 1927.)

As ever, when Godard found himself without a theme to orient a project, he turned to the cinema: the fourth version of *Eloge de l'amour,* dated May 1998, had a new title, *Voulez-vous faire du cinéma?* (Do You Want to Do Cinema? or Do You Want to Be in Pictures?). It comprised two sections, the first with that title, the second to be called *Eloge de l'amour.* And it began with the story of a young couple, Ludovic and Isabelle, who are engaged to be married.

In the first section, Ludovic and Isabelle quarrel and separate after an acrimonious weekend at the home of Isabelle's grandparents. The grandparents, who had been illustrious activists in the French Resistance, have received an offer from Steven Spielberg to buy the rights to their life story. Isabelle, a beginning actress, approves, hoping there might be something in it for her; the young man disapproves, breaks the engagement, and leaves.

In the second section, a man in Paris, who is heard but not seen, is seeking actors for a project called *Eloge de l'amour.* His assistant helps him look for a young woman he had once known, a waitress who "seemed interesting to him, very demanding but without arrogance." It turns out to be the same Isabelle. The man finds her working as a cleaning woman, but fails to persuade her to take part in the film, and accompanies her to the métro. They pass before a plaque dedicated to the memory of a "keeper of the peace officer [a policeman] killed by the Germans" and she declares, "It shouldn't be written like that." He never sees her again; sometime later, he learns that she has died of tuberculosis.

This version of *Eloge de l'amour,* much of which went into the final film, is transfigured by history: Godard streamed into it an extraordinary amount of political history, personal history, and the history of cinema. He selected Brittany as the site of the grandparents' house for reasons both personal and

political. That part of France is where he went on his childhood summer vacations with his family ("I think that childhood vacations have unconscious
and psychological repercussions in a man's life").[19] It also has special significance for the French Resistance, as Godard explained: "I chose Brittany in
reference to Breton sailors who were the first to leave for London and join de
Gaulle. Land of Catholicism, it also is the cradle of Colonel Rémy, the great
resister and founder of the Confrérie Notre-Dame," a Catholic resistance
group.[20]

The new story was also marked by an encounter that had affected Godard a few years earlier. After seeing *Hélas pour moi* in 1994, a young woman
from Bordeaux, Isabelle C., wrote to him. In response, Godard asked to meet
her. She was a young woman in difficult straits; having broken with her family as a teenager, she had not finished her schooling. She was a prodigious autodidact of literature and cinema; she had an unusual speculative aptitude
and an intense, peremptory tone of voice. She wrote with an energized emotional immediacy. She was hardly working, getting by with odd jobs and
manual labor. She came to Paris to see Godard and wondered why he chose
to respond to her letter among the hundreds that he must surely receive; he
answered that he found her writing "exalted." He asked her why people seek
to make personal contact with artists they admire: "If I saw Dostoyevsky in
the street, I wouldn't invite him to have a coffee." She asked Godard for a job.
He told her, "It's not that easy," and asked her what type of work she thought
she could do for him. After hours of discussion, much of it centered on literature, the meeting ended, with Godard offering to pay for her ticket back to
Bordeaux.[21] Much of what Godard saw in Isabelle C. made its way into the
film.

The other crucial addition to Godard's fourth version of the story is the
figure of the artist, the man in Paris, who appears only in the shadows—a
stand-in for Godard. *Eloge de l'amour* became a film about Godard attempting to make a film about people who were involved with Steven Spielberg.
The actual shadow-"project" of the shadow-creator resembled the third version of *Eloge de l'amour*, concerning three couples, young, adult, and elderly,
but with one caveat, which he wrote into the new scenario: though he had no
trouble identifying young people and old people, depicting "adults," he said,
was difficult.

If one sees them at a protest, for instance, one doesn't say, 'There go adults
protesting.' One says: truck drivers, teachers, nurses. One must add their role
(their job) in society to define the adult. That's not so for the young or the old.
So, farewell documentary and hello Hollywood.

Meaning, farewell to a film based on Godard's own personal experience of reality, and hello to a film that is governed not by the facts but by a scripted preconception.

The question of youth and age followed on the problem, suggested in *Hélas pour moi*, regarding the handing-down of an artistic tradition. In *For Ever Mozart*, Godard had filmed age differences despairingly, as the old director in effect cannibalized the young to nourish his art, and the young, uninformed by the artistic practice of their elders, made poor use of their noble passions. Now, in *Eloge de l'amour*, Godard began with a story of predatory youth—a reflection of Bérangère Allaux's devastating effect on him—and ended up making a film about the tragic burden of his artistic legacy as endured by the young.

THE WITHDRAWAL OF Allaux and Bonnaffé in early 1997 had left Godard in a state of doubt and the project dangling. He soon met, through an agent, the young actress Marie Desgranges, and considered her for the part of Eglantine, but then told her that the shoot was off. Two years later, he asked her to come to his office, listened to her read a text by Brecht, and signed a contract with her for a shoot that would run from September through November 1999.[22] His expectations went far beyond the usual: he told Desgranges that he wanted to learn how an actress "enters the inner life," and so, he asked her personal questions (warning her, "You must tell me everything, or else it's worthless") and wanted her to question him frankly in return. She spoke freely with him and considers that she fell into his "trap."[23] Godard fired her shortly before the start of the shoot.

Marie Desgranges's name does not appear in the credits of *Eloge de l'amour*, but two shots of her appear in the film—camera tests, done by the crew in Godard's absence, on a bench in the streets of Paris. In those images, she resembles, with her furtive, wounded look, lean angularity, and involuted ferocity, Isabelle C. These two images, live-action pentimenti, have a valedictory quality, reflecting Godard's nostalgic curiosity about the film that might have been made with Desgranges as well as a farewell to the woman, who, in a single brief meeting, left such a deep and substantial mark on the film.

Godard filled the role of the assistant to the unnamed artist with a non-actor who had made a big impression on him in another domain. In late 1998, Godard wrote to Philippe Loyrette, the writer who had sent him a videocassette of his chant of Robert Brasillach's "Testament," the performance on which the video *Adieu au TNS* was based. He admitted that he had lost Loyrette's cassette but said that he had recently recovered it—and had clipped a moment of the incantation into a re-edited version of *Histoire(s) du cinéma*, a cassette of which he enclosed.[24] In addition, he invited Loyrette to play the role of Philippe, the assistant in *Eloge de l'amour*, and to intone Brasillach's text on-screen in the course of the film.[25]

But the actor who would play the young creator proved hard to find. In February 1999, Godard saw a film by Jean-Claude Guiguet, *Les Passagers* (The Passengers), was impressed by its young lead, Bruno Putzulu, and invited him to his Paris office. When Putzulu arrived, Godard immediately asked whether he might videotape him while they spoke. He gave Putzulu a text to read aloud; after the recitation, Godard praised him for having delivered it "without adding anything." The next day, Godard called to offer him the part—explaining that the actor would remain off-screen and be only heard on the sound track in discussion with other performers.

Putzulu was an authentic young star—he had just received the 1999 César award for "jeune espoir masculin" (most promising actor).[26] Yet he had no objection to Godard's plan, which, ultimately, was abandoned, since Putzulu appears on-screen in a true starring role.[27]

Having hired his actor, Godard fired his actress, and auditioned, according to his assistant Fleur Albert, fifty others, calling back six of them to read with Putzulu. Cécile Camp was chosen. "On Monday he called me to tell me I'd got it," Camp reported. "We started to shoot on Wednesday."[28]

ELOGE DE L'AMOUR is centered on a young man's work on a "project"—in effect, a film without its apparatus—and his relationship with a young woman whom he seeks to enlist in it. The film is constructed as a flash-back: its first section, which runs an hour, takes place two years after the second, shorter section. As a result, many of the events in the film's first half remain unclear until the flashback provides retrospective clarity. Yet the film's initial ambiguities serve an unusual function: having elaborated the story over such a long period of time and woven into it so many strands of history and personal associations, Godard leaves many loose narrative threads, as if to invite an unusually free interpretive viewing. More than any of his prior films, *Eloge de l'amour* derives its significance from the wealth of particular incidents, lines of dialogue, gestures, and nuances of which it is composed; despite the intellect that the film embodies and the ideas it reflects, *Eloge de l'amour* is Godard's most concrete and analogical work, the one which is most closely identifiable with the events that take place within it.

The first section, which is filmed in black and white, is set in Paris. A young man, Edgar (Putzulu), is seeking actors to play Eglantine and Perceval for a "project" regarding the four stages of love: "the encounter," "physical

passion," "separation," and "reunion." Among the candidates are a young
woman from North Africa, who listens to Edgar tell the story of Eglantine
being beaten at a protest while wearing a yellow star, and a pale and fragile
woman and a gentle, elfin man who jointly audition for the roles of Eglantine
and Perceval by reciting lines from Walser's *La Rose*. (The scene, a real audition at an office, was filmed in February 1999, well before the actual shoot
had begun. In the scene as filmed, Godard himself was heard off-camera in
discussion with the candidates, but Putzulu's voice was later dubbed in
speaking Godard's lines.)

Periodically, Edgar visits an older man, an art dealer named Rosenthal,
who supports him and subsidizes his project. The family connections between Edgar and Rosenthal run deep: Rosenthal's father and Edgar's grandfather were partners in a gallery; both were both deported to concentration
camps, and Rosenthal was also in love with Edgar's mother, who married another man and eventually committed suicide. Now Rosenthal is in frequent
discussion with his attorney—Paul Forlani, played in fact by Godard's longtime acquaintance Rémo Forlani—over the restitution of artwork stolen
from his family by German occupiers. (Godard's choice of the name Rosenthal also runs deep: in Renoir's *Rules of the Game*, it is the name of the
mother of the Marquis de la Chesnaye, the owner of the manor, who is identified as a Jew; and it alludes to Paul Rosenberg, a French Jewish art dealer
who was, at the time, involved in just such a suit.) Rosenthal asks Edgar
about his "project"; Edgar explains its subject, the three ages of love—youth,
adulthood, old age—and the impossibility of finding adults, and he mentions his difficulty in finding an actress for it. Rosenthal encourages Edgar to
seek out a particular woman whom the young man had once known and had
described as "not very attractive, but she dared to say things."

Following up on rumors he'd heard, Edgar tracks the woman down to a
depot on the outskirts of Paris, where she is working the night shift cleaning
trains. When he approaches her, she refuses him outright. He wants to speak
with her more, but she still has offices to clean and on the weekend will have
to drive her son to see an uncle in the provinces.

Edgar continues to audition performers, but is dissatisfied with them all.
To explain to one of them what is missing from her recitation of a text, he
asks his assistant, Philippe, to show her how it should be done, and Philippe
intones the Brasillach poem. Ultimately, Edgar finds the young woman
again, at a bookstore in a Montparnasse passageway, where she is attending a
conference with the American journalist Mark Hunter (a real journalist living in Paris) on the subject of Kosovo, specifically on "the judgment of war
crimes."

After the conference, Edgar and the as-yet-nameless young woman walk through Paris from night until morning, stopping at a plaque on the Pont Neuf that reads, "Here, René Revel, keeper of the peace of the 15th arrondissement, Knight of the Legion of Honor, was killed by the Germans on August 19, 1944." She says, "It should not be said like that. Neither 'keeper' nor 'peace,' nor 'the Germans.'" The next day, the two face the île Seguin, an islet in the Seine and the site of a former Renault plant, now closed and empty—"the empty fortress," the woman calls it—where she tells the story of her parents, who (like Edgar's mother) committed suicide. (Her father killed himself in 1970, she says, when she was five years old.)

She asks Edgar what he thinks of "what happened" in Brittany (referring—as is not yet clear from the film's action—to their prior relationship, which ended two years earlier). Edgar says that she was right, then, to say that "the Americans"—those of the North, she specifies, "not the Mexicans, not Brazil"—"have no memory of their own, or very little. Their machines do, yes, maybe, but not them personally, so they buy that of others, especially of those who resisted." After their discussion, Edgar returns to town—first entering and leaving a train at a station marked "Drancy-Avenir" (Drancy-Future). Drancy is a town north of Paris where the Vichy regime had established a staging area for transports to Auschwitz.

Having planted in the film a vast and intricate set of political, historical, and personal references, Godard then offers the most breathtakingly intimate love scene in his entire body of work: a single shot, almost three minutes long, of the young woman sitting at the desk of the bookstore, talking on the telephone to Edgar. His voice is heard only in the first sentence ("I wonder who had the brilliant idea to speak of the future at Drancy"). The rest of the shot, in which the woman is far from the camera and hidden in shadow, features only her voice, her side of the conversation. She refuses to reveal where she lives; she tells him to write to her care of the bookstore; she asks why he no longer speaks of his project; she says that she wants nothing to do with it—"I'm not pretty enough"—and, seemingly in response to his protest, adds, "On the contrary, I think that's what you think." She tells him, "You win, I was just smiling," and asks him to repeat slowly the phrase that had made her smile, which she then recites back to him: "Each thought should recall the ruins of a smile." Then she makes a confession, the significance of which becomes retrospectively clear only during the film's second part: "You know, when I drove you after your meeting with Jean Lacouture, I left too, they've had no news of me since then. I was in the same train as you, I saw you at Montparnasse, I said to myself that one must let things take their course."

Rosenthal and Philippe join Edgar for something like a staging of the "project" at a homeless shelter, where the two young actors seen auditioning

for Eglantine and Perceval perform a scene in which they reunite while soap-
ing a man's back. The scene is enacted for no camera and no audience, as a
sort of private or command performance for the creators themselves.

Finally, in a flash forward, Edgar meets the woman's grandfather (along
with an unidentified man) at a café, to learn what has become of her. The
grandfather tells him, "We received a letter from Amsterdam; there are people over there who help those who want to put an end to things." He brings
several books from among which she had wanted Edgar to take one; Edgar
chooses *Le Voyage d'Edgar*—a 1938 adventure book by Edouard Peisson,
mentioned by Johnny Hallyday in *Detective*, that Godard had loved as a
child.

Her grandfather reproaches Edgar for not having pursued his "project"
and tells him that she believed in it. Edgar responds, "One doesn't kill oneself
for that." He asks Edgar, "Did you know her well?" Edgar answers, "I didn't
even know her name, nor yours, for that matter. In your hotel, we talked for
seven or eight minutes, and the same when we saw each other again, no
more. The tone of her voice interested me, the ideas often became very lively;
for the rest, she was a disappointment." The old man tells him, "You're the
disappointment."

This seems like the end of the film, but it is only the one-hour mark. After a close-up of the book *Le Voyage d'Edgar*, the film bursts from black-and-
white into brilliant, acidic color, a seascape with the sea a fiery orange and
the sky an acrid yellow, an image that introduces the title card "Two Years
Earlier."

Edgar walks down a country road and a car stops for him. The driver
identifies himself as (and in fact is) Jean-Henri Roger, a filmmaker and Godard's associate in the Dziga Vertov Group. Roger plays, in his own name, a
regional cultural counselor in Brittany. (He is recognizable as the man who
accompanied the woman's grandfather at the café.) Edgar explains that he
has come to do research about Catholics in the Resistance, in preparation for
"a cantata about Simone Weil"—the Jewish philosopher who converted to
Catholicism and sought to be active in the Resistance. Roger offers to show
him archives left by his own great-uncle, Gilbert Renaud, the famed resister,
"Colonel Rémy" of the Confrérie Notre-Dame.

Almost from the beginning of the sequence, Godard's attention is fixed
on the United States, as a car pulls up beside Roger's and a brassy African-
American woman impatiently asks for directions. Roger tells Edgar that she
is "one of the Americans who are bugging us." It soon becomes clear which
Americans Roger is referring to, when he and Edgar arrive at their destina-
tion: a hotel belonging to an elderly couple, where Edgar has been invited to
meet and interview Jean Lacouture, the historian and journalist (who also

plays himself), about the Catholics and the Resistance. Lacouture explains that the hotel's proprietors are "two former Resisters who have sold their memory to Hollywood" in order to keep their hotel running.

At the hotel, the owner's wife, Madame Bayard, has a meeting with two people from Hollywood—the African-American woman and a man, Lemmy (played by Lemmy Constantine, the son of Eddie Constantine)—as well as one man from Washington, "Sumner Welles Jr." (The young woman from the first part of the film, referred to in passing as Berthe—not Isabelle—is also present.) Welles explains his presence at the gathering, in response to a question from Berthe: "Do please understand, my dear young lady, that Washington is the real director of the ship, and that Hollywood is—forgive me, Lemmy—only the steward."

While this meeting takes place upstairs, Edgar is downstairs with Jean Bayard, who owns the hotel. Jean explains that his granddaughter, Berthe, "got sick, stopped everything, and now works in Paris in a lawyer's office." Jean also talks about his wartime past, telling Edgar that the "intelligence service" of their Resistance network had asked him to work for the Gestapo as a double agent, and that as a result, "many people died." As Edgar later learns from Berthe, Jean had been ordered to denounce Madame Bayard, as a result of which she was sent to Ravensbrück; they married upon her liberation.

The Hollywood meeting upstairs continues. The grandmother listens to Lemmy read the contract: "Our company, Spielberg Associates and Incorporated [*sic*], has acquired the rights . . . to tell this man and woman's story from the terrible years of '41, '42, '43 and '44." The film would be called *Tristan and Isolde*, the name of the network of resisters; the script would be written by William Styron, and the role of the young Madame Bayard would be played by "Juliette Binoche, who has just received an Oscar."

Berthe interrogates the young executive—"objection, your honor"—on his description of William Styron as an "American writer," asking, "Which 'American' do you mean?" He says, "Obviously, someone from the United States." "Obviously," she answers, "but Brazil is also made up of united states." He says "of North America," and she responds, "Mexico is also made up of united states of North America, and those people are called Mexicans; Canada too, and they are called Canadians."

She continues: "So what is the name of what you call your United States? You see, you have no name. This agreement has been signed with the representative of a country the inhabitants of which have no name. It's no surprise that they need other people's stories, other people's legends," and she suggests that "since you don't have a long history, you go looking for it from others, in Vietnam, in Sarajevo." Lemmy Constantine reminds her that the

Bayards have cashed their first check, for fifty thousand dollars. Berthe reads another clause—"In all the films, all the young girls must get undressed and roll around with their lovers"—and asks her grandmother, "Is that really your story with Grandfather?" Lemmy says, "Steven gave me a cassette of his film, *Schindler's List,* so that Madame Bayard can verify the seriousness of his intentions."

Berthe and Edgar (who have seen each other for an instant, through a window, in an astonished glance that seems like love at first sight) meet after the discussion has broken up. She has come downstairs to search for a video-cassette recorded by her grandfather. "There is a terrible image there," she says, "the gaze of the guilty upon the innocent," and Godard includes a clip of it on-screen: an image of a man, who resembles Hitler, gazing at a pile of naked corpses. When she enters the room downstairs, Jean and Edgar are talking at a table, with books before them, and Jean reads several passages, including one from Sartre: "Today, August 20, 1945, in this deserted and starving Paris, the war has ended but the peace has not yet begun."

As Edgar goes to take his leave, Berthe pulls him aside to ask, "When did the gaze founder?" Edgar answers, "Ten years ago, fifteen, perhaps fifty years ago, before television." The two continue to talk, and Edgar asks about the contract discussion. Berthe answers, "Jean wants money because the hotel is failing. As for her, I don't know, I think that she wants to be a star the way she was sixty years ago, with the Tristan network."

Berthe goes back to see her grandmother and brings a book from Jean Lacouture ("Godfather Jean"): Robert Bresson's *Notes on Cinematography,* from which Berthe reads aloud. She then asks her grandmother about her wartime experiences; the grandmother says that when she was a young girl traveling in the United States and was asked about the concentration camps, she "babbled always the same memories, and people reacted as they do now, before their television screens," but, she adds, "I didn't inhabit my words." Berthe then asks why she herself has her father's family name, Samuel, whereas her grandmother still calls herself by her nom de guerre, Bayard. The grandmother does not answer.

After two children in folkloric costumes come to the hotel door with a petition "seeking signatures to get *The Matrix* shown in Breton," Berthe drives Edgar to the train station for his return to Paris. In the car, Edgar tells her that he separated recently from a woman he had been with for ten years, and adds, "It's strange, how things take on meaning when they're finished." She tells him, "You know the saying of Saint Augustine, 'The measure of love is to love without measure.' "

Edgar arrives at Montparnasse Station in Paris and remains in the train with a copy of Chateaubriand's *Mémoires d'outre-tombe* open in front of him, and says, "This is how everything in my story vanishes, how I am left only with images of what happened so quickly. I will go down the Champs-Elysées with more shadows than any man ever brought along." As he crosses the platform, words spoken at the beginning of the film, taken from Edgar's audition with a candidate for a role in his "project," are heard in voice-over: "Do you remember the names? Perhaps we didn't say it. Perhaps we didn't say it. Perhaps we didn't say it. Perhaps we didn't say it."

WITH THE FILM'S casting, a crucial element of its emotional and historical import, Godard initiates his elaborate play of associations. The only professional actors are Bruno Putzulu, Cécile Camp, and Jean Davy (the grandfather). The grandmother is played by Françoise Verny, a venerable editor at Gallimard, who was ill and struggling for breath. Godard said of Verny, "She'd been one of the queens of Paris literary production, a bit like Lucie Aubrac was a queen of the Resistance."[29]

Jean Lacouture, who plays himself, had known Godard since 1967, when the writer served as what he called a "political adviser" on the collective project *Far from Vietnam,* but they had not seen each other for many years. In mid-1999, Godard invited Lacouture to his office, explained that an important aspect of his new film concerned the relations of Catholics and Communists during the Resistance, and asked Lacouture to appear on-camera and talk on the subject, in his own name. Lacouture agreed, on the condition that he speak in his own words. Godard agreed, and then, after telling him the story of the film, added that there would be a scene in which Lacouture would have to take a stand on whether the pair of aged Resistance heroes had the "right" to sell their story to Steven Spielberg. Lacouture told Godard at once that he would advise them to do it—he admired *Schindler's List* and considered Spielberg "a great artist"—provided that the couple had the right to approve the screenplay.[30]

Lacouture had obviously given the wrong answer, as he discovered when he arrived for the shoot in Brittany with his text in favor of Spielberg. First, Godard induced him to play a short scripted scene with Davy; then Godard filmed Lacouture saying his speech on behalf of Spielberg, which, of course, ended up on the cutting-room floor. Then Godard videotaped an hourlong interview with Lacouture about Simone Weil's request to General de Gaulle that he let her parachute into France for the Resistance. De Gaulle had refused; soon thereafter, Weil died of hunger in London, and, as Lacouture later said, "Godard considers de Gaulle guilty of that."[31]

The rest of the cast was filled out with non-actors who were of both historical and personal significance to Godard. Philippe Loyrette, Jean-Henri
Roger, and Lemmy Constantine were all connected to his past. Rosenthal
was played by Claude Baignères, the longtime film critic for Le Figaro.[32]
Rémo Forlani, who played Rosenthal's attorney, had written the faux script
for Pierrot le fou. In a scene in the passageway to the Montparnasse bookstore, a crowd gathers around a magician: Bruno Mesrine, the son of the
legendary gangster Jacques Mesrine, about whom Godard had wanted to
make a film with Jean-Paul Belmondo in the late 1970s. Outside a movie
theater in the same arcade, two people are on line to see Bresson's Pickpocket: Noël Simsolo, the critic who had done fifteen radio interviews with
Godard concerning Histoire(s) du cinéma in 1989 and 1998; and Marceline
Loridan-Ivens, whom Godard had known for decades[33] and who was herself a survivor of Auschwitz.[34]

These personal relations produced an unusual degree of calm during
the shoot. When Godard called Roger about a role in the film, they hadn't
spoken since 1990, when, shortly after the death of Roger's wife, Juliet Berto
(whom Godard had "discovered" as an actress in 1966), he invited the
grieving man to visit him. At the time, Godard told Roger, "I don't have the
desire to make films anymore; it takes the crew, the people, the money."
Roger thought that Godard preferred "to tinker with video" in a studio that
seemed to him to resemble in its isolation "a submarine." While casting Eloge, Godard called Roger to suggest that they "talk together again." Roger
found him more open than before and the working environment in Brittany
conducive to "a rapport of discussion." Roger attributed this openness to the
fruitful exchange that took place between Godard and Putzulu: "It's been a
long time since he had an actor with whom he could speak. He speaks with
Putzulu."[35]

Indeed, Putzulu (born in 1967) and Godard had an extraordinarily
frank working relationship. Some on the set wondered how the two would
get along, given Godard's intellectual inclinations and Putzulu's reputation as
a man's man of an actor. Superficially, their point of contact was sports: the
athletic Putzulu had played soccer and boxed, and the two often discussed
sports when they had a free moment. But, more important, Putzulu is a serious, thoughtful, and dedicated actor, whose great admiration for Godard's
films translated into an intense devotion to the practical and contemplative
demands of the text and the situations his performance involved. The two
often exchanged letters, before and after the shoot, and had long conversations about acting.

Prior to the beginning of the shoot, Godard had expressed his respect for Putzulu, seeking the actor's input regarding the six actresses

who were candidates to take over the lead female role.[36] Moreover, Godard drew upon the substance of his discussions with the actor for the film's dialogue. As Putzulu later recalled: "One day, he asked me, 'How are you?' I said, 'Not very well.' He said, 'Why?' I said, 'I separated from a woman with whom I had been together for ten years. It's only afterwards, when things are finished, that they take on sense.' And he put that in the film."[37]

Putzulu approached his work with Godard not only with a deep respect for the filmmaker, but also with a craftsmanlike pride in his own performance, which prompted him to speak to Godard with an unusual directness. The concrete result of this was Godard's air of controlled calm during the shoot. During the first scene with Putzulu and Cécile Camp, Godard, according to the actor, "did not really know what to do." The scene, which was set on a train in the yard, involved extras, and Godard had trouble organizing it. As Putzulu later recalled:

> He yelled, and so I yelled too: "If that's how it's going to be, I don't see how I'm going to put up with it!" The next day, he asked me to come to his office. I thought he was going to fire me. He said, "You yelled." I said, "You yelled too." He laughed and said, "But *why* did you yell?" I told him, "Conflict is natural in the cinema, on a shoot, it comes by itself and one deals with it, but I had the impression that you created conflict and were working against the film." And afterward, he didn't yell.[38]

Despite the collegial atmosphere, however, the familiar tensions of a Godard shoot flared with one performer—Camp, who played Berthe.

Camp has a commanding, oracular voice that seemed to rise from deep in her chest yet also as if from outside her. She knew that Godard had chosen her mainly for her voice, and thought that the lines in the film about Berthe, such as "She's not very attractive" and "She was a disappointment," were meant for her personally. As she recalled: "During the shoot, he told me, 'I don't want people to say that I change actors all the time, but if I had had more money, I might have changed.' " Camp also took the fact of her having been filmed almost exclusively in shadow as proof that Godard found her unattractive.[39] Moreover, Camp is visibly taller than Putzulu and, as she recalled, Godard told her that "it's important. That's how it's clear that it isn't physical or carnal love, that you aren't a couple."

Both Putzulu and Fleur Albert observed the tension between Godard and Camp. Albert thought that Camp was paying the price for Godard's frustrations with Marie Desgranges; Putzulu thought that it had to do with Godard's "woman problem" as such.[40] In practical terms, Camp had done overtime work in Brittany for which she was supposed to be paid, and Godard told her, "But you worked badly, so I can't do it."[41]

Indeed, Camp's performance has little of what usually constitutes, in a film by Godard or anyone else, an actor's accomplishment: she has no close-ups and is almost always seen at oblique angles or in obscuring shadows. Yet in one crucial respect—the intellectual and moral power with which she infuses her character—Camp is the strongest female performer in Godard's cinema. For the first time, in *Eloge de l'amour*, he filmed a female character in supreme command of her intellect, a woman of exceptional determination and philosophical insight. The only woman of comparable strength in Godard's work is Anne-Marie Miéville herself.

THE ENTIRE SHOOT of *Eloge* took place under the sign of memory. For Godard, merely filming in black and white on the streets of Paris was a plunge into memory, an active reminiscence of the early days of the New Wave. Godard chose locations that held personal significance, places where he had lived or filmed, including Montparnasse and the place de la Concorde (which figures in *Breathless*), yet to get them on film, Godard sent the crew without him—as if to find images that were not only his own recollections but also derived from a shared or collective memory.

The café where Edgar meets Berthe's grandfather and Jean-Henri Roger, La Favorite, on the boulevard St.-Michel, was where Godard and Roger had coffee every morning during the Maoist years.[42] Another café that features in the film, La Liberté, is the one that Sartre frequented in his last years (at the moment that the café appears, Forlani says, "Tout va bien"—the name of the film Godard made at a time when he joined Sartre in militant activity). The next shot shows the café L'Odessa, across the boulevard Edgar-Quinet from La Liberté, at the intersection of the rue du Montparnasse, the rue Delambre, the rue d'Odessa, and the rue de la Gaîté; this intersection is known as the "crossroads of Erostratus," from Sartre's story "Erostratus" (in the collection *The Wall*, published in 1939), in which a young man named Paul Hilbert plots random murders around the possibility of escape from that very junction.

Godard gives himself a cameo in Montparnasse, showing himself sitting on a bench at night and reading a book as a lighthearted young couple sits back-to-back with him and the busy nocturnal circulation of people and traffic swirls behind him; overhead, a large neon sign for a Gaumont movie theater dominates the opposite corner. This cameo of near-immobility is actually a pointed exposition of Godard's method and of his mode of self-presentation, which turns on a small moment of urban life and a keen attention to details that, once noticed, alters perception forever: a Parisian film critic erroneously described Godard filming himself in the "Place Montparnasse," when in fact the official name for the great and fabled crossroads is the place du 18 juin 1940. June 18, 1940, is the date of General Charles de Gaulle's epochal speech on the BBC, popularly titled L'Appel, the Call, exhorting the French people to resist German rule. Godard places himself in the spot of the date of the call; his preferred form of resistance is to read—and to film himself doing so.

THE FIRST LINE of Eloge, spoken to a young woman being interviewed for a project, is: "Do you remember the names? Perhaps we didn't mention it." The film is constructed around the significance of a young woman's name, which is mentioned so casually that viewers of the film often fail to identify it. While the granddaughter's name is Berthe Samuel, she is never actually called that. Her first name is said only twice, in passing.[43] At first, Godard told Cécile Camp that her character was called Iphigenia—who is prepared for sacrifice by her father, Agamemnon. That name was replaced simply by "she," and only later by Berthe. The name had appeared in a book published in September 1999 (just as the shoot was getting under way) by the French historian Annette Wieviorka, Auschwitz expliqué à ma fille (Auschwitz Explained to My Daughter), in which the survivor of Auschwitz who recounts her experiences is an elderly woman named Berthe.

Berthe's last name, Samuel, a conspicuously Jewish one, is the actual family name of Raymond Aubrac and the married name of Lucie Aubrac, before the war. In the film, the young woman's last name is revealed only when she asks her grandmother why she kept her nom de guerre, Bayard. Though the grandmother does not answer, Godard himself posed the same question during interviews: why did many French Jews, such as Marcel Bloch, the French aviation pioneer, who took the name Dassault during the war, or Jean-Pierre Grumbach, who called himself Melville in the Resistance, keep their new names after the Liberation?

Berthe's explanation for her grandmother's name is that Madame Bayard is attempting to keep the war going, at least for herself, since the Resistance provided the most meaningful years of her life. In interviews, Godard offered another answer, that for people who lived through such persecution, perhaps, the war never really ended—("No doubt because the war didn't change anything at the time for those who had a Jewish name").[44] But he also had a more invidious explanation in mind, which he expressed at the time of the film's release, in May 2001:

Many French Jews who came back from the camps thought of themselves as French first, then of the Jewish religion, like me—I'm of the Protestant religion. It's afterwards that the singularity of Judeity was constructed and they didn't want to make a big deal out of it, which explains why they made use of their nom de guerre. The idea of the Holocaust came much later. Then Claude Lanzmann launched the name of the Shoah, so to speak.[45]

Godard's interpretation suggests that, despite having been deported to concentration camps because they were Jewish, some French Jews took the high moral and political ground by not "making a big deal out of it." He reproached Jews who instead claimed the "singularity" of their background and experience by assigning to the German program of extermination the names "Holocaust" and "Shoah." In the specific case of Madame Bayard, his suggestion is, in effect, that being a resister takes moral primacy over being Jewish as the cause of deportation to a concentration camp—and indeed he showed her repenting for having been, shortly after the war, in effect a "too dreadful martyr" for having "babbled always the same memories."

The Jews of *Eloge de l'amour* are not enlightened or ennobled by historical memory, but burdened and scourged by it, as with Jean Bayard's self-justifications regarding his wartime conduct, his wife's unwillingness to let go of her wartime of adventure and sacrifice, Edgar's indecisive artistic dilettantism, and the dark vortex of Berthe's solitary martyrdom. These complexities of character mirror the film's political ambiguities: Brasillach's text is read alongside tributes to the Resistance, and discussions with Jean Bayard and Jean Lacouture in Brittany suggest that the Communist resistance was in cahoots with the German occupiers.

Yet, *Eloge de l'amour* is both Godard's cinematic tribute and rebuttal to *Shoah,* and at the same time his refutation of *Schindler's List:* he rejects naturalistic reconstructions of the Holocaust and instead sees history, as Lanzmann does, in its present-day traces—but not in terms of testimony. *Eloge de l'amour,* made in the aura of the ongoing discussion, actual and virtual, with Lanzmann, seeks to uncover the Holocaust, in its historical specificity, as a contemporary presence. By the time of the editing of *Eloge de l'amour,* Godard was able to say of Lanzmann and *Shoah:* "He made a very great film," but Godard shifted his admiration away from its most distinctive element, its first-person survivor accounts: "Especially when he shows himself with the Germans, he is very hard on them, he did a very important thing."[46]

Godard, in *Eloge de l'amour,* approached the situation of Jews in the present day as one marked, scarred, determined by their sufferings at the hands of Germans and French collaborators, as a result of crimes that continue to stain humanity as a whole—but about which they do best not to speak. They should rather let the images of the cinema testify mutely for them.

Throughout the film, Godard managed not to say the words *Israel* and

Palestine. Although the film was possibly his lacunary tribute to the Jewish experience—he held his tongue on a matter regarding which he would not be able to avoid blaming Jews—he also avoided mentioning Israel in a context that could have served to justify its existence.

THE FILM IS marked by aspects and forms of the past that live in the present. When Rosenthal tells Forlani of having been in love with Edgar's mother, the sound track features, at that moment, a snippet of the sound track of *American Beauty,* from the moment when an adult man (Kevin Spacey) meets the young girl who becomes the object of his obsession. This citation, indicating the desire of an older man for a young girl, suggests that Rosenthal has preserved Edgar's mother in memory as a similarly young girl, whereas he, who still loves her, is not the young man he was but the old man he now is.

The shots of *Eloge de l'amour* are neither monumental like those of *Nouvelle Vague* nor highly inflected like those of *Hail Mary, Soigne ta droite,* or *King Lear.* Rather, its black-and-white images are infused with a nostalgia for the present: they embody history in each moment while instantly transforming each moment into a part of history, as if the present not only slips into the immediate past but is absorbed as well by the distant past.

The texts from which *Eloge de l'amour* is composed are more exposed than in Godard's other films; they are less overwhelmed by music and less obscured by other texts or other sounds. The dominance of text marks a significant application of the hard-won method of *Histoire(s) du cinéma. Eloge de l'amour* is, principally, the setting of texts in images and performances and situations that reveal the full extent of their emotional power and intellectual significance. The film's script is not richer than in *For Ever Mozart* or in *Hélas pour moi*; it is clearer, simpler, and more direct. The film is purified of complications, as if to bring to the fore the historical elements and artifacts, the controlled chains of associations and the layers of time, of which it is comprised.

IN THE SECOND part of the film, shot in Brittany, Godard used a new piece of equipment, mini-DV cameras. Albert, his assistant, recalled that Godard had originally intended to do all of the DV camerawork himself, together with her. He then asked the cameraman Christophe Pollock to join them (along with a sound recordist)—but instructed him to "film the landscape like a Japanese tourist." According to Albert, "His idea was that with the little video camera it would be like an amateur personal archive, a family archive, like images that Berthe herself would have made or could have made."[47]

The shots with the little digital video cameras indeed came out casual and playful, and Godard did playful things with them. For instance, he used his little DV camera like a spy camera; when riding in a car with his actors, he refused the proffered courtesy of sitting in the front seat and insisted on sitting in the back, in order to videotape his actors as the car rolled. He occasionally filmed others from behind, such as Pollock and a passerby, and used Putzulu's voice-over to create the illusion that the actor himself was in the shot.

And yet, in *Eloge de l'amour*, Godard used video more like film than he had before. He used few video-editing effects such as superimposition or slow motion—though he shifted the color of the video images to harsh and bright tones that he likened to Fauvist paintings. The similarity of the DV shoot to a film shoot is not coincidental: Godard's first choice of equipment for the Brittany sequence was the 70mm camera, which offers a hyper-vivid image and extraordinary detail. However, that equipment was too expensive, so he went in the opposite direction, toward simplicity.

Here, too, Godard imbued the film with memory: the film's color scheme, with the present shot in black and white and the flashback in color, is derived from Otto Preminger's *Bonjour Tristesse*, from 1958, the film that Godard had taken as his principal model for *Breathless*. In making *Eloge de l'amour*, he had come full circle.

ELOGE DE L'AMOUR aroused, in advance, unusual curiosity. Expectations ran high. Significantly, *Eloge* had been invited to premiere, in competition, at the Cannes Film Festival in May 2001. It was Godard's first new feature film since *For Ever Mozart,* which had been released in October 1996. Its distributor, ARP (the company of Michèle Halberstadt, the journalist who had played herself in *King Lear*), had big plans for the film's release: it would open in eight theaters in Paris on May 16 (the day after its Cannes screening), ranging from small art houses to mall-like multiplexes.

With its wide release and young star, and with much of the film having been shot in Paris, *Eloge de l'amour* was anticipated by many as something of a return (which is, of course, what many of Godard's fans had been hoping for ever since *Breathless*). The high expectations were stoked by an intense press campaign; in advance of the release, Godard submitted to an astonishing number of interviews. He appeared on the cover of many publications in the week of the film's release, from *Télérama* to *Epok* (published by the book chain FNAC), and he spoke to the major newspapers and magazines as well as to many minor ones. Godard, who was seventy years old, went to the task like a person invigorated, responding with inspired literary expatiations that went on for spoken paragraphs. Indeed, he did most of the talking.

When *Eloge de l'amour* went to Cannes, Godard went with it. Putzulu and Camp came to help promote the film. Putzulu was also interviewed by a wide range of journalists; Camp, whose extraordinary but unusually composed performance was so crucial to the film, was interviewed by none.

The reviews came in, and they were generally favorable, but ineffectually so. Most of the leading French critics admired the film but did not discuss it as a love story; they lauded Godard's interest in history but neglected its web of historical references. One critic, Serge Kaganski, writing in the youth-oriented *Les Inrockuptibles,* dismissed *Eloge:* "Despite its spare beauties, *Eloge de l'amour* is a film that doesn't really get it up, that is dominated by a sensation of fatigued recycling, in which the artist serves up to us again all his old numbers, but without splendor, without vigor."[48]

Even with Putzulu's increasing prominence as an actor, and despite the romantic promise of the title, which the film richly fulfilled, the theaters were, for the most part, nearly empty.[49] Several months later, when Jean-Marie Straub's new film, *Operai, contadini* (Workers, Peasants), opened in Paris, Godard commiserated with him: "I hope your film is doing better than mine."[50]

Meanwhile, in Paris, two theaters in the Latin Quarter ran Godard retrospectives to accompany the release of *Eloge:* one showed his films of the 1960s; the other offered those of the 1980s and '90s. Screenings at both theaters were sparsely attended.[51] Yet in June, he was photographed attending the French Open, where his presence made news.[52]

Some years after the release of *Eloge de l'amour*, a journalist, François Gorin, ruefully recalled its opening:

> [There were] several good reviews, the ritual press conference, a handful of spectators, and silence. It's a film by Jean-Luc Godard that, for practical purposes, did not exist . . . It's as if Godard, between an excess of praise and a lack of love, had disappeared.[53]

Godard's first first film, *Breathless,* and his second first film, *Sauve qui peut,* were successful with the public and won well-deserved acknowledgment and, occasionally, even thoughtful exegesis from the critics. *Eloge de l'amour,* Godard's third first film, found him on the highest of pinnacles—and, as he had foreseen in his many dire diagnoses of the state of the world, there were fewer and fewer people to seek out his rarefied view. Exalted,

Godard resembled a sort of holy survivor, a living treasure, a symbol of the miraculous endurance of a grand and ancient artistic tradition. Yet Godard had passed through the other side of the cinema, so to speak, and as he had become sacred, his work, with its complexities, demands, and ambiguities, had acquired the aura of something taboo.

thirty

NOTRE MUSIQUE

"Today I have fallen from that margin"

W HEN *ELOGE DE L'AMOUR* CAME OUT, IT WENT largely unrecognized, both for its intrinsic artistic importance and its significance in Godard's oeuvre. The work that reflected the self-surpassing creative renewal of one of the century's leading artists instead fell into oblivion; although Godard was willing to take the high road of posthumous honor, he nonetheless had been recognized in his time and was aware of the energy and the opportunities that recognition had brought him. On the threshold of old age, Godard had changed directions audaciously, yet his tour de force went unnoticed. The effect on Godard of the short-term failure of his third first film was rapidly apparent in his new work.

In some ways, the fate of *Eloge de l'amour* had been foretold in the reception given to another project with which Godard was intimately associated during the long gestation of *Eloge,* Anne-Marie Miéville's film *Après la réconciliation* (After the Reconciliation). As with *Eloge de l'amour,* the substance of Miéville's film was subordinated—by critics and audiences—to Godard's involvement, resulting in a lack of appreciation of its intrinsic artistic merits.

Après la reconciliation, which Miéville had initially written as a play, is essentially a chamber work for four characters: two women (one, an older unnamed intellectual, the other, Cathos, a young dancer) and two men (Robert, an intellectual, and Arthur, a young sailor). Miéville had originally wanted the actor Pierre Richard to play Robert. He withdrew from the project, however, and Godard offered to take on the role. As Miéville recalled, "Jean-Luc felt himself to be in harmony with the script, he wanted to say those words, to participate in this enterprise. He insisted on acting. I was not in favor of it, because we had already done the previous one together, be-

In Sarajevo, Rony Kramer and Godard talk about Israel.
(TCD-Prod DB © Les Films Alain Sarde / DR)

cause his name was a burden and because I was reproached for using it as a kind of advertising."[1] Godard's "harmony with the script" was no surprise: Miéville had modeled the dialogue between Robert and the unnamed woman on the dialogue between Jean-Paul Sartre and Simone de Beauvoir in *La Cérémonie des adieux*.

The shoot was scheduled to take place in the spring of 2000, so Godard interrupted the editing of *Eloge de l'amour* for it. Though he had previously stepped in at the last minute to play the lead role in Miéville's *Nous sommes tous encore ici* in 1996, that performance required little preparation on his part; as he recalled, "I was able to find much of myself in it, so it sufficed to pay attention, to concentrate, to be serious, to be as I am."[2] For *Après la réconciliation*, Miéville put Godard through a month of rehearsals. Several days before the start of the shoot, when the actress slated to play the first, unnamed woman withdrew from the project, Miéville herself decided to take on the role, which was closely paired with Godard's part.

In the film's principal story, the older couple, riding in a car in the city (she, Miéville, is driving; he, Godard, is the passenger), meet by chance a friend, Cathos, and bring her to their calm and subtly luxurious apartment. The group lacks beverages; the first woman, Miéville, goes to get them. While she is out, she meets a solitary wanderer named Arthur; she kisses him and brings him along with her. Meanwhile, Cathos attempts to seduce Robert, unsuccessfully. Miéville arrives with Arthur; in a long and sharp-edged conversation that soon turns to insult, Arthur leaves, and Cathos leaves to pursue him.

Left alone with Robert, the first woman confesses that she kissed Arthur. Robert withdraws to a bedroom, where she finds him crying. Their confrontation is horrific and moving, as Robert tells her, "But really, at your age, you don't need to be loved anymore." Miéville reviews with him the story of their life together, starting when they were young, when "the whole soul, the whole heart, and also the imagination desired that something happen, thought it possible," whereas now "the heart has started to weigh heavily, so heavy and large that it finally fills the whole body." Robert sits silently, unwilling to respond to Miéville's litany of recriminations, until she challenges him, "Dirty bastard! It would take just one sentence for you to set me free! Say it! Say the sentence!" Robert can only respond with, "Oh la la, how painful it is to finish interminable sentences." Miéville can take no more. "Then beat it!" she yells. "Say your fucking sentence and beat it, Robert, please, my good Robert, but say your sentence." He breaks down in brutalized, deeply rising sobs, considers leaving and not coming back, and finally, exhausted, tells her, "You see, you want me to talk but you don't want to hear what I'm saying . . . In the end, you're so tyrannical."

In an epilogue, they are together and, going out for a drink, run into Cathos and Arthur. The two couples go to the theater and discuss, with fragile serenity and Apollonian good cheer, life "after the reconciliation."

While less spontaneous and less naturally intimate than *Nous sommes tous encore ici,* which has the feel of permutations of Godard and Miéville's actual domestic discussions, *Après la réconciliation,* with its dancelike formality and its highly constructed dialogue and situations, lays bare inner lives, ravaging fears, suppressed ecstasies, and frightening desires, with an extraordinarily controlled gracefulness.

Yet as if to set the theatrical drama in its authentic context, Miéville begins *Après la réconciliation* with an agonized prologue, a kind of home movie of herself visiting her grandchildren, accompanied by her own voice-over confession: "On this day in '99, I have an appointment with the maid to bring the youngest girl a dress I made for her birthday." She continues, "I only see them rarely. The door seems to be closed, but I must stay there in case it opens, in case it doesn't." Miéville made it clear that she could visit her grandchildren only when her daughter was not at home.

Godard had already made this estrangement public, in the second volume of *Jean-Luc Godard by Jean-Luc Godard.* As Alain Bergala was editing the book, Godard, without further explanation, gave him a copy of a letter for inclusion. The letter is eight pages long, handwritten, dated August 2, 1995. Though the names are blackened out, initials remain, and it begins, "Very dear A—," a reference to Miéville's daughter, Anne. The letter is Godard's plea for permission to see her children (she had four). He admits that he is "only the friend of the grand parent [*sic*] of [the] small children," and acknowledges with sadness that neither she nor her "companion" want him to know them—despite his having been named godfather of one of them.

The alienation had been established for years. Anne-Marie Faux, who worked as what she called the "secretary" to Miéville and Godard in the Paris office of Peripheria from 1990 through 1995, recalled, "Anne-Marie Miéville's relations with her daughter were full of conflict. While I was working with them, her daughter did not see her—and so [Miéville] did not see her grandchildren either. . . . nor did Godard."[3] Godard himself later attested to the troubled state of Miéville's family relations—"She had difficulties with her daughter to have the right to see her grandchildren"[4]—and even credited this problem with inspiring his own work regarding the bond of grandparents and grandchildren in *Eloge.*[5] Miéville, however, bravely framed her work of fiction with an explicit glimpse of her real and intimate grief.

Après la réconciliation is a significant work of art, but for all of Miéville's accomplishment, it was received as a film dominated by the image of Godard, as if it were a star vehicle. Indeed, the interest in Godard's person at the expense of his and Miéville's cinema was not only nourished by this project, but was also heightened by Godard's efforts on the film's behalf. *Après la réconciliation* was scheduled to be released in Paris on December 27, 2000, and Godard worked with Miéville to help promote it, granting joint interviews and accompanying her and the film at a screening and discussion with high-school students in rural Sarlat, a widely reported event. Though *Après la réconciliation* was taken seriously, Godard's on-screen tears were its most generally remarked element.

Miéville's work with Godard did draw some admirers, however. When Mary Lea Bandy of the Museum of Modern Art in New York decided to commission a video about MOMA from Godard, Colin MacCabe of the British Film Institute, a partner in the enterprise, said that he preferred Godard's recent work with Miéville to what Godard was doing on his own. "That's why," he recalled, "when we were commissioning *The Old Place*, I specified that he do it with her."[6] The film was budgeted at $500,000, which Godard assumed would be easy money. "Well, I thought, $500,000 for a film that we'll finish in two weeks, not bad," he recounted. "But it took us a year to figure out what to do, to find the images, to choose the texts, et cetera. Then after taxes, the cost of production, what's left?"[7]

Rather than come to New York to film at MOMA, Godard and Miéville filmed at home, on the subject of art, using reproductions as well as their own documentary footage of contemporary art installations (including a machine by Jean Tinguely and a vast installation of used clothing by Christian Boltanski). Through their voice-over dialogue, Godard and Miéville explore their ideas on the virtues of classical art and modern art's fallen status, linking the critical failure of the movies to document the Holocaust to the process of artistic devolution that ran from painting to photography to cinema. In the process, they considered, art itself had been emptied of its documentary virtues.

The central idea of *The Old Place* is to unify political morality with visual aesthetics. Godard and Miéville use texts and works by artists in order to analyze art visually into two components: a lesson in looking at the world, whether a field of flowers or the way the light hits one's living-room furniture, and the documentation of suffering; and their argument is that the two are inseparable.

The point was amplified in a second short film by Godard, *Dans le noir du temps* (In the Dark of Time), which was premiered at the Pompidou Center in Paris on November 28, 2001, together with *The Old Place* (MOMA did not show the film until 2002). *Dans le noir du temps* had been made on commission from British producers for a series called *Ten Minutes Older,* in which a number of directors made a film of their choice exactly ten minutes long. (The directors included Bernardo Bertolucci, Claire Denis, and István Szabó.) Godard took the commission at its word: he showed brief moments from his own films in order to illustrate "the last minutes" of essential qualities of existence. For the last minutes of youth, he showed Jean-Pierre Léaud in *Made in USA,* who is asked, "If you had to die, would you prefer to know in advance or to die immediately?" Léaud says, "Immediately," and gets shot. The final minutes of compassion feature a montage that joins documentary footage from the war in the former Yugoslavia and pornography. The last minutes of thought are shown by black garbage bags being filled with books as Godard reads the titles, then the bags sitting in an alley and being picked up and thrown into a garbage truck (the only image actually shot for the film, Godard said). For "the last minutes of memory," there is an image of naked, emaciated bodies thrown onto a pile, archival footage from the liberation of a concentration camp. The last minutes of silence are suggested by a scene of torture from *Le Petit Soldat.* The last minutes of beauty, from Godard's *King Lear,* show Burgess Meredith and Molly Ringwald approaching the sea, moments before the death of Cordelia. The last minutes of cinema are shown by an art installation of a white screen writhing in agony (an image that had been included both in *The Old Place* and *Histoire(s) du cinéma*).

Miéville explained to the audience, "I told Jean-Luc that the film was too dark, I would have wanted to add something more optimistic, the last ten minutes of hypocrisy" or something else that people would be pleased to see come to an end; but Godard answered her, "We weren't able to do it. It's bin Laden's fault." The screening took place some two months after the attacks of September 11, 2001, which Godard spoke of as a "horror." However, in an interview, he criticized American and, for that matter, French television for showing the same footage, of the towers in flames and collapsing, repeatedly, but not showing victims leaping from the towers and falling to their death.[8] As with the Holocaust, so with 9/11: Godard wanted photographic evidence of human suffering in order to be certain of its reality.

Yet another short film, *The Origin of the 21st Century,* which had been commissioned by the Cannes festival for the year 2000, suggested the coexistence of the cinema with the political reality that, in his view, it existed to document. It was a brief synopsis of the twentieth century, recursively, from the end back to the beginning, as reflected in Godard's own films and others. For the last decade, Godard included the image from *Hélas pour moi* of the violinist as Ludovic, walking in uniform, on his way to war, is followed by television images of a bus leaving Kosovo with fleeing refugees.

The year 1960 is shown by footage from the Algerian War, together with Jean Seberg at the end of *Breathless* asking, in response to Jean-Paul Belmondo's dying words, "What does that mean, 'disgusting'?" The film ends at a fictionalized 1900 with a scene from Max Ophüls's *Le Plaisir* (from 1951), of an old man disguised as a young man, dancing himself to collapse, followed by a famous line from the same film: "Le bonheur n'est pas gai"—Happiness is not gay (also cited in *Eloge*). The century of cinema, and Godard's thumbnail résumé of it, suggests the inverse: that the cinema's gaiety reflects anything but happiness.

BY LATE 2001, when Godard had completed his three short commissions, the experience of *Eloge de l'amour*'s poor reception by audiences and critics had been fully absorbed. As in the past, a political vehemence came to mask a personal crisis of cinema: in the wake of *Eloge*, in his next film, Godard turned to doctrinaire political advocacy, which served a purpose comparable to that of his earlier hortatory work: it reconnected him with youth.

At the premiere of *Eloge de l'amour,* Godard announced plans for a film called *Notre Musique* (Our Music), about Manfred Eicher and ECM Records, and the influence of that music on Godard's work. He also intended to make an abridgment of *Histoire(s) du cinéma* for Gaumont to release theatrically, *Moments choisis* (Chosen Moments). In addition, he was hoping to work with the young producer Emmanuel Benbihi, who announced at Cannes a compilation film called *Paris je t'aime* (Paris, I Love You), in which twenty directors would each film a short love story in one of the twenty arrondissements of Paris. Among the directors recruited for the project along with Godard included Woody Allen, Agnès Varda, Bertrand Tavernier, and Emir Kusturica.[9] Godard's idea was to make a film called *Champ Contre Champ* in the eleventh arrondissement. The title was a pun on the French for "shot-countershot" (the classical pattern for filming dialogue) as well as on the (peculiar) proper names, "Shot Versus Shot" (as in *Kramer Versus Kramer*). The love story would be grounded in a study of the use of shot and countershot to represent the differing views of a man and a woman on love.[10]

The first intimations of the effect of *Eloge de l'amour*'s failure were evident in Godard's abridgment of *Histoire(s) du cinéma*, transferred to 35mm film for theatrical release and presented at Beaubourg on November 29, 2001. This eighty-four-minute work differed significantly from the six-hour project on which it was based; it was an act of self-revisionism. Excerpted moments from *Histoire(s)* had been recast in an entirely new political framework. Godard removed his opening praise of the Hollywood producers Irving

Thalberg and Howard Hughes, whose creative energy and outlaw imagination he had extolled in his initial synoptic introduction to the *Histoire(s)* as the precondition of the movies' stories, as the story of all stories. In fact, Godard voided the film of its predominantly Jewish character. He removed the specific references to the Holocaust from the essays and, instead, oriented the distillation toward the failures of the cinema in recent days to document and to prevent massacres in Sarajevo, Kosovo, and elsewhere, atrocities perpetrated principally against Muslims. Yet instead of considering the role of Christian Serbs and Croats in the massacre of Muslims in the former Yugoslavia, Godard turned his attention once more to the confrontation between Muslims and Jews in the Middle East.

Even before the attacks of September 11, 2001, political conflict in the Middle East had become reinflamed by the breakdown of Israeli-Palestinian negotiations and by Ariel Sharon's 2000 visit to Jerusalem's Temple Mount. Palestinians began a new campaign of violence against Israel, which caused, in turn, large-scale military incursions by Israel into Palestinian cities, towns, and refugee camps.

As if in response, Godard's plans for *Notre Musique* underwent a transformation. Instead of making a film about ECM Records, he now wanted to base it on the novel *Le Silence de la mer,* by Vercors,[11] written in 1943, which had been the basis for Jean-Pierre Melville's first feature film in 1947. The novel and the film are a story of France under German occupation, in which a German officer—an intellectual and a Francophile—is quartered in the house of a French family. Godard's idea, he later said, was to adapt *Le Silence de la mer,* but with "an Israeli officer, from the occupying army, who speaks in a proper and polite way with a family in their living room." The conversation would involve the Bible, or perhaps also the Bible and Homer, but Godard dropped the idea, he said, because he didn't think he had the necessary "book learning."[12]

Then he came up with another way to film his notion of the conflict in the Middle East:

> We're in an apartment, and then someone comes and says "God has chosen me, from now on this is my apartment." I wanted to make a film about that with Marcel Ophüls, where we would show ourselves together in this apartment. And then we would have a discussion, we would try to resolve the question among ourselves, as if we were actually in power. But it didn't work out.[13]

Then coincidence intervened: Godard was invited by Francis Bueb, the director of the Centre André-Malraux in Bosnia, to take part in the second annual "Rencontres Européennes du Livre," literary encounters that Bueb organized in Sarajevo. Bueb, a former bookstore executive, had gone to Sarajevo at the height of the war and founded the center in order to provide cultural support to the besieged city. With a sort of peace restored after the Dayton accords of 1995, Bueb remained there to help with the city's reconstruction.[14]

During Godard's first visit, he presented *Eloge de l'amour,* and he also engaged a group of young cinephiles and film students in several seminars. He returned to the center in June 2002 to present the premiere of a new short film, *Liberté et patrie,* which had been commissioned by Expo 02, a cultural festival of the Jura region of Switzerland. The title of the film, which means "Freedom and Fatherland," is the slogan of the canton of Vaud and is featured on the canton's flag.

The film is based on the novel *Aimé Pache, peintre vaudois* (Aimé Pache, Painter from the Vaud), by Ramuz, from 1911. It is a twenty-one-minute capsule autobiography; in title cards, Godard declares that Expo 02 has commissioned "from him, Aimé Pache, painter from the Vaud, a painting called 'Liberté et Patrie.'" Godard illustrates the film's brief sections with excerpts from his own films—*For Ever Mozart, King Lear, Eloge de l'amour, Weekend, Band of Outsiders*—to recount the voyage of young Aimé from the countryside near Lausanne to Paris, where he lived in poverty and visited many art exhibits, and went to the Louvre to copy "the works of the great masters." The images of Paris, in black and white, are from *Eloge de l'amour;* but the screen bursts again into full color with the return trip to Switzerland, with a glorious sunset over the hills and the lavish foliage of the countryside. ("And then he leaves, and that's liberty, and he comes back, and that's fatherland.") After the death of Pache's parents and his abandonment of painting for a time (which, according to the commentary, came "after '68"), he resumes his work on "le grand tableau," the great painting. To bring the self-portrait definitively around to Godard's primal artistic identity, it features on the sound track no mood music from ECM but the slow movement from the Opus 132 string quartet of Beethoven.

The latest panel of the "great painting," by which Godard's reputation would be secured once more, was yet to come; but the trip to Sarajevo played an important part in its creation.

Alain Bergala, who went to the Centre André-Malraux several days after this screening, missed Godard there but collected accounts of his visit:

He was invited for an evening; he stayed three days. They offered to show him around the city. He said, "No, I see better from here." There was a window from which one could see a corner of the market where there had been the explosion, and there were all the young people, and the young women, who came to the Center . . . and he was happy there—he was glad that nobody was disturbing him—and he came home and sent them a check for 100,000 francs for "space rental."[15]

The project of *Notre Musique* was reconceived on the basis of his visits to Sarajevo.

NOTRE MUSIQUE IS a triptych. The first section, "Hell," is a collage of war footage, culled from documentaries, television news, and fiction films. The second and longest section, "Purgatory," is organized as a visit by Godard to the Centre André-Malraux for the purpose of giving a seminar. Upon his arrival at the airport, he is greeted by his translator, Ramos Garcia, who identifies himself as a French Jew of Egyptian origin whose father had been an anti-Zionist Communist but whose mother had been a Zionist. The section features a second track of action, revolving around the French embassy in Sarajevo. A young Jewish woman named Judith Lerner, a journalist from Israel, has come to the embassy in the hope of speaking with the French ambassador to Bosnia, Ambassador Naville (Godard's maternal grandmother's maiden name), about a project of peace between Israelis and Palestinians. She hopes to enlist, as she puts it, "not the ambassador but the man"—the man who had, as a young student, hidden her own grandfather from the Gestapo during wartime and in whose garret her mother had been born.

Several other writers have come to Sarajevo for the seminar, including Pierre Bergounioux from France, the Spanish novelist Juan Goytisolo (whose *Cahier pour Sarajevo* Godard had cited in his video *Je vous salue, Sarajevo* in 1993 and in *JLG/JLG*), and the Palestinian poet Mahmoud Darwish.

Judith Lerner (who is played by the Franco-Israeli actress Sarah Adler) interviews Darwish in the lobby of the Holiday Inn, where he says:

Do you know why we Palestinians are famous? Because you are our enemy. The interest is in you, not in me. So we have the misfortune of having Israel as an enemy, because she has strong allies. So many we can't even count them. And we have the good fortune of having Israel as our enemy. Because Jews are the center of interest of the world. That's why you've brought us defeat and renown.

Speaking of Darwish's on-screen remarks, Godard amplified the idea in a subsequent interview: "What does 'the center of the world' mean? I understand this. The Israelites"—here Godard revives an old word, one commonly used in France before World War II to designate Jews—"have something very original, but in that thing that is 'original' they introduced the idea of 'origin.' The origin, meaning that one is the first. They had a theory about that, and so it is completely normal that what happened to them happened to them, and it's because this happened to them that they were able to theorize it."[16]

In Godard's shocking interpretation of Darwish's remarks, he suggests that Jews saw themselves as the first people among the nations, the chosen people, and thus rendered themselves odious to the rest of the world; that if Jews are persecuted, they made themselves so, through their pride; that if they are hated, they incited that hatred—and then, thanks to their persecutors, they could be admired for their ability to "theorize" about persecution, as in the work of Hannah Arendt, which Godard cites in *Notre Musique*.

GODARD FILMED AT the ruins of the Sarajevo library, where two million books had been destroyed in the bombing though the building's stone shell remained standing. In an upstairs hall, converted into an improvised book exchange, two Native Americans in traditional dress appear and lament their historic losses in literary declamation (and reappear later in the film). The reference is not incidental: in the film's credits, Godard lists the Palestinian writer Elias Sanbar, who had written about Native Americans in his own work, as the film's "memory."

Sanbar was born in Haifa in Palestine in 1947; Godard had met him in the Palestinian territories while filming there with Jean-Pierre Gorin in 1969–70.[17] In *Le Bien des absents* (The Absentees' Goods), an autobiographical and historical work, Sanbar, a longtime activist in the Palestinian cause and a former negotiator for the PLO, discusses the alliance between Israel and the United States:

> We had the habit of saying: "The Palestinians are the Israelis' Jews." But what if, in reality, they were their Redskins?
>
> This line of questioning rapidly turned into a path of research. It allowed me to approach the circumstances of the creation of Israel from the perspective of episodes from the birth of the United States, and I touched upon the profound connection that underlies the mirror-game between *Americanism* and *Zionism*.[18]

Godard's allusion in *Notre Musique* to Sanbar's view suggests his endorsement of the idea that Israel and the United States, alone among nations, developed by conquest and forced displacements, and were thus fundamentally illegitimate and tainted. This rhetorical trick—of Sanbar, who wrote it, and of Godard, who filmed it—lent intellectual respectability

and a progressive profile to the conjunction of the ancient right-wing bug-
bears of the European right: the United States and Jews.

In *Notre Musique,* Godard's seminar at the Centre André-Malraux is
based on the lectures that Godard in fact gave there during his earlier visits.
In the second draft of his scenario, dated November 2002, Godard wrote a
scene in which he engaged the students in a reflection on the shot and the
countershot (as in the short film *Champ Contre Champ* that he had planned
to make for the compilation film *Paris je t'aime*). Among the examples that
he intended to use were: "A photo of Jewish refugees in 1948 on the beach in
Tel Aviv, and the same photo but with Palestinian refugees the same year, on
the beach at Haifa"; another pairing was "a Jewish cadaver dragged by the
feet in Auschwitz, and to whom the German language gives the name of
'Muslim.'" His idea was, as it had been in *Ici et ailleurs, JLG/JLG,* and elsewhere, to juxtapose the two pairs—German/Jew and Jew/Muslim—as if in
the relation of shot and countershot. (Godard also planned to revive his former argument about Jews as the primal enemies of the visual, by referring to
"Moses, who saw the bush in flames and who came down from the mountain
and didn't say, 'This is what I saw,' but 'Here are the tablets of the law.'")

In the film as he actually shot it in the spring of 2003, Godard's seminar
was indeed centered on the concept of shot and countershot: "The shot and
the countershot are very well-known figures of cinema. But if you look atten-
tively at these two photos from the Hawks film"—two stills from *His Girl
Friday,* one showing Cary Grant, the other Rosalind Russell—"you'll see that
in fact it's the same thing twice, because the director is incapable of seeing
the difference between a man and a woman." He adds, "The worst thing is
when it's a question of two similar things"—and then shows two images, one
a news photo of refugees on the road, which he labels "Kosovo," and the
other, a painting of Mary and Joseph's Flight to Egypt, labeled, "Egypt":

> Take, for example, two news photographs which show the same moment in
> history. One sees that in truth, truth has two faces. If you want my opinion, it's
> because those who keep the books are only accountants. What's more, Balzac
> talks in his book about the Great Ledger. The tables of the Law, the Holy
> Scriptures, the people of the book.

Here, Godard shows an image of an inmate in a concentration camp and
labels it "Jew," then (after a shot of a student's hand and arm holding a
photo) he shows another labeled "Muslim." The commentary continues:

> For example, in 1948, the Israelites walked in the water toward the Promised
> Land. The Palestinians walked in the water toward drowning. Shot and counter-

shot. Shot and countershot. The Jewish people rejoined fiction. The Palestinian people, documentary. One says that the facts speak for themselves, but Céline said, "Alas, not for long." He said that already in 1936. Because already the field [*champ*, also meaning "shot"] of text had covered up that of the image.

Godard once again dragged out the riff he had used in *Ici et ailleurs* and cited in person to Yasser Arafat in 1970, making much of the fact that Jews in Auschwitz referred to the near-dead as "Muselmen"—a word for Muslims. However, in interviews regarding *Notre Musique*, Godard took pains to distance himself from the implication in the film that Israel does to Palestinians what Germany did to Jews:

> But look out: because of two photos, people have been suggesting that I wanted to say that Muslims are enduring the same thing as the Jews did sixty years ago. But I slipped a shot in between these two photos. One must not be over-hasty in making associations.[19]

The shot that he "slipped in" (of a student's arm and hand) does briefly separate the two images and does blur, in Godard's stringently literal definition, the connection of the two as shot and countershot, or as "the same thing twice." In another interview, Godard went even further to deny that he was making such "associations."

> I bring together two situations and they say: "Godard asserts that the Shoah that the Jews endured and the Nakba that the Palestinians endured are the same thing." Of course not! That's completely idiotic. The shot and the countershot do not signify any equivalence, any equality, they merely pose a question.[20]

In these interviews from 2004, Godard says exactly the opposite of what he says in the film to the students in Sarajevo. The idea that he might have seemed to equate Palestinian exile with the extermination of Jews was clearly troubling to Godard; yet in fact the rest of his remarks in the seminar is at least as inflammatory. The charge that "the people of the book" are "the accountants" whose insensitive and self-interested record of history causes it to be understood wrongly bears the unmistakable overtone of rhetoric against the Jewish demons of legend, one classic and the other modern: the Jewish usurer and the Jewish media.

As the second part of the film progresses, Judith Lerner travels to Mostar to view the ruins of the bridge, the beginning of its reconstruction, and a presentation by the French architect Gilles Pecqueux to a group of school-children on the history of the bridge and its rebuilding. There, she sees a group of Native Americans who stand sentinel at the banks of the Neretva River. She also takes note of another woman, whom she thinks she recognizes without ever having seen her before. This is a Jewish woman of Russian origin and French nationality named Olga (played by Nade Dieu), the niece of Godard's translator, Ramos Garcia (Rony Kramer). She has arrived in Sarajevo en route to Jerusalem and talks to her uncle of her plans for suicide.

Godard returns to Switzerland and is working in his garden when he receives a call from Ramos Garcia. He learns that in Jerusalem, a woman entered a movie theater with a backpack and gave the patrons five minutes to leave, but invited any who were willing "to die for peace" to stay with her. Garcia reported that the theater emptied out and Israeli sharpshooters gunned down the woman, whose backpack was found to contain only books. This woman, he was sure, was his niece, Olga, and the false bomb threat was her form of suicide.

Originally, Godard said, he had intended this deed to be done by Judith Lerner, the Israeli character, but the actress, Sarah Adler, refused. So Godard created a different character to do it and brought in another actress to play her.

The film's third and concluding section, "Paradise," features U.S. Marines guarding a fenced-in wooded area near the sea. Olga arrives, and a marine pretends to stamp the inside of her wrist, letting her pass through the gate. In this "paradise," young people frolic in bathing suits and a young man reads a book by David Goodis, *Sans espoir de retour (Street of No Return;* literally, "without hope of return"). She finds another young man at the edge of the water. He is eating an apple and offers her a bite.

NOTRE MUSIQUE IS a film of prewar prejudices adorned with postwar resentments—and, like much else in the history of anti-Semitism, with personal frustrations. Godard attempted to explain his motives in making the film in the course of interviews he gave at the time of its Cannes screening in 2004.

> I wanted the film to bear the trace of the Israel-Palestine conflict, a conflict I have felt close to for a long time, together with Anne-Marie Miéville . . . As marginals, expelled from our cinematographic garden by what is called the American cinema, I feel close to them, the Vietnamese, the Palestinians . . . As creators, we have become homeless. For a long time I said that I was on the margin, but that the margin is what holds the pages together. Today I have fallen from that margin, I feel that I'm between the pages.[21]

As Godard suggested, Palestinian dispossession had personal symbolism for him. This is also true of Sarajevo, the importance of which lay, for him, in its burned-out library, its usefulness in representation, its symbolic significance as a victimized city. In the end, he sees nothing in Sarajevo, whereas the glimpse that he provides of himself cultivating his garden in Switzerland conveys the sense of relief at his restored distance from that fallen, chaotic, struggling world—from the torments of modernity. In *Eloge de l'amour,* Godard attempted to reconcile himself with the city, in which he had not filmed in decades; in *Notre Musique,* Godard returned to agrarian fantasy.

Godard attributed the triptych structure of *Notre Musique* to an inclination that he shared with Miéville, who was credited with the film's "artistic direction," and whose *Nous sommes tous encore ici* and *Après la réconciliation* were also in three parts. The film's hectoring tone is itself réminiscent of the dogmatic partisanship of Miéville (such as she expressed in *Ici et ailleurs, France tour détour deux enfants,* and *Soft and Hard*).

Notre Musique is a diatribe under the guise of a meditation, a work of vituperative prejudice disguised as calm reflection, a work of venom dressed up as a masque. After the rejection of his best, loftiest, most conciliatory work, *Eloge de l'amour,* Godard took his rejection out on the old targets, Jews. Following *Eloge de l'amour,* Godard was isolated; he needed to reconnect with a milieu of French intellectuals and French youths and he found a recognizable group of sympathizers at a time that paroxysms of anti-American and anti-Israeli rhetoric swept through France as the war in Iraq seemed inevitable. (Virtually all protests there were not only against war in Iraq but brought together Palestinian demands and the indemnity of Saddam Hussein, with whom Yasser Arafat had sided in the Gulf War.) The film, which identified Godard with that line, was successful. With its ethnic politics, unambiguous rhetoric, and intellectual demagogy, *Notre Musique* put Godard back in the limelight.

The film was invited to the Cannes festival in 2004. (In his press conference there, Godard criticized the festival for requiring the subtitling of films in English, and claimed that non-Francophones would only be able to grasp "five or six percent" of *Notre Musique.*) Although it did not win a prize at Cannes, the film was the subject of immediate, favorable attention, receiving reviews such as few works by Godard had won. It earned Godard a nomination for Best Screenplay and Sarah Adler one for Best Actress at the European Film Awards, and the film won the Grand Prix for Best Film of the Year from FIPRESCI, the international film critics' circle. *Notre Musique* was warmly received at the 2004 New York Film Festival; Manohla Dargis of the *New York Times* simply denied its doctrinaire content:

Like a benevolent pedagogue, [Godard] draws dotted lines between his preoccupations, points in many directions, suggests various means of interpretation and delivers multiple references. But what he adamantly refuses to do,
both in this film and elsewhere, is draw our conclusions for us, which may be
the highest compliment a filmmaker can pay his audience.[22]

It was released theatrically in New York on November 24, 2004, to enthusiastic reviews. Andrew Sarris, however, writing in the *New York Observer,* criticized the film's tendentious politics.

In *Notre Musique,* Mr. Godard talks about Jews as if they'd emerged tri-
umphantly from the death camps to promptly drive the Palestinians out of
their homeland . . . I am frankly surprised that most of my colleagues haven't
seen through Mr. Godard's evasive paradoxes, the banal anti-"Zionist"/anti-
American prejudices that he shares with his countrymen, whether French or
Swiss.[23]

But Godard was, in his own way, again relaunched. He returned to
Sarajevo, this time in the company of Sanbar, in September 2003. He
joined Sanbar, at the writer's request, at the opening of an exhibit of pho-
tographs of Palestine at a theater in Le Havre, where Godard also arranged
screenings of several films of his choosing (including *Demi-Tarif* by Isild
Le Besco, *The Brown Bunny* by Vincent Gallo, *Level Five* by Chris Marker,
Du Soleil pour les gueux by Alain Guiraudie, *Saltimbank* by Jean-Claude
Biette, *Les Naufragés de la D 17* by Luc Moullet, and three films by Jean-
Pierre Gorin: *Poto and Cabengo, Routine Pleasures,* and *My Crasy Life*).
Gorin (as well as Le Besco and Guiraudie) was present. Asked about the
attacks of September 11 by a spectator who said that they were "staged by
a demon," Godard responded, "I don't think anything about September
11. On the other hand, the word 'demon' makes me think of Maxwell's
equations."

Prior to the release of *Notre Musique,* Godard had been widely—albeit
wrongly—received as a filmmaker who was out of touch with the contemporary world. In 2001, Jean-Michel Frodon, former film critic at *Le Monde* and
editor in chief of *Cahiers du cinéma,* considered Godard's subject no longer
to be "ici et ailleurs," here and elsewhere, but merely "ici et ici," here and
here.[24] But now Godard was hailed as an engaged artist, and he pursued that
engagement, trotting himself out as a celebrity symbol of the Palestinian
cause. Thus, unlike his militancy in the wake of 1968, when he sacrificed his
public profile and his artistic activity to pursue with a Spartan self-denial his
principles, he now enjoyed with his social activism a favorable and promi-

nent profile that he could no longer maintain through his best artwork alone. The fault was that of the times, which had grown blind and deaf to the deep and subtle virtues of that work; but Godard was no longer ready or able to endure the isolation that this obstinate artistic quest now cost.

WHEN NOTRE MUSIQUE was released, Godard announced his next project: a museum collaboration with Beaubourg, to be called "Collages de France"— Collages of France, but also a pun on "Collège de France" (the research institution that had spurned him in the mid-1990s). He described the collaboration as "courses 'exhibited' by Jean-Luc Godard," a nine-month series, intended to run from October 2005 through June 2006, to comprise Godard's discussions with scientists, philosophers, artists. Each episode would also feature gallery installations of images and texts, together with videotapes made specifically for each monthly installation, as well as daily updates.

In his statement of purpose for the exhibit, he brought up what he called "a question" by the philosopher Emmanuel Levinas: "in the 'I think, therefore I am,' is the 'I' of 'I am' no longer the same as the 'I' of 'I think,' and why?" He then suggested, "The project Collages de France will seek to respond to this kind of question, more profoundly than the philosopher, in a sort of proof by nine courses." The intellectual ambition and philosophical scope of the enterprise by which Godard intended "to show and to demonstrate several aspects that have made and unmade 'la cinématographie'" was grand. Once again, what Godard conceived as the cinema's privileged relation to both reality and the imaginary made it the subject of subjects, the means by which all things and all ideas could be considered in their entirety.

However, practical issues intervened, notably with the administration of the museum and the conventions of its installations. After conflict with curators, particularly with Dominique Païni, Godard refused to work with the museum's officials and put the exhibit together on his own, with the help of staff. The exhibit, retitled *Voyage(s) en utopie* (Voyage(s) in Utopia), *Godard, 1946–2006*, was reconceived: no longer would it feature Godard's frequent appearance, but rather three rooms filled with images and documents, as well as a new video, *Vrai Faux Passeport* (Real Fake Passport), that would play on a screen. Yet even in its truncated version, the exhibit provided proof, as if more were needed, of Godard's claims for the cinema and its inseparability from his own identity. According to Godard, the cinema was, is, more than itself; it is both a supreme aspiration and an impossibility, a repository of history and intimate memory in an age of celebrity and forgetting, a lost golden age of self-transcendence, self-discovery, and a noble, doomed mission of folly for those who would attempt, as Godard himself continues to do, to recover it and restore it.

A complete retrospective of Godard's work, shown at Beaubourg con-currently with the exhibit, was a great success, with a full house at most of its screenings. As had long seemed clear to those who followed Godard's career, and to Godard himself, the oeuvre transcended the confines of the movie in-dustry; now, it officially took its place in the house of art—precisely the claim with which the New Wave had demanded its place in the sun.

EPILOGUE

ROLLE AND ITS SURROUNDINGS ARE A NATURAL PARA-
dise. The fifteenth-century castle perches on the shore of the
dark blue waters of Lake Geneva. A hundred yards out into the
lake, a rounded islet with arcs of dense foliage pierced by a proud, solemn
obelisk resembles a Fragonard come to life. The setting is so timeless, it is as
if Godard has found shelter in a most un-Swiss form of paradise, one in
which the clocks seem to have stopped.

Godard dines here often with Anne-Marie Miéville in the shadow of the
medieval castle at the Hostellerie du château (where he filmed Michel Piccoli
in *2 × 50 Years of French Cinema*), as he did during my visit to the town in
June 2000. In the busy restaurant, even the nearest voices melt into the rever-
berant din of table talk and kitchen sounds, yet one could discern the high,
flutelike voice of Anne-Marie Miéville: "Brigitte Bardot . . . Cannes . . . to drop
off his screenplay . . . he's waiting . . . budget . . . doing the color timing before
the editing . . ." Occasionally, when Miéville paused, Godard murmured haltingly before she resumed the steady flow of energized observations. One of the
restaurant's waitresses described the evening as typical: "He hardly ever speaks.
She speaks, not him."[1] Godard seemed to be enjoying a kind of cinematic sere-
nade, an intimate update from the realm of movies, pronounced by the one
trustworthy messenger who was not of that fallen world.

Earlier, Godard had spoken to me of filmmakers whose work he loves and
who kept working at a high artistic level, late in life, even after the collapse of
the studio system—Howard Hawks, John Ford—and he likened himself to
them: "They were also producers. They had their own production houses,
that's how they managed—like me, I've got my production house too."

The cinema has always been his "gauge," his "means of measurement—even for politics . . . We were for Mao," he said, "but when we saw the films he was making, they were bad. So we understood that of necessity there was something wrong with what he was saying . . . Even today, there are lots of people protesting globalization or things like that, but when I read their texts or their books, I find them bad, or when I see their films, I say to myself, 'They're no good either.' It's not good if what they do is bad. The cinema has always been a touchstone . . . a reference of moral and artistic measure."[2]

It follows, then, that Godard's negative view of the current state of the cinema should lead him to dismay regarding contemporary life as a whole. Young filmmakers, he said, "don't know the past," and Godard finds this loss of connection to the past embodied—of course—in the cinema, notably in film technology: "With digital, there is no past, not even technically." To see a previous shot, one strikes a key, he explains. "It doesn't take any time to get there, the time to unspool in reverse, the time to go backward. You're there at once. There's an entire time that no longer exists, that has been suppressed."

Godard's self-imposed isolation in Rolle, his calculated distance from the ordinary modes of modern life, even his continued use of analog video equipment, are strenuous forms of resistance to the suppression of the past. Yet at our meeting in June 2000, he spoke of a change, in both his life and his films: "I'd like to come back to what I would call a classical film, even with fewer resources, but calmly." He thought that a change of scenery might help, and talked about leaving Rolle: "We have had our fill . . . we have to find something else."

But when he told me this, I knew that he would not be likely to leave Rolle, nor to make what he would call a "classical film"—a film reminiscent of the Hollywood movies of the 1940s and '50s, which were his first love when he was starting out in the cinema. It seems reasonable for Godard to dream, from the standpoint of his artistic solitude, of a return to classical film, yet inconceivable that he would actually do so. Indeed, if there is no longer a classical cinema for him to come back to, it's largely as a result of his own efforts.

In the twilight of a summer evening, the lakefront at Rolle is redolent of many of the crucial elements of Godard's later films: the lapping of water on rocks; the constant and startlingly various voices of birds; the rhapsodic blue of the sky; the vapor trail of a small, fast airplane; the rustle of leaves in the wind; the saturated purples, reds, yellows, pinks of the flowers; the agile starts and stops of solid little cars in small parking lots and narrow roads; the short, hollow peal of an ancient church bell; the presence of man in nature and of nature in man; and most of all, the sense of a last refuge, a place where the new melts imperceptibly into the old, where the press of commerce, the noise of show business, the simulated miracles of technology recede quietly behind settled traditions and natural consolations. Where can Godard go, when even the radical timelessness of Rolle is not enough?

In that unlikely outpost, he still considers the burden of cinema, its future, to be his. "If nobody makes good films, if nobody can make good films, then it will disappear. But as long as I'm alive, it will last. I still have ten or twenty more years to make it last a little longer."

The cinema will live on for as long as Godard's films are seen, or Godard himself is remembered.

ACKNOWLEDGMENTS

This book developed from a profile of Jean-Luc Godard that was published in *The New Yorker* magazine. That profile grew from a twenty-five year fascination with Godard's films, throughout which time I had been discussing them, often with David Remnick, who, as friend and editor, enlisted me to write what I had been talking about, gave me the confidence and taught me the skills with which to attempt to do so, and delivered me to the magazine's magnificent mechanism for helping writers to surpass themselves. As the book progressed, his encouragement, advice, editorial insight, devotion, and practical efforts of many sorts were indispensable to its coming into being. Joining him at *The New Yorker* has been a privilege and a delight. The joyful exertions and the stimulating conversations have nourished me and the book apace. David is a great editor; he is a greater friend. My gratitude is boundless on both counts.

Riva Hocherman of Metropolitan Books asked me to expand the profile into a book. Her suggestions were unfailingly golden. She said all the right things to get it going and to keep it growing, and she also knew when, at a crucial moment, it needed to shrink. Her exacting and insightful editing has been essential to the project's development. This book is unimaginable in its current form without her engaged, informed, and impassioned attentions. Her deep knowledge of the subject (and of so much more), as well as her unfailing approach to the author—her wise words and her equally wise silences—are essential to the work at hand. A surer hand at the tiller—and a more farsighted navigation—are hard to imagine. I am deeply grateful for her guidance, empathy, and friendship.

I'm also grateful to Sara Bershtel, the associate publisher of Metropolitan Books, for her energetic and caring support for this project from beginning to end; to Grigory Tovbis for his cheerful attention to all the moving parts; to Meryl Levavi for her exquisite taste and vision; and to Rita Quintas for her extraordinary care and patience under the wire. Their concerted efforts, along with those of everyone at Metropolitan, have brought the elusive ideas into reality.

As agent and friend, Deborah Karl went far downfield for me like a wide receiver, protected me like an offensive lineman, threaded the needle like a quarterback, and guided me like a coach. I'm endlessly grateful for her friendship, advocacy, and authoritative experience.

At *The New Yorker,* Alice Truax devoted exceptional care and energy to this tyro writer's first pieces; I am deeply indebted to her for her skill, knowledge, devotion, and enthusiasm.

My colleagues—my friends—at *The New Yorker* continue to sustain, inspire, and astonish me. The ongoing conversations with David Denby and Anthony Lane have enriched my work, and my life, as the book sped toward completion; their erudition, passion, encouragement, and probing questions have helped me to keep going. Ben Greenman's editorial judgment and insights have been a key point of reference in the later stages of the work, his treasure trove of oblique angles a stimulating delight; Shauna Lyon, John Donohue, Russell Platt, and Andrea Scott have endured my labor pains with sympathy and good humor. Michael Specter brought care, energy, and practical support when they were needed most, as well as the joy of new friendship. Elisabeth Biondi and the entire photo department, former and latter—Paula Gillen, Melissa Goldstein, Asha Schechter, and Cassandra Jenkins—helped out and pitched in, wisely, generously, indispensably, and graciously.

Michael Witt was kind enough to invite me to submit a proposal for the For Ever Godard conference in London in June 2001; he, Michael Temple, and James Williams graciously accepted it and flew me over to participate in the program; Chris Darke generously put me up (and put up with me). Fourouzan Deravi offered sympathetic conversation and generous introductions. Thomas Elsaesser, in an evening's riverside stroll, adjusted my philosophical compass more decisively than he may realize.

Gilberto Perez, my professor at Princeton and my friend, gave me a crucial vote of confidence when it was needed; talks with Jonathan Rosenbaum, to whom he introduced me, were a great impetus and inspiration in getting the project off the ground.

Much of my research was done in Paris, where Chloé Guerber-Cahuzac, Philippe Collin, Etienne Féau and Alexandra Quien, Laurence Crémière and

Gérard Gromer, and Patrice Martinet welcomed me and opened doors, personal and professional, without which the book couldn't have become what it is. Sabine Trébinjac and Olivier Kyburz, Vesna Jovović, Voutch, and Michelle Seawell made me feel at home. I am especially grateful to Simone Nikolić for good lodgings, good food, and good company.

In addition to the many people who granted interviews, among those who generously made archival materials available were: Alain Bergala, Manette Bertin, Jacques Bonnaffé, Antoine Bourseiller, Bernard Cohn, Romain Goupil, Jean-Pierre Laubscher, Hugues Le Paige, Madeleine Morgenstern, Bruno Putzulu, Philippe Rony, Barney Rosset, Michel Royer, and Rafael Vela. In inspired fashion, Jean-Pierre Beauviala brought a camera to lunch. Chris Babey volunteered to send a tape, and sent it.

Michael Chaiken, the cinephilic star of his generation, provided, provided, and provided.

Much of this book was written in the sanctuary of the New York Public Library's Allen Room, a true New York treasure. I'm deeply grateful to Wayne Furman, its benevolent dictator and guardian angel, for letting me in just when I needed it most.

At the Bibliothèque du Film, Régis Robert made sure that I knew what to look for and that I found it. The Cinémathèque Suisse welcomed me like family. Oksana Dykyj at Concordia University made long-forgotten videos come to life again. Mary Lea Bandy led me to the library of the Museum of Modern Art, where Charles Silver spread the treasures out before me. Jackie McAllister, at the Swiss Institute in New York, and Gareth James, who curated a wonderful exhibit of Godard's videos there in 2000, helped get the ball rolling. Jonas Mekas and Robert Haller opened the doors to the superb library at Anthology Film Archives. The CNC graciously invited me to consult the archives of the Commission de contrôle.

Junji Hori offered a copious bibliography and batch of Japanese texts; Maki Noda delivered heroic, expert, and generous translations and synopses.

Warren Niesluchowski talked with me about iconoclasm and then introduced me to an icon.

Tom Luddy has been a rock of encouragement and wisdom, as well as a font of good conversation and generous suggestions.

Conversation and correspondence with Isabelle Clavé, who lives the cinema with a rare passion, were a crucible for many of the book's ideas.

It is a special pleasure to have made dear friends in the course of research. Véronique Godard, a true friend to the cinema, has been a true friend to me and to my family; she is deeply missed in New York since she brought her wondrous fervor back to Paris. Jean-Pierre Gorin is a philosopher of cinema and a born teacher from whom I learn endlessly, about movies and far more. With Michel Vianey and his wife, Marie-Laurence, the empathetic understanding was immediate and joyous.

Jean-Luc Godard graciously received me at his office, showed me videos, and invited me to dinner. The day and evening I spent with him are unforgettable; this book would have been far poorer without the frank insights that he so generously and so unsparingly shared. Even if "at the cinema, we do not think, we are thought," Jean-Luc Godard has done more for thinking at, about, and by means of the cinema than anyone, ever. This book can never repay what his films and videos have meant to me and to my way of thinking, about movies and about life.

Andrew Mendelsohn was there when this all got started.

When the book was in its Starbucks phase, Carl Titolo nourished it with old-school wisdom and creative faith. His unflagging sense of purpose and artistic dedication are an inspiration.

Jasenka Redzić provided peace of mind and all the time that was needed.

My sister, Jane Brody, has been a steadfast source of confidence and encouragement through the years, even when it was least justified; so were our late parents, Bernard and Carol Brody.

My darling daughters, Juliette and Louise, grew along with the book, and endured my absences, distractions, sleepless nights, and sleepy mornings. I hope they'll think it's all worth it. They never cease to amaze, delight, and inspire me; they have opened my world to wondrous new dimensions.

My beloved wife, Maja Nikolić, has changed my life, expanded my horizons, made me more than I could imagine, made possible more than I dared to dream. I dedicate this book to her.

NOTES

G par G refers to *Jean-Luc Godard par Jean-Luc Godard*, Alain Bergala, ed. (Paris: *Cahiers du Cinéma*, 1998).

CS refers to the clipping files of the Cinémathèque Suisse, Lausanne.

Preface

1. Susan Sontag, *Styles of Radical Will* (New York: Farrar, Straus and Giroux, 1966), p. 150.
2. *Paris Match*, March 9, 1968.

Chapter One: "We do not think, we are thought"

1. *La Gazette du cinéma*, September 1950.
2. Au cinéma, nous ne pensons pas, nous sommes pensés.
3. Thomas Edison's movies were first shown publicly in 1894; the Lumière brothers first displayed their work to a paying audience in 1895. However, Edison's work remained at the level of mere recording, whereas the Lumière brothers' efforts reflected the concepts and choices of works of art.
4. Godard withdrew his authorization when MacCabe was seven years into his project; the resulting book features generous views of young Godard's family life.
5. Jean-Pierre Laubscher, interview by author, February 21, 2003.
6. Papers of Jean-Pierre Laubscher.
7. *Lire*, May 1997.
8. *Télérama*, October 4, 2000.
9. *Le Nouvel Observateur*, February 1, 1985.
10. *Introduction à une véritable histoire du cinéma*, p. 59; *Le Monde de l'Education*, November 1997; in *G par G*, vol. 2, p. 443.
11. *L'Autre Journal* no. 2, January 1985, in *G par G*, vol. 1, p. 599–600.
12. *Studio*, May 2001.
13. Gilles Perrault, *Paris sous l'Occupation*, pp.152–53; cited in clicnet.swarthmore.edu/aobajtek/ultras_litt.html.
14. *Studio*, May 2001; *Télérama*, October 4, 2000.
15. *Studio*, May 2001.
16. *Libération*, December 3, 1996.
17. *Lire*, May 1997.
18. Roland Tolmatchoff, interview by author, March 20, 2002.

19. Godard would later borrow Parvulesco's name for a character in a film, and Eric Rohmer would—in 1995—cast Parvulesco himself in a role.

20. *Paris-Match,* March 25, 1961.

21. *Télérama,* July 8, 1978.

22. G. P. Langlois and G. Myrent, *Henri Langlois* (Paris: Denoël, 1986), p. 175.

23. *Sartre,* a film by Alexandre Astruc and Michel Contat (text published by Gallimard, 1977).

24. "La Fin de la guerre," *Les Temps Modernes,* October 1945; in *Situations, III,* p. 65.

25. De Gaulle had suspected that Blum, a Jew who had survived Buchenwald and other German concentration camps, would be able to make a special appeal to the Jewish financiers of Wall Street.

26. Despite the accord's apparent disadvantage for the French film industry—as noted at once by industry representatives—it was issued apart from the main accord because the latter was subject to Congressional approval, and Byrnes assumed that Congress would never approve a bill that placed any limit at all on the export of American films.

27. *Le Monde,* June 16–17, 1946.

28. *L'Humanité,* June 8, 1946.

29. *L'Humanité,* June 16, 1946.

30. The new constitution took effect on October 24, 1946.

31. *L'Humanité,* October 11, 1947.

32. *La Revue du cinéma,* January 1947, in Antoine de Baecque, *La Cinéphile* (Paris: Fayard, 2003).

33. "Quand Hollywood se met à penser," trans. Dana Polan, in *Post Script,* vol. 7 no. 1, Fall 1987, as "Citizen Kane."

34. *Les Temps Modernes,* February 1947.

35. André Bazin did not hesitate to write, late in 1943, "I will perhaps shock some readers by asserting that of all French artistic activities since the war the cinema is the only one that is progressing."

36. André Bazin, "The Ontology of the Photographic Image," in *What is Cinema?* vol. 1, trans. Hugh Gray (Berkeley and Los Angeles: University of California Press, 1967).

37. *La Revue du cinéma,* June 1948, in Rohmer, *Le Goût de la beauté* (Paris: Etoile, 1984).

38. *Le Temps Modernes,* September 1948.

39. Ibid., June 1949.

40. *Télérama,* July 8, 1978.

41. *Les Inrockuptibles,* June 5, 1996.

42. Richard Roud, A *Passion for Films* (New York: Viking, 1983), p. 68.

43. Ibid., p.67.

44. Huguette Marquand Ferreux, *Musée du Cinéma Henri Langois* (Paris: Moeght/Cinémathèque Française, 1991).

45. In a later article, from 1952, Godard characterized the film as "anti-cinema."*Cahiers du cinéma,* September 1952, in *G par G,* vol. 1, p. 84.

46. Hélène Frappat, *Jacques Rivette, secret compris* (Paris: Cahiers du cinéma, 2001), p. 55.

47. Anne-Marie Cazalis, *Mémoires d'une Anne,* Paris: Stock, 1976, p 95. 16mm film was the amateur format, which was not controlled by government or union strictures.

48. Alexandre Astruc, *Le Montreur d'ombres* (Etrepilly: Bartillat, 1996).

49. *Jean-Luc Godard ou le cinéma au défi,* directed by Hubert Knapp (French television, 1964).

50. *Réalités,* January 1964.

51. *Art Press, Spécial Godard,* December 1984 and January–February 1985.

52. Suzanne Schiffman was then known by her maiden name, Suzanne Klochendler.

53. *Lire,* May 1997.

54. Suzanne Schiffman, videotaped interview by Bernard Cohn, September 15, 1999.

55. *Lire,* May 1997.

56. That is, it was the equivalent of slide film: there was no negative and no print, and the film on which the images were recorded was edited and projected.

57. Jacques Rivette, interview by author, March 11, 2002.

58. Laubscher, interview by author, February 21, 2003.

59. Schiffman, videotaped interview by Bernard Cohn, September 27, 1999.

60. Rivette, interview by author, March 11, 2002.

61. Greil Marcus, *Lipstick Traces* (Cambridge, Mass.: HUP, 1990).

62. Mourre soon wrote a book, *Malgré la blasphème* (Despite the Blasphemy), to this effect. He subsequently made his living as a lay writer of Catholic treatises.

63. François Truffaut, Correspondence, 1945–1984 (Farrar, Straus and Giroux, 1990), p. 24.

64. Claude Chabrol, *Et pourtant je tourne . . .* , Paris: Robert Laffont, 1976, p. 86.

65. Charles Bitsch, interview by author, September 19, 2001. On Christmas Eve 1983, when Gégauff and his second wife were together alone in a cabin in rural Norway, she stabbed him to death.

66. Momo: short for Maurice, as in Schérer, whose friends also called him "Le Grand Momo"—Big Momo, or Momo the Great, both in reference to his height, his seniority, and his seigneurial grandeur. He is tall, but he was also very much of a grandee among his younger acolytes.

67. *Chambre 12, Hôtel de Suede*, a documentary film by Claude Ventura and Xavier Villetard, in Criterion DVD set of *Breathless* (2007).

68. *Le Journal du cinéma*, broadcast December 13, 1970 (DVD *Claire's Knee*, Criterion, 2006).

69. Rivette, interview by author, September 11, 2001.

70. The cancellation itself then became the occasion of another odd stunt: a speaker addressed the crowd, which was assembled to see the film nonetheless. To announce its cancellation, the speaker declared that the version of the film delivered was, erroneously, the British remake, which was both philo-Semitic and a very bad film, and therefore did not merit screening.

71. *Le Monde*, October 14, 1950. In November, after further legislative debate, the minister explained apologetically that the screenings were protected by freedom of the press, and added, "In the current state of the law, apology for collaboration cannot be the object of any judicial pursuit." *Le Monde*, November 4, 1950.

Chapter Two: "A matter of loving or dying"

1. There was also a special issue published in 1949.

2. Tolmatchoff, interview by author, March 20, 2002.

3. Colin MacCabe, *A Portrait of the Artist at Seventy* (New York: Farrar, Straus and Giroux, 2003).

4. Tolmatchoff, interview by author, March 20, 2002.

5. *Le Nouvel Observateur*, December 31, 1964–January 6, 1965.

6. Bitsch, interview by author, September 19, 2001.

7. Godard later said that Bazin didn't consider the film "faithful to Maupassant." *Télérama*, July 15, 1978. Indeed, in September 1952, Bazin reviewed another film, *Trois Femmes*, directed by André Michel, which, like *Le Plaisir*, was based on three stories by Maupassant; he stated that he considered Michel's film to be a more faithful adaptation of Maupassant.

8. "Découpage" means the sequence of shots in a film, the after-the-fact "storyboard."

9. *Cahiers du cinéma*, April 1951.

10. *Cahiers du cinéma*, September 1952; *G par G*, vol. 1, pp. 80–84.

11. It was held under the sponsorship of Jean Cocteau, who sought to avoid the group's threatened disruption of the official event.

12. *Construire*, no. 24, June 12, 2001. www.construire.ch.

13. Laubscher, interview by author, February 21, 2003.

14. Ibid.

15. Tolmatchoff, interview by author, March 20, 2002.

16. Laubscher, interview by author, February 21, 2002.

17. *Schweizer Film Suisse*, July 7, 1955.

18. Sometimes he was driven there by Tolmatchoff, in whose Opel with a broken windshield Godard would ride and freeze; Tolmatchoff recalled that Godard once thawed himself out by lying underneath the car and smearing himself with the warm oil that dripped from it.

19. Actor Jean-Claude Brialy described Rohmer as "more or less the pope" of the young *Cahiers* critics (*Le Journal du cinéma*, broadcast December 13, 1970 (DVD *Claire's Knee*, Criterion, 2006).

20. *The Guardian*, December 4, 2001.

21. *Cahiers du cinéma*, December 1984.

22. Jean-Luc Godard, interview by author, June 2000.

23. Fereydoun Hoveyda, interview by author, October 30, 2001.

24. Michel Dorsday, telephone interview by author, May 21, 2001.

25. *Cahiers du cinéma*, April 1957.

26. Ibid.

27. Ibid.

28. *L'Humanité,* November 26, 1952, December 2–6, 1952.

29. Michel Marie, *A bout de souffle* (Paris: Nathan, 1999), p. 30.

30. Truffaut cited the example of Michelangelo Antonioni, who was at the same time denied permission to film in Paris a story about juvenile delinquency.

31. The opening image that Truffaut conceived in his first scenario was the Eiffel Tower, seen from afar through a train window—and indeed the opening image of Truffaut's first feature, *The 400 Blows,* was of the tower, but seen from close by, within Paris.

32. Truffaut archives, BiFi.

33. In the event, Becker's next film, *Le Trou,* was released in 1960, and its unusual length made it impossible for it to be shown with a short film; by that time, however, Godard was already a feature-film director—and Becker had died.

34. Tolmatchoff, interview by author, March 20, 2002.

35. Ibid.

36. *Realités,* January 1964.

37. *Le Nouvel Observateur,* January 6, 1984.

38. Hoveyda, interview by author, October 30, 2001.

39. http://www.suntimes.com/includes/ebert/chabrol.html; *Chicago Sun-Times,* "Flashback: Chabrol and Ebert talk in 1971," January 24, 1971.

40. *New York Post,* August 30, 1984.

41. *Cahiers du cinéma,* November 1957.

42. The literal translation is "a whorishness" [*une saloperie*]; in different versions of the story, Godard is said to have called the film "shit," or *dégueulasse,* disgusting.

43. *Arts,* April 22, 1959, in *G par G,* vol. 1, pp. 193–95.

44. *L'Express,* October 3, 1957.

45. Vadim's *Et Dieu . . . créa la femme* (*And God Created Woman*), a sex drama that made Brigitte Bardot an instant international sensation, was highly praised by the *Cahiers* critics and by Godard. But Godard's praise proved a short-lived enthusiasm, as Vadim soon showed himself to be a clever purveyor of titillation rather than a chronicler of mores.

46. *Arts,* April 22, 1959, in *G par G,* vol. 1, pp. 193–95.

47. Jean Douchet, *French New Wave* (New York: D.A.P., 1998).

48. To be precise, *A Bout de souffle* should be translated as "Out of Breath": "Breathless" has a positive quality of joyful astonishment or satiety with pleasure that is absent from "à bout de souffle," which refers to a state of exhaustion.

Chapter Three: *Breathless*

1. Jean-Paul Belmondo, *Trente Ans et vingt-cinq films* (Paris: Union Générale d'Editions, 1963), p. 59.

2. *Arts,* March 12, 1958.

3. Truffaut archives, BiFi.

4. David Richards, *Played Out: The Jean Seberg Story* (New York: Random House, 1981), pp. 84–85.

5. *Les Nouvelles Littéraires,* July 7, 1982.

6. November 26, 1958; *G par G,* vol. 1, p. 150.

7. Philippe Durant, *Belmondo* (Paris: Robert Laffont 1993), p. 149.

8. Capitalized to make a pun on the title of *Les Temps de Paris,* a short-lived daily newspaper intended to rival *Le Monde,* on which Truffaut was able to get Godard work writing gossip; the paper was published from April 17 to July 3, 1956. (www.quid.fr/2000/INFORMAT/Q037010.HTM)

9. A double reference: on the one hand, Sagan was the author of *Bonjour Tristesse,* and the hiring of Jean Seberg brought the association inevitably to mind; but Sagan was also staying in St.-Tropez not far from Truffaut.

10. Belmondo, *Trente Ans et vingt-cinq films,* p. 60.

11. Minister of State in Charge of Cultural Affairs.

12. *Echéances*—the due date for a payment. Chantal de Beauregard, *Georges de Beauregard* (Nîmes: Lacour, 1991), p. 89.

13. Ibid.

14. The version that Truffaut gave Godard, in *La Lettre du cinéma*, no. 3; Godard's version, in *L'Avant-Scène Cinéma*, March 1968.

15. An ingenious way of staying faithful to the original newspaper accounts of the real incident (which ended with the man's arrest and trial) while avoiding the conventional cinematic resolution of a courtroom drama.

16. This story, an experience also shared by Paul Gégauff, would become the basis for Eric Rohmer's first feature, *The Sign of Leo*, which he too filmed in the summer of 1959, immediately before Godard's shoot of *Breathless*. Godard has a cameo role in Rohmer's film, as a party guest who puts on the record player a record of a Beethoven quartet (op. 132) and repeatedly places the needle at the same passage. It was a gesture taken from something that Godard's friends had seen him do.

17. *L'Avant-Scene Cinéma*, no. 79, March 1968.

18. Letter from Godard to Truffaut (undated, July 1958), courtesy of Madeleine Morgenstern.

19. Ibid.

20. Raoul Coutard, interview by author, April 27, 2001.

21. *Le Nouvel Observateur*, September 22, 1965.

22. In a 35mm film camera, shooting 24 frames per second, one foot produced sixteen frames, or two-thirds of a second.

23. Pierre Braunberger, *Pierre Braunberger, producteur: cinéma mémoire* (Paris: C.N.C., 1987).

24. *Filmkritik*, July 1983.

25. Braunberger, *Pierre Braunberger*.

26. The difference is sometimes noticeable.

27. The main character of that film, a gangster named Bob Montagné, is mentioned in *Breathless* as a friend of Poiccard.

28. *Film Culture*, no. 35, 1964–1965.

29. Richards, *Played Out*, p. 85.

30. Seberg complained about Godard's lack of hygiene; he wore his only suit, and she claimed that it smelled (Jean Clay, *Réalités*). Godard may have been relatively poor compared to professional filmmakers, but he is said to have had certainly enough money to buy decent clothing; he was simply neglectful of his appearance and had the habit of owning only one suit, wearing it out, and then replacing it. Seberg also complained that Godard had written a line indicating that her character had stolen money from her concierge; Godard removed the line.

31. Jean-Paul Belmondo, *Trente Ans et vingt-cinq films*, texte recueilli par Gilles Durieux (Paris: Union Générale d'Editeurs, 1963), p. 61.

32. Jean-Luc Godard, *Introduction à une véritable histoire du cinéma* (Paris: Albatros, 1980), p. 86.

33. *Filmkritik* (Munich), July 1983.

34. *France-Observateur* was the precursor to the contemporary *Le Nouvel Observateur*.

35. *France-Observateur*, October 29, 1959.

36. An expression that means something like "wild oats," the not-atypical troubles of a spirited youth.

37. *L'Express*, December 23, 1959.

38. In French, *propédeutique*.

39. Rui Nogueira, ed., *Melville on Melville* (New York: Viking, 1972), p. 76.

40. What he decided at random, however, was the cutting of a scene where Belmondo drives and Seberg is the passenger. Godard had filmed both, separately, from the perspective of the back seat of the car, and had originally intended to cut back and forth between the characters in a traditional shot-reverse shot schema. But he decided that instead of trimming the shots of both characters, he would reduce the scene radically by flipping a coin to see which of the characters would be completely edited out.

41. There was the added psychological effect of suggesting that Michel was on the verge of doing himself in, symbolically, as well.

42. Concordia University, Montreal, March 12, 1977.

43. *The Enforcer* is credited to Bretaigne Windust but was directed in significant part by Raoul Walsh.

44. From a privately recorded audio cassette.

45. Jean Collet, *Jean-Luc Godard* (Paris: Seghers, 1963).

46. *Réalités*, January 1964.

47. Ibid.

48. *Breathless* failed to win the Louis Delluc Prize from French film critics for best film of the year because "only four or five jurors, out of about fifteen, had seen Godard's first feature film." The others did not even take the trouble to attend a private screening. "Thus it could not get a majority." G.S. (Georges Sadoul), *Les Lettres françaises,* January 20, 1966, p. 31. (The prize went instead to *On n'enterre pas le dimanche* [We Don't Bury on Sunday], directed by Michel Drach.)

49. This was understood by some to be an elegant deflection.

50. *Positif,* April 1960.

51. Gérald Devries, *Démocratie 60,* March 25, 1960.

52. Gilbert Salachas, *Radio-Cinéma-Télévision,* April 3, 1960.

53. Jacques Siclier, "*A Bout de Souffle,* Le manifeste de la 'Nouvelle Vague.' "

54. This is the newspaper that goes by that name today.

55. Simone Dubreuilh, *Libération,* March 23, 1960.

56. Pierre Marcabru, *Combat,* September 3, 1960.

57. D and F, *Nouveaux Jours,* March 25, 1960.

58. Siclier, "*A Bout de Souffle,* Le manifeste de la 'Nouvelle Vague.' "

59. Dorsday, interview by author, May 21, 2001.

60. *Le Monde,* March 18, 1960.

61. André Bessèges, *France Catholique,* March 25, 1960.

62. This was known as the "Jaccoud affair."

63. *Tribune de Genève,* February 3, 1960.

64. *Philippe de Broca,* ed. Alain Garel (Paris: Veyrier, 1990).

65. Chantal de Beauregard, *Georges de Beauregard: " . . . Premier sourire de Belmondo . . . dernier de Bardot . . ."* (Nîmes: Lacour/Colporteur, 1991), pp. 99–102. (The title is taken from Godard's eulogy for Beauregard.)

66. Ibid.

67. Quoted in Michel Vianey, *En attendant Godard* (Paris: Grasset, 1967), p. 196.

68. Ibid., p, 197.

Chapter Four: *Le Petit Soldat*

1. *El-Moudjahid* (Algiers), February 7, 1967.

2. René Cortade, *Arts,* March 23, 1960.

3. Raymond Borde, Freddy Buache, and Jean Curtelin, *Nouvelle Vague* (Paris: SERDOC, 1962), p. 21.

4. Louis Seguin, *Positif,* April 1960.

5. Borde, Buache, and Curtelin, *Nouvelle Vague,* p. 64.

6. Ronald Aronson, *Camus and Sartre* (Chicago: University of Chicago, 2004), pp. 213–14.

7. Capdenac, CS *Petit Soldat* clipping.

8. Ibid., February 1960.

9. The subject of brainwashing had received great attention in January and February of 1958, when *L'Express* published as a cover story a three-part series of the first-person account of Lajos Ruff, a young Hungarian who, in the dark days of Stalinist oppression in the early 1950s, had committed the crime of plotting to emigrate, and who, while incarcerated for his offense, was subjected to psychological torture. A loud headline announcing the series as "the first first-person account of brainwashing" was angled onto the upper edge of the cover photo, a close-up of the actor Maurice Ronet in his starring role in Louis Malle's *Elevator to the Gallows;* at first glance, the cover seems to suggest that the photo of Ronet illustrated the brainwashing story—that Ronet was starring in a film that would be the first first-person account of brainwashing. It is not hard to imagine Godard, and indeed many other readers, envisaging such a film—a film that only Godard, of course, sought to make.

10. *Jean-Luc Godard,* vol. 1, pp. 219–20; *Cahiers du Cinéma,* December 1962.

11. *Libération,* April 26, 1960.

12. *L'Express,* June 16, 1960.

13. *L'Humanité,* March 21, 1960.

14. *France-Observateur,* April 14, 1960.

15. CS *Petit Soldat* clipping.

16. Godard's original notion was that the action would last "fifteen days;" a radio broadcast heard in the last scenes of action specify the next day to be Thursday, May 22 (1958), yet only four days of

action are explicitly shown on-screen. The scenes of torture, in which days and nights are not seen elapsing, are of unspecified duration.

17. CS *Petit Soldat* clipping.
18. Ibid.
19. *France-Observateur*, March 17, 1960.
20. Agnès Guillemot, *Cahiers du Cinéma* special issue, *Nouvelle Vague*, 1999, p. 45. Nadine Marquand was the first replacement for Decugis, but soon left the production (to join the actor Jean-Louis Trintignant, whom she would marry, on a shoot).
21. A complex reference: "Veronica" was the main character of the Russian film *The Cranes Are Flying*, which, in a roundabout way, had resulted in *Breathless* (and which was shown at Cannes in May 1958, where Godard and Truffaut were at the time of the May 13 putsch); "Véronique" also is the name of Godard's younger sister, who is approximately the same age as Anna Karina, and who at the time was a student in Paris; and "Dreyer" is, of course, a wink to Carl Theodor Dreyer, the Danish director.
22. Fontana's wife, Carmen, is the woman who calls to Godard from the window in *Une Femme coquette*.
23. Schiffman, videotaped interview by Bernard Cohn, September 27, 1999.
24. Ibid.
25. *La Tribune de Genève*, May 7–8, 1960.
26. Laubscher, interview by author, February 21, 2003.
27. Michel Subor, interview by author, November 26, 2001.
28. CS *Petit Soldat* clipping.
29. Michel Subor, interview by author, November 26, 2001.
30. *L'Express*, June 16, 1960.
31. Jean-Luc Godard, interview by author, June 9, 2000.
32. Godard, *Introduction à une Véritable Histoire du cinéma*, p. 60.
33. The French phrase is "le cinéma c'est 24 fois la vérité par seconde" (the cinema is 24 times truth per second).
34. *Libération*, October 2, 2001.
35. Ibid.
36. *Film* (London), May 1973.
37. Paul Gégauff, in *Godard*, Jean-Luc Douin (Paris: Rivages, 1989), p. 21; Bérangère Allaux, interview with author, April 15, 2001.
38. *Les Lettres françaises*, January 31, 1963.
39. *Le Monde*, September 13, 1960.
40. *L'Express*, June 16, 1960.
41. Ibid.
42. As in ballet.
43. Subor, interview by author, November 26, 2001.
44. Godard, *Introduction à une véritable histoire du cinéma*, p. 53.
45. Godard, interview by author, June 9, 2000.
46. As in *Breathless*, one brief scene was filmed in direct sound with the Nagra tape recorder that Tolmatchoff had procured for Godard: aboard a train, Tolmatchoff himself tells Laubscher a convoluted joke.
47. Guillemot, *Cahiers du cinéma, Nouvelle Vague*, special issue, 1999, pp. 45–46.
48. *G par G*, vol. 1, p. 221; *Cahiers du cinéma*, December 1962.
49. "The only way to stay out of trouble is to grow old, so I guess I'll concentrate on that. Maybe I'll live so long that I'll forget her. Maybe I'll die tryin.'"
50. *L'Express*, June 16, 1960.
51. *Cahiers du cinéma*, vol. 1, p. 582.
52. *Arts*, March 23, 1960.
53. *Le Monde*, September 13, 1960.
54. Actually the sentences are not identical: in the scene of torture, Laszlo of the FLN says, "Quelquefois il faut avoir la force de frayer son chemin avec un poignard," whereas at the end, Jacques of the Red Hand says, "Il faut avoir la force quelquefois de frayer son chemin avec un poignard."
55. *Libération*, April 4, 1960.

56. *L'Express,* June 16, 1960.
57. *Paris-Presse,* September 14, 1960.
58. Quoted in Beauregard, *Beauregard,* p. 118.
59. Criterion DVD *of Breathless,* 2007.
60. CS *Petit Soldat* clipping (Sylvain Zegel).
61. *Les Lettres françaises,* January 31, 1963.
62. The system is still in effect. To this day, some officials of the CNC are sensitive about the use of the word *censorship* and prefer to talk about the "control" of films.
63. Instead of removing the shot, Resnais painted over the officer's cap.
64. *Le Monde,* March 11, 1960.
65. CS *Petit Soldat* clipping.
66. *Cinéma 61,* no 52 (January 1961), p. 19.
67. *L'Express,* June 16, 1960.
68. *Le Monde,* September 14, 1960.
69. Ibid., September 16, 1960.
70. *Paris-Presse,* September 14, 1960.
71. CS *Petit Soldat* clipping.
72. *Le Nouvel Observateur,* May 10, 1989; *G par G,* vol. 2, p. 176.
73. Signoret had just won the Oscar for Best Actress in a Leading Role for her performance in *Room at the Top.*
74. Truffaut, despite his association with the right wing in the 1950s, had mollified his political views, in large measure under the influence of his father-in-law, Ignace Morgenstern, and considered himself a "Mendésiste," a supporter of the moderate leftist Gaullism of Pierre Mendès-France.
75. *L'Express,* October 6, 1960.
76. Madeleine Morgenstern, interview by author, February 16, 2003.
77. *Les Lettres françaises,* May 14, 1964.
78. *G par G,* vol. 2, p. 413.
79. Beauregard, *Beauregard,* p. 119.
80. http://www.ornitho.org/ornitho/imprim.php3?id_article=24; Pierre Vidal-Naquet, April 20, 2001.
81. Beauregard, who supported French control of Algeria, hid the film director Jacques Dupont, a member of the OAS, from the French authorities.

Chapter Five: *A Woman Is a Woman*

1. According to CNC documents from the Commission de Contrôle. In 1960, the French currency was revalued by a factor of 100 (the former 100 francs would now be 1 new franc).
2. The aspect ratio was 2.35:1; it was achieved by the use of anamorphic lenses in shooting and projection.
3. For some of the street scenes, Coutard would indeed use a handheld Cameflex with Cinemascope lenses, and for those sequences, Godard would dub the sound.
4. It was recorded onto a separate reel of 35 mm film, not the one that passed through the camera.
5. Godard later told Vlady that he needed to have Beauregard's rejection of well-known actresses whose fees were too high in order to have the producer's authorization to make the film with Karina. Marina Vlady, *24 Images/Seconde* (Paris: Fayard, 2005), pp. 159–60.
6. In Beauregard, *Beauregard,* p. 119, Karina retrospectively scoffed at Godard's interest in Collins, saying, "There's no one more artificial than Joan Collins . . . Jean-Luc always says that he doesn't want make-up, that he likes the natural"; she did not consider that, prior to her first performance with Godard in *Le Petit Soldat,* there had been no one more artificial than Anna Karina either, who had been a made-up, coiffed model and cover girl. It was only Godard's antitheatrical minimalism and repudiation of the artifices of makeup, coiffure, and theater-bound technique that allowed her own character and irrepressible nature to shine through the thin scrim of her performance.
7. Rousseau, like Godard, was Swiss, and originally from Geneva—and the Ile Rousseau was featured prominently in *Le Petit Soldat* as well as in the short film *Une Femme coquette.*
8. *L'Express,* January 12, 1961.
9. *Cahiers du cinéma, Spécial Godard* (1991).

10. Raoul Coutard, in *Jean-Luc Godard* (Munich: Carl Hanser Verlag, 1979), p. 63.

11. *Cahiers du cinéma, Spécial Godard, Trente ans depuis* (1991).

12. *Le Nouvel Observateur,* September 22, 1965.

13. *Films and Filming,* September 1961.

14. *Cahiers du cinéma,* December 1962; *G par G,* vol. 1, p. 222.

15. *Télérama,* May 22, 1961.

16. *L'Express,* July 27, 1961.

17. Jean-Claude Brialy, *Le Ruisseau des singes,* p. 162. Anna Karina, however, considers the actor's remarks one-sided and sensationalizing. She told me, "Brialy said, 'They fought.' Why didn't he say, 'They came to my chateau; Jean-Luc ate bread and jam'?" (Anna Karina, interview by author, June 18, 2001.)

18. *Tribune de Lausanne,* February 4–5, 1961.

19. *L'Express,* January 12, 1961.

20. *Cinema 65: dossier du mois,* Ciné-Club d'Annecy, November 1964.

21. Ibid.

21. Peter W. Jansen and Wolfram Schütte, eds., *Jean-Luc Godard* (Munich: Carl Hanser Verlag, 1979), p. 71.

23. *Herald Tribune,* February 5, 1961.

24. *Paris-Match,* March 25, 1961.

25. Agnès Varda, interview by author, March 16, 2001.

26. Beauregard, *Beauregard,* p. 112.

27. Ibid., p.120.

28. *Cahiers du cinéma,* December 1962; *G par G,* vol. 1, pp. 225–26.

29. Coutard, interview by author, April 27, 2001.

30. *Cahiers du cinéma,* December 1962.

31. *L'Express,* April 13, 1961.

32. *L'Express,* July 27, 1961.

33. *The Golden Coach.*

34. The record was never made available, but a transcript of its text was published in 1968 in *Jean-Luc Godard par Jean-Luc Godard.* It is now available as an extra on the Criterion DVD of *A Woman Is a Woman.*

35. Agnès Varda, *Varda par Agnès* (Paris: Cahiers du cinéma, 1994), p. 56.

36. Morvan Lebesque, *L'Express,* September 14, 1961.

37. Michel Aubriant, *Paris Presse-L'Intransigeant,* in Beauregard, *Beauregard,* pp. 124–25.

38. Jean de Baroncelli, *Le Monde,* September 14, 1961.

39. Jacques Siclier, *Télérama,* September 1961.

40. Claude Mauriac, *Le Figaro littéraire,* September 6, 1961.

41. *Cahiers du cinéma,* December 1962.

42. *Positif,* July 1959.

43. Paule Sengissen, *Radio-Cinéma-Télévision,* in *Cahiers du cinéma,* February 2001, p. 69.

44. René Cortade, *Arts,* March 23, 1960.

45. François Truffaut, *Correspondence, 1945–1984* (New York: Farrar, Straus and Giroux, 1990), p. 165.

46. *France-Observateur,* October 19, 1961.

47. Ibid.

48. *Cahiers du cinéma,* December 1962; *G par G,* vol. 1, p. 216.

49. Ibid., p. 232.

50. *France-Observateur,* October 19, 1961.

51. *Cahiers du cinéma,* December 1962, p. 50.

52. *Sight and Sound* 32, no. 1 (Winter 1962–63), p. 10.

53. A right-wing French writer who had looked favorably upon the German occupation.

54. *L'Express,* July 27, 1961.

55. Barthes's remark is in *Les Lettres Nouvelles,* March 11, 1959; Godard recalled it in a roundtable discussion on *Hiroshima mon amour,* in *Cahiers du cinéma,* July 1959. The actual quote from Barthes: "Recalling the first images of *Le Beau Serge,* I say to myself once more that, here in France, the talent is on the right and the truth is on the left; that it is this fatal disjunction between form

and meaning that suffocates us; that we are unable to escape from aesthetics because our aesthetic is always the alibi for a conservatism." Quoted in *Oeuvres complètes,* vol. 1, 1993, p. 787.

56. Truffaut, *Correspondence,* p. 165.
57. *France Soir,* November 24, 1961.
58. Beauregard, *Beauregard,* p. 141.
59. *France-Soir,* November 23 and 24, 1961.
60. *Paris-Presse–L'Intransigeant,* November 24, 1961.
61. Ibid., January 9, 1962.

Chapter Six: *Vivre sa vie, Le Nouveau Monde, Les Carabiniers*

1. Rozier wanted his largely improvised dialogue to be recorded with direct sound. Beauregard said that the budget didn't allow it. To aid with dubbing, Rozier recorded the dialogue on portable, non-sync-sound equipment, which malfunctioned. Rozier couldn't understand the dialogue and called in a lip-reader to transcribe it.
2. Marin Karmitz, interview by author, April 27, 2001.
3. *Combat,* September 11, 1962.
4. *Cahiers du cinéma,* December 1962; *G par G,* vol. 1, p. 227.
5. *Combat,* September 11, 1962.
6. *G par G,* vol. 2, *1984–1998,* edited by Alain Bergala (Paris: Cahiers du cinéma, 1998), p. 298. *Limelight* no. 34, January, 1995.
7. *Cinéma 65,* March 1965.
8. The French word for "master of ceremonies" is "bonimenteur."
9. *Le Monde,* September 20, 1962.
10. Ibid.
11. *Cinématographie française,* February 17, 1962.
12. *Sight and Sound* 32, no. 1, Winter 1962–63.
13. *Cahiers du cinéma,* December 1962; *G par G,* vol. 1, p. 227.
14. *Le Monde,* September 20, 1962.
15. *Cahiers du cinéma,* December 1962; *G par G,* vol. 1, p. 228.
16. Schiffman, in *Le Nouvel Observateur,* May 6, 1965.
17. *Le Nouvel Observateur,* December 3, 1964.
18. *Libération,* January 22, 2005.
19. *Cahiers du cinéma,* December 1962; *G par G,* vol. 1, p. 221.
20. This image comes after the credits, which are superimposed over backlighted silhouette close-ups, in profile and facing the camera, of Anna Karina.
21. *Cinéma 65,* March 1965.
22. Ibid.
23. *Cahiers du cinéma,* December 1962; *G par G,* vol. 1, p. 227.
24. *France-Observateur,* October 19, 1961.
25. Author's translation of the Baudelaire translation, which Godard used in the film.
26. *Tribune de Genève,* April 26, 1962.
27. Gilles Deleuze, in his two books, *L'Image-Mouvement* and *L'Image-Temps,* uses the same paradigm of space and time. But Deleuze's books are only loosely historical; he does in general suggest the switch in paradigm to coincide with the New Wave and does write more about Godard under the second than the first rubric, but he does not see a moment of enlightenment and revolution; we do.
28. Files of Jean-Pierre Laubscher, undated interview by Patrick Thévénon, *France-Soir.*
29. *La Cinématographie française,* September 8, 1962.
30. *France-Observateur,* September 6, 1962.
31. *Candide,* September 12, 1962, in *L'Avant-Scène Cinéma,* no. 19, October 15, 1962.
32. *Le Figaro littéraire,* September 22, 1962.
33. *Les Lettres françaises,* September 13, 1962.
34. *Télérama,* September 30, 1962.
35. *Cahiers du cinéma,* October 1962.
36. *Combat,* September 24, 1962.

37. *Le Film français,* February 21, 1964.
38. Jean Clay, "Le Paradoxe de Jean-Luc Godard," *Réalités,* September 1963.
39. Beauregard, *Beauregard,* p. 141.
40. Ibid.
41. *Cahiers du cinéma,* December 1962; *G par G,* vol. 1, pp. 228–29.
42. Alain Bergala, *Godard au travail* (Paris: *Cahiers du cinéma,* 2006), p. 108.
43. Godard, *Introduction à une véritable histoire du cinéma,* p. 67.
44. Ibid., p. 69.
45. *New York,* September 1964; published in *Objectif* 65 (Quebec, Canada), August–September 1965; in *Bande à Part,* ed. Yellow Now, p. 136.
46. He played the male lead in Agnès Varda's *Cléo de 5 à 7.*
47. Antoine Bourseiller, interview by author, November 16, 2001.
48. Ibid.
49. Anna Karina, interview by author, June 18, 2001.
50. Coutard, interview by author, April 27, 2001.
51. *Sight and Sounds,* vol. 32, no. 1 (Winter 1962–1963).
52. The company's investment was a prepurchase of distribution rights.
53. They called him "Gaspard-Zero" (*huit* means "eight").
54. Coutard, interview by author, April 27, 2001.
55. Pierre Braunberger, letter to François Truffaut (undated, March 1968); Truffaut archives, Bifi; *Correspondence, 1945–1984,* p. 387.
56. Hélène Frappat, *Jacques Rivette, secret compris* (Paris: Cahiers du Cinéma, 2001), p. 129.
57. *Journal de Genève,* May 12–13, 1962.
58. *Télérama,* clipping from Bibliothèque André Malraux, Paris.
59. *Sight and Sound,* vol. 32, no. 1 (Winter 1962–1963).
60. *Cahiers du cinéma,* July 1963, in *La Politique des auteurs* (Paris: Champ Libre, 1972), p. 98.
61. Jean Gruault, *Ce que dit l'autre* (Paris: Julliard, 1992), pp. 225–26.
62. Published in *L'Avant-Scène cinéma* in 1976.
63. *G par G,* vol. 1, p. 238.
64. José Luis Guarner, *Rossellini* (New York: Praeger, 1970), p. 104.
65. *Cahiers du cinéma,* December 1962; *G par G,* vol. 1, p. 230.
66. In a later interview, Godard oddly misattributed the story to H. P. Lovecraft: "I took up the theme of a book by Lovecraft, *I Am a Legend.* One day, upon waking, a man notices that the world has changed and that he is the only one to have remained a man. Thus, he becomes a legend." *Le Monde,* May 6, 1965.
67. The details on the page, however, are from the edition of November 17.
68. Rossellini's episode is called *Illibatezza*; Pasolini's episode, *La Ricotta,* stars Orson Welles as a fictional director of the Passion. Gregoretti's episode is called *Il pollo ruspante.*
69. Bitsch, interview by author, September 19, 2001.
70. *Cahiers du cinéma,* December 1962; *G par G,* vol. 1, p. 230.
71. *Réalités,* September 1963.
72. *L'Avant-Scène Cinéma,* July–September 1976, p. 7.
73. Bitsch, interview by author, September 19, 2001.
74. *Combat,* June 5, 1963, in *L'Avant-scéne cinéma,* July–September, 1976.
75. *Réalités,* September 1964.
76. Collet, *Jean-Luc Godard,* p. 107.
77. The other films were made by Claude Chabrol, Ugo Gregoretti, Hiromichi Horikawa, and Roman Polanski.
78. Tag Gallagher, *The Adventures of Roberto Rossellini* (New York: Da Capo, 1998), pp. 557–58.

Chapter Seven: *Contempt*

1. *Lire,* May 1997.
2. Catherine Rihoit, *Brigitte Bardot, un mythe français* (Paris: Oliver-Orban, 1966), p. 165.
3. Brigitte Bardot, *Initiales B.B.* (Paris: Grasset, 1996), pp. 308–9.
4. Ibid.

5. The name Javal is an unusual choice, being the name of one of the leading Jewish families in Paris in the nineteenth century (Esther Benbassa, *Histoire des Juifs de France* (Paris: Seuil, 2000), p. 164); in Moravia's book, the character was named Riccardo Molteni. The name Moravia is a pseudonym; the author's family name was Pincherle, and he was in fact Jewish.

6. Collet, *Jean-Luc Godard*, p. 105.

7. *G par G*, vol. 1, p. 242; BiFi archive, SCEN, 1732.

8. Collet, *Jean-Luc Godard*, p. 100.

9. This story, perpetuated by Lang himself, is apocryphal; Lang's departure seems to have taken a little longer to organize. (Patrick McGilligan, *Fritz Lang: The Nature of the Beast* (London: Faber and Faber, 1997), p. 180.

10. Raoul Coutard, *Filmkritik*, July 1983, p. 333.

11. Tolmatchoff, interview by author, March 20, 2002.

12. Laubscher, interview by author, February 21, 2003.

13. Bitsch, interview by author, September 19, 2001.

14. "Pour le Plaisir," for French television, 1965.

15. Karina, interview by author, June 18, 2001.

16. Bardot, *Initiales B.B.*, p. 327.

17. Tolmatchoff, interview by author, March 20, 2002.

18. Schiffman, videotaped interview by Bernard Cohn, September 27, 1999.

19. Beauregard, *Beauregard*, p. 169.

20. BiFi archive, *Le Mépris*, SCEN, 1732.

21. *Réalités*, September 1963.

22. Ibid.

23. The other two minutes were filmed later—see below.

24. Karina, interview by author, June 18, 2001.

25. *Libération*, October 14, 1981.

26. *Lui*, July 1965.

27. Michel Vianey, "En Attendant Homère," *L'Express*, May 30, 1963.

28. Schiffman, videotaped interview by Bernard Cohn, September 27, 1999.

29. Vianey, "En Attendant Homère," *L'Express*, May 30, 1963.

30. *Le Figaro littéraire*, December 26, 1963.

31. Vianey, "En Attendant Homère," *L'Express*, May 30, 1963.

32. Schiffman, videotaped interview by Bernard Cohn, September 27, 1999.

33. Truffaut, *Correspondence*, letter to Godard, 1973.

34. Collet, *Jean-Luc Godard*, pp. 97–98.

35. Ibid.

36. *G par G*, vol. 1, p. 16.

37. Godard, *Introduction à une véritable histoire du cinéma*, p. 67.

38. Michel Vianey, interview by author, June 16, 2000.

39. Agnès Guillemot, *Jean-Luc Godard* (Munich: Carl Hanser Verlag, 1979), p. 73.

40. *Les Lettres françaises*, December 25, 1963.

41. The book was titled *Entrez sans frapper* (Enter Without Knocking); Godard placed it so that the title faced the camera; before the cameras rolled, Piccoli turned the book so that its title was upside down, to spare Bardot the vulgarity. "Godard was furious, but after the rushes, he came to tell me that I was right." Robert Chazal, *Michel Piccoli le provocateur* (Paris: France-Empire, 1989), p. 63.

42. *Le Film français*, August 23, 1963.

43. *Le Monde*, February 15, 1966.

44. Godard did in fact film an added scene of Prokosch watching a nude Camille getting dressed, but it did not make the final cut. (Michel Marie, *Le Mépris* [Paris: Nathan, 1990], p. 20.)

45. *Les Lettres françaises*, December 25, 1963.

46. *Le Figaro littéraire*, December 26, 1963.

47. *Cinéma 65*, March 1965.

48. Examples include such avowedly Godard-ophobic critics as Samuel Lachize, *L'Humanité;* Robert Benayoun, *France-Observateur;* Judith Crist, *New York Herald Tribune;* and Frances Herridge, *New York Post.*

49. Godard mentioned this, in print and on television. See *Les Lettres françaises*, December 25, 1963, and Godard interview by François Chalais, in the Criterion DVD set of *Contempt*.

50. *L'Express*, in an unsigned piece, declared this first version of *Contempt* to be "an attempt at synthesis between the young cinema and the elements theoretically sure of success." *L'Express*, September 5, 1963.

51. *G par G*, vol. 1, p. 16.

52. *Sight and Sound*, September 1996.

53. Godard, interview by author, June 9, 2001.

54. *Films and Filming*, September 1961.

55. Jean-Luc Godard, interview by François Chalais, on the *Contempt* DVD.

56. *G par G*, vol. 1, p. 222; *Cahiers du cinéma*, December 1962.

57. David Bordwell, Janet Staiger, and Kristin Thompson, *The Classical Hollywood Cinema* (New York: Columbia University Press, 1985).

58. In the long bedroom scene, Paul walks around the apartment in his Dean Martin hat and a white toga, and Camille sits in the tub reading aloud from an interview with Fritz Lang about Greek tragedy.

59. Jean-Louis Bory, *Arts*, December 27, 1963.

60. *Paris-Presse-L'Intransigeant*, December 25, 1963.

61. *Le Monde*, December 22–23, 1963.

62. Gérard Legrand, *Positif*, March 1964.

63. *France-Observateur*, December 24, 1963.

64. *Les Lettres françaises*, December 25, 1963.

65. *Les Lettres françaises*, February 6, 1964.

66. Plus "143,704 in the seven key provincial cities": Marie, *Le Mépris*, p. 21.

67. *Cinématographie française*, January 4, 1964.

68. Quoted in Calvin Tomkins, *The New Yorker*, September 16, 1967.

Chapter Eight: *Montparnasse et Levallois, Band of Outsiders*

1. *La Cinématographie française*, October 12, 1963.

2. Albert Maysles, interview by author, May 31, 2000.

3. *Cahiers du cinéma*, October 1965; *G par G*, vol. 1, p. 259.

4. *Cahiers du cinéma*, December 1963–January 1964, p. 19.

5. Godard had been paid fifty thousand dollars to make *Contempt*, a high-budget film.

6. Jean-Luc Godard, *Interviews*, David Sterritt, ed. (Jackson: University Press of Mississippi, 1998), p. 17; from *Los Angeles Free Press*, March 15, 1968.

7. *Télérama*, August 16, 1964.

8. Anouchka, a Russian nickname for Anna, is pronounced "Anoushka."

9. Barthélemy Amengual, *Bande à Part de Jean-Luc Godard* (Crisnée, Belgium: Yellow Now, 1993), p. 115.

10. BiFi archives.

11. Sami Frey, interview by author, March 8, 2002.

12. Raoul Coutard, in *Bande à Part*, ed. Yellow Now, p. 114.

13. Ibid.

14. *Télérama*, August 16, 1964.

15. Karina, interview by author, June 18, 2001.

16. *Le Nouvel Observateur*, December 3, 1964.

17. *Télérama*, August 16, 1964.

18. *Paris-Match*, June 13, 1964.

19. *Cinéma 65*, March 1965.

20. Unifrance Film, no. 268 (Cinémathèque Suisse).

21. *Cahiers du cinéma*, June 1964.

22. Ibid., October 1964.

23. *L'Express*, August 22, 1964.

24. *Les Lettres françaises*, August 20, 1964.

25. *Cahiers du cinéma*, October 1965; *G par G*, vol. 1, p. 263.

26. Literally, *The Eleven O'Clock Demon*.

27. Unifrance Film, no. 268, p. 148.
28. Jean-Luc Godard, interview by Gérard Guégan and Michel Pétris, *Les Lettres françaises,* November 19, 1964.

Chapter Nine: *A Married Woman*

1. *La Cinématographie française,* "Rendez-vous de Cannes" (1964), CS clipping.
2. In another account, Chiarini decided not to premiere the film.
3. *France-Soir,* June 16, 1964.
4. Letter from Godard to François Truffaut, undated. Courtesy of Madeleine Morgenstern.
5. Godard, *Introduction à une véritable histoire du cinéma,* p. 129.
6. *Ch* in French is pronounced like *sh* in English; thus the actress's first name is pronounced "Masha."
7. *Cinémonde,* August 1964.
8. Macha Méril, interview by Aimé Patri, *Preuves,* April 1965.
9. *L'Express,* September 7, 1964.
10. The camera pans down the sign, which is arranged vertically to end on the word *main* and then pans left to the word *de*—rather than "demain," it reads, "main de," "hand of," making the title read: "Yesterday, Today, Hand of . . ."—signifying what is learned a few minutes later in the film: that the actor, Robert, is not the married woman's first lover. (Indeed, three months earlier her husband had had her followed by a detective and learned of that previous infidelity, which is why she now takes such extraordinary precautions about seeing her lover.)
11. *Arts,* May 5, 1965.
12. *Les Lettres françaises,* September 17–23, 1964.
13. Gaston Bounoure, *Alain Resnais* (Paris: Seghers, 1974). (Resnais used watercolor to paint over it.)
14. Macha Méril, interview by author, March 27, 2002.
15. Roud, *A Passion for Films,* p. 95.
16. Georges Langlois and Glenn Myrent, *Henri Langlois* (Paris: Denoël, 1986), p. 234.
17. Roud, *A Passion for Films,* p. 101.
18. Langlois and Myrent, *Henri Langlois,* p. 289.
19. "And about 800 in 1976": but of course this is another part of the story. René Bonnell, *Le Cinéma exploité* (Paris: Seuil, 1978), p. 292.
20. *Cinématographie française,* June–July 1964.
21. *France-Observateur,* March 1, 1962.
22. Ibid., July 25, 1963 (italics in original).
22. *Les Lettres françaises,* September 17–23, 1964.
24. *France-Soir,* September 10, 1964.
25. *Lire,* November 1998.
26. *Le Temps* (Geneva), June 7, 2001.
27. Sterritt, *Godard Interviews,* p. 46.
28. *L'Express,* September 14, 1964.
29. *Le Monde,* September 10, 1964.
30. *Cahiers du cinéma,* October 1964.
31. *France-Observateur,* October 8, 1964.
32. Ibid.
33. *France-Soir,* October 15, 1964.
34. Ibid.
35. Ibid.
36. *New York Times,* December 4, 1964.
37. Ibid.
38. Méril, interview by author, March 27, 2002.
39. Cendrars, *La Gazette de Lausanne,* January 16, 1965.
40. *New Yorker,* October 9, 1965.
41. *Les Lettres françaises,* December 10, 1964.
42. Gérard Guégan, interview by author, March 14, 2002.
43. Godard, interview by Gérard Guégan and Michel Pétris, *Les Lettres françaises,* November 19, 1964.
44. Guégan, interview by author, March 14, 2002.

45. Ibid.
46. Ibid.
47. Jean Daniel, *Oeuvres autobiographiques,* (Paris: Grasset, 2002), p. 249.
48. Ibid.
49. Ibid., p. 429.
50. "Les copains" was the code word by which the young French rock generation referred to each other.
51. Guégan, interview by author, March 14, 2002.
52. Daniel, *Oeuvres autobiographiques,* p. 942.
53. Ibid., p. 942.
54. The first British translation of the book was *Words;* the second, American, was *The Words;* I favor the former on the grounds of meaning: the book is not about particular words but about the author's youthful and lifelong obsession with words.
55. Claude Lévi-Strauss, *La Pensée sauvage* (Paris: Plon, 1962).
56. *Les Lettres françaises,* November 19, 1964.
57. *Cahiers du cinéma,* December 1962; *G par G,* vol. 1, p. 233.
58. *Le Monde,* April 18, 1964.
59. *Cinéma 65,* March 1965.

Chapter Ten: The American Business

1. *Cahiers du cinéma,* December 1962, p. 90.
2. In an unpublished essay, "The American Critical Reception of Jean-Luc Godard, 1959–1968," Rafael Vela also argues that Godard's films in the United States depended upon the importation of auteurism through the work of Andrew Sarris. Rafael Vela, interview by author, 2004.
3. *DGA Magazine* 25, no. 5 (January–March 2001).
4. Ibid.
5. Sarris is often unjustly maligned for having adapted the *politique des auteurs* as the auteur *theory,* as if a theory were any less heuristic or malleable than a policy or a politics.
6. Such films would eventually come, but they would be not his; rather they were those of such American neoclassicists as Martin Scorsese, Brian De Palma, and Bogdanovich himself.
7. A British auteurist publication.
8. "Incredible Shrinking Hollywood," *Holiday,* March 1966, p. 86; in Louis Menand, "Finding It at the Movies," *New York Review of Books,* March 23, 1995.
9. Pauline Kael, *I Lost It at the Movies* (Boston: Little Brown, 1965), pp. 14–15.
10. She "would not recommend" Godard's 1965 *Pierrot le fou* either. Pauline Kael, *Kiss Kiss Bang Bang* (Boston: Little Brown, 1968), pp. 17 and 130.
11. "The Perils of Being Pauline, Francis Davis Interviews Pauline Kael," *The New Yorker,* October 22, 2001.
12. *New York Times,* September 27, 1964.
13. No. 2 (Summer–Autumn 1964), p. 9.
14. *New Republic,* September 11, 1965.
15. *The New Yorker,* August 21, 1965.
16. David Newman, National Film School of Denmark, EuroScreenwriters 1998–1999, Conversation at Hotel Chelsea, New York, October 1, 1998.
17. Robert Benton, interview by author, September 17, 2004.
18. Ibid.
19. Truffaut, *Correspondence,* pp. 251–52.
20. Collection of Madeleine Morgenstern.
21. Robert Benton, interview by author, September 17, 2004.
22. Ibid.
23. *The Bonnie and Clyde Book,* ed. Sandra Wake and Nicola Hayden, eds. (New York: Simon and Schuster, 1972), p. 23.
24. Godard, interview by author, June 9, 2000.
25. Benton, interview by author, September 17, 2004.
26. Louis Menand, "Paris, Texas," *The New Yorker,* February 17, 2003; *The Bonnie and Clyde Book,* p. 23.

27. Ibid.
28. Louis Menand, "Paris, Texas," *The New Yorker*, February 17, 2003.

Chapter Eleven: *Alphaville*

1. Interview with André Michelin by P. G., undated and unreferenced, from file at Bibliothèque André-Malraux, Paris.
2. Ibid.
3. Bitsch, interview by author, September 19, 2001.
4. As Bitsch recalled, when the film was done, "Michelin had to reimburse the Germans because they said that it wasn't what was in the screenplay."
5. *Les Alphabètes*: the Alphabets (the Literates).
6. *Analphabète: An-Alphabet* (Illiterate).
7. *Le Nouvel Observateur*, December 3, 1964.
8. *Cinématographe*, December 1980.
9. The title is a nod to Aldiss, whose novella *Equator* (published in French in 1963) features space travelers from the planet Alpha.
10. Jean-Luc Godard, interview by Jean Collet (*Télérama*), from a clipping file at Bibliothèque André-Malraux, Paris.
11. A nod to Harry Dickson, a detective from a French pulp fiction series of the 1930s.
12. The name that Godard had scripted was Leonardo Davinci (*sic*); the change of the scientist's and his daughter Natasha's last name to von Braun reinforced the film's specific references to the present day as an already alienating future.
13. *Cinématographie française*, January 30, 1965.
14. *Les Lettres françaises*, April 22, 1965.
15. Ibid.
16. Godard, *Introduction à une véritable histoire du cinéma*, p. 109.
17. John Ardagh, *The New France*, 3rd edition (London: Penguin, 1977), p. 605.
18. *Cinématographe*, December 1980.
19. *Le Nouvel Observateur*, May 6, 1965.
20. Schiffman, videotaped interview by Bernard Cohn.
21. Ibid.
22. Godard, interview by Collet.
23. Ibid.
24. *L'Express*, July 27, 1961.
25. Godard, interview by Collet.
26. Bernanos distinguished the French Revolution from the Russian Revolution, which he characterized as the revolt of urban and cosmopolitan Jews who "exploited" the Christian "muzhiks" rooted in the land and in authentic Russian culture (George Bernanos, *La France contre les robots* [Paris: R. Laffont, 1947], pp. 84–85).
27. Ibid., p. 139.
28. This role was played by Christa Lang, a German actress living in Paris, who would soon meet and later marry the American film director Samuel Fuller.
29. The heroine of *Le Nouveau Monde* keeps a dagger in the same place.
30. Paul Eluard, *Capitale de la douleur*, edited with an introduction and notes by Vera J. Daniel (Oxford: Blackwell French Texts, 1985), pp. 42, 114, 115.
31. *Paris-Presse*, May 12, 1965.
32. Ibid.
33. *Le Monde*, December 29, 1965.
34. *Cinématographe*, December 1980.
35. *New York Review of Books*, October 28, 1965.
36. *The New Yorker*, October 9, 1965.
37. *Village Voice*, September 16, 1965.

Chapter Twelve: *Pierrot le fou*

1. *France-Soir*, February 25, 1964.
2. Philippe Durant, *Belmondo* (Lausanne: Ed. Pierre-Marcel Favre, 1987), p. 110.

3. *Cahiers du cinéma,* October 1965; *G par G,* vol. 1, p. 265.
4. Rémo Forlani, *Toujours vif et joyeux* (Paris: Denoël, 2003), p. 472.
5. Godard, *Introduction à une véritable histoire du cinéma,* p. 146.
6. www.arkepix.com/kinok/Raoul%20coutard/coutard_interview1.html, text of an interview from May 1, 1999.
7. *Lui,* July 1965.
8. "Le Tourbillon de la vie" (The Whirlwind of Life).
9. Serge Rezvani, *Les Années–lumière (Le Testament amoureux)* (Arles: Actes Sud, 1997), p. 1166.
10. Alain Bergala, *Nul mieux que Godard,* pp. 5–6. Bergala would later be a critic and editor at *Cahiers.*
11. Claude Lanzmann, interview by author, February 26, 2003.
12. *Le Nouvel Observateur,* July 21, 1965.
13. Ibid.
14. Luc Moullet, interview by author, November 17, 2001.
15. Alain Jouffroy, interview by author, June 27, 2002.
16. Jean-Paul Belmondo, interview with Rex Reed, *New York Herald Tribune,* October 17, 1965.
17. Vianey, *En attendant Godard* (Paris: Grasset, 1987), p. 119.
18. Schiffman, taped interview by Bernard Cohn, September 27, 1999.
19. *Cahiers du cinéma,* October 1965.
20. *Le Monde,* April 22, 1966.
21. *Cahiers du cinéma,* October 1965; *G par G,* vol. 1, p. 265.
22. *Cahiers du cinéma,* October 1965; *G par G,* vol. 1, p. 263.
23. The film was never made.
24. The 1962 Ford Galaxie that Godard sank in the sea was in fact his own; and he had acquired it through the good offices and better contrivances of his friend Roland Tolmatchoff: "The '62 Galaxie—because I had a '61—which I just sold, by the way—the big white American car—which I had gone to New York to buy—then I went to his home on the rue Niccolo. French customs knocks on the door—'That car, is it yours?' He says, 'No, it's his.' By chance, I had on me the papers for import into Switzerland, and the temporary registration—they said, 'Make sure you bring it back to Switzerland.' That's the car that he dunked in the water." Tolmatchoff, interview by author, March 20, 2002.
25. *New York Times,* March 18, 1965.
26. She is wearing a T-shirt that reads "Mic Mac," and as they dance to music coming from a portable record player, Marianne murmurs along: "Oh, quel micmac!" (Oh, what a mess!) The moment, of a passing insignificance, is strikingly significant: it is a pentimento, alluding to a third song that is not in the film but is inseparable from it. The song, "Mic et Mac," with lyrics by Rémo Forlani and music by Antoine Duhamel (who wrote the film's score), told the story of two men, Mic and Mac, who are in love with the same woman, and of the woman, who cannot choose ("Mic wants to kill Mac, Mac wants to kill Mic, oh, quel micmac!"). Forlani was of course alluding to the triangle of Godard, Karina, and Maurice Ronet, but Godard, finding the allusion to his private life too direct, suppressed the song from the film, and yet leaves in the film just enough of it for those in the know to know that Godard too was in the know.
27. *Pariscope,* October 13, 1965, p. 26. To a journalist from the *New Yorker,* when he was presenting *Alphaville* at the New York Film Festival in September, Godard reported Truffaut's response: "He said it's a startling film, and he said, 'I hope everybody doesn't start to make movies like this, because then I'll have to give up making movies.'" *The New Yorker,* October 9, 1965, p. 45.
28. *Pariscope,* October 13, 1965.
29. Godard's press conference from Venice, CS clipping.
30. Louis Marcorelles, *Les Lettres françaises,* September 2, 1965.
31. Yvonne Baby, *Le Monde,* August 31, 1965.
32. Michel Cournot, *Le Nouvel Observateur,* September 1, 1965.
33. *Les Lettres françaises,* September 9, 1965.
34. *Le Nouvel Observateur,* November 3, 1965.
35. *L'Humanité,* November 6, 1965.
36. Bernard-Henri Lévy, interview with author, May 24, 2004.
37. http://www2.bifi.fr/cineregards/article.asp?sp_ref=233&ref_sp_type=2&revue_ref=26 cineregards, March 27, 2003.

38. http://www.fluctuat.net/cinema/interview/akerman2.htm. In 1968, she made her first film, a short film, *Saute ma ville* (Blow Up My City), which was precisely that, a version of the ending of *Pierrot le fou* in which a young woman does to herself in her kitchen in Brussels the same thing that Ferdinand did to himself on the promontory of the island of Porquerolles.

39. Vianey, *En attendant Godard*, p. 189.

40. Ibid., p. 28.

41. Rezvani, *Les Années-lumière (Le Testament amoureux)*, p. 1210.

42. *Arts,* March 30, 1966.

Chapter Thirteen: *Masculine Feminine*

1. *L'Avant-Scène Cinéma,* May 1965; *G par G,* vol. 1, pp. 257–58.

2. *Cahiers du cinéma,* October 1965; *G par G,* vol. 1, p. 263.

3. Vianey, *En attendant Godard,* p. 19.

4. Vianey, interview by author, June 7, 2000.

5. Vianey, *En attendant Godard,* p. 56.

6. Jacques Gerber, *Anatole Dauman: Pictures of a Producer,* Paul Willemen, trans. (London: BFI, 1992), p. 104. The word "fuck" is rendered "f . . . "

7. Dauman, p. 96.

8. Jacques Gerber, *Anatole Dauman: Pictures of a Producer,* p. 97.

9. Though Truffaut did intend to make more films about Antoine Doinel, it was only Godard's plans for his own film that prompted Truffaut, in the summer of 1965, to start work on a new script for the character. (Truffaut, *Correspondence,* p. 172.)

10. Vianey, *En attendant Godard,* p. 69.

11. *Les Lettres françaises,* April 21, 1966.

12. *Masculine Feminine* (New York: Grove Press, 1969), p. 220.

13. Vianey, *En attendant Godard,* p. 27.

14. *Masculine Feminine* (Grove Press), p. 235; *24 Heures,* December 29, 1965.

15. Duport had a small role in Truffaut's *The Soft Skin.*

16. Jean-Luc Godard, interview by Pierre Daix, *Les Lettres françaises,* April 21, 1966.

17. Ibid.

18. Vianey, *En attendant Godard,* pp. 73–74.

19. A French imitation of *The New Yorker,* down to the typeface and the cartoons.

20. *Masculine Feminine,* p. 235.

21. Christian Jelen, "Les Commandés," *Les Temps Modernes,* September–October 1965.

22. Vianey, *En attendant Godard,* p. 106.

23. Ibid.

24. Ibid.

25. The novel was awarded the Prix Renaudot, a major French literary prize, on November 22, 1965, the first day of the shoot of the film.

26. The three lines of on-screen typography (the children / of Marx / Coca-Cola) could make the possessive *de* apply together or separately to the two objects: "the children of Marx / of Coca-Cola"; here too is another example of the understanding of the film and its substance being determined by Godard's remarks in the press.

27. *Le Monde,* April 22, 1966.

28. When Charles de Gaulle became president in the new president-centered Fifth Republic in 1958, his "election" to the seven-year term of office was by a yes-no referendum. That new constitution called for future presidential elections to be held only among a council of "notables," the approximately seventy-five thousand elected officials at all levels of government throughout France. It was not amended to require a popular vote until September 1962.

29. And indeed, in late 1967, the National Assembly voted to lift the ban.

30. Godard saw the play at the Théâtre de Poche, in Montparnasse, which belonged to Godard's friend Antoine Bourseiller, and which Godard had helped him buy. Godard had requested that Bourseiller allow him to attend rehearsals; Godard cast one of the play's actors, Yves Afonso, in a bit part; he also had Bourseiller play a scene alongside Brigitte Bardot, in which Bourseiller, playing himself, was discussing lines from a play with Bardot, also as herself.

31. The adaptation is close, not identical, to the corresponding lines from Jones's play.
32. Vianey, *En attendant Godard,* p. 173.
33. *Elle,* February 10, 1966.
34. *Masculine Feminine,* p. 59.
35. *Elle,* February 10, 1966.
36. Vianey, *En attendant Godard,* p. 172.
37. *Elle,* February, 10, 1966.
38. *Le Monde,* April 23, 1966.
39. Vianey, *En attendant Godard,* p. 82.
40. *Pariscope,* January 19, 1966.
41. *Les Lettres françaises,* April 21, 1966.
42. Eustache did not write for the magazine; his wife was a secretary there, and Eustache was a regular presence at the office.
43. *Pariscope,* March 16, 1966.
44. *Les Lettres françaises,* April 21, 1966.
45. *Cahiers du cinéma,* July 1966; in *Masculine Feminine,* pp. 261–62.
46. *Les Inrockuptibles,* September 25, 1991.
47. *Candide,* no. 261.
48. *Candide,* May 23, 1966.
49. *Village Voice,* September 29, 1966.
50. *Village Voice,* October 6, 1966.
51. *The New Republic,* November 19, 1966, in Kael, *Kiss Kiss Bang Bang,* p. 127.
52. Vianey, interview by author, June 7, 2000.
53. *Le Figaro littéraire,* January 19, 1967.
54. *Le Monde,* supplement, February 1, 1967.
55. Willy Kurant, interview by author, September 10, 2001.
56. *Le Nouvel Observateur,* August 26, 1993.
57. Anne Wiazemsky, interview by author, February, 20, 2003.
58. *Le coup de foudre*—the French expression for "love at first sight."
59. Wiazemsky, interview by author, February 20, 2003.

Chapter Fourteen: *Made in USA, Two or Three Things I Know About Her*

1. At such liberal publications as *Les Lettres françaises* and *La Cinématographie française.*
2. *France-Soir,* April 2, 1966.
3. Cited in *Le Monde,* April 13, 1966.
4. The sites of particularly brutal sieges by the French army in Algeria.
5. *Le Monde,* April 3–4, 1966.
6. *Mémoires intérieures* is the title of a 1959 book of memoirs (followed by the *Nouvelles mémoires intérieures* in 1965) by the novelist François Mauriac, also a supporter of de Gaulle.
7. *Le Nouvel Observateur,* April 6, 1966. Godard's signature was followed by a postscript: "Read and approved by François Truffaut, obliged to shoot in London, far from Paris, *Fahrenheit 451,* the temperature at which books burn."
8. *Le Monde,* April 24, 1966; (the other being Claude Lelouch's *A Man and a Woman*). The Council did, however, reject Alain Resnais's *La Guerre est finie* because the film, concerning a Spanish opponent of Franco in exile in France, was feared to give offense to the Spanish government, and Malraux accepted this decision too. Resnais's film was nonetheless shown at the festival, but unofficially.
9. *L'Express,* April 11–17, 1966.
10. Specifically, he accepted the commission's original decision to allow its release.
11. Vlady, *24 Images/Seconde,* pp. 162–63.
12. Ibid., p. 159.
13. "The Handstand and the Fox: Ten Days with Godard," *Eiga Geijutsu,* July 1966.
14. Ibid.
15. *Eiga ni Me ga Kurande* (Mesmerized by Movies) by Shigehiko Hasumi (Tokyo: Chuo-Koron-Sha, 1995).

16. Junji Hori, e-mail to author, August 6, 2002.
17. "The Ten Days in Japan of the Director Godard," *Kinema Junpo,* June 1966 (no. 416).
18. Ibid.
19. *Le Nouvel Observateur,* March 23, 1966.
20. *Le Nouvel Observateur,* May 4, 1966.
21. Called in French the *grands ensembles* or *HLM, habitations à loyer modéré* (moderate-rent dwellings).
22. *G par G,* vol. 1, p. 17: "I was in Nice, I was vaguely in love, at that time, with Marina Vlady, with whom I was going to shoot *Two or Three Things* and I had gone to see her in Saint-Paul-de-Vence without much success."
23. *Le Nouvel Observateur,* October 12, 1966.
24. Vianey, *En attendant Godard,* pp. 210–11.
25. Cofounder of the Cinémathèque and director of *La Tête contre le mur* and *Eyes Without a Face.*
26. Bernard Violet, *L'Affaire Ben Barka* (Paris: Editions Fayard, 1991), p. 197.
27. *France-Soir,* January 20, 1966.
28. Violet, *L'Affaire Ben Barka,* p. 197.
29. *Le Monde,* November 7–8, 1965.
30. Jacques Derogy and Frédéric Ploquin, *Its ont tué Ben Barka* (Paris: Fayard, 1999), p. 150.
31. It would not be his only version; however, much of his account is consistent with the later findings of investigative journalists and historians.
32. Despite suspicions that he was killed by the French government.
33. *France-Soir,* January 29, 1966.
34. *Le Nouvel Observateur,* October 12, 1966.
35. In the novel, his name is Tiftus.
36. Lászlo Szabó, interview by author, January 31, 2002.
37. *Le Figaro littéraire,* February 2, 1967; *L'Avant-Scène* 70, p. 48.
38. *Les Lettres françaises,* December 22, 1966.
39. Ibid., February 2, 1967.
40. *G par G,* vol. 2, p. 25.
41. Georges Sadoul, *Ecrits 1* (Paris: October 18, 1979), pp. 367–74; *Les Lettres françaises,* December 29, 1966.
42. *Cahiers du cinéma,* January 1967.
43. *Le Monde,* January 27, 1967.
44. *Cet été-là,* p. 185.
45. *2 ou 3 choses que je sais d'elle* (Paris: Seuil/Avant-Scène, 1971), pp. 15–16.
46. Vlady, *24 Images/Seconde,* p. 163.
47. *L'Express,* August 8, 1966.
48. Vlady, *24 Images/Seconde,* p. 164.
49. Interview with Marina Vlady, *Film* (Velber bei Hannover, Germany), March 1969.
50. Jansen and Schütte, *Jean-Luc Godard,* p. 78.
51. *Cahiers du cinéma,* October 1967; *G par G,* vol. 1, pp. 325–26.
52. Bitsch, interview by author, September 19, 2001.
53. Jansen and Schütte, *Jean-Luc Godard,* p. 78.
54. Ibid., p. 78. The best days of her career were behind her. She soon married Russian poet, singer, and hero Vladimir Vysotsky. Although she continued to act, she neither achieved her former level of stardom nor took on any roles of enduring interest.
55. Ibid., p. 81.
56. *Le Nouvel Observateur,* October 12, 1966.
57. Bercholz had produced the 1961 compilation film *The Seven Deadly Sins,* which included Godard's sketch, "Sloth."
58. The other directors and their themes: Claude Autant-Lara (the modern day), Mauro Bolognini (Rome), Philippe de Broca (French Revolution), Franco Indovina (the prehistoric age), Michael Pfleghar ("La belle époque").
59. *Le Nouvel Observateur,* October 12, 1966.
60. *Télérama,* April 2, 1967; in *Deux ou trois choses,* Seuil / Avant-Scène, p. 116.

61. CS [*Télérama*], December 27, 1966.

62. *Cahiers du cinéma,* February 1967.

Chapter Fifteen: *La Chinoise, Weekend*

1. Marie-Pierre Ulloa, *Francis Jeanson, un intellectuel en dissidence de la Résistance à la guerre d'Algérie* (Paris: Berg, 2001), p. 231.

2. Richard Gombin, *Les Origines du gauchisme* (Paris: Seuil, 1971).

3. *G par G,* vol. 1, p. 293; *Cahiers du cinéma,* November 1966.

4. Bourseiller, *Les Maoïstes* (Paris: Plon, 1996), p. 33.

5. Jean-Pierre Gorin, interview by author, March 18, 2005.

6. Lévy, interview by author, May 24, 2004.

7. Gorin, interview by author, March 18, 2005.

8. Press conference at Venice, *Jeune Cinéma,* October 1967 (MOMA collection).

9. Ibid.

10. The manager refused to project the film unless a second person showed up; Gorin called his friend Rafael Sorin, who hastened to the movie theater.

11. *Jump Cut,* no. 3, 1974, pp. 17–19. In particular, Gorin took the new film *Not Reconciled,* by Jean-Marie Straub, an adaptation of Heinrich Böll's *Billiards at Half-Past Nine,* to be a crucial example of new possibilities in political cinema. Godard had given Straub some financial help to make the film and then, when Böll and his publisher contested the distribution of the film—Straub made it without securing rights to the novel—Godard defended the film in the German press and helped to bring about its release. Godard then helped to finance Straub's *The Chronicle of Anna Magdalena Bach.*

12. *Combat,* August 17, 1967.

13. *El-Moudjahid,* February 7, 1967.

14. Truffaut Archives, BiFi, file Jean-Luc Godard 551 B 313, folder 8 of 12: press clippings (interviews): *Cinéma International* no. 16, Château d'Echandens (Vaud, Switzerland).

15. Wiazemsky, interview by author, February 20, 2003.

16. Godard had met Semeniako at Grenoble while presenting *Masculine Feminine* at the student ciné-club there. Semeniako recalled: "When he returned to Paris, he had someone call to see whether I had a month free to work with him. I didn't at all know what I was going to do, whether I was being hired as an extra or as a camera assistant, but I accepted immediately." Michel Semeniako, "Tourner avec Godard," interview with François Albéra (BiFi, Truffaut archives).

17. *Cahiers du cinéma,* October 1967; *G par G,* vol. 1, p. 326.

18. Sholokhov, who won the Nobel Prize in 1965 for novels that included *And Quiet Flows the Don,* was a leading figure of socialist realism.

19. *Cahiers du cinéma,* October 1967; *G par G,* vol. 1, p. 310.

20. Michel Semeniako, "Tourner avec Godard," interview with François Albéra (BiFi, Truffaut archives).

21. *G par G,* vol. 1, p. 311; *Cahiers du cinéma,* October 1967.

22. Alain Jouffroy, *Le Roman vécu* (Paris: Robert Laffont, 1978), p. 349.

23. This poster is in the collection of Antoine Bourseiller.

24. Wiazemsky, interview by author, February 20, 2003.

25. Sterritt, *Jean-Luc Godard: Interviews,* p. 48 (*Los Angeles Free Press,* March 29, 1968).

26. Godard, interview by author, June 9, 2000: "Yes, but that's typical of the unconscious, because I was naively on Anne Wiazemsky's side and I made her say my own ideas in regard to Jeanson, but today, what remains is that Jeanson is rather correct. So my unconscious was correct, but it's the cinema that got things right, more or less right, what is said isn't necessarily right, often what the author says is even less right, because the author is present in what he does, not in what he says."

27. *Le Nouvel Observateur,* August 7, 1967.

28. Bourseiller, interview by author, November 16, 2001.

29. *Le Monde,* August 8, 1967.

30. Wiazemsky, interview by author, February 20, 2003.

31. *Les Letters françaises,* September 1, 1967.

32. *Le Nouvel Observateur,* September 20, 1967.
33. Ibid.
34. Ibid.; *Paris-Presse,* September 10, 1967.
35. *Le Figaro littéraire,* September 10, 1967; in *Avant-scène cinéma,* May 1971.
36. *Le Monde,* September 6, 1967.
37. William Klein, interview with author, May 26, 2000.
38. *France Catholique,* August 25, 1967.
39. *France-Soir,* September 10, 1967.
40. *Combat,* September 5, 1967.
41. *France-Soir,* September 10, 1967.
42. *G par G,* vol. 1, p. 312; *Cahiers du cinéma,* October 1967.
43. *Cahiers du cinéma,* October 1967.
44. Ibid.
45. *France-Soir,* September 10, 1967; radio interview, Europe 1.
46. Bitsch, interview by author, September 19, 2001.
47. Bitsch was not among them, he was directing his first feature, *The Last Man,* produced by Godard.
48. *Cahiers du cinéma,* October 1967; *G par G,* vol. 1, p. 327.
49. Wiazemsky, interview by author, February 20, 2003.

Chapter Sixteen: *Revolution (1968–1972)*

1. Alain Bergala, *Godard au travail* (Paris: Cahiers du cinéma, 2006), p. 372.
2. Wiazemsky, interview by author, February 20, 2003.
3. *Les Inrockuptibles,* May 13, 1998. *Cahiers du cinéma,* March 1968, contains an important, detailed chronology of the controversy's first days, as well as a transcript of the press conference.
4. *Le Monde,* February 11–12, 1968.
5. Ibid., February 14, 1968.
6. Ibid., February 16, 1968.
7. *Cahiers du cinéma,* March 1968.
8. Roud, *A Passion for Films,* pp. 157–59; Langlois and Myrent, *Henri Langlois,* p. 337.
9. *The Globe and Mail* (Toronto), March 2, 1968.
10. Cine Cubano 48.
11. Godard, interview by author, June 9, 2000.
12. Cine Cubano 48.
13. Wiazemsky, interview by author, February 20, 2003.
14. *Eye,* September 1968.
15. Joseph Gelmis, *The Film Director as Superstar* (New York: Doubleday, 1970), p. 186.
16. Ibid., p. 29.
17. *Newsweek,* February 12, 1968.
18. Gene Youngblood, *Los Angeles Free Press,* March 8, 1968; Sterritt, *Jean-Luc Godard Interviews,* p. 10.
19. *Sight and Sound,* Summer 1968.
20. *Combat,* April 17, 1968.
21. *Newsweek* clipping, Museum of Modern Art clippings file.
22. *Sight and Sound,* Summer 1968.
23. Ibid.
24. *Daily Texan,* March 8, 1968.
25. *Eye,* September 1968.
26. *Kansas City Star,* March 17, 1968.
27. *The Globe and Mail* (Toronto), March 2, 1968.
28. Abnormally long projects appealed to Godard at this point, likely, as Norman Mailer suggested, under the influence of Andy Warhol's films. Mailer and Godard met in New York around that time: "When I was making my three underground films we walked together for a block or two at one point, we were going from, I think, from one party to another, and he said, 'I hear you've made a forty-five-hour film,' and I said, 'Yes, the problem's gonna be to cut it down,' and he said, 'No, don't cut it down, show all of it.' That was in the '60s, when Andy Warhol was, you know, cutting quite a swath with *his* underground films." Norman Mailer, interview by author, July 10, 2000.

29. Gorin, interview by author, March 18, 2005.
30. The title was something of a pun on the title of the French film-industry journal, *Le Film français*.
31. Gorin, interview by author, March 18, 2005.
32. D. A. Pennebaker, interview by author, February 19, 2001.
33. Jonathan Rosenbaum, interview by author, May 27, 2000.
34. Richard Roud, *Godard*, 1970, p. 148.
35. Mim Scala, *Diary of a Teddy Boy* (London: Review, 2001), pp. 104–5.
36. Wiazemsky, interview by author, February 20, 2003.
37. Anne Wiazemsky had dropped out of the university in 1967.
38. One participant recalled that it was the denial of a room to a group of militant filmmakers to show footage shot at a recent Berlin protest that actually caused the demonstration to turn into an occupation. Elisabeth Salvaresi, *Mai en héritage* (Paris: Syros/Alternatives, 1988), p. 148.
39. Alain Peyrefitte, *C'était de Gaulle* (Paris: Editions de Fallois-Fayard, 1994), vol. 3, March 25, 1968.
40. *Le Monde*, May 16, 1998.
41. *Le Nouvel Observateur*, special issue, May 1968.
42. Daniel Cohn-Bendit, *Le Grand Bazar* (Paris: Belfond, 1975), p. 33.
43. *Le Monde*, May 16, 1998.
44. Jouffroy, interview by author, June 27, 2002.
45. Freddy Buache, *Le Cinéma français des années 70* (Renens: Five Continents, 1990), p. 6.
46. www.bopsecrets.org/French/graffiti.htm.
47. A traditional consultative body convened by the King; the last was in 1789.
48. Interview with Godard in August 1968, *Film* (Velber, West Germany), April 1969.
49. Truffaut archives, BiFi.
50. Ibid.
51. Archival footage of the event.
52. Truffaut archives, BiFi.
53. Freddy Buache, interview by author, March 18, 2002. Marcel Ophüls remembered the events somewhat differently: "In 1968, at the Cannes festival, while François Truffaut and Louis Malle, somewhat pathetically, were hanging onto the curtain of the festival hall to prevent further screenings in the face of de Gaulle's riot police, Jean-Luc was seen to be negotiating a deal with the Hakim brothers in the lobby of the Hotel Martinez." *American Film*, September 1984.
54. Godard, *Introduction à une véritable histoire du cinéma*, p. 294.
55. Hervé Hamon and Patrick Rotman, *Génération* (Paris: Seuil, 1987), vol. 1, p. 531.
56. Claude Mauriac, *Le Figaro littéraire*, June 14–23, 1968.
57. Gorin, interview by author, March 18, 2005.
58. *Génération*, vol. 1, p. 481.
59. Gorin, interview by author, March 18, 2005.
60. This incident and its significance figure in Philippe Garrel's film, *Les Amants Reguliers* (Regular Lovers), a drama from 2004 about the uprising and its aftermath.
61. Yves Afonso, interview by author, November 11, 2001.
62. *Le Nouvel Observateur*, May 30, 1968.
63. Patrice Martinet, interview by author, October 23, 2004.
64. Gorin, interview by author, March 18, 2005.
65. Wiazemsky, interview by author, February 20, 2003.
66. Bourseiller, interview by author, November 16, 2001. Bourseiller offered the pathetic epilogue to this story: "Two years later, he rang the bell: 'Is there any soup?' And there was soup, and he ate his soup, and we talked as if nothing had happened—and I never saw him again."
67. Schiffman, videotaped interview by Bernard Cohn, September 27, 1999.
68. Moullet, interview by author, November 17, 2001.
69. *Oz*, August 1968.
70. *Sunday Times* (London), June 23, 1968.
71. Gorin, interview by author, March 18, 2005.
72. Alain Jouffroy, *Le Roman vécu* (Paris: Robert Laffont, 1978), p. 376.
73. Gorin, interview by author, March 18, 2005.
74. Godard, *Introduction à une véritable histoire du cinéma*, p. 268.

75. Dated May 10. (Cohen-Solal, *Sartre*, p. 789).

76. August 1968, Jean-Luc Godard, interview by members of the Frankfurt Film Coop, *Film* (Velber), April 1969.

77. *Cinéma vu pour vous,* Centre d'initiation au cinéma, no. 5, p. 10, Locarno, 1968 [CS].

78. Wiazemsky, interview by author, February 20, 2003.

79. CNC documents.

80. *Le Gai Savoir* (Paris: L'Union des écrivains, 1969).

81. *Sunday Times* (London), June 23, 1968.

82. Roud, p. 148.

83. Wiazemsky, interview by author, February 20, 2003.

84. Mick Jagger, 1995; http://www.timeisonourside.com/SOSympathy.html.

85. *Sunday Times* (London), June 23, 1968.

86. Wiazemsky, interview by author, February 20, 2003.

87. Pennebaker, interview by author, February 19, 2001.

88. Leacock-Pennebaker, distributed *Un film comme les autres,* pairing it with a documentary of Godard's NYU appearance in April, *New York Times,* December 30, 1968; *Variety* (undated clipping). D. A. Pennebaker claimed that the real problem was a technical one: "We had [the translation] as a mag track on a 16 print. I had [the translator] do it on one track of a stereo print, the idea was to show it with a stereo projector at Lincoln Center. Well, they didn't even know what a fucking stereo projector is. The sound was all muddled, you couldn't understand a thing. . . . They began to tear up the seats. Lincoln Center tried to sue us for $3,500." Pennebaker, interview by author, February 19, 2001.

89. *Manchester Guardian Weekly,* August 1, 1968.

90. Michael Chaiken identified the correlation between the film's dialogue and Mailer's interview.

91. Wiazemsky, interview by author, February 20, 2003.

92. *Times* (London), November 29, 1968.

93. *Times* (London), November 30, 1968; *Films and Filming,* February, 1969; *Le Monde,* December 1–2, 1968.

94. *New York Times,* March 7, 1970.

95. *Village Voice,* April 30, 1970.

96. Alain Jouffroy, *Le Roman vécu* (Paris: Laffont, 1978), pp. 486–87.

97. *Le Monde,* October 15, 1968.

98. Pennebaker, interview by author, February 19, 2001.

99. Godard, *Introduction à une véritable histoire du cinéma,* p. 296.

100. Pennebaker, interview by author, February 19, 2001.

101. Grace Slick, *Somebody to Love?* (New York: Warner Books, 1998), p. 179.

102. *New York Times,* November 20 and December 6, 1968. In the commotion, Rip Torn and David McMullin of Leacock-Pennebaker were arrested. When the police learned that the production was for PBL, they let the two go with a summons.

103. Wiazemsky, interview by author, February 20, 2003.

104. *Mai en décembre (Godard en Abitibi),* a film by Julie Perron (2000).

105. Wiazemsky, interview by author, February 20, 2003.

106. Ibid.

107. In 2000, Montreal filmmaker Julie Perron made a noteworthy documentary film, *Mai en décembre (Godard en Abitibi),* to reconstruct the traces of this abandoned project.

108. Isabelle Pons, interview by author, March 9, 2002.

109. Collection of Madeleine Morgenstern, p. 389.

110. Jean-Henri Roger, interview by author, June 14, 2001.

111. Wiazemsky, interview by author, February 20, 2003.

112. Ibid.

113. *Village Voice,* April 30, 1970.

114. *Film Quarterly,* Winter 1970–71.

115. MacCabe, *Portrait of the Artist at Seventy,* p. 219.

116. *Tribune Socialiste,* January 23, 1969.

117. *Rolling Stone,* June 14, 1969.

118. Ibid.

119. *Village Voice,* April 30, 1970.

120. Cohn-Bendit, *Le Grand Bazar* (Paris: Pierre Belfond, 1975), p. 62.

121. Wiazemsky, interview by author, February 20, 2003.

122. Cohn-Bendit: *Le Grand Bazar,* p. 62.

123. Gorin, interview by author, March 18, 2005.

124. Wiazemsky, interview by author, February 20, 2003.

125. Gorin, interview by author, March 18, 2005.

126. *Le Monde,* April 27, 1972.

127. Press release from Grove Press, cited by Andrew Sarris in *Village Voice,* April 30, 1970.

128. Gorin, interview by author, March 18, 2005.

129. Raphaël Sorin, interview by author, March 25, 2002.

130. Gorin, interview by author, March 18, 2005.

131. Jules Feiffer, interview by author, January 19, 2002.

132. http://www.elliottgould.net/archive/fortune.htm (article by Martin Mayer, "Elliott Gould as 'The Entrepreneur,'" *Fortune,* 1970).

133. Michael Goodwin and Greil Marcus, *Double Feature* (New York: Outerbridge and Lazard, 1972), p. 37.

134. Robert Benton, interview by author, September 17, 2004.

135. *Le Nouvel Observateur,* February 16, 1970.

136. Gorin, interview by author, March 18, 2005.

137. *Jump Cut,* no. 3, 1974.

138. Roger, interview by author, June 14, 2001.

139. Armand Marco, interview by author, September 17, 2001.

140. Ibid.

141. Elias Sanbar, "Vingt et un ans après," *Trafic,* no. 1, 1991.

142. Elias Sanbar, interview by author, June 16, 2001. Excerpts from the script have been published in Goodwin and Marcus, *Double Feature.*

143. "Godard chez les feddayin," *L'Express,* July 26–August 2, 1970.

144. Sanbar, "Vingt et un ans après."

145. Godard, interview by author, June 9, 2000.

146. Ibid.

147. *Jump Cut,* no. 3, 1974.

148. *Evergreen Review,* October 1970.

149. Ibid.

150. *Double Feature,* p. 18.

151. Barney Rosset, interview by author, 2000.

152. *Evergreen Review,* October 1970.

153. Godard thought of making an even more burlesque version of the trial—featuring Abbie Hoffman himself doing a tap dance number—but this project, too, went unrealized. Marco, interview by author, September 17, 2001.

154. *Vladimir and Rosa* came out in New York in April 1971; though criticized by Vincent Canby of the *New York Times,* it was cited by Stuart Byron in the *Village Voice* (April 29, 1971) as "the best thing Godard has done since *Le Gai savoir,*" which he meant equivocally. It was praised unequivocally by Michael Goodwin in *Rolling Stone;* Goodwin was involved in a book-length interview of Godard, *Double Feature,* that was made during the 1970 tour.

155. *Le Nouvel Observateur,* February 16, 1970.

156. Ibid., June 15, 1970.

157. Claude Mauriac, *Le Figaro Littéraire,* July 20–26, 1970.

158. *Village Voice,* April 9, 1970; *The New Yorker,* May 30, 1970; *Village Voice,* June 4, 1970; *New York Times,* September 12, 1970.

159. *Village Voice,* April 30, 1970. In 1973, Sarris explained his position even more bluntly: "I got off the Godard bandwagon with *Weekend,* and I have not been on since . . . It is as if Godard had indeed died and been reborn in a new form. Certainly, his cinema is now completely dead." *Village Voice,* February 22, 1973.

160. *J'Accuse,* no. 00, November 1, 1970.
161. Wiazemsky, interview by author, February 20, 2003.
162. Gorin, interview by author, March 15, 2005.
163. Buache, interview by author, March 18, 2002.
164. Pierre Jeanneret, *Popistes* (Lausanne: Editions D'en Bas, 2002); at www.republique.ch/archives/2002–04/gauchistes/rupture.
165. MacCabe, *Portrait of the Artist at Seventy,* p. 240.
166. Pons, interview by author, March 9, 2002.
167. *New York Times,* April 16, 1971.
168. Godard returned to Paris instead of going on to Turin to introduce a screening of *Le Gai Savoir. Variety,* March 31, 1971.
169. MacCabe, *Portrait of the Artist at Seventy,* p. 232.
170. Gorin, interview by author, March 18, 2005; Tolmatchoff, interview by author, March 20, 2002.
171. Gorin, interview by author, March 18, 2005.
172. Wiazemsky, interview by author, February 20, 2003.
173. Marco, interview by author, September 17, 2001.
174. Vianey, interview by author, June 7, 2000.
175. Wiazemsky, interview by author, February 20, 2003.
176. Martin Even, interview by author, January 10, 2003.
177. *New York Times,* December 24, 1972.
178. "Producteurs, sauvez-vous vous-meme."
179. Montreal, Concordia University, March 11, 1977.
180. *Filmkritik,* September 1979.
181. *Christian Science Monitor,* December 12, 1972.
182. Erik Ulman, "Die Froehliche Wissenschaft," in *The Hidden and the Plain,* Viennale, Vienna International Film Festival, 2004.
183. Gorin, interview with author, March 18, 2005.
184. *G par G,* vol. 1, p. 22.
185. Ibid.

Chapter Seventeen: Restoration (1973–1977)

1. Document in Truffaut archives, la BiFi, Paris.
2. Published in 1969.
3. *L'Express,* December 23, 1959.
4. Truffaut claimed in June that Godard had received it; but Godard's name does not appear on published lists of advances on receipts awarded in the first seven months of 1973.
5. The successor to *Le Cinéma chez soi* (Home Movies), a copy of which was featured in *A Woman Is a Woman.*
6. The French reads: 20 million, 10 million, and 5 million francs, respectively. Godard, like many of his generation, and indeed many publications, including, for instance, *Cinématographe,* was still in the habit of referring to old francs, 1/100 the value of the new ones. Truffaut, writing back, also calculated in old francs.
7. Truffaut, *Correspondence, 1945–1984,* pp. 385–91.
8. Collection of Madeleine Morgenstern.
9. Specifically, he made films from 1937 to 1954.
10. Antoine de Baecque and Serge Toubiana, *François Truffaut* (Paris: Gallimard, 2001), p. 713.
11. The company name came from Aton, the primal Egyptian god cited in Freud's *Moses and Monotheism,* but it was spelled with two As so it would come first in the professional telephone listings.
12. Freddy Buache, *Le Cinéma français des années 70* (Remens: Five Continents), p. 6.
13. Ibid.
14. Ibid., p. 7.
15. Ibid.
16. Jean-Pierre Beauviala, interview by author, March 21, 2002.

17. The seed money for Sonimage had come from the producer Jean-Pierre Rassam, from money that had been put into *Tout va bien* by Gaumont, and from Godard's and Miéville's own funds (which Richard Roud reported as "inheritances"). (Richard Roud, *Guardian,* August 16, 1975.)

18. Montreal conference, March 11, 1977.

19. *Le Monde,* September 17 and October 14, 1976.

20. *Le Monde,* September 18, 1976; *Libération,* October 22, 1976; *Le Quotidien de Paris,* September 20, 1976.

21. *Le Film français,* March 14, 1975.

22. *Politique hebdo,* September 24, 1975.

23. Ibid.

24. The French nickname Beauregard used was "Jeannot."

25. *Le Monde,* May 8, 1975.

26. Ibid.

27. CS, May 1975.

28. *Libération,* May 24, 1975.

29. *Le Nouvel Observateur,* October 6, 1975. *Newsweek's* Edward Behr reported from Paris on Godard's "truly revolutionary development in technique" by which, "once more, Godard has called into question the very nature of the art." *Newsweek,* October 20, 1975.

30. *Le Film français,* March 14, 1975.

31. *Libération,* September 15, 1975.

32. Portugal's army had staged a coup in 1974 to put an end to rightist dictatorship and establish a socialist state; elections a year later brought to power a democratic socialist with no intention of installing an orthodox Communist government. The protesting soldiers were joined by twenty thousand "Marxist-Leninist" revolutionaries, to whom *Libération* was sympathetic.

33. *Libération,* September 17, 1975.

34. This is the diminutive of Odile, Godard's mother's name.

35. As one editor said, "There's Godard and there are all the others."

36. *Le Monde,* May 11, 1976.

37. Alain Bergala, *Nul mieux que Godard* (Paris: Cahiers du cinéma, 1999), pp. 27–31; *Cahiers du cinéma,* July–August, 1978.

38. *Variety,* March 17, 1976.

39. In fact, exactly ten hours.

40. *Le Monde,* July 18–19, 1976.

41. Manette Bertin, interview by author, February 18, 2003.

42. *Le Monde,* July 18–19, 1976. The contract specified that the company would deliver a series of programs "on communication." Godard quipped that he thought of it rather as "on, under, beside, across" communication, and indeed the ten hours of programming are alternately called *Sur et Sous la Communication* (On and Under Communication).

43. *Libération,* July 23, 1976.

44. Godard, *Introduction à une véritable histoire du cinéma,* p. 100.

45. William Lubtchansky, interview by author, September 12, 2001.

46. Ibid.

47. Bertin, interview by author, February 18, 2003.

48. *Le Nouvel Observateur,* August 2, 1976.

49. *Le Monde,* August 9, 1976.

50. Jonathan Kandell, "The Talk of Paris; 'Morose' Describes It All: Weather, Politics, Crime," *New York Times,* August 1, 1978.

51. *Filmkritik,* September 1975.

52. Ibid., February 1977.

53. *Le Devoir* (Montreal), July 19, 1968.

54. Ibid., March 10, 1977.

55. Tape summary by March 9, 1977.

56. March 12, 1977.

57. *Le Devoir,* August 25, 1977.

Chapter Eighteen: *France Tour Détour Deux Enfants*

1. Bertin, interview by author, February 18, 2003.
2. *Politique hebdo,* September 24, 1975.
3. *Télérama,* September 27–October 3, 1975.
4. He was also leaving behind unfulfilled business obligations; with Godard leaving and Gérard Martin, a co-signatory for Sonimage, remaining, Martin, aware of Gorin's tribulations after Godard's departure from Paris, refused to stay on the hook: he sued Godard successfully for 400,000 francs relating to the company's outstanding debts. (Jean-Pierre Gorin, interview by author, March 18, 2005.)
5. *Machin* means both "thingamajig" and "whatsisname."
6. *Le Cinéma français,* no. 15, 1977.
7. Bertin, interview by author, February 18, 2003.
8. He had told Philippe Rony the same thing. Rony, interview by author, February 17, 2003.
9. All quotations by Camille Virolleaud are from my interviews with her on April 16, 2001, April 22, 2001, November 22, 2001, and March 28, 2002.
10. Martine Virolleaud, interview by author, April 22, 2001.
11. François Virolleaud, interview by author, April 22, 2001.
12. Manette Bertin papers.
13. Cohn-Bendit, *Le Grand Bazar.*
14. *L'Express,* February 22, 2001.
15. *Libération,* February 23, 2001.
16. *L'Express,* February 22, 2001.
17. *L'Express,* March 1, 2001.
18. Ibid.
19. *Libération,* February 23, 2001.
20. Ferré is the songwriter whom Godard had asked in 1970 to write a song about the ban on *La Cause du peuple.*
21. Bertin, interview by author, February 18, 2003.
22. http://www.fluctuat.net/cinema/interview/bergala.htm; February 22, 2002.
23. *Le Monde,* May 3, 1979.
24. Bertin, interview by author, February 18, 2003.
25. Ibid.
26. Serge Losique, interview by author, January 22, 2003. However, one student who was present, Kent Jones, recalls that the sessions were sparsely attended.
27. Godard, *Introduction à une véritable histoire du cinéma,* p. 59.
28. Ibid., p. 81.
29. Ibid., p. 82.
30. Ibid., p. 201.
31. *Le Cinéma francais,* no. 22, 1978.
32. And later for such films as *The Tin Drum, The Return of Martin Guerre,* and *The Unbearable Lightness of Being.*
33. Jean-Claude Carrière, interview by author, November 22, 2001.
34. *Le Cinéma français,* no. 24, 1978.
35. *Women's Wear Daily,* October 8, 1980.
36. Ibid.
37. Catherine Verret, interview by author, June 29, 2000.
38. Tom Luddy, interview by author, February 1, 2001.
39. As proven by its eventual publication, *G par G,* vol. 1.
40. *Ça cinéma,* no. 19, 1980.
41. *Le Matin de Paris,* May 20, 1980.
42. *Nouvelles litteraires,* August 1978.
43. *Kuxa Kanema,* a documentary film (2003, Morgarida Cardoso).
44. RAI broadcast [unidentified].
45. *Kuxa Kanema.*
46. Ibid.
47. Letter to Carole Roussopoulos, *Cahiers du cinéma,* no. 300.

48. Jean-Claude Carrière, http://www.revolver-film.de/Inhalte/Rev3/html/Carriere.htm; Carrière interview, by Jens Börner and Benjamin Heisenberg, December 17, 1998 in Munich, edited by Börner and translated into German by Eva Pampuch.

Chapter Nineteen: *Sauve qui peut (la vie)*

1. *Minneapolis Star,* February 23, 1981.
2. Godard, *Introduction à une véritable histoire du cinéma,* p. 109.
3. Carrière, interview by author, November 22, 2001.
4. *Travelling* (Lausanne), Documents Cinémathèque Suisse, no. 56–57, Spring 1980.
5. Press book, *Sauve qui peut (la vie),* CS; New York Public Library.
6. Nathalie Baye, interview by author, June 21, 2002.
7. Véronique Godard, interview by author, December 12, 2001.
8. At the time, he had written to Godard to seek his help making a film (Godard indeed sponsored it).
9. Goupil, interview by author, June 15, 2001.
10. *Quotidien de Paris,* December 6, 1979.
11. *Ça cinéma* (Paris: Albatros, 1979).
12. Ibid., p. 108.
13. *Politique hebdo,* April 27, 1972; *G par G,* vol. 1, p. 374.
14. *Le Point,* March 24, 1980.
15. *Le Matin,* May 21, 1980.
16. Lubtchansky, interview by author, September 12, 2001.
17. Cécile Tanner, interview by author, November 13, 2001.
18. As Paul waits on line, a furious patron storms out of the theater complaining that the film has no sound. Godard had wanted Jacques Tati to play the role of the patron; when Tati refused, Godard hired an unfamiliar actor who played the part with a child perched on his shoulders—exactly like a character from a memorable scene in Tati's 1967 film *Playtime.*
19. Isabelle Huppert, interview by author, April 2, 2002.
20. *Le Point,* March 24, 1980.
21. *Etabli* refers to the left-wing activist who "established" himself in the factory and also to the workbench itself.
22. Goupil, interview by author, June 15, 2001.
23. *Travelling,* no. 56–57, Spring 1980, Symposium de Lausanne (June 1–4, 1979).
24. Godard, interview by author, June 9, 2000.
25. *Filmkritik,* September, 1981.
26. *Los Angeles Reader,* January 23, 1981.
27. *Le Progrès dimanche* (Lyon), August 3, 1980.
28. *Le Point,* March 24, 1980.
29. *Le Matin,* May 23, 1980.
30. *Le Figaro,* May 23, 1980.
31. Karmitz, interview by author, April 27, 2001.
32. *Le Monde,* October 16, 1980.
33. *New York Times,* June 1, 1980.
34. *Village Voice,* June 2, 1980.
35. *New York Times,* May 4, 1981.
36. *The New Yorker,* November 24, 1980; she also criticized Godard for what she considered to be an *excessive* deference to feminist sensibilities, specifically referring to a scene of amicable complicity between Isabelle and Denise.
37. Karmitz bought the rights to Thompson's novel from a French agent and planned to produce Godard's film adaptation of it but soon discovered that the agent was not in fact entitled to sell those rights. The director Bertrand Tavernier (who had been Godard's publicist, working for Beauregard, for the release of *Les Carabiniers*) wanted to make a film based on the same book and had gone to the United States and purchased the rights directly from the representatives of Thompson, who had died in 1977. Godard suggested to Tavernier that both of them could make a film from the same book, splitting the purchase price. "He would make a big film, I would make a little one," Godard said. Tavernier refused (claiming that his purchase of rights allowed the making of one film, not two); his film,

Coup de torchon (*Clean Slate*) was released in France in 1981 and in the United States in 1982. Godard, interview by author, June 9, 2000; Bertrand Tavernier, interview by author, July 21, 2000.

38. http://binomat27.1.free.fr/ptt/resume_camp_2.htm.

39. André Halimi, *Coluche victime de la politique* (Paris: Edition 1, 1994), p. 23.

40. Ibid., p. 61.

41. Ibid., p. 68. Coluche did not actually endorse Mitterrand until April 6.

Chapter Twenty: *Passion* and *First Name: Carmen*

1. *Le Nouvel Observateur,* May 22, 1982.

2. Huppert, interview by author, April 2, 2002.

3. Karmitz, interview by author, April 27, 2001.

4. *New York Times,* March 21, 1980.

5. Sterritt, *Jean-Luc Godard: Interviews,* p. 111.

6. CS clipping.

7. *Le Matin* (undated CS clipping).

8. Ed Lachman, interview by author, April 20, 2002.

9. *New York Times,* February 2, 1981, March 23, 1981.

10. *Los Angeles Herald Examiner,* May 27, 1984.

11. *Cahiers du Cinéma,* October 2001.

12. *Sight and Sound* 52, no. 2 (Spring 1983).

13. *Filmkritik,* July 1983.

14. Huppert, interview by author, April 2, 2002.

15. Lachman, interview by author, April 20, 2002.

16. *Variety,* October 8, 1980.

17. *Point de rencontre,* television interview, TF1, 1982.

18. *Sight and Sound* 52, no. 2 (Spring 1983).

19. Jean-Luc Bideau, interview by author, February 15, 2003.

20. Carrière, interview by author, November 22, 2001.

21. Hanna Schygulla, interview by author, June 11, 2005.

22. Ibid.

23. Coutard, interview by author, April 27, 2001.

24. Karmitz, interview by author, April 27, 2001.

25. Coutard, *Filmkritik,* July 1983.

26. Huppert, interview by author, April 2, 2002.

27. *Le Monde,* May 26, 1982.

28. *Ouvert le dimanche,* broadcast on FR3, June 6, 1982.

29. Huppert, interview by author, April 2, 2002.

30. Ibid.

31. *Libération,* May 25, 1982.

32. *Sight and Sound* 52, no. 2 (Spring 1983).

33. *Ouvert le dimanche,* FR3, June 6, 1982.

34. This includes the footage of Schygulla and Radziwilowicz working at love through Mozart.

35. *Violette & François* and *The Brontë Sisters.*

36. *New York Times,* August 15, 1985.

37. He had founded and run the International Festival of Theater in Nancy, and, in 1972, was appointed the director of the National Theater of Chaillot, in Paris (formerly the Théâtre National Populaire).

38. *TLM* (Swiss), January 9, 1982.

39. *New York Times,* February 21, 1983.

40. *Variety,* May 18, 1988, p. 18.

41. *Le Matin,* December 12, 1983.

42. *G par G,* vol. 1, pp. 574–582: interview from *Le Monde de la Musique,* April 1983.

43. Claude Chabrol, for his part, had never stopped filming the most arrantly commercial projects, and his trajectory was essentially unaltered by the changed circumstances.

44. de Baecque and Toubiana, *François Truffaut* (Paris: Gallimard Folio, 2001), pp. 727–28.

45. *L'Avant-Scène Cinéma,* 323/324, March 1984.

46. Ibid.

47. *Le Matin,* January 9, 1984.

48. *Libération,* 25 May, 1982.

49. Myriem Roussel, interview by author, February 26, 2003.

50. *Art Press, Spécial Godard,* December 1984 to January–February 1985.

51. Collection of Jacques Bonnaffé.

52. "For *First Name: Carmen,* I tried to check myself into a hospital that I knew in order to be able to prepare my screenplay in peace and quiet. I kept a trace of this in the film, I had to prove that I was sick, I couldn't do it, so they wouldn't have me." Jean-Luc Godard, *Apostrophes,* 1985.

53. *Framework 21,* interview on April 25, 1983, Salsomaggiore. At the 1982 Cannes Festival, Godard and Wiazemsky met by chance. She told him that she had found *Passion* "moving." He responded that he didn't want her to be moved by him, and he walked away. Wiazemsky, interview by author, February 20, 2003.

54. *Cinéma 84,* January 1984.

55. Roussel, interview by author, February 26, 2003; *Art Press,* December 1984 to January–February 1985, vol. 4, Godard special.

56. *G par G,* vol. 1, p. 561.

57. Jacques Bonnaffé, interview by author, June 12, 2001.

58. *Revolution,* January 6, 1984.

59. *Le Matin,* September 17–18, 1983.

60. *Télérama,* January 25, 1984.

61. Ibid.

62. Ibid.

63. *Revolution,* January 6, 1984.

64. *Les Nouvelles,* January 5–11, 1984.

65. Ibid.

66. *Le Figaro,* January 11, 1984.

67. CS clipping.

68. *Cinema 84,* January 1984.

69. *G par G,* vol. 2, pp. 574–82; interview from *Le Monde de la Musique,* April 1983.

70. *L'Express,* January 6, 1984.

71. *Revolution,* January 6, 1984.

72. Bonnaffé, interview by author, June 12, 2001.

73. *Le Nouvel Observateur,* December 30, 1983.

74. *Revolution,* January 6, 1984.

75. Martine Bianco, interview by author, March 21, 2002.

76. The discussion ran in two parts in *Cahiers du cinéma* in July–August and September 1983.

77. *G par G,* vol. 1, p. 556; *Cahiers du cinéma,* August 1983.

78. Beauviala, interview by author, March 21, 2002.

79. Ibid.

80. Bonnaffé, interview by author, June 12, 2001.

81. *Le Matin,* January 9, 1984.

82. *Le Nouvel Observateur,* December 30, 1983.

83. *Le Monde,* September 9, 1983.

84. *Libération,* September 9, 1983.

85. *Libération,* January 19, 1983.

86. *Le Matin,* January 9, 1984.

87. *Cinématographe,* no. 95, December 1983; press conference from the Venice Film Festival, September 1983.

Chapter Twenty-one: *Hail Mary*

1. *Le Nouvel Observateur,* July 17, 1982.

2. *Révolution,* February 1, 1985.

3. *Art Press,* no. 88, January 1985: Conversation between Jean-Luc Godard and Philippe Sollers (from the film by J. P. Fargier, November 21, 1984).

4. *Revolution,* February 1, 1985.
5. *La Croix,* January 24, 1985.
6. Ibid.
7. In an interview several years later Godard offered a striking explanation for his choice of subject. In that interview, he stated his belief that his path through life paralleled that of Bob Dylan—he highlighted their motorcycle accidents, and added, "I have a great deal of sympathy for him when I read critics who eviscerate him, who call him a 'has-been.' Sometimes I read *Rolling Stone* to get news of him, I want to see whether he's on the charts. I tried to get him to act in who-knows-which film, a project in the United States, and then all of a sudden he turned toward Christ and I said to myself, 'That will happen to me too.' I forgot all about it, but when I made *Hail Mary,* I remembered: 'Look, Dylan warned me.' " (*Actuel,* January 1988.)
8. *Cinématographe,* April 1986.
9. Lévy, interview by author, May 24, 2004.
10. Roussel, interview by author, February 26, 2003.
11. *New York Post,* October 15, 1983.
12. *France-Soir,* January 23, 1985.
13. Roussel, interview by author, February 26, 2003.
14. *Le Nouvel Observateur,* December 30, 1983.
15. *Libération,* January 23, 1985.
16. Ibid.
17. Roussel, interview by author, February 26, 2003.
18. *Art Press, Spécial Godard,* December 1984 and January–February 1985; Conversation between Jean-Luc Godard and Philippe Sollers (from the film by J. P. Fargier, November 21, 1984).
19. Ibid.
20. *Art Press, Spécial Godard,* December 1984 and January–February 1985.
21. Roussel, interview by author, February 26, 2003.
22. *Libération,* January 23, 1985.
23. Godard spoke of Artaud's *Letters from Rodez* as an influence (*Art Press, Spécial Godard*).
24. *Libération,* January 23, 1985.
25. *New York Times,* October 14, 1983.
26. *Cinématographe,* no. 100, May 1984.
27. *Tristesse et beauté,* by Joy Fleury, alongside Charlotte Rampling.
28. "Before John Paul II no Pope had devoted as much space and emphasis to Mary both in catechesis and liturgy." *Inside the Vatican,* May 1996. Cited in www.wayoflife.org/fbns/mostmarian.htm.
29. *Le Monde,* May 4, 1985; *New York Times,* May 4, 1985.
30. *New York Times,* May 11, 1985.
31. Sterrit, *Jean-Luc Godard: Interviews,* p. 168; Katherine Dieckmann, "Godard in His 'Fifth Period': An Interview," *Film Quarterly* 39, no. 2 (Winter 1985–1986), p. 2.
32. *Variety,* October 9, 1985.
33. *Le Figaro* magazine, January 26, 1985 ("Il faut longtemps pour aller chercher loin").

Chapter Twenty-two: *Detective* and *Soigne ta droite*

1. *Journal du dimanche,* January 20, 1985.
2. A droll reversal of the philological point that "martyr," in Greek, indeed means "witness."
3. *Cahiers du cinéma,* June 1985.
4. Nathalie Baye, interview by author, June 21, 2002.
5. *France-Soir,* May 18, 1985.
6. Ibid.
7. *Le Temps* (Geneva), January 12, 2000.
8. *Le Nouvel Observateur,* January 8, 1998.
9. *Le Monde,* October 21–22, 1984.
10. *Cahiers du cinéma,* June 1985.
11. As Nuytten recalled, Godard resisted any attempt to add lighting to the available light on location. Then, Nuytten said, came the blowout: "It was a scene where Johnny was filmed from behind, in

front of a window. Across from him there was a building façade that was in full sunlight, bright white, which must have been f/64, while the interior was f/1.4. I asked Jean-Luc, 'What do you want to see?' Silence. Then Godard said, 'There you go, he hasn't read the script, it's always the same thing, nobody gives a shit . . .' and that's how it started." (http://www.objectif-cinema .com/webmag/horschamp/film/questionsa/f14f.htm)

Godard raised the argument to a harsh, ad hominem level, challenging Nuytten's competence, knowledge, and politics. Yet despite Godard's disagreeable and exaggerated way of saying so, he was right about the question at hand and its relation to the substance of the scene. In the scene Hallyday is overlit, unnaturally bright in front of the daylight-bright exterior, without any play of contrasts or shadows. The line that Hallyday speaks in the shot indeed relates directly to the problem at hand.

12. *Observer Magazine—Life,* February 7, 1995; (www.jaybabcock.com/observer.html).
13. *New York Post,* October 8, 1985.
14. *Le Nouvel Observateur,* May 17, 1985.
15. MacCabe knew Godard, having interviewed him on several occasions and published a book-length study of Godard's work of the late 1960s and 1970s, *Godard: Images, Sounds, Politics.*
16. Colin MacCabe, interview by author, January 31, 2001.
17. Alain Bergala, interview by author, May 20, 2001.
18. Ibid.
19. *Quotidien de Paris,* January 26, 1985.
20. Caroline Champetier, interview by author, June 27, 2001.
21. *Cahiers du cinéma,* Godard special issue, 1990.
22. Champetier, interview by author, June 27, 2001.
23. Hervé Duhamel, interview by author, December 3, 2002.
24. Ibid.
25. Even, interview by author, January 10, 2003.
26. He had a cameo role in *First Name: Carmen.*
27. The turn of events is Godard's unambiguous reference to the mysterious murder—to this day unsolved—of Gérard Lebovici, the founder of the French talent agency Artmédia and the associate of Guy Debord. On March 7, 1984, Lebovici was found dead, shot in the back of the head, behind the steering wheel of his car in the underground parking lot of his office building.
28. *G par G,* vol. 1, pp. 574–82; *Le Monde de la Musique,* April 1983.
29. Beauregard, *Beauregard,* pp. 249–50.
30. *G par G,* vol. 1, pp. 610–11; *Le Film Français,* September 21, 1984.
31. *Libération,* December 30, 1987.
32. *Le Monde,* August 8, 1998.
33. *Le Nouvel Observateur,* March 13, 1997.
34. *Best,* January 1988.
35. *Cahiers du cinema, Musiques au cinéma,* special issue, 1995.
36. www.ritamitsouko.com; *Le Figaro,* December 1985.
37. *7 à Paris,* December 30, 1987.
38. Malraux's autobiographical *Le Miroir des limbes* is the source of the recited text (p. 859).
39. *New York Times,* November 25, 1978.
40. *Cahiers du cinéma,* December 1987.
41. *Télérama,* December 30, 1987.
42. *Cahiers du cinéma,* Godard special issue, 1990.
43. Duhamel, interview by author, December 3, 2002.
44. *Variety,* April 16, 1986.
45. Duhamel, interview by author, September 8, 2001.
46. *Best,* January 1988.
47. Robert Goldberg, "Eleven Things He Knows About Godard," *Wall Street Journal,* January 21, 1987.
48. *Le Journal du dimanche,* January 3, 1988.
49. *Le Monde,* December 30, 1987.

50. Ibid.
51. *L'Evènement du jeudi,* December 24–30, 1987.
52. *Le Nouvel Observateur,* January 1–7, 1988.

Chapter Twenty-three: *King Lear*

1. Karmitz, interview by author, April 27, 2001. Godard was afraid to call Duras himself because he thought that she was angry at him. When Karmitz called Duras on Godard's behalf, she asked what reason she might have to be angry with him. "Because," the producer replied, "he sent you a letter and enclosed a daisy [*une marguerite*]," but received no response. "There was no daisy," Duras said, "there was a button, the kind you find on underwear." It turned out that Godard had sent Duras a little round clip that was used for recording on large-format video cassettes; with its four leaves, it looked like both a daisy and an underwear button.
2. Menahem Golan, interview by author, July 12, 2000.
3. Luddy, interview by author, February 1, 2001.
4. Norman Mailer, interview by author, July 10, 2000.
5. Roger Ebert, *Chicago Sun-Times,* May 16, 1985.
6. Tom Luddy, e-mail to author, January 30, 2001.
7. Mailer, interview by author, July 10, 2000.
8. Ibid.
9. Ibid.
10. Duhamel, interview by author, December 3, 2002.
11. Viviane Forrester, *La violence du calme* (Paris: Seuil, 1980), p. 68.
12. http://ouvrir.le.cinema.free.fr/pages/mon-coin/JLG-KingL.html (Club de l'Etoile, November 24, 1987); transcribed by Alain Bergala.
13. *Le Monde,* July 24, 1986.
14. Le *Nouvel Observateur,* March 28, 2002.
15. *Actuel,* September 1986.
16. Luddy, interview by author, February 1, 2001.
17. *Sunday Times* (London), May 18, 1986.
18. Ibid., September 28, 1986.
19. Mailer, interview by author, July 10, 2000.
20. Godard, interview by author, June 9, 2000.
21. Ibid.
22. Duhamel, interview by author, September 8, 2001.
23. Mailer, interview by author, July 10, 2000.
24. Godard, interview by author, June 9, 2000.
25. Mailer, interview by author, July 10, 2000.
26. Golan, interview by author, July 12, 2000.
27. *Le Monde,* April 2, 1987.
28. Mailer, interview by author, July 10, 2000.
29. *Le Monde,* April 2, 1987.
30. *Le Nouvel Observateur,* November 21, 1986.
31. http://ouvrir.le.cinema.free.fr/pages/mon-coin/JLG-KingL.html (Club de l'Etoile, November 24, 1987).
32. Luddy, interview by author, February 1, 2001.
33. http://ouvrir.le.cinema.free.fr/pages/mon-coin/JLG-KingL.html (Club de l'Etoile, November 24 1987); transcribed by Alain Bergala.
34. Godard, interview by author, June 9, 2000.
35. Woody Allen, interview by author, June 23, 2000.
36. Jean-Luc Godard, *L'Humanité du Cinéma* (unpublished book); interview with Noël Simsolo (France-Culture, "A Voix nue," 1989–1998), tenth interview.
37. Allen, interview by author, June 23, 2000.
38. *Le Monde,* February 4, 2002.
39. Molly Ringwald, interview by author, June 28, 2000.
40. Godard, interview by author, June 9, 2000.

41. Michèle Halberstadt, "J'ai tourné avec Godard," May 1987, unidentified clipping, Bibliothèque André-Malraux, Paris.
42. Ringwald, interview by author, June 28, 2000.
43. *Le Monde*, April 2, 1987; Duhamel, interview by author, September 8, 2001.
44. *Le Monde*, April, 1987.
45. *Variety*, May 20, 1987.
46. Ibid.
47. *Le Figaro*, May 16–17, 1987.
48. *Variety*, May 20, 1987.
49. *Le Monde*, May 7, 1987.
50. Mailer, interview by author, July 10, 2000.
51. *Libération*, July 23, 1987.
52. *New York Times*, January 22, 1988.
53. *Time*, February 1, 1988.
54. Agence France Presse, January 21, 2004.
55. She had received advance financing for it from Gaumont and the CNC in 1985 but had to wait two years for production funds from Switzerland, where the film was made. This funding ultimately came from a small company, Xanadu, and its producer, Ruth Waldburger, who had worked with Godard as a production manager on *Passion*.
56. *24 Images* (Canada), Spring 1995.
57. René Bonnell, interview by author, June 25, 2002. *Libération* reported in 1988 that Canal Plus had, at its inception, financed *Histoire(s)* directly with an investment of 4 million francs; but according to Bonnell, who was in charge of film production at the station, Canal Plus did not invest directly in the series until 1987.

Chapter Twenty-four: *Histoire(s) du cinéma*, Part 1

1. Champetier, interview by author, June 27, 2001.
2. It is now, there, commonly called the Shoah.
3. *Cahiers du cinéma*, August 1963.
4. *Le Matin Magazine*, May 10–11, 1980.
5. Ibid.
6. *G par G*, vol. 1, p. 603; *L'Autre Journal*, January 1985.
7. Barbie was imprisoned and died in jail in 1991.
8. Interview with François Albéra, *CinemAction*, no. 52, 1989.
9. Godard, *L'Humanité du cinéma* (unpublished manuscript); *A voix nue*, radio interviews with Godard by Noël Simsolo.
10. That transcription occurred in 1999, when the sound track of *Histoire(s)* was released as a set of audio CDs, accompanied by a "libretto" featuring the text in the original French, plus English, German, and Italian translations. Also, *Le Monde* published excerpts from Godard's voice-over as if it were an essay; December 15, 1994.
11. Duhamel, interview by author, September 8, 2001.
12. *Libération*, May 11, 1987.
13. *Le Monde*, May 21, 1988.
14. Nicolas Seydoux, interview by author, February 19, 2006.
15. Ibid.
16. Bonnell, interview by author, June 25, 2002.
17. Ibid.
18. *Le Monde*, May 6, 1989.

Chapter Twenty-five: *Nouvelle Vague*

1. *Le Matin*, March 9, 1987.
2. Karmitz, interview by author, April 27, 2001.
3. *Le Monde*, December 30, 1987.
4. Karmitz, interview by author, April 27, 2001.
5. Godard, interview by author, June 9, 2000.

6. Seydoux, interview by author, January 19, 2006.

7. *Le Monde,* December 30, 1987.

8. Duhamel, interview by author, September 8, 2001.

9. "I found, I still find, nothing more admirable than the word of Valentin Feldman to the German soldier who insulted him while taking him to be shot: "Imbecile, it's for you that I die." (Claude Roy, *Moi je,* p. 469).

10. Cinémathèque Suisse.

11. *G par G,* vol. 2, p. 190.

12. Godard, interview by author, June 9, 2000.

13. *Libération,* May 18, 1990.

14. Ibid.

15. *Cahiers du cinéma,* April 1996.

16. *Libération,* August 24, 1996.

17. Lubtchansky, interview by author, September 12, 2001.

18. *G par G,* vol. 2, pp. 193–94.

19. Press conference from Cannes, 1990 (*Cahiers du cinéma,* June 1990).

20. Here Godard uses the words of the famous Hemingway/Fitzgerald repartee but revises their meaning: the daughter doubts the difference on the basis of a common humanity, while the mother asserts the fact of the rich having more money as a significant and real difference.

21. Press conference, Toronto Film Festival, September 1996: http://www.mediapolis.com/ecm-cgi-bin/background?1600.

22. *Télérama,* November 1996. http://www.mediapolis.com/ecm-cgi-bin/background?1600.

23. In *Nouvelle Vague,* Godard also included excerpts of Schoenberg's *Transfigured Night* and chamber music by Paul Hindemith, but it was the music of ECM's group of contemporary composers (including Darling, Pärt, Heinz Holliger, and Meredith Monk) that dominated.

24. Jean Schwarz, interview by author, February 17, 2003. Schwarz's music also figured in *Detective* and *Comment ça va.*

25. *Cahiers du cinéma,* June 1990.

26. *L'Humanité,* May 19, 1990.

27. *The Nation,* February 18, 1991.

28. *New York Times,* September 29, 1990.

29. June 6, 1989; broadcast in November and December 1989 on France Culture radio.

30. *Le Monde,* September 5, 1991.

31. CS clipping.

Chapter Twenty-six: *Germany Year 90 Nine Zero*

1. In the end, Godard and John Boorman made films in the series, which was to comprise Italian and Russian films as well (but did not). *Le Monde,* November 4, 1991.

2. *Le Monde,* September 5, 1991.

3. Ibid., August 9, 1993.

4. *Construire* (Zurich), October 23, 1991.

5. The title of a book by critic Lotte Eisner about the German cinema of the Weimar era.

6. *Le Monde,* September 5, 1991.

7. Ibid.

8. Text from collection of Romain Goupil.

9. Goupil, interview by author, June 15, 2001.

10. Text from collection of Romain Goupil.

11. Goupil, interview by author, June 15, 2001.

12. *Le Monde,* September 5, 1991.

13. Goupil, interview by author, June 15, 2001.

14. *Réalités neuchâteloises* (Geneva), September 3, 10, 17, 1992.

15. *Le Monde,* September 5, 1991.

16. The French is *plaques de ceinturon.*

17. Jean Girandoux, *Siegfried et le Limousin* (Grasset/Lirre de Poche, 1962), pp. 145–46.

18. This quote from Raymond Chandler had figured in *Grandeur et décadence.*

19. *Le Monde,* September 13, 1991.
20. Ibid., September 5, 1991.
21. Goupil, interview by author, June 15, 2001.
22. Anne-Marie Faux, interview by author, November 28, 2001.
23. *Le Nouveau Quotidien* (Swiss), April 2, 1992; *Le Matin* (Swiss), April 2, 1992; *Schweizer Handelszeitung* (Zurich), April 29, 1993.
24. *Komsomolskaya Pravda,* February 29, 1992 (French translation in CS).
25. *Kultura* (Moscow), February 15, 1992 (CS).
26. *Le Monde,* July 5, 1992.
27. *L'Humanité,* April 23, 1993; *Variety,* April 16, 1993.
28. Neither did Russell.
29. Champetier, interview by author, June 27, 2001.

Chapter Twenty-seven: *Hélas pour moi, JLG/JLG, Histoire(s) du cinéma,* Parts 2 and 3

1. Jean-Luc Godard, *L'Humanité du cinéma; A voix nue,* radio interviews with Noël Simsolo.
2. As early as 1975, when he planned to make a film about cancer, he had sought financing from the Centre National de recherche scientifique (CNRS) but was rejected.
3. *Télérama,* September 4, 1985
4. *G par G,* vol. 2, p. 280; *Cahiers du cinéma,* October 1993.
5. Bergala, interview by author, November 27, 2001.
6. *G par G,* vol. 2, pp. 219, 280.
7. *Le Monde,* October 8, 1991.
8. http://www.scerern.fr/revueTDC/907-77658.htm (an interview with Serge Toubiana); *Le Monde,* October 30, 1992.
9. Yet Godard did not return the funds advanced to him for the first year of affiliation with La fémis, and nobody asked about it—for the time being. And when somebody did, late in the decade, his *Histoire(s) du cinéma* would come back into the equation.
10. *G par G,* vol. 2, p. 250.
11. Bergala, interview by author, November 27, 2001.
12. *Le Figaro,* December 11, 1990.
13. *G par G,* vol. 2, p. 36.
14. Ibid., p. 269.
15. Ibid., p. 274.
16. Ibid., p. 271. Remarkably, the poem concludes with a lament for the "happy people" in the "California woods" whose innocent bliss is destroyed by the arrival of Europeans, i.e., a complaint about the United States.
17. *La Croix,* September 1, 1993; the actual line from the book: "For a woman who loves her man, is not every man the shadow of God?"
18. *G par G,* vol. 2, p. 278; *Cahiers du cinéma,* October 1993.
19. Champetier, interview by author, June 27, 2001.
20. *G Par G,* vol. 2, p. 274; *Cahiers du cinéma,* October 1993.
21. *G par G,* vol. 2, p. 322.
22. *G par G,* vol. 2, p. 274; *Cahiers du cinéma,* October 1993.
23. Champetier, interview by author, June 27, 2001.
24. *G par G,* vol. 2, p. 283.
25. *Les Inrockuptibles,* October 1993.
26. *Première,* November 1999.
27. Champetier, interview by author, June 27, 2001.
28. *L'Evènement du jeudi,* September 2–8, 1993.
29. Godard had considered filming *L'Histoire du Soldat* in 1962.
30. *Liberation,* September 8, 1993.
31. *Le Monde,* August 26, 1993.
32. Ibid., September 10, 1993.
33. *Les Inrockuptibles,* October 1993.

34. Ibid.
35. *New York Times,* March 18, 1994.
36. Godard, *L'Humanité du cinéma* (unpublished); interview with Noël Simsolo, *France-Culture, À Voix nue,* 1989–1998.
37. Ibid.
38. *Film Journal* (New York), July 1994.
39. *Le Matin,* January 23, 1985.
40. L'Invité du jeudi, September 17, 1981, "maudit"—cursed, despised.
41. Even if it is arguable that the leaders of the American film industry in the nineteen thirties and forties, who were predominantly Jewish, critically failed the Jews of Europe who were facing extermination—that Hollywood producers didn't flood the market with exposés of the Nazi regime, which came to power in 1933—Godard does not make this point in such terms.
42. *Women's Wear Daily,* October 8, 1980.
43. It was also the occasion for a postponement of another publication: *Son + Image* featured a biographical sketch of Godard by MacCabe of the British Film Institute, who had been working on an authorized biography; but the sketch contained information that Godard and Miéville claimed not to have given him, and Godard de-authorized MacCabe. MacCabe, interview by author, January 31, 2001. (After a seven-year hiatus, MacCabe resumed work on his book, which, as *A Portrait of the Artist at Seventy,* was published in 2003.)
44. *Film Comment,* March–April 1995.
45. He uses titles referring to the abbé Sieyès's comments on the Third Estate during the French Revolution: "What is the cinema? Nothing. What does it want? Everything. What can it do? Something."
46. *Le Monde,* August 13, 1995. Indeed, Godard's expressions of displeasure at the caliber of the discussion were sufficiently strong for one of the more experienced spectators, Jean-Michel Frodon, then the film critic of *Le Monde* (now editor of *Cahiers du cinéma*), to consider Godard to have displayed "a need to break the possibility of meaning and to break the possibility of dialogue." Jean-Michel Frodon, interview by author, September 14, 2001.
47. *G par G,* vol. 2, p. 404.

Chapter Twenty-eight: *For Ever Mozart, Histoire(s) du cinéma,* Part 4

1. Webern stepped outside his door to smoke a cigar; in violation of the curfew, he was shot. This occurred not in Vienna but in Mittersill, a town near Salzburg.
2. Press conference, "Films d'un peu partout causant français," Film Festival, Beaujolais, 1996.
3. *Le Monde,* May 20, 1994.
4. Press conference, "Films d'un peu partout causant français," Film Festival, Beaujolais, 1996.
5. Bérangère Allaux, interview by author, April 15, 2001.
6. Goupil, interview by author, June 15, 2001.
7. Frédéric Pierrot, interview by author, April 16, 2001.
8. Allaux, interview by author, April 15, 2001.
9. Ibid.
10. Ibid.
11. The French words are *nichons, nibars, roploplos.*
12. Allaux, interview by author, April 15, 2001.
13. Ibid.
14. Godard, interview by author, June 9, 2000.
15. Jean-Louis Martinelli, interview by author, March 29, 2002.
16. Gill Holland, interview by author, June 6, 2002.
17. On the ostensible grounds of Godard's insistence that the festival director, Richard Peña, view the film at a screening in Paris, and his refusal to send a video for the entire selection committee to review (Rob Tregenza, e-mail to author, May 30, 2002). When Gill Holland called Peña to complain of this rejection on formalities, the festival director responded, "He never comes, he says he'll come, then he doesn't come" (Gill Holland, interview by author, June 6, 2002).
18. Holland, interview by author, June 6, 2002.
19. Ibid.
20. Paul Otchakovsky-Laurens, interview by author, June 13, 2000.

21. *Nulle part ailleurs,* February 25, 1998, 2nd part, Marie Darrieussecq; www.cyberpresse.ca/reseau/arts/xp/art_p1056130.html, May 15, 2001, Boudé en salle, Jean-Luc Godard fêté sur la Croisette, par Didier Saltron, Agence France-Presse, Cannes.

22. *Nulle part ailleurs,* February 25, 1998, 2nd part, Marie Darrieussecq.

23. Ibid.

24. Otchakovsky-Laurens, interview by author, June 13, 2000.

25. *Journal de Genève / Gazette de Lausanne,* November 30 / December 1, 1996.

26. At the same time, Otchakovsky-Laurens also released Godard's similar "versification" of the text of *JLG/JLG.*

27. Though *Inside/Out* was accepted to the "Un Certain regard" section of the 1997 Cannes Film Festival and received favorable reviews, it was not picked up for distribution in the United States. Tregenza has not made another feature film since then. Meanwhile, Tregenza, as per his agreement with Godard, had resold American distribution rights in *For Ever Mozart* to New Yorker Films. (The film was not released commercially and had only a brief run at the Walter Reade Theater of Lincoln Center.)

    From April 1997 on, Tregenza heard nothing more from Godard—until July 2001, when Godard left a message on Tregenza's answering machine, a message that Tregenza calls "polite and friendly," regarding a "collaboration." Tregenza was out of town at the time and did not get the message until ten days later. When he called Godard back, Godard said that he had changed his mind.

28. Allaux, interview by author, September 16, 2001.

29. *Libération,* December 3, 1996.

30. Delphine Chuillot, interview by author, March 29, 2002.

31. Martinelli, interview by author, March 29, 2002.

32. Allaux, interview by author, September 16, 2001.

33. Bonnaffé, interview by author, June 12, 2000.

34. Allaux, interview by author, September 16, 2001.

35. *G par G,* vol. 2, p. 399.

36. Bergala, interview by author, May 20, 2001. Godard did, however, allow Bergala to publish the text in the second volume of the book *Jean-Luc Godard par Jean-Luc Godard.*

37. Buache, interview by author, March 18, 2002.

38. *L'Express,* May 3, 2001.

39. Maillot, interview by author, April 23, 2001.

40. Bergala, interview by author, November 27, 2001.

41. Ibid.

42. *Télérama,* October 4, 2000.

43. *Epok,* May 2001.

Chapter Twenty-nine: *Eloge de l'amour*

1. *Les Inrockuptibles,* October 21, 1998.

2. "Seminar with Claude Lanzmann, 11 April, 1990," *Yale French Studies,* no. 79 (1991).

3. *Les Inrockuptibles,* October 21, 1998.

4. *Le Monde,* December 3, 1998.

5. Bergala, interview by author, November 27, 2001.

6. Bernard-Henri Lévy, *Comédie* (Paris: Grasset, 1997), p. 55.

7. Lévy, interview by author, May 24, 2004.

8. Claude Lanzmann, interview by author, February 26, 2003.

9. *Le Monde,* June 27, 1999.

10. Lévy, interview by author, May 24, 2004.

11. Lévy, interview by author, May 23, 2004.

12. *Le Monde,* June 27, 1999.

13. Lévy, interview by author, May 23, 2004.

14. Ibid.

15. Lanzmann, interview by author, February 26, 2003.

16. *Libération,* December 3, 1996.

17. The four versions described here are published in *G par G,* vol. 2, pp. 447–69.

18. Godard, interview by author, June 9, 2000.

19. *Le Télégramme* (Bretagne), December 1, 1999.

20. Ibid., November 30, 1999.

21. Isabelle C., discussions and correspondence with author, 1995–2002.

22. Marie Desgranges, interview by author, June 27, 2001.

23. Ibid.

24. Philippe Loyrette, interview by author, March 30, 2002.

25. Loyrette, interview by author, June 27, 2001.

26. For the film *Petits disorders amoureux,* directed by Olivier Péray.

27. Bruno Putzulu, interview by author, March 30, 2002.

28. Cécile Camp, interview by author, May 18, 2001.

29. http://www.dvd.reviewer.co.uk/news/interview.asp?Index=5664 (Jean-Luc Godard, interview by Michèle Halberstadt).

30. Jean Lacouture, interview by author, June 15, 2000.

31. Ibid.

32. Godard had wanted the painter Pierre Soulages to play the role as himself, but the artist refused.

33. Marcelline Loridan-Ivens, interview by author, April 23, 2001.

34. Loridan-Ivens talked about this experience in 1960 in the film by Jean Rouch and Edgar Morin, *Chronicle of a Summer.*

35. Roger, interview by author, June 14, 2001.

36. Putzulu, interview by author, March 25, 2002.

37. Putzulu, interview by author, June 18, 2001.

38. Putzulu, interview by author, March 25, 2002.

39. Camp, interview by author, May 18, 2001.

40. Fleur Albert, interview by author, May 19, 2001; Putzulu, interview by author, June 18, 2001.

41. Putzulu, interview by author, March 25, 2002.

42. Roger, interview by author, June 14, 2001.

43. Her grandfather tells Jean Lacouture, "Berthe is inside looking at the contract" before we actually know who is looking at the contract, and he tells Edgar, "Berthe was a superb swimmer" when she is not seen on-screen. Also, Edgar refers to her obliquely as "no Berthe Morisot," Manet's model.

44. *Le Film Français,* May 15, 2001.

45. Ibid.

46. Godard, interview by author, June 9, 2000.

47. Albert, interview by author, May 19, 2001.

48. *Les Inrockuptibles,* May 15–21, 2001.

49. As I can attest, having been present at each of them for shows at different times of the day and evening in the first two weeks of its run.

50. Jean-Marie Straub, interview by author, September 23, 2001.

51. I was one of ten people in the audience for an evening show of *Two or Three Things I Know About Her,* one of five for a screening of *First Name: Carmen.*

52. *Le Figaro Magazine,* June 9, 2001.

53. *Télérama,* May 12, 2004.

Chapter Thirty: *Notre Musique*

1. *Libération,* December 27, 2000.

2. Godard, interview by author, June 9, 2000.

3. Faux, interview by author, November 28, 2001.

4. *Epok,* May 2001.

5. Along with his own relations with his grandparents, and particularly with his maternal grandfather. *Studio,* May 2001.

6. MacCabe, interview by author, January 31, 2001.

7. Godard, interview by author, June 9, 2000.

8. *Libération,* April 7, 2002.

9. None of whom actually had a film in the series when it was completed in 2007.

10. This was likely the project for which Godard called Rob Tregenza to do camera work, given Tregenza's repudiation of shot-countershot.

11. "Vercors" was a pseudonym for Jean Bruller.
12. *Le Monde,* supplement "Aden," May 19–25, 2004; and *L'Humanité,* May 20, 2004. Tregenza, e-mail to author, May 30, 2002.
13. *Le Monde,* May 12, 2004.
14. Ibid., September 29, 2004.
15. Bergala, interview by author, June 21, 2002.
16. *Le Monde,* May 13, 2004.
17. Sanbar recalled that meeting in a 1991 article in the first issue of *Trafic* (to which Godard contributed a brief poetic text) and again in his book *Le Bien des absents* (The Absentees' Goods), published in 2001.
18. Elias Sanbar, *Le Bien des absents* (Arles: Actes Sud, 2001), p. 95.
19. http://www.lavoixdunord.fr/loisirs/cinema, Propos recueillis par Gi.D., June 2004 (http://www.geocities.com/glen_norton/interviews.html).
20. *Cahiers du cinéma,* May 2004.
21. *Les Inrockuptibles,* May 5–11, 2004.
22. *New York Times,* October 2, 2004.
23. *New York Observer,* December 2, 2004.
24. Frodon, interview by author, September 14, 2001.

Epilogue

1. Ghislaine Moutote, interview by author, June 11, 2000.
2. Godard, interview by author, June 9, 2000.

INDEX

JLG = Jean-Luc Godard

ABOUT THE AUTHOR

RICHARD BRODY is an editor and writer at *The New Yorker*. *Everything Is Cinema* is his first book. He lives in New York City.